# Economic Analysis
## Theory and Application

Irwin Publications in Economics
*Advisory Editor*   Martin S. Feldstein   *Harvard University*

1982 ● FOURTH EDITION

# Economic Analysis

## Theory and Application

### S. Charles Maurice
Professor of Economics
Texas A&M University

### Owen R. Phillips
Assistant Professor of Economics
Texas A&M University

### C. E. Ferguson
Late Professor of Economics
Texas A&M University

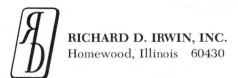 RICHARD D. IRWIN, INC.
Homewood, Illinois   60430

ISBN 0-256-02614-9

Library of Congress Catalog Card No. 81–85252

*Printed in the United States of America*

1 2 3 4 5 6 7 8 9 0 MP 9 8 7 6 5 4 3 2

To: Jillian, Dana, Ross
and two Lori's

# Preface

This textbook is designed for undergraduate courses in basic microeconomics—the theory of value and distribution. The fourth edition has two major objectives. The primary purpose is to present the basic fundamentals of price theory. The secondary, but quite important, purpose is to illustrate how the fundamentals of price theory can be applied to the solution of real-world, decision-making problems and to give students experience in solving these problems.

Over the past several years, we have noticed that students in economics courses have become increasingly interested in applications of theories they learn in class. For this reason, instructors in these courses are demanding a considerable number of applications in the texts. While we have reduced the number of applications in this edition, the new applications are longer and more forceful. The number of pages devoted to applications of the theory remain virtually unchanged. Moreover, to give students more practice in problem solving, we increased the number of questions at the end of the chapters by about 50 percent. Approximately 75 percent of the problems are new.

Nonetheless, *Economic Analysis* remains a fundamental text in the basics of microeconomic theory. It presents and uses the essential theoretical tools. While in this edition we have slightly increased the level of difficulty and have added some new concepts, no calculus is used.

Some of the most important new concepts added are in Chapter 7, which is almost all new, covering market dynamics that determine consumption, production, and investment over time. To give students tools to study how prices behave over time, we introduce the concepts of future value, present value, and, of course, the rate of interest. The tools are used to analyze how consumers optimally allocate income over time and how producers make investment decisions. The effects of inflation on investment are analyzed. Also included are analyses of the optimal rate of depleting a natural resource, technology conversion, and the effects of risk and uncertainty.

Chapter 10, dealing with imperfect competition, has been almost completely rewritten to reflect new developments in industrial organization. We deal with monopolistic competition and oligopoly in terms of amount of monopoly power possessed by firms in these market structures. Nonprice competition in imperfectly competitive markets—advertising, product quality, and location—are more thoroughly explored. We introduce the prisoner's dilemma to show how firms interact when they are recognized rivals. Also discussed in this chapter are tacit collusion, barriers to entry, and the incentives for cartel members to break agreements.

A third major change is the introduction of the applied economic tools of consumer's and producer's surplus. These concepts are covered in a rigorous but understandable fashion and then used in a variety of contexts, both in the basic material and in the applications, to provide a more complete explanation of important economic issues.

A large number of important yet less sweeping changes have been made. Among these are the following. In Chapter 3 we make a stronger distinction between cardinal and ordinal utility. That chapter also includes a new section on nonlinear budget lines and nonconvex indifference curves in order to show how budget lines can be affected by policy and why economists use convex indifference curves. Chapter 4 introduces compensated demand curves and compares them to ordinary schedules. Compensated demand is then used to motivate consumer's surplus. Several pages are devoted to an intuitive definition of consumer's surplus and how it is used.

The chapters developing the theories of production and cost have also been improved. We try to make a much stronger distinction between efficiency and profit maximization. The transition between Chapter 5 on production theory and Chapter 6 on cost has been made smoother. We show how short-run and long-run cost come from the production function. The material on producer's surplus is introduced in Chapter 8, the theory of perfect competition. Applications showing how total surplus can be used in policy analysis are used in this and later chapters. Despite their rarity, decreasing cost industries are discussed for perfectly competitive markets.

We begin the chapter on monopoly with a discussion of monopoly power and its measurement. The causes of monopoly and limit pricing are discussed in more detail, as are discriminatory pricing strategies and multiplant and multiproduct monopolies. Also bilateral monopoly is discussed in detail in Chapter 11. Finally, in Chapter 12—efficiency and competition—we make the connection between Pareto efficiency and total surplus as indicators of welfare. That chapter also discussed at length how externalities and public goods result from market failure.

While these are the most substantive changes, many other minor changes and additions have been made. We have eliminated the exercises and asides in the text. Since these may have tended to distract students, most have been rewritten into the text or reserved for the problems at the end of the chapter. We have also extensively edited the text to make it easier to read.

While *Economic Analysis* remains primarily a theory text, we feel the applications contribute greatly to students' understanding of the theory. To make it easier to separate theory from the applications, the applications have been set apart. Most applications deal with analysis of current real-world, decision-making problems. As noted, the number of problems at the end of each chapter has been substantially increased. These problems are separated into two sections: (1) technical problems, where the solution is somewhat mechanical, and (2) analytical problems, which involve the application of theory to analyze problems in a thought-provoking manner. The increased number of questions and analytical problems is in response to suggestions from many users of the earlier editions.

The text effectively lends itself to several teaching approaches. Chapter 2 is a review of supply and demand, subjects generally covered in principles courses. Some instructors may wish to omit this chapter or cover only the applications. For some classes, the interest may be only in theory and not in applications. Since all applications are set apart, they can be omitted without loss of continuity.

Some instructors may wish to cover production and cost theory as well as the theory of the firm before developing the theory of consumer behavior. Chapters 3 and 4, consumer theory, can be left until later, allowing the students to skip from Chapter 2 to Chapter 5, the theory of production. Nothing in Chapters 3 and 4 is necessary for understanding the material in these later chapters. Finally, individual instructors may wish to cover the material in the final chapter immediately after the theory of perfect competition, Chapter 8.

We wish to thank several of our colleagues at Texas A&M for help with this revision. Among these are Carl Enomoto, Mike Ormiston, Rich Anderson, Steve Wiggins, Dub Lane, Charles Smithson, and Ray Battalio. We are also grateful for the many suggestions we have received from students and from instructors who have used *Economic Analysis* in their courses. In the later category, Bob Ekelund of Auburn University has been particularly helpful.

*S. Charles Maurice*
*Owen R. Phillips*

# Contents

*lateral monopoly.* (APPLICATION: Monopsony in the military.) Capital input markets: *Demand for capital.* Summary.

Introduction. Social welfare: *The difficult concept of social welfare. Pareto optimality. Consumer's surplus and Pareto efficiency.* Perfect competition and Pareto optimality: *Edgeworth Box diagram. Equilibrium of exchange.* (APPLICATIONS: Uses of the theory of trade: Goods-in-kind and water rationing.) *Equilibrium of production. General equilibrium. Equilibrium in perfect competition.* Perfect competition and social welfare: *Public goods. Imperfect competition. Information.* Ownership externalities: *Definition of externalities.* (APPLICATION: Externalities and urban renewal.) *Property rights and externalities. Nonowned or community-owned property.* (APPLICATION: A common property problem.) *Private ownership and externalities. Some solutions.* Summary. Epilogue.

# Chapter 1

## Scope of economics

### 1.1 INTRODUCTION

You are beginning a course in microeconomic theory and analysis. Some of you have had a beginning Principles course; for others, this is your first course. In the Principles course, you were concerned with some economic theory, but you were also probably taught a great deal about economic institutions, such as how government operates, characteristics of businesses, and so forth.

In this course, you will be concerned with learning the basics of economic theory—the fundamental tools used by economists—and with using the theory to analyze real economic problems. The theories you will learn in this course are relatively simple but very relevant and applicable to the solution of many important economic problems. Let us emphasize at the very beginning that, simple as the theories may be, they are very similar to those theoretical methods used by highly paid professional economists in government, business, and universities to analyze important real-world problems. The mathematical and statistical techniques used by these economists are more advanced, but the fundamentals of the theoretical structure are frequently quite similar.

You will apply the theories you learn to analyzing such problems as the impact of OPEC (Organization of Petroleum Exporting Countries), the reasons for shortages of natural gas, and the effect of divestiture of integrated oil companies. These are the same types of questions now being analyzed by recent winners of Nobel Prizes in economics, such as Paul Samuelson and Milton Friedman. You will analyze problems quite similar to those that now concern economists who, at this time, are high-ranking government officials. You will be concerned with decision-making problems similar to those that are now being considered by top financial analysts employed by the nation's largest banks and industrial firms.

This is a different situation from that encountered by undergraduate students in other fields. Students in undergraduate chemistry and physics courses do not work on the same types of problems being addressed by Nobel Prize winners in chemistry and physics. Beginning mathematics students are many years away from using the techniques employed by their professors to solve problems. This, however, is not the case with beginning or intermediate economics students.

Let us reemphasize: *the basic theoretical tools, the fundamental methods of analysis, and the overall approaches to the solution of economic problems for the professional economist are those that you will learn and use in this course.* Economic theory is essentially a way of thinking about problems. The economic way of thinking does not change fundamentally as one acquires more sophisticated tools.

## 1.2 THE SCIENCE OF ECONOMICS

Thomas Carlyle, a Scottish historian of some repute, was fond of criticizing economists. It was he who referred to Malthus and Ricardo as "the respectable professors of the dismal science," thereby giving economics a name it has never quite overcome— possibly, as John Kenneth Galbraith has said, because it has never quite deserved to. In one sense, economics remains a dismal science in that economists all note that there is no such thing as a free lunch, even though most economists no longer make the dire predictions about the inevitable poverty of society that were being made at the time Carlyle coined his phrase.

The dismal nature of economics stems from the definition of economics. As most beginning texts avow, economics is a study of the method of allocating scarce physical and human resources among unlimited wants or competing ends. In other words, economics is the study of scarcity, which results when people want more than can be produced. Since wants are unlimited for society, and the resources used to produce things to satisfy the wants are finite or limited, all wants cannot be satisfied. To satisfy some wants, the satisfaction of other wants must be sacrificed. Alternative uses for resources makes them valuable, and this is what leads to cost.

Those who know economics tend to be a somewhat cynical lot. They have a habit of asking what something will cost—cost in the sense of what will have to be sacrificed. People with some economic expertise tend to scoff a bit when politicians promise more schools, more police, more buildings, more of everything, at no additional cost to society. They frequently respond to the promise that society can have many more military goods along with more consumption goods with "nonsense." To have more of some goods, society must give up other goods.

Thus, economics has become fundamentally the science of making choices. Most, if not all, basic theory is designed to aid in making decisions and in understanding the consequences of economic decisions made by others. These economic decisions are necessary because of scarcity. Societies and individuals must make choices between desirable goals. All goals cannot be met. How nice it would be if society and individuals could have more of the good things without having to give up anything. To the extent that economists continually point out the costs of these "good things," economics still merits the title "dismal science."

From another point of view, however, those who know some economics have a rather cheerful or optimistic outlook. Economists have recently begun to present arguments counter to the current fad of "doomsday" philosophies. Those who espouse the doomsday approach are fond of pointing out that some natural resource or group of natural resources will be totally depleted in a specific number of years if society continues to use the resources at the current rate. Or they prophesy shortages of many resources in the future. That is, they say that, in a few years, society will need a certain amount of the resource, but this amount will not be available.

Economists are quick to point out flaws in such doomsday arguments. The major flaw, they say, is ignoring the functioning of the market. As society uses up some resource, the amount of that resource decreases, causing the resource to become more and more scarce. This increasing scarcity, as we know, drives up the price of the resource. The increased price causes consumers to economize on their consumption of the resource. The increased price also induces increased exploration for additional deposits. It causes deposits that were unprofitable to exploit under the lower prices to become profitable, thus adding to the amount available. Finally, the higher price brings about research and development in other areas in search of a substitute commodity. Much of our theoretical analysis in the text deals with the fundamentals behind such processes. In any case, those who understand the operation of economic markets argue that, when something becomes scarcer, prices rise to ration the commodity among buyers and bring forth increased quantities from producers. Thus, when a "crisis" occurs, economists often point out that there are fundamental economic forces at work which offer a solution.

## APPLICATION

### The development of synthetic rubber

The economic history of the development of synthetic rubber provides a fascinating application of how the market finds a solution to the burdensome problem of scarcity. True, prices and costs, the elements of any market, are a result of scarcity, but when prices rise and prevent some buyers from participating in the market, they look for substitutes. The search for substitutes is often the silver lining in an otherwise dismal economic cloud.

As early as 1909, the German Bayer Company demonstrated the possibility of making a synthetic rubber. Unfortunately, the finished product lacked the strength and flexibility of natural rubber. Despite these handicaps, the product was invaluable to a resource-starved Germany during World War I. For tires, cables, and especially submarine storage batteries, the substitute was indispensible. The commercialization of the 1909 development did not come about until Germany was at war and natural rubber was virtually impossible to obtain. After the war, moreover, when the price of natural rubber returned to normal levels, the future of synthetic substitutes looked dim. Synthetic rubber was more expensive and of lower quality than natural rubber, so the product fell into obscurity.

In the mid-1920s, the price of natural rubber rose again. Demand for crude rubber was increasing dramatically because of the growth of the automobile industry. Great Britain had also formed a rubber cartel to restrict worldwide natural rubber supply. In 1926, Thomas Midgley, a research scientist at General Motors, approached Alfred Sloan, president of the company, concerning a research project on synthetic rubber. General Motors was interested. In the words of Sloan, natural rubber was "most unsatisfactory from the standpoint of erratic costs. . . ."[1] In other words, prices were often too high for the company's tastes.

---

[1] S. Leslie, "Thomas Midgley and the Politics of Industrial Research," *Business History Review*, Winter 1980, p. 490.

For two years, Midgley investigated the properties of natural rubber in an effort to duplicate them, but the investigation was commercially unsuccessful. General Motors canceled the project in 1928.

Then in 1933, at almost the same time that Great Britain was attempting to form a second rubber cartel, General Tire and Goodyear began separate investigations into the feasibility of a synthetic rubber tire. After a year of research, both companies lost interest. General's final report on the research concluded that synthetic rubber was unsuitable for "handling in standard factory equipment, and the quality of the product was definitely inferior to natural rubber."[2] But, in 1937, Standard Oil Development Company, the research branch of Standard Oil of New Jersey, perfected a synthetic rubber christened "Butyl." The quality was comparable to that of natural rubber, yet it was much too expensive (relative to natural rubber) to produce. Until World War II, it was believed there was no way to commercially develop a high-quality synthetic at a price close to that of natural rubber.

At the outbreak of World War II, the U.S. War Department was worried about threatened supplies of natural rubber and the increased demand for the substance if the United States should get involved in the war. In 1939, the five largest tire companies in the United States were contacted about the impending danger; natural rubber prices were rising quickly. The companies were encouraged to look for a commercially feasible synthetic. Research support was provided by the War Department. By 1942, the rubber companies had commercially developed several kinds of high-quality synthetic rubber. Natural rubber was virtually impossible to obtain at this time because of the war with Japan. Interestingly, the price of synthetic rubber was not higher than that of natural rubber. In 1947, standard-grade natural rubber ranged from 9.9 to 23 cents per pound, while "Buna-S," the standard grade of synthetic rubber, was priced between 15 and 20 cents per pound.

## 1.3 USES OF ECONOMICS

The major reason for studying economic theory is that it is practical. Very few students who take this course go on to become Ph.D.s in economics. Everyone, however, must make economic decisions every day. We all will continue to face the problems of scarcities and, consequently, must continue to make choices.

---

[2] F. Howard, *Buna Rubber* (New York: D. Van Nostrand, 1947), p. 39.

All students will, therefore, find economics useful in their private and professional lives. Students who choose business as a career will find economics particularly helpful. (Students who become doctors or lawyers or who enter other professions are in business also.) A knowledge of economics is extremely important in business decision making if profit is a motivation. For example, one way economics is useful in business is in predicting what the effect will be of an external change that affects the business. What would be the effect of gasoline rationing? A change in the tax laws? Stricter antitrust laws? An increase in the minimum wage? Further, economics is useful in deciding whether or not to expand a business and whether to sell an asset or hold it in anticipation of a future price increase. Decisions concerning whether or not to stay open extra hours or produce additional output are basically economic decisions. The decision whether or not to change jobs is based on economics.

More and more students are going to work in government— federal, state, or local. A knowledge of economics is of great use in many of these occupations. A frequent duty of people who work for all branches of government is to forecast the effect of some action to be taken by the branch of government for which they work. At the local level, for example, what will be the effect of a change in zoning regulations? Stricter pollution standards? Changes in tax rates? Increased urban renewal? At the state level, decisions on allocation of funds between education and highways is of great importance. And what would be the effect of a state minimum wage higher than the federal minimum? At the federal level, economic theory is used when considering the effect of changes in income tax and welfare laws. And, for another example, what would be the effect of stricter enforcement of laws concerning illegal drugs? Economic theory is probably the most important tool used by policymakers in making predictions. Throughout this text, we will develop and apply many of the tools needed to analyze questions relevant to government policymakers.

Many students take positions in nonprofit institutions other than government—in hospitals, universities, and foundations. Since these institutions are greatly affected by economic forces, the decision makers must have a good economic understanding. Because these institutions are not basically motivated by profit does not mean that they must not make decisions based on economic variables. Often times, nonprofit groups work with a fixed budget. Managers desire to maximize the quantity and quality of their service subject to keeping expenditures within their budget. Choices must be made, and economic theory has a good deal to say about the best way to make them.

Finally, a good understanding of economics is important in a person's private life also. Obviously, to be a well-informed citizen and voter, one needs to know economics. But a knowledge of economics is also useful in the private decision-making process. After all, we stressed that economics is the science of decision making; people make decisions in their private lives, as well as in their business lives, based on economic factors. The type of home appliance to install is, in large part, based upon economic variables, such as the interest rate. Economic factors, such as predicted employment opportunities for women, influence the decision of families to have children. This does not, of course, mean that other, noneconomic variables do not affect such decisions, but economic forces play an important part. The decision concerning leaving a job and returning to school in order to train for a different job requires economic analysis, as does the decision to go on to graduate school.

We have barely skimmed the surface, mentioning only a few types of decisions for which economic reasoning is extremely useful in making the correct choice. We will bring up many more examples and actually analyze these problems throughout the entire text. As you increase your expertise in applying economics, in using the tools to make an analysis, you will have the satisfaction of actually solving the problems yourself. It is through practice that you increase your ability to solve problems.

## 1.4 PURPOSE OF THEORY

Since this course is basically concerned with microeconomic theory, we might take the time to explain what theory is. No doubt you have heard statements such as "That's OK in theory, but how about the real world?" The fact is that theory is designed to apply to the real world; it allows us to gain insights into the economy that would otherwise be impossible. We can make predictions from theory that hold in the real world even though theoretical structures abstract from most actual characteristics of the world. Theory is abstraction—a way of simplifying things—its purpose is to make sense out of confusion. The real world is a very complicated place. There are an infinite number of variables that are in continual change. Theory is concerned with knowing which variables are important to the issue at hand and which are not. Theoretical structures allow us to concentrate on a few important forces and ignore the many, many variables that are not important. In other words, when using theory, we ignore the irrelevant.

It is this ability to abstract—to cast aside all factors insignificant to the problem—that allows us to come to grips with the issue at hand without becoming bogged down in unimportant issues. We reach conclusions using very simple assumptions, while ignoring forces that *could* affect the consequences but in all likelihood will not. Not only economists, but people in business, government, and everyday life make predictions using similar principles. With the use of economic theory, we have a more formalized structure, or method of analysis, for handling economic questions.

Using a formal but simple theoretical model, we can answer thousands of questions, such as those noted above. These questions are important both to individuals and governments; and they can be given answers that are *approximately* correct. In carrying out our analysis, we must remember that, while everything depends on everything else, most things depend in an essential way upon only a *few other things*. We usually ignore the general interdependence of everything and concentrate only upon the *close interdependence* of a few variables. If pressed far enough, the price of beef depends not only on the prices of pork and other meats and fowls, but also on the prices of butane, color televisions, and airline tickets. But, as a first approximation, we ignore the prices of butane, TVs, and so on. We temporarily hold *other things constant*, and concentrate our attention on a few closely related variables.

In this text, we adopt that basic approach. We assume that *most*, but not all, of the economic interrelations can be ignored. We analyze our problems and realize that our answers are first approximations. We carry out our analysis from assumptions based on real-world conditions, and then we go through a purely logical analysis. Before we make any definite statements or predictions about the real world, we must go through the interpretation stage. Here, it is necessary to realize that we have held many "other things" constant. Thus, we must conclude that a freeze in Florida, for instance, will *tend* to cause an increase in the price of oranges. If our theory is sound, the answers, even though first approximations, will be qualitatively correct. This is about all one can demand of economic theory. Quantitative results are up to the econometricians; that is, those interested in testing economic theories. This text consists mostly of the theory and applications, but the testing aspect will not be totally ignored.

## 1.5 STRUCTURE OF THE COURSE

We might briefly examine what types of material will and will not be covered in this text. Economic theory is generally divided into two major branches—macroeconomics and microeconomics. Microeconomics, the subject of this book, is concerned with organizing individual behavior, or the behavior of small groups of individuals. Some examples are analyses of the forces that determine the price and the amount of beef consumed by a group of customers, the reasons for a natural gas shortage, why the price of hand calculators has fallen as most other prices have been rising, and why price must increase for firms to be induced to supply more output. Macroeconomics, on the other hand, is concerned with aggregates over the economy as a whole; for example, the total level of unemployment in a society, the rate of inflation, the effect of changing the supply of money in a society, the forces affecting the level of interest rates, per capita rates of consumption, and so on.

By way of contrast, in microeconomics we study the forces that affect relative prices—why the price of oil rises relative to the price of coal, even though both are increasing. Macroeconomics courses analyze why the entire price level, the "cost of living," rises or falls. In this course, we will study the reasons why wage rates in a particular industry change relative to rates in other industries. This contrasts with the macro approach, which analyzes reasons for changes in the wage level for the whole economy. To summarize, we will be concerned with analyzing behavior of individuals and groups of individuals but not the behavior of aggregates in the economy as a whole, such as all households or all businesses. And we will concentrate on the causes and effects of changes in relative prices, knowing that inflation may be causing all prices to rise in a given period.

Typically, a course in microeconomics is divided into three major sectors. This text follows that approach. The first area is the behavior of individual consumers and groups of consumers. Such behavior determines the demand for goods and services. The second major area is the theories of firms and industries. Among these are the theories of production and cost. The behavior of firms and industries determines the supplies of goods and services. The third major area is theories of distribution. In this area, we study the forces that affect the payment to the owners of resources—labor, capital, land, management. The owners of these resources receive wages, salaries, rents, profits, and interest from those firms that purchase the resources.

Sometimes economists simplify the economy by thinking of it as being divided into two sectors: (1) households composed of individuals who purchase and consume commodities produced by the other sector; (2) firms. But the households must have income to purchase the goods and services produced and sold by the firms, which must in turn hire the resources owned by the households if they are to produce the goods. Thus, we can think of the economy as consisting of resource owners who sell their resources to firms in order to attain income with which they buy their consumption goods. This is a rather simplistic view, of course, but one does get from such a view a beginning idea of how the economy functions.

The major factor limiting the amount of goods and services that such a society produces and consumes is the amount of resources in the society available to produce goods and services. Clearly, as either the technology improves or as the resources owned by the society increase, the society can have more of some goods without giving up some other goods. But during any one period of time, the total supply of resources limits the total amount of goods possible; and if the society wishes more of certain things, it must give up some other things that are also desired. Thus, the society experiences scarcity, and scarcity is the subject of study for economists. We shall deal with this concept more completely in Chapter 5 with an analysis of this limit to the amount of goods and services a society can have at any one time, that is, with the production possibilities of the society as a whole.

## 1.6 STYLE OF TEXT

We have tried to make this text as easy to understand as possible. This is not to say that everything you read will be simple. On the contrary, you will encounter some difficult concepts, but in the most understandable fashion.

To help you grasp the important ideas presented in each chapter, we have identified and classified them as *definitions, relations,* or *principles.* Often, these concepts will be listed at the end of a chapter as a summary. They are very important in your study of microeconomics.

You will also encounter sections in each chapter set aside as *applications.* You encountered your first one a few pages ago. The purposes of applications are to emphasize the value of the theory and to stress the importance of the arguments presented just before the application. There is a connection between the real world and the curves and symbols used in abundance throughout this text. Occasionally, an application will even extend the theory in the context of a real-world issue.

Finally, each chapter, except Chapter 1, ends with two sets of problems. The first set falls under the heading of "technical problems." Here, the solutions are generally expressed in quantities or a money unit. They are designed to ensure your understanding of market mechanics. The second set is given the name "analytical problems." These problems are more thought provoking. They are intended to make you apply the theory presented in the chapter in a wide variety of market contexts. These problems you will undoubtedly find the more difficult. You might not be able to answer all of the analytical problems. They are learning tools intended to keep you thinking. We hope you will find them interesting enough to discuss with your fellow students and instructor.

Of course, each chapter, including this one, will conclude with a summary to help you tie things together.

## 1.7 SUMMARY

We emphasized at the beginning of this introductory chapter that economics is the science of decision making. These decisions arise because of this important concept of scarcity. If it were not for scarcity, there would be no problems of economic decision making. No decision about what to produce and what to consume would be necessary. Everyone could have everything desired. But because scarcity does exist, economic decisions are necessary; people make such decisions about production and consumption every day. The study of economics enables us to understand how and why individuals make these decisions. It allows us to predict the consequences of such decisions, and it helps us in actually making better decisions.

We have thus far discussed only the scope and structure of economics. We have mentioned what economics is and what it can do. Now we will begin developing the basic theory and applying that theory to problems. We will show how economists have used theories as simple as those to be developed here to solve interesting, sophisticated, and highly relevant business and social problems. We will be dealing with problems as vast as the pollution question, the conservation of natural resources, and the consequences of an oil embargo. We will also discuss how economics is used in business decision making, and how it is applicable to the decisions of households. There will be many examples of both types.

We should stress that the purely theoretical sections make up a large part of the text and form a self-contained unit. Very little new theoretical material is introduced in the applications. Thus, the applications can even be omitted—they are easily spotted because they are marked off—if one is interested only in theory. But the applications are designed to show how theory is used. They are offered primarily to give you practice in using the theory. After all, in economics, as in mathematics, riding a bike, playing baseball, dancing, speaking a foreign language, and so on, one learns how to do something by actually doing it. If practice doesn't make perfect, it will at least make you better. Finally, the applications are designed to give you some fun, as you become better and better at doing the analysis yourself. At the end of each chapter, you will find some problems that will allow you plenty of practice.

# Chapter 2

# Demand and supply

## 2.1 INTRODUCTION

In Chapter 1, we emphasized that economics is concerned with the problem of scarcity. Goods are scarce because they have alternative uses. Markets evolve to enable exchange to take place. In these markets, goods sell for a price. Therefore, a fundamental task of economics is to analyze the factors that determine the price and purchase of commodities. The more important determinants of price and quantities sold are usually separated into two categories: those affecting the demand for a good and those affecting supply. The purpose of this chapter is to explain what demand and supply are and to show how they determine price and quantity in markets. We shall also show how the concepts of demand and supply can be used to solve problems.

Thomas Carlyle, mentioned in Chapter 1 as the man who gave economics the name "the dismal science," said about economists also, "It is easy to train an economist: teach a parrot to say Demand and Supply." This is another epigram that has survived because it is humorous and contains a certain amount of truth. Demand and supply are, in fact, such important tools of analysis that we will devote several chapters to investigating the underlying forces behind these two concepts. In this chapter, however, we take many of the underlying forces as given in order to discuss what demand and supply are and, more specifically, how they determine prices in markets. We will separately examine the determinants of demand and supply, then put the two together to investigate how they determine price and quantity sold in markets.

The basic concepts to be developed in Chapter 2 are

1.  The determinants of demand and the elasticity of demand.
2.  The determinants of supply and the elasticity of supply.
3.  How price and quantity are determined in the market.
4.  The effect of floor and ceiling prices.
5.  The effect of excise taxes.

## 2.2 INDIVIDUAL AND MARKET DEMAND SCHEDULES

An individual's (or a household's) demand schedule for a specific commodity is the quantity of that commodity the person is willing and able to purchase at each possible price during a particular time period. For example, if someone is willing and could afford to buy during some time period (say, a week), 6 units of a particular item at $6 each, 10 units at $5 each, and 15 units at $4 each, these combinations would be part of the demand schedule for the commodity. Of course, we would have to extend the list of prices upward and downward to get a complete schedule.

Consumers are usually willing and able to buy more at lower prices. Such behavior is so pervasive it is referred to as the *law of demand*. If you doubt the law of demand, try to think of a specific item you would buy in larger amounts if its price were higher. A major reason for the law of demand is that consumers tend to substitute and buy more of the relatively less expensive and fewer of the high-priced goods when prices change. Since considerable portions of Chapters 3 and 4 are devoted to analyzing the law of demand and this "substitution effect," we now simply assume that the following is correct: people are willing and able to buy more at lower than at higher prices.

**Principle.**  An individual's demand schedule is a list of prices and corresponding quantities that an individual is willing and able to buy in some time period. Quantity demanded per time period varies inversely with price.

### Aggregating and graphing demand schedules

Suppose a very large group of people gathers together to buy its weekly supply of some commodity. Suppose also that an auctioneer in the market has all the people turn in a list indicating the amount of the good they are willing and able to purchase that day at each price, $1, $2, $3, $4, $5, $6, and so forth. The auctioneer then adds up the amounts that each person is willing and able to buy at each of the prices and gets the figures shown in Table 2–1. The table shows

**TABLE 2–1**
**Market demand schedule**

| Quantity demanded | Price per unit (dollars) |
| --- | --- |
| 2,000 | 6 |
| 3,000 | 5 |
| 4,000 | 4 |
| 5,000 | 3 |
| 5,500 | 2 |
| 6,000 | 1 |

a list of prices and corresponding quantities that consumers demand per period of time at each price in the list. This list of prices and quantities is called a *market demand schedule*. It is the *sum* of the demand schedules of all the individuals in the market. Again, since people are willing to buy more at lower prices than at higher prices, quantity demanded and price vary inversely in the market.

**Principle.** The market demand schedule is the sum of the quantities that all individual consumers in the market demand at each price. In the market, quantity demanded varies inversely with price.

Some people not particularly well trained in economic reasoning accuse economists of saying that price is the only thing that affects the purchases of consumers. They say economists are not aware of style, taste, and so on, which also influence purchases. This accusation can be concisely stated by using the letter "$f$" for the symbol "function of" or "depends upon." If we let $X$ represent the quantity of a certain good and $P$ its price, then the accusation is that economists think $X$ is only a function of $P$, or

$$X = f(P).$$

This accusation is not really valid. All economists recognize that many forces other than price determine the quantity demanded.

Recall from Chapter 1 that a fundamental analytical method used in economics is to hold all other influences constant and focus attention on one important variable. Economists do not say price is the *sole* influence upon purchases; they do say that price generally has a *very important effect* upon quantity purchased. Therefore, in order to analyze the effect of price, economists hold constant those other variables and concentrate upon the relation between quantity demanded and price—a relation shown by demand curves. In this way, attention can be focused strictly upon the effect of price. But, when using demand curves, you should be aware of the other things that influence quantity demanded but are held constant when deriving demand.

First, a consumer's income affects the amount demanded at any price. For some consumers, an increase in income would cause them to demand more of a particular commodity at a particular price. For other commodities, an increase in income would cause consumers to demand less at some given price. Thus, we generally hold income constant when deriving demand.

Second, the prices of *other* goods must be held constant, because they affect how much of a good is purchased at a given price. For example, suppose both beef and pork sell for $1 a pound; now let the price of beef fall to 50 cents per pound. Consumers would probably buy less pork at $1 a pound when beef is 50 cents than when beef is $1 a pound.

Third, changes in consumers' tastes can affect how much of a good is demanded at a given price. If some influential movie or television stars are photographed wearing a certain style of clothing, consumers who wish to imitate them would probably be willing to buy more of that style at the prevailing price. Since changes in tastes affect the demand for commodities, economists hold tastes constant when deriving demands.

Finally, people's expectations affect demand. When people think the price of a good is going to rise, they have an incentive to increase their rates of purchase before the price rises. On the other hand, expecting prices to fall causes some purchases to be postponed.

Therefore, economists do not believe that quantity demanded is simply a function of price; but, if we let $M$ represent the consumer's income, $\tilde{P}$, the prices of other goods, $T$, tastes, and $V$, expectations, then economists know fully well that

$$X = f(P, M, \tilde{P}, T, V).$$

Moreover, when economists draw up demand schedules such as the one shown in Table 2–1, they do so *ceteris paribus*, or under the assumption that other things remain the same. The other things are, of course, (1) consumer's incomes (and the income distribution among consumers); (2) tastes; (3) the prices of other goods; and (4) expectations. It is not that economists think price is the sole determinant of the quantity that people purchase, but they are interested in *isolating* the effect of price changes.

Quite often, it is more convenient to work with the graph of a demand schedule, called a *demand curve*, rather than with the schedule itself. Figure 2–1 is the graph of the schedule in Table 2–1. Each price-quantity combination ($6–2,000, $5–3,000, and so on) is plotted; then the six points are connected by the curve labeled *DD′*. This curve indicates the quantity of the good consumers are willing and able to buy per unit of time at *every* price from $6 to $1. Since consumers demand more at lower prices, the curve slopes downward.

**FIGURE 2–1**
**Market demand curve**

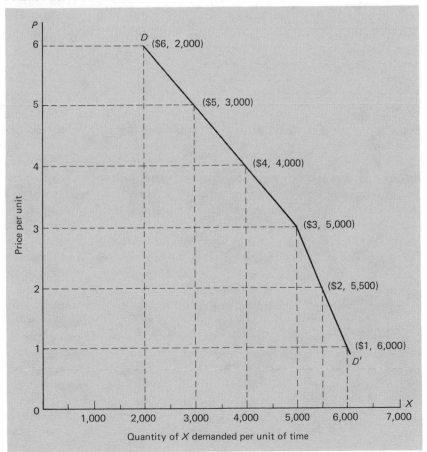

Quantity of *X* demanded per unit of time

Note that, when deriving a demand curve from a set of price-quantity data given by a demand schedule, one assumes that price and quantity are infinitely divisible. Price can be *any* number between $6 and $1; quantity demanded can also be any number. This assumption is not too unrealistic when we consider that the quantity is *per unit of time*. In any case, the sacrifice in realism is more than counterbalanced by the gain in analytical convenience.

We must emphasize that, when drawing market demand curves, we draw them sloping downward to conform with the law of demand. Since individuals are assumed to demand less as price increases, less is demanded in the entire market as price rises. Furthermore, as price increases, some individuals may purchase nothing at all, again causing the quantity demanded to decrease. Whenever we draw a demand curve, price will be on the vertical axis and quantity on the horizontal axis. By convention, the variable on the vertical scale is dependent on the one measured by the horizontal scale, so we have reversed the role of $P$ and $X$ in our $f$ notation above. Technically, the curve in Figure 2–1 is an inverse demand curve. We will continue, however, to refer to it as simply the demand curve.

### Changes in demand

When price falls (rises) and consumers purchase more (less) of a good, other things remaining the same, we say that *quantity demanded* increases (decreases). We do not say that demand increases or decreases when price changes. Recall that demand is a *list* of prices and quantity demanded at each price on the list.

Demand increases or decreases only if one or more of the factors held constant when deriving demand changes. For example, if incomes of consumers change, causing them to demand more of a good at each price than they did previously, the demand for that good increases. If the change in income causes consumers to demand less of a good than they did before at each price, then demand decreases.

Figure 2–2 illustrates changes in demand. Assume that the demand curve for a good is at first $D_0D'_0$; at a price of $12 per unit, consumers purchase 2,100 units per period of time. If price falls to $8, *quantity demanded* increases to 2,500 units. Now, begin with demand at $D_0D'_0$ and a price of $12. Assume that tastes change and demand decreases (shift to the left) to $D_1D'_1$. Now consumers demand only 1,000 units per period of time at the price $12. In fact, it is easy to see that, at every price, consumers are willing and able to buy less of the good after the shift than before. This shows a *decrease in demand*. Now, let something previously held constant

**FIGURE 2–2**
**Shifts in demand**

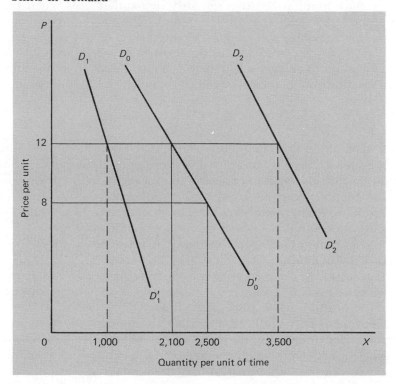

change, causing demand to increase (shift to the right) to $D_2D'_2$. At
$12, consumers purchase 3,500 units per period; and at every other
relevant price they buy more than before. This shows an *increase in
demand.* It is worthwhile to repeat, if demand is $D_0D'_0$ and price
falls from $12 to $8, other things remaining the same, we say that
*quantity demanded* changes from 2,100 to 2,500. These relations
may be summarized as follows:

**Relation.**   When price falls (rises), other things remaining the same, quantity demanded rises (falls). When a factor held constant in deriving the
demand curve changes, demand increases or decreases. An increase
in demand indicates consumers are willing and able to buy more at
each price in the list. A decrease in demand indicates they are willing
and able to buy less at each price. Changes in demand are represented by shifts in the demand curve; changes in quantity demanded are shown by movements along the original demand curve.
Do not confuse changes in quantity demanded with increases or decreases in demand.

## 2.3 DEMAND ELASTICITY

We have emphasized that quantity demanded rises when price falls, and vice versa—the law of demand. Those who use economics in decision making are frequently interested in the shape of the demand schedule, because this determines how total expenditures on a commodity change when there is a movement along the curve. Total expenditure or total revenue $(R)$ is simply price times quantity demanded, or

$$R = P \cdot X.$$

Note that, along a demand curve such as the one shown in Figure 2-1, $P$ and $X$ move in opposite directions and, consequently, have offsetting effects on $R$. For example, an increase in price alone would tend to increase expenditures, whereas the resulting decrease in quantity would tend to decrease expenditures. Thus, we would assume that the effect on total expenditure depends upon which force dominates, the increase in price or the decrease in quantity demanded.

The change in price dominates if the percentage increase in price exceeds the percentage decrease in quantity demanded; in this case, total expenditure rises. Total expenditure falls, however, if the percentage increase in price is less than the percentage decrease in quantity demanded. Similarly, if the percentage decrease in price exceeds (is less than) the percentage increase in quantity demanded, total expenditure falls (rises). We see, then, that the effect of a price change depends upon the relative sensitivity of quantity demanded to price along a demand curve. The measure of this relative sensitivity along a given demand curve is called the *elasticity of demand.*

This concept is of great interest to both economists and business decision makers. Obviously, in business, one would like to know the effect of a change in price on sales revenue and what determines such an effect. For some products, a small change in price over a certain range of the demand curve results in a significant change in quantity demanded. In this case, quantity demanded is very responsive to changes in price, and the total revenue collected by a seller falls when price increases. For other products, or perhaps for the same product over a different range of the demand curve, a relatively large change in price leads to a correspondingly smaller change in quantity demanded. That is, quantity demanded is not particularly responsive to price changes.

A graph can help us visualize how price and quantity interact to determine the effect on total revenue of a movement along the demand curve. In Figure 2–3, suppose a seller sets a price of $p_0$, sells quantity $x_0$, and then raises price to $p_1$. As shown, the quantity sold

**FIGURE 2–3**
**Change in revenue from a price increase**

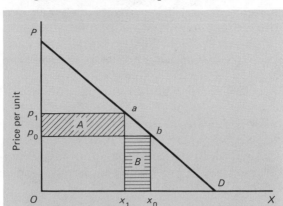

Quantity of $X$ per unit of time

falls to $x_1$. Before the price change, revenue or total expenditure on the seller's commodity was

$$R_0 = p_0 x_0 = \text{area } Op_0 bx_0.$$

After the price change, it became

$$R_1 = p_1 x_1 = \text{area } Op_1 ax_1.$$

The difference in revenue is easily seen to be the difference between shaded areas $A$ and $B$ in Figure 2–3. For a price increase, total revenue rises if area $A$ is greater than area $B$; it falls if area $A$ is less than area $B$; and stays the same if area $A$ equals area $B$.

Economists have a precise way of classifying demand according to the responsiveness of quantity demanded to a price change and the effect of changes in price on total expenditure. They classify demand as elastic or inelastic according to its degree of responsiveness. More specifically, demand is said to be elastic if revenue falls with a price increase and rises with a price decrease; it is inelastic if total revenue rises with a price increase and falls with a price decrease.

Thus, we can talk about changes in total revenue or total expenditure in response to changes in price through the concepts of demand elasticity or inelasticity. First, suppose the price change "outweighs" the quantity change in terms of percent; that is, quantity demanded is not particularly responsive to price. In this case, when price rises and quantity falls, total expenditure increases. Demand is said to be inelastic. If price decreases and quantity demand increases under the inelastic demand, total expenditure falls. On the other hand, if demand is elastic, the percentage change in quantity demanded exceeds the percentage change in price. In this case, when price rises and quantity falls, total revenue falls because of the greater quantity effect. Clearly, a price decrease leads to an increase in quantity demanded, and, with an elastic demand, total revenue rises.

Finally, we classify a demand as having unitary elasticity when the percentage change in price is exactly offset by the percentage change in quantity demanded. In this case, a change in price results in no change in total expenditure. All of these relations are summarized in Table 2–2. In the table the terms $|\% \Delta P|$ and $|\% \Delta X|$ are the absolute values of the percentage changes in price and quantity. The $\Delta$ symbol means "the change in."

**TABLE 2–2**
**Relations between demand elasticity and total expenditure ($TE$)**

|  | Elastic demand $\|\%\Delta X\| > \|\%\Delta P\|$ | Unitary elasticity $\|\%\Delta X\| = \|\%\Delta P\|$ | Inelastic demand $\|\%\Delta X\| < \|\%\Delta P\|$ |
|---|---|---|---|
| Price rises ................. | $TE$ falls | No change in $TE$ | $TE$ rises |
| Price falls ................. | $TE$ rises | No change in $TE$ | $TE$ falls |

**Computation of elasticity**

We have thus far talked of elasticity and inelasticity only in very general terms. It is useful, at times, to have a specific measure of relative responsiveness rather than merely speaking of demand as being elastic or inelastic. We should emphasize, however, that it is not accurate to say that a given demand curve is elastic or inelastic. In many cases, demand curves have both an inelastic and an elastic range, along with a point or range of unitary elasticity. We can only speak of demand as being elastic or inelastic over a particular range of price or quantity magnitudes. We might wish to determine, over a certain range of prices, which of two demand curves is more elastic. For this we need a measuring device. That device is the coefficient of price elasticity ($E$):

$$E = -\%\Delta X / \%\Delta P = -\frac{\Delta X/X}{\Delta P/P} = -\frac{\Delta X}{\Delta P} \cdot \frac{P}{X},$$

where $\Delta$ is "the change in," and $P$ and $X$ denote price and quantity demanded.

Since price and quantity vary inversely, a minus sign is used in the formula to make the coefficient positive. From the formula, we see that the relative responsiveness of quantity demanded to changes in price measures the ratio of the proportional change in quantity demanded relative to that of price. If $E$ is less than one, demand is inelastic, $|\%\Delta X| < |\%\Delta P|$. If $E$ is greater than one, demand is elastic, $|\%\Delta X| > |\%\Delta P|$. If $E = 1$, demand has unitary elasticity, $|\%\Delta X| = |\%\Delta P|$.

We can return to Figure 2–3 and show that, for a price increase, if total expenditure goes up, then demand is truly inelastic. If total revenue rises in Figure 2–3, then area $A$ > area $B$ or

$$x_1 \cdot (p_1 - p_0) > p_0 \cdot (x_0 - x_1),$$

and, using the $\Delta$ sign again, this means

$$x_1 \Delta p > p_0 \Delta x.$$

Dividing the right side by the left side gives

$$1 > \frac{\Delta x}{\Delta p} \cdot \frac{p_0}{x_1} = E.$$

Indeed, when total expenditures rise, demand elasticity is less than one. If total revenue goes down, then we reverse the inequality; area $A$ < area $B$, and

$$x_1 \Delta p < p_0 \Delta x.$$

Again, dividing the right side by the left side

$$1 < \frac{\Delta x}{\Delta p} \cdot \frac{p_0}{x_1} = E.$$

So demand elasticity is greater than one when total revenue falls for a price increase. It is left as an exercise for the student to show $E = 1$ when area $A$ = area $B$.

The process of deriving the coefficient of elasticity between two price-quantity relations involves a simple computation; certain problems, however, are involved in selecting the proper base. As an example, let us consider the demand schedule given in Table 2–3. Suppose price falls from $1 to 50 cents; quantity demanded rises

**TABLE 2–3**
**Demand and elasticity**

| Price | Quantity demanded | Total expenditure | Elasticity |
|---|---|---|---|
| $1.00 . . . . . . . . . . . . . . | 100,000 | $100,000 | ELASTIC |
| .50 . . . . . . . . . . . . . . | 300,000 | 150,000 | UNITARY |
| .25 . . . . . . . . . . . . . . | 600,000 | 150,000 | INELASTIC |
| .10 . . . . . . . . . . . . . . | 1,000,000 | 100,000 | |

from 100,000 to 300,000 and $P \cdot X$ or $TE$ rises to $150,000. By the above analysis, demand is elastic since total expenditure increases.

Let us now compute $E$:

$$E = -\frac{\Delta X/X}{\Delta P/P} = -\frac{(100{,}000 - 300{,}000) \div 100{,}000}{(\$1 - \$0.50) \div \$1} = -\frac{-2}{1/2} = 4.$$

As expected, the coefficient is greater than one. But some caution must be exercised. $\Delta X$ and $\Delta P$ are definitely known from Table 2–3, but we really do not know whether to use the value $X = 100{,}000$ or $X = 300{,}000$ and the value $P = \$1$ or $P = \$0.50$. There are four combinations of $P$s and $X$s we might use, all giving a different $E$. Try the computation with $P = .50$ and $X = 300{,}000$:

$$E = -\frac{(300{,}000 - 100{,}000) \div 300{,}000}{(\$0.50 - \$1) \div \$0.50} = \frac{2}{3}.$$

It actually looks as though demand is inelastic, despite the fact that we know it is elastic from the total expenditure calculation.

The difficulty lies in the fact that elasticity has been computed over a wide arc of the demand curve but evaluated at a specific point. We can get a much better approximation by using the *average* values of $P$ and $X$ over the arc. That is, for large changes such as this, we should compute elasticity using the "arc formula." Arc elasticity $\overline{E}$ is

$$\overline{E} = -\frac{X_1 - X_0}{(X_1 + X_2)/2} \div \frac{P_1 - P_0}{(P_1 + P_0)/2} = -\frac{X_1 - X_0}{X_1 + X_0} \div \frac{P_1 - P_0}{P_1 + P_0},$$

where subscripts 0 and 1 refer to the initial and the new prices and quantities demanded. Using this formula, we obtain

$$\overline{E} = -\frac{(100{,}000 - 300{,}000) \div (100{,}000 + 300{,}000)}{(\$1 - \$0.50) \div (\$1 + \$0.50)} = \frac{3}{2}.$$

Demand is indeed elastic when allowance is made for the very discrete or finite change in price and quantity demanded.

**Principle.**  Demand is said to be elastic, of unitary elasticity, or inelastic according to the value of $E$. If $E > 1$, demand is elastic; a given percentage change in price results in a greater percentage change in quantity demanded. Thus, small price changes result in more significant changes in quantity demanded. When $E = 1$, demand has unit elasticity, meaning that the percentage changes in price and quantity demanded are precisely the same. Finally, if $E < 1$, demand is inelastic. A given percentage change in price results in a smaller percentage change in quantity demanded.

## Graphical computation of elasticity

The formulas developed above are not conducive to comparing the relative elasticity of two demand curves; neither do they permit us to estimate price elasticity by a visual inspection of the demand curve. A graphical computation of point elasticity allows us to judge immediately the relative price sensitivity of two schedules and provides us with a way of estimating elasticity at any point on a curve.

First, consider the case of a linear demand curve such as that shown in Figure 2–4. The point elasticity at any price and quantity, such as $P$ and $X$ at point $B$, can be computed as the ratio of $XC/OX$, or $OP/AP$. These ratios are both estimates of the elasticity at a point for very small changes in price and quantity, and each proves useful in different contexts.

It is not difficult to show that these ratios do measure the elasticity of the demand curve in Figure 2–4 at point $B$. Recall that $E = \Delta X/\Delta P \cdot P/X$. The ratio $P/X$ is geometrically $OP/OX$, but, since $OX = PB$, $P/X = OP/PB$. The slope of the demand curve is $\Delta P/\Delta X$, just the inverse of $\Delta X/\Delta P$. Referring to Figure 2–4, $\Delta P/\Delta X = AP/PB$, so $\Delta X/\Delta P = PB/AP$. Therefore,

$$E = \frac{\Delta X}{\Delta P} \cdot \frac{P}{X} = \frac{PB}{AP} \cdot \frac{OP}{PB} = \frac{OP}{AP}.$$

Similarly, since we may also write $OP = BX$, $OP/OX = BX/OX$ and the slope $\Delta P/\Delta X = BX/XC$, giving

$$E = \frac{\Delta X}{\Delta P} \cdot \frac{P}{X} = \frac{XC}{BX} \cdot \frac{BX}{OX} = \frac{XC}{OX}.$$

**FIGURE 2–4**
**Estimation of point elasticity**

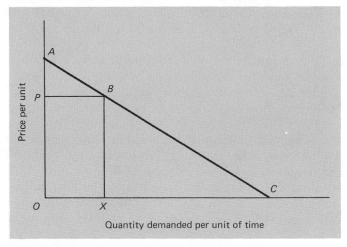

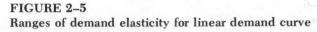

**FIGURE 2–5**
**Ranges of demand elasticity for linear demand curve**

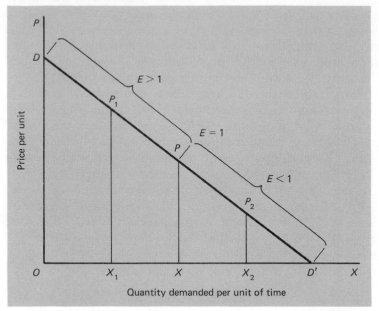

Quantity demanded per unit of time

Thus, we can locate a point on $DD'$, the linear demand curve in Figure 2–5, such that $OX = XD'$; at the midpoint of a linear curve, demand has unitary price elasticity, or $E = 1$. Next, consider any point to the left of $X$ such as $X_1$. At $X_1$, $E = X_1D'/OX_1 > 1$. Thus, the coefficient of price elasticity is greater than unity at any point to the left of $X$. Finally, at any point to the right of $X$, say $X_2$, the coefficient of price elasticity is $E = X_2D'/OX_2 < 1$. Over this range, demand is inelastic. These observations deserve to be highlighted:

**Relation.** For a linear demand curve: (a) demand is elastic at higher prices, (b) has unit elasticity at the midpoint, and (c) is inelastic at lower prices. Thus, in the case of linear demand, elasticity declines as one moves downward along the curve.

When demand is not linear, such as the case of $DD'$ in Figure 2–6, we can easily approximate point elasticity in the following manner. Suppose we want to compute the elasticity of $DD'$ at point $R$. First, draw the straight line $AB$ tangent to $DD'$ at $R$. For very small movements away from $R$ along $DD'$, the slope of $AB$ is a relatively good estimate of the slope of $DD'$. Hence, we may esti-

**FIGURE 2–6**
**Computation of point elasticity for nonlinear demand curve**

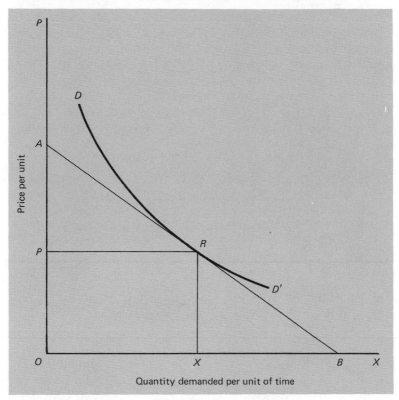

mate the elasticity at $R$ by using either of the above elasticity ratios

$$E = \frac{XB}{OX} = \frac{OP}{AP}$$

These formulas also help us compare the relative elasticities of two or more demand schedules. Figure 2–7 illustrates two intersecting demand curves. To intersect, they must have different slopes. While elasticity is not the same as slope, it is possible to show, in this example, that the demand curve with the higher magnitude of slope is more inelastic. It is a straightforward application of the geometric ratios for elasticity. By applying either formula, $D_1D_1'$ is more inelastic at $P_0$ than is $D_2D_2'$.

The curves in Figure 2–8 do not intersect. By now, observation should tell us which curve is more elastic. At price $P_0$, for $D_1D_1'$, $E_1 = OP_0/P_0D_1$, but for $D_2D_2'$, $E_2 = OP_0/P_0D_2$. The numerators are equal

**FIGURE 2–7**
**Relative elasticities of two intersecting
demand curves**

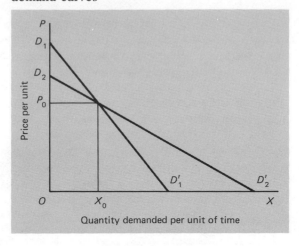

Quantity demanded per unit of time

**FIGURE 2–8**
**Relative elasticities of two nonintersecting
demand curves**

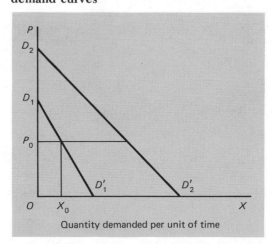

Quantity demanded per unit of time

for both ratios, but the denominator is smaller for $D_1D_1'$. Hence, at any given price $D_1D_1'$ is the more elastic schedule. That is, $E_1 > E_2$. As long as linear schedules do not share the same endpoints, the curve with the smaller quantity demanded at every price has the greater elasticity at any given price.

These results may be·summarized by the following principle:

**Principle.**   Slope is not elasticity. Demand curves with different slopes
may have the same elasticity at any price, while curves with the same
slope may have different elasticities.

### Factors affecting demand elasticity

Whether demand is elastic or inelastic is an important consideration in making government policy and business decisions. For example, suppose the demand for wheat is elastic. An increase in the
price of wheat would accordingly result in a proportionately greater
reduction in quantity demanded. Farmers would thus obtain
smaller total revenue from the sale of wheat. Now, suppose the
government establishes a minimum wheat price above the market
equilibrium price. Wheat sales would be reduced, as would farmers' incomes, unless the price support were accompanied by a minimum sales guarantee. On the other hand, if the demand for wheat is
inelastic, as it probably is over the relevant range, a minimum price
above the equilibrium price would increase farmers' total revenue.

Price elasticities can take a wide range of values. For any given
demand curve, two basic factors determine price elasticity: the
availability of good substitutes and the time period of adjustment.
These factors are related because, the longer the time period of
adjustment, the more time consumers have to shop around for suitable substitutes in the event of a price increase. If the adjustment
period is sufficiently long, substitutes can even be developed when
none were present earlier. These two factors are discussed in turn.

The more and better the substitutes for a specific good, the
greater its price elasticity will be at a given set of prices. Goods with
few and poor substitutes—wheat and salt, for example—will always
tend to have low price elasticities. Goods with many substitutes—
wool, for which cotton and man-made fibers may be substituted, for
instance—will have higher elasticities.

Substitutability implies that there is a great deal of difference
between the market elasticity of demand for a good and the elasticity of demand faced by one seller in the market. For example, if all
of the gasoline stations in a city raised the price of gasoline 5 cents a
gallon, the total sales would undoubtedly fall off some but, in the
absence of close substitutes, probably not much. If all of the Gulf
stations—but no others—raised the price a nickel, the sales of Gulf
gasoline would probably fall substantially. There are many good
substitutes for Gulf gasoline at the lower price. If one service station
alone raised price, its sales in the long run would probably fall
almost to zero. Some might continue buying there, perhaps the

owner's wife and mother, but the availability of so many easily accessible substitutes would encourage most customers to trade elsewhere, since the cost of finding a substitute service station is so small.

Finally, we should discuss to some extent the effect of time upon the demand for a commodity. To illustrate, let us consider the following application: the deregulation of natural gas. There is pressure in Congress to deregulate the price of gas piped across state lines. Prices for an average cubic foot of natural gas would increase. What predictions would you make, using your knowledge of demand theory and information about the real world, about the effect of such a change upon the quantity of natural gas demanded immediately after deregulation, a few years afterward, and in a rather long period of time, say a decade or two?

We examine first the very near future, say within a year after deregulation. Our theory says that, when the price of something increases, people demand less. But, in most cases, people already have their gas-using appliances installed. Manufacturing plants that use gas are already built. But some can still change rapidly. In the last 10 years, many industrial and utility boilers have, in fact, been designed so as to be able to use two fuels interchangeably. One of the two is always gas; the other is either coal or oil. These utilities could change from gas to coal rapidly. Furthermore, even during a very short period of adjustment, people will respond by decreasing somewhat the temperature setting in their homes. This decreases the gas usage to some extent. Possibly, those who use gas to heat water can decrease the use of hot water somewhat. But the point is that, over a fairly short period, the use of natural gas will not be particularly responsive to the increase in price, even though the use will be somewhat responsive. For the most part, however, people do not suddenly change from gas to electricity in response to a reasonably small increase in prices. Consumers are rather limited in their form of adaptation. While people do respond to some extent, demand is rather inelastic when the time period of adjustment is short.

Given a longer period of adjustment, users of natural gas can decrease consumption even more. Builders of new homes can insulate better. People can increase the insulation in older homes; they can install storm windows. Businesses can find alternative fuels. An even longer period of time results in gas appliances wearing out and substitution being made where it is economically feasible. In summary, if people think the price increase is permanent, the longer the time period in which consumers have to adapt to a price change, the more elastic is the demand for the product. This adaptation can be in response to a price increase or a price decrease.

---

## APPLICATION

### Some uses of demand elasticities

Many important business and policy decisions require the estimation of demand elasticities. This application shows the value of such estimates.

One obvious use of demand elasticity in decision making is forecasting changes in price from projected changes in quantity, or changes in quantity from projected changes in price. For example, the Japanese government, at the request of the U.S. government, has put a limit on the number of automobiles it will export to the United States. Certainly governmental policymakers would wish to know the effect of the decreased imports upon price. Suppose the best estimate of the elasticity of demand for automobiles is approximately 1.5—a 1 percent increase in price leads to a 1.5 percent fall in quantity purchased. The expected percentage reduction from voluntary import restrictions is 9 percent. Assuming American manufacturers do not make up the difference, what is the expected increase in the average price of automobiles? Using our definition of elasticity

$$E = -\frac{\%\Delta X}{\%\Delta P},$$

we can solve for

$$\%\Delta P = -\frac{\%\Delta X}{E} = \frac{.09}{1.5} \cong .06,$$

where the sign $\cong$ means "approximately equal to." This indicates that a 6 percent increase in price from the 9 percent reduction in the number of new automobiles sold each year. We know that American manufacturers will attempt to increase sales, so the 6 percent hike in real prices is an upper bound. The change in prices may be negligible if Americans view domestically built automobiles as good substitutes for Japanese imports.

Another example from the automobile industry involves the neglect of demand elasticities to the detriment of government policy. In the spring of 1977, President Jimmy Carter during a speech to the nation released his plan to conserve energy. There were several points, but one of the more important was a large tax on the purchase of "gas guzzlers," automobiles that had rather low miles-per-gallon ratings, this to be combined with a subsidy on the purchase of new automobiles that had miles-per-gallon ratings higher than a particular level. The plan was designed to raise the price of gas guzzlers and lower the price of small cars that were gas efficient.

This would, in the long run, effectively increase the average gasoline mileage of automobiles being driven in the United States. This increase in average mileage would, it was alleged, decrease gasoline consumption in the country over the long run.

No one questioned this postulated effect for some time. The major argument was about the effect on the automobile industry. But most analysts had neglected the effect of demand elasticity on automobile sales.

In an article appearing in the May 23, 1977, issue of the *National Observer,* it was pointed out that, when relative demand elasticities are taken into account, the heavy tax on large cars combined with the subsidy on small cars may cause *more rather than less* gasoline to be consumed even though the tax-subsidy scheme would increase the average gasoline mileage of cars on the road.

This article pointed out several problems with the program, most of which we shall neglect here. The principal argument was based upon the difference in demand elasticities for small cars and large cars. First, it was pointed out that most studies indicated that the demand for large, gas-inefficient cars was relatively inelastic. But studies also showed that the demand for small, gas-efficient cars was relatively elastic.

If this is the case, people would, in response to the higher price, decrease their purchases of larger cars as is predicted by demand theory. But potential Cadillac or Lincoln purchasers would not move all the way to Toyotas or Pintos. They may step down a little in response to higher prices caused by taxes. But, if the demand for the large cars is not very elastic, even inelastic, the purchase of the larger cars would not fall much.

On the other hand, the subsidy on smaller cars would tend to lower their prices. If the demand for small cars is rather elastic, this lower price would cause a rather substantial increase in the purchase of small cars. People would perhaps be induced by the lower price to buy a second car. Some who previously used public transportation would be marginally induced to buy a car.

Thus, if the sales of the "gas guzzlers" did not fall much while the sales of small cars increased significantly, the *number* of cars on the road might well increase even though the average gas mileage increased. Thus, more cars being driven, even with higher gas mileages, might well, it was predicted, *increase rather than decrease the total gasoline consumption.*

The question is, of course, an empirical one. The point we want to make here, however, is that the difference in relative demand elasticities should have at least been considered. That difference could make a policy designed to have one effect, conserving gasoline, have an entirely different effect, increasing the use of gasoline.

A third example of the use of demand elasticity comes from a recent court case. The case involved a very large brick-making firm in Texas and the Internal Revenue Service. The brick maker owned a very large deposit of extremely fine clay, which it used to make bricks. This type of clay, which was of much better quality than that ordinarily used for brick-making, also served as the primary ingredient for ceramic goods. However, the brick-making firm did not sell the clay on the market but rather used it as an ingredient in bricks. A problem for the IRS was determining what should be the permitted price of the clay for tax purposes. Since none of the clay was sold at any price, the market price had to be estimated. The estimated price would determine the profitability of the firm and, consequently, the taxes it paid.

The firm in question used, for tax purposes, the average price of similar clay sold by other firms for use in ceramics. The IRS challenged their deduction on the following grounds: over the years in question, the amount of clay used by the brick-making firm was large enough that, had it been marketed in the Southwest, the price of that type of clay would have been significantly lowered. The answer centered around two figures: the amount of clay used by the brick-making firm relative to the total amount of that type of clay sold in the Southwest and the elasticity of demand for the clay.

The firm commissioned an elasticity study, and the judge used the results in making the decision. The elasticity of demand was estimated as approximately 1. Had the brick maker sold its clay in the market, the amount of clay marketed in the Southwest would have increased by 20 percent, indicating a 20 percent reduction in price. But the attorneys for the firm argued that the transportion advantages that the Texas firm would have had over the other firms that sold in the area—they were located primarily in Tennessee and Kentucky—would have given it a cost advantage that would have offset the reduced price. That is, the increase in quantity would have displaced some of the other clay sold and price would not have been significantly affected. The judge ruled that, while a 20 percent increase in quantity would have reduced the price by 20 percent, the transportation saving would have offset this reduction and the market price was the relevant price for the purpose of taxation.

## 2.4 SUPPLY SCHEDULES

To gain an understanding of supply, suppose a large number of farmers sell cabbage in the same market. One particular farmer is willing to grow and sell 1,000 cabbages per season if the price per head of cabbage is 25 cents. If the price of cabbage was 35 cents, he would be willing to grow more, say, 2,000 heads. The higher price induces the farmer to take land out of the cultivation of other crops and put it into the cultivation of the now relatively more lucrative cabbage. A still higher price, 50 cents perhaps, would be required to induce him to market 3,000 cabbages, and so on. That is, the farmer allocates time and land so as to make as much money as possible. Higher and higher prices are required to induce him to reallocate more and more time and land to cabbage production.

A portion of the farmer's cabbage supply schedule might, therefore, be as follows:

| Price | Quantity supplied |
|-------|-------------------|
| $0.25 | 1,000 |
| .35 | 2,000 |
| .50 | 3,000 |
| .75 | 4,000 |
| 1.25 | 5,000 |

This schedule shows the *minimum price* that induces the farmer to supply each amount on the list. Note that, in contrast to demand analysis, price and quantity supplied are directly related. We must postpone the explanation of why price and quantity vary directly until Chapter 8, after we have analyzed cost and production. For the present, we assume that the supply schedule shows the minimum price necessary to induce producers voluntarily to offer each possible quantity for sale. We also assume that an increase in price is required to induce an increase in quantity supplied.

Just as the market demand schedule is the sum of the quantities demanded by all consumers, the market supply schedule shows the sum of the quantities that suppliers (firms) would supply at each price. If all cabbage farmers had the same supply schedule as that shown in the above table and there were 10,000 cabbage farmers, then 10 million heads would be supplied at 25 cents, 20 million at 35 cents, and so on. Thus, our definition of supply is analogous to that of demand.

**Definition.** Supply is a list of prices and the quantities that a supplier or group of suppliers (firms) would be willing and able to offer for sale at each price in the list per period of time.

### Graphing supply schedules

Consider the supply schedule in Table 2–4. This table shows the minimum price necessary to induce firms to supply, per unit of time, each of the six quantities listed. In order to induce greater

**TABLE 2–4**
**Market supply schedule**

| Quantity supplied (units) | Prices (dollars) |
|---|---|
| 7,000 | 6 |
| 6,500 | 5 |
| 6,000 | 4 |
| 5,000 | 3 |
| 4,000 | 2 |
| 3,000 | 1 |

quantities, price must rise; or, in other words, if price increases from $4 to $5, firms will increase quantity supplied from 6,000 units to 6,500 units. Remember that we are assuming a large number of competing firms; in the case of a single firm supplying the entire market, a different principle applies (as shown in Chapter 9). Figure 2–9 shows a graph of the schedule in Table 2–4.

**FIGURE 2–9**
**Market supply curve**

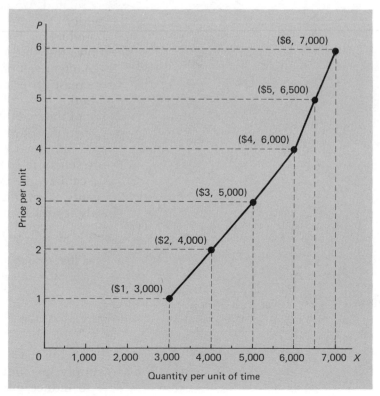

## Factors influencing supply

As in the case of demand, we might ask why the supply schedule in Table 2–4 is what it is. Why, for example, does a price of $5 rather than a price of $4 induce a quantity supplied of 6,500? Or why is not a lower quantity supplied at each price in the list? A much more thorough discussion of supply is undertaken in Chapter 8. For now, we will only mention briefly four factors that affect supply. These are the factors generally held constant when drawing a supply curve.

First, technology is assumed to be unchanged. If a more efficient method of production is discovered, firms generally change the amounts they are willing to supply at each price. Second, the prices of factors of production are usually held constant. For example, a change in wage rates or in the prices of raw materials will change the supply curve. Third, the prices of related goods (in production) are held constant. If the price of corn rises while the price of wheat

**FIGURE 2–10**
**Shifts in supply**

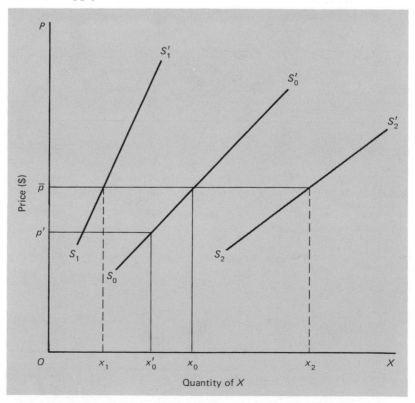

Quantity of X

remains the same, some farmers will switch from growing wheat to growing corn, and less wheat will be supplied. Fourth, the expectations of producers are assumed not to change.

## Changes in supply

When price rises and firms are induced to offer a greater quantity of a good for sale, we say *quantity supplied* increases. When one or more of the factors mentioned above change, firms are induced to offer more or less at each price in the schedule; in this case, we say supply changes. Consider Figure 2–10 in which $S_0S'_0$ is the initial supply curve. If price falls from $\bar{p}$ to $p'$, the quantity supplied decreases from $x_0$ to $x_0'$, other things remaining the same. If technology changes and supply consequently changes from $S_0S'_0$, to $S_2S'_2$, we say supply increases. Firms now wish to offer $x_2$ at price $\bar{p}$, and they wish to offer more units for sale at each price in the entire range of prices. A movement from $S_0S'_0$ to $S_1S'_1$ indicates a decrease in supply. Firms then wish to offer less for sale at each price in the range.

**Relation.** When price rises (falls), other things remaining the same, quantity supplied rises (falls). When something held constant in deriving supply changes, for example the prices of inputs, supply increases or decreases. If firms are induced to offer more (less) at each price, supply has increased (decreased).

## 2.5 SUPPLY ELASTICITY

As is the case for demand, the coefficient of supply elasticity measures the relative responsiveness of quantity supplied to changes in price *along a given supply schedule*. The computation technique is essentially the same as that used for demand elasticity.

## Computation

The coefficient of supply elasticity is defined as

$$E_s = \frac{\Delta X/X}{\Delta P/P} = \frac{\Delta X}{\Delta P} \cdot \frac{P}{X},$$

where $\Delta X$ is the change in quantity supplied, $\Delta P$ is the change in price, and $P$ and $X$ are price and quantity supplied. Since $X$ and $P$ are assumed to change in the same direction, the coefficient is positive. One can use an averaging technique like that discussed for demand, when the changes are discrete; that is, when differences in the bases used affect $E_s$.

If the percentage change in quantity supplied exceeds the percentage change in price, supply is elastic and $E_s > 1$. If the two percentages are equal, supply has unitary elasticity and $E_s = 1$. If the percentage change in price exceeds the percentage change in quantity, supply is inelastic and $E_s < 1$. Therefore, the more elastic is supply, the more responsive is quantity supplied to price changes. Note, however, that, in contrast to demand, we cannot relate supply elasticity to positive or negative changes in total dollar value supplied; that is, changes in price times quantity supplied at that price. Since price and quantity vary directly, an increase in price increases quantity supplied and, hence, increases the dollar value of quantity supplied whether supply is elastic or inelastic. A fall in price likewise decreases the dollar value of quantity supplied.

Geometrically, it is possible to tell whether a supply curve at a certain point is elastic, inelastic, or unitary at a glance. Consider the curve in Figure 2–11, with points $e, f$, and $g$ along with the corre-

**FIGURE 2–11**
**Calculating the elasticity of supply**

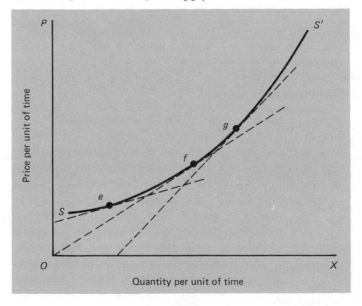

sponding tangent lines. Each of the tangent lines is of the form $P = aX + b$.

For such simple linear forms, we know that the slope, $\Delta P / \Delta X$, is "$a$" and the intercept is "$b$." We also know that, if we divide both sides of the linear equation by $X$, then

$$\frac{P}{X} = a + \frac{b}{X}.$$

Since the elasticity of the supply curve at each point approximately equals the elasticity of the tangent at that point, this information helps us determine the elasticity of a supply curve. Observe for $a > 0$:

$$E_s = \frac{\Delta X}{\Delta P} \frac{P}{X} = \frac{1}{\Delta P/\Delta X} \frac{P}{X} = \frac{1}{a}\left(a + \frac{b}{X}\right) = 1 + \frac{b}{aX}.$$

At point $e$ in Figure 2–11, $b > 0$, thus $E_s = 1 + b/aX > 0$ and the supply curve is elastic. More generally, if the tangent at a point intercepts the vertical axis, supply is elastic at that point. If we knew "$a$" and "$b$", we could even estimate the elasticity. At point $f$, $b = 0$; so $E_s = 1$. If the tangent line goes through the origin, the elasticity of supply is unitary. Finally, at point $g$, $b < 0$ for the tangent line and $E_s < 1$. A tangent cutting the horizontal axis means the supply curve is inelastic. These results are captured in the following principle:

**Principle.** For any point on a supply curve, if the tangent line intersects the vertical axis, supply is elastic at that point; if it passes through the origin, it is unitary; and if it cuts the horizontal axis, supply is inelastic.

### Determinants of supply elasticity

The responsiveness of quantity supplied to changes in price depends, in very large measure, upon the ease with which resources can be drawn into the production of the good in question, in case of a price increase, or withdrawn from production of that good and attracted into production of other goods, in case of a price decrease. If additional quantities can be produced only at much higher costs, then a very large increase in price is needed to induce more quantity supplied. In these cases, supply is rather inelastic. On the other hand, if more can be produced at a very small increase in cost, quantity supplied is quite responsive to price changes, and supply is rather elastic. To summarize, suppose the price of a particular good increases. If the resources used to produce that good are readily accessible without increasing their prices much, and if production can physically be increased easily, supply is more elastic than if the opposite is the case; that is, supply would be less elastic if the additional resources are obtainable only at rapidly increasing prices. For a price decrease, elasticity depends upon how rapidly resources can be released from production of the good in question and moved into the production of other goods.

One can also think of the elasticity of the supply of persons to an occupation. For some occupations, a small increase in the average wage or salary induces rapid entry into that occupation. Thus, supply is elastic if entry is easy. For other occupations, the supply is more inelastic because entry is induced only at a much higher wage.

Possibly, it is difficult to train for the occupation. In any case, the elasticity of persons to an occupation depends upon how easily people can enter the occupation after a wage increase and how willing they are to enter that occupation. In the case of wage decreases, elasticity depends upon how rapidly people leave the occupation.

As you have probably deduced by now, the length of the time period of adjustment is a crucial determinant of supply elasticity, either in the case of goods and services or entrants into an occupation. Clearly, the more time permitted suppliers to adapt to a change in price, the more responsive is quantity supplied, and hence the more elastic is supply. Obviously, over a very short period of time, supply would generally be quite inelastic.

Economists frequently distinguish between momentary, short-run, and long-run supply elasticity. As an example, let us consider the supply of people in a particular profession, say lawyers. Three supply curves for lawyers are shown in Figure 2–12. $L_M L'_M$ is the

**FIGURE 2–12**
**Effect of time of adjustment on supply elasticity**

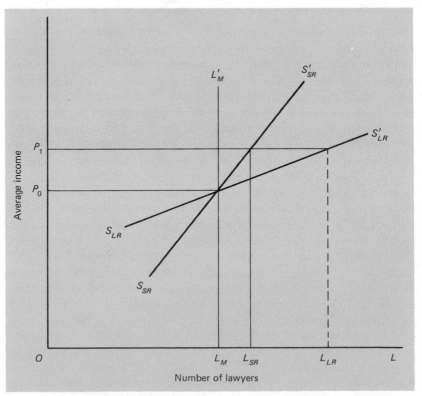

momentary supply of lawyers. At a moment of time, there are $L_M$ lawyers, and this number cannot be instantaneously changed. Suppose the average income of lawyers rises from $p_0$ to $p_1$; at that moment, or over a very short period of time, the number of lawyers cannot be increased. Since quantity does not respond at all, the vertical supply curve $L_M L'_M$ is infinitely inelastic.

Within a reasonably short period of time, however, the increase in the average income of lawyers will induce an increase in the number of lawyers, perhaps from $L_M$ to $L_{SR}$. The increase in income will induce some retired lawyers to begin practice again; some businesspeople with law degrees will be induced to leave their companies and enter practice. The resulting short-run supply curve is $S_{SR} S'_{SR}$, the supply curve when a reasonably short period of adjustment is permitted. This curve is more elastic than is $L_M L'_M$, because, when some adjustment time is permitted, quantity supplied is more responsive to price changes.

The long-run supply curve is $S_{LR} S'_{LR}$, which allows sufficient time for *all* adjustments to be made. (We shall define short run and long run more precisely in Chapters 5 and 6.) In our example, higher average incomes will induce more college graduates to enter law school, and the period of adjustment is long enough to permit them to begin practicing law. Alternatively, if average income declines relative to other professions requiring similar periods of training, the number of lawyers will decline appreciably. Thus, the long-run supply curve $S_{LR} S'_{LR}$ is more elastic than is $S_{SR} S'_{SR}$, because quantity is more responsive to price when sufficient adjustment time is permitted.

## 2.6 MARKET DETERMINATION OF PRICE AND QUANTITY

The purpose of studying supply and demand is to prepare us to analyze their interaction, which determines market price and quantity. A primary reason for separating them is to isolate the factors that determine each so that we can anlyze the market effects of changing these factors. Before further analyzing, in later chapters, the underlying forces behind the two schedules, we will examine the interaction of supply and demand in the market.

### Equilibrium

Suppose that in the market for a good, demanders and suppliers have the particular schedules set forth in Tables 2–1 and 2–4 respectively. These schedules are combined in Table 2–5. Suppose also that an auctioneer, who does not know the schedules, is assigned the task of finding a price that clears the market; that is, a

**TABLE 2–5**
**Market demand and supply**

| Price (dollars) | Quantity supplied | Quantity demanded | Excess supply (+) or demand (−) |
|---|---|---|---|
| $6 ................ | 7,000 | 2,000 | +5,000 |
| 5 ................ | 6,500 | 3,000 | +3,500 |
| 4 ................ | 6,000 | 4,000 | +2,000 |
| 3 ................ | 5,000 | 5,000 | 0 |
| 2 ................ | 4,000 | 5,500 | −1,500 |
| 1 ................ | 3,000 | 6,000 | −3,000 |

price at which quantity demanded equals quantity supplied. The auctioneer does not know the market-clearing price, since the schedules change from time to time. The auctioneer begins by picking some price at random and announcing this price to the demanders and suppliers, who then tell him the amounts they wish to purchase or sell at that price. The first price chosen may or may not clear the market. If it does, exchange takes place; if not, the auctioneer must choose another price, but this time does not proceed purely at random.

The auctioneer knows from long experience that, if quantity demanded exceeds quantity supplied (we call this situation excess demand), an increase in price will cause quantity demanded to decrease and quantity supplied to increase; that is, excess demand will decrease when price rises. The auctioneer also knows that, if quantity supplied exceeds quantity demanded (called excess supply), a reduction in price causes a reduction in quantity supplied and an increase in quantity demanded; that is, a price reduction reduces excess supply.

Suppose the first price chosen is $5; 3,000 units are demanded, but 6,500 units are offered for sale. There is an excess supply of 3,500 units at that price. To reduce excess supply, the auctioneer reduces price, say to $1. Now, since consumers demand 6,000 but producers are willing to supply only 3,000, excess demand is 3,000. The auctioneer raises price to $4, and quantity supplied exceeds quantity demanded by 2,000. He therefore reduces price to $3. Quantity demanded equals quantity supplied, and the market is cleared. The equilibrium price and quantity are $3 and 5,000 units.

We can also express the equilibrium solution graphically. In Figure 2–13, $DD'$ and $SS'$ are the market demand and supply curves. (These are not graphs of the schedules in Table 2–5.) It is clear that $p_e$ and $x_e$ are the market-clearing, or equilibrium, price and quantity. Only at $p_e$ does quantity demanded equal quantity supplied. In this model, we need not make our assumption about the auctioneer.

**FIGURE 2–13**
**Market equilibrium**

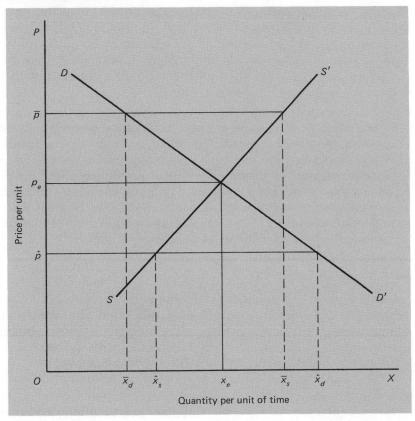

Consumers and producers themselves bid the price up or down if
the market is not in equilibrium.

Suppose price happens to be $\bar{p}$, greater than $p_e$. At $\bar{p}$, producers
supply $\bar{x}_s$, but only $\bar{x}_d$ is demanded. An excess supply of $\bar{x}_d\bar{x}_s$ develops. This surplus accumulates for the producers. When this hap-
pens, producers are induced to lower price in order to keep from
accumulating unwanted surpluses. (This is the same thing our auctioneer would have done.) Note that at any price above $p_e$, there is
an excess supply, and producers will lower price. On the other
hand, suppose price is $\hat{p}$. Demanders are willing and able to purchase $\hat{x}_d$, while suppliers are only willing to offer $\hat{x}_s$ units for sale.
Some consumers are not satisfied; there is an excess demand of $\hat{x}_s\hat{x}_d$
in the market. Since their demands are not satisfied, consumers bid
the price up. Again, this is what our auctioneer would have done if a
shortage existed. As consumers continue to bid up the price, quan-

tity demanded decreases and quantity supplied increases until price reached $p_e$ and quantity is $x_e$. Any price below $p_e$ causes a shortage, and the shortage causes consumers to bid up the price. Given no outside influences that prevent price from being bid up or down, an equilibrium price and quantity are attained. This equilibrium price is the price that clears the market; both excess demand and excess supply are zero in equilibrium. Equilibrium is attained in the market because of the following:

**Principle.**   When price is above the equilibrium price, quantity supplied exceeds quantity demanded. The resulting excess supply induces sellers to reduce price in order to sell the surplus. If price is below equilibrium, quantity demanded exceeds quantity supplied. The resulting excess demand causes the unsatisfied consumers to bid up price. Since prices below equilibrium are bid up by consumers and prices above equilibrium are lowered by producers, the market will converge at the equilibrium price-quantity combination.

### Demand and supply shifts

So long as the determinants of demand and supply do not change, the price-quantity equilibrium described above will not change. Before finishing our study of the market, we must see how this equilibrium is disturbed when there are changes in one or more of the factors held constant in deriving demand and supply.

A bit of intuitive reasoning may ease the transition to the somewhat complicated graphical analysis that follows. Consider the career you plan after graduation. Suppose you plan to become an economist. Suppose also that prior to your graduation, Congress passes a law requiring that everyone who buys a share of stock or a bond must, for protection, consult with an economist. Would this law please you? Why, or why not? Does it not seem logical that economists' salaries would rise after this law is passed? People now must consult economists when previously they did not have to. How could they bid away the necessary economists from jobs in academics or government? They would do so simply by offering higher salaries. Before long, economists' salaries would have generally risen since universities, government, and businesses must meet the increasing bids of potential investors. Or, in terms developed in this chapter, the demand for economists rises. With a given supply of economists, salaries must rise. Of course, after a while, the higher salaries may lure others into the profession and drive salaries back down again.

Consider another example. Does a cotton farmer bringing his crop to market want a large or small amount of cotton marketed at the same time? Obviously, a small amount because the larger the amount of cotton available, the lower will be the price of cotton. It should thus be intuitively clear that, with a given demand, the greater the supply, the greater will be the quantity sold but the lower the price will be. In like manner, the greater the demand—for economists, cotton, or anything else—the greater both *quantity* and *price* will be. These relations are intuitively clear; but they can be refined by graphical analysis, to which we now turn.

In panel A, Figure 2–14, $p_0$ and $x_0$ are the equilibrium price and quantity when demand and supply are $D_0D'_0$ and $SS'$. Suppose in-

**FIGURE 2–14**
**Changes in equilibrium prices and quantities**

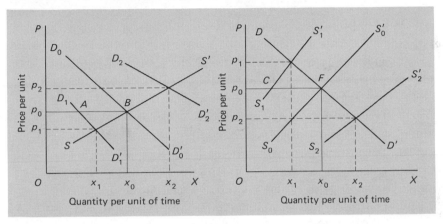

| Panel A | Panel B |

come falls and demand decreases to $D_1D'_1$. At $p_0$, quantity supplied exceeds the new quantity demanded by $AB$; that is, excess supply at $p_0$ is $AB$. Faced with this surplus, sellers reduce price until the new equilibrium is reached at $p_1$ and $x_1$. Now, suppose the price of some substitute good increases so that demand increases to $D_2D'_2$. At price $p_1$, quantity demanded far exceeds quantity supplied, and, hence, a shortage occurs. The excess demand causes consumers to bid the price up until the new equilibrium at $p_2$ and $x_2$ is reached. We can see that, if supply remains fixed and demand decreases, quantity and price both fall; if demand increases, price and quantity both rise. This direct relation between price and quantity would be expected when we consider that the movements take place *along* the supply curve, which is positively sloped.

Panel B, Figure 2–14, shows what happens to price and quantity when demand remains constant and supply shifts. Let demand be

$DD'$ and supply $S_0S'_0$. The original equilibrium occurs at price $p_0$ and quantity $x_0$. Now, let input prices rise so that supply decreases to $S_1S'_1$. The shortage of $CF$ at $p_0$ causes consumers to bid up price until equilibrium is reached at $p_1$ and $x_1$. Now, let technology improve so that supply increases to $S_2S'_2$. The surplus at $p_1$ causes producers to lower price. Equilibrium occurs at $p_2$ and $x_2$. Thus, we see that, if demand remains constant and supply decreases, price rises and quantity falls; if supply increases, price falls and quantity increases. This inverse relation is expected, since the movement is *along* a negatively sloped demand curve.

The direction of change is not always immediately apparent when both supply and demand change simultaneously. In panel A, Figure 2–15, $D_0D'_0$ and $S_0S'_0$ are the initial demand and supply

**FIGURE 2–15**
**Effects of supply and demand shifts**

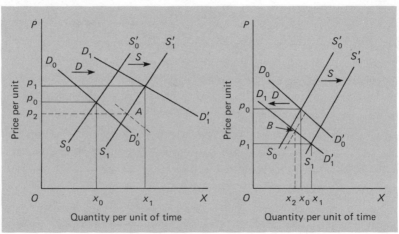

Panel A                                    Panel B

curves. Their intersection determines the equilibrium price and quantity, $p_0$ and $x_0$. Now, suppose supply increases to $S_1S'_1$ and demand increases to $D_1D'_1$; price rises to $p_1$ and quantity rises to $x_1$. While quantity always increases when both demand and supply increase, price may increase, decrease, or even remain the same. Suppose supply shifts to $S_1S'_1$, but demand shifts only to the position indicated by the dashed demand curve crossing $S_1S'_1$ at $A$. With this shift, quantity still rises (although by a lesser amount), but price falls to $p_2$. Furthermore, by constructing the change in supply or demand still differently, we can cause price to remain at $p_0$ while quantity increases.

To see the effect of a decrease in both supply and demand, consider $D_1D'_1$ and $S_1S'_1$ in panel A as the original schedules. Next, let them both decrease to $D_0D'_0$ and $S_0S'_0$. Quantity and price decrease from $x_1$ and $p_1$ to $x_0$ and $p_0$. While quantity always decreases when both curves decrease, price need not fall.

Panel B, Figure 2–15, shows the effect of an increase in one curve accompanied by a decrease in the other. Let supply *increase* from $S_0S'_0$ to $S_1S'_1$, and let demand *decrease* from $D_0D'_0$ to $D_1D'_1$. Price falls from $p_0$ to $p_1$ and quantity rises from $x_0$ to $x_1$. While price *must* fall when supply increases and demand decreases, quantity need not increase. Suppose that, while demand went to $D_1D'_1$, supply increased only to the position indicated by the dashed line crossing $D_1D'_1$ at B. The new equilibrium entails a price reduction (although not so large as before), but now quantity decreases to $x_2$ rather than rising to $x_1$. To see the effect of a decrease in supply accompanied by an increase in demand, simply assume that demand shifts from $D_1D'_1$ to $D_0D'_0$ and supply from $S_1S'_1$ to $S_0S'_0$. Price must rise. In this illustration, quantity decreases, but, depending upon the size of the shifts in the curves, quantity may change in either direction.

**Principle.** (1) When demand increases (decreases), supply remaining constant, both price and quantity increase (decrease). (2) When supply increases (decreases), demand remaining constant, price falls (rises) and quantity rises (falls). (3) When both demand and supply increase (decrease) quantity increases (decreases), but price can either increase or decrease, depending upon the relative magnitude of the shifts. (4) When supply and demand shift in opposite directions, the change in quantity is indeterminant, but price always changes in the same direction as demand.

## 2.7 SUPPLY AND DEMAND IN REAL MARKETS

Some students may question the relevance of demand and supply analysis to real-world problems. What if sellers do not know the demand or the supply schedules? In fact, do they even know what demand and supply are? It may, therefore, be useful to show how demand and supply determine price and allocate output in the absence of perfect knowledge about the schedules.

It should be apparent that prices have two social functions. Prices are a rationing device among consumers of the product, and they serve as an inducement for producers to produce more or less of a product. High prices restrict consumption to those who have a willingness and ability to pay a price at least equal to the going price. The higher the price, the more restricted consumption. For the producer, since supply is upward sloping, a higher price causes more to be produced; a lower price causes less to be produced. An example should help clear up these points.

### Theoretical example

Suppose one day the newspapers all print a scientific report stating that eating rhubarb makes people more healthy. Now we know, having gone through the first part of this chapter, that the demand for rhubarb probably increases. But perhaps the grocers, some of whom have not read this chapter, do not know this. How can the market allocate under these conditions?

First, consider what happens to the rhubarb on the grocers' shelves. Assuming that demand in fact increases, grocers find that what had previously been a week's supply of rhubarb at the established price now lasts only until Thursday morning. Customers complain that they cannot get rhubarb. We can use demand analysis to examine the situation *even though buyers and sellers are completely unaware of demand and supply analysis.*

**FIGURE 2–16**
**Supply and demand analysis of real markets**

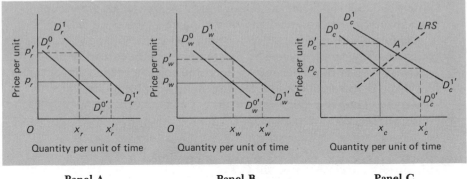

| Panel A | Panel B | Panel C |
| Retail market | Wholesale market | Commodity market |

Panel A, Figure 2–16, shows what happens in the retail market. Price is $p_r$, and $x_r$ per week is the rate of sales when demand is $D_r^0 D_r^{0'}$. Demand increases to $D_r^1 D_r^{1'}$. At $p_r$, consumers now want $x'_r$ units per week. Grocery stores consequently run out of rhubarb before the week is over. The profitable thing for grocers to do is order more rhubarb from wholesalers. When they do, the wholesalers sell more rhubarb and their stocks begin to run low. This is shown in panel B. The original demand is $D_w^0 D_w^{0'}$; this is the demand by grocers for wholesale rhubarb. When demand at retail increases, demand at wholesale also increases. Before the shift in demand, retail grocers wanted $x_w$ at a wholesale price of $p_w$; they now want $x'_w$.

As their inventories run low, wholesalers instruct their buyers in the commodity market to buy more rhubarb. At any one time, however, there is a limit to the amount of rhubarb available. Therefore, as the buyers try to increase their purchases, they bid against one another and force price up. Panel C indicates what happens in the commodity market. The old demand of wholesalers for rhubarb was $D_c{}^0D_c{}^{0'}$ and price was $p_c$. Suppose the quantity available is $x_c$ (the supply at the moment). When wholesalers' demand rises to $D_c{}^1D_c{}^{1'}$, a shortage of $x_cx'_c$ develops at price $p_c$. Price rises to $p'_c$ to ration the available rhubarb among the competing buyers. (It might be well to note that the scales of the graphs in Figure 2–16 are different.)

Wholesalers now pay a higher price in the commodity market and, consequently, raise their price to grocers, to $p'_w$. As they tell the grocers, their costs have risen and they are forced to raise prices. Since grocers now pay the wholesale price of $p'_w$, they raise the retail price to $p'_r$. As they tell their complaining customers, costs have risen so they are forced to raise prices. Costs to the grocers and to the wholesalers have, of course, risen, but ultimately it was the increased demand that caused the price rise. And price must rise until it rations the available rhubarb to those prospective buyers who are both willing and able to pay the price.

Everything that occurs in the transition period occurs not because we draw some curves, but because of individual actions in the market. We use demand and supply curves only to analyze more clearly what takes place in the market.

We can take the analysis a few steps further. Suppose the higher price in the commodity market induces farmers to increase their rhubarb crop or induces farmers growing other crops to switch to rhubarb. Remember $x_c$ and $p_c$ make up only one point on the long-run supply curve. Assume that there is an upward sloping long-run supply ($LRS$) passing through point $A$ in panel C. In the commodity market, price falls and quantity increases after all adjustments are made (point $A$, panel C). The increased quantity supplied causes price to fall and quantity sold to rise in the wholesale and in the retail market.

## APPLICATION

### Market effects of rising energy prices

The energy industry over the past decade gives us a good example of how markets respond to changing prices and the difference between long-run and short-run supply. The 1973–74 Arab oil embargo caused a tremendous increase in energy prices. Between December 1973, and December 1980, the price of domestic crude oil rose 308 percent. The price of natural gas increased 575 percent and the price of coal 118 percent.[1] Such large price increases did not just happen without cause.

Certainly, the world supply of oil was drastically restricted by the OPEC cartel. The Iranian crisis in 1979 had a similar effect. Domestically, price regulation has, until recently, discouraged investment in the natural gas and petroleum industries.[2] As a result, the quantity of oil sold on the world market did not increase as significantly as it would have otherwise. Over the same period, the demand for energy has been increasing. We would have predicted substantial price increases in the short run with less rapid increases as long-run adjustments are made.

Let us examine what has happened. During 1974, the prices of oil, coal, and gas rose at an average rate of 37 percent. By 1978, they rose at an average annual rate of only 6.3 percent. The Iranian crisis and U.S. price deregulation raised prices substantially in 1979 and 1980, but by mid-1981, real fuel prices were practically stable.

When oil prices began to increase rapidly, firms had difficulty adapting in the short run. But over the long run, firms in the oil industry, in response to the higher prices, began to increase investment and exploration in markets that were not subject to price regulation. Also, energy users began to shift from oil to gas and coal, increasing demand and, hence, price in those areas.

Some statistics can show this response. Richard Greene in the May 1981, *Monthly Labor Review*, reported that from the end of 1973 to the end of 1980, employment in the petroleum, natural gas, and coal industries had increased by 91 percent, almost six times the growth rate of jobs in the private, nonfarm economy. The biggest increase occurred after 1979 and was concentrated in the oil and gas industries—those areas for which the price increase has been the greatest. By 1980, employment in the three fuel industries was expanding at the rate of 6,600 jobs per month.

Thus, while it took some time for firms to respond to the price increase, they have made dramatic adjustments over time. Likewise, the rapidly increasing energy prices have encouraged conservation by consumers. Clearly, consumers could not adapt immediately, but given sufficient time, conservation, encouraged by the

---

[1] R. Greene, "Employment Trends in Energy Extraction," *Monthly Labor Review*, May 1981, pp. 3–8.

[2] P. MacAvoy, "The Effectiveness of the Federal Power Commission," *Bell Journal of Economics and Management Science* 1, no. 2 (Autumn 1970): 271–303.

higher prices, reduced the rate of increase in consumption. While total consumption has increased due to growth, per capita consumption has declined. All of these forces combined have slowed the rate of increase in energy prices.

## 2.8 FLOOR AND CEILING PRICES

As we noted, excess demand or excess supply can occur after a demand or a supply shift. But market forces over time tend to eliminate these. In fact, it is the very existence of these excess demands and supplies, reflecting changes in market conditions, that allows the market to work. There are, however, certain shortages (excess demands) and surpluses (excess supplies) that market forces do not eliminate. These are more permanent in nature and result from interferences with the market mechanism.

If there are two things that governments know how to do, they are (1) how to create a shortage, and (2) how to create a surplus. Shortages and surpluses can be created simply by legislating a price below or above equilibrium. Governments have, in the past, and probably will in the future, decide that the price of a particular commodity is or will be either "too high" or "too low" and proceed to set the "fair" price. Without evaluating the desirability of such interference, we can use demand and supply curves to analyze the economic effects of the two types of interference: the setting of minimum and maximum prices.

### Theory

If the government imposes a maximum, or ceiling, price on a good, the effect is to cause a shortage of that good (and frequently to create a black market that rations the quantity available). In Figure 2–17, a ceiling price, $p_c$, is set on good $X$. No one can legally sell $X$ for more than $p_c$ per unit, which is below the equilibrium price, $p_e$. At the ceiling price, only $x_e$ is offered for sale; that is, the *momentary* supply is the vertical line at $x_e$. Over a period of time, the shortage grows worse. After a suitable time period of adjustment, suppliers decrease the quantity supplied still more, to $x_s$. Excess demand is now $x_s x_d$. Since quantity supplied is less than quantity demanded at the ceiling price, there must be some method of allocating the limited quantity among all those who are willing and able to buy a larger amount. The sellers may devise the method, perhaps consumers have to stand in line, with suppliers deciding who comes first in the line on the basis of under-the-counter offers. Black mar-

**FIGURE 2–17**
**Effect of ceiling price**

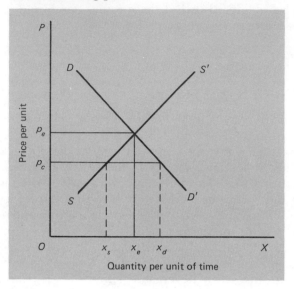

kets may develop. In any case, the market does the allocating, but, when restricted by outside requirements, the allocation is either based upon nonmarket considerations or the market mechanism functions less effectively outside the law.

In contrast, the government may feel that the suppliers of the good are not earning as much income as they "deserve" and, therefore, sets a minimum, or floor, price. We can see the results of such actions in Figure 2–18. Dissatisfied with the equilibrium price and quantity, $p_e$ and $x_e$, the government sets a minimum price of $p_f$. Since the law of demand could not concurrently be repealed, consumers demand less ($x_d$), and, immediately, a surplus of $x_d x_e$ develops. In order to maintain the price $p_f$, the government must find some way to limit supply, or it must agree to purchase the surplus. As firms are induced to supply more and as new firms are enticed into the industry by the higher price, the quantity supplied at $p_f$ increases. If $SS'$ is the long-run supply curve, the increased quantity supplied causes a greater surplus, $x_d x_s$, which the government must now buy or allocate among producers; that is, the government could simply restrict production to $x_d$. The vertical dashed line at that point then becomes the new supply. A price of $p_f$ now clears the market.

We should recognize that certain temporary shortages or surpluses may not all be governmentally caused. For example, sev-

**FIGURE 2–18**
**Effect of floor price**

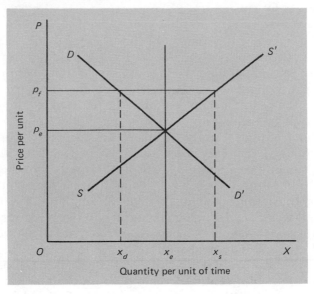

eral northern cities have recently experienced serious gas shortages during extreme cold spells. Many people have blamed these shortages on the fact that gas shipped interstate is subject to a regulated ceiling price below the market equilibrium. It is true that more households and firms use gas than would be the case with a market-determined price rather than the artificially low price. But some shortages probably would, and even should, occur with no ceiling price.

Why? Well, consider when the gas shortages occur; always during an extreme cold spell—for example, a 50-year low in temperatures. Clearly, a publicly or privately owned gas company would not construct pipelines and storage capacity to accommodate all users during such a cold spell. This would simply not be economical. Also think of the political implication if the city or even a private utility drastically raised prices to consumers during a freezing blizzard. People would march on city hall. Therefore, cities or utilities rely upon a gas capacity sufficient to handle the vast majority of winters. When one of the rare, extremely cold periods occurs, they generally ration by eliminating or reducing some industrial users and asking for voluntary reductions by consumers.

The situation is analogous to the snow removal situation in the small Texas city where we live. About every eight or nine years, this city experiences some snow—light by any northern standards, paralyzing by our standards. Practically everything comes to a standstill until the snow melts. Would snow removal equipment be economical? Of course not. Such an expense to alleviate some inconvenience every eight or nine years would be terribly wasteful.

Similarly, during the summer of 1980, Dallas, Texas, experienced the hottest two months in its recorded history. Heavy air conditioning usage caused periodic shortages of electricity. Should the electric company have increased prices to consumers? Over 100 people died from the heat. What do you think the reaction would have been to a large price increase?

Similar conditions apply to businesses. Movie theaters sometimes turn away customers from a popular movie. They also have a surplus, sometimes a very large surplus, of seats for other movies. Prices could be used more effectively to ration seats, but theaters would be constantly changing them depending upon the movie and the time it was shown. Such behavior would likely cause poor public relations. Moviegoers, uncertain of the price they would pay, might prefer entertainment with more stable prices. The long-run profits of theaters could fall. Similarly, retailers face the problem of the proper size of inventory to hold. Too much stock can get very costly to store, too little turns customers away. Over the long run, an inventory is held to maximize profits, but because there is a cost of storage, shortages can occur at the going price.

The fact that markets are not always in equilibrium by no means invalidates our theory. Markets do *tend* toward equilibrium when they are not regulated, even though temporary shortages and surpluses occur. Our theory simply explains why there is this tendency toward equilibrium, and it gives us an excellent insight into the way real markets function. Most important, the theory enables us to make accurate predictions about the real world using general and rather simple assumptions. Thus, our theory of market equilibrium is quite a useful tool of analysis.

## APPLICATION

### Price supports for peanuts[3]

The U.S. peanut program is designed to help peanut farmers. Each year, the Department of Agriculture decides what the size of the peanut crop in the coming season should be, then tells the approximately 53,000 growers, who hold the legal right to grow

---

[3] This application is based on an article appearing in *Business Week*, "Cuts in Farm Supports Face a Peanut Test," July 6, 1981, pp. 96–97.

peanuts, how much acreage they can plant. Anyone who markets peanuts commercially without an "allotment" can be fined or sent to jail.

Loans, which essentially guarantee that farmers receive a set price for their peanuts, are also provided by the government. As of 1981, the government would lend a peanut farmer $455 per ton of peanuts if the crop could not be sold for at least that amount on the open market. Later, if the crop could be sold for $455 or more per ton, the loan had to be repaid. But if prices stayed below $455 a ton, the government took the crop, and the farmer did not have to repay the loan. In essence, the government set a price floor for peanuts at $455 per ton.

The federal peanut program can be modeled in a simple supply and demand setting. Figure 2–19 shows the main features of the

**FIGURE 2–19**
**Price floors for peanuts**

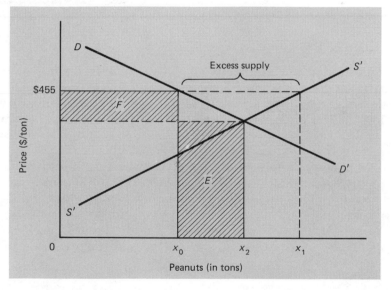

program. We can easily see why the Department of Agriculture restricts the acreage that can be put into peanuts. At $455 per ton, there would be an excess supply, equal to $x_0 x_1$, which the government would have to purchase at the agreed upon price if there were no restrictions.

Does the income of peanut farmers rise from the price floor? On the surface, it appears that it does. But the answer really depends upon the elasticity of demand. Suppose the acreage restriction is just sufficient to limit quantity supplied to $x_0$; there is no excess supply. Clearly, peanut farmers gain if the area $F$ in Figure 2–19 exceeds area $E$. We know that this situation occurs if demand is inelastic over the relevant range. Thus, under our assumption, peanut farmers would want price supports and restrictions if and only if demand is inelastic. Otherwise they are better off in nonregulated markets.

But the situation is, in reality, a bit more complex. Even with the restrictions, farmers with acreage allotments have become very successful at increasing their yield per acre. The average restriction notwithstanding, price floors have brought about excess supply in the market as farmers have increased productivity. In fiscal 1981, the government expected to pay an estimated $51 million in "loans" for peanut crops that could not be sold. The government then has to take the crops and store them. This shows that, even with restrictions, excess supply can occur if the restrictions are not exactly accurate.

## 2.9 EXCISE TAXES

An excise tax is a tax directly related either to the number of units sold or the price of a particular commodity. Excise taxes are always collected through the seller. If the tax is based on the number of units sold, it is often called a unit tax. The classic example of a unit tax is the excise tax collected on gasoline sold to motorists. It is not based upon the price of gasoline, but strictly on the number of gallons pumped. Alternatively, the tax may be a fixed percent of the sales price, in which case the excise tax is also known as an ad valorem tax. Sales taxes on consumer goods in most cities and states are examples of ad valorem taxes.

We will use supply and demand to study the market effects of excise taxes, looking first at the unit tax and then turning to ad valorem taxes.

### The market effect of a unit tax

Suppose your state legislature is debating the establishment of a state excise tax on gasoline. Claims are made that such a tax will cause motorists to conserve on gasoline, and the added tax revenue is necessary for road improvement and construction. On the other hand, some lawmakers may oppose the tax on grounds that sellers will just pass it on to the consumer, and they are taxed heavily enough already. Economic tools we have already developed can help us evaluate these arguments.

**FIGURE 2–20**
**Price effect of an excise tax**

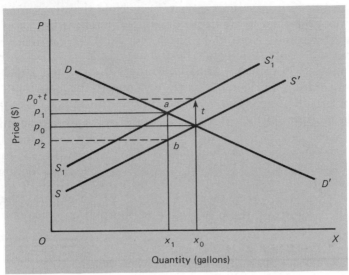

Let us turn to a theoretical analysis of the problem using the tools of supply and demand. Suppose $DD'$ in Figure 2–20 is the state economy's demand for gasoline. $SS'$ is the present supply of gasoline prior to the tax imposition. Thus, $x_0$ and $p_0$ are, respectively, the equilibrium quantity and price.

Now, a unit tax simply means that for every gallon of gasoline sold, the seller must pay a stipulated amount to the state. This payment shifts the supply curve upward (decreases supply). Demand does not shift. The consumer who pays $1.50 for a gallon of gasoline presumably does not care what portion of the price goes to the seller and what portion goes to the government. Consumers demand so much at $1.50 and at every other price, no matter what part goes to the government. But sellers do care what portion of the price goes to the government and what portion they can keep. For example, suppose at a price of $1.50 a gallon, stations are induced to supply a million gallons per week to the market. This means that they themselves must receive $1.50 a gallon to supply this amount. Let a tax of 10 cents a gallon be imposed. In order to induce suppliers to supply 1 million gallons a week, the price must be $1.60 a gallon, because only in this way can suppliers keep $1.50 for themselves. Moreover, at every other quantity, suppliers must receive 10 cents a gallon more to induce them to supply the same amount.

In terms of Figure 2–20, suppose the unit tax being debated is $t$ cents per gallon. By the argument presented above, the original supply $SS'$ shifts upward by $t$ cents to $S_1S_1'$. Thus, at the old price of $p_0$, there is excess demand; consequently, price is bid up to $p_1$. The new quantity sold declines from $x_0$ to $x_1$. Note that the extent of the price rise and quantity decrease depends upon the elasticity of supply and demand. Note also that price does not rise by the full amount of $t$ cents. Price rises by the amount $p_1 - p_0 = \Delta p$, which, you can see, is less than $t$. Thus, consumers absorb some of the tax in the form of higher prices, and producers absorb the remainder of the tax. In fact, the *burden* or *incidence* of the unit tax on consumers is simply the portion they pay:

$$\text{Tax incidence} = \frac{\Delta p}{t} \le 1.$$

The only time consumers pay the entire tax is when demand is perfectly inelastic, as shown in Figure 2–21. In general, the more inelastic is demand, the heavier the tax burden on consumers.

**FIGURE 2–21**
**Price effect of an excise tax when demand is perfectly inelastic**

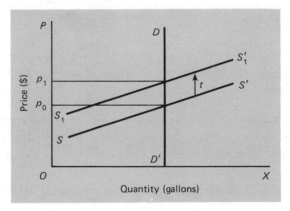

This is not a surprising conclusion. Inelastic goods are insensitive to price; in other words, when prices rise, consumers are willing to pay the increase rather than forego the commodity. Suppose demand was elastic. Now the quantity purchased is sensitive to price. Rather than pay the tax, consumers reduce consumption. It stands to reason that, under these conditions, the seller ends up paying most of the tax.

In summary, the more inelastic is demand the greater is the tax burden on consumers and the smaller is the change in quantity purchased. Conversely, the more elastic is demand the smaller is the tax burden on the buyer, and the greater is the change in quantity purchased.

That the tax burden depends upon the elasticity of demand is a difficult concept for students to accept. Too frequently, it is claimed that taxes are fully passed on to consumers; that is, the tax is added to the old price $p_0$ and everyone is forced to pay it. But suppose gasoline dealers did this. Returning to Figure 2–20, dealers would surely like to charge a price of $p_0 + t$, yet if they did, excess supply would result. Inventories would build up and eventually price would fall to $p_1$. The willingness of consumers to pay does not allow suppliers to sell $x_0$ at $p_0 + t$.

Turning now to the effect of supply elasticity, the more inelastic is the supply curve, the less is the burden of a unit tax on consumers, or conversely, the heavier it is on suppliers—someone must pay the tax. Figure 2–22 is similar to Figure 2–20 except that the supply

**FIGURE 2–22**
**Price effect of a unit tax when supply is relatively inelastic**

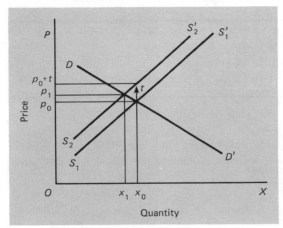

curve is noticeably steeper. The demand curves have exactly the same slope. Comparing the two figures reveals that the difference between $p_0 + t$ and $p_1$ is greater in Figure 2–22. In other words, the consumer pays a smaller portion of the tax.

Although this is easy to see in the graphs, the reasoning behind this conclusion is worth putting into words. The key to understanding why price does not change much when supply is inelastic, as shown in Figure 2–22, is to realize that when a unit tax is imposed there is not much of a leftward (as opposed to upward) shift in the supply curve. As a consequence, there is only a small movement along the demand curve, and there tends to be little overall change in price and quantity exchanged. By comparing Figures 2–20 and

2–22 you can see what happens when supply is relatively elastic as shown in Figure 2–20. The leftward shift is larger the more elastic is supply. We observe that when supply is elastic, sellers are more willing to adjust the quantity supplied rather than pay the tax themselves. In contrast, when supply is inelastic, the quantity sold adjusts very little, so sellers tend to absorb the tax.

### Ad valorem taxes

The analysis is conceptually the same for an ad valorem tax. The tax shifts the supply curve upward, and the incidence of the tax depends upon the elasticity of demand and supply. With a percentage tax, the amount of tax depends upon the price of the commodity. Let us focus our attention on the supply curve. Recall that it tells us how much sellers offer at each possible price. If we placed a 10 percent ad valorem tax on sellers, they would need their old price plus 10 percent to supply the same amount.

Supply curves have a positive slope, meaning that higher prices are necessary for sellers to offer larger quantities in a market. As prices rise to induce larger quantities, the absolute amount of the tax, $t$, must rise. Remember $t$ is a constant percentage of the sales price; as the price rises, so does the amount of tax paid. For example, if the sales tax on a bicycle is 10 percent, then a $100 price tag means

**FIGURE 2–23**
**The market effect of an ad valorem tax**

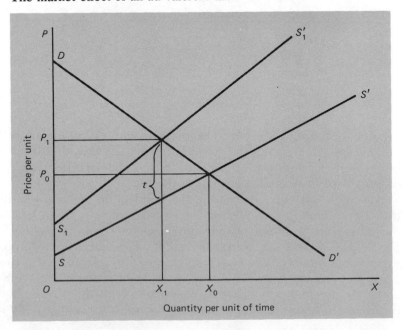

the tax is \$10; but if the price jumps to \$150, the tax becomes \$15.

Figure 2–23 shows a market supply and demand schedule. With an ad valorem tax, $t$ gets larger as we move up the supply curve $SS'$. The new equilibrium is defined by the intersection of $S_1S_1'$ and $DD'$. Compared to the old equilibrium, prices are higher, and the quantity sold is less.

The incidence of the tax does not fall entirely on the buyer. Figure 2–23 shows that $\Delta p = p_1 - p_0 < t$ at the new equilibrium. The rise in price would get closer to $t$ as demand got more inelastic or supply more elastic at $p_0$. Unlike a unit tax, however, as demand becomes more inelastic, both the incidence of the tax on buyers and the total amount of the tax rises. Consumers would pay a higher percentage of a larger tax.

### Government revenue

The amount of tax revenue collected by the government is always equal to the tax, $t$, times the numbers of units sold. Letting $T$ be tax revenue, then

$$T = t \cdot x.$$

In Figure 2–20, $T$ is the rectangular area $abp_2p_1$. For any $t$, tax revenue is less, the greater the fall in quantity sold when the tax is imposed. Tax authorities prefer to tax goods that are not sensitive to tax rates, e.g., gasoline, cigarettes, and liquor. These kinds of goods represent reliable sources of income to governments, because they tend to have market demand schedules that are relatively inelastic.

**FIGURE 2–24**
**Revenue depends on the elasticity**
**of demand**

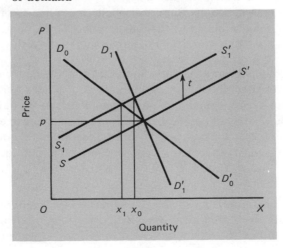

The point can be made more forcefully by comparing the tax revenue collected on a good with two contrasting elasticities of demand. Figure 2–24 illustrates the relative revenue-generating power of a commodity when demand is elastic as opposed to when it is inelastic. In both cases, the same tax is collected on the units sold, but when demand is relatively inelastic, more units are sold, hence, tax revenue is higher. The difference in revenue collected is clearly $t(x_0 - x_1)$ in Figure 2–24.

## 2.10 SUMMARY

In this chapter we have analyzed the following principles:

**Principle.**   Demand is a list of prices and of the corresponding quantities that consumers are willing and able to buy at each price. Quantity demanded varies inversely with price. Demand (that is, the entire schedule) changes when something held constant in deriving demand changes. Among these are income, tastes, the prices of other goods, and expectations.

**Principle.**   Demand elasticity measures the responsiveness of quantity demanded to price changes. The more (less) responsive quantity demanded is to price, the more elastic (inelastic) is demand. An increase in price causes total revenue to increase if demand is inelastic and to decrease if demand is elastic. The effects are opposite for a price decrease. In case of unitary elasticity, there is no change in total revenue for a change in price. Elasticity is affected by the availability of substitutes, the number of uses, and adjustment time.

**Principle.**   Supply is the list of prices and the corresponding quantity that will be supplied at each price on the list. Changes in technology, the price of inputs, and the prices of related (in production) goods will shift the entire schedule. Supply elasticity measures the responsiveness of quantity supplied to changes in price. The time period of adjustment is one of the principal determinants of elasticity.

**Principle.**   When price in a market is such that quantity demanded equals quantity supplied, the market is in equilibrium. Prices below equilibrium cause excess demand (or shortages). If prices are not artificially fixed, they will be bid up. Prices above equilibrium cause excess supply (or surpluses). If prices are not fixed, they will be bid down. When supply and demand change, equilibrium price and quantity will change.

Every day, economists use simple demand and supply analysis to solve complex problems and to answer questions dealing with the

real world. In fact, demand and supply are probably the most frequently used tools in the economist's bag.

Therefore, much of the remainder of this book is devoted to demand and supply and to the factors that influence demand and supply. As we shall see, however, one must be able to decide *which*
demand and *which* supply are relevant for the solution of a particular problem before being able to use these tools fruitfully.

In all cases, a fundamental concept to remember is that when the
price of something falls, more is taken; when the price of something
rises, less is taken. In the next two chapters we turn to the theory of
consumer behavior to see why this is so.

## TECHNICAL PROBLEMS

1.  In Table 2–3, compute $E$ for a change in price from $.25 to $.10
    and from $.50 to $.25. Use the arc elasticity formula.
2.  Assume the following demand and supply functions:

    $$X_d = 100 - 2P$$
    $$X_s = 10 + 4P$$

    *a.* What are equilibrium price and quantity?
    *b.* Supply shifts to

    $$X_s = 28 + 4P$$

    What are the new equilibrium price and quantity?
    *c.* Suppose you were appointed the chief of the government
    agency that regulates this industry; you wished to create a
    shortage of 13 units. What ceiling price would you set?
    Recall that a shortage is an excess demand equaling $X_d - X_s$. Use the first supply equation.
3.  Can a price clear the market in the sense that sellers sell every-
    thing they offer and the market still not be in equilibrium?
    Explain.
4.  The following are the demand and supply functions for a
    hypothetical product

    $$X_d = -.6P + 3.0$$
    $$X_s = .4P + 2.0$$

    *a.* Plot these functions on a graph.
    *b.* Find the equilibrium price.
    *c.* Calculate the elasticity of demand and supply at the
    equilibrium.
    *d.* At what price and quantity is the demand elasticity equal
    to $-1$?

5. *a.* Consider an increase in the demand for petroleum engineers in the United States. Describe exactly what would happen in the momentary situation, the short run, and the long run.

   *b.* Consider a decrease in the demand for elementary school teachers. What would happen in the momentary situation, the short run, and the long run?

6. "I earn $20 a week and spend it all on beer no matter what the price of beer is." Exactly what is this person's elasticity of demand for beer?

7. "Federal Officials would be quite happy if severe weather reduced the size of the [1980 grain] crop," says Russel Arndt, president of the National Corn Growers' Association. "The pickup in price would bail [farmers] out." [*Business Week,* July 21, 1980.] If Mr. Arndt means a rise in income would bail farmers out, what must be true about the elasticity of demand for grain?

8. Casio, a large Japanese watchmaker, aims to win market share by slashing prices to the bone. This spring, Casio unwrapped its new F-7 model, which retails for $15.75. "Our per-unit profits may be going down, but the increase in volume compensates for that," claims Kazno Kashio, executive managing director at Casio. What can an economist say about the elasticity of Casio's demand schedule? As Casio's market share increases, show what happens to its price elasticity.

9. Seltzer Company sells spring water at a desert oasis; its costs are virtually zero. Seltzer knows that its demand function is $Q_d = 25 - (3/2)P$. Presently, it charges a price of $2 per gallon of water. You are hired as a consultant to help Seltzer increase profits. Do you recommend a price change? If so, calculate and explain at what price the firm ought to sell its water.

10. Suppose the demand schedule for umbrellas is $X_d = 50 - (4/5)P$, where $X_d$ is the quantity demanded in millions of umbrellas and $P$ is price in dollars per umbrella. Calculate the price elasticity of demand for umbrellas. If you have trouble, what piece of information is missing? Can you prove that you need to know more?

11. Suppose a unit tax is placed on sellers in a market. Describe the change in price and quantity sold, and carefully explain why price usually does not rise by the full amount of the tax.

12. Excise tax authorities find themselves torn between the need to tax items that promise a high and steady flow of revenue but

not tax "necessities." Explain the conflict. On items that provide a good tax base, who bears the burden? Explain.

13. A subsidy is clearly the opposite of a tax; that is, the government gives a certain payment to each purchaser of a good which the government for some reason or another thinks people should consume more of. Begin with an original set of supply and demand curves. Show equilibrium. Next show graphically the effect of the subsidy on market price and on equilibrium quantity. Discuss the way that the slopes of demand and supply affect the change in equilibrium price and quantity.

**FIGURE E.2–1**

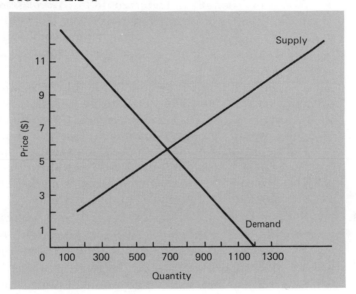

14. Use Figure E.2–1 to answer the following questions:
    a. In equilibrium price is $_____, and quantity sold in the market is _____ units.
    b. A governmentally mandated price of $4 will cause a _____ of _____ units.
    c. A governmentally mandated price of $8 will cause a _____ of _____ units.
    d. The imposition of a $2 per unit excise tax will change equilibrium price to $_____.
    e. $_____ of the tax is paid by producers, and $_____ is shifted to consumers of the good.

## ANALYTICAL PROBLEMS

1. Insurance agents receive a commission on the policies they sell. The recent state hearings on insurance rates in Texas were attended by agents from all over the state. Would higher or lower rates raise the income of agents? Distinguish between the short-run and long-run effects.

2. Some cities license taxi cabs. The cities also fix the rate that taxis may charge. If, after several years, no new licenses are issued, an "unofficial" market for licenses generally rises.
   a. Discuss the factors that determine the price of a license.
   b. Would a change in the allowed fare raise or lower the price of a license?
   c. Who would benefit and who would lose from an expansion in the number of licenses issued by the city?

3. Between August of 1979 and August of 1981, the price of housing rose approximately 18 percent, while money income rose only 14 percent. Interest rates for mortgage loans during the same period rose from 10 percent to roughly 15 percent. Thus payments on a $60,000, 30-year mortgage went from $526.54 to $895.23 per month, a 70 percent increase. Given this information, what would you expect happened to
   a. The demand for owner-occupied housing?
   b. The size of houses built during this period?
   c. The demand for rental housing?
   d. The demand for household appliances?

4. Prostitution is illegal. But in most cities there is a black market for prostitution. Is the *black market* price for prostitutes higher, lower, or the same as it would be if prostitution were legal? Explain your answer.

5. Some people say that, without government price support programs, farmers could not afford to grow some crops like cotton; therefore, the country would have no cotton without the support program. Analyze.

6. a. The destruction of much of Brazil's coffee crop a few years ago increased the price of tea. Why?
   b. The coffee minister of Colombia (a country that also grows coffee) was quoted as saying that he hoped the U.S. coffee boycott over the next couple of years (during which time the Brazilian trees would be back to normal) would be a success in keeping down coffee prices during the period. Why would the minister of a coffee-producing country want a boycott to keep coffee prices down over the next two years? (This is a tough one; do not neglect the effect of price on quantity supplied.)

7.  Some legislators want to put higher taxes on liquor and cigarettes because they assert that people, particularly poor people, spend too much of their income on liquor and cigarettes and not enough on other goods, such as food. Thus, if extra taxes are levied on liquor and cigarettes, people would spend less on the "bad" things and more on other "good" things. Evaluate.

8.  Assume first an effective government-imposed maximum price is placed on a particular good. The price is set below equilibrium. Let the price ceiling be removed. Consumer spending on the good will increase only if demand is inelastic. Evaluate. (This is another tricky one.)

9.  Much higher tuition was recently imposed in state universities in Texas. High school counselors are advising high school seniors to expect lower admission standards in state universities and higher standards and tuition in private universities. Do you agree? Why or why not?

10. Several members of the economics faculty were standing in a rather long line at the student union cafeteria during one lunch hour. Some were heard to remark that they wished that the cafeteria would increase prices. Why?

11. The president signed an executive order deregulating petroleum products. Before this, the price of gasoline was set by law below the equilibrium. As a result of the order, what do you expect to happen to price and the quantity sold?

12. If you manage a grocery store, how could you tell whether the price of a given item is too high or too low? What does "too high" or "too low" mean?

13. The airline industry is now deregulated. Previously, the Civil Aeronautics Board (CAB) kept a price floor on airline fares. When a price floor is eliminated, predict the effect on market price and output. Are your predictions consistent with your observations of what occurred in the airline industry?

14. Consider the U.S. market for automobiles. Use demand and supply analysis to predict the effect on price and quantity sold of the following policy measures:
    a.  Quotas on imports of Japanese automobiles.
    b.  An import tariff on all foreign automobiles.
    c.  Quotas on imports of foreign steel.
    d.  A large increase in the tax on gasoline.
    e.  A drastic reduction in air fares.
    f.  A depression in the economy.
    g.  A large decline in interest rates.
    h.  Much more severe safety regulations and pollution restrictions on automobile exhausts.

# Chapter 3

## Theory of consumer behavior: Preferences and constraints

### 3.1 INTRODUCTION

In the discussion of demand and supply in Chapter 2, we postulated downward-sloping demand curves without formally deriving them. Since demand itself is directly related to the way consumers are willing and able to act, it is necessary to understand consumer behavior in order to understand the determinants of demand. This chapter and the following describe the theory of consumer behavior and the relations between that theory and the theory of demand. First, the tools of analysis are developed; then these tools are used to analyze the way in which consumer behavior determines demand, with particular emphasis upon explaining why market demand curves are negatively sloped.

#### Principles of maximization

The purpose of this chapter is to analyze the determinants of consumer behavior. We will explain why a consumer chooses a particular group of goods and services and not some other group. Why does one person consume none of some good, like a motorcycle, while someone else with about the same income may own two or three motorcycles?

The method of analysis is really quite simple. You, as a consumer, have a given income and you desire goods. Most likely, your income prohibits you from purchasing everything you desire. Therefore, you must make decisions about which goods you purchase during a given week or any other period of time. You have an allocation problem: how do you make the most of your income?

If you wish to consume more of some good in some future period than you are consuming now, you must give up other goods. A new car this semester will cost you your trip to Europe next summer. An additional movie will cost you a trip to McDonald's. Say you are now seeing about 10 films a month. Why do you not see another? The obvious answer is that you value another movie less than you value what you would give up to purchase the ticket. Similarly, you do not choose to consume only 8 movies a month because you value the 9th and 10th more than you value what you would purchase from the money you saved by giving up the films.

If your two alternatives are the new car or the trip to Europe, the decision is the same. If you value the new car more than you value the trip, then you give up the trip; if not, you give up the car.

Or suppose you would like a new 10-speed bike. Why would you not choose to purchase one? Don't say you can't afford one. Clearly you could if you give up enough other things. The reason you do not purchase a bicycle is simply that the added value or satisfaction you think you would receive from owning one is not sufficient to compensate you for what you would be forced to give up.

The fundamental analytical tool is the concept of *marginal analysis*. Marginal means "a small change in." For someone to choose more of one good and less of some others, the marginal gain must outweigh the marginal loss from giving up the other goods. In economics, we are concerned with small changes rather than all-or-nothing decisions. Consumers start at a particular plan of consumption, then make changes in order to reach more preferred levels.

This is our basic theory. Consumers are constrained or restricted by limited incomes and the prices that must be paid for the goods. They attempt to reach the most preferred level of consumption possible, given these constraints. Once they attain this level, they cannot become better off by giving up some goods in order to get others.

The basic concepts developed in Chapter 3 are

1.  What determines the amount of any good a consumer chooses to consume.

2. The fundamentals of indifference curves, indifference maps, and budget lines.
3. Why a consumer may choose to purchase none of some good.
4. The consequences of a change in the constraints.

## 3.2 BASIC ASSUMPTIONS

As is the case with any theory, the theory of consumer behavior makes some simplifying assumptions in order to go directly to the fundamental determinants of behavior. These assumptions allow us to abstract away from less important aspects of the decision process.

First, we assume that each consumer has complete information on all matters pertaining to consumption decisions. A consumer knows both the full range of goods available in the market and the capacity of each good to satisfy a want. Furthermore, the exact price of each good is known, and the consumer knows these prices will not be changed by his or her actions in the market. Finally, the consumer knows what his or her income will be during the planning period. Given all this information, each consumer tries to maximize satisfaction from consumption *given* a limited income. More precisely, economists say a consumer maximizes utility subject to an income constraint. Utility, a term frequently used in this chapter and Chapter 4, is defined as follows:

**Definition.**   Utility is a consumer's perception of his or her own happiness or satisfaction.

Admittedly, to assume perfect information is an abstraction from reality. Consumers have only a fairly accurate notion of what income will be for a reasonable planning period, not perfect knowledge. They only have a notion of the capacity of a good to satisfy a want, not precise knowledge of its capacity to satisfy. No consumer actually succeeds in the task of spending a limited income so as to maximize satisfaction. This failure is attributable to the lack of accurate information. Yet the more or less conscious effort to attain maximum satisfaction given imperfect information determines an individual's demand for goods and services, so the assumption of complete information does not distort the relevant aspects of the economic world. It allows us to concentrate on how consumption choices are made.

Second, we assume that each consumer is able to rank all conceivable bundles of commodities. That is, when confronted with two or more bundles of goods, a consumer is able to determine the order of preference among them. For example, assume that a person is confronted with two choices: (*a*) five candy bars, six pints of ice cream, and one soft drink; or (*b*) four candy bars, five pints of ice cream, and three soft drinks. The person can say one of three things; (*a*) I prefer the first bundle to the second; (*b*) I prefer the second to the first; or (*c*) I would be equally satisfied with either.

Therefore, when evaluating two bundles of goods, an individual either prefers one bundle of goods to the other or is indifferent between the two. Since we will use the concepts of preference and indifference frequently, it is essential to understand them thoroughly now. If a consumer prefers one group of goods to another group, he or she obviously believes a higher level of satisfaction will be gained from the preferred group. The less preferred bundle would, in the opinion of the consumer, give less utility than the other. If a person is indifferent between two bundles, he or she would be perfectly willing to let someone else (or perhaps the flip of a coin) determine the choice. An economist would say that, in the consumer's mind, either bundle would yield the same level of utility.

Much of what follows is based upon the consumer's ability to rank groups of commodities. This is a relatively weak requirement. It is important to understand what we are *not saying* about consumer preference and indifference.

First, we do not say that the consumer estimates *how much* utility or *what level* of satisfaction will be attained from consuming a given bundle of goods. Only the ability to *rank* is required; the ability to measure utility is not necessary.

Second, we do not imply that an individual can say by *how much* one bundle of goods is preferred to another. Admittedly, a consumer might be able to say one group of goods is desired a great deal more than another group, and perhaps just a little more than still another group. But "great deal" and "just a little" are imprecise; their meanings differ from one person to another. Therefore, at this level of abstraction, the theory of consumer behavior is not based upon the assumption that the consumer is able to state the amount by which one bundle is preferred to another.

Third, we do not say we think consumers *should* choose one bundle over the other, or that we believe they will be better off if they did so. It is only necessary that consumers be able to rank bundles according to the order of expected satisfaction. More explicitly, when we say a consumer can rank bundles of goods, we assume that the consumer's preference pattern possesses the following characteristics:

   *a.* Given three bundles of goods (A, B, and C), if an individual prefers A to B and B to C, then A is preferred over C. Similarly, if an individual is indifferent between A and B and between B and C, he or she must be indifferent between A and C. Finally, a consumer who is indifferent between A and B and prefers B over C, must prefer A over C. This assumption obviously can be carried over to four or more different bundles. It therefore follows that, if individuals can rank *any pair* of bundles chosen at random from all conceivable bundles, they can rank *all conceivable bundles*.

b. If bundle A contains at least as many units of *each commodity* as does bundle B, and more units of at least one commodity, A must be preferred over B.

Note, we did not say that a real-world consumer who *purchases* one good rather than another must prefer the chosen good. If you drive a Ford rather than a Rolls Royce, we cannot infer that you prefer a Ford to a Rolls. If the Rolls costs less than the Ford at the time of purchase, and you were aware of this, then we could make this inference. If, as was probably the case, the Rolls costs more, we can say nothing. If the two goods are presented at equal cost, and you choose one over the other, we could say that you prefer that good. Or, if two goods are priced differently and you choose the higher-priced good, we could again deduce that you prefer that good. But if you choose the lower-priced good, we could say nothing.

### Ordinal versus cardinal utility

To put things into perspective, we should note that the present theory of consumer behavior went through a very long period of development. Our discussion will touch on the highlights of the historical development of consumer theory in order to emphasize the difference between cardinal and ordinal utility.

The earliest psychological approaches to the theory of demand were based on the notion of a subjective and precisely measurable utility. This concept can be found in the works of Herman Gossen (1854), William S. Jevons (1871), and Leon Walras (1874). Just as modern theorists do, these early writers assumed that any good or service consumed provides utility. In contrast to modern theorists, however, they also took it for granted that utility was cardinal, additive, and independent of the rate of consumption of any other good.

Cardinal measurability implies that the difference between two numbers is itself numerically significant. For example, apples are cardinally measurable; four apples represent twice as much as two apples. On the other hand, measurement is ordinal if items can only be ranked. For example, if one item is ranked second and another fourth it does not mean the item with a rank of 2 is twice as desirable as the item with a rank of 4. Both ordinal and cardinal measures rank items. The difference is that, in an ordinal system, one can say only that $x$ is greater than $y$; in a cardinal system, it is possible to say by how much $x$ exceeds $y$.

Historically, it was not much later that economists such as F. Y. Edgeworth (1881), G. B. Antonelli (1886), and Irving Fisher (1892), objected to the additivity assumption. Instead, they argued that, while utility was cardinally measurable, it was not simply the sum of the independent utilities obtained from the consumption of each good. These theorists related the level of total utility to the rates of consumption of all goods simultaneously. For example, the utility from eating ice cream depends upon, among other things, the amount of pie consumed and the kind being served.

A development that came directly from the work of these later economists on cardinal utility theory is the notion of marginal utility. The more of a good consumed, the greater the total utility associated with it. Each additional unit of a good consumed per unit of time adds to total utility, but it is generally assumed that each unit adds less than the previous one added. For example, a scoop of ice cream might yield 5 units of utility; two scoops, 9 units; and three, 11 units of utility. The marginal utility of the second scoop is four, while the marginal utility of the third scoop is three units of utility. Marginal utility declines as consumption increases. More formally, we define marginal utility as follows:

**Definition.**   Marginal utility is the addition to total utility that is attributable to the addition of one unit of a good to the current rate of its consumption. The marginal utility of good X depends upon its rate of consumption as well as the rates of consumption of other goods.

This definition will be very helpful in later sections of this chapter, as we develop the theory of utility maximization.

The last major step in the development of modern utility theory enabled economists to use the concept of utility without resorting to the assumption of cardinal measurability. This final step, which is essentially attributable to Vilfredo Pareto (1906), led to the use of indifference curves in analyzing consumer behavior. We now turn to a study of such curves. It is important to keep in mind that indifference curves depend only on ordinal preference measures. That is, their existence comes from consumers having a preference pattern that:

1. Establishes a rank ordering among all bundles of goods.
2. Compares bundles of two and indicates that A is preferred to B, B is preferred to A, or the consumer is indifferent between the two goods.

3. In three- (or more) way comparisons, if A is preferred (indifferent) to B and B is preferred (indifferent) to C, A must be preferred (indifferent) to C.
4. A greater bundle in the sense of having at least as much of each good and more of another is always preferred to a smaller one.

## 3.3 INDIFFERENCE CURVES

Using the assumptions set forth above, we can now analyze two concepts that are fundamental to the theory of consumer behavior: indifference curves and indifference maps.

**Definition.** An indifference curve is a locus of points—or particular bundles or combinations of goods—each of which yields the same level of total utility or satisfaction.

**Definition.** An indifference map is a graph that shows a set of indifference curves.

For analytical purposes, let us consider a consumer who can use only two different goods, $X$ and $Y$, each of which is continuously divisible or infinitesimally variable in quantity.[1] Figure 3–1 shows a portion of this consumer's indifference map consisting of four indifference curves labeled I–IV. Our consumer considers all combinations of $X$ and $Y$, on indifference curve I to be equivalent (for example, $20X$ and $42Y$, and $60X$ and $10Y$); these combinations yield the same satisfaction, and, thus, the consumer is indifferent among them. Because of indifference between the two specified combinations, the consumer is obviously willing to substitute $X$ for $Y$ in order to move from point $a$ to point $b$. In other words, he or she is willing to give up 32 units of $Y$ to obtain 40 additional units of $X$. Conversely, if the present bundle of goods is situated at $b$, the consumer is willing to forego 40 units of $X$ to obtain an additional 32 units of $Y$, and thus, is willing to substitute at the *average* rate of $4/5$ units of $Y$ per unit of $X$.

All combinations of goods on indifference curve II (say $30Y$ and $50X$) are superior to *any* combinations of goods on I. Likewise, all

---

[1] Admittedly, the possibility of continuous variation in quantity *is* perhaps less frequently encountered than "lumpiness," but this assumption permits a great gain in analytical precision at the sacrifice of very little realism. The assumption that bundles consist of no more than two separate goods enables us to analyze the problem of consumer behavior with two-dimensional graphs. This assumption is made, therefore, purely for simplicity of exposition. With the use of the differential calculus, bundles of any number of different goods can be handled. But the analytical results based on two goods are exactly the same as those based upon more than two. Here, again, the gain in simplicity outweighs the loss of realism.

**FIGURE 3-1**
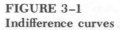
Indifference curves

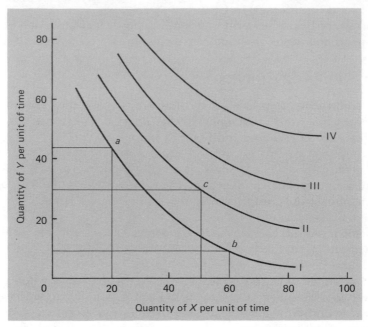

combinations on III are superior to any combination on II. Each indifference curve that lies above a given indifference curve represents combinations of X and Y that are considered superior to, or capable of yielding more utility than, every combination on the lower curve. At every utility level designated by a particular indifference curve, the consumer is willing to substitute X for Y or Y for X at some rate so as to be on the same curve (that is, with the same satisfaction or utility level) but consuming different combinations of goods.

Since X and Y are assumed to be continuously divisible, each indifference curve specifies an infinite number of combinations that yield the same amount of satisfaction. Further, it is important to note that the specific utility numbers attached to I, II, III, and IV are immaterial. The numbers might be 5, 7, 12, 32, or 96, 327, 450, 624 or any other set of numbers that *increase*. For the theory of consumer behavior, only the shape of the indifference curves matters. That is to say, only the ordinal ranking of commodity bundles is important. Since a precise measurement of utility is unnecessary, the theory of consumer behavior does not have to be based on the questionable concept of measurable utility. The indifference curves and the concept of preference are all that are required—all bundles of goods situated on the same indifference curve are equivalent; all combinations lying on a higher curve are preferred.

**Relation.**   A consumer regards all bundles yielding the same level of utility as equivalent. The locus of such bundles is called an indifference curve because the consumer is indifferent as to the particular bundle consumed. The higher, or further to the right, an indifference curve, the greater is the underlying level of utility. Therefore, the higher the indifference curve, the more preferred is each bundle situated on the curve.

## 3.4 CHARACTERISTICS OF INDIFFERENCE CURVES

Indifference curves have four characteristics that are important in our discussion of consumer behavior. All but the fourth property are based on the consumer's ability to rank consumption bundles and on the assumption that the consumer always prefers more to less.

For simplicity, assume once more that there are only two continuously divisible goods, X and Y. The X-Y plane is called *commodity space*. The first property is that each point in commodity space lies on one, and only one, indifference curve. This property is, of course, derived from the prior assumption that X and Y are continuously divisible. Each point in commodity space represents some specific combination of the two goods and, hence, some level of utility. As mentioned above, it is possible to take away Y and add X or take away X and add Y in an infinite number of ways and leave the consumer with the same level of satisfaction. Thus, each point in commodity space lies on an indifference curve. Since all bundles can be ranked, each lies on only one indifference curve. For obvious reasons, when graphing an indifference map, only a relatively few curves are used to represent the entire map. But remember, an infinite number of indifference curves lie between any two indifference curves that are drawn.

Second, indifference curves are negatively sloped. This notion is based on the assumption that a consumer prefers a greater bundle of goods to a smaller one. An upward-sloping indifference curve would indicate that a consumer is indifferent between two combinations of goods, one of which contains more of *both* goods. The fact that a positive amount of one good must be added to the bundle to offset the loss of another good (if the consumer is to remain at the same level of satisfaction) implies negatively sloped indifference curves.

Third, indifference curves cannot intersect. This property is a logical necessity, as illustrated in Figure 3–2. In this graph, I and II are indifference curves, and the points P, Q, and R represent three different bundles (or combinations of X and Y). R must clearly be

**FIGURE 3–2**
Indifference curves cannot intersect

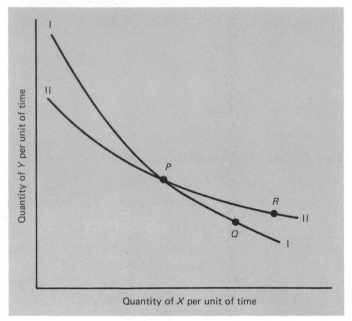

Quantity of X per unit of time

preferred to $Q$ because it contains more of both goods. $R$ and $P$ are equivalent because they are situated on the same indifference curve. In like manner, the consumer is indifferent between $P$ and $Q$. Indifference is a "transitive" relation—that is, if a consumer is indifferent between $A$ and $B$ and between $B$ and $C$, he must be indifferent between $A$ and $C$. In our case, $R$ and $P$ are equivalent, as are $P$ and $Q$. Hence, $R$ must be equivalent to $Q$. But, as previously mentioned, $R$ is preferred to $Q$ because it contains more of both goods. Hence, intersecting indifference curves, such as those shown in Figure 3–2, are logically impossible.

The fourth property is that indifference curves are *convex*—that is, an indifference curve must lie above its tangent at each point, as illustrated in Figure 3–3. The convexity of indifference curves does not follow from the capability of consumers to consistently order consumption bundles, but comes from empirical observations that show consumers diversify and consume a number of different commodities. If the indifference curve were not drawn as pictured in Figure 3–3, as will later become clear, utility maximization would lead to specialization rather than diversification in consumption. The predictions of our model would contradict common observation.

**FIGURE 3–3**
Indifference curves are convex

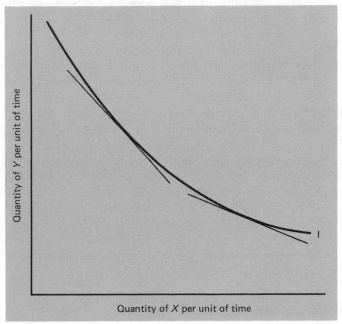

It is worthwhile to mention that we could apply the definition of marginal utility and get convex indifference curves. If we assume that the more of a commodity a consumer has, the less valuable an additional or marginal unit becomes—that is, marginal utility declines—preferences would have to be described by convex indifference curves. As the consumer moves along a particular curve, he or she would require increasingly more of the abundant good to maintain the same level of utility. For example, a person at a football game with four hot dogs and one soft drink might be willing to trade two hot dogs for another soft drink. On the other hand, if the same person had only two hot dogs and two soft drinks, he or she would be much less willing to give up another dog. In all likelihood, several soft drinks would be required to coax another hot dog away.

The results of this section may be summarized in the following:

**Relation.**   Indifference curves have the following properties: (*a*) some indifference curve passes through each point in commodity space; (*b*) indifference curves slope downward to the right; (*c*) indifference curves cannot intersect; and (*d*) indifference curves are convex.

## 3.5 MARGINAL RATE OF SUBSTITUTION

As previously emphasized, one essential feature of subjective value theory is that different combinations of commodities can give rise to the same level of utility. In other words, the consumer is indifferent as to the particular combination obtained. Therefore, as market prices might dictate, one commodity can be substituted for another in the right amount so that the consumer remains just as well off as before. He or she will, in other words, remain on the same indifference curve. It is important to know the rate at which a consumer is willing to substitute one commodity for another in consumption.

The reason for analyzing this rate of substitution so carefully lies in the concept of utility maximization. As we shall see later in this chapter, a consumer attains maximum satisfaction from a limited money income when choosing a combination of goods such that the rate at which he or she is *willing* to substitute goods is the same as the rate at which market prices *permit* substitution. Therefore, to understand utility maximization, one must understand the rate of substitution in consumption.

### Substitution in consumption

Consider Figure 3–4. An indifference curve is represented by I. The consumer is indifferent between bundle R, containing 4 units of X and 18 of Y, and bundle P, containing 11 units of X and 8 of Y. The consumer is willing to substitute 7 units of X for 10 of Y. The *rate* at which the consumer is willing, on average, to substitute X for Y is therefore

$$\frac{\Delta Y}{\Delta X} = \frac{RS}{SP} = \frac{18 - 8}{4 - 11} = - \frac{10}{7},$$

where, again, $\Delta$ means "the change in." This ratio measures the average number of units of Y the consumer is willing to forego in order to obtain one additional unit of X (over the range of consumption pairs under consideration).[2] Thus, the consumer is willing to give up $1^3/_7$ units of Y in order to gain one more unit of X. Stated alternatively, the ratio measures the amount of Y that must be sacrificed ($1^3/_7$ units) per unit of X gained if the consumer is to remain at precisely the same level of satisfaction.

In our subsequent use, we would find it very cumbersome to have the minus sign on the right-hand side of the equation above.

---

[2] The ratio is, of course, negative, since the change in Y associated with an increase in X is negative. This type of relation results directly from the postulate of negatively sloped indifference curves.

**FIGURE 3–4**
**The marginal rate of substitution**

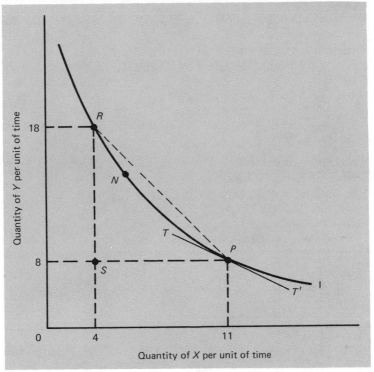

Thus, we define the rate of substitution as

$$-\frac{\Delta Y}{\Delta X} = \frac{10}{7}.$$

The rate of substitution given by the ratio above is obviously the negative of the slope of the broken straight line joining points $R$ and $P$. The ratio could be quite different between two alternative points, say $N$ and $P$. But, as point $R$ moves along I toward $P$, the ratio $RS/SP$ approaches closer and closer to the slope of the tangent $TT'$ at $P$. In the limit, for extremely small movements in the neighborhood of $P$, the negative of the slope of I, which is the negative of the slope of its tangent at $P$, is called the *marginal rate of substitution of X for Y.*

**Definition.** The marginal rate of substitution of X for Y measures the number of units of Y that must be sacrificed per unit of X gained so as to maintain a constant level of satisfaction. The marginal rate of substitution is given by the negative of the slope of an indifference curve at a point. It is defined only for movements along an indifference curve, never for movements among curves.

We shall hereafter use the letters MRS to denote the marginal rate of substitution of X for Y in consumption or, more generally, the marginal rate of substitution of the variable plotted on the horizontal axis for the variable plotted on the vertical axis. Also, since we wish the $MRS_{X \text{ for } Y}$ to be positive, and since $\Delta Y / \Delta X$ is necessarily negative, the minus sign must be attached.

### Diminishing MRS

The requirement that indifference curves be convex implies that the MRS of X for Y diminishes as X is substituted for Y along an indifference curve. This is illustrated in Figure 3–5.

**FIGURE 3–5**
**Diminishing marginal rate of substitution**

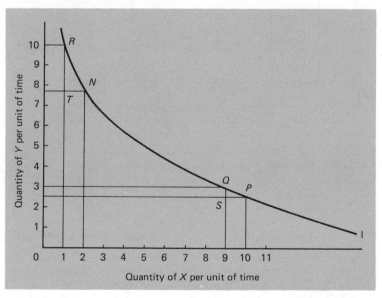

I is an indifference curve; R, N, Q, and P are four bundles situated on this curve. Consider a movement from R to N. In order to maintain the same level of utility, the consumer is willing to sacrifice slightly more than two units of Y to gain one unit of X. Now consider the consumer situated at Q. To move to P and gain one unit of X, the consumer now is willing to give up approximately ½ unit of Y.

**FIGURE 3–6**
**Diminishing** *MRS*

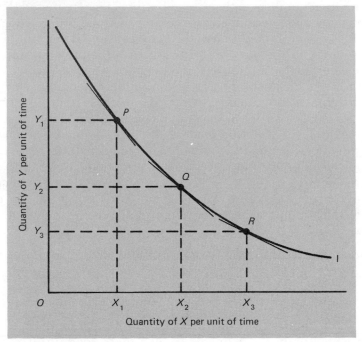

Diminishing *MRS* is further illustrated in Figure 3–6. I is an indifference curve, and *P*, *Q*, and *R* are three bundles situated on this curve. The horizontal axis is measured so that $OX_1 = X_1X_2 = X_2X_3$. Consider first the movements from *P* to *Q*. If *P* is very close to *Q*, or the amount $X_1X_2$ is very small, the *MRS* at *Q* is

$$\frac{OY_1 - OY_2}{OX_2 - OX_1} = \frac{Y_1Y_2}{X_1X_2}.$$

Similarly, for a movement from *Q* to *R*, the *MRS* at *R* is

$$\frac{OY_2 - OY_3}{OX_3 - OX_2} = \frac{Y_2Y_3}{X_2X_3}.$$

By construction, $X_1X_2 = X_2X_3$, but, very obviously, $Y_1Y_2 > Y_2Y_3$. Hence, the *MRS* is less at *R* than at *Q*. This is also shown by the absolutely decreasing slopes of the tangents at *P*, *Q*, and *R*.

**Marginal utility approach**

Earlier approaches to the theory of consumer behavior, as noted above, used the concept of marginal utility. In fact, this approach is still frequently used by many theorists.

Recall that the earliest economists who used the concept of utility assumed that utility was actually measurable and that one could assign actual numbers to the value of utility. They reasoned that the more of one good consumed, the greater the total utility associated with it. Each *additional* unit of the good consumed per unit of time adds to total utility, but each adds less than the previous unit.

We can quite easily relate the concept of marginal utility to the marginal rate of substitution along an indifference curve. Note first that marginal utility can be either (*a*) the increase in utility attributable to a small increase in the rate of consumption of a commodity, holding the level of consumption of all other commodities constant; or (*b*) the decrease in utility attributable to a small decrease in the rate of consumption under the same assumption.

Assume now that utility ($U$) is measurable and depends upon the rate of consumption of two goods, $X$ and $Y$. Next, let the consumption of both $X$ and $Y$ change very slightly. We can represent the total change in utility resulting from the changes in $X$ and $Y$ as

$$\Delta U = [(MU \text{ of } X) \times \Delta X] + [(MU \text{ of } Y) \times \Delta Y].$$

For example, if $X$ increases by 2 units, and the average marginal utility of each is 5, while $Y$ increases by 3 units and the average marginal utility of each is 4, utility increases by 22 units $= (2 \times 5) + (3 \times 4)$. Or, under the same marginal utility assumptions, if $X$ increases by 4 units and $Y$ decreases by 5 units, total utility remains constant; $(5 \times 4) + (4 \times -5) = 0$.

Since an indifference curve represents the locus of all combinations of $X$ and $Y$ among which the consumer is indifferent, utility must remain constant along any indifference curve. Thus, $\Delta U$ equals zero for any movement along an indifference curve. From the equation above, if, for very small changes in $X$ and $Y$, $\Delta U$ equals zero

$$\frac{MU_x}{MU_y} = - \left( \frac{\Delta Y}{\Delta X} \right),$$

where ($\Delta Y / \Delta X$) is the slope of the indifference curve. Recall that the slope of an indifference curve is the marginal rate of substitution; thus, we can interpret

$$MRS_{x \text{ for } y} = \frac{MU_x}{MU_y}.$$

A marginal utility interpretation of a previous hot dog–soft drink example might help. First, remember that we assume the marginal utility of any commodity is smaller the greater the rate of its consumption. Now picture a graph (or construct one for yourself) in which the number of hot dogs is plotted on the vertical axis, the number of soft drinks on the horizontal.

When the number of hot dogs a football fan has is great, the marginal utility of hot dogs is relatively low. Similarly, when the number of soft drinks is low, their marginal utility is relatively high. Thus, the *MRS*, which is the ratio of the marginal utility of soft drinks to that of hot dogs, is relatively high. Now let the football fan substitute soft drinks for hot dogs (*X* for *Y*, in the previous notation). Increasing the rate of consumption of soft drinks decreases their marginal utility, while reducing the rate of consumption of hot dogs increases theirs. Thus, the substitution of soft drinks for hot dogs must lead to a decrease in the *MRS* of soft drinks for hot dogs.

### The value of indifference curve theory

Although the theory of indifference curves is very useful in developing the theory of demand, measuring and plotting actual indifference curves for real people is extremely difficult. This is not to say that economists have not attempted such measurement. They have done so—with both people and animals—with varying levels of success. But the *actual measurement and graphing* of indifference curves are not really relevant methods of analysis for people who use economics in business, in government, or in other everyday decision making.

In fact, there is considerable controversy among economists at this time over the meaning of indifference curves for groups of consumers, such as an indifference curve for an entire community or state or nation. Some say such indifference curves have no meaning at all. Others say they have meaning only under very restrictive assumptions. Still others say that such community indifference curves are very useful tools of analysis under some circumstances.

Notwithstanding the tremendous difficulty of estimating indifference curves, the *concept* of these curves is rather useful in decision making. A decision maker in a business must recognize that employees have subjective rates of trade-off between income and the package of working conditions. It is possible to obtain certain goals by trading off between the two types of employee benefits. For example, some of the recent Ph.D.s in economics from our department have gone to work in business departments such as finance departments, while others have joined economics departments. The teaching load——number of classes to be taught—for young Ph.D.s has been on average higher in business than in economics departments, but the total income earned has been somewhat lower in the economics departments. Thus, there is a trade-off between the faculty working conditions and income. University officials recognize this. They also recognize that faculty are willing to trade some amenities such as preferred seating at football games and preferred parking facilities for income. All the results depend upon a comparison of utilities.

Any business must make its decisions about working conditions based on comparison of utilities. Government decision makers must attempt to balance utilities. Consumers of government products—constituents—do not want zero schools and perfect streets or perfect schools and no streets. Government officials must realize that there is a trade-off between the two that would be preferred. Even within a school system, there is a trade between teaching and classroom facilities.

Finally, and perhaps most important, any student of economics must realize that all goods have some substitutes. There are very few goods—probably no goods—that you are now consuming that you would not give up some amount of in order to obtain other goods. Do not say, I would not give up food because I would die. We did not say you would give up *all consumption* of a large group of goods. We only said that there is some group of other goods for which you would be willing to give up some amount of the food—or some type of food—you are now consuming. Any consumers will make trade-offs among goods.

In very few cases is it *essential* that someone consumes exactly the same amount of that good as is being consumed now. We can think of some examples, of course, mostly medical, such as a given amount of medicine without which the patient would die, or a weekly treatment on a kidney machine. But these absolute essentials are rare.

Therefore, do not make the mistake, unless you are trying to convert someone to your point of view, of making statements like, "It is essential that the school increase classroom space by 20 percent"; "The city must double its recreational area in five years." Each of these "essentials" has some substitutes in the minds of consumers. The concept of the indifference curve allows us to analyze this concept of substitution. We shall return to a discussion of this below.

### Summary

The concept of indifference curves is extremely important to the theory of consumer behavior and, therefore, to the theory of demand. Indifference curves show equally preferred combinations of goods. A higher curve designates more preferred levels of consumption. Indifference curves slope downward, reflecting the assumption that, when the consumption of one good increases, the consumption of the other good must be decreased in order to keep the consumer indifferent between the two combinations.

The marginal rate of substitution is the rate at which one good is substituted for another good along an indifference curve. The *MRS* can be interpreted as the ratio of the marginal utilities of the two goods, marginal utility being the additional utility obtained from the consumption of an additional unit of the good. *MRS* diminishes as one moves downward along an indifference curve. This decrease in *MRS* reflects the assumption that, as one has less of one good relative to a second good, the consumer is willing to give up less and less of that good in order to obtain an additional unit of the second good.

## 3.6 BUDGET LINES

Thus far in this chapter, we have set forth a method to analyze what a consumer is willing to do or wishes to do. But recall from Chapter 2 that demand indicates both what consumers are *willing* or wish to do and what they are *able* to do. We will now set forth a method to analyze what a consumer can do.

### Income constraints

If all consumers had an unlimited money income—in other words, if there were an unlimited pool of resources—there would be no problem of "economizing," nor would there be "economics." But, since this utopian state does not exist, even for the richest members of our society, people are compelled to determine their behavior in light of limited financial resources. For the theory of consumer behavior, this means that each consumer has a maximum amount that can be spent per period of time. The consumer's problem is to spend this amount in the way that yields maximum satisfaction.

Continue to assume that there are only two goods, $X$ and $Y$, bought in quantities $x$ and $y$. Each individual consumer is confronted with market-determined prices, $p_x$ and $p_y$, of $X$ and $Y$ respectively. Finally, the consumer in question has a known and fixed money income $(M)$ for the period under consideration. $M$ is the maximum amount the consumer can spend, and we assume that it is all spent on $X$ and $Y$.[3] Thus, the amount spent on $X$ $(xp_x)$ plus the

---

[3] In more advanced models, saving may be considered as one of the many goods and services available to the consumer. Graphical treatment limits us to two dimensions; thus, we ignore saving. This does not mean that the theory of consumer behavior precludes saving—depending upon preference ordering, a consumer may save much, little, or nothing. Similarly, spending may, in fact, exceed income in any given period as a result of borrowing or from using assets acquired in the past. The $M$ in question for any period is the total amount of money to be spent during the period. We will analyze borrowing and saving in Chapter 7.

amount spent on $Y$ ($yp_y$) is equal to the stipulated money income. Algebraically,

$$M = xp_x + yp_y. \tag{3-1}$$

This equation can be expressed as the equation for a straight line. Solving for $y$—since $y$ is generally plotted on the vertical axis—one obtains

$$y = \frac{M}{p_y} - \frac{p_x}{p_y} x. \tag{3-2}$$

Equation (3–2) is plotted in Figure 3–7. The first term on the right-hand side of equation (3–2), $M/p_y$, shows the amount of $Y$ that can be purchased if no $X$ is purchased at all. This amount is represented by the distance $OA$ in Figure 3–7; thus, $M/p_y$ (or point $A$) is the ordinate intercept of the equation.

In Equation (3–2) ($- p_x/p_y$) is the slope of the line. Consequently, the slope of the budget constraint is the negative of the price ratio. To see this, consider the quantity of $X$ that can be purchased if $Y$ is not bought. This amount is $M/p_x$, shown by the distance $OB$ in Figure 3–7. Since the line obviously has a negative slope, its slope is given by

$$-\frac{OA}{OB} = -\frac{\dfrac{M}{p_y}}{\dfrac{M}{p_x}} = -\frac{p_x}{p_y}.$$

The line in Figure 3–7 is called the budget line.

**Definition.** The budget line is the locus of combinations or bundles of goods that can be purchased if the entire money income is spent. Its slope is the negative of the price ratio.

Note again our assumption that the consumer spends all income on $X$ and $Y$. This implies that the bundle purchased must lie on the budget line.

### Shifting the budget line

In much of the analysis that follows, we are interested in changes in quantities purchased resulting from changes in price and money income, both of which are represented graphically by shifts in the budget line. Consider first the effect of a change in money income, the prices of the goods remaining constant.

Any given budget line represents the set of all possible consumption bundles for a consumer at a given set of relative prices and

**FIGURE 3-7**
**Budget line**

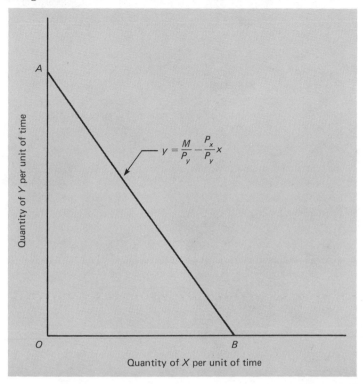

Quantity of X per unit of time

money income. If the consumer has an increase in money income at the original set of commodity prices, the set of possibilities must increase. Since the increase in money income allows the consumer to buy more goods, the budget line is pushed outward, but the slope of the budget line is the ratio of prices, which does not change when money income changes. Hence, the slope of the line is the same. Thus, an increase in money income causes an outward parallel shift in the budget line. Similarly, a decrease in money income, the price ratio held constant, causes a parallel inward shift in the budget line. In Figure 3-8, budget line $AB$ is associated with a lower income than is budget line $A'B'$. Since the slopes of $AB$ and $A'B'$ are equal, the price ratio remains constant as the change in money income shifts the budget constraint upward or downward. Note that the endpoint of the budget line is income divided by the prices of $X$ and $Y$. So distances $OA = M/p_y$; $OA' = M'/p_y$; $OB = M/p_x$; and $OB' = M'/p_x$, where $M'$ is the larger income.

Figure 3-9 shows what happens to the budget line when the

**FIGURE 3–8**
Changing money income

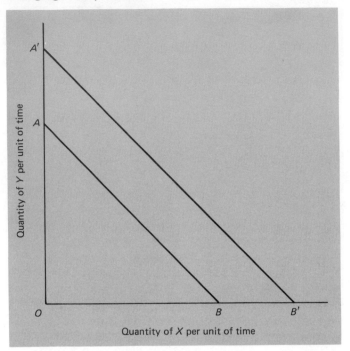

price ratio changes, money income held constant. Assume that money income and the prices of $X$ and $Y$ are such that the relevant budget line is $AB$. The slope of the line is $-(p_x/p_y)$. Hold money income and the price of $Y$ constant, then let the price of $X$ increase. Since $p_x$ increases, $p_x/p_y$ increases also. Thus, the budget line becomes steeper, in this case the line $AB'$. The intercept on the $Y$ axis remains the same because $M/p_y$ remains constant. In other words, if income and the price of $Y$ remain constant, the consumer can purchase the same amount of $Y$ by spending the entire income on $Y$ regardless of the price of $X$. Thus, we can see that an increase in the price of $X$ rotates the budget line backward, the $Y$-intercept remaining fixed. Of course, a decrease in the price of $X$ pivots the budget line outward, in Figure 3–9, from $AB'$ to $AB$.

Alternatively, and perhaps more directly, the price change can be explained as follows. At the original price, $p_x$, the maximum purchase of $X$ is $M/p_x$, or the distance $OB$. When the price rises to $p'_x$, the maximum purchase of $X$ is $M/p'_x$, or the distance $OB'$. Thus, an increase in the price of $X$ is shown by pivoting the budget line clockwise around the ordinate intercept. A decrease in the price of $X$ is represented by a counterclockwise rotation.

**FIGURE 3-9**
**Changing the price of X**

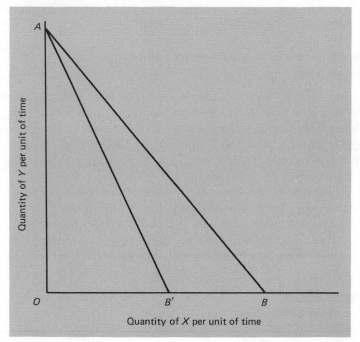

Relation. (a) An increase in money income, prices unchanged, is shown by a parallel shift of the budget line—outward and to the right for an increase in money income, and in the direction of the origin for a decrease. (b) A change in the price of X, the price of Y and money income constant, is shown by rotating the budget line around the ordinate intercept—to the left for a price increase, to the right for a decrease.

## 3.7 UTILITY MAXIMIZATION

All bundles of goods (combinations of X and Y) designated by the budget line are available to consumers in the sense that their income allows them to purchase these bundles if they wish. This line is established by the fixed money income and the given prices of the commodities available. A consumer's indifference map shows the rank ordering of all conceivable bundles of X and Y. The principal assumption upon which the theory of consumer behavior is built is that *a consumer attempts to allocate a limited money income among available goods and services so as to maximize satisfaction or utility.* Given that assumption and the concepts developed in this chapter, it is a relatively simple matter to determine the way a consumer will allocate income; that is, select the most preferred bundle of goods available with the given level of income and prices.

### Maximizing satisfaction subject to a limited money income

Graphically, we can visualize the consumer as being constrained by the fact that a limited money income permits consuming only bundles of goods along the budget line. The consumer chooses the particular bundle along the line that is on the highest attainable indifference curve. In this way, the highest possible preference level is achieved.

The problem is depicted by Figure 3–10. The portion of the indifference map represented by the four indifference curves drawn in that figure indicates preferences among different combinations of goods. Similarly, the budget line specifies the different combinations the consumer can purchase with the limited income, assuming

**FIGURE 3–10**
**Consumer optimization**

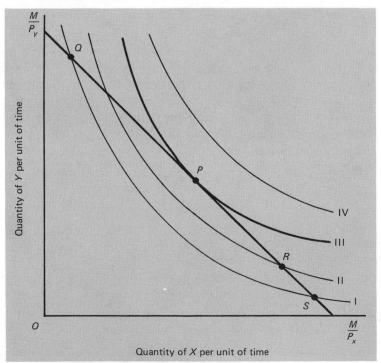

all income is spent on $X$ and $Y$. Thus, the choice of combinations is limited by the given income.

Clearly, the consumer cannot purchase any bundle lying above and to the right of the budget line and, hence, cannot consume any combination lying on indifference curve IV. Some points on curves I, II, and III are attainable. Moreover, as already observed, an infinite number of indifference curves lie between curves I and III. Therefore, all points on the budget line between $Q$ and $S$ are touched by some indifference curve, and, if we extend the map to include curves below I, all points above $Q$ and below $S$ are touched by some curve. Thus, each point on the budget line yields some specific level of utility. Four of the infinite number of attainable combinations are represented by points $Q$, $P$, $R$, and $S$.

Suppose the consumption bundle is located at $Q$. Without experimenting, the consumer cannot know for certain whether $Q$ represents a maximum position or not. Let the individual experimentally move to combinations just to the left and right of $Q$, along the budget constraint. Moving to the left lowers the level of satisfaction to some indifference curve below I, but moving to the right leads to a higher indifference curve. And continued experimentation will lead the consumer to move at least as far as $P$, because each successive movement to the right leads to a higher indifference curve. Continuing to experiment, however, by moving to the right of $P$, the consumer would locate upon a lower indifference curve with its lower level of satisfaction and would accordingly return to the point $P$.

Similarly, if a consumer were situated at $R$, experimentation would cause the substitution of $Y$ for $X$, thereby moving in the direction of $P$. No point except $P$ is optimal, because each successive substitution of $Y$ for $X$ brings the consumer to a higher indifference curve. Hence, the position of maximum satisfaction—*or the point of consumer optimization*—is attained at $P$, where an indifference curve is just tangent to the budget line.

As you will recall, the slope of the budget line is the negative of the price ratio, the ratio of the price of $X$ to the price of $Y$. As you will also recall, the slope of an indifference curve at any point is called the *MRS* of $X$ for $Y$. Hence, the point of utility maximization is defined by the condition that the *MRS* must equal the price ratio.

The interpretation of this proposition is very straightforward. The *MRS* shows the rate at which the consumer *is willing to substitute* $X$ for $Y$. The price ratio shows the rate at which prices permit substitution of $X$ for $Y$. Unless these two are equal, it is possible to change the combination of $X$ and $Y$ purchased so as to attain a higher level of satisfaction. For example, suppose the *MRS* is two—meaning the consumer is willing to give up two units of $Y$ in order to obtain one unit of $X$. Let the price ratio be unity, meaning that one unit of $Y$ can be exchanged for one unit of $X$. Clearly, the consumer will benefit by trading $Y$ for $X$, since he or she is willing to give up two $Y$ for one $X$ but only has to give up one $Y$ for one $X$ in the market. Generalizing, unless the $MRS$ and the price ratio are equal, some exchange can be made so as to move the consumer to a higher level of satisfaction.

**Principle.** The point of consumer equilibrium—or the maximization of satisfaction subject to a limited money income—is defined by the condition that the $MRS$ of $X$ for $Y$ must equal the ratio of the price of $X$ to the price of $Y$.

### Marginal utility interpretation of optimization

Recall that, at the beginning of this chapter, we gave a rather simplified intuitive explanation of utility maximization subject to a budget constraint. We argued that, if a consumer could give up some good and gain more satisfaction from purchasing other goods for the same total expenditure, such substitution would occur. We can set forth this explanation a bit more formally now, using the marginal utility interpretation of indifference curves.

Recall from Section 3.5 that, along an indifference curve

$$MRS_{x \text{ for } y} = \frac{MU_x}{MU_y}.$$

Writing the condition for utility maximization symbolically,

$$MRS_{x \text{ for } y} = \frac{p_x}{p_y}.$$

Thus, in equilibrium

$$\frac{MU_x}{MU_y} = \frac{p_x}{p_y},$$

or

$$\frac{MU_x}{p_x} = \frac{MU_y}{p_y}.$$

This relation provides an alternative view of the condition for consumer equilibrium. Dividing the marginal utility of a commodity by its price gives the marginal utility per dollar's worth of the commodity bought. In this light, we can restate the condition for utility maximization as the following:

**Principle.** To attain maximum satisfaction, a consumer must allocate money income so that the marginal utility per dollar spent on each commodity is the same for all commodities purchased.

This principle is certainly plausible, and explaining why it is plausible illustrates a method of analysis that is used pervasively in economic theory. Suppose, at the current allocation of income, the marginal dollar spent on $X$ yields a greater marginal utility than the marginal dollar spent on $Y$. That is, suppose

$$\frac{MU_x}{p_x} > \frac{MU_y}{p_y}.$$

Reallocating one dollar of expenditure from $Y$ to $X$ will, therefore, increase total utility; and it must do so until the marginal utility per dollar's worth is the same for both commodities.

Alternatively, if

$$\frac{MU_x}{p_x} < \frac{MU_y}{p_y},$$

a dollar taken away from $X$ will reduce utility less than the increase in utility obtained from spending the dollar on additional consumption of $Y$. The consumer will continue to substitute away from $X$ toward $Y$ until the marginal utilities per dollar expenditure are equal. Thus, our intuitive definition is theoretically sound.

### Zero consumption of a good

To this point, the discussion has implied that the consumer chooses to consume some positive amount of both $X$ and $Y$, regardless of relative prices. This circumstance obviously need not be the case. A consumer might choose to spend the entire income and purchase none of some specific good.

One set of theoretical circumstances under which a consumer would choose to spend the entire income on (say) good $Y$ and none on $X$ is depicted in Figure 3–11. Given the budget line, $LM$, and the indifference map represented by curves I, II, III, and IV, the highest level of satisfaction attainable from the given money income is at point $L$ on indifference curve III. The consumer chooses to purchase $L$ units of $Y$ and no $X$. This point need not be a point of tangency at which the $MRS$ equals the price ratio (although it could be such a point). Note that an equilibrium situation exists even though there is no point (at both non-negative $X$ and non-negative $Y$) where the $MRS$ equals the price ratio. Economists call such a situation a *corner solution*. Note also, however, that for a sufficiently large decrease in the price of $X$ relative to the price of $Y$ (say to a

**FIGURE 3–11**
Corner solution

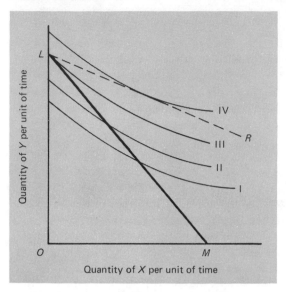

price ratio depicted by budget line *LR*), the budget line could become tangent to some indifference curve above III (curve IV) at a point where both *X* and *Y* are bought. Hence, the consumer will purchase some positive amount of *X* if its relative price decreases sufficiently.

In other words, a corner solution, in which the consumer purchases none of some good *X*, results when

$$\frac{MU_x}{p_x} < \frac{MU_i}{p_i} = \cdots = \frac{MU_j}{p_j}$$

for all goods *i, j*, etc., where the *i*th and *j*th goods are purchased in positive amounts. The consumer spends the entire income, yet the marginal utility per dollar of *X* is less than the marginal utility per dollar spent on any other good that is purchased. This is generally what we mean when we say that "we cannot afford something." Perhaps you do not own a Cadillac. You say you cannot afford one. Conceivably you could buy one (perhaps by borrowing). So, if you do not own one, it must be that the alternative expenditure on goods that you consume gives more utility *per dollar* than would a Cadillac, even though a Cadillac would give *more* total utility than your present automobile. Stated differently, one does not consume some good *X* when the $MRS_{x \text{ for } y}$ (where *Y* is any other good that is consumed) is less than the price ratio, $p_x/p_y$, and total income is exhausted.

## APPLICATION

### Economics of philanthropy

It would be a serious mistake if you have acquired the impression, as many people have, that economic theory necessarily assumes humans are coldly calculating individuals concerned only with their personal well-being and, therefore, totally uninterested in the welfare of others. This is by no means the case. In fact, we can use the simple analytical techniques developed in this chapter to examine the causes of charitable contributions.[4]

Begin by assuming that an individual's utility depends upon both the amount of his or her own consumption and the level of consumption enjoyed by other people. Let us assume, for simplicity, only two individuals, A and B. A's utility is a function of his or her own consumption and of B's. Assume also that it is costless for A to transfer income to B. We need not worry about *why* A's utility depends partly upon B's consumption, our only interest is that it does.

Equilibrium for A is depicted by Figure 3–12. Indifference curve $I_A$ is one of the family of A's indifference curves between A's own

**FIGURE 3–12**
**Philanthropy**

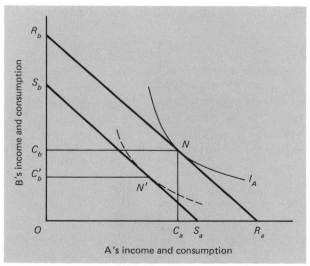

---

[4] Much of this application is based upon the article by R. A. Schwartz, "Personal Philanthropic Contributions," *Journal of Political Economy*, November/December 1970, pp. 1264–91.

consumption and B's consumption, where B's consumption is measured along the vertical axis and A's along the horizontal. This curve
is drawn to reflect A's diminishing marginal rate of substitution between his or her consumption and B's in the neighborhood of $N$.
That is, around $N$, the smaller A's consumption becomes relative to
B's, the less consumption A is willing to give up to B and remain at
the same level of utility.

The budget constraint of A is $R_b R_a$. The distance $OR_b = OR_a$ is
A's income. If A gave all income to B and consumed nothing, B
would have $OR_b$ income. If B got nothing, then A would have $OR_a$
income. Since we assume that transfers are costless, the slope of
$R_b R_a$ is unity; that is, a dollar of income transferred from A to B costs
A one dollar. Let A begin with an income of $OR_a$. Person A can
reach a higher level of utility by transferring $C_a R_a$ to B, attaining
equilibrium at point $N$. Person B now consumes $C_b$ and A consumes
$C_a$. If A's initial income were less, say $OS_a$, the budget line would
shift to the left, $S_b S_a$. Person A would now transfer less income
($C_b'$) to B in order to arrive at $N'$, the point of A's highest attainable level of utility. Thus, the theory of utility maximization is quite
applicable to philanthropy.

## 3.8 INDIFFERENCE CURVES AND BUDGET LINES: SOME DIFFERENT TWISTS

We now want to talk about some special cases that may make you
more comfortable with the tools of utility maximization and may
help you use these tools to analyze economic problems more effectively. We will look at several cases in which indifference curves are
not convex; this should help convince you that convexity is the most
reasonable shape for indifference curves. We will also examine
budget lines more carefully. Certain income and price changes can
lead to some "bent" and "broken" constraints.

### Unusual preference maps

Earlier it was mentioned that, empirically, consumers prefer variety in their consumption bundle. Of course, theoretically, this does
not always have to be true; in fact, we have just used indifference
curves and budget constraints to show that corner solutions can
exist. Figure 3–11 illustrates, for example, the case in which a consumer prefers to consume only $Y$ and no $X$.

Consider some indifference maps that are not strictly convex.
Figure 3–13 shows two such maps. In panel A, the indifference

**FIGURE 3–13**
**Indifference maps that are not convex**

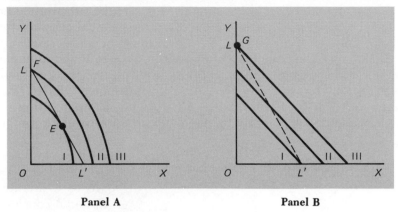

Panel A                                    Panel B

curves are strictly concave—they lie below their tangent lines at each point. The budget line is $LL'$. The consumer optimizes by seeking the highest indifference curve touching the budget line. Usually, this is where the indifference curve and income line are tangent; but at point $E$, the tangency of indifference curve I and $LL'$ in Figure 3–13 (A), the consumer actually minimizes utility. The highest indifference curve is reached by moving to the left along $LL'$ until the consumer eventually hits $F$. At this point, the consumer purchases no $X$ and only $Y$. It will always be the case when indifference curves are strictly concave that corner solutions are the point of consumer equilibrium. Consumers will never choose a variety of products when they maximize satisfaction. A small amount of reflection on how people actually do behave leads to the conclusion that this is not an appropriate way of modeling behavior.

Panel B shows some linear indifference curves. The budget line is dashed to avoid confusing it with an indifference curve. Here, the marginal rate of substitution is constant—that is, the consumer is always willing to trade $X$ and $Y$ at the same rate no matter how much the consumer has of each good. Now that both the constraint and indifference curves are linear, there can be no optimizing tangency. If the lines have different slopes, then the consumer maximizes utility at a corner again, like point $G$ in panel B. The problem could get unmanageable if the budget line and indifference curves had the same slope. Imagine the situation; there would be one indifference curve that was perfectly superimposed over the budget line. No other indifference curves would even touch the constraint. The consumer would certainly know what level of utility was optimal but would not know which mix of goods to consume on that indifference curve; there would be an infinite number of optimal consumption bundles. Behavior would be arbitrary and uncertain. Once again, this kind of model does not accurately describe the real world. Consumers, by and large, appear to have definite ideas about what they want to purchase.

Finally, we can gain more understanding about how indifference maps reflect the tastes of consumers by briefly observing three more sets of indifference curves in which consumers avoid substitution between $X$ and $Y$. Figure 3–14 (A), (B), and (C) show some odd configurations. Interpreting them should be a fruitful exercise.

**FIGURE 3–14**
**Indifference maps with no substitution**

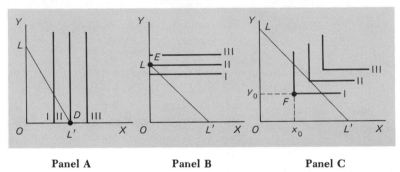

Panel A                    Panel B                    Panel C

Perfectly vertical indifference curves tell us that the consumer's utility depends only upon the amount of $X$ possessed. Good $Y$ has absolutely no influence on utility. It is only reasonable, then, that when we view such an indifference map with an income constraint, as shown by $LL'$ in Figure 3–14 (A), that the consumer would maximize satisfaction by consuming only good $X$ (at point $D$). The consumer should not spend any income on $Y$ if it does not contribute any satisfaction.

Panel B shows just the opposite case. Now $X$ contributes nothing to utility. Satisfaction depends entirely on how much $Y$ the consumer has. The consumer maximizes utility at point $E$, another corner solution in which the consumer's entire income is spent on $Y$.

The consumer whose indifference map is shown in panel C of Figure 3–14 at least enjoys some variety. Such indifference curves have the property that, at any point on the curve, increasing $X$ without increasing $Y$ or increasing $Y$ without increasing $X$ leaves the level of utility unchanged. For example, at the combination $x_0$ and $y_0$, the consumer could receive increased $X$ and experience no additional utility as long as the quantity of $Y$ remains at $y_0$. Or $Y$ could be increased indefinitely with no increase in utility as long as the quantity of $X$ remains $x_0$. In other words, the consumer wishes to consume the two goods in fixed proportions; for example, one left shoe and one right shoe or two left shoes and two right shoes. Any movement away from the fixed proportion by increasing one good without increasing the other keeps the consumer on the same indifference curve. Hence, it should come as no surprise that, when we add the budget line to Figure 3–14 (C), the consumer optimizes at the corner of the highest attainable indifference curve, point $F$ in the figure. Both $X$ and $Y$ are consumed, but no substitution takes place along the curve.

We have explored all of the basic forms indifference curves might take other than the smooth convex shapes we have been using in our discussion. The result of our investigation is that the indifference maps in Figures 3–13 and 3–14 allow the consumers in equilibrium little or no variety in their consumption of goods and services and little or no substitution. We know this is by and large not true of most consumers, so we will continue working with the smooth convex indifference curves we introduced at the beginning of this chapter.

### Bent and broken budget lines

The budget line need not always be a straight line. Frequently, consumers are confronted with pricing structures in markets in which the price they pay depends upon the amount they purchase. Sometimes, too, the government will tax or subsidize the marginal units of a good a consumer buys, causing a kink in the budget line.

As an example, suppose you visit an amusement park. Typically, there is a fixed fee at the entrance plus a charge for each ride taken. Let the price at the gate be $F$ and the price for a ride be $P$. Such a pricing scheme is commonly known as a two-part tariff. The average price you pay ($\overline{P}$) depends upon the number of rides you take, $X$. That is, since total expenditure is $F + PX$, the average price is

$$\overline{P} = \frac{F}{X} + P.$$

The more rides you take, the lower the average price of a ride. The budget line looks like the solid curve in Figure 3–15. It is similar to our conception of an indifference curve. As you can see, this presents a more complicated picture for utility maximization. It is possible that a tangency may occur at a point like $A$ in Figure 3–15, but the highest indifference curve may also be reached at an intersection with the budget constraint—and without being a corner solution.

**FIGURE 3–15**
The budget line when a consumer pays
a two-part tariff

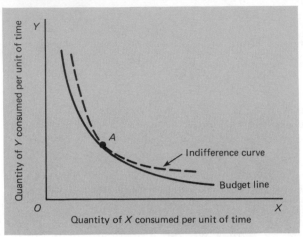

Discrete bends in the budget line are brought about by price decreases or increases after a consumer buys a specific amount of a good. For example, in Texas, grocery stores will frequently put Blue Bell ice cream, a very popular brand of ice cream, on sale but limit purchases at the reduced price to three quarts per customer. Consumers pay the sale price for the first three quarts and a higher price for additional amounts. Such a budget constraint is pictured in Figure 3–16, panel A. Good $Y$ has a fixed price for any amount purchased. Consumers can purchase $X$ at a reduced price until the amount $\bar{x}$ is purchased. Beyond $\bar{x}$, they pay a higher price. This pricing structure is represented by a flatter budget line until $x$, becoming steeper beyond that amount to reflect the higher price. The price paid for the final unit depends upon whether the highest attainable indifference is tangent to the flatter or the steeper segment of the budget line.

The budget line can bend the other way, as shown in panels B and C, Figure 3–16. These shapes results from a price decrease after a certain quantity is purchased. Suppose the government thinks people ought to eat more bagels. To induce individuals to eat more, it gives customers a subsidy for every bagel they purchase after the fifth. So the price of the first five may be $1, but thereafter 75 cents because of the subsidy. Bagels become cheaper after five are purchased. The slope of the budget line becomes less steep at the fifth bagel to reflect the price discount.

Does such a subsidy cause consumers to consume more or less than they would otherwise? The answer depends upon the indiffer-

**FIGURE 3–16**
Bends in the budget line

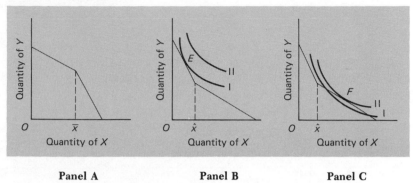

Panel A                    Panel B                    Panel C

ence map. In Figure 3–16, panels B and C, good $X$ becomes less expensive after $\hat{x}$ is purchased, giving the budget line a kink at that quantity. The consumer whose preferences are shown in panel B attains utility maximizing equilibrium at point $E$. This consumer does not benefit from the subsidy. The preference pattern of the consumer depicted in panel C is such that utility maximization occurs at $F$. Thus, this consumer benefits from the subsidy and purchases more with the subsidy than without it.

Compensation policies by employers or income transfers from the government or other institutions can create gaps in the budget line. To illustrate this, let us say you can receive a small scholarship at the school you attend. The grant pays some of your expenses but not all of them; you receive the grant only if you attend classes full time at your college. The net result is that, to receive the scholarship, you must make a specified expenditure on your own, only then do you get the grant. Figure 3–17 shows your budget constraint. On the vertical axis $Y$ now are noneducational expenditures, while $X$ represents expenditures on education. You must spend at least $OR$ (or $LM$) out of your own pocket to be eligible for the scholarship. If you do not spend that much, you do not receive the scholarship. The distance $RP$ (or $NL'$) represents the amount of the scholarship. If you pay at least amount $OR$ on education (reduce your noneducational expenditure by $LM$), you receive the scholarship, and your budget line shifts outward by that amount. Without the scholarship, the budget line is $LN$. With it, the budget line is the broken line $LWZL'$.

Is a student better off with such a grant? The answer is yes, if he or she would have spent at least $OR$ on education anyway. The student with preferences reflected by indifference curves I and II is unambiguously better off. Without a grant, the student would

**FIGURE 3–17**
**The effect of a partial scholarship on a student's budget constraint**

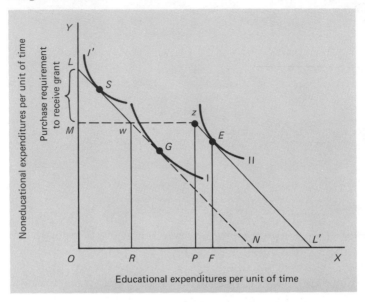

Educational expenditures per unit of time

maximize utility at *G* on I. With the grant, the student maximizes at *E* on II, spending *OR* plus *PF* on education in addition to the scholarship of *RP* (the total educational expenditure is *OF*).

If the student would not have spent at least *OR* on education, the answer is unclear. Suppose that, without the possibility of a grant, another student would attain equilibrium at *S* on indifference curve I. Even with the possibility of a scholarship, this point may represent the highest attainable level of utility. On the other hand, the shift in the line might permit the student to reach a higher indifference curve, tangent to the segment *ZL′*. Thus, in this case, the answer is ambiguous.

## APPLICATION

### Fringe benefits and taxation

Fringe benefits—goods and services received by employees and paid for by employers—are an important part of employees' total income. In 1979, they made up approximately one third of the average employee's compensation. We can use the tools developed here to analyze why employees might prefer increased fringe benefits rather than an equivalent increase in salary.

**FIGURE 3–18**
The effects of fringe benefits on
utility maximization

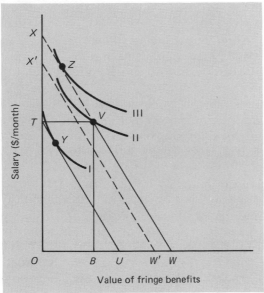

Value of fringe benefits

In Figure 3–18, an employee's salary is measured along the vertical axis; the value of the fringe benefits (in dollars) is measured along the horizontal scale. For simplicity, we assume that the employee could purchase these benefits—insurance, automobile usage, education, travel, etc.—at a price equal to their value. Initially, assume no fringe benefits and a total monthly salary of $OT$. The employee, who can purchase these fringes as desired, faces a budget constraint of $TU$. Some benefits are purchased, and the employee maximizes utility at point $Y$ on indifference curve I.

Now let the salary remain at $OT$ but let the employer give fringe benefits equal in value to $OB$. The new budget line is $TVW$. The employee clearly can now reach a higher indifference curve and is, therefore, better off. Suppose the employee chooses to purchase no additional benefits; equilibrium is attained at point $V$ on indifference curve II. The question is, would the employee be better off receiving the value of the benefits in salary rather than the fringe benefits themselves? Under the assumptions made here, the answer is the employee could not be made worse off and could be made better off by receiving money rather than benefits.

To see this point, assume that the value of the benefits, $OB$, is paid in salary. The employee receives additional salary of $TX$ and no fringes. We simply extend the budget line above point $V$. The new budget line is now $XW$. The person who previously maximized utility at V is clearly now better off, attaining equilibrium at Z on the higher indifference curve III. Thus, anyone who chose a solution at V under the benefit package can be made better off by receiving the value of the benefits as income. These people will choose some point on the segment XV. Anyone who chose a combination on the segment VW with the benefit package will continue to maximize at that position if the benefits are paid as salary.

Why would employers sometimes prefer to offer fringe benefits to more salary? The answer could be, in part, because employers can purchase the fringe benefits at a lower price than is available to employees, for example, group insurance plans are less expensive than are policies purchased by individuals. A more important answer is the existence of taxation. To get at this point, return to Figure 3–18 with the employee receiving fringe benefits of OB and choosing the combination represented by point V. In general, fringe benefits are not subject to taxation. Let us assume this is the case here, but let us also assume that the increase in salary, if fringe benefits are relinquished, is taxed at a rate of 25 percent. Thus, the employee receives an additional TX' after taxes rather than TX. The new budget line is X'W'. Clearly, the employee prefers combination V to any combination along X'W'. Thus, fringe benefits are prefered to the increased salary.

Notice that the relative value of untaxed fringe benefits increases as an employee's marginal tax rate increases. If the tax rate increases, X'W' moves closer to TU. Thus, we would expect employees whose salaries are increasing, and who consequently are moving into higher tax brackets, to take larger proportions of the increased compensation in untaxable fringe benefits. Thus, employers can make their employees better off at a lower cost than that of equivalent salary increases. We should emphasize that we are not saying that incomes do not increase. They do. All we are saying is that, as salaries increase, we would expect some increase in the proportion of nonpecuniary benefits to salary.

An important implication of our theory is that, if cost-of-living wage increases push workers into higher tax brackets, employees will opt for more benefits at the margin rather than take the entire increase in wages. As matters stand now, a typical four-member family earning $20,000 pays about $2,013 in federal income taxes. If the family gets just enough of a pay raise to offset 10 percent inflation, that raise will nudge the breadwinner into a higher tax bracket and raise the family's tax bill to $2,346. The hidden tax of inflation reduces the family purchasing power by $333. Thus, inflation, during which salaries increase at the same rate as the cost of living, actually increases taxes by moving people into higher marginal tax brackets. Nontaxable benefits should increase relative to total income during inflation.

**TABLE 3-1**

**Weekly earnings and fringe benefits for workers in the United States, 1969-1979**

| Benefits | 1969 | 1979 | Percent change |
|---|---|---|---|
| Old-Age, Survivors, Disability and Health Insurance (FICA taxes) .......................... | $6.44 | $16.87 | +162% |
| Insurance (life, hospital, surgical, medical, etc.) ..... | 5.00 | 16.56 | +231 |
| Pensions (nongovernment) ......................... | 5.88 | 15.87 | +170 |
| Paid vacations ................................. | 6.17 | 13.63 | +121 |
| Paid rest periods, coffee breaks, lunch periods, etc............................. | 4.12 | 10.37 | +152 |
| Paid holidays .................................... | 3.85 | 9.27 | +141 |
| Workers' compensation ............................ | 1.29 | 4.90 | +280 |
| Unemployment compensation taxes ................. | 1.10 | 4.40 | +300 |
| Profit-sharing payments ........................... | 1.63 | 4.15 | +155 |
| Paid sick leave ................................... | 1.25 | 3.60 | +188 |
| Christmas or other special bonuses, suggestion awards, etc. .......................... | 0.67 | 1.23 | + 84 |
| Salary continuation or long-term disability .......... | n.a. | 0.88 | n.a. |
| Thrift plans ....................................... | 0.23 | 0.83 | +261 |
| Dental insurance ................................. | n.a. | 0.77 | n.a. |
| Employe education expenditures ................... | 0.12 | 0.48 | +300 |
| Employe meals furnished free ..................... | 0.29 | 0.44 | + 52 |
| Discounts on goods and services purchased from company by employe ...................... | 0.17 | 0.27 | + 59 |
| Other employe benefits ........................... | 1.25 | 2.40 | + 92 |
| Total employe benefits .......................... | 39.46 | 106.92 | +171 |
| Average weekly earnings ........................ | 141.44 | 292.13 | +107 |

n.a. = Data not available.
Source: *Nation's Business*, October 1980, p. 78.

Table 3-1 shows evidence that this trend did in fact occur during the 1970s, a period of high inflation in the United States. This table shows the estimated value of fringe benefits for the typical employee in the United States between the years 1969 and 1979. Employee benefits increased 171 percent while earnings increased 107 percent over the period. Thus, the evidence supports our theoretical conclusions.

## 3.9 SUMMARY

In this chapter, we have developed the basic tools necessary to analyze consumer demand theory. Foremost are the concepts of indifference curves and budget lines. An indifference curve shows combinations of goods among which consumers are indifferent. Several indifference curves make up an indifference map. The slope of an indifference curve shows the rate at which a consumer is willing to substitute one good for another in order to remain at a constant level of utility. The slope is called the marginal rate of substitution.

The marginal rate of substitution can be related to marginal utility, which is the addition to total utility attributable to the addition of one unit of a good to current consumption. The marginal rate of substitution between two goods is the ratio of the two marginal utilities.

The budget line indicates the combinations that the consumer is able to purchase with a given money income. The price ratio given by the market is the slope of the budget line. An increase in money income moves the budget line outward, parallel to the old line. A change in commodity price pivots the budget line.

From this relation we develop the following principles:

**Principle.** The point of consumer optimization—or the maximization of satisfaction subject to a limited money income—is defined by the condition that the MRS of X for Y must equal the ratio of the price of X to the price of Y.

Alternatively,

**Principle.** To attain maximum satisfaction, a consumer must allocate money income so the marginal utility per dollar spent on each commodity is the same for all commodities purchased.

## TECHNICAL PROBLEMS

1. Assume that an individual consumes three goods, X, Y, and Z. The marginal utility (assumed measurable) of each good is independent of the rate of consumption of the other goods. The prices of X, Y, and Z are respectively \$1, \$3, and \$5. The total income of the consumer is \$65, and the marginal utility schedule is as follows:

| Units of good | Marginal utility of X (units) | Marginal utility of Y (units) | Marginal utility of Z (units) |
|---|---|---|---|
| 1 | 12 | 60 | 70 |
| 2 | 11 | 55 | 60 |
| 3 | 10 | 48 | 50 |
| 4 | 9 | 40 | 40 |
| 5 | 8 | 32 | 30 |
| 6 | 7 | 24 | 25 |
| 7 | 6 | 21 | 18 |
| 8 | 5 | 18 | 10 |
| 9 | 4 | 15 | 3 |
| 10 | 3 | 12 | 1 |

a.  Given a $65 income, how much of each good should the consumer purchase to maximize utility?

b.  Suppose income falls to $43 with the same set of prices; what combination will the consumer choose?

c.  Let income fall to $38; let the price of X rise to $5 while the prices of Y and Z remain at $3 and $5. How does the consumer allocate income? What would you say if the consumer maintained that he now does not buy X because he can no longer afford it?

**FIGURE E.3–1**

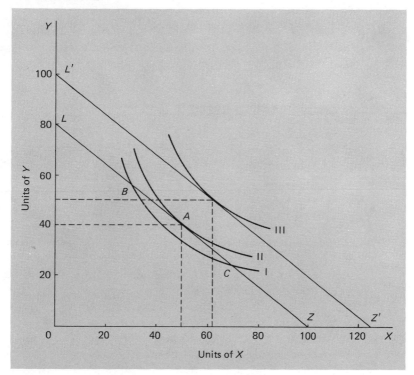

2.  In Figure E.3–1, suppose a consumer has the indicated indifference map and the budget line designated LZ. You know the price of Y is $5 per unit.

a.  What is the consumer's income?

b.  What is the price of X?

c.  Write the equation for the budget line LZ.

d.  What is the value of the slope of LZ?

e.  What combination of X and Y will the consumer choose? Why?

      *f.*  What is the marginal rate of substitution in equilibrium?

      *g.*  Explain precisely in terms of *MRS* why the consumer would not choose combinations designated by *B* or *C*.

      Suppose the budget line shifts to *L'Z'*.

      *h.*  At the same prices, what has happened to money income?

      *i.*  What combination is now chosen?

      *j.*  Draw the relevant budget line if money income remains at the original level (designated by *LZ*), the price of *Y* remains at \$5, but the price of *X* rises to \$10.

      *k.*  Draw in an indifference curve showing the new equilibrium.

      *l.*  What are the new equilibrium quantities?

3.  Suppose $MU_x = ay$ and $MU_y = ax$; $M = $ Income $= P_x X + P_y Y$.

      *a.*  Fill in the following columns with answers that maximize consumer utility.

| | (1) | (2) | (3) | (4) | (5) |
|---|---|---|---|---|---|
| | $M = 100$<br>$P_x = 10$<br>$P_y = 10$ | $M = 200$<br>$P_x = 20$<br>$P_y = 20$ | $M = 150$<br>$P_x = 10$<br>$P_y = 10$ | $M = 150$<br>$P_x = 10$<br>$P_y = 20$ | $M = 150$<br>$P_x = 10$<br>$P_y = 30$ |
| *x* | | | | | |
| *y* | | | | | |
| *x/y* | | | | | |

      *b.*  Using a preference map, graph each of the five utility-maximizing equilibria.

      *c.*  Explain your results when prices and income double between columns (1) and (2).

      *d.*  Explain the change in consumption between columns (1) and (3) when income is increased by 50.

      *e.*  In columns (3), (4), (5), do your results seem reasonable after prices are doubled and then tripled?

4.  Use indifference curves to analyze the effect of the following policies on the quantity demanded of some good, *X*.

      *a.*  Government gives the individual \$500.

      *b.*  Government places a 5 percent tax on good *X* only.

      *c.*  Government places a 5 percent tax on both goods.

5.  If $MU_x/MU_y < P_x/P_y$, the individual would (increase, decrease) the consumption of *X* relative to *Y*. Explain your answer.

6.  Define the marginal rate of substitution and relate it to the older concept of marginal utility.

7. Suppose the following table represents points on one indifference curve.

| Point | Quantity of pizzas | Quantity of hamburgers |
|-------|--------------------|------------------------|
| A.................... | 10 | 1 |
| B.................... | 8 | 3 |
| C ................... | 6 | 6 |
| D ................... | 4 | 10 |
| E ................... | 2 | 15 |

   a. Draw this indifference curve, putting quantity of pizzas on the vertical axis and quantity of hamburgers on the horizontal axis. Label points A, B, C, D, and E.

   b. Does this indifference curve show diminishing MRS? Defend your answer by calculating the MRS between points A and B and between B and C.

8. Let Mary Jones have the utility function $U = X + Y$; her spending is limited to $100 per period, while the price of X is $10 and the price of Y is $5. Mary's behavior is one of extremes; she detests variety. Does utility maximization support this assertion? (*Hint:* $MU_x$ is the change in utility when X changes by one unit. $MU_x = \Delta U/\Delta X = [(X + 1) + Y] - (X + Y) = 1$. The same is true for Y).

9. Suppose that consumers in Dallas pay twice as much for grapefruit as for oranges, and consumers in Houston pay three times as much for grapefruit as for oranges. If consumers in both cities maximize utility, how much larger will the marginal rate of substitution of oranges for grapefruit be in Dallas relative to Houston?

10. An individual consumes two goods, A and B. The price of A is $5 per unit; the price of B is $7 per unit. The marginal utility of A is 10; the marginal utility of B is 21. The consumer spends the entire income on A and B.

    a. What should the consumer do?

    b. The marginal utility of B falls to 14; what should the consumer do now?

11. Figure E.3–2 shows a portion of an individual's indifference map between pizzas and hamburgers. Explain in terms of MRS why you think this person likes _____ relative to _____.

12. "If the price of X equals the price of Y, then the utility-maximizing consumer will always buy equal amounts of X and Y." Analyze.

FIGURE E.3–2

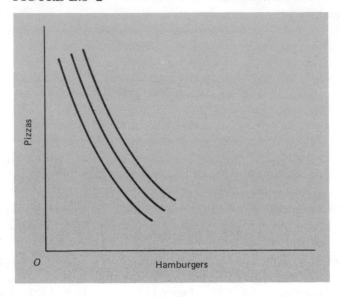

13. Suppose the price of X is $2 and the price of Y is $6. If the marginal utility of X is 12, then the marginal utility of Y for a consumer in equilibrium is _____. Why?

14. A person's marginal rate of substitution between X and Y ($\Delta Y/\Delta X$) is 4. The person is in equilibrium with the price of X at $12 and the price of Y at $3. The price of X rises to $15 and the price of Y rises to $5. Income is varied to restrict the consumer to the same indifference curve. Does the consumer substitute more X for Y or more Y for X? Explain.

15. Economists admit that people have greatly differing taste patterns. But they say that, for any two goods consumed by any two people picked at random, the marginal rates of substitution must be equal even though tastes differ. How can this be so?

## ANALYTICAL PROBLEMS

1. Business executives generally receive their salary in money income and in goods in kind, such as stock options, nice offices, free trips, and so on. If the income tax is replaced by a sales tax, how do you think the general ratio of money income to nonpecuniary income would change? Explain.

2. The fact that wants can be synthesized by advertising, catalyzed by salesmanship, and shaped by the discreet manip-

ulation of the persuaders shows that they are not very urgent.
Analyze.

3. "Researchers are intrigued by the fact that many of those moving to small towns or into the country have willingly ignored
   economics to do so—passing up both better jobs and bigger
   paychecks. A lot of people are putting other concerns above
   jobs—quiet place, scenic, safe for children, less noise and congestion, a slower pace of life" [*Newsweek,* July 6, 1981]. Are
   those people who move to small towns really ignoring economics? Use a preference map, plotting income on the vertical axis
   and small-town quality of life on the horizontal axis, to show
   how tastes are changing. Could you argue that the "price" of
   income is rising relative to quality of life in a small town?

4. If higher sales tax was imposed on all automobiles in a particular state, *every one* of the automobile salespeople in the state
   would have been opposed to the tax increase. Evaluate the
   conclusion under the following conditions:
   
   *a.* The tax is a fixed dollar amount per car sold.
   
   *b.* The tax is a given percentage of the purchase price.
   
   *c.* The tax is progressive, the percentage increasing with the
   price of the automobile.

5. Suppose government is considering a lump sum tax on
   cigarette smoking. Anyone who smokes must pay a flat amount
   regardless of the amount smoked. Use cigarettes as one good
   and expenditures on all goods other than cigarettes as the
   other.
   
   *a.* What would the new budget line under the lump sum tax
   look like? (The price of cigarettes remains constant.)
   
   *b.* What would probably happen to the amount of cigarettes
   purchased?
   
   *c.* Compare the conclusion with those under the assumption
   of a per-unit excise tax.

6. Explain what effect firms would like the advertising of their
   products to have on the indifference maps of potential customers. Why would you think firms advertise?

7. What would the budget lines look like if consumers received a
   lower price the more they purchased during a particular period? The reduction varies continuously over the entire range
   of quantities of the good. Would the utility-maximizing
   equilibrium condition be substantially changed from those
   that prevail under fixed prices?

8. At this time, major league baseball players are on strike, and
   many think there will be no major league baseball all summer.
   If this conclusion is correct, how might the strike affect the

indifference maps of consumers (considering major league games attended are one good) over the next few years? Explain. What might happen to the demand for tickets in the future?

9. Explain why indifference curves might turn upward or bend backward, as shown in Figure E.3–3. Why would people never choose a combination on these portions of their indifference maps?

FIGURE E.3–3

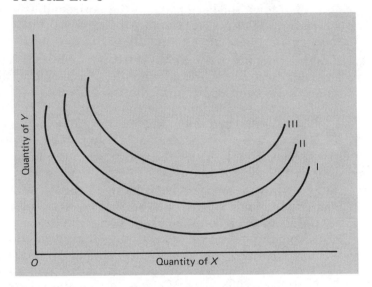

10. Increasingly, employees are being allowed to choose benefit packages from a menu of items. For instance, workers may be given a package of benefits that includes "basic" and "optional" items. Basics might include modest medical coverage, life insurance equal to a year's salary, vacation time based on length of service, and some retirement pay. But then employees can use credits to choose among such additional benefits as full medical coverage, dental and eye care, more vacation time, additional disability income, and higher company payments to the retirement fund. How do you think flexible benefit packages will affect the employee's choice between higher wages and more benefits? Before you answer, review the application on fringe benefits in the text.

# Chapter 4

## Theory of consumer behavior: Changes in income and price

### 4.1 INTRODUCTION

Having developed the concept of utility maximization, we are now prepared to analyze the effect of changes in two important determinants of the amount demanded—the consumer's income and the price of the good. Recall from Chapter 2 that the theory of demand is concerned primarily with the effect of changes in price, other things held constant. One of the factors held constant was income, but we know that, when prices change, there is a change in purchasing power. More precisely, when we discussed the budget line, the maximum amount of good $X$ a consumer could purchase with income $M$ was $M/p_x$. If prices fall to $p'_x$, then he or she could purchase more: $M/p'_x$ units; there was an increase in purchasing power, or what is frequently called real income. Hence, with a constant money income, real income cannot be held constant when prices change, and, as a consequence, when a price does change, economists identify an "income" effect as well as a price effect.

In this chapter, we will examine these two types of changes in some depth. We shall also analyze in depth the reasons that economists assume demand curves slope downward.

## Basic principles

The effects of changes in income and price are really rather simply analyzed. First, consider the effect of an increase in money income, prices held constant. You will recall from Chapter 3 that this increase involves a parallel shift outward in the budget line. If the consumer was in equilibrium before the increase in income, after the increase, there will be a new equilibrium on the higher budget line tangent to a higher indifference curve. The increase in income simply extends the set of the consumer's consumption possibilities, thereby making the consumer better off. The new equilibrium on the higher curve is attained under exactly the same conditions—the marginal rate of substitution equals the price ratio. The effect of a decrease in money income is analyzed similarly. In this case, the budget line shifts downward; equilibrium is attained on a lower indifference curve since the set of consumption opportunities is decreased.

Now recall that a change in the price of a good, money income held constant, rotates the budget line—outward for a decrease in price, inward for an increase. The adjustment principle is simple. Begin in equilibrium. Let the price of the good decrease. Since the budget line rotates outward, the set of consumption opportunities available to the individual is increased. In other words, the consumer is made better off. The good for which the price decreased is now less expensive relative to other goods. Thus, the consumer tends to substitute consumption away from other goods to the now relatively cheaper good. Economists call this effect on consumption the "substitution effect." The fall in price also increases the consumer's consumption opportunities. More goods can be bought with the same money income; this includes all goods, but in particular the less expensive commodity. Economists call this effect the "income effect."

The combination of these two effects leads to a new equilibrium situation; the new budget line, which has rotated outward, is tangent to a higher indifference curve. The entire effect combines both income and substitution effects. After the change, the marginal rate of substitution equals the new price ratio.

The effect of an increase in price is symmetrical. The budget line rotates inward, leading to a new tangency on a lower indifference curve. The income effect follows, because the consumer now has a smaller set of consumption possibilities and is therefore worse off. Since the price of the good increases relative to that of other goods, the substitution effect involves a shift in consumption away from the now more expensive good to other goods.

Thus, you see that the principles involved in analyzing the effects of changes in income and prices are quite straightforward. There are, however, several implications of the theory that are made more apparent with the use of graphical analysis. Of particular interest is the relation of the principles discussed above to demand theory. We shall devote considerable space in this chapter to developing that relation and using the analysis to see why economists assume that demand slopes downward.

The basic concepts to be learned in Chapter 4 are

1. The definition and determinants of income elasticity.
2. The derivation of a demand curve from indifference curves and budget lines.
3. The definition and identification of the income and substitution effects.
4. How the slope of demand is determined by the income and substitution effects.
5. The relation between consumer surplus and indifference curves and budget lines.
6. How to develop labor supply theory from indifference curves and budget lines.

## 4.2 CHANGES IN MONEY INCOME

### Income-consumption curve

To analyze graphically the effect of changes in money income we will, as before, plot the quantity of some good, $X$, along the horizontal axis. But, rather than plotting the quantity of some other good, $Y$, along the vertical, we plot expenditure on all goods other than $X$. Thus, the unit of measure along the vertical axis is dollar expenditure. In Figure 4–1, each indifference curve, I–IV, indicates the various combinations of $X$ and expenditures on other goods that yield the same level of utility. Higher levels of utility are indicated by the higher-numbered indifference curves. Assume that the price of $X$ is fixed at \$10 per unit and that, initially, the consumer has an income of \$1,000, indicated by budget line $L''Z''$. A consumer can spend all income on $X$ and purchase 100 units, buy no $X$ and spend all income on other goods, or can purchase any combination on $L''Z''$. We know from Chapter 3 that utility is maximized at $R$ on indifference curve III, indicating that the highest available level of utility comes from 40 units of $X$ and \$600 spent on other goods.

When we decrease income to \$700, the new budget line is $L'Z'$. Equilibrium is now at $Q$, with 30 units of $X$ and \$400 spent on other goods. An income of $400 causes the consumer to purchase 20 units of $X$ and spend $200 on other goods. Finally, if income is increased to $1,400, $L'''Z'''$ is tangent to IV at 70 units of $X$ and $700. As income changes, the point of consumer equilibrium changes, as well. The line connecting the successive equilibria is called the *income-consumption curve,* indicated by $AB$ in Figure 4–1. This

**FIGURE 4–1**
**Income-consumption curve**

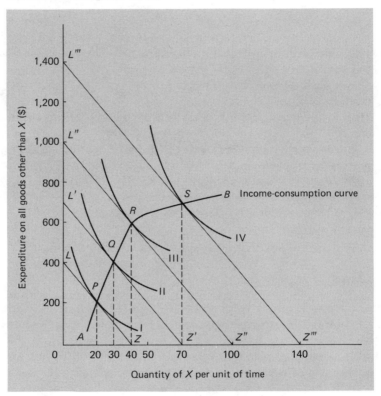

curve shows the *equilibrium combinations* of $X$ and expenditures on goods other than $X$ at various levels of money income, nominal prices remaining constant throughout. That is, it shows the various equilibria corresponding to various income levels; it thus shows the effects of changes in money income at constant commodity prices.

**Definition.** The locus of points showing consumer equilibria at various levels of money income at constant prices is called the income-consumption curve.

### Engel curves and income elasticity

Now we can relate the income-consumption curve to Engel curves. Engel curves, named for a 19th-century German statistician, show the relation between money income and the consumption of some good, other things, including the price of the good, held constant. These curves are closely related to a good's elasticity of income and are important for applied studies of economic welfare and for the analysis of family expenditure patterns.

The Engel curve derived from the income-consumption curve in Figure 4–1 is constructed in Figure 4–2. Here, the quantity of good $X$ is plotted along the horizontal axis, money income along the vertical. Hence, the slope of an Engel curve is defined for a small change in $X$ and $M$, where $M$ is money income, as before. Algebraically, we write the slope as $\Delta M / \Delta X$. Point $LZ$ in Figure 4–2, showing that,

**FIGURE 4–2**
**Engel curve**

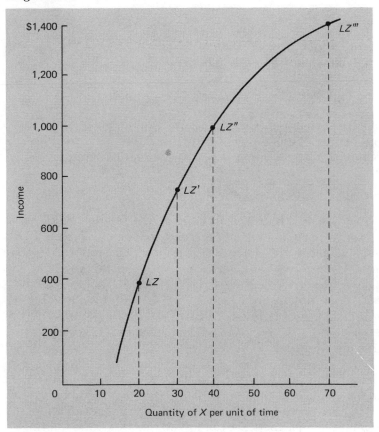

with an income of $400, the consumer purchases 20 units, is associated with point $P$ in Figure 4–1. It follows that $LZ'$, 30 units of $X$ at an income of $700, is associated with point $Q$. Likewise, $LZ''$ and $LZ'''$ are equivalent to $R$ and $S$, respectively. As we shall see, not all income-consumption curves and Engel curves have the same general slope as this.

**Definition.**   An Engel curve is a locus of points relating equilibrium quantity of some good to the level of money income. Such curves are readily derived from income-consumption curves.

The responsiveness of quantity demanded to income changes, other things remaining the same, is measured by the coefficient of income elasticity $(E_M)$. Specifically, the income elasticity of demand is the ratio of the percentage change in quantity demanded to the percentage change in money income. Symbolically

$$E_M = \frac{\Delta X / X}{\Delta M / M} = \frac{\Delta X}{\Delta M} \cdot \frac{M}{X} \gtreqless 0.$$

Note that we do not know the sign of $E_M$. It depends upon the term $\Delta X / \Delta M$, which may be positive, negative, or zero. We can write this term somewhat differently. Observe

$$\frac{\Delta X}{\Delta M} = \frac{1}{\Delta M / \Delta X}.$$

The denominator in the right-hand expression is the slope of the Engel curve. Thus, $E_M$ is positive, negative, or zero, whenever the slope of the Engel curve is positive, negative, or zero.

### Normal and inferior goods

Note that in Figures 4–1 and 4–2, the relation between money income and the amount of the good consumed is such that, as income increases, the amount of the good consumed increases, the prices of all goods held constant. That is, in this case, the income-consumption curve does not bend backward; neither does the Engel curve slope downward. Such a good is called a *normal good* over the relevant income levels. That is, more $X$ is purchased as money income increases; the income-consumption curve and the Engel curve are positively sloped for a normal good.

In the case of a normal good, the income elasticity of the good is positive. That is, $(\Delta X / X) \div (\Delta M / M) > 0$. Normal goods are given that name because economists in the past seemed to believe that, in the majority of cases, an increase in income causes an increase in the consumption of a good; they believed that this is the "normal" situation. However, an increase in income may well cause a decrease in the consumption of certain commodities at certain price ratios. These commodities are called *inferior* goods. In other words, an inferior good is a commodity for which the income elasticity is negative over a range of incomes.

**Definition.**   A good is normal if its income elasticity is positive; it is inferior if its income elasticity is negative. A normal good's Engel curve is positively sloped. The Engel curve for an inferior good is negatively sloped over its range of inferiority.

Figure 4–3 illustrates a good that is inferior over a certain range of incomes. Note that, in this figure, the quantity of Y, rather than expenditure on all goods other than X, is plotted on the vertical axis. The analysis is the same in either case. The quantity of good X is plotted along the horizontal axis.

Begin with an income shown by budget line $LZ$. Point $P$, indicating $x_1$ consumed, is the point of equilibrium for the consumer. Next,

**FIGURE 4–3**
**Illustration of an inferior good**

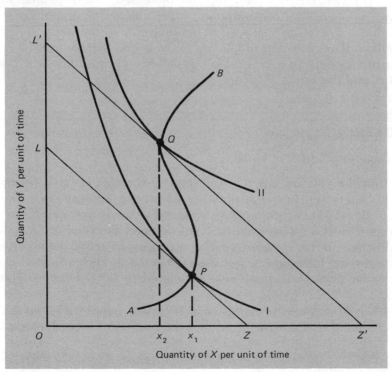

let income increase to the level shown by $L'Z'$, prices held constant. After the change, the position of consumer equilibrium shifts from point $P$ to point $Q$. The consumer is better off by being on a higher indifference curve. But the increase in income leads to a *decrease* in the consumption of $X$. For this reason, we say that $X$ is inferior over the range of incomes denoted by $LZ$ and $L'Z'$. Over this range, the income consumption curve bends backward. Since this curve bends backward, the income elasticity of demand, $(\Delta X/\Delta M)(M/X)$, is negative. We might note that, over some ranges of income, the good may be normal for the consumer, such as movements from $A$ to $P$ and from $Q$ to $B$.

We should emphasize in passing that it is clear from the above exposition that inferiority and normality—and therefore, of course, income elasticity—vary over different ranges of income. Hamburger may be a normal good for one family over a particular range of incomes. It may be an inferior good over still another range of incomes. Furthermore, the classification of goods as inferior or normal depends upon the price ratio. At one price ratio, a good may have an income elasticity substantially different from the income elasticity at another price ratio. We might also note that economists frequently point out examples of inferior goods such as margarine, hamburgers, and Volkswagens. As their income increased, many people may have reduced their consumption of these goods. Many others may not have. Therefore, it is well to remember that inferiority and normality are not inherent properties of the goods themselves. Income elasticities depend upon preference patterns of consumers, the price ratio, and the range of incomes.

## APPLICATION

### Income elasticities of housing

Branches of the federal and state governments have become quite interested in the availability of private housing. In making their development plans, governmental officials are naturally interested in the income elasticity of demand for housing. A study published in 1971 estimated the elasticity of rental expenditure with respect to income as between 0.8 and 1.0. The estimated elasticity for owner-occupants was estimated to lie between 0.7 and 1.5.[1]

In making plans over the next 10 years, people who work for government might wish to predict the increase in the demand for

---

[1] See F. de Leeuw, "The Demand For Housing: A Review of Cross Section Evidence," *The Review of Economics and Statistics* 53 (February 1971): 1–10.

housing (rental and owner-occupied) due to increases in yearly real per capita income, which is expected to increase between 2 and 3 percent a year. Those making predictions generally realize that they cannot come up with a precise single estimate. Using your knowledge of elasticities and the figures given above, how would you estimate the increase in housing demand due to increases in real income?

First, we must estimate the expected increase in real per capita income 10 years hence. If income increases 2 percent per year, then income at the end of the first year will be 1.02 times that at the first of the year; at the end of the second year it will be (1.02) times (1.02) times income at the beginning of year one. To generalize, at the end of the 10th year, income will be $(1.02)^{10}$ times income at the beginning of the period. Since $(1.02)^{10}$ equals 1.218, real per capita income will increase by 21.8 percent, if income increases 2 percent a year. (Note that, for simplicity, we have not resorted to averaging.)

If income increases 3 percent a year, income in 10 years will be 34.3 percent higher, since $(1.03)^{10}$ equals 1.343. Using estimates for the elasticity, we can solve for the percent of increase in the demand for rental housing because of income increases over the 10-year period with the formula

$$E_M = \frac{\% \Delta X}{\% \Delta M}.$$

We can summarize the results for rental housing in a table showing the percentage change in quantity under each possible combination.

| | | Percent increase in income | |
|---|---|---|---|
| | | 21.8% | 34.3% |
| Income elasticities | 0.8 | 17.4% | 27.4% |
| | 1.0 | 21.8% | 34.8% |

Thus, the range of increase lies between 17.4 percent and 34.3 percent.

The estimates of the percent of increase in the demand for owner-occupied housing due to increases in income are summarized in the following table.

| | | Percent increase in income | |
|---|---|---|---|
| | | 21.8% | 34.3% |
| Income elasticities | 0.7 | 15.3% | 24.0% |
| | 1.5 | 32.7% | 51.5% |

Note that the range of estimation is far greater in the case of owner-occupied housing, because the range of elasticities is greater.

We must emphasize that these estimates are estimates of the increase in the amount that would be demanded at a given real price. A person trained in economics would hedge by pointing out that increases in price would curtail, to some extent, the increase in quantity demanded.

## 4.3 DEMAND CURVES

The effect of price on the consumption of goods is even more important to economists than is the effect of changes in income. In this section, we hold money income constant and let price change in order to analyze the fundamentals of demand theory.

### Price-consumption curves

Just as was the case for Engel curves, demand curves are derived by moving the budget line and observing the various points of tangency to indifference curves. In this case, rather than a parallel shift in the budget line, there is a rotation of the line, as was noted in the introduction to this chapter.

Figure 4–4 contains a portion of an indifference map for a consumer who can consume $X$ (measured in units along the horizontal axis) and goods other than $X$. (The total expenditure on these is measured in dollars along the vertical axis.) The consumer has money income of $1,000. When $X$ is priced at $25 per unit, the consumer's budget line is $LZ$. He or she can spend the $1,000 on other goods, spend the entire $1,000 on 40 units of $X$ at $25 per unit, or spend at any point along $LZ$. By the analysis developed above, the consumption represented at point $P$, where $LZ$ is tangent to indifference curve I, is optimal. He or she consumes 24 units of $X$, thereby spending $600 on this commodity. The remaining $400 is spent on other goods.

Assume that the price of $X$ falls to $10. Now, if the consumer wishes to spend all income on $X$, he or she can purchase 100 units. The budget line at the new price is $LZ'$, with a slope of $-10$ rather than $-25$. The new equilibrium point of tangency is designated by $Q$, at which he or she consumes 70 units of $X$ at a total expense of $700 and spends the remaining $300 on other goods. If price falls to $8 per unit, other things remaining the same, the new budget line is $LZ''$, with a slope of $-8$. At equilibrium point $R$, he or she purchases 87.5 units of $X$. Note that $700 is still spent on $X$ and $300 on all other goods. Finally, the price of $X$ falls to $5. The new budget line,

**FIGURE 4-4**
Price-consumption curve

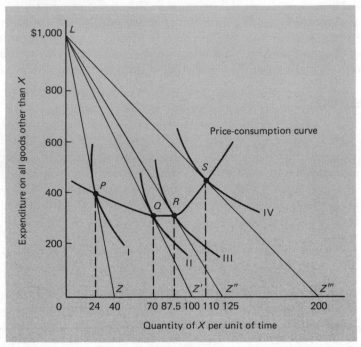

*LZ'''* is tangent to indifference curve IV at point S. The maximum utility level is attained by spending $550 on 110 units of *X* and $450 on goods other than *X*. Thus, each price decrease causes the consumer to purchase more units of *X*. The line joining points *P*, *Q*, *R*, and *S* (and all other equilibria) is called the *price-consumption curve*. For a given money income, it shows the amount of *X* consumed as its price changes, other prices remaining the same.

**Definition.** The price-consumption curve is a locus of equilibrium points relating the quantity of *X* purchased to its price, money income and all other prices remaining constant. In the case treated above, the price-consumption curve also shows how expenditure on all goods other than *X* changes as the price of *X* changes.

### Derivation of demand curves from price-consumption curves

The individual's demand curve for a commodity can be derived from the price-consumption curve, just as an Engel curve is derivable from the income-consumption curve. The price-quantity relations for good *X* at points *P*, *Q*, *R*, and *S*, and presumably for all other points on the price-consumption curve in Figure 4–4, are plotted in Figure 4–5. The horizontal axis is the same (units of $X$), but the vertical axis now shows the price of $X$. When the price of $X$ is given by the slope of $LZ$ ($25), 24 units of $X$ are purchased, indicated by point $P'$ in Figure 4–5. If the price if $10, 70 units are purchased (point $Q'$), and so forth. All other points on the curve are derived similarly. The locus of these points is called the demand curve for $X$.

**FIGURE 4–5**
**Demand curve**

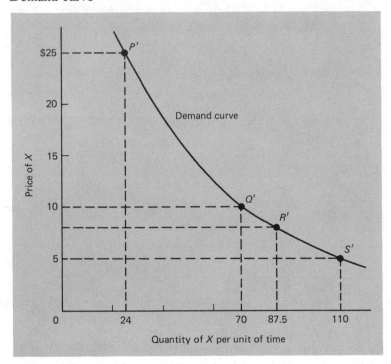

**Definition.** The demand curve of an individual for a specific commodity relates equilibrium quantities bought to market price, money income and nominal prices of all other commodities held constant. The slope of the demand curve illustrates the law of demand: quantity demanded varies inversely with price—income and the prices of other commodities held constant.

## Demand elasticity and the price-consumption curve

Using our knowledge of the relation between the change in total expenditure on a good and whether that good's demand is elastic, inelastic, or unitary, we can show from the shape of the price-consumption curve in Figure 4–4 that the demand curve in Figure 4–5 is elastic between $25 and $10, of unitary elasticity between $10 and $8, and inelastic between $8 and $5.

First, recall that, if the price of a good falls, total expenditure on the good increases (decreases) if the demand is elastic (inelastic). Total expenditure remains constant if the demand is of unitary elasticity. When price falls from $25 to $10, money income remaining constant at $1,000, equilibrium moves from point $P$ to $Q$. From the graph, it is clear that the movement involves a *decrease* in expenditure on all goods other than $X$. Thus, expenditure on $X$ must rise and demand must be in the elastic range. The fall in price from $10 to $8 moves equilibrium from $Q$ to $R$. Since expenditure on all other goods stays the same, with money income constant, expenditure on $X$ must stay the same as well. Thus, elasticity is unitary over the range $10 to $8. The fall in price from $8 to $5 moves equilibrium from $R$ to $S$; expenditure on all other goods increases. Thus, expenditure on $X$ decreases and demand is necessarily inelastic over this range. The demand curve in Figure 4–5 is elastic at higher prices, becomes unitary, then becomes inelastic at lower prices.

We might note that the relation between the slope of the price-consumption curve and demand elasticity holds only when expenditure on all other goods is plotted along the vertical axis. When the quantity of some other good, say $Y$, is along the vertical axis, the relation does not hold unless $Y$ stands for all other goods with a fixed price.

### Problems in estimation of demand and some methods of estimation

While theoretical or graphical derivation of consumer demand is simple, the statistical estimation of actual demand curves is quite difficult. It is, however, these real-world demands in which decision makers are interested. Those in business are willing to pay large amounts of money to have the demand for their products estimated. Certainly, a knowledge of this type of demand is of primary importance in business decision making. Anyone in business wishes to know how sales will vary when price varies.

Governmental decision makers make many important decisions based upon statistical estimates of commodity demand curves. Estimates of demand elasticities for gasoline and petroleum had a significant impact on government policy concerning these commodities. As it turned out, in some cases, the estimates proved accurate; in other cases, the results were far off. Estimates of demand play an important role in the decision to levy taxes on certain commodities.

Those working for nonprofit institutions make long-range plans based upon estimates of demand also. For example, the demand for hospital services plays an important role in the plans of hospital administrators. University presidents like to have good estimates about the demand for classroom space. We could go on and on, but the situation should be clear. Decision makers can frequently make better decisions when they have a reasonably accurate estimate of the demand for the relevant goods and services.

The problem is, however, that statisticians simply do not have available the indifference curves of individuals. They must use actual data. Furthermore, in theory, we hold everything but price and quantity constant when deriving demands; in actual investigations, economists may have strong reason to believe that other things have changed during the time over which they have collected their data. It is not enough to go out into the world and gather data on price and quantity sold, plot these data, and from those plotted points estimate a demand curve. A series of price-quantity observations collected over time may give the series of points plotted in Figure 4–6. The line drawn through the points appears to fit the data rather well. Its positive slope, however, is not evidence that the market demand for X is upward sloping. The points plotted in the figure may well designate different points of equilibrium. Supply and demand could have shifted many times during the period of observation

**FIGURE 4–6**
**Price-quantity observations from a time series**

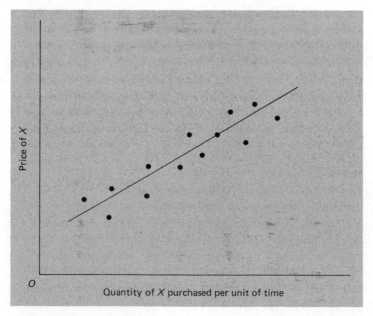

because of changes in other variables. Each indicated point would then be a point of equilibrium. Without knowledge of the way that these other variables change and the way that they affect supply and demand, one cannot really say what the line indicates. For example, supply and demand may have shifted over time in the way illustrated by Figure 4–7. $S_1$ and $D_1$ determine equilibrium point $A$, $S_2$

**FIGURE 4–7**
**Changing equilibria over time**

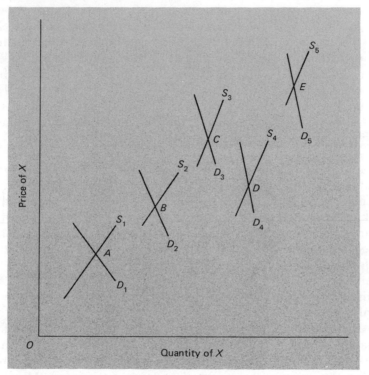

and $D_2$ determine $B$, and so forth. From five observations, we observe only points $A$ through $E$. We cannot tell simply from the observations how these points were generated.

Even though some observed points actually indicate an inverse relation between price and quantity, these points do not necessarily set forth a demand curve. Again, they may simply be points of equilibrium. There are, however, some techniques that economists and statisticians have used to estimate actual demands from actual data.

One obvious extension of the technique of estimating demand

solely from price-quantity data is to consider statistically those variables that would have been held constant in a controlled experiment. This technique is called multiple regression. Economists or statisticians set up a model of equations with two or more independent variables. They solve the model to obtain estimating equations. One example of this type is

$$Q_D = b_0 + b_1P + b_2W + b_3P_0,$$

where $Q_D$ is the total quantity demanded, $P$ is per-unit price of a good, $W$ is an average wage rate, and $P_0$ is some index of related prices. The $b$'s are the parameters to be estimated by multiple regression techniques. (Such techniques are generally taught in beginning statistics classes.) In this way, the effect of changes in $W$ and $P_0$ can be isolated while one attempts to analyze the effect of $P$ on $Q_D$. Of course, the effect of any other variables that affect supply and demand is not isolated. This omission could cause misleading interpretation. Another problem is the frequent difficulty of obtaining sufficient and accurate data so that meaningful results can be obtained.

In using the above method, the economist must assume that the relations are reasonably linear and that the estimating equation specifies what is actually happening. The problems concerned with making such types of estimates make up an entire branch of economics. This branch is known as econometrics—the use of statistics in economic theory. In any case, you should be aware that such techniques are available. Many government agencies and large businesses employ their own group of econometricians. Private firms of econometricians are available to answer questions for smaller businesses.

An interesting, though expensive and difficult, technique for estimating demand and demand elasticity is the controlled market experiment. The experimenter attempts to hold everything constant during the experiment except the price of the good. Many such experiments have been undertaken to gain information for the agricultural sector of the economy.

Those carrying out these market experiments display the products in several different grocery stores over a period of time. They make sure that there are always sufficient amounts available at each price to satisfy demand. In this way, the effect of changes in supply is removed. There is generally no advertising. During the period of the experiment, price is changed in reasonably small increments over a range, and sales are recorded at each price. Thus, many of the effects of changes in other things can be removed, and a reasonable approximation of actual demand is estimated. We must mention again, however, that this is a difficult and expensive process.

As we noted above, in market experiments to determine demand, advertising is generally omitted. Frequently, however, retail merchants are interested in the effect of both price and advertising. One such controlled experiment was carried out by the Agricultural Experiment Station of Oregon State University.[2] A grocery chain of 20 stores participated in the experiment, which lasted about five years.

The experiment was designed to determine whether sales revenue was higher from advertising a particular good, in this case fish, with or without a price reduction. Clearly a store advertises a good in the hope of increasing revenue from that good. But if, in conjunction with the ad, the price of the good is reduced, revenues may be either larger or smaller than if the good is advertised without a price decrease. The result, as you know, would depend upon price elasticity in connection with advertising.

Over the five-year period, several types of fish were advertised in the 20 stores. Sometimes there was no price reduction. At other times, the advertising was done in connection with price reductions that varied over the relevant range. In this way, the retailers learned the price response for various items. The results were rather surprising (to us, at least). For some fish—for example, salmon—advertising with a price discount created more revenue than advertising without a price decrease; for others—sole and snapper—revenue from advertising was greater without a price discount than with one.

We put in this example only to show that there are many ways to estimate the effect of price changes on sales under various circumstances, and there are many groups, public and private, that specialize in such estimation. This example is simply a means of showing the application of statistical methods to economic theory in making business decisions.

An alternative method of derivation, the questionnaire or survey approach, is a much cheaper method, but far less reliable. Potential or actual consumers are simply questioned about how much of certain goods they *would* buy at several prices; or what they consider a "reasonable" price. These surveys may provide some useful indirect information, but the imprecision and ambiguity is, as you probably would expect, extremely high. What consumers say they would do or would buy often differs from how they would actually act. In fact, consumers may not even know their future reactions. What people being questioned say may also depend upon the images they wish to convey to the questioner. That is, they may not wish to appear miserly and, therefore, say price would not affect their pur-

---

[2] *Fresh Fish Sales as a Function of Promotion in a Portland, Oregon, Grocery Chain,* Agricultural Experiment Station, Special Report 372. Corvallis: Oregon State University, October 1972).

chases. According to marketing experts, these techniques are not very reliable.

A relatively new technique, laboratory experiment, is a compromise between market experiments and surveys. In some types of laboratory experiments, volunteers are paid to simulate actual buying conditions without going through real markets. Volunteer "consumers" are given money to go on simulated market trips. The experimenter changes relative prices between trips. After many "shopping trips" by many "consumers," an approximation of demand is obtained. The volunteers have the incentive to act as though they are really shopping, because there is always the probability that they may keep their purchases. We might note that, in every case about which we have read, demand was deduced to be downward sloping.

Going a step further, some economists—with the help of psychologists—have conducted experiments on consumer behavior in mental institutions and in drug centers, by setting up token economies, which, incidentally, are supposed to have therapeutic value. Patients receive tokens for jobs performed. They can exchange these tokens for goods and services. The experimenters can change prices and incomes and, thus, generate demands and Engel curves. These are compared with the theoretical properties of such curves. These types of experiments are in very early stages. Some economists are going even further by emulating psychologists and conducting economic experiments on animals.

This discussion is not meant to teach you how to estimate actual demands. This is the task of your marketing and econometrics classes. In these classes, you will actually be shown how estimates are made. But, in order to do such estimating, one should have acquired a thorough foundation in the theoretical underpinnings of demand theory. The purpose of this chapter is to provide that foundation.

## 4.4 SUBSTITUTION AND INCOME EFFECTS

Let us now turn to a more complete analysis of why demand curves slope downward. Recall from the introduction that there are two effects of a price change. If price falls (rises) the good becomes cheaper (more expensive) relative to other goods, and consumers substitute toward (away from) the good. This is the substitution effect. Also, as price falls (rises), the consumer's purchasing power increases (decreases). Since the set of consumption opportunities increases (decreases), the consumer changes the level of consumption; the direction of change is not self-evident. This effect is called the income effect. Let us analyze each effect in turn, then combine the two in order to see why demand is assumed to slope downward.

### Substitution effect

We begin our analysis of the substitution effect with a definition:

**Definition.**  The substitution effect of a price change is the change in the consumption of a good resulting from a price change while the consumer is forced to stay on the same indifference curve.

Consider Figure 4–8, panel A. Assume $LZ$ is the original budget line, giving an equilibrium at point $A$ on indifference curve I. The equilibrium consumption of $X$ is $x_1$. Let the price of $X$ *decrease* so that the new budget line is $LZ'$. We know from our theory that the consumer will now move to a new equilibrium tangency on the new budget line $LZ'$.

But suppose we conduct the following experiment: after the decrease in the price of $X$, we reduce the consumer's money income just enough to force tangency on the original indifference curve I. That is, at the new price ratio given by the slope of $LZ'$, reduce income so that a budget line with the same slope (same price ratio) as $LZ'$ is tangent to I. This new budget line is shown as $RS$, parallel to $LZ'$ and tangent to I. With the new budget line $RS$ showing the new price ratio, the consumer maximizes at point $B$, consuming $x_2$ units of $X$. The consumer is neither better nor worse off, being on the same indifference curve as before. Thus, there is no income effect. The movement from $A$ to $B$, or the change in consumption from $x_1$ to $x_2$, is the pure substitution effect, designated by the arrow labeled $S$.

Note that, considering only the substitution effect along an indifference curve, a decrease in price must lead to increased consumption of the good. That is, a fall in the price of $X$ reduces the slope of the budget line. Because of the typical slope of indifference curves, the less steeply sloped budget line must become tangent to the original indifference curve at a greater quantity of $X$.

Panel B shows the substitution effect for an *increase* in the price of $X$. As above, begin with budget line $LZ$ tangent to indifference curve I at point $A$; $x_1$ of good $X$ is consumed in equilibrium. The price of $X$ now rises, causing the budget line at the given money income to rotate to $LZ''$. Again we know that, money income held constant, the new equilibrium will now be along $LZ''$.

Now we *increase the consumer's income* at the new price ratio, shown by the slope of $LZ''$, until a budget line with the new slope is just tangent to the original indifference curve I. This is shown by the budget line $ED$, tangent to I at point $C$. In this case, the consumption of $X$ is $x_3$ units. Thus, the pure substitution effect in this case is the movement from $A$ to $C$, or the change from $x_1$ units of $X$ to $x_3$, designated again by the arrow labeled $S$.

**FIGURE 4–8**
Substitution effects

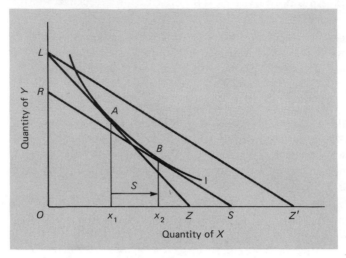

**Panel A**

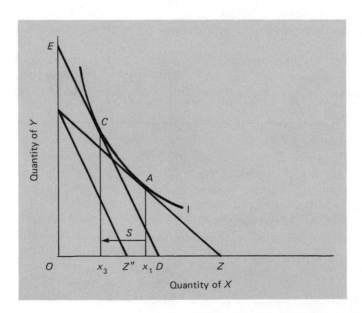

**Panel B**

Considering the substitution effect only, the *increase* in the price of X causes a reduction in the consumption of X. This must always be the case. An increase in the price of X makes the budget line steeper. The new point of tangency must come where the indifference curve is steeper. Thus, after a price decrease, tangency must come at a lower consumption of X, using normally sloped indifference curves.

We have established the following principle:

**Principle.** The substitution effect is the change in the consumption of a good after a change in price, when the consumer is forced by a change in money income to consume at some point on the original indifference curve. Considering the substitution effect only, the amount of the good consumed must vary inversely with its price. That is, utility held constant, $(\Delta X/\Delta P_X) < 0$.

### Income effect

We now have established the direction of the substitution effect. We cannot be as certain about how the income effect influences the quantity purchased. Before we study the income effect, let us define it:

**Definition.** The income effect from a price change is the change in the consumption of a good resulting strictly from a change in purchasing power, i.e., real income.

In Figure 4–9, begin with budget line LZ. The consumer is in equilibrium at point P on indifference curve I, consuming $x_1$ of X. Next, let the price of X fall, causing the budget line to rotate outward to LZ'. As before, we can isolate the substitution effect by reducing money income and forcing the new budget line at the new price ratio to move back until a new line with the same slope as LZ' is just tangent to I. Such a budget line is AB, tangent to I at Q, where the consumer chooses $x_2$ units of X. Thus, in this case, the substitution effect of the price decrease shows an increase in the consumption of X from $x_1$ to $x_2$, shown as S in Figure 4–9.

Now that we have isolated the substitution effect, let us return the money income to the original level. This simply involves a shift of the budget line from AB back to LZ'. Assuming that the good X is normal, the increase in money income from the level shown by AB to that shown by LZ' causes the consumption of X to increase. This result is shown by the movement from Q on indifference curve I to R on indifference curve II, or the increase in X from $x_2$ to $x_3$. This is the income effect. The income effect causes more X to be consumed

**FIGURE 4–9**
**Substitution and income effects for a decrease in the price of X**

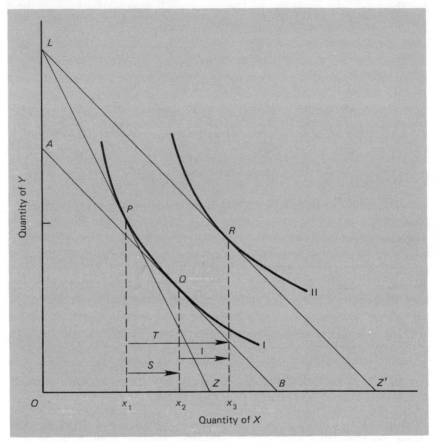

and, hence, reinforces the substitution effect, when the good is normal.

From our previous analysis, we can see that the total effect of the decrease in price that rotated the budget line from $LZ$ to $LZ'$ is the movement from $P$ to $R$, or the increase from $x_1$ to $x_3$. The total effect is broken up into the substitution effect, the distance $x_1x_2$, plus the income effect, the distance $x_2x_3$, resulting from returning the money income theoretically taken away when isolating the substitution effect.

In this example, the income effect was added to the substitution effect because the good was assumed normal. Had the good been inferior, however, the shift from $AB$ back to $LZ'$ would have caused a reduction in the consumption of $X$; that is, a decrease from $x_2$. Such a situation is shown in Figure 4–10, in which $X$ is inferior over the

**FIGURE 4–10**
Substitution and income effects for an inferior good

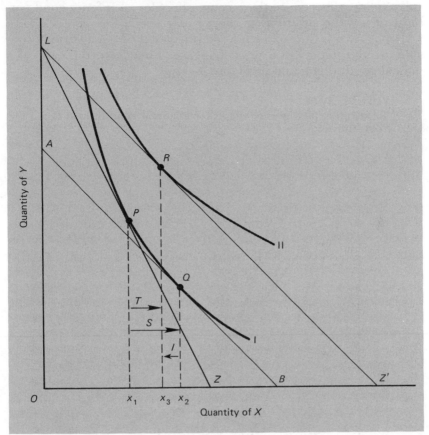

relevant range. Again, begin with budget line $LZ$; equilibrium is again at $P$, with $x_1$ being consumed. The decrease in the price of $X$, as before, rotates the budget line to $LZ'$, and, as before, the pure substitution effect of the decrease in price is the increase from $x_1$ to $x_2$, or the movement from $P$ to $Q$. Next, let the income be returned for the inferior good. As the budget line shifts from $AB$ back to $LZ'$ the consumption of $X$ is reduced from $x_2$ to $x_3$ by the return of the money income. Thus, the income effect is the movement from $Q$ back to $R$. The total effect is the change in $X$ from $x_1$ to $x_3$. But the total effect is less than the substitution effect alone because the income effect offsets, to some extent, the substitution effect. In other words, the decrease in price makes the consumer better off. Since the good is inferior, the shift between indifference curves, considered alone, causes less $X$ to be consumed.

Note that the total effect is still negative; a lower price of X increases the consumption of X. But this change results from the substitution effect, since the income effect for an inferior good partially offsets the substitution effect.

Let us review this somewhat complicated analysis by briefly considering the effects of a price increase. First, take the case of a normal good, illustrated in Figure 4–11.

**FIGURE 4–11**
**Substitution and income effects for a normal good in case of a price rise**

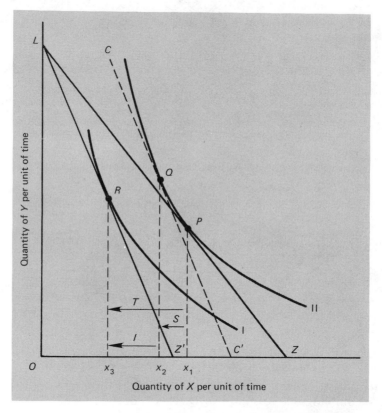

The original price ratio is indicated by the slope of $LZ$. The consumer attains equilibrium at point $P$ on indifference curve II, purchasing $x_1$ units of X. When the price of X rises, as indicated by shifting the budget line from $LZ$ to $LZ'$, the consumer moves to a new equilibrium position at $R$ on indifference curve I, purchasing $x_3$ units of X. The total effect of the price change is indicated by the movement from $P$ to $R$, or by the reduction in quantity demanded from $x_1$ to $x_3$. In other words, the total effect is $Ox_1 - Ox_3 = x_1x_3$. This is a negative total effect, because quantity demanded is reduced by $x_1x_3$ units when price increases.

Coincident with the price rise, the consumer is given an amount of additional money just sufficient to compensate for the loss in real income otherwise sustained. That is, he or she is given a compensatory payment just sufficient to make the consumer choose to consume on indifference curve II under the new price regime. This new imaginary budget line is $CC'$; it is tangent to the original indifference curve II at point $Q$, but it reflects the new price ratio.

The substitution effect is shown by the movement from $P$ to $Q$, or by the reduction in quantity demanded from $x_1$ to $x_2$. Now, let the consumer's real income *fall* from the level represented by the fictitious budget line $CC'$. The movement from $Q$ to $R$ (the decrease in consumption from $x_2$ to $x_3$) indicates the income effect. Since $CC'$ and $LZ'$ are parallel, the movement does not involve a change in

**FIGURE 4–12**
**Substitution and income effects for an inferior good in case of a price rise**

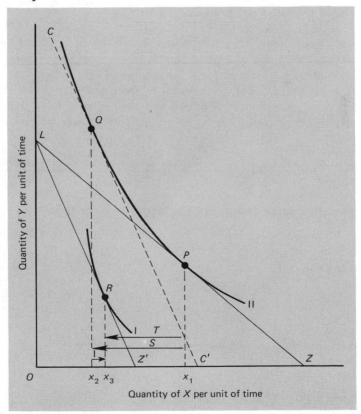

relative prices. It is once more a real income phenomenon, since the reduction in quantity demanded measures the change in purchases attributable exclusively to the decline in real income. The change in relative prices already has been accounted for by the substitution effect. Note that $X$ is a normal good; the decrease in real income causes a decrease in consumption. In this case, the income effect reinforces the substitution effect, as is always the case for a normal good.

Turn now to the situation in which the good is inferior. In Figure 4–12, an increase in price rotates the budget line from $LZ$ to $LZ'$. Following the now-familiar analysis, the consumer moves from point $P$ to point $R$, decreasing consumption of $X$ from $x_1$ to $x_3$ (the total effect). The substitution effect, derived by giving the consumer just enough additional money income to compensate for the decrease in real income occasioned by the price rise, is from $P$ to $Q$ (from $x_1$ to $x_2$). The income effect is from $Q$ to $R$ (an *increase* in consumption from $x_2$ to $x_3$). This partial offset to the substitution effect is to be expected, since $X$ is an inferior good; a decrease in income causes an increase in the consumption of $X$.

We have established an additional principle:

**Principle.** Considering the substitution effect alone, an increase (decrease) in the price of a good causes less (more) of the good to be demanded. For a normal good, the income effect—from the consumer's being made better or worse off by the price change—adds to or reinforces the substitution effect. The income effect for an inferior good offsets or takes away from the substitution effect to some extent.

## APPLICATION

### The consumer price index and the real effects of inflation

One of the most frequently encountered—and misunderstood—concepts in economics is the consumer price index (CPI), computed by the Bureau of Labor Statistics (BLS). Huge labor contracts hinge on changes in the CPI, as do purchasing and construction contracts. Changes in the payment of social security and welfare benefits are based on the CPI. Politicians are elected or defeated on favorable or unfavorable reports of the index. We can use the tools developed thus far to see how well increases in the CPI actually measure the impact of inflation.

First, let us define the CPI. In computing this index, the BLS uses a *Laspeyres price index,* which is the ratio of the cost of purchasing a specified bundle of goods in one year relative to the cost of purchasing the same bundle during some specified base year. For example, suppose there are two goods $X$ and $Y$, and the base year is 1970. The amount of each good consumed by a typical household in 1970, and, hence, the bundle used for weighting, consists of $X_0$ and $Y_0$. For 1982, the Laspeyres index $(L)$ is

$$L = \frac{p_x^{82}X_0 + p_y^{82}Y_0}{p_x^{70}X_0 + p_y^{70}Y_0} \gtreqless 1.$$

Note that the quantities in each year are the same, even though the consumption patterns might have changed. The superscripts on the prices represent the years. If there has been no change in prices, $L = 1$, because $p_x^{82} = p_x^{70}$ and $p_y^{82} = p_y^{70}$. If prices, on average, have risen, $L > 1$, if they have fallen, $L < 1$.

The BLS, of course, uses many more than two goods in computing the CPI. In fact, it now uses a market basket that an average urban family of four consumed in 1967. More generally we may write $L$ as

$$L = \frac{\Sigma p_i' X_i^0}{\Sigma p_i X_i^0},$$

where $p_i$ and $p_i'$ are, respectively, the price of the $i$th good in the base year and its price in the year for which the index is calculated; $X_i^0$ is the typical consumption of the $i$th good in the base period. Inflation, as measured by the change in the CPI, was 6.8 percent in 1977, 9 percent in 1978, 13.3 percent in 1979, and 12.4 percent in 1980. Looking at 1980, what the CPI is telling us is that it took 12.4 percent more income to buy the same bundle of goods at the end of the year than it did at the beginning of the year. The question is, does this description give us a very accurate picture of the true effect of inflation? An indifference map and some budget lines will show that the answer depends upon how much *relative* prices have changed over the year.

Let us return to the hypothetical two-good $(X$ and $Y)$ analysis. Figure 4–13 shows a particular individual's or household's equilibrium during the base period at point $A$ on budget line $LZ$ and indifference curve II. Next, let the prices of both goods increase, but let the price of $X$ rise relative to the price of $Y$. We know that, if money income is held constant and the quantity of $X$ is plotted along the horizontal axis, the budget line will shift backward and become steeper, reflecting the assumption that the ratio $p_y/p_x$ increases. This new line is shown as $L'Z'$ in the figure. If the household had the same money income after prices changed, it would choose to consume at combination $B$ on indifference curve I. The household is clearly worse off.

The CPI tells us how much additional income, or expenditure, the household needs to enable it to consume the original bundle at

**FIGURE 4-13**
Inflation and the consumer price index

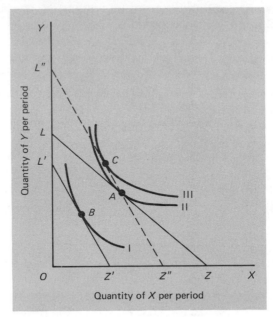

the new prices; i.e., to allow consumption at the old equilibrium, point $A$. As we noted, in 1980 this would take a 12.4 percent increase in income. In Figure 4-13, an increase in income just enough to shift the budget line to $L''Z''$ is needed. Suppose this shift requires a 12.4 percent increase. Does this increase in income represent the true incidence of inflation? In this case the answer is, it does not. It overestimates the impact of the price increase.

We know from our analysis of substitution effects that, with budget line $L''Z''$, the combination shown at $A$ would not be chosen. The household could increase utility by substituting $Y$ for $X$, because the price of $Y$ has decreased *relative* to that of $X$, even though both prices increased. The household would choose point $C$ on the higher indifference curve III and would be better off. Because of the possibility of substitution, an increase of 12.4 percent, the increase needed to return to $A$, would make the household better off than it was before. Thus, in this case, the change in the CPI overestimates the effect of inflation.

To carry the analysis further, assume that both prices rise, but this time the price of $Y$ increases by a greater percentage than the price of $X$; i.e., $p_x/p_y$ decreases. With money income constant, the budget line moves downward but now becomes less steep than $LZ$.

Next, move the budget line with the lesser slope outward so that it passes through the original point A. The required increase in money income is the change in the CPI. Now the household can move to a higher indifference curve than II by substituting X for Y. In this case also the change in the CPI overestimates the effect of inflation.

Finally, let both prices increase by the same percentage. The budget line shifts downward, but the slope does not change; $p_x/p_y$ remains constant. Now increase money income by the change in the CPI so that the line passes through A. This budget line is the same as LZ. The household cannot reach a higher indifference curve by substituting either X for Y or Y for X. Utility is still maximized at the combination given by A.

Thus, we can see that the only time the percentage increase in the CPI measures the amount that income must increase to make consumers exactly as well off as they were before, but no better off, is when prices all change in the same proportion. Otherwise, the change in the CPI exaggerates the impact of inflation, because of consumers' ability to substitute. The closer the price increase is to a proportional change, the more closely the change in the consumer price index reflects the real impact of inflation.

### Why demand slopes downward

In the case of a normal good, it is quite clear why price and quantity demanded are negatively related. From the substitution effect alone, a decrease in price is accompanied by an increase in quantity demanded, and an increase in price decreases quantity demanded. As we have shown, for a normal good, the income effect must add to the substitution effect. Thus, both effects push quantity demanded in the same direction, and demand must be negatively sloped.

But in the case of an inferior good, the income effect does not move in the same direction as, and to some extent offsets, the substitution effect. In the analysis set forth in the previous subsection, we hedged a little bit by saying that, in the case of an inferior good, the income effect *partially* offsets the substitution effect. Thus, in these cases, demand is still downward sloping. You might ask whether, under some circumstances, the income effect could dominate or more than offset the substitution effect, thereby causing price and quantity demanded to be directly rather than inversely related.

In other words, in Figure 4–10, could the indifference map be such that the income effect is so great that the equilibrium point on budget line $LZ'$ falls to the left of $x_1$ rather than at $R$? In this case, could not the income effect dominate the substitution effect, causing demand to slope upward?

Theoretically at least, such a circumstance is possible. In fact, economists call such theoretical cases in which the domination of the income effect for an inferior good causes an upward sloping demand *Giffen's Paradox*, named for a 19th-century British civil servant who collected data on the effect of price changes.

But just because such cases are theoretically possible does not mean that they are very likely or occur frequently, or even that they occur at all in the real world. Some economists have noted that one way a young economist could advance rapidly in the profession is by discovering a Giffen good. No one has yet, to our knowledge, done so. Thus, such cases involving positively sloped demands are probably just theoretical curios. They certainly are not important in the real world.

In fact, it is easy to see that in most if not all conceivable cases, the substitution effect would tend to dominate the income effect. In the first place, an increase in the price of a good makes this good more expensive relative to all other goods. In the sense that all goods compete for a consumer's income, all other goods are substitutes. Furthermore, it would be extremely unusual if a good did not have reasonably close substitutes. People can and do change consumption patterns in response to changes in relative prices by substituting to and from other goods.

Moreover, it would be an unusual case in which an increase in the price of a good consumed substantially reduced a consumer's real income. Furthermore, the effect of the probably slight reduction in real income would be felt not only in the case of a good with the increase in price, *but it would be spread over all other goods as well.* Thus, the impact of the change in real income from a price change for *any single good* would be rather small, if not minute. It, therefore, would appear that the slight change in real income from most relevant price changes in the case of inferior goods, combined with that slight change in real income being spread over all goods, make it extremely unlikely that the income effect from a change in the price of an inferior good would overcome the substitution effect and cause demand to slope upward.

Economists feel so strongly about the domination of the substitution effect over the income effect that they speak of the law of demand, in which quantity demanded varies inversely with price, ceteris paribus.

Marketing experts have pointed out several examples from the business world that supposedly violate the law of demand. Evidence of these alleged departures is that some goods have sold better at higher prices than at lower prices. Marketing experts call such departures from the law of demand "psychological pricing." Let us take a look at a few examples, then analyze them.

One example pointed out is a new nasal spray that did not sell well when introduced at a price lower than the price of well-known national brands. An increase in the price of the new spray increased sales. Another case of a firm's raising price of the new spray increased sales. Another case of a firm's raising price to increase sales involved the pantyhose manufactured by a national hosiery firm. The particular brand of pantyhose sold better when the price was increased to the range at which the competition was selling.

The marketing literature also points out other examples, such as a car wax, the sales of which increased after a price increase. There was a marketing experiment in which a particular brand of ink was displayed at 25 cents and 15 cents. Everything but the price and the name was the same. The ink sold better at 25 cents than at 15 cents.[3] There are many other examples available.

The question is, do these and similar empirical examples mean that the law of demand does not hold under these circumstances? The answer is, "No, these examples imply no such thing." The problem is one of ignorance.[4] Again, ask yourself the question: Is there anything you buy that you would be willing to buy more of if the price rises? Your answer is probably no; but you may well judge quality by price when you are uncertain (ignorant) about product quality. This is not irrational behavior; in fact, it is quite easy to explain why this type of behavior (products that sell better at higher than at lower prices) does not violate the law of down-sloping demand.

First of all, your time is valuable. Since time is scarce, no one takes the time to become an expert on every item available. While you are shopping around gaining information about products, you could be working or consuming leisure. The time that you spend shopping has value in the sense that you are allocating time (a scarce resource) away from other activities. Thus, economists say that the time spent shopping has an opportunity cost, and the total

---

[3] For these and other instances, see Chapter 10, "Demand Curve Estimation and Psychological Pricing," in F. C. Sturdivant et al., *Managerial Analysis in Marketing* (Glenview, Ill.: Scott, Foresman, 1970).

[4] Do not equate ignorance with stupidity. Ignorance means lacking knowledge about something. Even the smartest people are ignorant about many, many things, possibly through lack of interest. If we value the use of our time more in some other alternative than in learning about the diet of the ancient Incas, we will remain ignorant in that area. As in all things, overcoming ignorance has a cost.

cost of a good is the price of that good plus the value of the time spent shopping for it.

Second, people note from past experience that frequently, although not always, price and quality are directly related. Thus, price is often used in lieu of quality research as an indicator of product quality. This would be expected when the monetary saving expected from buying the lower rather than the higher-priced item is low compared to the cost (in time) of gaining information that might save a little money. When absolute price variations among products are low relative to income, as would be expected in the case of relatively low-priced items, one would expect people to do less systematic research and to judge quality more by prices. The absolute price variation among higher-priced goods is greater. Since the absolute difference is greater for higher-priced than for lower-priced goods, the cost of judging quality by price is greater relative to the cost of systematic quality research for higher-priced goods. Thus, as one would expect, consumers do depend more upon research and less upon price as an indicator of quality when purchasing high-cost (relative to income) items, such as housing, automobiles, and major household appliances. In other words, as the cost of taking price as an indicator of quality rises, people do it less.

Furthermore, as the returns to quality research rise, we should expect people to rely more on research and less on price as an indicator of quality. This, again, would be the case for higher-priced goods where the cost of making a purchasing mistake is greater. The penalty for misjudging quality in an automobile is greater than that for misjudging a 25-cent bottle of ink. All of the examples given above are for low-priced goods. One would guess that, if the price of the goods in these examples had been increased much above the going price, sales would have fallen substantially. The ink at $1 a bottle would not have sold well when other brands were selling at around 25 cents. In almost every example about which we have heard, the lower-priced good was well below the average price of similar goods, leading consumers to think it was not as good. In each case, the price was increased only to about the "going" price, never well above it, or the price increase was accompanied by a vigorous marketing campaign.

Finally, when consumers believe that quality differences among different brand names are great, they will be more likely to buy higher-priced brands than when they expect little quality difference. That is, when consumers believe they will gain little quality at higher prices, they tend to pay lower prices. Marketing experiments on brands of razor blades, floor wax, cooking sherry, mothballs, salt, aspirin, and beer tend to verify this hypothesis.[5]

---

[5] See Sturdivant et al., *Managerial Analysis*, for a description of such experiments.

Thus, we can easily explain apparent exceptions to the law of demand. If consumers *know* two goods are exactly alike in every way (including prestige) and choose the higher-priced good, it would be an exception. For some goods, the imputed quality is judged by price when the cost of other research on quality is high relative to expected return. These are different goods at different prices in the minds of some consumers, and the cases cited are not violations of the law of demand.

### Ordinary and compensated demand curves

Recall from Figure 4–11 that the total effect of a price increase is a decrease in the quantity consumed from $x_1$ to $x_3$, or a movement from point $P$ to point $R$ in the figure. Points $P$ and $R$ are also part of the price-consumption curve discussed in Section 4.3. It is from the price-consumption curve that we derived a demand curve. As a review, Figure 4–14 shows a demand curve based on Figure 4–11; it is the solid schedule with points P′ and R′; it is called an *ordinary demand curve*, perhaps because it is more frequently used than a related curve called a *compensated demand curve*.

Ordinary demand curves include both the substitution and income effects. When prices rise and pivot the budget line from $LZ$ to $LZ′$, the total effect is a decrease in consumption from $x_1$ to $x_3$, as shown in both Figures 4–11 and 4–14.

Compensated demand curves, on the other hand, include only

**FIGURE 4–14**
**Ordinary and compensated demand curves for a normal good**

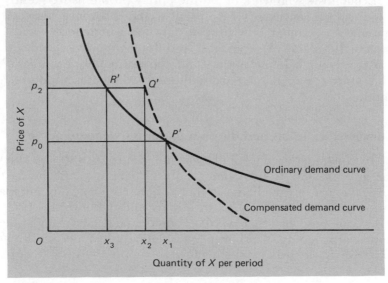

the substitution effect. When prices rise in Figure 4–11, the quantity consumed changes from $x_1$ to just $x_2$, or there is a movement along the compensated curve from $P'$ to $Q'$. We can see, therefore, that compensated demand curves are steeper than ordinary demand curves *for normal goods*. In order to derive a demand curve that has only the substitution effect, the consumer must, by definition, be held on the original indifference curve. Hence, when prices increase, the consumer must be "compensated" to move from budget line $LZ'$ to $CC'$ in Figure 4–11. This is how we get point $Q'$ in Figure 4–14. For price increases, the compensation must be positive, for price decreases it is negative—when prices fall, income is taken away to keep the consumer on the same indifference curve. Of course, when this happens, there is a smaller increase in the quantity demanded if the good is normal over the income range. Notice in Figure 4–14, that, when prices fall below $p_0$, there is indeed a smaller increase in the quantity demanded in the case of the compensated demand curve. Whenever a good is normal, the compensated schedule will always be more inelastic than the ordinary demand curve.

In the case of inferior goods, the income effect to some extent offsets, rather than reinforces, the substitution effect. Thus, if we take away the income effect, the substitution effect exceeds the total effect and the ordinary demand curve is steeper than the compensated demand curve. For inferior goods, then, the compensated demand curve is more elastic than the ordinary demand curve.

## 4.5 CONSUMER'S SURPLUS

Economists who work on public policy problems frequently use a tool called consumer's surplus. It is the difference between the amount a consumer is willing to pay for a commodity and what is actually paid. We can use indifference curves and budget constraints to help us understand the notion of consumer's surplus. Once it is explained, we will observe how it is applied in economics.

### Consumer's surplus and the area under the demand curve

To illustrate the concept of consumer's surplus, suppose you visit the grocery store to buy some apples. There is a sufficiently high price the grocer can charge so that you do not make any purchases, but at lower prices you will buy apples, and the lower the price the more you buy. In other words, your demand curve for apples is downward sloping. We show a hypothetical consumer's willingness to pay in Table 4–1. We do this for each apple, because it varies for

**TABLE 4–1**
**A consumer's willingness to pay for apples**

| Apple | Willingness to pay for the last apple | Grocer's price | Consumer's surplus |
|---|---|---|---|
| 1 ................................... | $1.00 | .40 | $ .60 |
| 2 ................................... | .80 | .40 | .40 |
| 3 ................................... | .60 | .40 | .20 |
| 4 ................................... | .40 | .40 | .00 |
| 5 ................................... | .20 | | |
| Total surplus .................... | | | $1.20 |

each one purchased. More precisely, a consumer has a high willingness to pay for the first apple, but as more apples are purchased, the willingness to pay declines. Additional apples are simply not as valuable. This is an obvious conclusion if the demand curve is downward sloping. Figure 4–15 illustrates a consumer's willingness to pay for the first five apples. Notice that the grocer's price is a constant 40 cents for the time period considered.

**FIGURE 4–15**
**Willingness to pay and consumer's surplus**

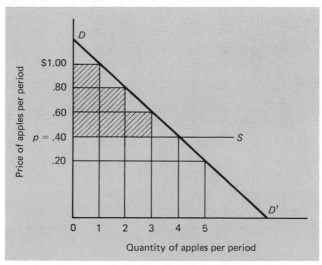

In Figure 4–15, the consumer buys four apples. This is where the grocer's supply curve intersects demand. As far as the consumer is concerned, the grocer stands ready to supply all the apples he or she could possibly want at 40 cents an apple. It is important to understand that the consumer does not buy four apples because four apples are valued at 40 cents each by the consumer. On the contrary, all but the fourth apple are valued more highly than 40′ cents. A consumer buys four because the consumer's willingness to pay for the fourth apple is just equal to the price of apples. The consumer does not buy more than four apples, because he or she is willing to pay only 20 cents for the fifth when the price is 40 cents.

It is the interpretation of demand as a schedule reflecting the willingness to pay that gives rise to the definition of consumer's surplus.

**Definition.** Consumer's surplus is the difference between a buyer's willingness to pay and the market price. It is estimated by the area between the demand curve and price.

Table 4–1 has actually subtracted price from the willingness to pay. Adding up these amounts tells us that the consumer's total surplus from buying four apples is $1.20. This is also represented by the shaded region in Figure 4–15. You can easily observe that, if we had taken the area under the demand curve above 40 cents, we would have overestimated the surplus by the four unshaded triangles between the price line and $DD'$. The estimate, however, becomes more exact as units of measure for the quantity become smaller. Say the grocer charged 20 cents for each apple half. The consumer depicted in Figure 4–15 would then buy eight halves. With units this small, the area between the price and the demand curve would become a much better estimate of consumer's surplus.

### Derivation of consumer's surplus from indifference curves

The theory of utility maximization lends credibility to the concept of consumer's surplus. For many years, economists were skeptical of using the area under ordinary demand curves as a measure of the value consumers put on a commodity. It has only been in the last 10 years that a rigorous derivation of consumer surplus from indifference-curve theory has convinced many economists of the reliability of consumer's surplus.[6]

We now want to show the relation between consumer's surplus and the theory of utility maximization using the tools we have developed in this chapter. This discussion will test your understand-

---

[6] See R. Willig, "Consumer's Surplus without Apology," *American Economic Review* 66, no. 4 (September 1976): 56–69.

ing of utility maximization; it is somewhat more difficult than the material we have presented so far. With some geometry, we will show that the area under an ordinary demand curve is not the best estimate of the willingness to pay of a consumer. Indeed, the best estimate of consumer surplus is the area under the compensated demand curve. Nevertheless, in applied economics, ordinary demand curves continue to be used because they are easier to estimate.

Let us begin with a preference map and budget lines that reflect a price increase, as shown in Figure 4–16. On the horizontal axis,

**FIGURE 4–16**
**Consumer's surplus and utility maximization**

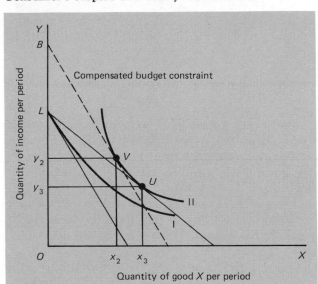

we plot good $X$ and assume $X$ is a normal good. On the vertical axis is income, $Y$. Thus, a consumer not wanting to buy any $X$ could keep the entire income. Otherwise, the consumer begins by maximizing utility at point $U$ on indifference curve II but, after the price increase, decides not to buy any $X$ and optimizes at point $L$ on indifference curve I. This is, of course, a corner solution. These two points give rise to the ordinary demand curve $DD'$ in Figure 4–17.

The compensated demand curve comes from just the substitution effect—a movement from $U$ to $V$ in Figure 4–16. This is demand curve $D_1D_1'$ in Figure 4–17.

Notice in Figure 4–17 that, as a result of the price increase, the consumer loses consumer's surplus equal to the area $p'up_0$, the

**FIGURE 4–17**
Consumer's surplus and compensated demand

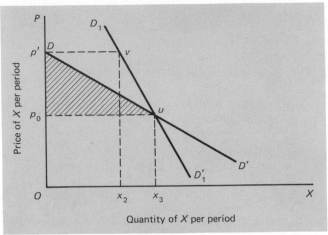

shaded region in the figure. This area reflects a loss of utility. How much would a consumer be willing to pay in order to avoid this hike in price? The answer comes from Figure 4–16. After the price increase, the consumer's utility declines to the level represented by indifference curve I. To return the person to the original level of utility, an increase in income equal to distance $BL$ is necessary. So a consumer would be willing to pay no more than $BL$ to avoid the higher price. Is $BL = p'up_0$? To see if it is, we need to compare the two figures.

First, at point $U$ in Figure 4–16, the consumer keeps $y_3$ in income and spends the remainder, $Ly_3$, on $X$. Hence, $Ly_3 = Op_0ux_3$. At point $V$, the consumer spends $By_2$ on $x_2$; remember the budget line is higher because of the compensation provided to return to indifference curve II. Looking at Figure 4–17, $By_2 = Op'vx_2$. Finally, let the consumer be at point $V$ again. A move from $V$ to $U$ is a move along the same indifference curve, and the $MRS_{X \text{ for } Y} = \Delta Y/\Delta X = y_2y_3/x_2x_3$. To gain $x_2x_3$ more $X$, the consumer is willing to pay income $y_2y_3$. In terms of Figure 4–17, this means that a movement from $v$ to $u$ on the compensated demand schedule is worth $y_2y_3$ to the consumer. Thus $y_2y_3 = x_2vux_3$, the area under the compensated demand schedule between $x_2$ and $x_3$.

Putting all this together, we get an area in Figure 4–17 that corresponds to $BL$, the amount of income equivalent to the value a consumer placed on the low price, $p_0$, as opposed to $p'$:

$$BL = By_2 + y_2y_3 - Ly_3.$$

Substituting:

$$BL = Op'vx_2 + x_2vux_3 - Op_0ux_3 = p_0p'vu.$$

Notice that $p_0p'vu > p'up_0$. The true loss is the area under the compensated demand schedule, not the ordinary demand curve. Thus, for a price increase, consumer's surplus represented by the area $p'up_0$ underestimates the amount of income the consumer would exchange in return for the right to purchase commodity $X$ at the lower price, $p_0$. If we repeated the analysis for a price decrease, we would deduce in a similar way that the area under the ordinary demand curve (consumer's surplus) overestimates the amount a consumer would pay for the right to purchase the commodity at the lower price rather than at $p_0$.

While we will not formally prove the point, it should be reasonably clear that, for an inferior good also, the area under the compensated demand, rather than the ordinary demand, represents the true loss or gain from a change in the price of the good. But if the good is inferior, the consumer's surplus overestimates rather than underestimates the loss from an increase in price and underestimates rather than overestimates the gain from a price decrease. This difference results from the difference in the direction of the income effect for a normal and an inferior good. Our graphical analysis in Figures 4–16 and 4–17 was carried out under the assumption that the income effect reinforces the substitution effect.

Deriving consumer's surplus from indifference curves tells us that income effects distort the surplus estimate. The stronger the income effect, the less reliable ordinary demand curves are for estimating the true consumer's surplus. Conversely, the smaller the income effect, the more reliable the estimate. For a price increases from $p_0$ to $p'$, the income effect reduces purchasing power and, thus, leads to a greater change in the quantity demanded than if demand were the compensated curve. But because of the gain in purchasing power, if prices were returned to $p_0$, consumers are willing to pay more for the price decrease than is shown by the area under the ordinary demand curve.

## APPLICATION

### The sale of gasoline rationing tickets

During the Carter administration, one plan to force consumers to conserve on energy was to ration gasoline. Motorists would be issued rationing tickets, which would be presented to the station attendant when they purchased gasoline. There was controversy among public officials over whether the tickets could be sold after they were issued. A major concern was that those people who could afford to buy tickets would benefit at the expense of those who could not. Consumer's surplus helps us analyze the question and decide whether the sale of ration tickets should be permitted in the event of rationing.

If tickets were sold, people could be divided into three groups: (1) those who sold tickets, (2) those who bought tickets, and (3) those who did neither. The last group is unaffected by the buying and selling of tickets, so they do not enter the analysis. The issue is whether those who buy and sell tickets are helped or harmed.

Suppose all motorists were issued their coupons each week, allowing them to purchase 10 gallons of gasoline. Mr. Adams and Ms. Jones drive the same amount each week, but for one reason or another—it could be Jones is richer—Jones is willing to pay more than Adams for the 10th coupon, even though they cost the consumer nothing. Figures 4–18 and 4–19 show, respectively, the amounts Adams and Jones would be willing to pay for each additional ration coupon. We can see that Adams is willing to pay $1.10 for the 10th coupon, while Jones is willing to pay $2.25.

**FIGURE 4–18**
**Adams's willingness to pay for rationing tickets**

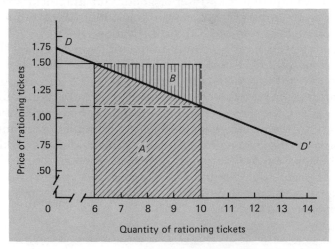

Now, suppose in the market for coupons, trading is allowed. After a few months, a price of $1.50 prevails. Adams would be willing to keep only 6 coupons at that price and would therefore wish to sell 4 of his 10 coupons. Jones would like to purchase four more tickets at this price. Clearly, trade would be beneficial to both. The benefit to Jones from being able to purchase four more tickets at $1.50 each is

**FIGURE 4–19**
Jones's willingness to pay for rationing tickets

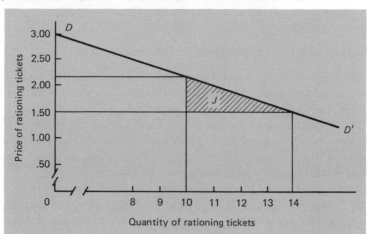

the consumer's surplus shown by the area *J*. This area represents the difference between what she is willing to pay for each additional ticket and what she actually pays (4 × $1.50 = $6.00).

Adams benefits also. Since the tickets cost him nothing, his consumer's surplus from tickets 6 through 10 is the area *A*. If he is not to be made worse off by selling the four tickets to Jones, he must receive an amount greater than or equal to the amount represented by *A*. He does, in fact, receive $1.50 × 4 = $6.00, which is represented by the sum of areas *A* and *B*. Thus, Jones is made better off from selling the tickets by an amount represented by the area *B*.

Hence, by applying the concept of consumer's surplus, we see that both the buyer and the seller of rationing tickets benefit regardless of who is richer or poorer. Those who do not trade are neither helped nor hurt by trading. The conclusion of this very simple benefit-cost study is that some groups of individuals are helped by trading, and no one is harmed. The trading of rationing tickets is therefore beneficial for motorists.

## 4.6 LABOR SUPPLY

The tools developed in this chapter can be easily adapted to analyze the theory of labor supply. We can consider that a person's willingness to supply a certain amount of labor time is the same as that individual's demanding leisure time. Thus, the analytical tools pertaining to demand theory are applicable to labor supply and to the economic problems associated with labor supply.

### Derivation of labor supply from indifference curves

Figure 4–20, panel A, contains a portion of an individual's indifference map between income and leisure. Instead of depending strictly upon the quantity of goods, utility is now regarded as a function of income and leisure. Note from the shape of the indifference curves that we have assumed that both income and leisure are considered desirable by the individual; that is, one does not become satiated with leisure within the relevant range.

Before considering the problem of how the consumer maximizes utility, a word of explanation about the unit of measurement for leisure and the vertical line at $L_m$ is in order. The unit of measurement along the horizontal axis can be hours per day, days per year, or any other period of time. Obviously, if the unit is hours per day, the maximum time for leisure is 24 hours. If the unit is days of leisure, the maximum is 7 per week or 365 per year. The line $L_m$ indicates the maximum attainable units of leisure per time period. If the individual chooses $C'$ units of leisure per period, he or she also chooses $C'L_m$ for work; or if he or she chooses $L_m$ of leisure, he or she does not work at all. The unit of measurement chosen for the horizontal axis clearly specifies the unit for the vertical. For example, when leisure is designated as hours per day, the vertical axis must measure income per day. Each indifference curve specifies the various combinations of income and leisure that yield the same level of satisfaction. For example, the consumer considers $C'$ leisure (and, hence, $C'L_m$ work) and income $C'H$ equivalent to $A'$ leisure (and, hence, $A'L_m$ work) and income $A'A$, since both points lie on the same indifference curve. The slopes of the curves indicate the rates at which an individual is willing to trade leisure for income. We assume, for analytical convenience, that both income and leisure are continuously divisible.

The budget lines are determined by the payment per unit of time. If the unit is hours per day, the budget line is determined by the individual's hourly wage rate; if days per year, by the earnings per day. Consider budget line $Y_1L_m$. If the individual works the entire time period (say 24 hours per day) and consequently takes no leisure, he or she could make $Y_1$ per time period. Assuming specialization in leisure and no work, income is zero. The slope of the budget line is the relevant wage rate or payment per unit of time. The "cost" of a unit of leisure is the sacrificed earnings for that

# FIGURE 4–20
## Indifference curve analysis of labor supply

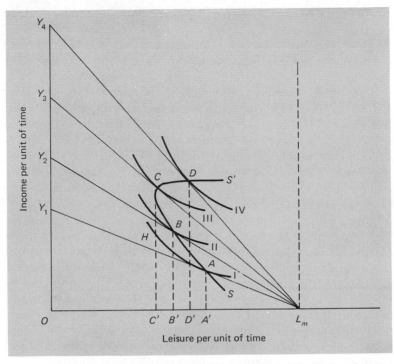

**Panel A**

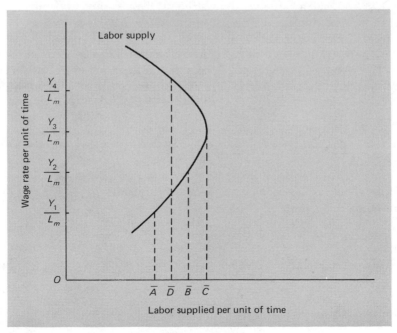

**Panel B**

period of time.[7] $Y_2L_m$, $Y_3L_m$, and $Y_4L_m$ are the relevant budget lines for higher wage rates, $Y_2/L_m$, $Y_3/L_m$, and $Y_4/L_m$, respectively.

With a given wage rate, the highest attainable level of utility is given by the point where the relevant budget line is tangent to the indifference curve. An individual with the wage rate indicated by the slope of $Y_1L_m$ achieves the highest attainable level of utility at point A. He or she chooses $A'$ leisure, $A'L_m$ work, and receives an income of $A'A$. If the wage rises to that level designated by budget line $Y_2L_M$, the highest attainable level of utility is at B, where the individual works $B'L_m$ for an income of $B'B$ and enjoys $B'$ leisure time. Points C and D indicate the equilibria leisure, work, and income for the other two budget lines, and $SS'$ connects these and all intermediate equilibria. Thus, $SS'$ indicates the amount of time the individual is willing to work (or the amount of labor he or she is willing to supply) at each of a series of wages.

Note that, at relatively low wages, the individual is willing to work more, or to consume less leisure, as the wage rate increases. Since an increase in potential earnings causes leisure to cost more (in lost earnings), he or she chooses less leisure and more work. After point C, however, further increases in the wage rate induce more leisure and less work. Leisure still costs the individual more as he or she moves from C to D, but the income effect means that the individual chooses to consume more leisure with the increased earnings.

Just as we can derive demand and Engel curves from price-consumption and income-consumption curves, we can derive a labor supply curve from curves such as $SS'$. Figure 4–20, panel B, shows the labor supply curve derived from the indifference map in panel A. The distance $\bar{A}$ in panel B equals $A'L_m$ in panel A and is the amount of work associated with wage rate $Y_1/L_m$, and so on. Since $SS'$ bends backward at C, the labor supply curve bends backward at $\bar{C}$.

## APPLICATIONS

### Some effects of an income tax and a minimum guaranteed income

Many times we cannot obtain a definitive answer to important policy questions by just using basic economic theory. We can only get the answer "It depends," or "The theory does not say," or "It's

---

[7] For simplicity, we assume a constant wage rate regardless of the amount of time worked. Certainly "overtime" work might be at overtime pay or a second job could be taken at a lower wage than the primary job pays. We also assume that the individual is free to choose the amount of working time; sometimes this may not be the case.

an empirical question." This is still, of course, a legitimate use of theory. Certainly a theory is useful in showing those who assert "obvious" answers that the answers are not so apparent.

We take two important policy questions as examples. These questions are even now being analyzed by government policymakers, because the solutions are certainly important for policy purposes. These problems are the effect on the incentive to work of an increase in the rate of income tax and the imposition of a government-supported guaranteed minimum income.

Turn first to the income tax, the results of which are much easier to analyze. Begin analysis under the assumption of no income tax. Consider the individual depicted by Figure 4–21. Before the in-

**FIGURE 4–21**
**Effect of an income tax**

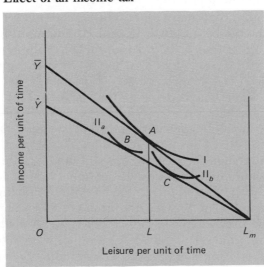

come tax, the income-leisure budget line is $\overline{Y}L_m$; the individual attains equilibrium on indifference curve I at $A$, working $LL_m$ and consuming $OL$ units of leisure per period of time.

The imposition of an income tax rotates the budget line downward to $\hat{Y}L_m$. The new budget line is very close to the old at low incomes, reflecting low taxation. Since high incomes are taxed more, the new line is further below the old at high incomes. Note that the before-tax income-leisure trade-off is the same. But the aftertax line rotates downward.

As Figure 4–21 indicates, the individual may choose to work more or work less. Points $B$ or $C$ on indifference curves $II_a$ or $II_b$ are equally possible, depending upon the indifference map. If point $B$ is the new equilibrium, more work time is chosen; if point $C$ is chosen, less work time and more leisure are chosen. Certainly other points on $\hat{Y}L_m$ are possible as well. Thus, our theory does not give a definitive answer. As noted, the solution must be empirical in nature.

Let us turn now to another implication of a possible government policy and analyze the effect of a guaranteed minimum income. Many discussions of guaranteed minimum income ignore the problem of work incentives. In its most familiar form, a guaranteed minimum income would allow people to work, but those who are unable to earn the minimum income would receive the difference between what they earn and the designated minimum from the government. It has been asserted that a person who could not make the minimum income would not work, but that anyone who could make more would choose to work. We can analyze the theoretical aspects of the problem rather simply.[8]

Consider an individual with an indifference map for leisure and earnings depicted by curves I, II, and III and earning possibilities shown by budget line $Y_eL_m$ in Figure 4–22. Following the type of analysis previously developed, we can see that equilibrium is at income $Y_0$, leisure $L_0$, and work time $L_0L_m$ per period of time. Now suppose the government declares that income $Y_m$ per period is a "necessary" income. No one should receive less. The government will make up any difference between what one earns and $Y_m$, assuming, of course, that one earns less than $Y_m$. Since the individual under consideration is earning more than $Y_m$, the question is whether the minimum will or will not affect him or her.

Note the way that the guaranteed minimum changes the set of possible incomes. The budget line from $C$ to $Y_e$ remains the same, but, since the individual can have at least $Y_m$ no matter how much he or she works and no matter what his or her wage rate, the income possibility line changes at point $C$. The new line becomes $Y_eCGL_m$. The individual can now attain the highest possible level of utility on indifference curve III by choosing $L_m$ leisure and no work. Since III is clearly higher than II, the utility-maximizing individual will move from $A$ to $G$ even though he or she could earn more than the guaranteed minimum.

Under the circumstances, three factors could change and cause the person to choose to work some portion of the time. First, the minimum income could be decreased to some level below the intersection of indifference curve II with the perpendicular at $L_m$; for

---

[8] This analysis is based upon an article by C. T. Brehm and T. R. Saving, "The Demand for General Assistance Payments," *American Economic Review*, December 1964, pp. 1002–18.

**FIGURE 4–22**
Indifference curve analysis of a minimum guaranteed income

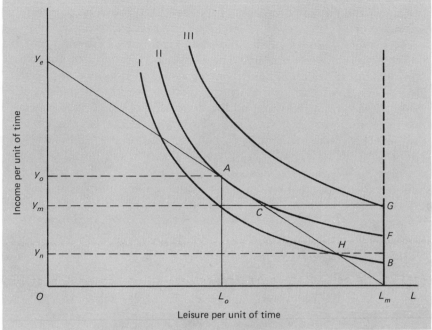

example, $Y_n$ may be the new minimum income. Then the person would choose point $A$ on II. Second, the wage or potential earnings rate could increase enough to induce him or her to work. A sufficient increase would raise the budget line at least enough for it to become tangent to indifference curve III. Third, the individual might not consider welfare payments as desirable as equal payments for work.

In any case, the answer must be reached empirically. Many types of tests have been done and are even now being carried out in order to reach a solution. However, no real conclusion has been reached yet. This example does show rather well how theory must be combined with statistical analysis to obtain answers to some problems.

## 4.7 SUMMARY

The basic principles of consumer behavior and demand have now been developed. The fundamental point of this chapter is that, if consumers behave so as to maximize satisfaction from a limited money income, quantity demanded (with one relatively unimportant exception) will vary inversely with price. An Engel curve is a locus of points relating equilibrium quantity to the level of money income at a specified set of relative prices. The Engel curve slopes upward if the good is normal over that range. If the good is inferior, the curve bends backward. Income elasticity is an alternative way of determining whether a good is normal or inferior. If the elasticity is positive, the good is normal; otherwise, it is inferior. The substitution effect of a price change upon the consumption of that good is always negative; that is, quantity demanded varies inversely with price, considering the substitution effect only. If the good is normal, the income effect reinforces the substitution effect. If the good is inferior, the income effect to some extent offsets the substitution effect.

After developing the concepts of the income and substitution effects, consumer's surplus was introduced. Consumer's surplus is the difference between what consumers are willing to pay and the market price. Indifference theory shows that the area under an ordinary demand curve is an estimate of consumer's surplus. How good an estimate depends upon the strength of the income effect.

The decision concerning the allocation of time and leisure can also be analyzed by using indifference maps. An individual's labor supply curve can be derived, and it may exhibit backward-bending tendencies.

## TECHNICAL PROBLEMS

1.  Consider the following table showing income, the quantity of the good demanded, and the price of the good.

| Quantity | Income | Price |
|---|---|---|
| 100 | $5,000 | $16 |
| 120 | 6,000 | 16 |

Compute the income elasticity of the good, using 100 as $X$ and $5,000 as $M$. Next, suppose the price of the good changes so that the schedule is now as follows:

| Quantity | Income | Price |
|---|---|---|
| 150 | $5,000 | $10 |
| 130 | 6,000 | 10 |

Compute again the income elasticity of demand, with $150 = X$ and $5,000 = M$. Why has it changed even though income is unchanged?

2.  If there is a single "all-important" commodity that absorbs all of the individual's income, what is its income elasticity? Explain your results using the definition of income elasticity.

**FIGURE E.4–1**

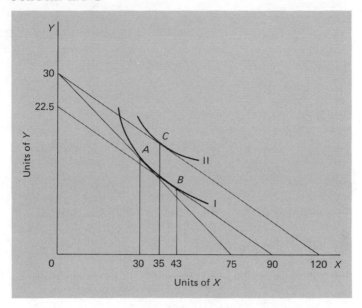

3.  Consider Figure E.4–1. Begin with the consumer in equilibrium with an income of $300 facing the prices $P_x = \$4$ and $P_Y = \$10$.
    a.  How much $X$ is consumed in equilibrium?
    Let the price of $X$ fall to $2.50, nominal income and $P_Y$ remaining constant.
    b.  What is the new equilibrium consumption of $X$?
    c.  How much income must be taken from the consumer to isolate the income and substitution effects?
    d.  The total effect of the price decrease is _____. The substitution effect is _____. The income effect is _____.
    e.  The good $X$ is _____, but not _____.
    f.  Construct the consumer's demand curve for $X$ with nominal money income constant; with real income (utility) constant.
4.  Figure E.4–2 shows an individual's indifference map between leisure and income. Ignore indifference curve III for now and assume that curves I and II make up the map. The unit of time is one day of 24 hours. The wage rate is $3 per hour.
    a.  How much does the individual choose to work? How much leisure does he or she consume?
    Let the wage rate rise to $5 an hour.

**FIGURE E.4–2**

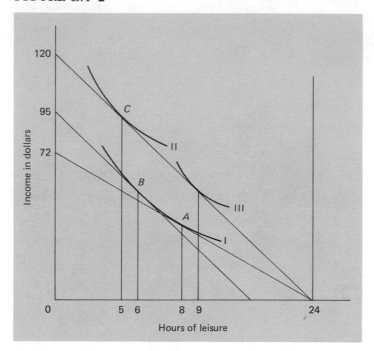

b. Ignoring III, what are his or her work and leisure time?
Suppose, at the wage rate of $5, the individual was taxed just
enough to make him or her choose a point on the original
indifference curve, I.
   c.   What is the substitution effect for the wage change from $3
        to $5?
   d.   Return the taxed income; what is the income effect?
   e.   What is the total effect?
   f.   In this example, leisure is a (normal, inferior) good, and the
        income effect (offsets, reinforces) the substitution effect.
   g.   Derive the associated supply curve for labor.
Now let the relevant indifference map be I and III.
   h.   Derive the new supply-of-labor curve.
   i.   Now the total effect of a wage increase from $3 to $5 is
        _____, the substitution effect is _____, and the income
        effect is _____.
   j.   Leisure is now a (normal, inferior) good.
   k.   What can you say about the classification of leisure and a
        backward-bending supply of labor?
   l.   Draw an indifference curve IV tangent to the budget line
        associated with $5 so that leisure is a normal good, but the
        supply of labor is not backward bending.

5. An individual can choose between income and leisure as depicted in Figure E.4–3. The maximum amount of time available in the period is $OT$. The first wage rate is indicated by the slope of $MT$; the new higher rate by the slope of $RT$. Regardless of the wage rate, the person works just long enough to earn income $OI$.

**FIGURE E.4–3**

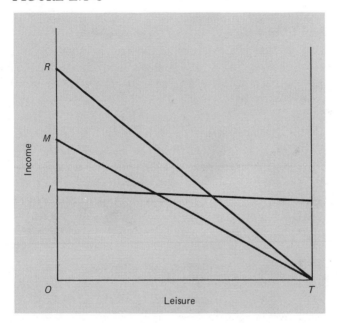

a. Draw in the indifference curves at the two points of equilibrium.
b. Is leisure a normal or an inferior good to the individual? Prove graphically.

6. Graphically derive a demand curve for a normal good. Start with indifference curves between goods $X$ and $Y$. Let the price of $X$ fall. Identify the income and substitution effects of this price decline on the graph. Identify two points on the resulting demand curve, showing where you got each of the points. Explain each step. Draw and label your diagrams clearly.

7. Draw an income-consumption curve and an Engel curve for good $X$, assuming that the price of $X$ is $10 and the price of $Y$ is $25, by examining incomes of $100, $200, and $300. Show your work. (Use conventionally shaped indifference curves.)

8. Calculate a Laspeyres price index for an individual who consumes 4 dozen eggs, 60 pounds of meat, 2 pairs of shoes, 1 pair

of jeans, and 30 movies per period. The years are 1975 and 1982. Prices are given below:

|                  | 1975    | 1982    |
|------------------|---------|---------|
| Eggs/dozen ....... | $  .60 | $  .80 |
| Meat/pound ....... | 1.25    | 1.65    |
| Shoes/pair ....... | 25.00   | 45.00   |
| Jeans/pair ....... | 13.00   | 38.00   |
| Movies ....... | 2.50    | 3.50    |

What percentage increase in income would this consumer need to buy the same bundle of goods in 1982?

9. Oscar Wilde once wrote, "A cynic is a man who knows the price of everything and the value of nothing." Explain the difference between price and value, using the concept of consumer's surplus.

10. Construct a graph with a demand curve. Show how consumer's surplus changes when price increases; when price decreases.

11. In the text, we showed that the change in the area under an ordinary demand curve underestimates a consumer's lost surplus for a price increase and overestimates the gain for a price decrease for a normal good. Show that, when the good is inferior over the relevant range, the change in the area under the ordinary demand curve overestimates the loss for a price increase and underestimates the gain for a decrease.

12. Verbally explain in terms of the substitution and income effects why an individual's supply of labor curve might bend backward.

13. The price of grapes is $1, and the price of oranges is $1.50. Someone who consumes both gets marginal utility of 20 for the last unit of grapes consumed and 25 for the last unit of oranges. What should the consumer do? Explain.

## ANALYTICAL PROBLEMS

1. Family size in the United States decreased for 50 years after 1900 while per capita income increased. Given constant tastes, children must be an inferior good. Evaluate.

2. Charitable contributions are deductible from income taxes. How would an increase in the tax rate affect charitable contributions? (Hint: consider both income and substitution effects.)

3. Suppose you are a government official given the job of estimating how a guaranteed annual income would affect labor-force participation. You have a very large budget. How would you carry out this research?

4.  For the entire United States, assume that real per capita income rises over the next few years. Assume also all *relative* prices remain the same. Draw what you think would be the appropriate Engel curve for the following commodities. Explain why you drew them with the shape you did.
    a.  Toyotas.
    b.  Cadillacs and Lincolns.
    c.  Water.
    d.  Fish.
    e.  All food.
    f.  College education.
    g.  Television sets.
    h.  Black and white television sets.

5.  If demand is perfectly inelastic, can you draw a graph to illustrate consumer's surplus? Suppose demand is perfectly elastic, is there any consumer's surplus if price is determined by the intersection of supply and demand?

6.  During the Great Depression, while per capita income was falling, movie theater receipts steadily rose. What does this tell you about the income elasticity of films? Are they normal goods?

7.  Explain the statement: "It is possible for all goods and services to be normal, but never can they all be inferior."

8.  Suppose you operate a very successful liquor store, and you are thinking about opening a second store elsewhere.
    a.  If the income elasticity of liquor is positive and large, in what kind of neighborhood would you want to put your new store?
    b.  Imagine that the area in which you sell is in a recession, what kind of income elasticity would you want your product to have?
    c.  As a business owner, would you want the income effects on your product to be small or large?

9.  Which type of country do you think would be more likely to have a backward-bending supply of labor for the economy as a whole: an advanced industrial country or a much less developed country? Explain.

10. Suppose prices increase by 10 percent over a 10-year period, say, 1970–79 in a certain country. Then, during 1980 alone, they increase another 10 percent. Would you expect changes in the consumer price index to overestimate the impact of inflation more or less from year to year or over a 10-year period?

11. Recently, the state of Texas outlawed the practice of scalping tickets just before major sport events and concerts. Scalping is

the selling of tickets to an event at a higher price than face value. The practice was considered "unfair" by legislators. Analyze who gains and loses from such a practice using the concept of consumer's surplus. Are you opposed to the practice?

12. Over the last decade, there is evidence showing that, as more medical doctors practice in a community, the real price of medical care rises. Could this be the result of a backward-bending supply curve among physicians? Can you think of other causes for this trend?

# Chapter 5

# Theory of production

## 5.1 INTRODUCTION

Now that we have completed demand theory, we have developed half of the theory of price. Let us turn to the other half of the theory, the theory of supply.

The basic foundation of the theory of supply is production theory. Production, in a general sense, refers to the creation of any good or service that people will buy. While we generally speak of production as being carried out by business firms, the theoretical structure is equally applicable to production of goods and services by agencies of government or by nonprofit institutions, such as hospitals and universities.

One can speak just as well about a doctor producing medical care as a city government producing police protection. Ford Motor Company produces automobiles, the Corps of Engineers produces dams, and Stanford University produces educated people. Most of the principles developed in this chapter apply to the production of either goods or services by private firms, branches of government, or nonprofit institutions.

We will, however, generally in this chapter concentrate upon the production of goods by business firms, only because it is simpler to specify the precise inputs and to identify the quantity of output. It is far easier to specify the number of automobiles produced by Ford or the amount of wheat produced by a farmer than it is to measure the amount of education produced by your school or the amount of defense produced by the federal government. But keep in mind at all times that the basic principles also apply to production by agencies other than private business firms and to services as well as to goods.

## Production-possibilities curves and the theory of production

The theory of production illustrates the economic problem faced by every society, the problem of scarcity. Recall our discussion in Chapters 1 and 2 in which we introduced the problem of scarcity. In order for a society to gain additional goods and services of one type, it must give up goods and services of other types. This is the cost to society of having more of one good or service.

Scarcity, the reason for such trade-offs, results from the fact that goods and services are produced by factors of production, such as labor, capital, natural resources, and so on. At any time in any society, these inputs or factors of production are limited. The limit is at a higher level for very rich societies, but the limit is still there. The basic point is that, in order to have some additional amounts of certain goods, the society must use inputs to produce these additional goods. Where do the added inputs come from? They must be taken away from the production of other goods and services. Consequently, these other goods must be given up.

If society is to get more cotton, then resources such as land and farm machinery must be withdrawn from the production of other crops. If government wishes to build more roads, labor and machinery must be taken from the construction of other things—houses, offices, and so on. Thus, the entire concept of scarcity is based upon this notion of production and the use of scarce inputs to carry out production. The problem of giving up some goods (or the inputs needed to produce these goods) in order to use the inputs to produce other goods exists in all economies regardless of their social makeup. The most totalitarian dictatorship, the most free democracy, and all societies in between face the same problem.

This problem is best illustrated with the concept of a production-possibilities frontier. This frontier illustrates the way societies must make trade-offs among different goods and services—publicly or privately produced.

To analyze the concept of a limit or a frontier to the available goods and services, let us for analytical simplicity assume that a society can produce and consume only two goods—call them food and shelter. Society's finite resources can be used to produce these two goods in many different combinations.

Figure 5–1 shows a hypothetical production-possibilities frontier or curve of a typically assumed shape. The curve *FRMS* shows the

**FIGURE 5–1**
**Production-possibilities curve**

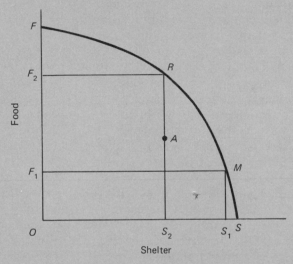

Shelter

combinations of the two goods possible for the society with a given amount of productive resources and technology. The figure shows that, if society chooses to produce no shelter, it can have *F* units of food per period; or if it chooses to produce no food, it can consume *S* units of shelter. Similarly, it can choose any other point on the curve, such as *R*, with $F_2$ units of food and $S_2$ units of shelter, or *M*, with a combination of $F_1$ and $S_1$ food and shelter.

Furthermore, the society could consume any combination inside of the curve *FRMS*, such as the combination indicated by point *A*. But at interior points such as *A*, society is not using all of its resources, or it is not using the resources efficiently. In this case, the society producing at *A* could increase its food consumption to $F_2$ without giving up any shelter, it could increase shelter with no sacrifice of food, or it could increase its consumption of both goods, moving to some point on *FRMS*. Scarcity exists simply because the society cannot consume any combination outside of the curve.

The shape of the curve reflects certain assumptions about the way in which the output of some goods can be substituted for other goods. In the first place, it is obvious that the production-possibilities curve slopes downward. This negative slope reflects the fact that, in order to have more of one good, society must give up some portion of the other good. Note also that the curve decreases at an increasing rate. For example, if the society decreases its food production from $F$ to $F_2$ units, it can increase shelter from zero to $S_2$. On the other hand, if there is very little food being produced, say $F_1$, and society moves from $F_1$ to zero food, it gains only the very slight increase in shelter from $S_1$ to $S$. We have drawn the distance $OF_1$ to equal the distance $F_2F$. It is easily seen that the increase in shelter from an equal decrease in food diminishes greatly as the amount of shelter rises relative to the amount of food. The *cost* of shelter increases as more shelter is produced. For the same sacrifice in food, less shelter is obtainable. Clearly, the situation holds for decreases in shelter relative to increases in food.

The changes in the production of goods, described above, reflect the fact that resources are better adapted to one type of production than to another. As the output of a good rises, less suitable resources must be used to increase its output. Even though we have been concerned here with only two goods, the same principles apply in a multiple-good world.

This chapter and the next deal with the theories of production and cost. As you go through these theories—and they are related quite closely—relate the concepts developed in these theories to this fundamental principle of scarcity, as illustrated by the production-possibilities frontier.[1]

The basic concepts to be learned in Chapter 5 are

1. How output varies with the services of one variable input.
2. The principle under which variable inputs can be substituted to produce output.
3. How to maximize the level of output obtainable at a given level of cost.
4. How to minimize the cost of producing a given level of output.
5. The principles and results of technological change.

---

[1] Those students who have already gone through consumer theory will note many similarities between the concepts discussed there and the theory of production. Several users of this text have pointed out that they choose to cover production and cost theory before consumer theory. Therefore, we will not dwell on these similarities in this and the next chapter. For those students who have already studied consumer-behavior theory, the relations should be rather obvious.

## 5.2 PRODUCTION FUNCTIONS

Production processes typically require a wide variety of inputs. They are not as simple as "labor," "capital," and "materials"; many qualitatively different types of each are normally used to produce an output. With a given state of technology, the quantity of output depends upon the quantities of the various inputs used. This relation is more formally described by a *production function*, associating physical output with physical rates of input.

**Definition.** A production function is a schedule (or table, or mathematical equation) showing the maximum amount of output that can be produced from any specified set of inputs, given the existing technology or "state of the art." In short, the production function is a catalog of output possibilities.

Mathematically, a production function can be written as

$$X = f(L_1, L_2, \ldots, L_m; K_1, K_2, \ldots, K_n; M_1, M_2, \ldots, M_s),$$

where $L_i$, $K_i$, and $M_i$ represent the various kinds of labor, capital, and materials that are used in the production of product $X$.

A hypothetical example of a very simple production function is the production of a student's test score from study time. This might take the form of a table such as:

| Expected percentage score | Minimum study time (hours) |
|:---:|:---:|
| 90 | 16 |
| 80 | 9 |
| 70 | 4 |
| 60 | 1 |
| 50 | 0 |

This table relates the expected score to the minimum time allocated to study. The production function could take the form of a simple equation such as

$$S = 10\sqrt{T} + 50,$$

where $S$ is the expected numerical grade, and $T$ is time spent studying. These functions make product (grade) depend only on one input (study time). Other functions relate output or product to two or more inputs. Still more complicated functions relate several different outputs to several different inputs. We will be dealing primarily with one output produced by either one or two inputs. The principles apply to more than two inputs, however.

### Economic efficiency in production

Economists are not engineers. So when economists work with production functions, they assume a producer knows how to technically derive the greatest amount of output from a given set of inputs. To put it another way, producers are assumed to be fully aware of the latest technological production processes, and economists consider this technology to even be a part of the production function. Thus, when producers are presented with input and output prices, the question at hand is not a technical one, but an economic question: how to produce a certain amount of output at the lowest cost, or, conversely, how to maximize output given total cost.

*Technical efficiency* exists when no more than the necessary amount of inputs are used in a production process. *Economic efficiency* takes technical efficiency and prices as given and seeks the maximization of output or the minimization of cost under these conditions.

We must not be too hasty about labeling a particular production process technically inefficient. A method of production is unquestionably inefficient if another method uses less of every input. But suppose a second process uses more of some inputs and less of others. Then the less expensive method of production depends upon input prices. The technology in the first method of production could be the economically efficient method under one set of input prices and the other process efficient under different prices. Both production processes are technically efficient. The choice of processes is an economic decision.

### Short and long runs

In analyzing the process of production, it is convenient to introduce an important distinction: classification of inputs as fixed or variable. Accordingly, a *fixed input* exists when the quantity of a production factor cannot readily be changed, even when market conditions indicate that a change in output is desirable. To be sure, no input is ever *absolutely* fixed, no matter how short the period of time under consideration. But frequently, for the sake of analytical simplicity, we hold some inputs fixed, reasoning perhaps that, while these inputs are in fact variable, the cost of immediate variation is so great as to take them out of the range of relevance for the particular decision at hand. Buildings, major pieces of machinery, and managerial personnel are examples of inputs that generally cannot be rapidly augmented or diminished. A *variable input,* on the other hand, is a factor of production of which the quantity may be changed quite readily in response to desired changes in output. Many types of labor services and the inputs of raw and processed materials fall in this category.

For the sake of analysis, economists introduce a distinction between the short and long runs. The *short run* refers to that period of time in which the input of one or more productive factors is fixed. Therefore, changes in output must be accomplished exclusively by changes in the use of variable inputs. Thus, if producers wish to expand output in the short run, they must usually do so by using more hours of labor service with the existing plant and equipment. Similarly, if they wish to reduce output in the short run, they may discharge certain types of workers; but they cannot immediately "discharge" a building or a diesel locomotive, even though its use may fall to zero.

In the long run, however, even this is possible, for the *long run* is defined as that period of time (or planning horizon) in which all inputs are variable. The long run, in other words, refers to that time in the future when output changes can be accomplished in the manner most advantageous to the producer. For example, in the short run, a producer may be able to expand output only by operating existing plant for more hours per day. In the long run, it may be more economical to install additional productive facilities and return to the normal workday.

### Fixed or variable proportions

Our attention here is restricted mainly to production under conditions of *variable proportions*. The ratio of input quantities may vary. The producer, therefore, must determine not only the optimal level of output to produce but also the optimal proportion in which to combine inputs.

There are two different ways of stating the principle of variable proportions. First, variable-proportions production implies that output can be changed in the short run by changing the amount of variable inputs used in cooperation with the fixed inputs. Naturally, as the amount of one input is changed, the others remaining constant, the *ratios* change. Second, when production is subject to variable proportions, the *same* output can be produced by various combinations of inputs—that is, by different input ratios. This may apply only to the long run, but it is relevant to the short run when there is more than one variable input.

Most economists regard production under conditions of variable proportions as typical of both the short and long run. There is certainly no doubt that proportions are variable in the long run. When making an investment decision, a producer may choose among a wide variety of different production processes. As polar opposites, an automobile can be practically handmade or it can be made by assembly-line techniques. In the short run, however, there may be some cases in which output is subject to fixed proportions.

*Fixed-proportions* production means that there is one, and only one, ratio of inputs that can be used to produce a good. If output is expanded or contracted, all inputs must be expanded or contracted so as to maintain the fixed-input ratio. At first glance, this might seem the usual condition: one man and one shovel produce a ditch, two parts hydrogen and one part oxygen produce water. Adding a second shovel or a second part of oxygen will not augment the rate of production. In such cases, the producer has little discretion about what combination of inputs to employ. The only decision is how much to produce.

In actuality, examples of fixed-proportions production are hard to come by. Certainly some "ingredient" inputs are often used in relatively fixed proportions to output. Otherwise, the quality of the product will change. There is so much leather in a pair of shoes of a particular size and style. Use less leather, and we have a different type of shoe. There is so much tobacco in a cigarette, and so on. In many cases, the producer has little choice in this regard. But fixed-ingredient inputs are really only a short-run problem. Historically, when these "necessary" ingredients have become very high priced or practically impossible to obtain, businesses, generally under the lure of profits, have invented new processes, discovered new ingredients, or somehow overcome the problem of a given production function and increasingly scarce ingredients.

The history of businesses is full of such examples. The oil crisis of 1973–74 was really the second oil crisis faced by the United States. The first was the whale-oil crisis of the middle 19th century. During that period, whale oil was absolutely necessary for lighting and lubrication, but the whales were disappearing under the pressure of increased hunting. The real price of whale oil quadrupled over a short period of time. Possibly spurred on by these higher prices, people discovered oil and how to use it for lighting and lubrication. Whales became almost redundant for oil production, and the price of whale oil fell drastically.

During the early days of the industrial revolution in England, charcoal, which was made from wood, was a necessary ingredient in the production of steel. The problem was that English mills were producing so much steel that the country was running out of trees. During this period, British newspapers constantly predicted that the manufacturing center of the world would move to Germany and Sweden, both of which had plenty of trees. But as wood became more expensive, manufacturers discovered that coke, made from coal, was better for steel production; England happened to be sitting on gigantic coal deposits.

These brief examples play no part in the basic theoretical structure of production theory. They emphasize that, in the long run, it is unlikely that an input must be used in fixed proportions. As a consequence, we will, in general, direct our attention to production in which the producer has some control over the mix of inputs. Thus, we concentrate on production with variable proportions.

## 5.3 PRODUCTION WITH ONE VARIABLE INPUT

We first introduce some simplifying assumptions in order to cut through the complexities of dealing with hundreds of different inputs. Our focus is upon the essential principles of production. To explore these principles, we assume that there is only one variable input which can be combined in different proportions with fixed inputs to produce various quantities of output. Note that this assumption still allows inputs to be combined in *various* proportions to produce the commodity in question. It is just that, in the short run, all but one input is fixed.

### Total, average, and marginal product: Arithmetic approach

Assume that a firm with a fixed plant can apply different numbers of workers to get output according to columns (1) and (2) of Table 5–1. Columns (1) and (2) define a production function over a specific range. They specify the product per unit of time for different numbers of workers in that period. The total output rises up to a point (nine workers), then declines. The *total output* is the *maximum* output obtainable from each number of workers with the given plant.

Average and marginal product are obtained from the production function. The *average product* of labor is the total product divided by the number of workers. (Here it rises, reaches a maximum at 15, then declines thereafter.) *Marginal product* is the additional output attributable to using one additional worker with a fixed plant (or with the use of all other inputs fixed). It first rises, then falls, becoming negative when an additional worker reduces total product.

Note that we speak of the marginal product of labor, not of the marginal product of a particular laborer. We assume all workers are the same in the sense that, if we reduce the number of workers from eight to seven, total product falls from 88 to 84 regardless of which of the eight workers is released. Thus, the order of hiring makes no difference; the third worker adds 20 units no matter who is hired.

Note also from the table that, when average product is rising (falling), marginal product is greater (less) than average. When average reaches its maximum, average equals marginal (at 15). This result is not a peculiarity of this table; it occurs for any production function in which the average product peaks. An example should illustrate this point. If you have taken two tests on which you have grades of 70 and 80, your average grade is 75. If your third test grade is higher than 75, say 90, your average rises, to 80. The 90 is the *marginal addition* to your total grade. If your third grade is less than 75, the marginal addition is below average, and the average falls. This is the relation between all marginal and average schedules. In production theory, if each additional worker adds more than the preceding worker, average product rises; if each additional worker adds less than the preceding worker, average product falls.

**TABLE 5–1**
**Total, average, and marginal products of labor**

| (1) Number of workers | (2) Total output per unit of time | (3) Average product | (4) Marginal product |
|---|---|---|---|
| 1 | 10 | 10 | 10 |
| 2 | 25 | 12.5 | 15 |
| 3 | 45 | 15 | 20 |
| 4 | 60 | 15 | 15 |
| 5 | 70 | 14 | 10 |
| 6 | 78 | 13 | 8 |
| 7 | 84 | 12 | 6 |
| 8 | 88 | 11 | 4 |
| 9 | 90 | 10 | 2 |
| 10 | 88 | 8.8 | −2 |

The short-run production function set forth in Table 5–1 specifies a very common assumption in production theory. Marginal and average products first increase then decrease, with marginal becoming negative after a point. Marginal reaches a peak before the peak of average is attained. At the peak of average, marginal equals average. These relations mean that total product at first increases at an increasing rate, then increases at a decreasing rate, and finally decreases. The graphical exposition in the next subsection will illustrate these points.

We summarize with two definitions:

**Definition.** The average product of an input is total output divided by the amount of input used. Thus, average product is the output-input ratio for each level of output and the corresponding volume of input.

**Definition.** The marginal product of an input is the addition to total output attributable to the addition of one unit of the variable input in the production process, all other inputs remaining constant.

### Total, average, and marginal product: Graphical approach

The short-run production function in Figure 5–2 shows the maximum output per unit of time obtainable from different amounts of the variable input (labor), given a specified amount of the fixed inputs. In Figure 5–2 and thereafter in this section, we assume that

**FIGURE 5–2**
**Derivation of average product from total product**

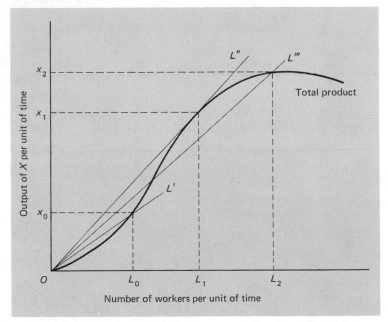

both the output and the variable input are continuously divisible. This assumption sacrifices little realism, yet adds a great deal of analytical convenience. As you will see, the product curve in this figure embodies the same assumptions about production given in the last subsection; both average and marginal product rise then fall, marginal product equaling average product at the maximum point of the latter.

In the figure, $x_0$ is the *maximum* amount of output obtainable when $L_0$ workers are combined with the fixed and ingredient inputs.

Likewise, $L_1$ workers can produce a maximum of $x_1$, and so forth. Certainly, the specified numbers of inputs could produce less than the amount indicated by the total product curve, but not more than that amount. First, total output increases with increases in the variable input up to a point, in this case $L_2$ workers. After that, so many workers are combined with the fixed inputs that output diminishes when additional workers are employed. Second, production at first increases at an increasing rate, then increases at a decreasing rate, until the maximum is reached.

The average product of $L_0$ workers is $x_0/L_0$, the slope of the ray from the origin, $OL'$. In like manner, the average product of any number of workers can be determined by the slope of a ray from the origin to the relevant point on the total product curve; the steeper the slope, the larger the average product. It is easy to see that the slopes of rays from the origin to the total product curve in Figure 5–2 increase with additional labor until $OL''$ becomes tangent at $L_1$ workers and $x_1$ output, then decrease thereafter (say, to $OL'''$ at $L_2$ workers). Hence, typical average product curves associated with this total product curve first increase and then decrease thereafter.

As with average product, we can derive a marginal product curve from a total product curve. In Figure 5–3, $L_0$ workers can produce $x_0$ units of output and $L_1$ can produce $x_1$. $L_0L_1$ additional workers in-

**FIGURE 5–3**
**Derivation of marginal product from total product**

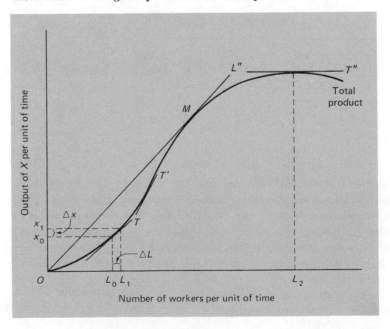

crease total product by $x_0 x_1$. Marginal product is therefore $x_0 x_1 / L_0 L_1$ or $\Delta x / \Delta L$. Let $L_1$ become very close to $L_0$; hence, $x_1$ is very close to $x_0$; $\Delta x / \Delta L$ approaches the slope of the tangent $T$ to the total product curve. Therefore, at any point on the total product curve, marginal product, which is the *rate of change of total product*, can be *estimated* by the slope of the tangent at that point.

On inspection, we see that marginal product first increases; note that $T'$ is steeper than $T$. It then decreases, $OL''$ at point $M$ being less steep than $T'$. Marginal product becomes zero when $L_2$ workers are employed (the slope of $T''$ is zero) and then becomes negative. At point $M$, the slope of the tangent $OL''$ is also the slope of the ray from the origin to that point. As noted above, average product attains a maximum when a ray from the origin is tangent to the total product curve. Therefore, marginal product equals average product at the latter's maximum point. To repeat, so long as marginal product exceeds average product, the latter must rise; when marginal product is less than average product, the latter must fall. Thus, average product must attain its maximum when it is equal to marginal product.

Figure 5–4 illustrates all these relations. In this graph, one can see not only the relation between marginal and average products, but also the relation of these two curves to total product.

**FIGURE 5–4**
**Total, average, and marginal products**

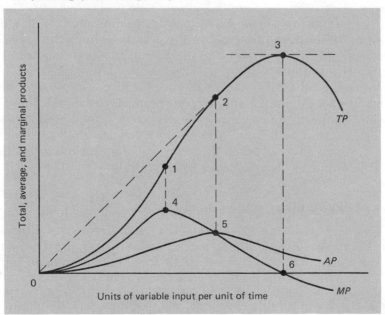

Consider first the total product curve. For very small amounts of the variable input, total product rises gradually. But even at a low level of input it begins to rise quite rapidly, reaching its maximum slope (or rate of increase) at point 1. Since the slope of the total product curve equals marginal product, the maximum slope (point 1) must correspond to the maximum point on the marginal product curve (point 4).

After attaining its maximum slope at point 1, the total product curve continues to rise. But output increases at a decreasing rate, so the slope is less steep. Moving outward along the curve from point 1, the point is soon reached at which a ray from the origin is just tangent to the curve (point 2). Since tangency of the ray to the curve defines the condition for maximum average product, point 2 lies directly above point 5.

As the quantity of variable input is expanded from its value at point 2, total product continues to increase. But its rate of increase is progressively slower until point 3 is finally reached. At this position, total product is at a maximum; thereafter, it declines. Over a tiny range around point 3, additional input does not change total output. The slope of the total product curve is zero; thus, marginal product must also be zero. This is shown by the fact that points 3 and 6 occur at precisely the same input value. And, since total product declines beyond point 3, marginal product becomes negative.

Most of the important relations have so far been discussed with reference to the total product curve. To emphasize certain relations, however, consider the marginal and average product curves. Marginal product at first increases, reaches a maximum at point 4 (the point of diminishing marginal returns) and declines thereafter. It eventually becomes negative beyond point 6, where total product attains its maximum.

Average product also rises at first until it reaches its maximum at point 5, where marginal and average products are equal. It subsequently declines, conceivably becoming zero if total product itself becomes zero. Finally, one may observe that marginal product exceeds average product when the latter is increasing and is less than average product when the latter is decreasing.

### Law of diminishing marginal product

The slope of the marginal product curve in Figure 5–4 illustrates an important principle, the law of *diminishing marginal product*. As the number of units of the variable input increases, other inputs held constant, after a point, the marginal product of the variable input declines. When the amount of the variable input is small relative to the fixed inputs (the fixed inputs are plentiful relative to the variable input), more intensive utilization of fixed inputs by variable inputs may increase the marginal output of the variable input. For instance, as you add more labor to a garden plot of fixed size, the marginal increase in vegetables you grow may at first rise. Nonetheless, a point is reached beyond which an increase in the use of the variable input yields progressively less additional product. Each additional unit has, on average, fewer units of the fixed inputs with which to work.

**Principle.**   As the amount of a variable input is increased, the amount of other (fixed) inputs held constant, a point is reached beyond which marginal product declines. This decline is often referred to as the law of diminishing marginal product.

**FIGURE 5–5**
**Stages of production**

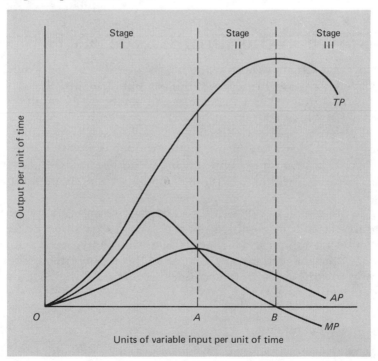

This is a simple statement concerning physical relations that have been observed in the real economic world. While it is not susceptible of mathematical proof or refutation, it is of some worth to note that a contrary observation has never been recorded. That is why it is called a law. Psychologists have even found that the law holds true for consecutive study time.[2]

### Three stages of production

Economists use the relations among total, average, and marginal products to define three stages of production, illustrated in Figure 5–5. Stage I covers that range of variable-input use over which average product increases. In other words, stage I corresponds to increasing *average returns* to the variable input. Stage III is defined as the range of negative marginal product, or declining total product. Additional units of variable input during this stage of production actually cause a decrease in total output. Even if units of the variable input were free, a rational producer would not employ them beyond the point of zero marginal product because their use entails a reduction in total output. Stage II includes the range over which marginal product is positive and less than average product.

## 5.4 PROFIT MAXIMIZATION WITH ONE VARIABLE INPUT

Now that we know how a variable input behaves, we would like to explore how much of it a producer ought to use to maximize profits. We already know that a firm will never use an input beyond the point at which marginal product becomes zero or negative, stage III of production. But we do not know how much of an input a firm would want to use when marginal product is positive. We shall discover that a producer with no influence over market prices, in other words, a price-taking firm, will choose to operate in production stage II.

The discussion in this section holds true for any number of variable inputs, but we continue, for the sake of exposition, to assume that only one input can be changed. For simplicity, we also assume that the producer can use any amount of this input without affecting its price, or the price of the producer's output. These assumptions are relaxed in Chapter 11.

### The profit-maximizing rule

A profit-maximizing producer is more concerned with the marginal revenue another unit of input brings than with the actual physi-

---

[2] Do not make the common mistake, however, of saying that you stopped studying because diminishing returns set in. The term *diminishing returns* is frequently heard in noneconomic usage and is almost as frequently misused. Diminishing returns may be set in with the first unit of study time, but you may continue studying. You cease studying when the marginal utility of the (expected) increase in grade (or of the pleasure of studying) from an additional unit of study time is less than the expected marginal utility of using that time for something else.

cal output it produces. Suppose you own a business and a worker applies for a job. Would you hire this worker? The answer depends on how much extra revenue the worker earns for your business. If the worker is expected to add more to revenue than you must pay in wages, the answer is yes. If the worker is expected to add less in revenue than the wages you pay, the answer is obviously no. The same reasoning applies to any factor of production. A producer would increase use of a particular input of any type if the additional unit of input is expected to add more to revenue than it adds to cost. If the additional unit increases cost more than it increases revenue, no more of the input would be added.

The amount that an additional unit of input adds to total revenue is called *marginal revenue product* (*MRP*). That is,

$$MRP = \frac{\Delta \text{ revenue}}{\Delta \text{ input usage}} = \frac{\Delta X \cdot P}{\Delta \text{ input usage}} = MP \cdot P$$

where $P$ is the given price of the producer's output and $MP$ is marginal product. We can also define marginal revenue product in words:

**Definition.**  The marginal revenue product (*MRP*) of a factor of production for a producer is the addition to total revenue attributable to the addition of one more unit of the factor. Thus, marginal revenue product is equivalent to marginal product multiplied by output price, when output prices are constant.

We shall often add a subscript to $MRP$ to denote the kind of input to which we are referring. For instance, $MRP_L$ is the marginal revenue product of labor.

Let the price of another unit of labor be $w$. The basic rule for hiring an extra unit is, if

$$MRP_L > w,$$

the producer would add more of the input. If

$$MRP_L < w,$$

the firm would add no more of the input; it would, in fact, decrease its use. Profit maximization requires

$$MRP_L = w.$$

The same rule applies to any factor of production. For instance, if we let $K$ be the symbol for capital, then it must also be true that a profit-maximizing producer sets

$$MRP_K = r,$$

where $r$ is the price of another unit of capital. In general, we have the following principle:

**Principle.** A profit-maximizing producer will employ units of a variable productive service until the point is reached at which the marginal revenue product of the input is equal to the input price.

While it is marginal revenue product that tells producers how to maximize profits, it is *average revenue product* (*ARP*) that tells them how much profit they earn. Average revenue product is simply total revenue divided by the amount of input used:

$$ARP = \frac{\text{revenue}}{\text{total input usage}} = \frac{X \cdot P}{\text{total input usage}} = AP \cdot P,$$

where $AP$ is average product and, once again, $P$ is the price of a producer's output. To see how $ARP$ determines the profitability of a good, suppose the only input used by a producer is labor, and this is the producer's only cost, then profit ($\Pi$) is

$$\Pi = \text{total revenue} - \text{total cost} = P \cdot X - w \cdot L.$$

$L$ is the total amount of labor hired by the producer, or the total amount of input used. Rearranging terms and applying the definition of $ARP_L$, we get:

$$\Pi = L \left[ \left( P \cdot \frac{X}{L} \right) - w \right] = L(ARP_L - w).$$

Hence, if $ARP_L \gtreqless w$, then profits are positive, negative, or equal to zero.

In sum, a producer uses $MRP$ to determine the amount of input to use in order to maximize profits, but uses $ARP$ to find out what profits are for the amount of input employed by the producer.

## Profits in stages I and II

To get some idea of whether a firm would operate in stage I or stage II in Figure 5–5, we alter the $TP$, $AP$, and $MP$ curves slightly by multiplying each point on the product curves by the price of the output. We continue to assume that the price of the output is constant, that is, the producer can sell all its output at the same price, $P$.

The boundaries separating stages I, II, and III remain unchanged at points $A$ and $B$. The units of measure have only changed from output to revenue on the vertical axis, and the names of the curves change from total product ($TP$) to total revenue ($TR$), average product ($AP$) to average revenue product ($ARP$), and marginal product ($MP$) to marginal revenue product ($MRP$). Figure 5–6 shows the transformation.

Once again, we see that a producer would never operate in stage III. Since input prices are positive, the producer could never follow the profit maximizing rule where $MRP < 0$.

**FIGURE 5–6**
**Stages of production in terms of revenue product**

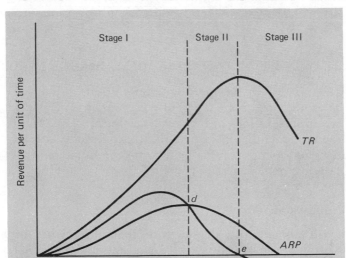

In stage I, notice that at every level of input, *MRP* is greater than average product. Thus, if a producer followed the profit-maximizing rule here—say the only input is labor—then in stage I for example, up to point $d$ in Figure 5–6

$$MRP_L = w > ARP_L.$$

But we know that if $w > ARP_L$, profits are negative. Hence, the firm would not choose to operate in stage I. It is important to keep in mind the two assumptions we have made in this section: the unprofitability of stage I critically depends on the producer's product price being held constant and on constant input prices. If one or both assumptions are not met, a firm may operate in stage I. When the output price and the input price are not constant, there is no longer a close correspondence between Figures 5–5 and 5–6. A switch from the output curves in Figure 5–5 to the revenue curves in Figure 5–6 could cause them to "drift" to the left, in which case there may be profitable points of operation in stage I.

Given constant input and output prices, however, stage II is the only level of production at which a producer could profitably operate. Now, when the producer sets $MRP_L = w$, it is also true that $w < ARP_L$, and, as a result, profits are positive at any point on $MRP_L$ between $d$ and $e$.

Stage II will play an important role in Chapter 11, when we discuss the demands for inputs. In that chapter we also study more carefully what happens when input and output prices are not held constant.

## 5.5 PRODUCTION WITH TWO OR MORE VARIABLE INPUTS

Here we consider the more general case of several variable inputs in production. For graphical purposes, we concentrate upon only two inputs, but all of the results hold for more than two. One may assume either that these two inputs are the only variable inputs, or that one of the inputs represents some combination of all variable inputs except one.

### Production isoquants

When analyzing production with several variable inputs, we cannot simply use several sets of average and marginal product curves such as those discussed above. Recall that these curves were derived holding the use of all other inputs constant and letting the use of only one input vary. Thus, when the amount of one variable input changes, the total, average, and marginal product curves of all other variable inputs shift. In the case of two variable inputs, increasing the use of one increases the amount of this input that is combined with the other input. This increase would probably cause a shift in the marginal and average product curves of the other input. For example, an increase in capital would quite possibly result in an increase in the marginal product of labor over a wide range of labor use.

This proposition is shown graphically in Figure 5–7. We show only the situation in which labor is in stage II. $TP_0$ in panel A and $AP_0$ and $MP_0$ in panel B are the original total, average, and marginal product curves of labor for a fixed amount of another factor, say capital. If the amount of capital increases, the three curves increase to $TP_1$, $AP_1$, and $MP_1$. This means that, for each amount of labor over the relevant range, total, average, and marginal products are greater. For example, for $L$ units of labor, an increase in capital increases total product from $T_0$ to $T_1$, average product from $A_0$ to $A_1$, and marginal product from $M_0$ to $M_1$.

If both labor and capital are variable, each factor has an infinite set of product curves, one for every amount of the other factor. Therefore, another tool of analysis is necessary when there is more than one variable factor. This tool is the *production isoquant*.

**Definition.** An isoquant is a curve or locus of points showing all possible combinations of inputs physically capable of producing a given level

**FIGURE 5–7**
Total, average, and marginal products for two different amounts of the
fixed factor

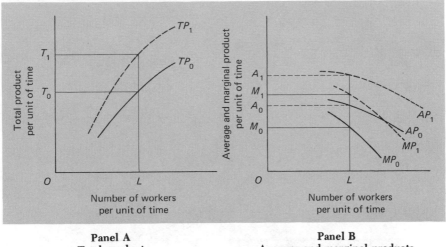

| Panel A | Panel B |
|---------|---------|
| **Total product** | **Average and marginal products** |

of output. An isoquant that lies above another designates a higher
level of output.

Figure 5–8 illustrates two isoquants of the shape typically assumed in economic theory. Capital use is plotted on the vertical axis
and labor use on the horizontal. Isoquant I shows the locus of combinations of capital and labor yielding 100 units of output. The
producer can produce 100 units of output by using 10 units of capital and 75 of labor, or 50 units of capital and 15 of labor, or by using
any other combination of inputs on I. Similarly, isoquant II shows
the various combinations of capital and labor that can produce 200
units of output.

Isoquants I and II are only two of an infinite number of isoquants
that are possible. In fact, there is an infinite number of isoquants
between I and II because there is an infinite number of possible
production levels between 100 and 200 units, provided, as we have
assumed, that the product is continuously divisible.

Isoquants have several important properties. First, as shown in
Figure 5–8, isoquants slope downward over the relevant range of
production. This negative slope indicates that, if the producer decreases the amount of capital employed, more labor must be added
in order to keep the rate of output constant. Or, if labor use is
decreased, capital must be increased to keep output constant. Thus,
the two inputs can be substituted for one another to maintain a
constant level of output.

**FIGURE 5–8**
**Typical isoquants**

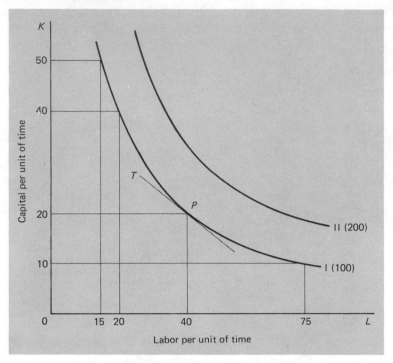

Great theoretical and practical importance is attached to the rate at which one input must be substituted for another in order to keep output constant. This rate at which one input is substituted for another along an isoquant is called the *marginal rate of technical substitution* (*MRTS*). It is defined as

$$MRTS = -\frac{\Delta K}{\Delta L},$$

where $K$ is the amount of the input measured along the vertical axis, capital, and $L$ is the amount measured along the horizontal, labor. The minus sign is added in order to make *MRTS* a positive number, since $\Delta K/\Delta L$, the slope of the isoquant, is negative.

Over the relevant range of production, the marginal rate of technical substitution diminishes; that is, as more and more labor is used relative to capital, the absolute value of $\Delta K/\Delta L$ decreases along an isoquant. This can be seen in Figure 5–8. If capital is decreased by 10 units, from 50 to 40, labor must be increased by only 5 units, from 15 to 20, in order to keep the level of output at 100 units. But if capital is decreased by 10 units, from 20 to 10, labor must increase by 35 units, from 40 to 75, to keep output at 100 units.

The fact that the marginal rate of technical substitution diminishes means that isoquants must be convex; that is, in the neighborhood of a point of tangency, the isoquant must lie above the tangent. This relation is seen at point $P$ in Figure 5–8. The slope of the tangent $T$ shows the rate at which labor can be substituted for capital in the neighborhood of point $P$, maintaining an output of 100 units. For very small movements along an isoquant, the negative of the slope of the tangent is the marginal rate of technical substitution. It is easy to see that the slope of the tangent becomes less and less steep as the input combination moves downward along the isoquant.

The concept of diminishing $MRTS$ is stressed again in Figure 5–9. $Q, R, S,$ and $T$ are four input combinations lying on the isoquant

**FIGURE 5–9**
**Diminishing marginal rate of technical substitution**

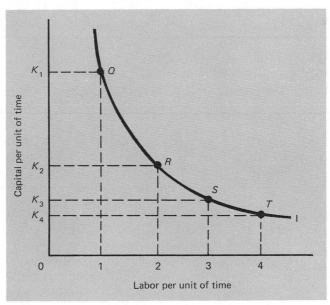

I. $Q$ has the combination $K_1$ units of capital and one unit of labor; $R$ has $K_2$ units of capital and two units of labor, and so on. For the movement from $Q$ to $R$, the marginal rate of technical substitution of capital for labor is, by the formula,

$$-\frac{K_1 - K_2}{1 - 2} = K_1 - K_2.$$

Similarly, for the movements from $R$ to $S$ and $S$ to $T$, the marginal rates of technical substitution are $K_2 - K_3$ and $K_3 - K_4$, respectively.

Since the marginal rate of technical substitution of capital for labor diminishes as labor is substituted for capital, it is necessary that $(K_1 - K_2) > (K_2 - K_3) > (K_3 - K_4)$. Visually, the amount of capital replaced by successive units of labor will decline if, and only if, the isoquant is convex. Since the amount *must* decline, the isoquant must be convex.

One final property of isoquants is that they cannot intersect one another. If they did, then one combination of $K$ and $L$ would yield two different levels of output. The producer's technology is inconsistent; we rule out such events.

### Relation of *MRTS* to marginal products

For very slight movements along an isoquant, the marginal rate of technical substitution equals the ratio of the marginal products of the two inputs. The proof is quite straightforward.

Let the level of output, $X$, depend upon the use of two inputs, $L$ and $K$. Assume that $L$ and $K$ are both allowed to vary slightly, and consider how $X$ must vary. As an example, suppose the use of $L$ increases by 3 units and that of $K$ by 5. If, in this range, the marginal product of $L$ is 4 units of $X$ per unit of $L$ and that of $K$ is 2 units of $X$ per unit of $K$, the change in $X$ is

$$\Delta X = (4 \times 3) + (2 \times 5) = 22.$$

In other words, when $L$ and $K$ are allowed to vary slightly, the change in $X$ resulting from the change in the two inputs is the marginal product of $L$ times the amount of change in $L$ plus the marginal product of $K$ times its change.[3] Put in equation form

$$\Delta X = MP_L \Delta L + MP_K \Delta K.$$

Along an isoquant, $X$ is constant; therefore $\Delta X$ equals zero. Setting $\Delta X$ equal to zero and solving for the slope of the isoquant, $\Delta K/\Delta L$, we have

$$-\frac{\Delta K}{\Delta L} = \frac{MP_L}{MP_K} = MRTS.$$

---

[3] Note that we have really violated our assumption about marginal product somewhat. The marginal product of an input is defined as the change in output per unit of change in the input, *the use of other inputs held constant*. In this case, we allow both inputs to change; thus, the marginal product is really an approximation. But we are speaking only of *slight*, or very small changes in use. Thus, the violation of the assumption is small, and the approximation approaches the true variation for very small amounts.

Since, as noted, along an isoquant $K$ and $L$ must vary inversely, $\Delta K/\Delta L$ is negative.[4]

Using the relations developed here, the reason for diminishing *MRTS* is easily explained. As additional units of labor are added to a fixed amount of capital, the marginal product of labor diminishes. Furthermore, as shown in Figure 5–7, if the amount of the fixed input is diminished, the marginal product of labor diminishes. Thus, two forces are working to diminish the marginal product of labor: (*a*) less of the other input causes a downward *shift* of the marginal product of labor curve; and (*b*) more units of the variable input (labor) cause a downward movement *along* the marginal product curve. Thus, as labor is substituted for capital the marginal product of labor must decline. For analogous reasons, the marginal product of capital increases as less capital and more labor is used. With the quantity of labor fixed, the marginal product of capital rises as fewer units of capital are used. But, simultaneously, there is an increase in labor input, thereby shifting the marginal product of capital curve upward. The same two forces are present in this case: a movement along a marginal product curve and a shift in the location of the curve. In this situation, however, both forces work to increase the marginal product of capital. Thus, as labor is substituted for capital, the marginal product of capital increases.

## 5.6 OPTIMAL COMBINATION OF RESOURCES

The core of production theory is concerned with how a producer should combine inputs when operating under a constraint. Any desired level of output can normally be produced by a number of different combinations of inputs. But nearly every producer has the goal of either maximizing output given an operating budget or minimizing cost given a required output to produce. This is the economic definition of efficiency; to pursue either goal is called constrained optimization. This is not profit maximization. A producer cannot maximize profits if costs or output are restricted.

Our task is to determine the specific combination of inputs a firm should select when it is constrained. We shall see in this section that a firm attains the highest possible level of output for any given level

---

[4] It is possible that, as more and more labor is used relative to capital, and labor goes into stage III, the isoquant bends upward. Or, as more and more capital is used relative to labor, and capital goes into stage III, the isoquant bends backward. Since both of these regions involve one input in stage III, production does not take place in that area. Thus, we shall ignore these noneconomic regions.

of cost or the lowest possible cost for producing any level of output when the marginal rate of technical substitution for any two inputs equals the ratio of input prices.

### Input prices and isocost curves

Inputs, as well as outputs, bear specific market prices. In determining the optimal input combination, producers must pay heed to relative input prices if they are to minimize the cost of producing a given output or maximize output for a given level of cost.

Input prices are determined, as are the prices of goods, by supply and demand in the market. For producers who are not monopsonists or oligopsonists (that is, the sole purchaser or one of a few purchasers of an input), input prices are given by the market, and their rates of purchase do not change prices even though many producers as a group can change them. Let us now concentrate upon a producer who faces fixed input prices.

Let us continue to assume that the two inputs are labor and capital, although the analysis applies equally well to any two productive agents. Denote the quantity of capital and labor by $K$ and $L$, respectively, and their unit prices by $r$ and $w$. The total cost, $\overline{C}$, of using any volume of $K$ and $L$ is $\overline{C} = rK + wL$, the sum of the cost of $K$ units of capital at $r$ per unit and of $L$ units of labor at $w$ per unit.

To take a more specific example, suppose capital costs \$1,000 per unit ($r$ = \$1,000), and labor receives a wage of \$2,500 per month ($w$ = \$2,500). If a total of \$15,000 is to be spent for inputs, the equation above shows that the following combinations are possible: \$15,000 = \$1,000$K$ + \$2,500$L$, or $K = 15 - 2.5L$. Similarly, if \$20,000 is to be spent on inputs, one can purchase the following combinations: $K = 20 - 2.5L$. More generally, if the fixed amount, $\overline{C}$, is to be spent, the producer can choose among the combinations given by

$$K = \frac{\overline{C}}{r} - \frac{w}{r} L.$$

This equation is illustrated in Figure 5–10. If \$15,000 is spent for inputs and no labor is purchased, 15 units of capital may be bought. More generally, if $\overline{C}$ is to be spent and $r$ is the unit cost, $\overline{C}/r$ units of capital may be purchased. This is the vertical axis *intercept* of the line. If 1 unit of labor is purchased at \$2,500, then 2.5 units of capital must be sacrificed; if 2 units of labor are bought, 5 units of capital must be sacrificed; and so on. Thus, as the purchase of labor is increased, the purchase of capital must decrease, if cost is held constant. For each additional unit of labor, $w/r$ units of capital must be foregone. In Figure 5–10, $w/r$ = 2.5. Attaching a negative sign, this is the *slope* of the line.

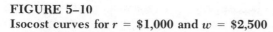

**FIGURE 5–10**
Isocost curves for $r = \$1,000$ and $w = \$2,500$

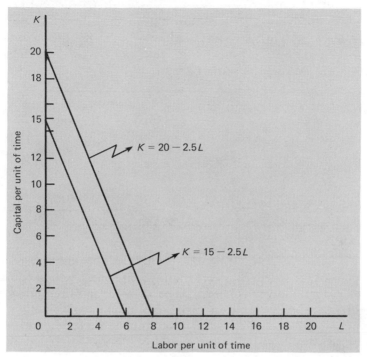

The solid lines in Figure 5–10 are called *isocost curves*, because they show the various combinations of inputs that may be purchased for a stipulated amount of expenditure. In summary:

**Relation.** At fixed input prices, *r* and *w* for capital and labor, a fixed outlay, $\overline{C}$, will purchase any combination of capital and labor given by the following linear equation:

$$K = \frac{\overline{C}}{r} - \frac{w}{r}L.$$

This is the equation for an isocost curve whose intercept $(\overline{C}/r)$ is the amount of capital that may be purchased if no labor is bought, and whose slope is the negative of the input price ratio $(w/r)$.

### Production of a given output at minimum cost

Whatever output producers choose to produce, they wish to produce it at the least possible cost. Or whatever expenditure the entrepreneur wishes to make, the highest output possible with that expenditure is desired. To accomplish this task, production must be organized in the most efficient way. The basic principles can be shown with the following problem: suppose that Transport Service, an airline, must produce a certain output of cargo and passenger service per year. The service is confronted with the following combinations of aircraft and mechanics that can be used to yield this required output over its route pattern.

| Combination | Number of aircraft | Number of mechanics |
|---|---|---|
| No. 1 ...................... | 60 | 1,000 |
| 2 ...................... | 61 | 920 |
| 3 ...................... | 62 | 850 |
| 4 ...................... | 63 | 800 |
| 5 ...................... | 64 | 760 |
| 6 ...................... | 65 | 730 |
| 7 ...................... | 66 | 710 |

If the cost resulting from the operation of another aircraft is $250,000, and if mechanics cost them $6,000 each, which combination of aircraft and mechanics should Transport Service use to minimize its cost? By trial and error, a solution of combination No. 4 is obtained. Or we could use the following method. Begin at combination 1. An additional airplane would cost $250,000 to operate, but 80 mechanics could be released at a saving of $480,000. A move to 2 would be beneficial. By moving to 3, the firm would save $420,000 in mechanics' salaries and add $250,000 in aircraft expenses. Following the same line of reasoning, the firm could save cost by moving to combination 4. It would not move to 5 since the $240,000 saved is less than the $250,000 added.

Let us analyze the problem graphically. Suppose, at given input prices $r$ and $w$, a firm wishes to produce the output indicated by isoquant I in Figure 5–11. Isocost curves $KL$, $K'L'$, and $K''L''$ represent the infinite number of isocost curves from which the producer can choose at the given input prices. Obviously the firm chooses the lowest one that enables it to attain output level I. That is, the firm produces at the cost represented by isocost curve $K'L'$. Any resource expenditure below that, for example, that represented by $KL$, is not feasible, since it is impossible to produce output I with these resource combinations. Any resource combinations above that represented by $K'L'$ are rejected because the entrepreneur wishes to produce the desired output at *least* cost. If combinations $A$ or $B$ are chosen, at the cost represented by $K''L''$, the producer can reduce costs by moving along I to point $E$. Point $E$ shows the optimal resource combination, using $K_0$ units of capital and $L_0$ units of labor.

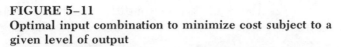

FIGURE 5–11

Optimal input combination to minimize cost subject to a given level of output

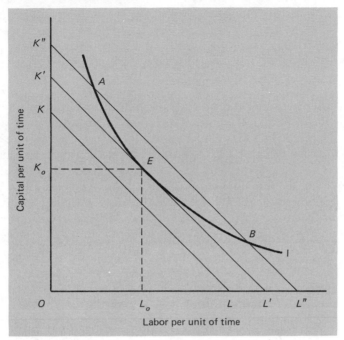

Equilibrium is reached when the isoquant representing the chosen output is just tangent to an isocost curve. Since tangency means that the two slopes are equal, least-cost production requires that the marginal rate of technical substitution of capital for labor be equal to the ratio of the price of labor to the price of capital. The market input-price ratio tells the producer the rate at which one input can be substituted for another *in purchasing*. The marginal rate of technical substitution shows the rate at which the producer *can substitute in production*. So long as the two are not equal, a producer can achieve a lower cost by moving in the direction of equality.

**Principle.** To minimize cost subject to a given level of output and given input prices, the producer must purchase inputs in quantities such that the marginal rate of technical substitution of capital for labor is equal to the input-price ratio (the price of labor to the price of capital). Thus,

$$MRTS = \frac{MP_L}{MP_K} = \frac{w}{r}.$$

We can analyze the equilibrium condition in another way. Assume the equilibrium condition did not hold, or specifically that

$$\frac{MP_L}{MP_K} < \frac{w}{r} \; .$$

In other words,

$$\frac{MP_L}{w} < \frac{MP_K}{r} \; .$$

In this case, the marginal product of an additional dollar's worth of labor is less than the marginal product of an additional dollar's worth of capital. The firm could reduce its use of labor by one dollar, expand its use of capital by less than one dollar, and remain at the same level of output but with a reduced cost. It could continue to do this so long as the above inequality holds. Eventually, $MP_L/w$ would become equal to $MP_K/r$ since $MP_L$ rises with decreased use of labor and increased use of capital, and $MP_K$ falls with increased capital and decreased labor. By the same reasoning, it is easy to see that firms substitute labor for capital until the equality holds if the inequality is reversed.

### Production of maximum output with a given level of cost

The most realistic way of examining the problem is to assume that the producer chooses a level of output and then chooses the input combination that permits production of that output at least cost. As an alternative, we could assume that the firm can spend only a fixed amount on production and wishes to attain the highest level of production consistent with that amount of expenditure. Not too surprisingly, the results turn out the same as before.

This situation is shown in Figure 5–12. The isocost line KL shows every possible combination of the two inputs at the given level of cost and input prices. Four isoquants are shown. Clearly, at the given level of cost, output level IV is unattainable. Neither level I nor level II would be chosen since higher levels are possible. Thus, the highest level of output attainable with a given level of cost is produced by using $L_0$ labor and $K_0$ capital. At point $A$, the highest possible isoquant, III, is just tangent to the given isocost. Thus, in the case of output maximization, the marginal rate of technical substitution of capital for labor equals the input-price ratio (the price of labor to the price of capital).

**Principle.**   In order either to maximize output subject to a given cost or to minimize cost subject to a given output, the producer must employ inputs in such amounts as to equate the marginal rate of technical substitution and the input-price ratio.

**FIGURE 5–12**
Output maximization for a given level of cost

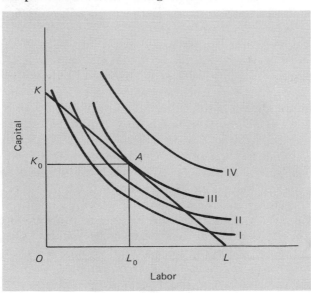

## Uses of constrained optimization in decision making

The concepts just developed are among the most applicable and useful tools for decision makers. Business and government decision makers use this type of analysis frequently in making important decisions. This would be expected because of the frequency of situations in which people are given a budget and are instructed to maximize something. Or just as frequently, they are given an objective and are told to minimize the cost of attaining that objective. Let us look at a few examples to see how the theory applies to daily decision making.

Agricultural agents, many of whom have training in agricultural economics, frequently must give advice such as how to blend fertilizers so as to give the maximum yield for a given level of cost. These fertilizers are a blend of several ingredients. The agent knows the general farming conditions and, equally important, the prices of the various ingredients. The formulas used are basically the same as those set forth here. In essence, the blend must be such that the marginal expected yield per dollar's worth is the same for each ingredient. Certainly the numerical solution is probably done by a computer, but the conditions are the same. Other very similar agricultural problems involve blending feeds so as to minimize the cost of a given weight gain in cattle or other stock. The same principles hold.

Businesses often hire efficiency experts in order to reduce the cost of running an office or increase the output from a particular plant operating at a given cost. Perhaps, in reorganizing an office, the expert would recommend reducing the number of secretaries and adding more word processors and copiers. Why such a recommendation? Clearly it was thought that the marginal product per unit of expenditure on secretaries was lower than the marginal products per unit of expenditure on word processors and copiers. The recommendation in the case of the factory would involve different inputs such as labor and machinery, but the solution is similar. You can certainly think of other business applications.

But the same method of analysis applies to nonprofit organizations. These organizations have objectives but have to operate within a budget also. Take, for example, a great medical center, perhaps the center in Houston with the famous heart surgeon Dr. Denton Cooley. The hospital administration must meet a budget, but it wishes to perform as many safe heart operations as possible. Clearly, there is some optimal operation mix consisting of Dr. Cooley, other assisting doctors, and equipment technicians. If you were told that Dr. Cooley and a few of the other most competent doctors were doing all of the work—preparing the patient, doing the operating, tending to the patient afterward—you could probably suggest that changes would decrease the cost of an operation and more operations could be performed. Additional nurses or less thoroughly trained doctors could perform some of the more routine tasks at which their marginal productivity per dollar expenditure was higher. This would free the most skilled doctors for more operations.

The administrators, regents, and faculty of some universities are currently debating an issue involving similar principles. Possibly officials of your school are. With the growth of universities, these officials are trying to decide how to give more education or training (however that is defined) within a given budget. The debate concerns substitution among very large classrooms with classes taught by very experienced professors, hiring more junior professors who teach smaller classes, using more graduate-student teachers, and so on. Clearly, there is a certain amount of added productivity per expenditure in each case. Of course, the really difficult thing in this case is how to measure the educational output of a university. How do you compare the returns from being taught in a large class by a professor or in a small class by a teaching assistant? Notwithstanding the measurement problem, the fundamental determinants in the decision-making process are the same as those set forth in the theory.

Turning to other types of government decisions, we have the

strategic and tactical decisions of the military. The navy, for example, has many options for attack—aircraft, submarines, cruisers. There is the problem of substitution among these weapons in order to obtain the maximum striking power from a given budget. The air force can use airplanes or missiles for defense. Here the problem may be to minimize the cost of a given level of air defense by substituting missiles for aircraft. Again, the principles are the same.

You can probably think of many more applications just as valid. Any time there is a given budget to carry out a specified task using two or more inputs, or a given task that is to be done at minimum cost, the same theory applies. In all cases, efficiency is attained when the marginal product per dollar expenditure on each input is the same. This type of analysis using the tools developed above occurs every day in many areas and in many jobs.

## APPLICATION

### The Averch-Johnson effect[5]

Government regulatory agencies that have the authority to prescribe prices generally use a "fair rate-of-return" criterion. Agencies allow the regulated firm to earn what they consider to be average profits on investment in plant and equipment. Suppose a state public-utility commission regulates an electric company. Then, if it followed the fair rate-of-return rule, the utility would be allowed to charge prices that gave it a normal return on its capital investment.

More specifically, suppose the allowed rate of return is 10 percent and the utility has two inputs, labor and capital. Let $D$ be the depreciation of capital during a given period. Rate of return regulation sets prices for the firm so

$$.10 \cong \frac{PX - wL - D}{rK} .$$

That is, $P$ is set in the numerator so the ratio on the right side is approximately equal to .10. The denominator, $rK$, is often called the *rate base*. If the rate base increases, then a regulator allows $P$ to increase so the ratio stays close to the target rate of return.

We can use production theory to show that rate-of-return regulation causes a firm to produce inefficiently. Without regulation, a firm would operate where

$$MRTS = \frac{MP_L}{MP_K} = \frac{w}{r} .$$

[5] H. Averch and L. Johnson, "Behavior of the Firm under Regulatory Constraint," *American Economic Review* 52, no. 5 (December 1962): 1052–69.

Rate-of-return regulation changes the price of capital to the firm and, consequently, the slope of the isocost line.

When a regulated firm buys another unit of capital, the price of the product is allowed to go up in order to give the firm a 10 percent return on the capital, so the price of a unit of capital is really $r -$ $.10(r) = r(1 - .10) = r(.9)$. The firm effectively gets a 10 percent discount on every unit of capital it buys. We can easily picture what happens to the isocost line under these circumstances.

**FIGURE 5–13**
**The Averch-Johnson effect**

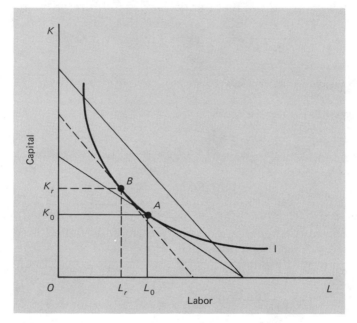

Figure 5–13 shows an unregulated firm optimizing at point $A$. This is the efficient point of production, given prices $r$ and $w$ for capital and labor. The firm employs $L_0$ and $K_0$ units of both inputs. Rate-of-return regulation lowers the price of capital to the producer, so the isocost line pivots upward along the vertical axis. If the regulated firm produced on the same isoquant as the unregulated firm, it would operate at point $B$, using more capital and less labor, $L_r$ units of labor and $K_r$ units of capital. This is an inefficient point of operation, caused by a distortion in the price of capital. For the same level of output, the cost of production is higher at $B$ than at $A$.

The excessive use of capital among firms subject to rate-of-return regulation is called the *Averch-Johnson (A-J) effect*. Several statistical studies have been done to determine the extent of overcapitalization among such regulated firms.[6] The results are mixed; the A-J effect has been difficult to verify in the real world. Part of the problem is that regulators are slow to make price adjustments once a firm has increased its rate base. During this *regulatory lag,* the firm is earning below normal rates of return which may not be recouped. Thus, regulated firms are cautious about overcapitalizing. Ironically, if regulatory agencies were more efficient, the A-J effect would probably be more pronounced.

### Expansion path

The expansion path in production theory shows the way in which factor usage changes when output changes, the factor-price ratio held constant. In Figure 5–14, curves I, II, III are isoquants depicting a representative production function; $KL$, $K'L'$, and $K''L''$ represent the least cost of producing the three output levels. Since the factor-price ratio does not change, they are parallel.

To summarize: first, factor prices remain constant; second, each equilibrium point is defined by equality between the marginal rate of technical substitution and the factor-price ratio. Since the latter remains constant, so does the former. Therefore, $OS$ is a locus of points along which the marginal rate of technical substitution is constant. But it is a curve with a special feature. Specifically, it is the locus along which output will expand when factor prices are constant. We may accordingly formulate this result as a

**Definition.**   The expansion path is the curve along which output expands when factor prices remain constant. The expansion path thus shows how factor proportions change when output or expenditure changes, input prices remaining constant throughout. The marginal rate of technical substitution remains constant also, since the factor-price ratio is constant.

As we shall see in the next chapter, the expansion path gives the firm its cost structure. That is, the expansion path shows the optimal input combination for each level of output at the given set of input

---

[6] See H. C. Petersen, "An Empirical Test of Regulatory Effects," *Bell Journal of Economics and Management Science* 6 (Spring 1975): 111–26; L. Courville, "Regulation and Efficiency in the Electric Utility Industry," *Bell Journal of Economics and Management Science* 5 (Spring 1974): 53–74; R. M. Spann, "Rate of Return Regulation and Efficiency in Production: An Empirical Test of the Averch-Johnson Thesis," *Bell Journal of Economics and Management Science* 5 (Spring 1974): 38–52; W. J. Boyes, "An Empirical Examination of the Averch-Johnson Effect," *Economic Inquiry* 14 (March 1976): 25–35.

**FIGURE 5–14**
Expansion path

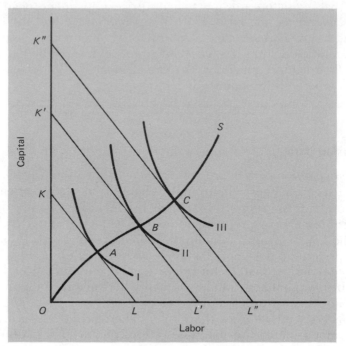

prices. Thus, it gives the minimum cost of producing each level of output from the cost associated with each tangent isocost curve.

In Figure 5–14, the two inputs, capital and labor, are called normal inputs because, as higher levels of output are produced, more of each input is used. In other words, the expansion path is positively sloped.

An input is called "inferior" if, over a range of outputs, the use of this input declines as production increases. Over this range, the expansion path is negatively sloped. In Figure 5–15, labor is inferior over the range of production between the outputs shown by I and II. At the lower output given by I, $L_0$ labor is used; labor is reduced to $L_1$ when the higher output represented by II is produced.

If capital had been the inferior input, the expansion path would have bent downward as capital becomes inferior. Clearly, both inputs cannot be inferior at the same time. No firm could increase output by reducing all inputs, therefore reducing total cost.

As mentioned at the beginning of this chapter, a production function could possibly be characterized by production under fixed proportions. In this case, all inputs must be used in the same proportion regardless of output. For example, if 2 units of labor and 5 of capital

**FIGURE 5–15**
Expansion path: One input inferior

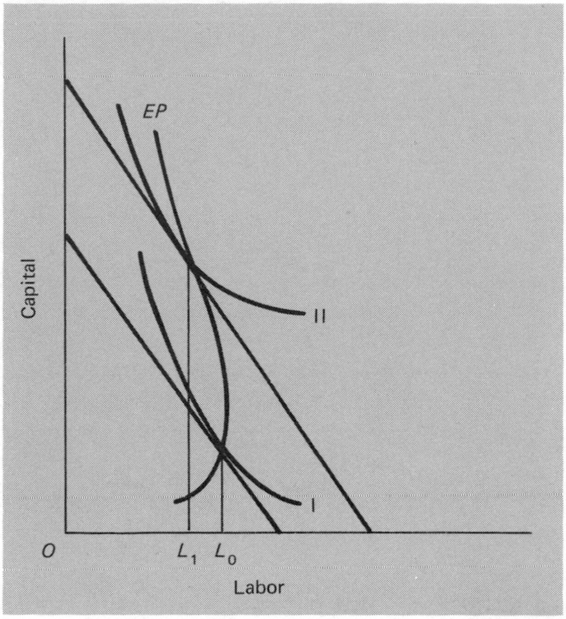

are necessary to produce 100 units of output, 200 units of output require 4 labor and 10 capital, 300 units require 6 labor and 15 capital, and so on. If labor is limited to 2 units, no matter how much capital is added beyond 5 units, only 100 units of output can be produced.

Figure 5–16 shows a set of isoquants and the expansion path for a fixed-proportions production function. The isoquants for outputs $X_1$, $X_2$, and $X_3$ form right angles. Take output level $X_1$; this output is produced by $K_0$ capital and $L_0$ labor. If labor remains at that level while capital is increased, no more output can be produced. Neither can an increase in labor increase output while capital remains fixed. Furthermore, $X_2$, $X_3$, and all other outputs require labor and capital to be used in the same ratio, $K_0/L_0$. This ratio is the slope of the expansion path, which is a straight line passing through the corner of each isoquant.

### Profit maximization and the expansion path

There is a relation between constrained optimization and profit maximization. It can easily be shown that a necessary condition for profit maximization is that the marginal rate of technical substitu-

**FIGURE 5–16**
Production with fixed proportions

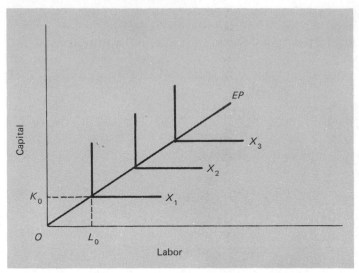

tion be equal to the ratio of input prices. And this is as it should be. A firm should not be able to maximize profits if it has not minimized costs for the output it produces, or has not maximized output given its cost of production.

A producer operates on its expansion path if, for any level of costs and output

$$MRTS = \frac{MP_L}{MP_K} = \frac{w}{r}.$$

This is the rule for optimal production. Take the same two inputs and let the producer maximize profits. We know that for both inputs

$$w = MRP_L,$$

and

$$r = MRP_K.$$

If we form two ratios, one for input prices and the other for the marginal revenue products, then

$$\frac{w}{r} = \frac{MRP_L}{MRP_K} = \frac{MP_L \cdot P}{MP_K \cdot P} = \frac{MP_L}{MP_K},$$

since, by definition, $MRP_i = MP_i \cdot P$ for a price-taking producer, and $i = K, L$. Hence, when a firm maximizes profits, it is operating on its expansion path. While all points on the expansion path represent efficient levels of production, only one point on the path is profit maximizing.

We may distinguish the profit-maximizing point on the expansion path somewhat further by rewriting the condition for constrained optimization as follows. We make the change from $MP_L/MP_K = w/r$ in three progressive steps. An arrow will be used to separate the steps; the arrow signifies "implies." Note:

$$\frac{MP_L}{MP_K} = \frac{w}{r} \rightarrow \frac{MP_L}{w} = \frac{MP_K}{r} \rightarrow P \cdot \frac{MP_L}{w} = P \cdot \frac{MP_K}{r} \rightarrow \frac{MRP_L}{w} = \frac{MRP_K}{r}.$$

The last ratio may take any positive value under constrained optimization, but at the profit-maximizing point, $w = MRP_L$ and $r = MRP_K$, so

$$\frac{MRP_L}{w} = \frac{MRP_K}{r} = 1.$$

Thus, the profit-maximizing point on the expansion path can be uniquely identified as that point where all of the ratios of an input's marginal revenue product to its price equal one.

### Returns to scale

Recall in Section 5.2 we wrote output, $X$, as a function of inputs. Specifically, for just two inputs, $K$ and $L$, we can write

$$X = f(L,K).$$

Suppose we increase the inputs by a constant proportion, say $\lambda$, and observe the proportionate change $(z)$ in output. We have

$$zX = f(\lambda L, \lambda K),$$

where $\lambda$ and $z$ represent proportionate increases in the scale of operation and level of output, respectively.

We have noted, in the case of fixed-proportions production functions, that, if inputs are increased by a constant percent, output rises by the same increase. More concisely, $z = \lambda$ in fixed-proportions production. This phenomenon is called *constant returns to scale*.

But returns to scale are often spoken of when dealing with variable-proportions production functions. If all inputs are increased by a factor of $\lambda$ and output goes up by a factor of $z$, then, in general, a producer experiences:

1. *Increasing returns to scale* if $z > \lambda$. Output goes up proportionately more than the increase in input usage.
2. *Decreasing returns to scale* if $\lambda > z$. Output goes up proportionately less than the increase in input usage.

3.  *Constant returns to scale* if $\lambda = z$. Output goes up by the same proportion as the increase in input usage.

Economists often refer to returns to scale in two contexts. Returns may exist at the plant level or at the firm level. Frequently, there are increasing returns to scale over ranges of output at the firm level, but not for plants. For a proportionate increase in output at the firm level, it often takes proportionately less of an increase in administrative and selling inputs, while, at the plant level, there may be constant or decreasing returns for the increase in output.

Do not deduce from this discussion of returns to scale that, with variable-proportions production functions, firms actually expand output by increasing input use in exactly the same proportion. As we have seen above, the very concept of variable proportions means that they do not necessarily expand in the same proportions; the expansion path may twist and turn in many directions. But, as stated, this concept of returns to scale is of great importance in the theory of cost, and, therefore, it should be at least mentioned in the theory of production.

## 5.7 INPUT PRICE CHANGES AND THE EFFECTS OF TECHNOLOGY

In Section 5.6, we showed how the optimal, or most efficient combination of inputs is derived for each level of output. Two things can occur to change the optimal level of input use for a given level of output: the prices of the inputs can change, and technological change can occur. Under either circumstance, the firm would probably, though not necessarily, change the input ratio.

### Input price changes

First, let us analyze the effect of a change in input prices, holding output constant. As we would expect, when the ratio of input prices changes, firms would substitute away from the relatively more expensive input toward the relatively cheaper input.

In Figure 5–17, let the output level be that given by isoquant $Q$. The original set of input prices is that given by the slope of isocost curve $KL$. Cost minimization occurs at point $A$; the ratio of input use is given by the slope of the ray $OR$. Now the price of labor rises relative to the price of capital. The budget line is $\bar{K}\bar{L}$, the steeper slope of which reflects an increase in the price of $L$ relative to the price of $K$. Thus, tangency, and hence, efficiency must occur at a steeper part of the isoquant, reflecting that, if output remains constant, capital, the now relatively cheaper input, is substituted for

**FIGURE 5-17**
Changing input prices

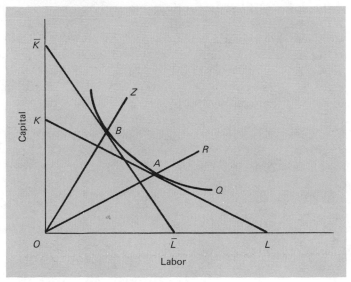

labor, now relatively more expensive. Equilibrium occurs now at point *B* on *Q*; the higher capital-to-labor ratio is shown by the steeper slope of the ray *OZ*. If the price of capital rises relative to that of labor, the isocost line becomes less steep and efficiency would then call for labor to be substituted for capital. In general, the factor demand curve must always be negatively sloped, the firm always substitutes away from the input that becomes relatively more expensive when the price ratio changes.[7]

There have been many dramatic changes in input proportions in response to changes in the relative prices of inputs. A historical example is a change beginning about 50 or 60 years ago, but lasting for a long period of time: the change from coal-powered transportation of freight to petroleum-powered transportation. This partial substitution or switch in proportions came in large measure because of the decrease in the price of petroleum relative to the price of coal over these decades. However, in the 1970s, the cost of oil rose relative to the price of coal, and a reversal of the process began, although not in transportation, but certainly in many other industries. Furthermore, businesses in many sections of the country are changing from gas to coal in anticipation of a relative increase in the price of gas.

[7] C. E. Ferguson, *The Neoclassical Theory of Production and Distribution* (Cambridge: Cambridge University Press, 1969).

We have seen a similar effect over the past decades in the home. As the job opportunities and salaries for women have improved, the labor of the housewife is becoming relatively more expensive in terms of lost earnings. We are witnessing a substitution away from labor-intensive housework and toward more capital-intensive, labor-saving devices, for example, wash-and-wear clothing and microwave ovens.

We see the same type of substitution among various countries. For example, agricultural methods vary greatly from one country to another. The French insist that American farmers are extremely inefficient compared to French farmers. They point out that French farmers plant crops much closer together and thus get a higher yield per acre than do American farmers; French farmers fertilize more carefully and weed much better, thereby growing larger vegetables. Americans plant, cultivate, and harvest by machine, which reduces yield per acre. Are French farmers more efficient than Americans? Clearly, the key point is that in the United States land is cheaper relative to labor, whereas in France, labor is cheaper relative to land. Thus, in France, farmers use a lot of the relatively cheap labor and try to conserve the relatively expensive land. They do this by planting crops close together, and so on. Farmers in the United States use a lot of land and capital to save on the relatively expensive labor. Technical efficiency is not the issue in this example; economic efficiency is. Input prices determine the relative mix of capital and labor. Producers in the United States and France are optimizing under different cost conditions.

## APPLICATION

### Oil as a fixed input

After the Arab oil embargo in late 1973 and a more than 35 percent increase in the price of crude oil, policymakers and economists were predicting massive income transfers from developed countries to the Mideast in exchange for petroleum. Economists predicted annual transfers of $40–$60 billion through the mid-1980s. These projections were based on the inability of petroleum users to substitute away from the relatively more expensive resource. That is, economists were assuming that oil was a fixed input for producers.[8]

In 1980, however, oil consumption in the industrial countries fell by slightly more than 7 percent, even while real output in the same countries rose, on average, by about 1 percent. This trend was pro-

---

[8] See J. Hein, "Oil Money and World Payments," *The Conference Record,* September 1974, pp. 7–11.

jected to be carried through the early 1980s.[9] The experience of the last two years suggests that higher oil prices can, in fact, lead to a major substitution for petroleum by other input factors in the production process.

There is clear evidence of interfuel substitution. Although most of the data have not taken into account the post-1979 increase in world crude prices, the percentage share of oil in total energy consumption shows significant declines (see Table 5–2). Remarkable

TABLE 5–2
Percentage share of oil in total energy use

|  | 1973 | 1977 | 1978 | 1979 | 1980 |
|---|---|---|---|---|---|
| United States ................ | 47 | 49 | 49 | 47 | 44 |
| Canada ..................... | 46 | 45 | 42 | n.a. | |
| Japan ...................... | 79 | 76 | 73 | 74 | |
| Western Europe ............. | 63 | 58 | 56 | 56 | |
| OPEC ...................... | 66 | 70 | 71 | n.a. | |

n.a. = Not available.
Source: J. Caldwell, "World Energy: In Uncharted Waters," *Crocker Bank Economic Report*, June 1981, p. 2.

substitution has occurred in Western Europe. In the United States, significant change did not occur until 1980. Before this time, domestic price controls prevents a full pass-through to users of higher world oil prices. Notice that OPEC has increased its percentage use of oil. Given that other forms of energy, i.e., coal and electric power, are expensive in the Mideast, we would expect these countries to use more of their relatively less expensive input.

The above trend in interfuel substitution away from petroleum has led to some dramatic forecasts of declines in the consumption of oil. Economists have predicted a 17 percent decline in U.S. consumption of oil between 1979 and 1985. For all developed countries, they see much the same picture.[10] OPEC's use of the fuel, on the other hand, is expected to double during this same period.

Obviously, oil is not a fixed input. While it has taken nearly eight years for producers to adjust to price increases, observation corresponds to theory. Producers will optimize by using less of an input whose price rises relative to other factors of production.

---

[9] J. Caldwell, "World Energy: In Uncharted Waters," *Crocker Bank Economic Report*, June 1981.

[10] Ibid.

## Technological change

A change in technology also can change input proportions. Technological change essentially involves a shift of the isoquant map toward the origin. This downward shift in the isoquants simply means that, at given input prices, each level of output can be produced at a lower cost (on a lower isocost curve) than was possible prior to the change in the level of technology. Thus, technological change involves an improvement in the state of knowledge—the knowledge of how to organize factors of production more efficiently. In terms of the production function, any given set of inputs in the relevant range can produce more output after the improvement in technology.

Technological change can, as noted, alter input proportions. Consider Figure 5–18. The given ratio of input prices is given by the

**FIGURE 5–18**
**Technological change**

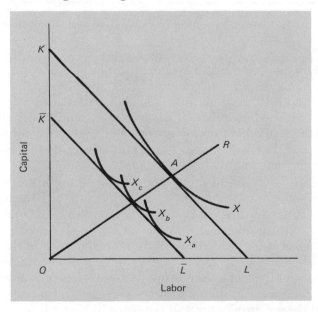

slope of budget line $KL$. Let isoquant $X$ represent some level of production. At the given input price ratio, cost minimization occurs at $A$; the slope of the ray $OR$ gives the capital-labor ratio.

Technological change from an improvement in knowledge shifts the isoquant representing output level $X$ toward the origin. It is now possible to produce $X$ with less capital and less labor. The isoquant representing an output of $X$ can shift in three possible ways, as shown by the three isoquants $X_a$, $X_b$, and $X_c$. These three possible isoquants represent the same level of output after technological change, as did isoquant $X$ before the change.

Let input prices remain constant; suppose $X$ shifts to $X_b$. Isocost $\overline{KL}$ gives cost minimization precisely at the original capital-labor ratio. True, there is less of each input used, but the proportions remain the same. If $X$ is shifted to $X_a$, the use of labor relative to capital is increased. On the other hand, if $X$ shifts to $X_c$, the use of capital increases relative to labor. Economists call these technological changes neutral, labor using, and capital using. Or sometimes the two nonneutral changes are referred to as capital saving (rather than labor using) and labor saving (rather than capital using). Thus, technological change over a given range of output can mean that, for any output level, capital is substituted for labor, labor is substituted for capital, or the proportion remains constant.

We would like to discuss briefly the relation between laborsaving technological change and unemployment. For more than 200 years, many groups have opposed technological change in industry on the grounds that such change would be labor saving and cause unemployment. But the effect of labor saving technology on industry employment is unclear. Employment in the industry may go up or down.

Any technological change lowers the cost of producing a given level of output. Hence, even though the amount of labor used per unit of output may fall, total labor employed may increase because output increases. Figure 5–19 illustrates the argument. Because technological change lowers the cost of production, producers are willing to offer their output to buyers at a lower price. In the exam-

**FIGURE 5–19**
**The market effects of technological change**

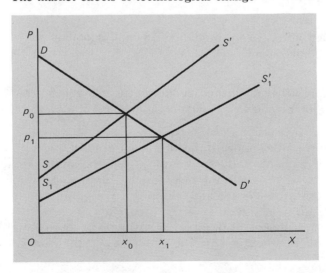

ple shown in Figure 5–19, technological change lowers cost and increases supply from $SS'$ to $S_1S_1'$. Since demand remains constant, price falls from $p_0$ to $p_1$ and quantity sold increases from $x_0$ to $x_1$. The effect upon price and quantity sold depends, of course, upon the strength of the shift in supply and the elasticity of demand. In any event, the increase in output—in this case $x_0x_1$—could certainly cause an increase in employment in the industry, despite the fact that firms use less labor in the production of each individual unit. While firms may substitute other inputs for labor, the output effect from increased production may well offset this substitution, causing more labor to be used.

The use of labor in the industry may, however, fall—especially if the supply does not shift much and the demand curve is rather inelastic. Then the change in output becomes relatively small. Economists generally argue that the reduction in labor in the affected industry can, in the long run, be spread over other occupations and, in effect, shift the production-possibilities frontier outward. Yet, in the short run, there is the problem—academic to those not directly affected, tragic to those who are—that some technological change can cause workers to become obsolete in their professions.

## 5.8 SUMMARY

This chapter has set forth the basic theory of production and the optimal combination of inputs under a given set of input prices.

We studied first the production function when only one input could be changed. We developed two important concepts captured by the following definitions:

**Definition.** The average product of an input is total output divided by the amount of input.

**Definition.** The marginal product of an input is the addition to total output attributable to the addition of one unit of the variable input.

We derived two more definitions, marginal *revenue* product and average *revenue* product, by multiplying the marginal and average products by the constant price of the output. With a fixed input price, the producer maximizes profit by equating the price of the input with its marginal revenue product.

Next we looked at production with two or more variable inputs. Our tools of analysis were the isoquant and the isocost curve.

**Definition.** An isoquant is a curve or locus of points showing all possible combinations of inputs physically capable of producing a given level of output.

The isocost curve is a linear schedule described by the following relation:

**Relation.** At fixed input prices, $r$ and $w$ for capital and labor, a fixed outlay, $\overline{C}$, will purchase any combination of capital and labor such that

$$K = \frac{\overline{C}}{r} - \frac{w}{r}L.$$

The firm, operating under either a cost or output constraint, maximizes the output that can be produced at any given level of cost, or minimizes cost at any given level of output, when

$$MRTS = \frac{MP_L}{MP_K} = \frac{w}{r},$$

or, more generally, when the marginal rate of technical substitution equals the ratio of input prices. This, of course, is a necessary condition for profit maximization.

Production functions can be described by returns to scale. A producer experiences increasing returns when output rises by a greater proportion than the increase in all the inputs, constant returns if the proportionate changes are equal, and decreasing returns if the increase in output is less than the proportional increase in the inputs.

Finally, we mentioned two ways the input ratio used to produce a product can change. If the relative price of an input rises, less of that input will be used. Technology, on the other hand, has a more ambiguous effect. Innovation usually leads to price decreases, and, as a consequence, output increases, offsetting to some extent, the decreased utilization of an input due to the change in technology.

## TECHNICAL PROBLEMS

1. Fill in the blanks in the following table.

| Usage of the variable input | Total product | Average product | Marginal product |
|---|---|---|---|
| 4 . . . . . . . . . . . . . . . . . . . . . | | 20 | — |
| 5 . . . . . . . . . . . . . . . . . . . . . | | | 14 |
| 6 . . . . . . . . . . . . . . . . . . . . . | 102 | | |
| 7 . . . . . . . . . . . . . . . . . . . . . | | | 10 |
| 8 . . . . . . . . . . . . . . . . . . . . . | | 14 | |
| 9 . . . . . . . . . . . . . . . . . . . . . | 126 | | |
| 10 . . . . . . . . . . . . . . . . . . . . | | 12 | |

2.  You are an efficiency expert hired by a manufacturing firm that uses two inputs, labor $(L)$ and capital $(K)$. The firm produces and sells a given output. You have the following information

$$P_L = \$4, \ P_K = \$100, \ MP_L = 4, \ MP_K = 40$$

  *a.*  Is the firm operating efficiently? Why or why not?
  *b.*  What should the firm do?

3.  Fill in all three columns in the following table. Make your numbers conform to the condition set forth below. Graph the average and marginal product curves.

| Units of variable input | Total product | Average product | Marginal product |
|---|---|---|---|
| 1............ | 100 | | |
| 2............ | | | |
| 3............ | | | |
| 4............ | | | |
| 5............ | | | |
| 6............ | | | |
| 7............ | | | |
| 8............ | | | |
| 9............ | | | |
| 10........... | | | |
| 11........... | | | |
| 12........... | | | |
| 13........... | | | |
| 14........... | | | |
| 15........... | | | |
| 16........... | | | |
| 17........... | | | |
| 18........... | 2,000 | | |

Make your numbers meet the following restrictions:
  *a.*  Marginal product first increases, reaches its maximum at 5 units of variable input, declines thereafter, and becomes negative after 17 units.
  *b.*  Average product first rises, reaches its maximum at 9 units, and declines thereafter.
  *c.*  Marginal product equals average product at approximately the maximum point of the latter.

4.  Use the table you derived in problem 3 to answer the following questions:
  *a.*  When average product is rising, marginal product is _____ than average product.
  *b.*  When marginal product is increasing, total product is increasing at a (decreasing, increasing) rate.
  *c.*  When marginal product is decreasing and positive, total product is increasing at a (decreasing, increasing) rate.

    *d.*  When marginal product becomes negative, total product _____ .

    *e.*  When average product is falling, marginal product is _____ than average product.

    *f.*  If the price of the product produced is $3 a unit, the maximum marginal revenue product is $_____ .

5.  A firm can produce a certain amount of a good using three combinations of labor and capital. Labor costs $2 per unit, capital $4 per unit. The three methods are:

|  | A | B | C |
|---|---|---|---|
| Labor (units) | 5 | 6 | 2 |
| Capital (units) | 7 | 5 | 9 |

    *a.*  Which method should be chosen?

    *b.*  The price of labor rises to $4 while the price of capital falls to $3, which method should be chosen?

    *c.*  Under the second price structure (part *b*) the labor is done by you and you hire capital at $3; now which method should be chosen? Why? (Can you even answer this? What information would you need?)

6.  Assume that a curve is drawn showing, along the horizontal axis, the amounts of a factor *A* employed in combination with a fixed amount of a group of factors called *B*, and, along the vertical axis, the amount of physical product obtainable from these combinations of factors (see Figure E.5–1).

**FIGURE E.5–1**

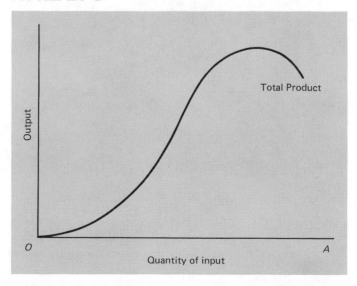

a.  How can you find (geometrically) the amount of $A$ for which the average physical product per unit of $A$ is a maximum?

b.  How can you find (geometrically) the amount of $A$ for which the marginal physical product of $A$ is a maximum?

c.  Between the two points defined in parts $(a)$ and $(b)$, will the marginal physical product of $A$ increase or decrease as more of $A$ is used?

d.  Between these two points, will the average physical product per unit of $A$ increase or decrease as more of $A$ is used?

e.  At the point defined in $(a)$, will the marginal physical product of $A$ be higher or lower than the average physical product per unit of $A$? Give reasons.

f.  At the point defined in $(b)$, will the marginal physical product of $A$ be lower or higher than the average physical product per unit of $A$? Give reasons.

g.  How can you find (geometrically) the amount of $A$ for which the marginal physical product of $A$ is zero?

**FIGURE E.5–2**

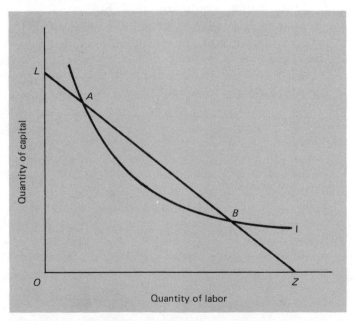

7.  In Figure E.5–2, $LZ$ is the isocost and I is a isoquant. Explain precisely why combinations $A$ and $B$ are not efficient. Explain in terms of the relation of the ratio of the marginal products to

the ratio of the input prices. Explain, in these terms, why the direction of substitution in each case, labor for capital or capital for labor, is optimal. Using the ratio of input prices given by *LZ*, find and label the least-cost combination of labor and capital that can produce the output designated by I. In the above terms, explain why this combination is optimal.

8. Explain precisely why *MP* exceeds (is less than) *AP* when *AP* is rising (falling).

FIGURE E.5–3

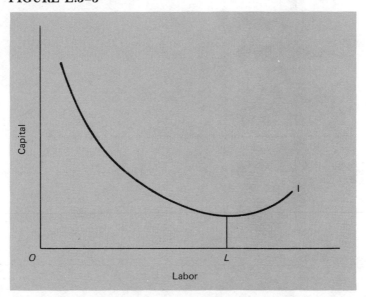

9. In Figure E.5–3, the isoquant turns upward at *OL* units of labor. Explain this upward turn in terms of labor going into stage III; i.e., negative marginal product.

10. A business executive claims a company should never hire another worker if the new person causes diminishing returns. Explain why this person is wrong and establish the profit-maximizing rule for hiring an input.

11. Cuddles Toy Company makes stuffed animals. There are two essential ingredients in the production of these animals: sewing machines (*K*) and machine operators (*L*). Can you offer any advice on the proper mix of these two factors of production?

12. Suppose that a steel plant's production function is $X = 5LK$, where $X$ is the output rate, $L$ is the amount of labor it uses per period of time, and $K$ is the amount of capital it uses per period

of time. Suppose that the price of labor is $1 a unit and the price of capital is $2 a unit. The firm hires you to figure out what combination of inputs the plant should use to produce 20 units. What is your answer? (Hint: $MP_L = 5K$ and $MP_K = 5L$.)

**FIGURE E.5–4**

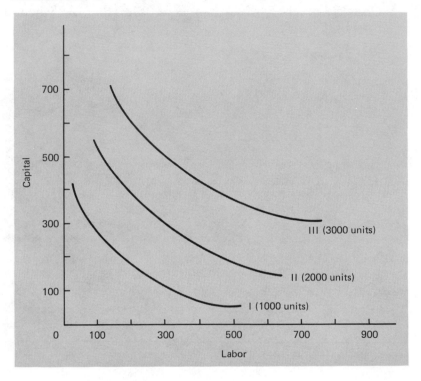

13. In Figure E.5–4, the isoquants I, II, and III are associated respectively with 1,000, 2,000, and 3,000 units of output. The price of capital is $2 a unit and the price of labor is $1 a unit.
    a. Construct an expansion path.
    b. How many units of each input are used to produce each level of output efficiently?
    c. What is the minimum cost of producing each level of output?
    d. Answer each question under the assumption that the price of labor is now $2 a unit and the price of capital is $1 a unit.

## ANALYTICAL PROBLEMS

1. Why do we say that a student should not stop studying after reaching diminishing returns? How much should a student study?

2.  The Meadowlark Country Club is a nonprofit organization. It collects only enough revenues from its members to cover the cost of operation. Explain why this club still ought to provide services at the point of tangency between the isocost line and a production isoquant, just like a profit-maximizing enterprise.

3.  An efficiency expert who examined a power company's plant said that he believed the mill was being operated inefficiently. When the president of the company asked for examples, the efficiency expert said that, for one thing, the crane operators who were unloading coal from barges were dropping an average of about 10 percent of the coal into the river. If you were the president of the company, would you necessarily consider this circumstance evidence of inefficiency? Why or why not? What questions would you ask?

4.  Several years ago, the United States was sending engineers and other technical experts to the more underdeveloped countries in order to advise these countries on the latest technological methods in manufacture and in agriculture. They also assisted these underdeveloped countries in instituting these modern technological methods of farming and manufacturing. Can you explain why in many, many of these countries the advice and help were utter failures, causing great cost to the poorer countries? Why do you think, in many instances, the old-fashioned methods worked better?

5.  If, over a long period of time in a country, considerable capital-using technological change occurs in agriculture, would you expect the birthrate to rise or fall for farm families? Why or why not?

6.  Explain why the marginal product of any input might become negative; that is, why would additional units of the input cause output to fall? Do not answer that the firm hires inferior inputs. Assume all units of the input are alike.

7.  The speed limit has been reduced to 55 miles per hour. The trucking industry competes with other means of transport in the time and cost of moving freight. Can you explain the increase of CB radios as a technological change in response to a change in relative prices?

8.  During the past 10 years, more and more business firms have been purchasing small computers and word processors. Provide an economic rationale for this. Can you think of more than one reason?

9.  Since 1973, the price of oil has risen relative to the price of most other resources. Clearly, there has been substitution. But can you think of any technological changes that have taken place in response to the change in relative prices? Can you

predict any possible future technological changes if the trend continues?

10. Suppose an economy experiences a considerable amount of technological change over a period. The changes have been strongly labor using or capital saving in most industries. What would you think would be the effect on the relative prices of labor and capital? What would be the effect upon the real price of capital and the real price of labor? Can you even answer this last question? If you cannot, why not?

11. Explain the following statement: "It is possible for a producer to be technically efficient and not economically efficient, but it is impossible for a producer to be economically efficient without being technically efficient."

12. Suppose we select three isoquants which describe a firm's technology. Each represents a doubling in output from the last, e.g., they represent output levels of 100, 200, and 400 units as they move outward. In relative terms, explain what the distance between the isoquants would be if the firm experienced:

    a.  Constant returns to scale.
    b.  Increasing returns to scale.
    c.  Decreasing returns to scale.

# Chapter 6

## Theory of cost

### 6.1 INTRODUCTION

As we noted in Chapter 5, the determinants of cost in production theory are the state of technology, characterized by isoquants, and input prices, described by isocost curves. The cost of producing or supplying goods and services is, as we shall see, the most important determinant of supply. This chapter develops the underlying theory of cost from the theory of production. It first sets forth the theory of cost in the long run when all inputs are variable, then turns to cost in the short run when some costs are fixed.

#### Opportunity costs

The cornerstone of cost theory is the concept of opportunity cost. Quite frequently, people ignore opportunity cost when discussing the cost of something. They generally think that cost simply means the price that must be paid for the item in question. To people in business, the cost of producing a good usually means the number of dollars that must be paid for raw materials, labor, machinery, and other inputs necessary to produce the good. In economics, however, cost means more.

Consider the cost of attending college for one year. As a first approximation, you might say that attending college for one year costs the year's tuition, room, board, book purchases, and incidental expenses. Using that approach, it would appear that the cost of attending a particular college is essentially the same for any two students. Under certain circumstances, that may not be quite correct. Assume that there are two students at the same school paying approximately the same tuition, board, and so forth. One student, however, is an exceptional tennis player who could turn professional and earn $50,000 on the tour in just the first year. The *real* cost of attending college is not only the sum of this person's expenses; it is also what he or she must forego to attend college. The athlete must *sacrifice* or *give up* the amount that would have been made by playing professional tennis in order to attend college.

The other student must also sacrifice something in addition to direct outlays for expenses. Assuming that this student is not so athletically inclined, perhaps the best alternative earning possibility might lie in working as a bank teller. This is what would have been done instead of enrolling in college; it is the sacrifice that must be made to attend school. Since bank tellers generally do not receive large salaries, the athlete must sacrifice a greater amount; hence, the *real* cost of attending college is greater for the tennis player than for the nonathlete. The athlete's *opportunity cost* is greater, so real total cost is greater.

Recall in Chapter 5, when we set out the production-possibilities curve, we emphasized that the cost of having more of one good is the amount of some other good that must be given up. This is the opportunity cost of production. Throughout this chapter, we shall attempt to stress the importance of this concept of opportunity cost.

**Definition.**   Opportunity cost is the value of the best alternative that must be given up to produce a good or service.

The talented tennis player in the above example must give up more, and therefore has a higher opportunity cost, than do less talented people in the production of educated college graduates.

### Private costs

Private cost is the amount producers actually pay to produce a good. Private cost often bears a close relation to opportunity cost, because a producer must pay a certain amount to the owners of productive resources in order to bid these resources away from their alternative uses.

Sometimes, however, private costs are not equivalent to opportunity cost because of market externalities. A market externality is simply a cost or benefit that is not paid because a market does not exist. Externalities are discussed in more detail in Chapter 12. For now, we want to mention that the actions of producers may result in uncompensated costs to others. For instance, an oil spill in the Gulf of Mexico pollutes the Gulf, killing sea life, which hurts the fishing industry and blackens beaches, thereby decreasing tourism. Fishermen and tourists are generally not compensated for their losses. The real cost of transporting oil to the Gulf Coast is higher than the private cost.

We must also be careful not to think of private costs as accounting costs. How the economist and accountant think of private costs are two different things. They agree on the *explicit* costs a producer incurs, but they differ on what economists call *implicit* costs in production. Private costs are equal to the sum of explicit and implicit costs. Implicit costs exist because accountants overlook inputs that do not have a clear price tag.

To aid in analyzing the nature of implicit costs, consider two firms that produce good $X$ and are in every way identical, with one exception. Both use identical amounts of the same resources to produce identical amounts of $X$. The first firm rents the building in which the good is produced. The second owns the building and, therefore, pays no rent. Whose costs are higher? An economist would say both are the same, even though the second firm makes lower payments to outside factors of production. The reason costs are the same is that using the building to produce $X$ costs the second firm the amount of income it could have received had it leased it at the prevailing rent. Since these two buildings are the same, presumably the market rental would be the same. In other words, a part of the cost incurred by the second firm is the payment from itself as producer to itself as the owner of a resource (the building).

If you are not convinced that implicit costs should be counted, think of the issue this way. Suppose the building owned by the second firm was destroyed. To continue production, a different structure is rented. Now an explicit payment is made to the input. What was once an implicit cost has been turned into an explicit cost.

Similarly, suppose an individual owns and manages a small business alone. Say at the end of the year, the business earns $60,000. This is not profit if the cost of the manager's time has not been taken into account. There is an implicit cost that must be subtracted from earnings to get profit. How should the owner's time be priced? We can answer with another question. What would the owner have paid to hire someone to manage the business equally well? If it would have taken $30,000 to hire a manager who could earn $60,000 at the end of the year, then the implicit cost of the owner's time is $30,000.

In sum, there are often inputs in a production process that are not explicitly paid. To an economist, these implicit costs should be valued at the price that would be paid to replace their contribution to output. Implicit costs must be added to explicit costs in order to obtain total private costs. Whatever private costs may be, however, they are not necessarily equal to opportunity cost.

The basic concepts that you will learn in this chapter are

1.  The fundamentals of long-run total, average, and marginal cost curves and what these curves look like.
2.  The fundamentals of short-run total, average, and marginal cost curves and what these curves look like.
3.  The relations between long-run cost curves and short-run cost curves.
4.  The relation between cost curves and the expansion path.
5.  The importance and effect of opportunity costs.
6.  The importance of the cost of time.

## 6.2 PLANNING HORIZON AND LONG-RUN COSTS

Let us begin our analysis of costs by assuming that an individual starts a firm in a particular industry. Since this person is just beginning the firm, it is in the long run. Recall from Chapter 5 that the long run is not some date in the future. The long run means that all inputs are variable to the firm. Therefore, one of the first things that must be decided upon is the *scale* of operation, or the *size* of the firm. To make this decision, the entrepreneur must know the cost of producing each level of output. We begin our analysis of cost with the long run rather than the short run, because the scale of the firm must be determined before an entrepreneur must decide upon different output levels from a fixed plant.

### Derivation of long-run cost schedules from a production function

Let us assume, for analytical purposes, that the individual knows the firm's actions will not affect the price that must be paid for the resources used. Further, assume that this person can estimate the production function for each level of output in the feasible range. Using the methods described in Chapter 5, the entrepreneur derives an expansion path. Assuming that the firm uses only two inputs, labor and capital, the characteristics of the derived expansion path are given in columns (1) through (3) of Table 6–1. Labor costs

**TABLE 6–1**
**Derivation of long-run cost schedules**

| (1) | (2) | (3) | (4) | (5) | (6) |
|---|---|---|---|---|---|
| | *Least cost usage* | | *Total cost at* | | *Long-run* |
| | | | *$5 per unit of* | *Long-run* | *marginal* |
| | *Labor* | *Capital* | *labor $10 per* | *average* | *cost* |
| *Output* | *(units)* | *(units)* | *unit of capital* | *cost* | *(per unit)* |
| 100 .............. | 10 | 7 | $120 | $1.20 | $1.20 |
| 200 .............. | 12 | 8 | 140 | .70 | .20 |
| 300 .............. | 20 | 10 | 200 | .67 | .60 |
| 400 .............. | 30 | 15 | 300 | .75 | 1.00 |
| 500 .............. | 40 | 22 | 420 | .84 | 1.20 |
| 600 .............. | 52 | 30 | 560 | .93 | 1.40 |
| 700 .............. | 60 | 42 | 720 | 1.03 | 1.60 |

$5 per unit and capital $10 per unit. Column (1) gives seven output levels and columns (2) and (3) give the optimal combinations of labor and capital for each output level at the prevailing input prices.

Column (4) shows the total cost of producing each level of output. For example, the least-cost method of producing 300 units requires 20 units of labor and 10 of capital. At $5 and $10, respectively, the total cost is $200. It should be emphasized that column (4) is a *least-cost schedule* for various rates of production. Obviously, the entrepreneur could pay more to produce any output by using less efficient productive processes or by paying some factors of production more than their market prices. The firm could not, however, produce an output at a cost lower than that given.

As noted above, the lowest total cost of producing any output consists of two components, the explicit costs and the implicit costs. The explicit costs given in Table 6–1, are the payments entrepreneurs must make to the factors of production. The implicit costs are the market values of the resources they own and use in production, including the wages they pay to themselves. We could assume, in Table 6–1, that the entrepreneur owns the capital. We could assume that implicit costs are zero. Or, we might just ignore them here. In any case, when entrepreneurs plan, they must consider payments to themselves since they cost what they would pay to replace themselves.

Two important cost schedules, derived from column (4) are average cost, shown in column (5), and marginal cost, shown in column (6). Average cost is simply the total cost of producing a given level of output divided by that output. Column (5) reflects an important assumed characteristic of average costs: average cost first declines, reaches a minimum, then rises.

Marginal cost is the change in total cost divided by the change in output; $MC = \Delta TC/\Delta X$. Moving from 100 to 200 units of output raises the total cost from \$120 to \$140. Twenty dollars divided by 100 gives a per-unit marginal cost of 20 cents. Thus, we can see arithmetically how the production function is related to the three important cost functions. Note that marginal cost first decreases then increases.

Let us now summarize the situation graphically. Consider Figure 6–1, in which we assume that output is produced by two inputs, $K$ and $L$. The known and fixed input prices give the constant input-price ratio, represented by the slope of the isocost curves $I_1I'_1$, $I_3I'_3$, etc. Next, the known production function gives us the isoquant map, partially represented by $x_1$, $x_3$, etc., in Figure 6–1.

As is familiar from Chapter 5, when all inputs are readily variable (that is, in the long run), the entrepreneur will choose input combinations that minimize the cost of producing each level of output. This gives us the expansion path $OP'Q'R'S'$. Given the factor-price ratio and the production function, the expansion path shows the combinations of inputs that enable the entrepreneur to produce each level of output at the least possible cost.

Now let us relate this expansion path to a long-run total cost ($LRTC$) curve with a shape frequently assumed by economists. Figure 6–2 shows graphically the least-cost curve for the good $X$, the expansion path of which was derived in Figure 6–1. The least cost of producing $x_1$ is $c_1$, of $x_2$ it is $c_2$, and so on.

The points $P$, $Q$, $R$, and $S$ in Figure 6–2 correspond exactly to the points $P'$, $Q'$, $R'$, and $S'$ respectively in Figure 6–1. For example, the cost, $c_1$, of producing $x_1$ units of output in Figure 6–2 is precisely the cost of using $K_1$ units of capital and $L_1$ units of labor to produce the output $x_1$ at the optimal combination represented by $P'$ in Figure 6–1. We assume that the implicit costs of production are included in the curve.[1] It is important to note that the firm may use different amounts and combinations of resources. Nothing is fixed except the

---

[1] Note that, since the cost curve begins at the origin and not at some positive amount on the vertical axis, we tacitly assume that the entrepreneur can readily vary the amount of time and other resources he or she "invests" in the business. That is to say, the implicit costs are as readily variable as the explicit cost when one is considering the long run, or planning horizon. It is only in the short run, as we shall see below, that implicit costs may be fixed.

**FIGURE 6–1**
**The expansion path and long-run cost**

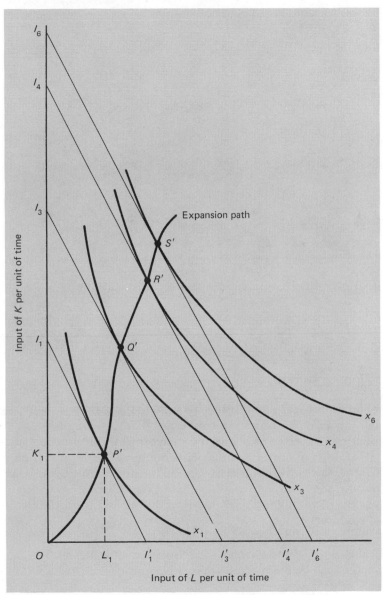

**FIGURE 6–2**
Long-run total cost curve

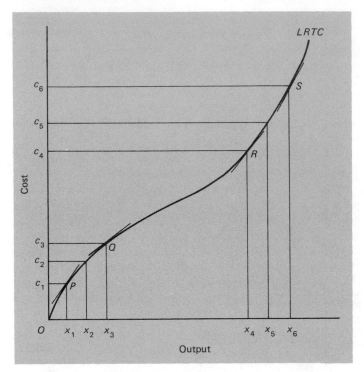

set of technological possibilities, or state of the arts, and the prices at
which the firm can purchase resources. Thus, completely different
production processes may be used to achieve minimum cost at (say)
$x_1$ and $x_2$ units of output. This "planning horizon" in which nothing
is fixed to the entrepreneur except factor prices and technology, is
called the long run, and the associated curve that shows the minimum cost of producing each level of output is called the *long-run
total cost curve.*

**Definition.**   Long-run total cost is the least cost at which each quantity of
   output can be produced when no resource is fixed in quantity or rate
   of use.

The shape of the long-run total cost (*LRTC*) curve depends exclusively upon the production function and prevailing factor prices.
The schedule in Table 6–1 and the curve in Figure 6–2 reflect some
of the commonly assumed characteristics of long-run total costs.

Two characteristics are apparent on inspection. First, costs and output are *directly related;* that is, the curve has a positive slope. It costs more to produce more, which is just another way of saying that resources are scarce, or that one never gets "something for nothing" in the real economic world. The second characteristic is that costs first increase at a decreasing rate and then at an increasing rate.

Recall from Table 6–1 that the cost of producing an *additional* 100 units at first decreases and then increases. For example, the first 100 units add $120 to cost, the second 100 units add $20 to cost, but the third 100 units add $60. Each 100 units thereafter adds more to costs than the preceding 100.

Figure 6–2 is constructed to reflect that incremental costs first fall, then rise. It is constructed so that $x_1 x_2 = x_2 x_3$, whereas $c_1 c_2$ is clearly greater than $c_2 c_3$. This means that the added total cost is greater when the entrepreneur moves from $x_1$ to $x_2$ than when output increases from $x_2$ to $x_3$. On the other hand, $x_4 x_5 = x_5 x_6$, but $c_4 c_5$ is less than $c_5 c_6$; over this range, the additional cost incurred by producing more output increases. Alternatively stated, the slope at $P$ (indicated by the tangent at that point) is greater than the slope at the larger output corresponding to $Q$. Incremental or marginal costs decrease over this range, even though total costs increase. The slope at $R$ is less steep than that at $S$, indicating that incremental costs are increasing over this range.

### Long-run average and marginal costs

Now we are prepared to examine graphically the relation between the long-run total cost curve and the long-run average and marginal cost curves. Recall the definitions used with Table 6–1:

**Definition.**  Long-run average cost is the long-run total cost of producing a particular quantity of output divided by that quantity.

**Definition.**  Long-run marginal cost is the addition to long-run total cost attributable to an additional unit of output when all inputs are optimally adjusted. It is thus the change in total cost as one moves along the expansion path or the long-run total cost curve.

The long-run average and marginal costs in Table 6–1 first fell then increased; the minimum marginal cost was attained at a lower level of output than the level at which minimum average cost was reached. As we shall show, these are the results forthcoming from the generally assumed long-run total cost curves such as that shown in Figure 6–2.

**FIGURE 6–3**
Derivation of average total cost curve

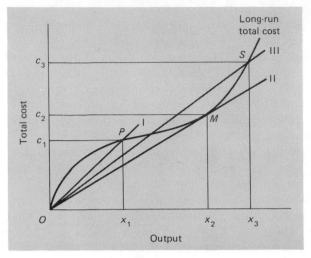

**Panel A**
**Long-run total cost**

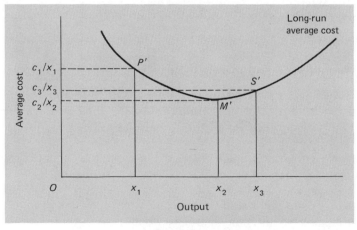

**Panel B**
**Long-run average cost**

Figure 6–3 shows graphically the relation between total cost (panel A) and average cost (panel B). Since average cost is total cost divided by the corresponding output, the average cost of a particular quantity is given by the slope of a ray from the origin to the relevant point on the total cost curve. For example, in panel A, the cost of producing $x_1$ is $c_1$. Average cost, $c_1/x_1$, is given by the slope of the ray designated I at point $P$. Average cost at $x_1$ is plotted in panel B at point $P'$. (Note that the vertical scales of the two graphs differ; the horizontal scales are the same.)

From inspection of the long-run total cost curve, it is clear that the slope of a ray to any point on the curve decreases as output increases from zero to $x_2$. Thus, average cost must fall as output increases from zero to $x_2$. This is shown in panel B. As output increases thereafter from $x_2$, the slope of a ray to any point on the total cost curve increases. For example, at $x_3$ the average cost is given by ray III at point $S$ in panel A. Average cost of $x_3$, $c_3/x_3$, is plotted at point $S'$ in panel B. Thus, minimum average cost is reached at $x_2$, where ray II is tangent to the cost curve at $M$ in panel A. Average cost is plotted at $M'$. Average cost rises thereafter.

**Relation.** For the generally assumed long-run total cost curve, long-run average cost ($LRAC$) first declines, reaches a minimum, where a ray from the origin is tangent to the long-run total cost curve, and rises thereafter. These relations are all shown in Figure 6–3.

The derivation of long-run marginal cost is illustrated in Figure 6–4. Panel A contains a total cost curve ($LRTC$) shaped similarly to the one in Figure 6–3. As output increases from $x'$ to $x''$, one moves from point $P$ to point $Q$ and total cost increases from $c'$ to $c''$. Marginal cost, the additional cost of producing one more unit of output, is thus

$$MC = \frac{c'' - c'}{x'' - x'} = \frac{QR}{PR}.$$

As $P$ moves along $LRTC$ toward point $Q$, the distance between $P$ and $Q$ becomes smaller and smaller, and the slope of the tangent $T$ at point $Q$ becomes a progressively better estimate of $QR/PR$. For movements in a tiny neighborhood around point $Q$, the slope of the tangent is marginal cost at output $x''$.

As one moves along $LRTC$ through points such as $P$ and $Q$, the slope of $LRTC$ diminishes until point $S$ is reached at output $x_m$. Therefore, the long-run marginal cost curve ($LRMC$) is constructed in panel B so that it decreases (as the *slope* of $LRTC$ decreases) until output $x_m$ is attained and increases thereafter (as the *slope* of $LRTC$ increases).

One point should be noted. As indicated in Figure 6–3, the slope of ray II gives minimum $LRAC$. But at this point, ray II is tangent to $LRTC$, hence the slope of II also gives $LRMC$ at point $M$. Thus, $LRMC = LRAC$ when $LRAC$ attains its minimum value. Ray V in Figure 6–4, panel A, also illustrates this point. Since the slope of $LRTC$ is less than the slope of a ray from the origin to any point on the curve to the left of $M$, $LRMC$ is less than $LRAC$ from the origin to $x_m$. Since the slope of $LRTC$ is greater than the slope of a ray from

**FIGURE 6–4**
Derivation of long-run marginal cost curve

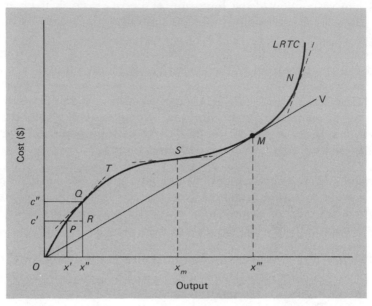

**Panel A**
**Long-run total cost**

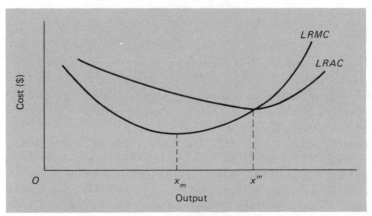

**Panel B**
**Long-run marginal cost**

the origin to any point on the curve to the right of $M$, say at point $N$, $LRMC$ is greater than $LRAC$ at outputs larger than $x_m$.

Following a line of reasoning similar to that set forth in the theory of production, the relations between marginal and average costs would be expected. If an additional unit of output adds more to cost than the average cost, the average must increase. Thus, average increases when marginal is greater than average. When the marginal cost is less than average, an additional unit of output adds less than the average; consequently, average must fall under this circumstance. When another unit adds exactly the average, average and marginal are equal.

**Relation.**   (1) *LRTC* rises continuously, first at a decreasing rate then at an increasing rate. (2) *LRAC* first declines, reaches a minimum, then rises. When *LRAC* reaches its minimum, *LRMC* equals *LRAC*. (3) *LRMC* first declines, reaches a minimum, and then increases. *LRMC* lies below *LRAC* over the range in which *LRAC* declines; it lies above *LRAC* when *LRAC* is rising.

### Economies and diseconomies of scale

We now want to draw attention to the long-run average cost schedule. The shape of this curve has far-reaching consequences for the profitability of firms and the prices they charge. Long-run average costs may be decreasing, constant, or increasing as output increases. If they are decreasing, then the firm is experiencing *economies of scale;* if they are rising, then the firm faces *diseconomies of scale;* and if long-run average costs are constant, the firm is simply said to have neither economies nor diseconomies. We can therefore characterize the long-run average cost schedule with the following definition:

**Definition.**   A firm is said to have economies of scale if the long-run average cost schedule is declining as output increases and diseconomies of scale if the long-run average cost schedule is rising.

Figure 6–5 illustrates the ranges of output for which an *LRAC* schedule exhibits economies and diseconomies. The firm experiences economies of scale up to $x_0$ units of output and diseconomies after $x_1$ units.

There is a relation between returns to scale and the shape of the long-run average cost curve. Recall from Chapter 5, our discussion of increasing and decreasing returns. When increasing returns exist, as output goes up, the increase in output is proportionately more than the increase in inputs. Thus, if the prices of all inputs are constant, *LRMC* is falling and this pulls *LRAC* down. Increasing returns to scale will lead to economies of scale. Long-run average cost declines if it takes less input at the margin to produce more output (i.e., less input than necessary to produce previous units) holding input prices constant. Similarly, if a producer experiences decreasing returns to scale, then proportionately more inputs are

**FIGURE 6–5**
The presence of economies and diseconomies of scale

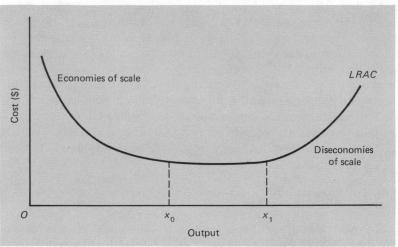

needed at the margin to increase output. *LRMC* is rising, and eventually this will cause *LRAC* to rise. Decreasing returns yield diseconomies if input prices are again unchanged. This description of the connection between returns is brief, but to be more specific about the relation between returns to scale and the shape of the average cost curve requires mathematics inappropriate for this text.[2] The point is, nonetheless, that the state of technology, expressed by the firm's isoquants, is a primary determinant of economies and diseconomies.

It is important to emphasize that economies and diseconomies occur in broader contexts than do returns to scale. Long-run average cost can be falling or rising when inputs are changed in various proportions—they do not have to vary by the same percentage. Thus, economies of scale and returns to scale are related but are not the same thing. It is possible for there to be economies of scale but no increasing returns to scale; but, if there are increasing returns, there must be economies if input prices do not rise as output increases.

What makes unit costs fall as output is increased? Adam Smith gave a major reason in 1776: specialization. Proficiency is gained by concentration of effort. If a plant is very small and employs only a

---

[2] See C. E. Ferguson, *The Neoclassical Theory of Production and Distribution* (Cambridge: Cambridge University Press, 1969), pp. 79–83, for the derivation of a measure of increasing and decreasing proportions. See pp. 158–63 of the same book for the relation to cost functions.

small number of workers, each worker will usually have to perform several different jobs in the production process. In doing so, he or she is likely to have to move about the plant, change tools, and so on. Not only are workers not highly specialized, but a part of their work time is also consumed in moving about and changing tools. Thus, important savings may be realized by expanding the scale of operation. A larger plant with a larger work force may permit each worker to specialize in one job, gaining proficiency and decreasing or eliminating time-consuming interchanges of location and equipment. There naturally will be corresponding reductions in the unit cost of production.

Technological factors constitute another force contributing to economies of scale. If several different machines, each with a different rate of output, are required in a production process, the operation may have to be quite sizable to permit proper "meshing" of equipment. Suppose only two types of machines are required, one that produces and one that packages the product. If the first machine can produce 30,000 units per day and the second can package 45,000, output will have to be 90,000 per day in order to utilize fully the capacity of each type of machine.

This example, in essence, shows that investment frequently must be made in "lumps." At the extreme, in some industries, nearly all of the capital investment must be made before any production can be undertaken. Such lumpiness leads to pervasive economies of scale. For example, suppose a railroad builds a line between two cities. Before the first run is made, tracks must be put down, stations built, and locomotives and cars purchased. To make 1 trip or 100 trips per period, the same capital investment is needed. Investment is virtually independent of the output. Clearly, the more trips made per period, the less is the capital cost per trip. Hence, lumpiness in the input leads to economies of scale.

Another technological element is the fact that the cost of purchasing and installing larger machines is usually *proportionately* less than the cost of smaller machines. For example, a printing press that can run 200,000 papers per day does not cost 10 times as much as one that can run 20,000 per day—nor does it require 10 times as much building space, 10 times as many people to work it, and so forth. Again, expanding size tends to reduce the unit cost of production.

A final technological element is perhaps the most important determinant of economies: as the scale of operation expands, there are qualitative changes in inputs. Consider ditch digging and the quality of capital. The smallest scale of operation is one laborer and one shovel. But, as the scale expands beyond a certain point, you do not simply continue to add workers and shovels. Shovels and workers are replaced by a modern ditch-digging machine. The capital-labor ratio rises with output; scale expansion permits the introduction of inputs that tend to reduce the unit cost of production.

Even without a change in the capital-labor ratio, studies have shown that, as labor produces more output, output per worker increases. Experience, or "learning by doing," improves the quality of labor. As cumulative output rises, the productivity of labor rises. This learning factor was discovered in the 1920s by the U.S. Air Force. From their work came what is known as the *learning curve* which shows that on-the-job experience lowers unit labor costs 10 to 15 percent each time output is doubled.[3]

Thus, two broad forces—specialization and technological factors—enable producers to reduce unit cost by expanding the scale of operation.[4] These forces give rise to the negatively sloped portion of the long-run average cost curve. But why should it ever rise? After all possible economies of scale have been realized, why doesn't the curve stay horizontal?

The rising portion of *LRAC* is usually attributed to diseconomies of scale, which generally implies limitations to efficient management. Managing any business entails controlling and coordinating a wide variety of activities—production, transportation, finance, sales, and so on. To perform these managerial functions efficiently, the manager must have accurate information; otherwise, the essential decision making is done in ignorance.

As the scale of plant expands beyond a certain point, top management necessarily has to delegate responsibility and authority to lower echelon employees. Contact with the daily routine of operation tends to be lost, and efficiency of operation declines. Red tape and paperwork expand; management is generally not as efficient. This increases the cost of the managerial function and, of course, the unit cost of production.

It is very difficult to determine just when diseconomies of scale set in and when they become strong enough to outweigh the economies of scale. In businesses where economies of scale are negligi-

---

[3] See *Perspectives on Experience* (Boston: Boston Consulting Group, 1972); and "Selling Business a Theory of Economics," *Business Week*, September 8, 1973, pp. 85–90.

[4] This discussion of economies of scale has concentrated upon physical and technological forces. There are pecuniary reasons for economies of scale as well. Large-scale purchasing of raw and processed materials may enable the buyer to obtain more favorable prices (quantity discounts). The same is frequently true of advertising. As another example, financing of large-scale business is normally easier and less expensive; a nationally known business has access to organized security markets, so it may place its bonds and stocks on a more favorable basis. Bank loans also usually come easier and at lower interest rates to large, well-known corporations. These are but examples of many potential economies of scale attributable to financial factors.

ble, diseconomics may soon become of paramount importance, causing *LRAC* to turn up at a relatively small volume of output Panel A, Figure 6–6, shows a long-run average cost curve for a firm of this type. In other cases, economies of scale are extremely important. Even after the efficiency of management begins to decline, technological economies of scale may offset the diseconomies over a wide range of output. Thus, the *LRAC* curve may not turn upward until a very large volume of output is attained. This case is illustrated in panel B, Figure 6–6.

**FIGURE 6–6**
Various shapes of *LRAC*

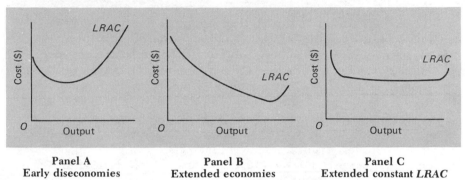

| Panel A | Panel B | Panel C |
|---------|---------|---------|
| Early diseconomies | Extended economies | Extended constant *LRAC* |

In many actual situations, however, neither of these extremes describes the behavior of *LRAC*. A very modest scale of operation may enable a firm to capture all of the economies of scale; however, diseconomies may not be incurred until the volume of output is very great. In this case, *LRAC* would have a long horizontal section, as shown in panel C. Some economists and businesspeople feel that this type of *LRAC* curve describes many production processes in the American economy. For analytical purposes, however, we will assume a "representative" *LRAC*, such as that illustrated in Figure 6–5.

## APPLICATION

### Estimating economies of scale

Many estimates have been made of the cost curves of various industries. Frequently, these studies are designed to find the point at which minimum long-run average cost is attained for firms in an industry. Most of these studies have used engineering data and the assumption that factors of production are available at a constant price. But when we examine actual industries, we observe that firms in the same industry frequently vary greatly in size. This leads us to believe that the short-run cost curves differ among firms in an industry. Some extremely small firms survive beside veritable giants, with many sizes of firms in between. This indicates that the minimum efficient size occurs at relatively small levels of output. That is, economies of scale are exhausted early. An interesting method of estimating the point of minimum average cost is called the "survivor technique."[5]

The survivor principle is based upon the following assumption: all firms in the industry are classified by size, and the share of total industry output is calculated; if the relative share of any class falls, that class is relatively inefficient, and is more inefficient the faster the share is falling. In this way, economists can consider not merely the technological composition of a firm's costs, but also the ability of the firm to solve its other problems—labor relations, innovation, regulation, and so on. In this way, one can tell the range over which economies of scale are attainable and points, if any, at which diseconomies are reached.

Examples of this method are G. J. Stigler's studies of the steel and automobile industries.[6] In the steel industry during the 1930s and 1940s, very small firms and the largest firms experienced a decline in relative share. Intermediate firms, in size classes from 2.5 to 25 percent of the industry's capacity, grew or retained their share. The smallest sizes lost shares most rapidly. It appears then that, over the period of measurement, the long-run average cost curve for the part of the steel industry that was measured looked somewhat like the curve in panel C, Figure 6–6. This change in distribution for the steel industry is shown in Table 6–2. Of course, this method cannot estimate how much higher than the minimum are the costs of the declining firms.

The analysis was extended from firm size to *plant size.* It was found that the share of the smallest plants—up to almost 1 percent of industry capacity—declined, with no tendency toward decline for plants above this size, even the very largest. It appears that the diseconomies of large firm size were due to diseconomies of multiplant operation and not to diseconomies of large plants.

The trend of the passenger automobile industry from 1936 to 1955 differed somewhat from that of steel. Over this span of time, the smallest automobile companies—under 5 percent of industry capacity—experienced a declining share. During periods of infla-

---

[5] This discussion is based upon two related papers: G. J. Stigler, "The Economies of Scale," *Journal of Law and Economics* 1 (October 1958): 54–71; and T. R. Saving, "Estimation of Optimum Size by the Survivor Technique," *Quarterly Journal of Economics* 75, no. 4 (November 1961): 569–607.

[6] Stigler, "Economies of Scale," pp. 54–71.

**TABLE 6-2**
**Distribution of output of steel ingot capacity**
**(by relative size of company)**

| Company size (percent of industry total) | 1930 | 1938 | 1951 |
|---|---|---|---|
| | 1. Percent of industry capacity | | |
| Under .5 ................. | 7.16 | 6.11 | 4.65 |
| .5 to 1 ................... | 5.94 | 5.08 | 5.37 |
| 1 to 2.5 ................. | 13.17 | 8.30 | 9.07 |
| 2.5 to 5 ................. | 10.64 | 16.59 | 22.21 |
| 5 to 10 .................. | 11.18 | 14.03 | 8.12 |
| 10 to 25 ................. | 13.24 | 13.99 | 16.10 |
| 25 and over ............. | 38.67 | 35.91 | 34.50 |
| | 2. Number of companies | | |
| Under .5 ................. | 39 | 29 | 22 |
| .5 to 1 ................... | 9 | 7 | 7 |
| 1 to 2.5 ................. | 9 | 6 | 6 |
| 2.5 to 5 ................. | 3 | 4 | 5 |
| 5 to 10 .................. | 2 | 2 | 1 |
| 10 to 25 ................. | 1 | 1 | 1 |
| 25 and over ............. | 1 | 1 | 1 |

Source: G. J. Stigler, "The Economics of Scale," *Journal of Law and Economics* 1 (October 1958): 58.

tion with price control, the data revealed diseconomies for the largest class, but substantial economies otherwise. That is, the long-run average cost is shaped like that in panel C, Figure 6–6, during inflation, but it does not rise with large size in other times. The petroleum industry from 1947 to 1954 showed essentially the same characteristics as steel in both firm size and plant size. The range of firm sizes from .5 percent to 10 percent of industry capacity contained all classes in the optimal range.

After examining these specific industries, Stigler investigated 48 manufacturing industries to isolate the most important determinants of the optimum size firm. In the past, economists had said that influences such as large advertising expenditures, complicated technology, research, and large plant size caused industries to be characterized by large-scale firms. After the optimum ranges of sizes for all industries were determined, the average assets of these firms were computed. This average size firm was regressed on advertising, technology and research, and plant size.[7] Advertising expenditure

---

[7] The ratio of chemists and engineers to total employment was used as a proxy variable for technology.

had no significant effect on average optimum size. The other two variables were quite significant. The range of optimum sizes was quite wide, indicating strongly that many *industry* (but *not* necessarily *firm*) cost curves are saucer-shaped, as in panel C, Figure 6–6.

One frequently hears that very large-scale plants are necessary for survival in manufacturing industries today. There are supposedly economies of large-scale production in manufacturing that make for large plant size. Evidence based upon the survivor technique does not verify this allegation.

T. R. Saving used this technique to investigate the minimum, average, and range of optimum size for plants in 89 manufacturing industries.[8] The data show wide variation in both average and minimum optimum sizes. The magnitudes, however, are quite small relative to total industry size. For example, 72 percent of all industries showed minimum optimum plant size—that is, they exhausted all economies of scale—at plant sizes that produced less than 1 percent of the industry's total output. Ninety-eight percent had an average optimum size below 10 percent of total, and 55 percent showed average optimum sizes at less than 1 percent. The ranges of optimum size tended to be small compared to the industry's size; 81 percent had ranges that were below 5 percent of total. The ranges, however, were large compared to average optimum size. It appears that economies of scale in plant size are rapidly exhausted in expansion.

After estimating optimum plant sizes, Saving looked at the causes of large or small average firm size relative to size of the industry. He hypothesized that average firm size is affected by optimum plant size and the extent of multiplant operation (as measured by the average number of plants per firm in the industry). Both variables significantly affected average firm size, accounting for about 87 percent of the variation, but the average number of plants was found to be a far more significant determinant. These economies may be more important than plant economies. That is, the optimum size plant is usually not so large as to cause industries to be characterized by a few very large firms.

Next, the determinants of optimum firm size were analyzed to examine why industries differ so greatly in the points at which plant economies of scale end and diseconomies begin. The hypothetical determining variables were (1) industry size, (2) rate of growth of the industry, (3) complexity of the productive process, and (4) the extent of capital intensiveness. These four variables explained approximately 50 percent of the variation in minimum and average plant size in the 89 industries tested. The two most important vari-

---

[8] Saving, "Estimation of Optimum Size," pp. 569–607.

ables in both tests were, in order of importance, industry size and capital intensiveness as measured by the capital-to-labor ratio. They accounted for about 80 percent of the explained variation. The rate of growth of the industry was not significant at all. The complexity of the productive process, measured by the proportion of chemists and engineers to total labor force, was not highly significant but was more significant in the case of the average optimum plant size than in the case of the minimum. The only important variables affecting the range of optimum plant size—that is, the length of the horizontal portion of industry long-run average cost—were the mean optimum plant size and the size of the industry.

Certainly there may be biases in the survivor technique from imperfections in data, but other methods of cost estimation must also use imperfect data. In any case, this technique gives some interesting insight into the nature of industry costs and the extent of long-run economies and diseconomies of scale.

Of course, the cost curve of primary interest to business decision makers is the cost structure of a particular firm, or of a specific project of the firm. This estimation involves a different technique. Certainly, engineering data would be of utmost importance, if one considers building a new plant or an entirely new operation. This can be obtained through consultation. Prices of inputs, particularly labor costs, are usually obtainable, at least over a range. Certainly the best tool of analysis is a lot of experience in the particular business.

## 6.3 THEORY OF COST IN THE SHORT RUN

Once entrepreneurs have investigated all possibilities open to them, they can decide upon a specific scale of output and, hence, build a plant to produce their output at the least possible cost. In order to find out how a firm maximizes profit once a scale of operation is selected, we must study costs in the short run.

### Short-run total cost

Prior to investing in buildings, machinery, and so on, the amounts of all resources are variable. That is, the use of each type of resource can be determined so as to obtain the most efficient (that is, the least-cost) combination of inputs. But once resources have been congealed into buildings, machinery, and other *fixed* assets, their amounts cannot be readily changed, although their rates of utilization can be decreased by allowing fixed assets to lie idle. (Note, however, that idle assets cost as much as, perhaps more than, utilized assets.) To summarize, in the *short run* there are certain resources whose amounts cannot be changed when the desired rate of output changes, while there are other resources (called variable inputs) whose use can be changed almost instantaneously.[9]

We can show the relation between short-run total cost ($SRTC$) and long-run total cost by returning to a producer's expansion path. Suppose there are only two inputs, capital and labor. Figure 6–7

**FIGURE 6–7**
**Short-run and long-run expansion**

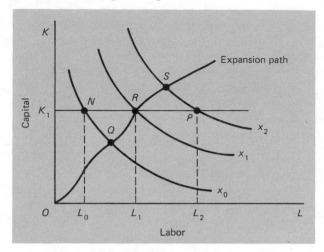

illustrates an expansion path with representative points $Q$, $R$, and $S$. These points are the least costly method of producing outputs $x_0$, $x_1$, and $x_2$ in the long run. They correspond to points $Q'$, $R'$, and $S'$ in Figure 6–8 on the $LRTC$ schedule.

Suppose an entrepreneur whose $LRTC$, or planning horizon, is that indicated in Figure 6–8, builds a plant to produce $x_1$ units of output. The producer should operate at point $R$ on the expansion path using $K_1$ and $L_1$ units of capital and labor in Figure 6–7. But once the plant is built, capital is fixed at $K_1$; if the producer decides to manufacture only $x_0$ units of output, $L_0$ and $K_1$ units of labor and

---

[9] It is not quite precise to say that the inputs of some resources cannot be changed. Certainly the firm could scrap a very expensive piece of capital equipment, buy another one twice as large, and have it installed before lunch, *if it is willing to pay the price*. In fact, the firm can probably change any input rather rapidly, given, once more, its willingness to pay. The short run is thus a convenient but important analytical device. It is frequently helpful in analyzing problems to assume that some inputs are fixed for a period of time. Moreover, it does not deviate too much from reality to make this assumption, since entrepreneurs often consider certain resources as fixed over a period of time. The student should not be overly concerned about the time factor in the short and long run. The fixity of resources is the important element.

**FIGURE 6–8**
Short-run total cost relative to long-run total cost

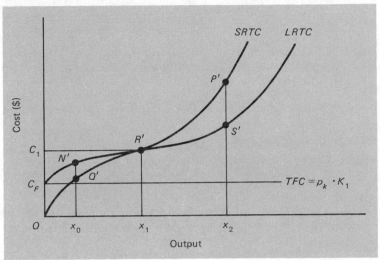

capital would be necessary. For $x_2$ units, $L_2$ and $K_1$ units of input would be needed. As you can see in Figure 6–7, this mix of inputs is not the lowest-cost method of operation. On the isoquant $x_0$, point $N$ represents a higher total cost than does $Q$; similarly, point $P$ is less efficient than $S$ on isoquant $x_2$.

This explains why the $SRTC$ schedule lies above the $LRTC$ schedule at every point except $R$. The entrepreneur has an input that is now invariant to output in the short run. The cost of this input is fixed. Total fixed costs ($TFC$) are $p_k \cdot K_1$, as shown in Figure 6–8. At $R'$, $K_1$ is just the right amount of capital, but when more or less of $X$ is produced, it is either too little or too much; the input mix is wrong. Thus, short-run total cost is higher than long-run total cost at every point except at $R'$. The more output diverges from $x_1$, the less efficient is the input mix and the higher $SRTC$ is relative to $LRTC$. Notice that, even if the entrepreneur produces nothing, costs are still $C_F = p_k \cdot K_1$ in Figure 6–8.

In discussing the short run, $SRTC$ is divided into total fixed cost ($TFC$) and total variable cost ($TVC$):

**Definition.** Total fixed costs are those costs invariant with respect to output in the short run.

**Definition.** Total variable costs are the amounts spent for each of the variable inputs used.

**Definition.** Total cost in the short run is the sum of total variable and total fixed costs.

In Figure 6–7, total variable cost is $p_L \cdot L$, where $L$ is the amount of labor employed and depends on the level of output.

Figure 6–8 shows both components of short-run total costs. Total fixed costs, $C_F$, must be paid regardless of output, and total variable costs ($TVC$) are the difference between $SRTC$ and $TFC$ at any level of output. $TVC$ changes as output changes, since variable costs are the payments to the resources that the firm can vary with output. In sum, we may write in symbols

$$SRTC = TFC + TVC.$$

### Average and marginal costs

The short-run total cost of production, including implicit cost, is very important to an entrepreneur. However, one may obtain a deeper understanding of total cost by analyzing the behavior of short-run average cost and marginal cost. The method used in deriving these curves is similar to that used to derive long-run average and marginal costs.

We assume a specific short-run situation, such as that developed in the last subsection. First, consider average fixed cost ($AFC$).

**Definition.**   Average fixed cost is total fixed cost divided by output.

Since average fixed cost is a constant amount divided by output, average fixed cost is relatively high at very low output levels and falls continuously as output decreases, approaching the horizontal axis as output gets very large. We picture $AFC$ in Figure 6–9 along with its associated TFC.

Now we examine average variable cost ($AVC$), a concept completely analogous to long-run average costs, since all costs are variable in the long run.

**Definition.**   Average variable cost is total variable cost divided by output.

Having spent considerable time developing the concept of long-run average cost, we need not spend much time deriving the average variable cost curve, since the two techniques are similar.

Figure 6–10 shows how $AVC$ is derived from $TVC$. As is true of all "average" curves, the average variable cost associated with any level of output is given by the slope of a ray from the origin to the corresponding point on the $TVC$ curve. As may easily be seen from panel A, the slope of a ray from the origin to the curve steadily diminishes as one passes through points such as $P$; and it diminishes until the ray is just tangent to the $TVC$ curve at point $Q$, associated with output $x_2$. Thereafter, the slope increases as one moves from $Q$

**FIGURE 6–9**
Average fixed cost and total fixed cost

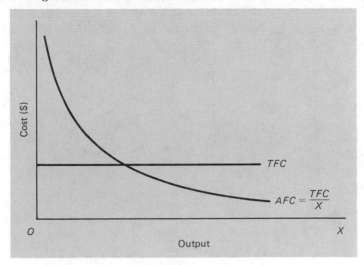

**FIGURE 6–10**
Derivation of the average variable cost curve

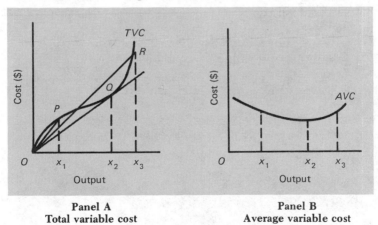

| **Panel A** | **Panel B** |
| Total variable cost | Average variable cost |

toward points such as $R$. This is reflected in panel B by constructing $AVC$ with a negative slope until output $x_2$ is attained. After that point, the slope becomes positive and remains positive.

Although the U-shapes of $AVC$ and long-run average cost are similar, the reasons for their decline and rise are different. The explanation for the curvature of $AVC$ lies in the short-run theory of production. Total variable cost at any output consists of the payments to the variable factors of production used to produce that output. $TVC$, therefore, equals the sum of the number of units of each variable input ($V$) multiplied by unit price ($W$) of that input. For example, at output $X$ produced by $n$ variable inputs, $TVC = W_1V_1 + W_2V_2 + W_3V_3 + \cdots + W_nV_n$. For the one-variable case, $TVC = WV$. Average variable cost is $TVC$ divided by output ($X$), or

$$AVC = \frac{TVC}{X} = \frac{WV}{X} = W\left(\frac{V}{X}\right).$$

The term ($V/X$) is the number of units of input divided by the number of units of output. In Chapter 5, we defined the average product ($AP$) of an input as total output ($X$) divided by the number of units of input ($V$). Thus

$$\frac{V}{X} = \frac{1}{(X/V)} = \frac{1}{AP},$$

and

$$AVC = W\frac{V}{X} = W\frac{1}{(X/V)} = W\left(\frac{1}{AP}\right).$$

Thus, average variable cost is the price of the input multiplied by the reciprocal of average product. Since, by the law of variable proportions, average product normally rises, reaches a maximum, then declines, average variable cost normally falls, reaches a minimum, then rises.

Figure 6–11 shows the derivation of short-run average total cost ($ATC$), which may be called average cost or unit cost.

**Definition.**   Average total cost is total cost divided by output.

**FIGURE 6–11**
**Derivation of the average total cost or unit cost curve**

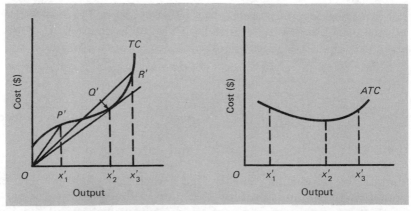

| Panel A | Panel B |
| Short-run total cost | Short-run unit cost |

Exactly the same analysis used for *AVC* holds for panels A and B, which show the derivation of *ATC* from *TC*. The slope of the ray diminishes as one moves along *TC* until point $Q'$ is reached. At $Q'$, the slope of the ray is at its minimum, so minimum *ATC* is attained at output level $x_2'$. Thereafter, the slope of the ray increases continuously, and the *ATC* curve has a positive slope. (Note: the output level $x_2'$ *does not* represent the same quantity as $x_2$ in Figure 6–10. As we shall see, *AVC* reaches its minimum at a lower output than that at which *ATC* reaches its minimum.)

*ATC* may also be computed by an alternative method. Since *TC* = *TFC* + *TVC*,

$$ATC = \frac{TC}{X} = \frac{TFC + TVC}{X} = \frac{TFC}{X} + \frac{TVC}{X} = AFC + AVC.$$

Thus, one may calculate average cost as the sum of average fixed and average variable cost.

This method of calculation helps to explain the shape of the average total cost curve. Over the range of values for which *AFC* and *AVC* both decline, *ATC*, the sum of *AFC* and *AVC*, must obviously decline as well. But even after *AVC* turns up, the decline in *AFC* causes *ATC* to continue to decline. Finally, however, the increase in *AVC* more than offsets the decline in *AFC*; *ATC*, therefore, reaches its minimum and increases thereafter. We will show this graphically below.

Finally, let us examine marginal cost in the short run.

**Definition.**  Marginal cost in the short run is the change in short-run total cost attributable to a one-unit change in output.

The definitions of long- and short-run marginal cost that we have given are virtually identical. The concepts are not quite the same, however. Long-run marginal cost refers to the change in cost resulting from a change in output when *all inputs are optimally adjusted*. Short-run marginal cost, on the other hand, refers to the change in cost resulting from a change in output when *only the variable inputs change*. Since the fixed inputs cannot be changed in the short run, input combinations are not optimally adjusted. Thus, the short-run marginal cost curve reflects suboptimal adjustment of inputs.

Although the concept of marginal cost differs slightly between the long run and the short run, the process of deriving marginal cost is similar. The marginal cost of, say, the second unit produced is the increase in the total cost caused by changing production from one unit to two units, or, $MC_2 = SRTC_2 - SRTC_1$. Since only variable cost changes in the short run, however, the marginal cost of producing an additional unit is the increase in variable cost. Thus, the marginal cost of the second unit is also $MC_2 = TVC_2 - TVC_1$.

**FIGURE 6–12**
Derivation of the marginal cost curve

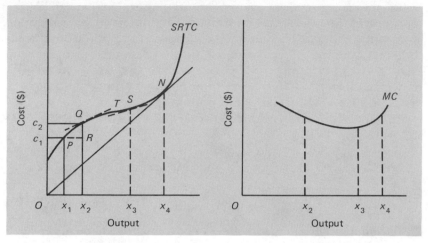

| Panel A | Panel B |
|---------|---------|
| **Short-run total cost** | **Short-run marginal cost** |

The derivation of marginal cost is illustrated in Figure 6–12. Panel A shows the short-run total cost curve $SRTC$. As output increases from $x_1$ to $x_2$, one moves from point $P$ to point $Q$, and total cost increases from $c_1$ to $c_2$. Marginal cost is thus $QR/PR$. As before, the slope of the tangent $T$ at point $Q$ becomes a progressively better estimate of $MC$ ($QR/PR$) as the distance between $P$ and $Q$ becomes smaller and smaller. Thus, for small changes, the slope of the total cost curve is marginal cost.

As $TC$ increases, the slope decreases ($MC$ decreases) until point $S$ is reached at output $x_3$. Thereafter, the slope increases ($MC$ increases). The $MC$ curve is constructed in panel B so that it decreases until output $x_3$ is attained, and increases thereafter.

Just as average variable cost is related to average product, marginal cost is related to marginal product. As before, consider the one-variable case in which $TVC = WV$. The price of the input is $W$, and $V$ is the amount employed.

$$MC = \frac{\Delta VC}{\Delta X} = \frac{\Delta(WV)}{\Delta X} = W\frac{\Delta V}{\Delta X},$$

where again $\Delta$ means "the change in." But, recall that marginal product is $MP = \Delta X/\Delta V$. Therefore,

$$MC = W\left(\frac{1}{MP}\right).$$

From this relation, as marginal product rises, marginal cost falls; when marginal product declines, marginal cost rises.

One final point concerning the relation of short-run marginal and average cost curves should be noted. As already implied, and as Figure 6–13 again illustrates, $TC$ and $TVC$ have the same slope at

**FIGURE 6–13**
**Relation of $MC$ to variable and total costs**

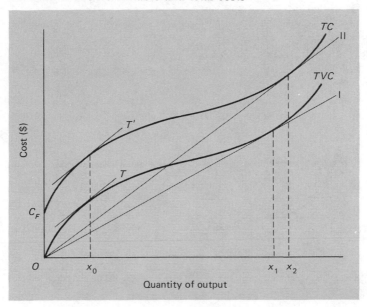

each output level. $TC$ is simply $TVC$ displaced upward by the constant amount $TFC$ (see Figure 6–13).

At output $x_0$, the tangent ($T$) to $TVC$ has the same slope as the tangent ($T'$) to $TC$. Since the slopes of the two tangents at output $x_0$ are equal, $MC$ at $x_0$ is given by the slope of either curve. The same holds true for any other output level. The slope of ray I from the origin gives minimum $AVC$. But at this point (output $x_1$), ray I is just tangent to $TVC$; hence, its slope also gives $MC$ at output $x_1$. Thus $MC = AVC$ when the latter attains its minimum value. Similarly the slope of ray II gives minimum $ATC$ (at output $x_2$). At this point the ray is tangent to $TC$; thus its slope also gives $MC$ at output $x_2$. Consequently, $MC = ATC$ when the latter attains its minimum value. Finally, as is easily seen from Figure 6–13, $AVC$ attains its minimum at a lower output than the output at which $ATC$ attains its minimum.

The properties of the average and marginal cost curves, as de-

**FIGURE 6–14**
Typical set of cost curves

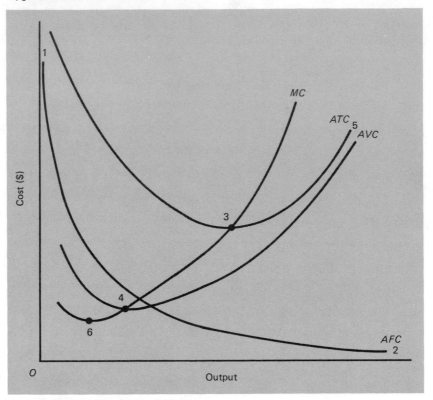

rived in this section, are illustrated by the traditionally assumed set of short-run cost curves shown in Figure 6–14. The curves indicate the following:

**Relation.** (a) *AFC* declines continuously, approaching both axes asymptotically, as shown by points 1 and 2 in the figure. (b) *AVC* first declines, reaches a minimum at point 4, and rises thereafter. When *AVC* attains its minimum at point 4, *MC* equals *AVC*. As *AFC* asymptotically approaches the horizontal axis, *AVC* approaches *ATC* asymptotically, as shown by point 5. (c) *ATC* first declines, reaches a minimum at point 3, and rises thereafter. When *ATC* attains its minimum at point 3, *MC* equals *ATC*. (d) *MC* first declines, reaches a minimum at point 6, and rises thereafter. *MC* equals both *AVC* and *ATC* when these curves attain their minimum values. Furthermore, *MC* lies below both *AVC* and *ATC* over the range in which the curves decline; it lies above them when they are rising.

**TABLE 6-3**
**Short-run cost schedules**

| (1) Output | (2) Total cost ($) | (3) Fixed cost ($) | (4) Variable cost ($) | (5) Average fixed cost | (6) Average variable cost | (7) Average total cost | (8) Marginal cost (per 100 units) | (9) Marginal cost (per unit) |
|---|---|---|---|---|---|---|---|---|
| 100 | $ 6,000 | $4,000 | $ 2,000 | $40.00 | $20.00 | $60.00 | $ 2,000 | $ 20.00 |
| 200 | 7,000 | 4,000 | 3,000 | 20.00 | 15.00 | 35.00 | 1,000 | 10.00 |
| 300 | 7,500 | 4,000 | 3,500 | 13.33 | 11.67 | 25.00 | 500 | 5.00 |
| 400 | 9,000 | 4,000 | 5,000 | 10.00 | 12.50 | 22.50 | 1,500 | 15.00 |
| 500 | 11,000 | 4,000 | 7,000 | 8.00 | 14.00 | 22.00 | 2,000 | 20.00 |
| 600 | 14,000 | 4,000 | 10,000 | 6.67 | 16.67 | 23.33 | 3,000 | 30.00 |
| 700 | 18,000 | 4,000 | 14,000 | 5.71 | 20.00 | 25.71 | 4,000 | 40.00 |
| 800 | 24,000 | 4,000 | 20,000 | 5.00 | 25.00 | 30.00 | 6,000 | 60.00 |
| 900 | 34,000 | 4,000 | 30,000 | 4.44 | 33.33 | 37.77 | 10,000 | 100.00 |
| 1,000 | 50,000 | 4,000 | 46,000 | 4.00 | 46.00 | 50.00 | 16,000 | 160.00 |

Table 6–3 illustrates numerically the characteristics of the cost curves we have thus far analyzed graphically. As seen in this table, average fixed cost decreases over the entire range of output. Both average variable and average total cost first decrease, then increase, with average variable cost attaining a minimum at an output lower than that at which average total reaches its minimum. Marginal cost per 100 units is the incremental increase in total cost and variable cost. Marginal cost (per unit) is below average variable and average total when each is falling and is greater than each when $AVC$ and $ATC$ are rising.

## APPLICATION

### Refinery cost functions from engineering data

In an earlier application, the survivor technique was discussed as a way of detecting economies of scale in an industry and getting a crude idea of how the $LRAC$ curve is shaped. But firms in an industry use different technologies and often face different input prices. The survivor technique is not very informative about the short-run costs of any single firm.

There are ways to estimate the average cost schedule for a particular firm. The two most popular methodologies employ either accounting data or an engineer's estimate of the production function. This application sets forth an example showing how the engineering approach is used to estimate short-run average cost.

An industry for which the engineering technique is used is petroleum refining. If a firm is considering the construction of a new refinery, it needs some estimates for the investment (fixed) and operating (variable) costs associated with the proposed refinery. In this application, we present a simplified example of the manner in which these estimates are obtained.[10]

At the outset, it must be noted that petroleum refineries are designed to handle a specific type and quantity of crude oil. In this example, let us assume that the refinery is designed to process 30,000 barrels per day (bpd) of a particular crude oil or mix of crude oils. The first process used in refining the crude oils is atmospheric distillation. On the basis of physical evaluation of the specific crude oils to be processed, the engineers estimate that this process will result in 8,000 bpd of finished products (e.g., gasoline and fuel oils) and 22,000 bpd of materials that require further processing. Part of

---

[10] This application is adapted from J. H. Gary and G. E. Handwerk, *Petroleum Refining* (New York: Marcel Dekker, 1975), pp. 214–27.

this amount (18,000 bpd) can be processed via vacuum distillation to yield the final products. The remainder (4,000 bpd) must be sent through a hydro-desulfurizer. As a result of this process, the engineers estimate an output of 561 pounds per day of sulfur, 1,000 bpd of finished products, and 2,900 bpd of materials that require still further processing. These materials are processed in a catalytic reformer to yield 2,700 bpd of finished products. This processing flow is illustrated in the following diagram:

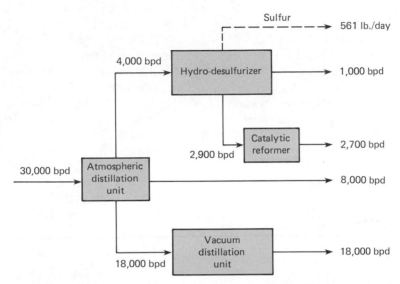

Given this knowledge of the production process, the firm then knows what types of capital are required and the necessary capacities for each (e.g., a catalytic reformer with a capacity of 2,900 bpd). It can then use available industry sources to obtain the cost of such capital equipment. In this way, the firm will be able to obtain estimates of the capital costs associated with this refinery. These are summarized below:

| Item | Capacity (bpd) | Cost* |
|---|---|---|
| Atmospheric distillation unit | 30,000 | $1,900,000 |
| Vacuum distillation unit | 18,000 | 1,200,000 |
| Hydro-desulfurizer | 4,000 | 625,000 |
| Catalytic reformer | 2,900 | 1,800,000 |
| Total | | $5,525,000 |

* All costs are as of 1973.

Thus, total fixed costs are $5,525,000.

The next task is to obtain an estimate of the variable costs associated with this refinery. These are normally calculated on an annual basis, assuming that the refinery is operating at capacity. The major variable inputs are crude oil, labor, cooling water, electric power, royalties, and catalyst replacement. Assuming that the refinery operates 340 days per year, the refinery will require 10,200,000 barrels of crude oil. If the crude oil to be used sells for $7 per barrel (1973 prices), crude oil costs will be $71,400,000. Using data obtained from other plants, the engineers calculate that this refinery will require a staff of 22 workers. Then, assuming an average annual wage of $18,000, annual labor costs would be $396,000. Required cooling water and electric power is determined from data on comparable refineries. Multiplying these requirements by the average current costs of the inputs, annual expenditures are obtained. Let us assume that these are, respectively, $16,000 and $14,000. Royalties are paid to patent owners on the basis of the throughput of the refinery. For example, if the royalty rate on the catalytic reformer is 4.5 cents per barrel, the annual royalty is $44,370 (i.e., $0.045 \times 2,900 \times 340 = 44,370$). Let us assume that total royalties amount to $66,000 annually. Finally, catalyst replacement is also determined by the amount of crude oil processed. We assume that the annual expenditures are $23,000. Combining these, the annual variable costs associated with this refinery are:

| | |
|---|---:|
| Crude oil | $71,400,000 |
| Labor | 396,000 |
| Cooling water | 16,000 |
| Electric power | 140,000 |
| Royalties | 66,000 |
| Catalyst replacement | 23,000 |
| Total | $72,041,000 |

While such an engineering approach to cost estimation is straightforward and useful, we must point out that using this approach involves several problems. An obvious difficulty is that the engineering production function may be based on the operation of a pilot plant and thus may not prove to be valid when the firm expands to a full-scale production facility. However, we feel that there is an even more serious problem. This problem results from the difference between the engineer's and the economist's view of efficiency. An example should illustrate our concern. Consider a very simple production process: Coal is moved from river barges to the loading hopper of a plant by means of a crane. Now, let us assume that in this process some coal is dropped into the river. Here, it is very likely that the engineer and the economist would differ as to their concept of efficiency. While the engineer might suggest mod-

ifying or replacing the crane to eliminate the "waste," the economist might take a very different view. If the price of coal is low
relative to the price of capital, it could be efficient (in the economic
sense) to drop coal into the water. The real problem is to determine
the optimal amount to drop. The point is that the technologically
efficient combination of inputs need not be the economically efficient combination.

## 6.4 RELATIONS BETWEEN SHORT-RUN AND LONG-RUN AVERAGE AND MARGINAL COSTS

Figure 6–8 showed the relation between short-run and long-run
total cost curves. Recall that the two curves are tangent at the output
for which the short-run is optimal. At every other level of output,
short-run cost exceeds long-run cost.

Figure 6–15 shows a long-run average and marginal cost curve.
Three short-run situations are indicated by the three sets of curves
$SRAC_1$–$MC_1$, $SRAC_2$–$MC_2$, and $SRAC_3$–$MC_3$. $SRAC_1$ and $MC_1$ are
the short-run curves for the plant size designed to produce output $x_s$
optimally. Since the short-run total cost curve is tangent to the long-

**FIGURE 6–15**
**Long-run and short-run average and marginal costs**

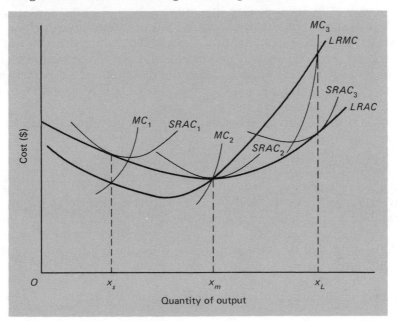

run total cost curve at this output, when we divide both cost curves by the same output, $x_s$, the two average cost curves will be tangent at this output also. Recall that marginal cost, $\Delta TC/\Delta X$, is shown by the slope of the total cost curve. Thus, long-run marginal cost equals short-run marginal cost at the output given by the point of tangency, $x_s$, since both total cost schedules have the same slope. Finally, short-run marginal cost crosses short-run average cost at the latter's minimum point. Note that, because $x_s$ is on the decreasing portion of $LRAC$, $SRAC_1$ must be decreasing also at the point of tangency.

$SRAC_3$ and $MC_3$ show another short-run situation. Here, tangency occurs at $x_L$ on the increasing part of $LRAC$. Thus, $SRAC_3$ is increasing at this point also. Again, the two marginal curves are equal at $x_L$, and $MC_3$ crosses $SRAC_3$ at the minimum point on the latter.

Finally, $SRAC_2$ is the short-run curve corresponding to the output level at which long-run average cost is at its minimum. At output level $x_m$, the two average curves are tangent. The two marginal costs, $MC_2$ and $LRMC$, are equal at this output, and since the two average curves attain their minimum at $x_m$, the two marginal curves equal the two average cost curves. Thus, all four curves are equal at output $x_m$.

In the situation shown in Figure 6–15, the firm must operate with one of the three plant sizes, large, medium, or small. But in the long run, it can build a plant of a size that leads to least average cost for any given output. Thus, it regards the long-run average cost curve as a planning device, because this curve shows the least cost of producing each possible output. Entrepreneurs, therefore, are normally faced with a choice among quite a wide variety of plants. In Figure 6–16, six short-run average and marginal cost curves are shown; but this is really far from enough. Many curves could be drawn between each of those shown. These six curves are only representative of the wide variety that could be constructed.

These many curves generate $LRAC$ as a planning device. Suppose the entrepreneur thinks the output associated with point $A$ in Figure 6–16 will be most profitable. The plant represented by $SRAC_1$ will be built, because it will allow production of this output at the least possible cost per unit. With the plant with short-run average cost given by $SRAC_1$, unit cost could be reduced by expanding output to the amount associated with point $B$ ($x_2$), the minimum point on $SRAC_1$. If demand conditions were suddenly changed so that this larger output was desirable, the entrepreneur could easily expand and would add to profitability by reducing unit cost. Nevertheless, when setting future plans, the entrepreneur would decide to construct the plant represented by $SRAC_2$, because

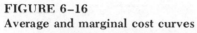

**FIGURE 6–16**
**Average and marginal cost curves**

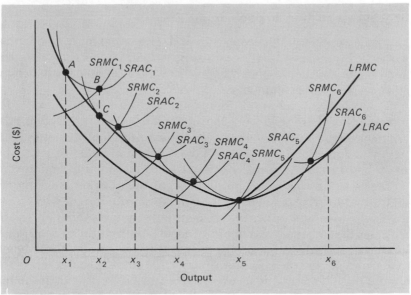

the firm could reduce unit costs even more. It would operate at point $C$, thereby lowering unit cost from the level at point $B$ on $SRAC_1$.

The long-run planning curve, $LRAC$, is a locus of points representing the least unit cost of producing the corresponding output. The entrepreneur determines the size of plant with reference to this curve, selecting the short-run plant that yields the least unit cost of producing the volume of output desired.

Figure 6–16 illustrates the following:

**Relation.** (a) $LRMC$ intersects $LRAC$ when the latter is at its minimum point. One, and only one, short-run plant has minimum $SRAC$ that coincides with minimum $LRAC$ ($SRAC_5$). $SRMC_5$ equals $LRMC$ at this common minimum. (b) At each output where a particular $SRAC$ is tangent to $LRAC$, the relevant $SRMC$ equals $LRMC$. At outputs below (above) the tangency output, the relevant $SRMC$ is less (greater) than $LRMC$. (c) For all $SRAC$ curves, the point of tangency with $LRAC$ is at an output less (greater) than the output of minimum $SRAC$ if the tangency is at an output less (greater) than that associated with minimum $LRAC$.

## APPLICATION

### Benefit-cost analysis in decision making

A crucial point in the economics of decision making, and one that we shall be making again and again, is that, in the short run, the decision maker should ignore fixed costs and rely on marginal costs: *fixed costs are irrelevant in the short run.*

This rule is critical in running your own business. It is also vastly important for those who work for someone else, in business, in government, or for nonprofit firms. The reason for such importance is the vast number of decisions that take the form of benefit-cost analysis. In most cases these are *marginal benefits* and *marginal costs.*

To illustrate, let us examine why airlines sometimes put on flights that incur losses when all costs are considered, or why trucking companies sometimes make seemingly unprofitable hauls. The reason is that the marginal benefit exceeds the marginal cost. It may be that a particular flight has so little passenger and freight demand that the total cost of the flight exceeds the total revenue when the cost of the plane is spread over this extra flight. But if the plane would be idle anyway, the real cost of the additional flight is the added labor and fuel costs, the added wear and tear on capital, and any other costs that would not be encountered if the flight was not made. In other words, *only the marginal costs matter.* If these marginal costs are expected to be less than the expected additional revenues from making the additional flight, the trip will be made. Exactly the same line of reasoning applies to the trucking companies' decisions about additional hauls.

Employees who manage departments or divisions of firms frequently use the same line of reasoning. Say you manage a department in a large department store. How do you convince your store manager that you need more advertising. (Always say "need" rather than want; "need" sounds much more crucial than "want".)[11] You know more advertising will increase sales and, therefore, your income. Convince the manager that the *additional returns from the additional sales will exceed the additional cost of additional advertising.* Use the same argument when you wish more sales help or more of any resource, like floor space, that will increase sales. Managers of offices or branches of plants can use much the same argument.

---

[11] Keep track of the number of times political figures at all levels of government use the term *need* when they really mean want. Need, which implies necessity, seems a little out of place when used in ways such as, "Los Angeles needs three new golf courses and a swimming pool" or "the state of New York needs legalized parimutuel betting at horse races."

Many, many governmental decisions are based upon marginal benefit–marginal cost analysis. For example, government agencies operate under a fixed budget; with this budget, they are assigned the task of carrying out certain operations—possibly building roads and highways. Obviously, there are more projects desired at any one time than can be undertaken with a given budget. Thus, the leading candidates for funding are analyzed as to the marginal benefit and the marginal cost involved in each. Theoretically (that is, political implications aside), the projects that should be undertaken are those in which the marginal gain exceeds the marginal cost by the greatest amount.

Even politicians make campaign decisions based upon marginal-cost considerations. If you plan to run for an elected office, your campaign funds will no doubt be limited—probably far below your desired level. Since you cannot saturate each area with expenditure, you will have to compare the marginal cost of political advertising (TV, etc.) with the marginal benefits in expected votes.

Possibly you will work for a nonprofit organization—a school or a hospital. Decision making using marginal cost is certainly relevant in either of these institutions. A hospital administrator, for example, would argue for additional facilities on the basis of a comparison between the marginal cost and the marginal gain, measured not necessarily in money income under these circumstances, but in more patients treated, better care per patient, and so on. School administrators use the same type of approach. Based on personal experience, we should warn you that such economically based arguments of marginal analysis may not always work if the upper level of management does not understand marginal analysis. Recently, one of the authors sent through a request for two new faculty members to be added to the economics department. Departmental income is based upon departmental student enrollment. The written request "proved" that the additional new faculty would cost less than the additional income from being able to offer the new classes. Thus, the department could teach more students at a lower net expenditure. The dean, who is an economist himself, approved the request. The top administrators, who were not economists, turned it down on the basis that fixed salary expenditure is already "too high." Moral: when using these arguments, hope that your superiors have had training in economics also, or give them some training in economics.

## 6.5 SUMMARY

The physical conditions of production and resource prices jointly establish the cost of production. If the set of technological possibilities changes, the cost curves change. Or, if the prices of some factors of production change, the firm's cost curves change. Therefore, it should be emphasized that cost curves are generally, although not always, drawn under the assumptions of *constant factor prices and a constant technology*.

We have distinguished between cost in the short run and in the long run. The chief distinction between the long and short run is the planning horizon. Some inputs are fixed in the short run, leading to fixed costs, as opposed to variable costs. The sum of variable and fixed costs is total cost in the short run. Average cost in either the long run or short run is found by dividing the relevant total cost schedule by output. Marginal cost is the change in total cost when output is increased by a small amount. Marginal cost in the long run is not the same as marginal cost in the short run, because some inputs do not change in the short run.

It is important to emphasize that the crucial cost to consider in decision making is marginal cost. When increasing the volume of any output or service, always compare marginal cost to the marginal gain. If the gain is greater than the cost at the margin, then expand. This rule is the foundation for profit maximization to be set forth in Chapter 8. Before we consider it further, however, we want to examine the behavior of cost and prices over time. This is the topic to which we turn in the next chapter.

## TECHNICAL PROBLEMS

1.  In the following table, total product is given; you must compute average and marginal product. You are also given the following information.

    1. Total fixed cost (total price of fixed inputs) is $220 per period.
    2. Units of the variable input cost $100 per unit per period. Using this information, complete the remaining columns in the table.

    a.  Graph the total cost curves on one sheet and the average and marginal curves on another.
    b.  By reference to table and graph, answer the following questions:
        (1) When marginal product is increasing, what is happening to:
            (a) Marginal cost?
            (b) Average variable cost?
        (2) When marginal cost first begins to fall, does average variable cost begin to rise?

| Units of vari-able input | Product | | | Cost | | | Average cost | | | Mar-ginal cost |
|---|---|---|---|---|---|---|---|---|---|---|
| | Total | Aver-age | Mar-ginal | Fixed | Vari-able | Total | Fixed | Vari-able | Total | |
| 1 ....... | 100 | | | | | | | | | |
| 2 ....... | 250 | | | | | | | | | |
| 3 ....... | 410 | | | | | | | | | |
| 4 ....... | 560 | | | | | | | | | |
| 5 ....... | 700 | | | | | | | | | |
| 6 ....... | 830 | | | | | | | | | |
| 7 ....... | 945 | | | | | | | | | |
| 8 ....... | 1,050 | | | | | | | | | |
| 9 ....... | 1,146 | | | | | | | | | |
| 10 ....... | 1,234 | | | | | | | | | |
| 11 ....... | 1,314 | | | | | | | | | |
| 12 ....... | 1,384 | | | | | | | | | |
| 13 ....... | 1,444 | | | | | | | | | |
| 14 ....... | 1,494 | | | | | | | | | |
| 15 ....... | 1,534 | | | | | | | | | |
| 16 ....... | 1,564 | | | | | | | | | |
| 17 ....... | 1,584 | | | | | | | | | |
| 18 ....... | 1,594 | | | | | | | | | |

(3) What is the relation between marginal cost and average variable cost wen marginal and average product are equal?

(4) What is happening to average variable cost while average product is increasing?

(5) What is average variable cost when average product is at its maximum? What happens to average variable cost after this point?

(6) What happens to marginal cost after the point at which it equals average variable cost?

    (a) How does it compare with average variable cost thereafter?

    (b) What is happening to marginal product thereafter?

    (c) How does marginal product compare with average product thereafter?

(7) What happens to total fixed cost as output is increased?

(8) What happens to average fixed cost as:

    (a) Marginal product increases?

    (b) Marginal cost decreases?

    (c) Marginal product decreases?

    (d) Marginal cost increases?

    (e) Average variable cost increases?

    (9)   How long does average fixed cost decrease?

   (10)   What happens to average total cost as:

        (*a*)   Marginal product increases?

        (*b*)   Marginal cost decreases?

        (*c*)   Average product increases?

        (*d*)   Average variable cost decreases?

   (11)   Does average variable cost increase:

        (*a*)   As soon as the point of diminishing marginal returns is passed?

        (*b*)   As soon as the point of diminishing average returns is passed?

   (12)   When does average cost increase? Answer this in terms of:

        (*a*)   The relation of average cost to marginal cost.

        (*b*)   The relation between the increase in average variable cost and the decrease in average fixed cost.

**2.**   Assume that labor—the only variable input of a firm—has the average and marginal product curves shown in Figure E.6–1. Labor's wage is $2 per unit of labor.

**FIGURE E.6–1**

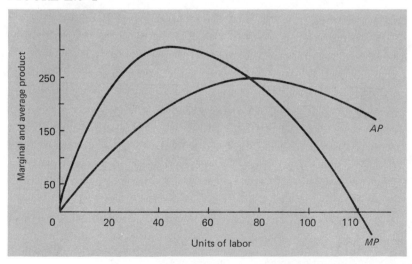

   *a.*   At how many units of labor does average variable cost reach its minimum? _____

   *b.*   What is average variable cost at this output? _____

   *c.*   At what level of output does marginal cost attain its minimum? _____

    *d.*    What is marginal cost at this output? _____
    *e.*    Suppose fixed cost is \$1,000. What is average total cost when average product is 200 and decreasing? _____
    *f.*    At the same fixed cost, what is average total cost when marginal product is 100 and falling? _____

3.    Why do long-run average cost curves first fall, then rise? Why do short-run average cost curves first fall, then rise?

**FIGURE E.6–2**

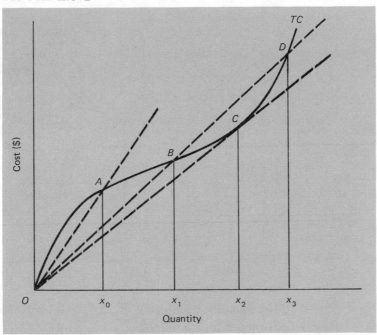

4.    Assuming the long-run total cost curve in Figure E.6–2, answer the following questions:
    *a.*    When output is $x_0$, average cost is the ratio _____ and is (greater than, less than, equal to) marginal cost.
    *b.*    At output $x_2$ average cost is the ratio _____ and marginal cost is the ratio _____.
    *c.*    Answer part (*a*) for output levels $x_1$ and $x_3$.
5.    In Figure E.6–3, *LRAC* and *LRMC* make up a firm's planning horizon. $SRAC_1$, $SRAC_2$, and $SRAC_3$ are the only three plant sizes available. These are called plant 1, plant 2, and plant 3.
    *a.*    Draw accurately the short-run marginal cost curves associated with each plant. Recall the relation between short- and long-run marginal costs.

**FIGURE E.6–3**

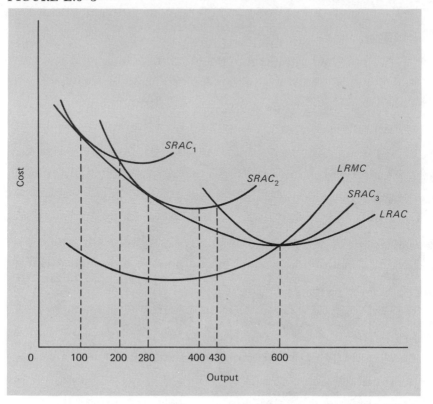

b. Plant 1 is designed to produce _____ units optimally, plant 2 is designed to produce _____ units optimally, and plant 3 is designed to produce _____ units optimally.

c. The firm would produce in plant 1 any output below _____. It would produce any output between _____ and _____ in plant 2.

d. $SRAC_2$ attains its minimum at 400 units. Suppose there was another plant (say 4) that could produce 400 optimally. Would the average cost curve associated with this plant attain its minimum above, below, or at 400 units?

e. The lowest possible per unit cost is attained at _____ units in plant _____. Why would the firm not use this plant to produce every other output since this is least per unit cost?

**6.** Consider the average and marginal curves shown in Figure E.6–4. Label properly the four curves, *LRAC*, *LRMC*, *SRAC*, and *SRMC*.

**FIGURE E.6–4**

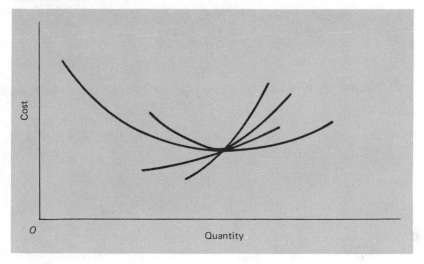

7. Fill in the blanks in the following table:

| Units of output | Total cost | Fixed cost | Variable cost | Average fixed cost | Average variable cost | Average total cost | Marginal cost |
|---|---|---|---|---|---|---|---|
| 1............ | $ | $100 | $ 900 | $ | $ | $ | $ |
| 2............ | | | | | 850 | | |
| 3............ | | | | | | | 700 |
| 4............ | | | | | 800 | | |
| 5............ | | | | | | 900 | |
| 6............ | | | | | | | 1,500 |
| 7............ | | | 7,900 | | | | |
| 8............ | | | | | | 1,300 | |
| 9............ | 14,000 | | | | | | |

8. Why does short-run marginal cost rise more rapidly than long-run marginal cost beyond the point at which they are equal?

9. If, at every level of output, average costs for a seller are equal to marginal costs, what can we conclude about the presence of fixed costs?

10. If average variable costs are constant, what must be true of marginal costs? Given that there are fixed costs, does the average cost schedule show that there are economies of scale?

11. Is it possible for the *AFC* curve to slope upward? Prove your answer by applying the definition of *TFC*.

12. Explain why short-run total cost can never be less than long-run total cost.

13. *a.* Suppose you own a commercial lot on a busy street. Your business is located on the lot. Last year your firm earned

$100,000. The lot next to yours rents for $30,000 a year. What is the implicit cost of your property? What is the opportunity cost?

b.  Now suppose Chris Evert Lloyd left professional tennis and opened a tennis shop that sold rackets and tennis wear. During the first year the shop was open, it earned $200,000. No payments were made to the owner. If Lloyd did not manage the shop, she would choose to continue playing professional tennis and earn at least $500,000 a year. What is the implicit cost of Lloyd's services to the tennis shop? What is her opportunity cost? In this case, are implicit and opportunity costs equal?

## ANALYTICAL PROBLEMS

1.  You are the adviser to the president of a university. A wealthy alumnus buys, then gives a plot of land to the university, which plans to use the land as an athletic field. The president says that, as far as the land is concerned, it does not cost the university anything to use the land as an athletic field. What do you say?

2.  Does it cost a doctor more to treat a rich person than a poor person? Explain. What information would you need to answer the question?

3.  Suppose you could somehow measure the output of education from a college or university. Why might the long-run average cost curve at first show economies of scale? Why, after some size, might diseconomies set in? How can you account for the fact that some of our most distinguished universities are rather small in terms of number of students, while other very distinguished universities are extremely large? How do you measure "distinguished?" The last part of this question may be very difficult to answer.

4.  We frequently hear several terms used by businesspersons. What do they mean in economic terminology?
    a.  Spreading the overhead.
    b.  A break-even level of production.
    c.  The efficiency of mass production.

5.  How much does it cost you to keep money in a checking rather than a savings account? If there is this cost, why do people keep money in a checking account? What would cause people to keep less in a savings account and more in checking?

6.  There is considerable debate in Congress at the present time about a proposal to eliminate some water projects, mainly

dams. If you were assigned the task, how would you go about estimating the marginal benefits and marginal costs of building a dam? What information would you need? Do you think it is readily available? (This is a hard question.)

7.  In his book on language, *Strictly Speaking*, Edwin Newman points out one of the more famous current clichés in the English language. "If we can fly men to the moon, why can't we eliminate the ghetto?" Or "If we can fly men to the moon, why can't we improve our school system?" Or "If . . . why can't we do something I want done?" Analyze such clichés using the concept of opportunity cost.

8.  Suppose that you manage a business and have to make business trips of two to four days at least once a month. What factors determine the total cost of a trip? What factors would you consider when deciding whether your salespeople should travel by automobile or airplane? Are these necessarily the same factors that determine the cost of your own travel?

9.  Given your answer to question 8, try this one: Airlines normally provide discounts to students or vacation travelers rather than to business travelers. While it may be the case that the airlines love students and families, it is somewhat more likely that there exists an economic rationale for such behavior. Provide this rationale.

10. Recently, a large number of automobile makers have idled or disposed of assembly plants. Describe the factors that must be considered in making such a decision.

11. A publisher of a new novel has spent $100,000 setting the type. It is now ready to print the book. For practical purposes, as many books as they like can be printed. In deciding how many copies to run, does the cost of typesetting have any influence on the publisher's decision? Explain your answer.

12. Suppose there are a large number of producers in an industry, and all of them produce identical products which sell for the same price. Suppose the firms experience economies of scale. Would they have the incentive to expand? Why? Explain what would eventually happen to the number of producers.

13. Let us return to our application dealing with an engineering cost function in petroleum refining.

    a.  Disregarding the output of sulfur, calculate the average variable cost associated with a barrel of finished products.

    b.  In such an approach, maintenance expense is normally calculated as a percent of total capital cost. Would such a cost be fixed or variable?

    c.  Note that fuel is not included as a cost of operation. This is because the firm does not purchase any fuel oils; rather, it simply burns some of its own output. Comment on such a practice and how it affects cost.

14. We have argued that engineering cost functions may not reflect the economically efficient combination of inputs. Could this be the case in the instance of the engineering cost function for petroleum refining described in one application in this chapter? Note that, in this production process, crude oil is completely utilized. Might there exist a circumstance in which it would be economically efficient to "waste" crude oil? Suggest the way in which this wastage would most likely occur.

# Chapter 7

## Dynamic markets: Decisions over time

## 7.1 INTRODUCTION

Thus far, the theories we have discussed have been basically static or timeless. Consumers have made purchasing and consumption decisions that take place during a single period. All income is received and spent during the same period. Likewise, we have assumed that managers hire inputs in one period to produce output during the same period. Thus, our theory has not had a time dimension. While it is probably safe to say that the majority of analysis by economists is carried out within a single-period framework, certain decisions do require multiperiod analysis.

This chapter sets forth a framework that allows us to study how multiperiod decisions are made. Decisions made now do affect the future. Often they involve investments or purchases that yield a stream of future returns, and perhaps require a stream of future payments. For instance, the decision to investment in capital equipment requires the producer to evaluate a stream of future returns and compare it to the present price of the equipment. Consumers purchase durable goods that yield services over several years—a home, an automobile, or an appliance. These goods have a price which consumers must weigh against the future services they provide. Consumption and particularly investment often involve the exchange of goods used for more than one period.

Whether you are a producer or a consumer, the decision to invest or not invest, to save or spend, to buy now or later, depends critically upon the rate of interest. This dependence is not difficult to understand. Interest rates are the opportunity cost of spending now. Income could be saved and spent later along with the interest payment. Thus, interest is forgone when income is spent. Also, an investment must yield a higher return than the alternative return earned by saving. High interest rates, for instance, raise the opportunity cost of investing. Investment tends to decline under such conditions.

Interest is inherently tied to the process of capital accumulation. If people are willing to defer consumption now and invest, they can later consume more than the amount originally foregone. If $C is invested in a productive process and $(C + r)$ is earned in the next period, then $r$ is interest and represents the opportunity cost of consuming now. To make the point stronger, consider a very simple example.

Suppose that, in a very primitive society, most of the people earn their living by fishing. Moreover, the state of technology is so primitive everyone fishes from the bank of a lake. One family deduces that if they had a boat, they could fish farther out in the lake and catch more fish. But in order to build the boat, the family must sacrifice some time that could be spent fishing and must, therefore, reduce consumption now in order to consume more later. This reduction in consumption represents an investment. Foregone consumption promises a higher return later. The opportunity cost of continued fishing from the bank is the extra fish that could be caught in a boat.

The family might decide that they do not want to decrease the amount of fish they consume while building the boat. They can still eat by finding other families who are willing to reduce their consumption now in order to give some of their fish to them. The problem is persuading other people to sacrifice some of their fish.

One method of persuasion is to agree to repay the fish after the boat is built and the catch becomes larger. But if they prefer consumption now to consumption in the future, the boat builders must agree to repay more fish than they receive in the present. The "lenders" of the fish require an additional amount to compensate them for the present consumption given up. The "borrowers" of the fish would be able to repay more than they borrowed, because future catches will be larger. The additional amount of fish repaid represents the rate of interest paid for the fish.

Combined, the facts that productive processes take time, and people prefer to consume today rather than tomorrow result in a positive interest rate for most societies. Furthermore, the rate of interest will be determined by the increase in output made possible by deferring consumption. Thus, the rate of interest represents the opportunity cost of current consumption compared to future consumption.

The idea that consumption some time in the future is worth less than consumption now is called *discounting*. It is the common thread tying the topics of this chapter together. Discounting is a simple but extremely important tool. When people make economic decisions that involve more than one period of time, they must consider a discount factor.

This chapter sets forth the theory necessary to analyze multiperiod consumption and investment. It first discusses the role of interest rates in such decisions by introducing the concepts of future and present value. It uses these concepts to analyze multiperiod choices. The effect of inflation and uncertainty on investment decisions are discussed next. Finally, we describe how managers determine the rate at which they should extract from the ground a natural resource such as oil, gas, or coal.

The important concepts to be understood in this chapter are

1. Discounting a future stream of expenditures and returns to a single *present value*.
2. How utility-maximizing consumers decide their consumption pattern over time.
3. When a profit-maximizing producer should invest in a project yielding returns over several periods of time.
4. The effects of inflation on investment.
5. The optimal rate of resource depletion.

## 7.2 FUTURE VALUE, PRESENT VALUE, AND THE RATE OF INTEREST

To introduce the role played by interest in making multiperiod decisions, let us begin by considering the rate at which an asset can appreciate in value over time, then determine the cost of holding the asset.

## Future value

First, suppose that the asset is $100 cash and that this amount can be invested at a 10 percent rate of interest. Clearly, since

$$\$100 + .10(100) = (1 + .10)(100) = 1.10(100) = \$110, \qquad (7\text{--}1)$$

the $100 will be worth $110 in one year. In two years the $100 will be worth

$$\$110 + .10(110) = (1 + .10)(110) = \$121,$$

because we had $110 at the end of the first year and the interest is still 10 percent. However, from (7–1) we can substitute an equivalent expression for $110:

$$(1 + .10)(110) = (1 + .10)[(1 + .10)(100)] = (1 + .10)^2(100) = \$121.$$

Similarly, in three years, the investment will be worth

$$\$121 + .10(121) = (1 + .10)(121) = (1 + .10)[(1 + .10)^2(100)]$$
$$= (1 + .10)^3(100) = \$133.10,$$

and in $n$ years it will be worth $100 (1 + .10)^n$. Generalizing, an investment of $A for $n$ years at a rate of return $r$ will, at the end of the period, be worth

$$\$A (1 + r)^n.$$

## The cost of holding assets

This approach is applicable to an analysis of the cost of holding assets. For simplicity of analysis, let us assume that storage costs are zero. We also assume that the assets yield no returns while being held, and neither do they give any utility. Assets that fit this requirement are a ton of coal, a case of wine, or an ounce of gold. Suppose someone owns an asset that can either be held in the hope of appreciation or sold. Should the person sell the asset or keep it, expecting its value to increase? The answer depends upon the rate at which the price of the asset is expected to increase and the rate of interest. Assume the asset could be sold now for $1,000 and the proceeds invested at a 12 percent rate of interest. The value in five years will be

$$\$1000(1.12)^5 = \$2,488.$$

If the alternative is holding the asset for five years in the hope of an increase in value, the person would be better off holding the asset if its value in five years is expected to exceed $2,488. If its value is expected to be less than $2,488, the asset should be sold. While we have assumed zero storage costs, if such costs should exist, they must be subtracted from the expected value of the asset. In this example, the asset should be held if its expected value *net of storage costs* exceeds $2,488.

We have established the following principle, which summarizes the above point:

**Principle.** The value of a monetary asset worth $A now in n years with a rate of interest equal to r is $V = $A(1 + r)^n$. The cost of holding an asset for a specified number of years is the return that could be gained by selling the asset now and investing the money over the time period in question. If the asset is expected to increase in value at a rate greater than the relevant rate of interest, the asset should be held. If the expected rate of increase is less than the relevant rate of interest, the asset should be sold.

### Present value

We have just shown how the future value of an asset can be determined through the use of interest rates. We can now reverse the analysis to consider how to translate future values into current or present values. To understand this economic tool, consider what you would pay now for the right to be paid $100 one year from now. You certainly would not pay a full $100 for the promise of $100 in one year, because you could invest a lesser amount today and have $100 in one year. Suppose the interest rate is 10 percent. The most you would pay for $100 in one year (i.e., the present value) is $90.91 because

$$\$90.91(1 + .10) = \$100.$$

Since

$$\$95.24(1 + .05) = \$100,$$

the present value of $100 in one year is $95.24, if the interest rate is 5 percent. Over longer periods:

$$\$82.64(1 + .10)^2 = \$100 \tag{7-2}$$

and

$$\$75.13(1 + .10)^3 = \$100, \tag{7-3}$$

when the interest rate is 10 percent, the present values of $100 in two and three years respectively are $82.64 and $75.13.

Or, dividing through by the $(1 + .10)$ term, the present values of $100 in two and three years with a 10 percent interest rate are

$$PV = \frac{\$100}{(1 + .10)^2} = \$82.64$$

and

$$PV = \frac{\$100}{(1 + .10)^3} = \$75.13$$

To generalize, if the interest rate is $r$, the present value of $R$ dollars to be paid in $t$ years is

$$PV = \frac{R}{(1 + r)^t} .$$

We can expand the analysis to calculate the present value of an expected set of future payments or stream of income. Consider the maximum amount that someone would pay for an investment expected to yield the following stream of returns or income, payable at the end of each year:

| Year | Income |
|------|--------|
| 1 | $1,000 |
| 2 | 1,200 |
| 3 | 1,500 |
| 4 | 2,000 |
| 5 | 1,500 |

While the sum of the incomes over the period is $7,200, no one would pay this amount for the stream. In fact, the maximum amount anyone would pay is the sum of the present values of the income in each year. If the going rate of interest in the economy is 8 percent, the present value of this stream is

$$PV = \frac{\$1,000}{(1.08)} + \frac{\$1,200}{(1.08)^2} + \frac{\$1,500}{(1.08)^3} + \frac{\$2,000}{(1.08)^4} + \frac{\$1,500}{(1.08)^5} = \frac{\$1,000}{1.08} +$$
$$\frac{\$1,200}{1.166} + \frac{\$1,500}{1.259} + \frac{\$2,000}{1.360} + \frac{\$1,500}{1.469} = \$925.92 + \$1,029.15 +$$
$$\$1,191.42 + \$1,470.58 + \$1,021.10 = \$5,638.14$$

To summarize, let $R_t$ be the expected income in year $t$, let $r$ be the expected rate of interest, and let the income be paid for years 1 through $n$; the present value of this stream is therefore,

$$PV = \frac{R_1}{(1 + r)} + \frac{R_2}{(1 + r)^2} + \frac{R_3}{(1 + r)^3} + \cdots + \frac{R_n}{(1 + r)^n} = \sum_{t=1}^{n} \frac{R_t}{(1 + r)^t} .$$

Thus far, we have established the following principle:

**Principle.** The present value of (the maximum amount that would be paid for) an income stream is $PV = \sum_{t=1}^{n} [1/(1 + r)]^t R_t$, where $R_t$ and $r$

are, respectively, the net incomes and the expected rate of interest in year $t$ and the time horizon goes from year 1 to year $n$.

We should note two points before concluding our discussion of present and future value. First, for a given stream of income and interest rate, the more heavily the stream is weighted toward present (future) income relative to future (present) income, the greater (lower) is the present value of the stream. To illustrate, consider the following two income streams, each of which totals $20,000.

| Year | Stream 1 | Stream 2 |
|------|----------|----------|
| 1 ................. | $2,000 | $6,000 |
| 2 ................. | 3,000 | 5,000 |
| 3 ................. | 4,000 | 4,000 |
| 4 ................. | 5,000 | 3,000 |
| 5 ................. | 6,000 | 2,000 |

If the interest rate is 10 percent, the present value of stream 1 (weighted more heavily toward the future) is

$$PV = \frac{\$2,000}{1.1} + \frac{\$3,000}{(1.1)^2} + \frac{\$4,000}{(1.1)^3} + \frac{\$5,000}{(1.1)^4} + \frac{\$6,000}{(1.1)^5} = \$14,446.40.$$

The present value of the second stream (weighted more heavily toward the present) is

$$PV = \frac{\$6,000}{1.1} + \frac{\$5,000}{(1.1)^2} + \frac{\$4,000}{(1.1)^3} + \frac{\$3,000}{(1.1)^4} + \frac{\$2,000}{(1.1)^5} = \$15,883.46.$$

We can see that the stream weighted more heavily toward the present is worth $1,437 more than the future-weighted stream, even though the undiscounted sums of each stream are the same. This is not a very surprising conclusion. It takes a smaller present value to equal an amount in the distant future, since the compounding effect of interest has more time to work. But amounts in the near future are discounted less because the interest earnings are less for the corresponding present value.

Second, the choice of the interest rate can affect the ranking as to present values of different income streams. For example, if we have two separate income streams, the present value of one might be higher than that of the other using one interest rate to discount, while a different interest rate might make the other greater in present value. Consider the following two streams of income or cash flows:

| Year | Stream 1 | Stream 2 |
|------|----------|----------|
| 1...................... | $ 8,700 | $ 8,000 |
| 5...................... | 5,000 | 7,300 |
| 10..................... | 4,300 | 4,000 |
| 15..................... | 8,000 | 3,000 |
| 20..................... | 1,000 | 4,700 |
| Sum .............. | $27,000 | $27,000 |

Each undiscounted flow sums to $27,000.

Next, we calculate the present value of each stream using a 5 percent rate of interest.

$$PV_1 = \frac{\$8,700}{1.05} + \frac{\$5,000}{(1.05)^5} + \frac{\$4,300}{(1.05)^{10}} + \frac{\$8,000}{(1.05)^{15}} + \frac{\$1,000}{(1.05)^{20}} = \$19,068.20$$

$$PV_2 = \frac{\$8,000}{1.05} + \frac{\$7,300}{(1.05)^5} + \frac{\$4,000}{(1.05)^{10}} + \frac{\$3,000}{(1.05)^{15}} + \frac{\$4,700}{(1.05)^{20}} = \$19,008.87$$

The present value of stream 1 is $59.33 greater than the present value of stream 2. If we use a 10 percent rate of interest, the two present values are

$$PV_1 = \$14,735.32$$

$$PV_2 = \$14,764.44$$

With the higher interest rate, the present value of stream 2 is now greater. While the difference is not great, the example illustrates the principle that the choice of an interest rate can affect relative present values. We can see in this case that, when interest rates were doubled, they had a relatively stronger discounting effect on returns in the distant future than in the near future. Enough so that it made $PV_2 > PV_1$. An increase in interest rates has more impact on the denominator in a discounted stream when the exponents are large. One thousand dollars discounted one year at 5 percent is $952.38; raise the discount rate to 10 percent, and it is $909.09. If the $1,000 is discounted three years at 5 percent and 10 percent, the respective

| | Discount rate | |
|---|---|---|
| Years | 5 percent | 10 percent |
| 1 .............. | $952.38 | $909.09 |
| 3 .............. | 864.30 | 751.31 |
| 5 .............. | 783.70 | 621.12 |
| 7 .............. | 710.73 | 513.12 |
| 9 .............. | 644.75 | 424.35 |
| 11 .............. | 584.80 | 350.51 |

present values are \$864.30 and \$751.31. As shown by the table above, the impact of interest rates increases the longer the discount period.

## 7.3 CONSUMPTION OVER TIME

Now that we have analyzed the way the interest rate determines how assets or income can be allocated over time, we can introduce multiperiod analysis into the consumption decision. Recall that our previous discussion of consumer behavior in Chapters 3 and 4 was restricted to consumers who receive income and spend it on goods during a single period. Consumers can obviously transfer income and expenditures between different periods by saving current income and spending in the future or by borrowing to spend now and reducing future consumption to pay back the loan. We can use the basic principles developed in Chapter 3 and the above discussion of the interest rate to analyze the principles of allocating consumption over time. We shall, for graphical simplicity, restrict our analysis to two periods, but the basic points are applicable to allocation over any number of periods.

### Income allocation over time

Consider first the specific case of a consumer who will receive \$10,000 income in period 1 and \$12,000 in period 2. The consumer can borrow or lend between periods at a 10 percent rate of interest. In Figure 7–1, consumption in periods 1 and 2 is plotted, respectively, along the horizontal and vertical axes. Indifference curves I, II, and III represent a portion of the consumer's indifference map for consumption in the two periods. The marginal rate of substitution along each curve is the rate at which the consumer is willing to trade added consumption in period 2 for more consumption in period 1.

The straight line between 23 on the vertical and 20.909 on the horizontal axis is the budget line. The slope represents the rate at which the consumer can transfer income between periods. The vertical intercept is the amount that could be consumed in period 2 if all income in period 1 is saved at a 10 percent rate of interest. In this case, the consumption in period 2 would be

$$\$12,000 + (1 + .10)\,\$10,000 = \$23,000.$$

If the consumer borrows so as to consume as much as possible in period 1, \$20,909 could be consumed. That is, consumption would be $10,000 plus the present value of $12,000 which is

$$\$10,000 + \frac{\$12,000}{(1 + .10)} = \$20,909.$$

Note that the slope of the budget line is $(1 + .10)$ since

$$\frac{\$23,000}{\$20,909} = 1.10.$$

Thus, this slope represents the rate at which income can be transferred between periods. The consumer's income stream determines the initial location on the budget line. In Figure 7–1, the initial location of the consumer is point $F$ on the budget line. But consumers can be lenders or borrowers to maximize utility; they can borrow or lend so their income stream matches their desired consumption stream.

Using the analysis of Chapter 3, optimization is attained where the budget line is tangent to the highest attainable indifference curve. At this point, the marginal rate of substitution equals $(1 + .10)$. In Figure 7–1, the consumer borrows $2,000 in order to consume $12,000 in period 1. In period 2, $2,000 plus 10 percent interest on this amount must be repaid leaving $12,000 − $2,200 = $9,800 for consumption.

**FIGURE 7–1**
**Allocation of consumption over time**

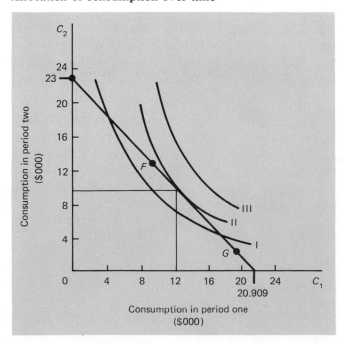

Consumption in period one
($000)

**FIGURE 7–2**
**Allocation of consumption over time**

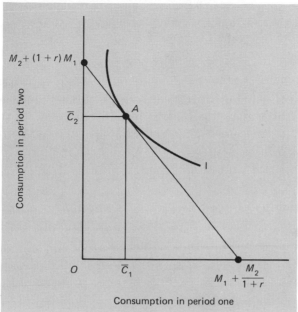

The general case is shown in Figure 7–2. Let $r$ be the interest rate, $M_1$ be income in period 1, and $M_2$ be income in period 2. If the consumer spends as much as possible in period 1, $M_1 + [M_2/(1 + r)]$ can be spent. This amount is the horizontal intercept. If consumption in period 2 is maximized, $M_2 + (1 + r)M_1$ is spent, which indicates the vertical intercept. The slope of the budget line is

$$\frac{M_2 + (1 + r)M_1}{M_1 + \dfrac{M_2}{(1 + r)}} = \frac{(1 + r)M_2 + (1 + r)^2M_1}{(1 + r)M_1 + M_2}$$

$$= \frac{(1 + r)[M_2 + (1 + r)M_1]}{[M_2 + (1 + r)M_1]} = (1 + r).$$

Thus, consumption can be transferred between periods at the rate $(1 + r)$. In other words, the price of consuming now rather than later is the interest rate.

Utility is maximized—the highest indifference curve is reached—at point $A$ on curve I. $\bar{C}_1$ is consumed in period 1, and $\bar{C}_2$ is consumed in period 2. If the consumer borrows in order to transfer income from period 2 to 1, $\bar{C}_1 = M_1 = B$, where $B$ is the amount borrowed from period 1 income and $\bar{C}_2 = M_2 - (1 + r)B$, since the loan must be repaid. If the consumer saves amount $S$ to spend more in period 2, $\bar{C}_1 = M_1 - S$ and $\bar{C}_2 = M_2 + (1 + r)S$.

In this section we have established the following principle:

**Principle.** A consumer can transfer income between periods at the rate (1 + r), where r is the rate of interest. Equilibrium is attained and utility maximized where the slope of the indifference curve for consumption in the two periods (the marginal rate of substitution) equals (1 + r), the rate at which the given interest rate permits the income transfer.

We want to emphasize that an income stream can place a consumer anywhere along the budget line. For instance, at point G in Figure 7–1, a consumer receives $19,000 in period 1 and only $2,000 in period 2. Utility is maximized by lending in this case rather than borrowing. Thus, both borrowing and lending allow consumers to reach a higher indifference curve.

## APPLICATION

### Discounting and consumption

The rate of interest and the concept of discounting have additional implications for consumer behavior other than determining the distribution or allocation of consumption over time. These tools of analysis are also frequently important in determining what goods to purchase and what methods of payment are least costly. In this application, we establish in three different contexts the value of discounting in making consumer decisions.

Consider first a recommendation made in the September 1980 issue of *Consumer Reports*. An article concerned with refrigerators made the point that, by choosing a refrigerator that is thrifty with electricity, you may save almost $400 over the appliance's lifetime. Since $400 is a significant portion of the price of a refrigerator, this figure would seem to represent a substantial saving. *Consumer Reports* arrived at the $400 figure by summing the monthly savings in electricity of $2.20 a month over the 15-year estimated lifetime of a refrigerator. From this type of analysis, it would appear that a purchaser would be wise to buy the energy-efficient appliance even though the price is almost $400 higher than that of an energy guzzler.

Clearly we can tell what is wrong with this advice. It is true that $2.20 saved each month for 15 years adds up to almost $400; but this is not the relevant figure. What should be estimated when comparison shopping is not the total saving but the present value of the saving, which is only $200.79, using a 10 percent interest rate (interest rates were around 12 percent at the time of the article); the estimate of the value of the energy savings made by *Consumer*

*Reports* was about double the actual value of the savings which should be used in making the purchase decision.

For another example of how discounting should enter the decision-making process, assume that someone is purchasing an air conditioning system for a house and is deciding among three systems. The three systems differ only in energy efficiency and in price. That is, let us assume that the three types will give the same amount of cooling, will require approximately the same amount of maintenance, and will have the same life expectancy—in this case, 15 years. The only difference is in the energy efficiency ratios (EER) of the systems. The higher the EER, the more energy efficient the system and the lower the electricity cost of a given amount of cooling. But the more efficient is the system, the higher its purchase price. Clearly, the prospective purchaser faces a present-value problem. Let us consider all costs and prices—including the rate of interest—as real values; that is, all values are net of inflation.

The *real rate* of interest (i.e., net of inflation) is expected to remain at approximately 5 percent over the 15-year time horizon. The electricity cost of running the least energy-efficient system (lowest EER) in real terms over the 15-year time horizon is expected to average $1,000 a month, or $12,000 a year. Thus, the total operating cost is expected to be $180,000. A more energy-efficient system has expected monthly operating costs of $800, or $9,600 a year; the total operating cost over the horizon is $144,000. Finally, the most energy-efficient system is expected to cost $700 a month, or $8,400 a year to operate. The total operating cost for the most efficient system would, therefore, be $126,000. The capital cost of the least efficient system is $15,000; of the more efficient system $30,000; and of the most efficient system $45,000. The total costs for each system are

Least efficient: $180,000 + $15,000 = $195,000
More efficient: $144,000 + $30,000 = $174,000
Most efficient: $126,000 + $45,000 = $171,000

While it would appear that the total cost of the most efficient system is lowest over the time horizon, these calculations are misleading. They do not take into consideration that the stream of operating costs must be discounted, because they are future costs. The present values of the operating costs for the three systems are

$$PV \text{ (least efficient)} = \sum_{t=1}^{15} \frac{\$12,000}{(1.05)^t} = \$124,558.99$$

$$PV \text{ (more efficient)} = \sum_{t=1}^{15} \frac{\$9,600}{(1.05)^t} = \$99,647.20$$

$$PV \text{ (most efficient)} = \sum_{t=1}^{15} \frac{\$8,400}{(1.05)^t} = \$87,191.30$$

When future costs are discounted, the most efficient, in an engineering sense, need not be the most efficient economically. As is shown below, the total present value of the cost of purchasing and operating the intermediate system is the lowest of the three and, under the assumptions made, that system should be chosen.

Present value of operating costs plus purchase price is

Least efficient: $124,588.99 + $15,000 = $139,558.99
More efficient: $ 99,647.20 + $30,000 = $129,647.20
Most efficient: $ 87,191.30 + $45,000 = $132,191.30

Finally, we can turn to the government's Truth in Lending Act to see how failure to distinguish the present value of a stream of payments from the stream itself leads to a distorted perspective. When lending consumers money for the purchase of items like automobiles, the lender is required to show in writing the *total* amount of interest that will be paid over the life of the loan. Thus, shorter-term loans for the same purchase price will obviously show a smaller total interest payment than will the longer-term loans—e.g., the total interest on a 24-month automobile loan is less than that shown for a 48-month loan of the same amount. But by now you know that payments three or four years from the purchase date have a lower value than payments in one or two years. Depending on the rate of interest, the difference could be significant, and the requirement as of now is misleading to the consumer. The Truth in Lending Act should require lenders to show the present value of interest paid on alternative loan plans.

## 7.4 THEORY OF INVESTMENT

The objective of any profit-maximizing firm making an investment is to obtain an aftertax stream of returns, the present value of which exceeds the cost of the investment. The firm first undertakes those projects with the greatest difference between present value and cost. Since the stream of returns and, generally, the stream of payments must be discounted, the concept of present value enters into each investment decision. The rate of interest is a key determinant of the amount of investment undertaken. It is important because a firm would invest in a productive asset only if the income stream the asset generated was larger than financially investing the same expenditure at the going interest rate.

### Investment decision making

To show the type of investment decision frequently made, consider the following example. Suppose a research and consulting firm is thinking about installing a small computer in its office. The total payments on the computer will be $250,000 a year for three years. Beginning in the second year, the net revenue (after subtracting operating costs) is expected to be, in real terms, $90,000 a year for the next 10 years. At the end of that period of time, the firm estimates that the computer will have a salvage value of $50,000. For calculation purposes, the firm uses a discount rate of 5 percent. Should the firm install the computer?

First, calculate the present value of the stream of purchase payments as

$$\frac{\$250,000}{1.05} + \frac{\$250,000}{(1.05)^2} + \frac{\$250,000}{(1.05)^3} = \$676,250.$$

Next, the discounted stream of net returns for 10 years, beginning in the second year, is

$$\frac{\$90,000}{(1.05)^2} + \frac{\$90,000}{(1.05)^3} + \ldots + \frac{\$90,000}{(1.05)^{11}} = \$745,740.$$

Finally, the present value of the salvage or resale is

$$\frac{\$50,000}{(1.05)^{11}} = \$29,200.$$

Thus, the research firm should purchase the computer, since the net present value is

$$PV \text{ (return + salvage } - \text{ cost)} = \$745,740 + \$29,200 \\ - \$676,250 = \$98,690.$$

Of course, a different discount rate will change the present value of a particular investment. For example, let us keep the same streams of cost and income as above, except the interest rate is now 12 percent. The present value of the purchase payments of $250,000 over three years is $600,457.82 with a 12 percent interest rate. The new present value of $90,000 a year for years 2 through 11 is $454,035.78. Finally, at a 12 percent interest rate, the present value of the $50,000 salvage price at the end of the 11th year is $14,373.81. Thus, with the higher interest rate, the present value of the investment is

$$PV = \$454,035.78 + \$14,373.81 - \$600,457.82 = -\$132,048.23$$

Since the investment has a negative value, it would not be made at the higher interest rate.

This example illustrates an important point. For most investments, the payments are made in early periods, while the returns are spread over a much larger period of time. Thus, the higher the interest rate, the lower the present value, and we would conclude that the high rates of interest discourage investment. We shall cover this principle in much greater detail later.

But discounting is helpful for making decisions other than whether or not to invest. It helps firms select investment alternatives. To take another example, assume that this research firm is considering buying an office building for $1 million—an investment—or renting the office space in the building for $60,000 a year for five years. For simplicity, assume that the rent would be paid at the end of each year. The firm estimates that, even with inflation, the wear and tear on the building will offset the appreciation in value. The building will sell for $1 million at the end of five years. Should the firm lease or buy the building? Assume the interest rate is 10 percent and, if the firm buys the building, the $1 million is payable now from assets owned by the firm.

The relevant stream is the discounted resale value of the building plus the present value of the stream of saving in rents (these savings add to profit—recall our discussion of opportunity costs) less the $1 million cost of the building:

$$PV = \sum_{t=1}^{5} \left(\frac{1}{1.10}\right)^t \$60,000 + \frac{\$1,000,000}{(1.10)^5}$$
$$- \$1,000,000 = -\$151,602.$$

Since the investment has a negative present value, the firm should not make the investment. It should invest the $1 million elsewhere, take the interest, pay the rent, and still have money left over. On the other hand, if the rate of interest is 5 percent, the present value of the investment is

$$PV = \sum_{t=1}^{5} \left(\frac{1}{1.05}\right)^t \$60,000 + \frac{\$1,000,000}{(1.05)^5} - \$1,000,000 = \$43,439.$$

Since the present value is positive, the firm should purchase the building.

To summarize our discussion, a firm undertakes investment to maximize aftertax discounted stream of net income. Obviously, a profit-maximizing firm wants any new capital purchased to have a flow of returns the present value of which is greater than, or at least equal to, the present cost of the capital. Therefore, the discounted income from an additional unit of capital to a firm and the cost of that unit are the key variables in the investment decision-making process. The present value of the expected stream of income from capital depends on several variables such as the market rate of interest, the price of goods produced, the expected lifetime and rate of deterioration of the capital, the flow of services or capital productivity, the prices of other inputs employed, and so forth. A firm should invest in assets that have a lifetime income stream with a positive (non-negative) present value; it should not invest in assets the income stream of which has a negative present value.

### Demand for investment

These principles allow us to develop a firm's demand for investment. Assume that a firm, during a particular time period, faces several investment opportunities, which can be ranked as to profitability. The firm may purchase capital goods either by selling debt instruments or by reducing its real money balances. We should note in passing that a firm's use of internal funds to finance investments does not change the cost of the investment. The opportunity cost of funds raised internally must be the relevant market rate of interest. We assume the firm may borrow or lend funds at the market rate of interest. While a firm may be restricted in its borrowing by its overall net worth, we will assume that this restriction is not a relevant barrier and ignore it in our analysis.

As noted above, the firm faces a given set of investment opportunities and can rank these according to expected rates of return, from the highest to the lowest. These rates of return are determined by the present values of the streams of net returns and the costs of the investments.[1] Figure 7-3 shows the firm's hypothetical situation. The amount of investment in a particular time period is plotted on the horizontal axis. The marginal rate of return from additional units of investment is plotted on the vertical. The down-sloping curve is the marginal return to investment (*MRI*), which shows the marginal rates of return forthcoming from each additional unit of investment.[2] Let us emphasize that the *MRI* curve does not show the return from the total amount of investment made; rather, it shows the rate of return from *each additional unit of investment.* The negative slope of the *MRI* curve reflects the assumption that firms can rank potential investments by rate of return from the highest to the lowest.

The theory of investment demand is relatively simple. The cost of an investment—whether financed externally or internally—is the

---

[1] Although rates of return can be calculated in various ways, a commonly employed formula is

$$\frac{PV - C}{C}$$

where *PV* is the present value of the future stream of net income and *C* is the (current) cost of the capital equipment.

[2] Recognizing that investments and the returns are in discrete amounts, we assume continuity for graphical simplicity.

**FIGURE 7–3**
**Marginal return to investment**

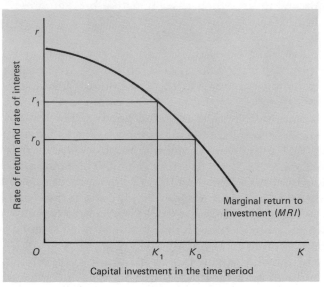

Capital investment in the time period

relevant rate of interest. If credit is unlimited, the firm would undertake all investments that have a rate of return that exceeds the rate of interest. If you can borrow funds at 10 percent, invest these funds, and earn 15 percent, you would do so. If you could earn only 8 percent on the investment, you would not make the transaction.

In Figure 7–3, assume the relevant rate of interest is $r_0$. The firm invests amount $K_0$ during the period, because at any level of investment less than $K_0$, the marginal rate of return from an additional unit of investment exceeds its cost, $r_0$; that is, $MRI > r_0$. The firm would not invest more than $K_0$, because the rate of return from any additional investment beyond this is less than $r_0$. If the rate of interest is $r_1$ rather than $r_0$, the firm would invest only $K_1$. Therefore, the $MRI$ curve or schedule shows the amount of investment forthcoming at each interest rate. This schedule is the firm's demand for capital during a particular period.

Before going any further, we should mention three points. First, the relevant rate of return is after taxation and not before taxation. Second, if the $MRI$ curve intersects the vertical axis below the relevant rate of interest, there is available no investment opportunity yielding a return greater than or equal to the rate of interest. Under this set of circumstances, the firm would undertake no investment. Finally, the firm might face credit limitations that do not allow investment to the point at which $MRI$ equals the interest rate.

The demand for investment by an entire industry is similar to the demand of a firm. We assume that the investment opportunities facing all firms in an industry can be ranked by potential rates of return, from highest to lowest. Thus, for the industry, the *MRI* curve slopes downward. But the *MRI* curve for the industry slopes downward for an additional reason. As we shall see in the next chapter, a competitive firm can invest and increase its output without lowering the price of the product. An entire industry cannot. If all firms undertake additional investment, the industry's output will increase and, because of down-sloping product demand, the price of the product will fall. Since the price of the product falls with additional investment, the rate of return from that investment is less than it would have been had output price not fallen. But the principle does not change. Firms invest until the marginal rate of return from investment equals the rate of interest. The lower the rate of interest, the more investment is undertaken.

Any change that affects the expected present value from investments, after taxation, shifts the *MRI* schedule and, therefore, the firm's demand for investment. For example, a large increase in wage rates would decrease present values (since it would decrease future net income), shift the marginal return on investment downward, and decrease the amount of investment forthcoming at any given interest rate. Technological change would have the opposite effect.

The effect of one such change, a change in the rate of taxation, on a firm's investment plans can be shown quite simply graphically. In Figure 7–4, *MRI* is the before-tax marginal rate of return on investment schedule. With no taxes and an interest rate of $r_0$, the industry would, with no credit restrictions, invest $K_0$. But any taxation lowers the present value of expected income from any investment and, therefore, shifts the *MRI* schedule downward. If taxation shifts this schedule to *MRI'* in Figure 7–4, investment would fall to $K_1$ at a rate of interest of $r_0$. We might note from *MRI* that the before-tax rate of return from the marginal investment equals the rate of interest. The difference reflects the magnitude of the tax and, of course, the proportion of the tax that firms can shift to consumers. The larger the tax, other things equal, the greater the effect on investment.

### Technological conversion

We have now set forth the foundation needed to analyze when it is profitable for a firm to switch technologies. Present-value calculations figure importantly in the analysis. The decision to change a technology or method of production is somewhat complicated. To give you an idea of how a producer makes this type of decision, we look at the conversion from gas and oil fuels to coal in production.

**FIGURE 7–4**
Effect of taxation on investment

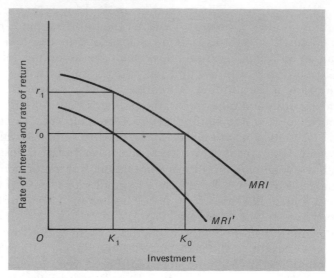

Since the mid 1970s, the federal government has put pressure on private businesses to convert plants from gas or oil to coal. Many electric utilities are required by law (Section 301 of the Fuel Use Act) to convert from gas by 1989. One might ask whether, if coal is a cheaper and a more certain energy source than oil or gas, total costs would not be reduced, and therefore the stream of profits be increased, by conversion to coal. The answer is that the stream of total profits may well increase, but it still may not be profitable to convert. We can use the concept of present value to analyze the problem of conversion from gas or oil to coal and, using this analysis, see why many firms are reluctant to convert.

To begin, let us assume a typical plant, say an electric utility, is currently using oil or gas as its source of energy. The firm owns all of its capital equipment. This plant and other equipment are expected to yield an income stream from the present period (call it year 1) through the final period in the horizon, year $H$. The present value of the income stream under existing conditions is

$$PV_1 = \sum_{t=1}^{H} \left( \frac{1}{1+r} \right)^t (R_t - C_t),$$

where

$r$ is the relevant rate of interest,
$R_t$ is total revenue in period $t$, and
$C_t$ is total cost in period $t$.

For simplicity let

$$Y_t = R_t - C_t$$

so that

$$PV_1 = \sum_{t=1}^{H} \left(\frac{1}{1+r}\right)^t Y_t.$$

The entire *undiscounted* stream of income is

$$Y = \sum_{t=1}^{H} Y_t.$$

Let us define a new concept, the *total discount* factor, $d_1$, as

$$d_1 = \frac{\sum_{t=1}^{H} \left(\frac{1}{1+r}\right)^t Y_t}{Y}.$$

Thus, the present value of the stream can be defined as

$$PV_1 = d_1 Y.$$

While the total discount factor depends upon the interest rate, the two are not equal. To show this, suppose $H$ is 20 years, $r$ is .12, and $Y_t$ is \$1,000 in each year. In this case

$$d_1 = \frac{\sum_{t=1}^{20} \left(\frac{1}{1+.12}\right)^t (\$1,000)}{\$20,000} = \frac{(7.462)(\$1,000)}{\$20,000} = .373.$$

The present value of this income stream is .373 times \$20,000 = \$7,460.

Next, suppose the firm purchases capital in order to convert to coal and let $E_t$ be the amount spent in certain periods on the conversion process. The value of $E_t$ depends upon the period in question and the type of conversion undertaken. For such new investments, one would assume that most such expenditures would come early in the time horizon. Therefore define

$$E = \sum_{t=1}^{H} E_t$$

and the total discount factor for energy conversion as $d_2$, where

$$d_2 = \frac{\sum_{t=1}^{H} \left(\frac{1}{1+r}\right)^t E_t}{E}.$$

Thus, the present value of the conversion expenditures is

$$PV_E = d_2 E.$$

Indicate the net revenue in any year $t$ (profit exclusive of conversion costs) when the capital is converted to save energy as $\overline{Y}_t$; thus,

$$\sum_{t=1}^{H} \overline{Y}_t = \overline{Y}.$$

Since energy conversion presumably lowers cost, $\overline{Y}$ would probably be greater than the other stream $Y$. Furthermore, one would not expect the total discount factor associated with $\overline{Y}$ to differ substantially from $d_1$, the discount factor associated with the old income stream, given similar time horizons and income distributions over time.

The present value of the net income stream with energy conversion is

$$PV_2 = \sum_{t=1}^{H} \left(\frac{1}{1+r}\right)^t \overline{Y}_t - \sum_{t=1}^{H} \left(\frac{1}{1+r}\right)^t E_t = d_1\overline{Y} - d_2E.$$

Note that $d_2$ does not equal $d_1$; in fact, $d_2$ would be expected to be considerably larger than $d_1$ because conversion expenditures would be made early in the horizon, while the returns would be spread over a considerably longer time horizon. Since the relation of $d_2$ to $d_1$ plays an important role in our analysis, we should ask why bias toward early expenditure increases the total discount factor.

Assume two $190 income streams spread over 4 years. The early-biased stream is distributed $100, $50, $30, $10; the future-biased stream is distributed $10, $30, $50, and $100. Continuing to assume an interest rate of 12 percent, the present value of the first stream is $158.31; the present value of the future-oriented second stream is $132.84. Since the total discount factor is present value divided by the total stream, the first discount factor is .833 and the second is .699. Thus, the discount factor associated with the more present-biased stream is .133 higher than the second. This brief example shows how the weighting of values toward the present or the future can change the discount factor.

In order to show the conditions under which it would be profitable for a firm to convert to coal, we compare present value under conversion, $PV_2$, to present value without conversion, $PV_1$. Dividing $PV_2$ by $PV_1$,

$$\frac{PV_2}{PV_1} = \frac{d_1\overline{Y} - d_2E}{d_1Y} = \frac{\overline{Y}}{Y} - \frac{d_2}{d_1}\frac{E_1}{Y}.$$

If conversion is to be profitable, $PV_2$ must exceed $PV_1$, or

$$\left(\frac{\overline{Y}}{Y}\right) - \frac{d_2}{d_1}\frac{E}{Y} > 1.$$

Note first that the relation of expenditures on conversion to either total cost or total revenue is irrelevant for decision-making purposes. To show what values are important, we write the above inequality as

$$(\overline{Y} - Y) > \frac{d_2}{d_1} E.$$

Obviously, the total increase in profits $(\overline{Y} - Y)$ must exceed the total expenditure on conversion, $E$. But this saving must exceed the expenditure by a much greater amount, since the up-front bias of the expenditures means $d_2/d_1$ is probably considerably larger than one. Thus, not only must the saving, $(\overline{Y} - Y)$, exceed the conversion expenditure, $E$, but it must be substantially greater, depending on the relative discount factors. Within this framework, one can analyze the profitability of conversion and the feasibility of enforced conversion.

In our original \$20,000 hypothetical income stream with $.373 = d_1$, suppose enforced energy conversion requires an expenditure of \$1,000, \$700 distributed in the first year and \$300 in the second. With the 12 percent interest rate, the total discount factor, $d_2$, is

$$d_2 = \frac{\dfrac{\$700}{1.12} + \dfrac{\$300}{(1.12)^2}}{\$1,000} = \frac{\$864.16}{\$1,000} = .864.$$

If the above inequality holds,

$$(\overline{Y} - \$20,000) > \frac{.864}{.373}(\$1,000) = \$2,316.$$

Thus, the \$1,000 conversion expenditure—5 percent of total net income—must increase total income by more than \$2,316—more than an 11 percent increase—for such an energy conversion to be economically feasible.

While we have described a way to estimate the economic feasibility of technological conversion in the context of fuel changeovers, analysts can use virtually the same methodology to predict the effect of changes in other variables, such as rates of taxation. The most important point of this discussion is that not only are present-value streams important in deciding when to alter a technology, but the way expenditures and incomes are distributed in the stream determines the profitability of conversion as well. It is possible for the present value of profits from the new technology to be greater than the discounted profits using the old technology and conversion to the new technology still not be profitable for the firm.

## 7.5 INFLATION AND INVESTMENT

Thus far in this chapter, we have used interest rates without distinguishing between the *real* rate and the *nominal* rate if there is inflation. The nominal interest rate is the money rate actually paid in the market. The real rate is the rate of interest after an inflation factor is subtracted from the nominal rate. It is net of inflation.

We now show that, under certain assumptions, it is unimportant to specify whether a nominal or real rate is used. For relatively low rates of inflation, as long as there is the same effect on interest rates as on the flow of returns, present value is unaffected.

### Theoretical effects of inflation

To begin, let $r$ be the *real* rate of interest and $R_t$ be the *real* return in period $t$ from an investment. The real present value of the stream is

$$PV = \sum_{t=1}^{H} \frac{R_t}{(1 + r)^t} \, .$$

If $i$ is the nominal, or money rate of interest, and $\pi$ is the rate of inflation, present value is

$$PV = \sum_{t=1}^{H} \frac{R_t(1 + \pi)^t}{(1 + i)^t} \, ,$$

under the assumption that the monetary returns increase at the same rate as the rate of inflation. Thus, if the real expected return next year is $R_1$, the money or nominal return will be $R_1(1 + .10)$, if the inflation rate is 10 percent.

But, if the real rate of interest is $r$, then to maintain $r$, the nominal rate of interest must be $i = r + \pi$. For example, suppose you have $100 and you want a 5 percent increase in the purchasing power of that money at the end of the year. If the inflation rate is 10 percent during the year, then you want at the end of the year

$$\$100 + .05(100) + .10(100) = (1 + .05 + .10)100 = (1 + r + \pi)100.$$

To increase purchasing power by 5 percent, the nominal rate of interest must be $i = r + \pi = 5\% + 10\% = 15\%$. Therefore, we may write the formula for present value as

$$PV = \sum_{t=1}^{H} \frac{R_t(1 + \pi)^t}{(1 + r + \pi)^t} \, .$$

Take a closer look at the denominator in the above equation. Notice that

$$1 + r + \pi = (1 + r)(1 + \pi) - r\pi.$$

The difference between $1 + r + \pi$ and $(1 + r)(1 + \pi)$ is the product $r\pi$. So, if $r = .05$ and $\pi = .05$, this term is .0025, a trivial difference. The lower the rate of inflation, the better $(1 + r)(1 + \pi)$ approximates $1 + i$. As the inflation rate gets larger, however, the poorer the approximation. For a 50 percent rate of inflation and a 5 percent real rate of interest, $r\pi = .025$, which is much larger than .0025. In this case, $(1 + r)(1 + \pi)$ overestimates the discount factor by a nontrivial amount. As a consequence, the $PV$ of investment is underestimated, using $(1 + r)(1 + \pi)$ as the discount factor.

Nevertheless, for low rates of inflation, we may write

$$PV = \sum_{t=1}^{H} \frac{R_t(1 + \pi)^t}{(1 + r + \pi)^t} \cong \sum_{t=1}^{H} \frac{R_t(1 + \pi)^t}{(1 + r)^t(1 + \pi)^t} = \sum_{t=1}^{H} \frac{R_t}{(1 + r)^t}.$$

It follows that investors would, under the assumption that inflation rates are low, pay the same amount for a particular stream of returns. We would, therefore, say that under these conditions, inflation is neutral with respect to investment because of the link between the nominal rate of interest and the rate of inflation.

But, with high rates of inflation, the present value

$$PV = \sum_{t=1}^{H} \frac{R_t(1 + \pi)^t}{(1 + r + \pi)^t} > \sum_{t=1}^{H} \frac{R_t(1 + \pi)^t}{(1 + r)^t(1 + \pi)^t} = \sum_{t=1}^{H} \frac{R_t}{(1 + r)^t}.$$

The nominal present value of a particular undiscounted stream of returns is greater than the real present value. We can see that, if the rate of inflation is high, the numerator is increasing faster than the denominator. Since nominal present value increases with inflation, investors would be willing to pay more for a given real stream of income than would be the case with little or no inflation. Investment is, therefore, not neutral with respect to high inflation rates.

## Actual effects of inflation

The above analysis is not meant to imply that, in reality, the amount of investment and the investment mix in an economy are not affected, or for that matter augmented, by inflation. This is far from the case. In the first place, inflation usually increases uncertainty, and increased uncertainty generally decreases the demand for investment. Investors may feel the returns would not keep up with inflation. Or they may believe that the rate of return and the allowable depreciation of the capital for tax purposes would not be sufficient to cover the replacement cost of the capital when the old capital wears out or is sold for salvage. While we have ignored to some extent capital replacement, this factor does play a significant role in investment decision making and tends to have a negative influence on investment.

Secondly, inflation and the tax structure interact unfavorably toward investment and the exchange of assets in general. Under our existing tax structure, nominal, not simply real, income is subject to taxation. Because of this, if a firm purchases an asset and resells it later, all gains are subject to taxation even though most or even all of the gains are due to inflation. For example, suppose a firm purchases an asset for $100,000. The value of the asset increases during a year at the same rate as the rate of inflation, 12 percent. Thus, the firm sells at $112,000, realizing a net gain of $12,000, which is taxed at the 48 percent corporate rate. The aftertax return is $6,240. The firm, in real terms, is $5,760 worse off, since the $112,000 is worth only $100,000 in year 1 dollars. In order to have $112,000 after taxation and merely break even, the rate of return must be 23 percent, almost double the rate of inflation.

Overall, inflation has increased the effective tax for corporations and stockholders. According to a study done by Martin Feldstein,[3] at the end of the 1960s, taxes paid by corporations either directly or indirectly by stockholders and creditors were 60 percent of the return on capital. By 1981, taxes took 70 percent of the return. Inflation had raised the effective tax rate by increasing nominal, but not real, earnings, capital gains, and inventory accounting profits. This increase in tax rates is partially responsible for a tremendous decline in net private investment. In the early 1980s, the United States had the lowest rate of new investment in the industrialized world. From the end of the 1960s to the early 1980s, net investment had fallen from 4.2 percent of GNP to 3 percent, a decline of nearly 30 percent.

In a world of perfectly anticipated inflation, free of institutional constraints and regulations, the nominal rate of interest and income streams would adjust in an inflationary economy so that firms would realize present values on earning streams approximately equal to those without inflation. The nominal rate of interest would include the rate of inflation and the real rate of interest. But in the actual world in which firms exist, there frequently is uncertainty and there exist constraints on the nominal returns firms may earn. Therefore, in this world, inflation can inhibit private investment.

## APPLICATION

### The effects of inflation on public utilities

Inflation has no effect on the present value of an income stream if the discount rate in the denominator and the periodic returns in the

---

[3] M. Feldstein, "Reviving Business Investment," *The Wall Street Journal*, June 19, 1981.

numerator are equally affected by the rate of inflation. Often this is not the case for industries whose prices are regulated. Publicly regulated utilities—for instance, electricity and telephone companies—must seek permission from a state regulatory board to increase their rates.

"Rate hearings" can last more than a year. For example, in 1978, the average length of time between a request for a price change and a regulatory decision was 13.6 months for electric utilities.[4] Such delays are called "regulatory lags." During this time, costs are rising as a result of inflation, while prices stay fixed unless an interim increase is granted.

Another problem for utilities is that regulators grant price increases at a pace less than the rate of inflation. Table 7–1 shows the

**TABLE 7–1**
**Price changes in regulated industries, 1961–1977**

| Industry | 1961– 1965 | 1965– 1969 | 1969– 1973 | 1973– 1977 | Average 1961– 1977 |
|----------|-----------|-----------|-----------|-----------|--------------------|
| Electricity and gas.......... | −0.1 | 0.2 | 4.3 | 11.3 | 3.9 |
| Telephone ................ | −0.5 | 0.2 | 2.5 | 2.9 | 1.3 |
| Railroad transportation ...... | −2.6 | 1.0 | 7.2 | 8.6 | 3.6 |
| Motor freight transportation ............ | 0.6 | 2.3 | 3.6 | 5.7 | 3.1 |
| Unregulated service industries ........ | 1.7 | 4.4 | 4.7 | 7.8 | 4.7 |

Source: Paul MacAvoy, *The Regulated Industries and the Economy* (New York: W. W. Norton, 1979).

price changes allowed several regulated industries compared to unregulated service industries between 1961 and 1977. We assume that the unregulated industries raise prices to keep up with inflation. For each industry, the average increase in price is less than that of the unregulated service sector. Rate of return regulation distorts the impact of inflation on the earning stream of a utility. While costs rise freely, prices are not allowed to adjust as rapidly. In the discount stream, the denominator is going up faster than the numerator.

The immediate implication of such regulation is that the profitability of investment is less in regulated utilities than in unregulated industries. Table 7–2 reveals that this is indeed the case. In the long run, investor-owned utilities will have trouble attracting capital to expand. In the past 20 years, the stock prices of utilities have been depressed, reflecting an unwillingness of investors to finance further utility growth.

---

[4] Paul MacAvoy, *The Regulated Industries and the Economy* (New York: W. W. Norton, 1979), p. 108.

TABLE 7-2
Rate of return on assets in regulated industries, 1962-1977

| Industry | 1962-1965 | 1966-1969 | 1970-1973 | 1974-1977 | Average 1962-1977 |
|---|---|---|---|---|---|
| Electricity and gas .......... | 5.0 | 5.1 | 5.2 | 5.7 | 5.3 |
| Telephone ................. | 5.2 | 5.2 | 5.4 | 5.8 | 5.4 |
| Railroad transportation ...... | 3.3 | 3.3 | 3.4 | 4.2 | 3.6 |
| Motor freight transportation ............. | 5.5 | 5.8 | 5.9 | 6.1 | 5.8 |
| Unregulated service industries ......... | 5.9 | 6.2 | 6.0 | 6.6 | 6.2 |

Source: Paul MacAvoy, *The Regulated Industries and the Economy* (New York: W. W. Norton, 1979).

## 7.6 DEPLETION OF NATURAL RESOURCES: PRICING OVER TIME

During the past decade, the topic of the depletion of natural resources has received a considerable amount of attention. We frequently hear that, because there are finite supplies of certain natural resources, such as oil, gas, and coal, the world will soon run out of these minerals if current rates of depletion continue. Economists assert that market forces can prevent such a disaster. Many policymakers argue that only governmentally imposed conservation will prevent or at least postpone such a doomsday. We can analyze the situation using the tools developed in this chapter.

### Rates of extraction

Assume that a firm owns a mineral deposit such as an ore body or oil field and knows approximately how much of the resource can be extracted. Suppose, also, that the firm expects the price of the natural resource to rise. Should the firm extract and sell some of the resource, or should it hold the resource for future sale? For analytical purposes, we will assume the relevant price for decision-making purposes is the sale price of the resource less the cost of extraction. We will also assume that the decision is simply whether or not to extract and not how much to extract. If the firm chooses to produce, we assume for now that the rate of extraction is predetermined. (The profit-maximizing rate of extraction is discussed in the next chapter.

We can deduce from our previous discussion on the future value of assets that the decision concerning whether or not to produce depends crucially upon the rate of interest. If the price is expected to rise at a rate lower than the rate of interest, the firm will produce.

That is, we know that under these conditions the firm could extract the mineral, sell it, then invest the returns at the market rate of interest and gain a larger return than could be realized by letting the deposit appreciate in value. Of course, if the firm expects the price of the resource to appreciate at a rate greater than the interest rate, the best course of action is to withhold extraction until the future.

Thus, we can condense the decision-making process into a single rule. If $P_t$ is the future price in time period $t$, then the future price under which the firm would be indifferent between producing and selling now or producing and selling in period $t$ is

$$P_t = P_0(1 + r)^t,$$

where $r$ is the rate of interest, and $P_0$ is the present price of the resource. If price in period $t$ is expected to exceed $P_t$, the firm should withhold production; if not, it should produce and sell.

Now let us examine what we would expect in the economy as a whole. Suppose the economy has a finite amount of a particular resource and this resource in the ground is owned by many private firms. Suppose also that the industry has been producing at some particular rate. Now let some firms notice that the economy is depleting its supply of the resource. These firms would deduce that the reduced supply would probably cause future prices to increase more rapidly; let us say at a rate greater than the rate of interest. These firms would, therefore, withhold extraction in present periods in order to shift it to the future when price is expected to be above the break-even price. Expected prices change the rate of extraction.

But the decrease in supply from the decrease in present production would, as we know, drive up current prices relative to future prices. How much would they be driven up? Suppose so many firms withhold production that the current price rises to the point that the future price is less than $(1 + r)^t P_0$; the future expected price does not exceed the present market price invested for $t$ periods. Some firms would then be induced to increase the current rate of extraction. We would expect the adjustment process to continue until the price expected in each future period equals the present price adjusted for interest.

Thus, when the price of the resource increases at the same rate as the rate of interest, firms would have no incentive to increase or decrease production. If there is, in fact, a finite amount of the resource, equilibrium requires price to increase at approximately the same rate as the rate of interest. If price is rising less rapidly than the interest rate, firms will increase production now, driving down present prices relative to future prices. If the price is rising more rapidly than the rate of interest, firms will tend to decrease production, driving up present prices relative to future prices. Thus, market forces tend to force prices along an equilibrium path set by market rates of interest.

But certain factors tend to disrupt this equilibrium path. Clearly, discoveries of new deposits of the resource lead firms to believe that future prices will be lower than they would have been otherwise. These discoveries lead to increased production and decreased prices. Also, increases in price tend to decrease the quantity demanded as consumers substitute away from the resource that is becoming more and more scarce and into resources with relatively lower prices.

In fact, the problem with this scenario of finite resource supply with prices increasing at the same rate as the rate of interest is that increasing prices lead to the development of products and technologies that can change the adjustment drastically. As we noted, increasing prices will decrease consumption of the resource. But the increased price will lead to research to discover substitutes; and, if such substitutes are discovered or invented, the demand for the resource will fall. Alternatively, if increased prices lead to new technologies, the supply of the resource can rise. Moreover, while all resources at any given time are, in fact, fixed in supply, the actual known reserves depend upon the price of the resource. Take, for example, oil fields that were uneconomical to produce from when the price was $10 a barrel for crude. When prices rose to $30 a barrel, some of these fields became very economical and quite profitable.

A good illustration of these effects is a field in East Central Texas called the Austin Chalk. When most domestic crude was regulated and this oil was selling at around $6 a barrel, no one could produce profitably from the field. The problem was that the Austin Chalk was of such low permeability that, under the available technology, it was unprofitable to drill in the area even though geologists knew oil was there. After price was allowed to increase, drillers developed a new technology that permitted profitable drilling in a previously unprofitable area. What had not been considered reserves a few years ago are now reserves; the Austin Chalk is one of the most rapidly developing oil fields in the country—and a very profitable one at that.

Oil shale gives us another example. There is a considerable amount of oil shale now in the Rocky Mountains, but with present oil prices and present technology, it is not profitable to extract oil from shale. However, firms are working now to improve the technology because, if oil prices get much higher, it will be profitable to do so. Thus shale, not now counted as reserves, may well be considered reserves in the future.

Another function of higher resource prices is that they increase the incentive to explore and develop new reserves. Exploration is similar to other inputs into the production process. Firms will carry out exploration to search for new reserves as long as the expected marginal gain exceeds the marginal cost. Given a particular probability of success from exploration, the higher the price of the resource, the higher the expected marginal gain and, hence, the more exploration that will be undertaken. And the more exploration, the greater will be the reserves.

**Principle.** If a mineral resource is known to be in finite supply, market forces will ensure that the price of the resource will increase at the same rate as the rate of interest. But the increasing price has two consequences. The higher price will induce firms to develop substitutes for the resource. Second, the higher price will induce more exploration, more production from previously unprofitable deposits, and the development of new technology to lower the cost of extraction.

## APPLICATION

### Historical resource price trends

We can easily see how well historical resource prices have followed the trend line set by the rate of interest. That is, we can examine whether mineral firms have extracted too rapidly or too slowly from a market point of view. Did producers withhold production too little or too much? We can use our simple price formula for extraction to examine the question. Let $P_t$ and $P_{t+1}$ be the historical prices of a resource in years $t$ and $t + 1$ respectively and let $r_t$ be the interest rate in year $t$. If

$$P_t(1 + r_t) > P_{t+1},$$

firms should have extracted more in year $t$ relative to year $t + 1$. Too much production was withheld. If the inequality is reversed, firms should have withheld more production in period $t$ because such stockpiling would have been profitable. Thus, if $P_t(1 + r_t) > P_{t+1}$, firms extracted too little in year $t$; if $P_t(1 + r_t) < P_{t+1}$, firms extracted too much in year $t$. Because of uncertainty, equality would practically never hold. But we would assume that disturbances would be random, and firms would have extracted too much of a resource in about half the years and too little in about half.

Let us examine changes in mineral prices in the United States from 1900 through 1975. In Table 7–3, column (1) lists 14 depletable resources and column (2) shows the total number of years from 1900 through 1975 for which data were available. Columns (3a), (4a), (5a), and (6a) show the number of years that additional "holdbacks" in extraction for one year would have resulted in a gain using four different rates of interest. That is, these columns show the

**TABLE 7–3**
**Number of years production holdbacks in anticipation of price increases would not have resulted in losses for 14 depletable resources from 1900 through 1975, using four interest rates**

| (1) | (2) | (3a) | (3b) | (4a) | (4b) | (5a) | (5b) | (6a) | (6b) |
|---|---|---|---|---|---|---|---|---|---|
| | Total number of years | R = AAA | | R = CPI + 2% | | R = CPI + 3% | | BTM | |
| Resource | | Number | Percent | Number | Percent | Number | Percent | Number | Percent |
| Aluminum | 75 | 21 | 28 | 22 | 29 | 20 | 26 | 6 | 8 |
| Bauxite | 75 | 18 | 24 | 23 | 30 | 21 | 28 | 5 | 6 |
| Coal | 75 | 26 | 34 | 25 | 33 | 21 | 28 | 9 | 12 |
| Copper | 75 | 38 | 50 | 34 | 45 | 33 | 44 | 14 | 18 |
| Crude petroleum | 71 | 26 | 37 | 25 | 35 | 24 | 34 | 11 | 15 |
| Gold | 75 | 7 | 9 | 13 | 17 | 12 | 16 | 5 | 6 |
| Iron ore | 75 | 25 | 33 | 28 | 37 | 24 | 32 | 9 | 12 |
| Lead | 75 | 31 | 41 | 31 | 41 | 29 | 38 | 15 | 20 |
| Lime | 70 | 18 | 25 | 18 | 25 | 14 | 19 | 4 | 5 |
| Magnesium | 57 | 14 | 24 | 13 | 22 | 13 | 22 | 3 | 5 |
| Nickel | 75 | 29 | 38 | 34 | 45 | 32 | 42 | 7 | 9 |
| Silver | 75 | 27 | 36 | 27 | 36 | 25 | 33 | 12 | 16 |
| Tin | 75 | 34 | 45 | 32 | 42 | 30 | 40 | 15 | 20 |
| Zinc | 75 | 36 | 48 | 32 | 42 | 30 | 40 | 11 | 14 |
| Average | | 24 | 34 | 25 | 34 | 22 | 32 | 8 | 11 |

*Number of years holdbacks would not have resulted in losses*

Source: G. Anders, W. P. Gramm, and S. C. Maurice, *Does Resource Conservation Pay?* International Institute for Economic Research, Paper 14, July 1978, pp. 23—29.

number of years that the increase in resource price exceeded the alternative investment yields at different rates of return. The interest rate used in column (3a) is the AAA corporate bond rate, the rates used in (4a) and (4b) are, respectively, the percentage change in the consumer price index (CPI) plus 2 and 3 percent. Column (6a) uses the before-tax rate of return in manufacturing. Columns (3b), (4b), (5b), and (6b) show the *percentage* of the total time additional extraction holdbacks at the various interest rates would have resulted in economic gains, i.e., $P_t(1 + r_t) < P_{t+1}$. That is, the columns show how often industries were extracting too rapidly.

Using the AAA corporate bond rate, in only 34 percent of the years would firms have gained by holding back extraction from one year to the next; 66 percent of the time they would have incurred losses. Obviously, if storage costs were encountered in holding the resource, the percentage of time that net gain would have been achieved by holdbacks could have been even lower. Employing the percentage change in the consumer price index plus 2 percent as a discount rate, 34 percent of the time firms again would have obtained gains. With the percentage change in consumer prices plus a 3 percent premium as a discount rate, the percentage of years during which production holdbacks would have resulted in economic gain drops to 32 percent. When the before-tax rate of return on manufacturing is employed as a discount rate, only 11 percent of the time would production holdbacks have resulted in an economic advantage for the decision maker.

The implication of these results is, if firms felt *certain* about the future, the returns from future price increases would be eliminated, because, if prices were expected with certainty to increase more rapidly than the rate of interest, firms would withhold production, driving up current prices relative to future prices. If the reverse were expected, firms would increase present rates of extraction relative to future rates.

One might expect profits from short-term holdbacks about half the time and losses about half of the time, with the average returns from holdbacks being about zero. From a profitability and social point of view, it appears that firms have exploited resources too slowly during the 20th century. Of course, this could have occurred because of the frequency of disruptions, such as technological change and new discoveries.

## 7.7 EFFECTS OF RISK AND UNCERTAINTY

With the exception of the brief discussion of the effect of inflation on investment because of the resulting uncertainty, we have ignored the effects on investment when risk and uncertainty exist. We have also ignored consumption decisions made under uncertainty. This section briefly analyzes the way risk and uncertainty can influence investment and consumption decisions.

Until now, our discussion of consumption and investment over time has generally assumed economic decision makers know future incomes, prices, and costs. This assumption is usually very useful for analytical purposes, but for some types of analysis, we need to assume future economic variables can take several possible values. For instance, a particular investment may have several possible income streams because there is uncertainty over the way future prices and costs will behave.

### Expected value

To keep things manageable, we assume that decision makers know the probability of an uncertain event occuring. While even this is not always true, it is a useful approximation in understanding the functioning in most markets. Suppose decision makers know the likelihood of some uncertain event occuring. With this information, consumers and investors can determine what will happen "on average," or what they can "expect" to happen if they had to make the same choice involving uncertain events many times. The expected outcome or the expected value is defined as follows:

**Definition.** If a particular event has several potential numerical outcomes, designated $X_1$, $X_2$, $X_3$, . . . , $X_n$ and the probability of each outcome is $p_1, p_2, p_3, . . . , p_n$ where $0 \leqq p_i \leqq 1$ for all $i$ and $\sum_{j=1}^{n} p_j = 1$, the *expected* value of the event is $\sum_{j=1}^{n} p_j X_j$. Thus, the expected value is the sum of the outcomes weighted by the probability of occurrence.

As an example of expected value, consider how much someone would expect to win from a lottery after playing a large number of times. In the lottery, the probability of winning \$10,000 is 1 percent; of winning \$5,000, 2 percent; and of winning \$1,000, 3 percent. Since the probability of winning some amount is 6 percent, the probability of winning nothing is 94 percent. After a large number of draws, a person could expect to win on average:

$$V = .01(\$10,000) + .02(\$5,000) + .03(\$1,000) + .94(0) = \$230.$$

Thus, a person who played many times would pay up to \$230 for the ticket.[5] This amount is the expected value of the investment.

---

[5] People do, of course, pay more than the expected value of lotteries such as in the numbers racket because they attach more weight (attach more utility to) the possible winnings than to the cost of the ticket.

The concept of expected value can help consumers maximize utility under uncertainty. A simple example can illustrate the usefulness of this tool. Imagine that during your next summer vacation you have a choice of visiting relatives—which can get dull, but you know with virtual certainty what will take place during your stay. On the other hand, you can visit an exotic Caribbean island. This is much more of an adventure, but things that could happen might be very unpleasant. For instance, you could catch malaria, be caught in a hurricane, or get stuck in the middle of a revolution. What should you do?

Compare the utility of visiting relatives $(U_R)$ with the *expected* utility of a vacation in the Caribbean. Without any disasters the, island vacation yields utility, $U_C$, where $U_C > U_R$. But there is much less satisfaction in the trip if you get malaria—call it $U_M$; suffer through a hurricane $(U_H)$; or witness a war $(U_W)$. So,

$$E(U_C) = P_M U_M + P_H U_H + P_W U_W + (1 - P_M - P_H - P_W) U_C,$$

where $P_M$, $P_H$, and $P_W$ are, respectively, the probabilities of malaria, hurricane, and revolution. If $U_R > E(U_C)$, then visit the relatives, but if $U_R < E(U_C)$, serious consideration ought to be given to the island trip. You still may not be sure about taking the trip because of *risk aversion*. Some consumers and investors value certainty in itself. Even though you might expect to be happier visiting the Caribbean, on average, over a large number of outcomes, the chance of a very unpleasant time during any single visit may bias your choice toward the relatives. We will discuss risk aversion more in the context of investment decisions.

### Risk effects in investment

Business decisions are also made under uncertainty. A potential investment could have many possible present values, each of which has a specific probability of occurrence, depending upon external circumstances. When considering potential investments, the firm would not simply make the decision using only one possible stream of income, but would use the expected present value of the possible streams. Moreover, the variance, or possible dispersion of the present values, enters the decision process also.

Consider the following investments with the possible present values given below:

Both investments have the same expected present value, $290,000, but the streams are distributed quite differently. For investment A, there is little variation around the present value—the minimum return possible is $100,000; the maximum, $500,000. In the case of investment B, $1 million can be made, but the investment could lose $300,000, or possibly make zero profit. One investor

| Investment A | | Investment B | |
| --- | --- | --- | --- |
| Probability | Possible present value | Probability | Possible present value |
| .10 ........... | $100,000 | .10 ......... | −$300,000 |
| .80 ........... | 300,000 | .25 ......... | 0 |
| .10 ........... | 500,000 | .25 ......... | 200,000 |
| | | .20 ......... | 500,000 |
| | | .15 ......... | 800,000 |
| | | .05 ......... | $1,000,000 |
| Expected present value ..... | $290,000 | Expected present value ... | $ 290,000 |

might prefer A, while another would prefer B, depending upon the
risk aversion of the investors. One may prefer the chance to make $1
million, even with the greater probability of making nothing or even
losing $300,000. Evidence of this type of optimistic behavior is the
opening of thousands of small businesses every year, even though

**FIGURE 7–5**
**Income distributions**

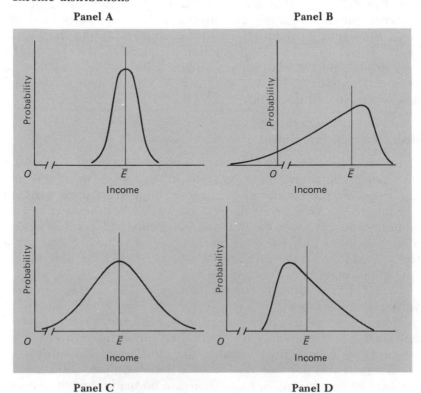

the vast majority fail in a year or two. The great success stories, few as they are, encourage the investors.

A few of the many possible distributions of income streams are shown geometrically in panels A, B, C, and D, Figure 7–5. In each panel, the possible distribution of discounted streams of income from a particular investment is graphed along the horizontal axis. For graphical exposition, we assume that the distribution is continuous. The probability of each stream is plotted along the vertical axis. The expected present value, $\bar{E}$, is the same for each investment.

Panel A shows a small symmetrical distribution around the expected value $\bar{E}$. While the investment cannot lead to incomes much above $\bar{E}$, it will not give incomes much below. Panel B shows a distribution that can lead to incomes far below $\bar{E}$, or even losses. Incomes much above $\bar{E}$ are not probable. Panel C indicates a symmetrical distribution around $\bar{E}$. But, in contrast to the distribution in panel A, incomes much higher and much lower than $\bar{E}$ are possible; that is, the variance is much higher. Finally, the distribution in D is such that incomes much lower than $\bar{E}$ are not too probable, but very high incomes are possible.

Thus, under uncertainty, investors must consider several factors. First, of course, is the expected present value. But they must also consider the variance of the distribution and how the distribution is skewed—i.e., contrast the distributions in B and D. But, for analytical purposes, we should emphasize that the most useful assumption is that investors consider only the expected present value, or that they know the prospective income stream.

## 7.8 SUMMARY

This chapter has used the concept of present value to develop the theories of consumption allocation over time, investment, and extraction of mineral resources. We can summarize the three theories in the following principles:

**Principle.** A consumer will allocate consumption expenditure between two consecutive periods so that the marginal rate of substitution between consumption in the two periods equals one plus the rate of interest $(1 + r)$. This rule maximizes utility for the consumer. If the periods are not consecutive, the MRS between consumption equals $(1 + r)^i$ where $i$ is the difference in the periods.

**Principle.** Firms would be willing to pay for an investment up to the present value of the stream of income from that investment. An industry's demand for investment is the marginal return from investment schedule. Firms invest up to the point at which the marginal return from the last investment equals the rate of interest.

**Principle.** If a natural resource is fixed in supply, firms will choose to extract the resource at a rate such that price (that is, selling price less the cost of extraction) rises at the same rate as the rate of interest. If price is expected to rise more rapidly, firms will increase present production, driving down current relative to future prices. The caveat is that resources are generally not fixed in supply. Higher prices lead to new technology, more exploration, and exploitation of reserves that were not previously available.

Finally, few economic choices are made by decision makers knowing with certainty future prices, incomes, and costs. Under uncertainty, consumers and business decision makers are helped by using the concept of expected value. Consumers are concerned with maximizing expected utility, and the variance in possible outcomes will affect the choices they make. Similarly, investors look at the expected present value of a stream of income from an investment. Variance in earning streams is an important influence on the choice of projects undertaken. A decision maker might make a choice with a lower expected present value over one with higher expectations, depending upon the variance.

## TECHNICAL PROBLEMS

1. An ice cream distributor is thinking about buying another ice cream truck. The price of the truck is $20,000, and it is estimated that the truck will increase profits $4,000 per year for 10 years. Explain how the distributor should decide whether or not to buy the truck.

2. You are hired as an economic consultant to a firm that produces and sells wine. Over a relevant period, the wine gets better as it ages; therefore, the longer it ages, the higher the price the wine maker can get for the wine. Explain precisely the method that you would use in order to advise the wine maker how long to age the wine before putting it on the market. Assume you have all the required technical information.

3. Assume the average price of oil is $30 a barrel and the interest rate is 10 percent. The government wants to stockpile oil in reservoirs (assume they are free). What is the cost of stockpiling this oil over the next 10 years? What if the interest rate is only 4 percent?

4. Explain why the stockpiling cost mentioned in problem 3 is just as real a cost to the government—the taxpayers—as the actual cost of purchasing the oil or of storing the oil if such costs are not zero. Who would benefit and who would lose if

these opportunity costs are ignored when making a stockpiling decision for strategic purposes?

5. Suppose you own a deposit of a natural resource, the price of which is $2 a pound (price net of costs). The rate of interest is 12 percent. What would the price of the resource have to be in five years to make extraction holdbacks economical over this period? Answer the question under the assumption that the interest rate is 5 percent.

**FIGURE E.7–1**

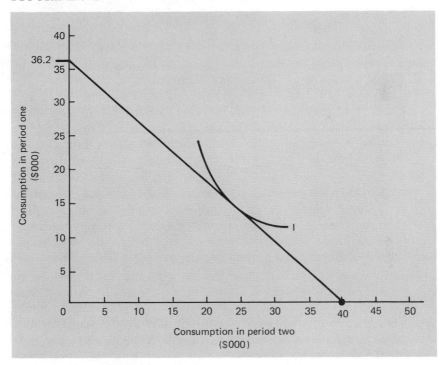

6. Use Figure E.7–1 to answer the following questions. Income in period 1 is $20,000:
   *a.* What is the rate of interest?
   *b.* What is income in period 2?
   *c.* The consumer spends $_____ in period 1 and $_____ in period 2.
   *d.* The consumer's marginal rate of substitution between consumption in periods 1 and 2 is _____.
   *e.* Suppose the interest rate increases by 5 percent. What happens to consumption in periods 1 and 2, if consumption in both periods is a normal good?

7.  The rate of interest is $r$. A consumer receives $A in both periods 1 and 2, and consumes $A in each period—i.e., the consumer maximizes utility by neither borrowing or lending. Use a graphical exposition to answer the following questions. (Hint: the consumer can continue to consume $A in each period regardless of the rate of interest.)

    a.  What happens to the consumer's utility if the interest rate increases?

    b.  If interest rates increase, does the consumer become a net (borrower, lender)?

    c.  What happens to the consumer's utility if the interest rate decreases?

    d.  If interest rates decrease, does the consumer become a net (borrower, lender)?

8.  The current return from an investment is $10,000 per year. The real rate of interest is 5 percent and the rate of inflation is 5 percent. Compare the present value of the return five years from now using the real and the nominal rates of interest. (The return is expected to rise at the same rate as the rate of inflation.) Make the comparison with a 50 percent rate of inflation.

9.  A firm can lease a piece of capital equipment for five years at $100,000 a year, or it can purchase the capital now, use it for five years, then sell it at the end of the period for one fourth of the purchase price. If the rate of interest is 10 percent, what is the maximum price of the capital at which it would be economical to purchase rather than lease?

10. In Figure E.7–2, MRI is an industry's marginal return on investment before taxation. If the interest rate is 10 percent, how much investment will be undertaken? At the same rate of interest, how much will investment decline if a tax of 20 percent is placed on the return to capital? If the interest rate rises to 13 percent and the tax rate increases to 50 percent, what happens to investment?

## ANALYTICAL PROBLEMS

1.  Nuclear power plants require large capital outlays to build and relatively small amounts of money to operate. During the many years of construction, they are producing no electricity revenues whatsoever. In light of the time lag between money outlays and electricity revenues, explain why long-term interest rates are so important to public utilities in deciding if and when to build such plants. If prices are fixed by regulation, how would you expect inflation to affect the development of power plants?

**FIGURE E.7–2**

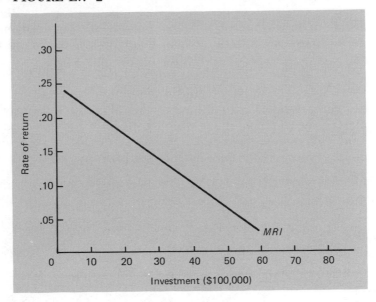

2. The president of a large chemical firm recently stated that it was more profitable for his firm to pirate the inventions of other companies than it was to engage in original research. How does this behavior affect the value of R&D spending?

3. Suppose you are a lawyer representing a person whose spouse was killed at work through proven negligence of the employer. The firm obviously cannot measure, and therefore compensate for, the grief of the survivor. It will compensate for the *economic* loss because of the lost earnings of the deceased, who, incidentally, was 50 years old at death. Mandatory retirement is at age 65. The firm is willing to make a flat cash settlement now if you can show the economic loss. What information do you need? How would you figure the economic loss if you had the information?

4. Bonds have a printed coupon rate and a face value. The face value is the amount the borrower pays the lender when the bond matures. Equal periodic payments are made to the lender. The amount of the payments is the coupon rate multiplied by the face value of the bond. If the market rate of interest is equal to the coupon rate, the bond sells for its face. Suppose the market rate of interest is higher than the coupon rate; what must happen to bond prices? What happens if the market rate is below the coupon rate?

5.  Explain how a college senior could use the principles of utility maximization under uncertainty developed in this chapter to decide upon what career to follow or to decide between entering business or continuing on in graduate school. Would the expected stream of future income be the only variable considered? If so, why? If not, what other variables would be relevant? How would you set up the problem?

6.  Answer question 5 with the framework of a high school senior making the decision about which college or university to attend. Did you use the method of analysis described here when making your school decision? If you did not, how did you decide?

**FIGURE E.7–3**

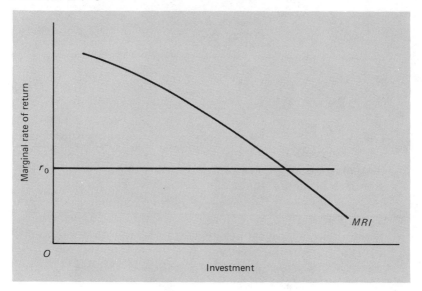

7.  Use Figure E.7–3 to answer the following questions: investment per period in the U.S. gadget industry is plotted along the horizontal axis. The relevant rate of interest is $r_0$. Explain what happens to investment in the gadget industry if the following events occur:

    a.  The government grants a subsidy to gadget producers.
    b.  A high tariff is placed upon imported gadgets.
    c.  Strict pollution and safety controls are placed upon the industry.
    d.  The FTC finds that gadgets may be hazardous to your health.

   *e.*  Sweeping technological change occurs in the widget in-
         dustry. (As you know, widgets are a good substitute for
         gadgets in most uses.)
   *f.*  The interest rate falls.
   *g.*  The rate of inflation increases.

8.  Is interest the price of money? Is it the opportunity cost of
    holding money?

9.  If interest rates were zero or negative, would individuals still
    save? Analytically support your answer. Suppose interest rates
    were zero. What factors would determine how much individ-
    uals saved?

10. Interestingly, as gasoline prices have gone up, so have prices
    of smaller, fuel-efficient automobiles relative to larger, less
    efficient automobiles. Suppose an automaker produces two au-
    tomobiles exactly alike except for the number of miles they
    travel per gallon of gas. Which automobile will be more ex-
    pensive? Explain.

11. At this time, the people in government are pushing programs
    designed to subsidize households that convert their heating
    systems from oil or gas to solar power.
    *a.*  Under what conditions would households voluntarily con-
          vert?
    *b.*  If households would not voluntarily convert, but govern-
          ment subsidizes the conversion, the fact that discounting
          represents the opportunity cost of capital means that sub-
          sidization is not optimal from a social point of view. Ex-
          plain.

# Chapter 8

## Theory of price in perfectly competitive markets

### 8.1 INTRODUCTION

In Chapter 2, we showed how demand and supply interact to determine prices and quantities sold in markets. Chapters 3 and 4 established the fundamentals of demand. This chapter will develop the basic determinants of supply. The foundations of supply theory are the concepts discussed in Chapters 5 and 6—the theories of production and cost.

Thus, Chapters 3 through 6 supply the framework upon which the theory of the firm is based. *Demand* establishes the revenue side of business operation. *Production and cost* establish the supply conditions. Brought together, revenue and cost for the individual business firm and demand and supply for the entire market determine the market price and output of the firm and industry. Furthermore, as we shall see in this and subsequent chapters, these forces also determine the allocation of resources among industries.

#### Why firms exist

Before developing the theory of the firm, we should discuss, at least briefly, why firms exist at all. We pointed out in Chapter 1 that economists, for analytical purposes, divide the economy into two sectors—households and business firms. Households sell their resources to firms in exchange for income with which they purchase goods and services produced by firms.

An economy could, of course, function without firms, and some have in the past; some do today. In the past, households produced practically everything they consumed. Frontier households in the United States were virtually self-sufficient. Clearly, this method of production is less efficient in the sense that society loses the advantage of specialization and households do not gain from trade. We could go one step further and let households specialize in one part of production and trade their products in the marketplace. This method would be more efficient than assembling all resources used to produce the household's goods under a single roof. But there would be large transportation and transaction costs involved in such exchanges. Some people would discover that it is more efficient to bring together all of the resources in one place and cooperate in the production of goods and services. This system of production would give the advantages of specialization and division of labor. If there were economies of scale, this cooperative form of organization would produce at a lower cost and drive out other organizational forms of production. Historically, this method of production did develop very quickly in the second half of the 19th century. It is often referred to as the *factory system.*

But mere cooperation of resources does not necessarily make a firm efficient. To see why, let us take a very simplified example. Suppose four of us chipped in and bought a boat in order to enter the fishing business. We agree to split the profits equally. Fishing is hard work. We know that if one of us goofs off a little, we catch fewer fish than if we fished hard all of the time. But every fish the loafer *does not catch* costs the person doing the loafing only one fourth of the value of that fish, because its value is divided into four parts. Thus, since the cost of goofing off is lower than if we received only the value of our product, we will goof off more. Production falls off. The same situation holds for a factory or a farm.

Someone would soon see the advantage of separating ownership from the operation of the business venture. A corporation would be formed. The owners would contract with workers for a fixed amount of their labor per period in return for a fixed payment per period. Owners would then claim any residual after the output was sold and the workers paid. They would also suffer the loss if that should result. The residual claimants could either assume the task of monitoring the workers to make sure they fulfilled their contract, or they could hire monitors, sometimes called managers, to do the job.

Firms of various types arise in an economy because they have been able to organize production more efficiently than other types of institutions could. Generally, we think of the owners of capital as doing the task of contracting with other resources and either hiring managers (monitors) or carrying out this task themselves. While this may be the most prominent form of organization, it is not the only one. In many countries, the labor-managed firm is a frequently used form of organization. Sometimes, but less frequently, we find the consumer-managed firm. But the point here is that most production takes place in business firms. These are not merely forced onto a helpless society. The institution of business firms exists because this is an efficient form for organizing production. If some other, more efficient, way of organizing production is discovered, that organization will replace the business firm. Until then, economics texts will treat production of goods and services as generally being organized in firms.

The basic concepts to be learned in Chapter 8 are

1. What determines the level of output for competitive firms in the short run and in the long run.
2. What factors determine the supply curve for a competitive firm and industry.
3. Why most supply curves are upward sloping.
4. How profits are competed away in the long run and how long-run equilibrium is attained.

## 8.2 THE CONCEPT OF PROFIT MAXIMIZATION

The fundamental point of this chapter is the way firms determine their output from cost curves, both in the long run and the short run. The basic analysis is really rather simple. We shall summarize the fundamentals here before going into the more rigorous formal analysis below.

### Principle of profit maximization

Our entire theoretical structure is based upon the simple assumption that entrepreneurs try to maximize profits. That is, other things remaining the same, they prefer more profit to less, profit being the difference between revenue and cost. This assumption does not mean that a businessperson may not seek other goals. Nonetheless, one who ignores profits or prefers less profit to more, other things equal, would be rather unusual. In any case, a business generally cannot remain in business very long unless some profits are earned. To be sure, there have been several criticisms of the profit-maximizing assumption, but this assumption provides a general theory of firms, markets, and resource allocation that is successful both in explaining and predicting firm behavior. In short, the profit-maximization assumption is used, first because it works well, and second because it describes, to some extent, the way that firms behave.

The basic principles of profit maximizing are straightforward. The firm will increase any activity so long as the *additional* revenue from the increase exceeds the *additional* cost of the increase. The firm will cease to expand the activity if the *additional* revenue is less than the *additional* cost.

Suppose that the activity or choice variable is the firm's level of output. As the firm increases its level of output, each added unit adds to the total revenue of the firm. The change in revenue per unit of change in output is called *marginal revenue*. This term will be used so frequently in this chapter and the next that it deserves to be highlighted.

**Definition.**   Marginal revenue is the change in total revenue when output is increased by one unit or by a small amount.

As the firm increases its level of output, each unit of increase in output increases the firm's total cost. As you will recall from Chapter 6, the added cost per unit increase in output is called *marginal cost*.

Thus, the firm will choose to expand output so long as the added revenue from the expansion (marginal revenue) is greater than the added cost of the expansion (marginal cost). The firm would choose not to increase output if the marginal cost of the increase is greater than the marginal revenue from the increase.[1] Profit maximization is, therefore, based upon the following principle:

**Principle.**   Profit is the difference between revenue and cost. If an increase in output adds more to revenue than to cost, the increase in output adds to profit. If the increase in output adds less to revenue than to cost, the increase in output subtracts from profit. *The firm, therefore, chooses the level of output at which marginal revenue equals marginal cost.* This level maximizes total profit.

### Profits and a price-taking firm

In this chapter, we are concerned with the special case in which the price of the produced commodity is given to the firm by the

---

[1] There is one extremely minor exception to this rule of behavior. The exception will be mentioned later in the text.

market. In this special case, marginal revenue equals price. That is, if the firm is a cotton farm, and the price of cotton is $500 per bale of cotton, the marginal revenue from each additional bale of cotton is $500. The owner of the farm would increase cotton production as long as the marginal cost of each additional bale is less than $500. It would not increase production if each additional bale costs more than $500 to produce.

This very simplified explanation provides the theoretical structure for a powerful predictive and explanatory theory. This theory is the theory of perfect competition. Throughout the formal exposition of the theory, do not forget that most of the structure is based upon the very simple notion that the firm maximizes profit by producing the output at which marginal revenue equals marginal cost.

Let us note in passing that the term *profit* means return over and above *all costs,* including implicit costs. Recall from Chapter 6 that implicit costs is included in total cost. Thus, if the owner manages the firm, the wages that would be paid to an equally qualified manager are included in the cost. Let us take another example. Suppose the entrepreneur has invested his or her own resources in capital used in the firm's production process. The return that could be earned from the use of the capital is an opportunity cost and is an implicit cost to the firm.

Economists frequently refer to the opportunity cost of using the entrepreneur's capital as a "normal return." Any return over and above the "normal" return is called "pure profit" or economic profit. To illustrate, suppose the entrepreneur has $1 million worth of capital invested in the firm. Suppose also that the normal or going return in the economy is 6 percent per year. If the entrepreneur earns 10 percent per year, the normal profit, included in cost, is 6 percent; the pure or economic profit is the additional 4 percent return. In this text, when we use the term *profit,* we shall mean pure or economic profit, over and above the normal return on the entrepreneur's resources.

## 8.3 PERFECT COMPETITION

The theory of the firm set forth in this chapter is based upon the exacting concept of *perfectly competitive markets.* Perfect competition forms the basis of the most important and widely used model of economic behavior. The essence of perfect competition is that neither buyers nor producers recognize any competitiveness among themselves; no *rivalry—direct* competition—among economic agents exists.

The theoretical concept of competition is diametrically opposed to the typical concept of competition. For example, someone in business might maintain that the automobile industry or the cigarette industry is quite competitive, since each firm in these industries must consider what its rivals will do before it makes a decision about advertising campaigns, design changes, quality improvements, and so forth.

That type of market is far removed from what the economist means when speaking of perfect competition. Perfect competition permits no personal rivalry (that is, personal in the sense that the firm considers the reaction of competitive firms in determining its own policy). All relevant economic magnitudes are determined by impersonal market forces.

Several important conditions define perfect competition. Taken together, these conditions guarantee a large, impersonal market in which the forces of demand and supply, or of revenue and cost, determine the allocation of resources and the distribution of income. The first of these conditions or assumptions has been discussed in Section 8.2 above. This assumption is that firms attempt to maximize profits. There are five additional restricting assumptions.

### Free markets

We assume that each market is free and operates freely in the sense that no external control of market forces exists. One form of external control is governmental intervention—for example, farm crop controls, public utility regulations, or minimum wages. All such controls establish artificial market conditions to which business firms must adjust. Another type of control is collective behavior or collusion of firms in a market. Such behavior limits the free exercise of market forces.

While many markets are not free in the sense used here, a large number are. The object is to analyze the efficiency of resource allocation in free markets. In cases in which the market is not free, one may draw inferences concerning the relative efficiency of free, as opposed to controlled, markets. Thus, the perfectly competitive market serves as a yardstick to measure the performance of other types of market structures.

Furthermore, we can use the competitive theory to analyze the consequences of externally imposed interferences with the free market. That is, we can use the competitive theory to generate equilibrium conditions in the absence of interferences. Then we impose such an interference—for example, some type of regulation—and see how this change affects the equilibrium. Thus, while the basic theory assumes free markets, external constraints can be imposed in order to study the results of the constraint.

## Small size, large numbers

Perfect competition requires that every economic agent be so small, relative to the market as a whole, that it cannot exert a perceptible influence on price. From the standpoint of buyers, this means that all consumers taken individually must be so unimportant that no one can obtain special considerations from the sellers. Perhaps the most familiar special consideration is the rebate, especially in the area of transportation services. But there can be many others, such as special credit terms to large buyers or free additional services. None of these can prevail if the market is perfectly competitive.

From the seller's standpoint, perfect competition requires that each firm be so small it cannot affect market price by changes in output. If all producers act collectively, changes in quantity will definitely affect market price. But if perfect competition prevails, each producer is so small that individual changes will go unnoticed. In other words, the actions of any individual firm do not affect market supply.

## Homogeneous product

A closely related provision is that the product of each seller in a perfectly competitive market must be identical to the product of every other seller. This ensures that buyers are indifferent as to the firm from which they purchase. Product differences, whether real or imaginary, are precluded by the existence of perfect competition.

To an economist, "product" has a much more detailed meaning than it does in ordinary conversation, in which one might regard automobiles or apparel as products. While it is appropriate to speak of industries in such a way, e.g., the automobile industry or the apparel industry, this is not an adequate way to describe a product. A product is a bundle of characteristics that are important to buyers—every changable feature of the good must be included in its definition. When buying an automobile, for instance, the product is defined by engine size, passenger room, trunk capacity, number of doors, fuel efficiency, upholstery, color, etc. Not only are the physical characteristics important, but the location and service reputation of the dealer also determine whether two automobiles are, in fact, the same product. To an economist, product homogeneity is a very exacting requirement.

It should be apparent that very few products are homogeneous, or perfectly standardized. For this reason, there are not many perfectly competitive markets. Even slightly differentiated products imply that buyers know who the seller of a certain product is. This leads to brand loyalties and gives sellers a degree of control over the price at which they sell their products. The producer can raise price without losing all its customers. This degree of control, or *market power* is not allowed in the model of perfect competition.

### Free mobility of resources

Another precondition for perfect competition is that all resources are perfectly mobile—each resource required can move in and out of the market very readily in response to prices.

The condition of perfect mobility is also exacting. First, it means that labor must be mobile, not only geographically, but among jobs. Next, free mobility means that the inputs are not monopolized by an owner or producer. Finally, free mobility means that new firms (or new capital) can enter and leave an industry without extraordinary difficulty. If patents or copyrights are required, entry is not free. Similarly, if vast investment outlays are required, entry certainly is not easy. In short, free mobility of resources requires free and easy entry and exit of firms into and out of an industry—a condition very difficult to realize in practice.

### Perfect knowledge about markets

Consumers, producers, and resource owners must possess perfect knowledge if a market is to be perfectly competitive. If consumers are not fully cognizant of prices, they might buy at higher prices when lower ones are available. Then there will not be a uniform price in the market. Similarly, if laborers are not aware of the wage rates offered, they may not sell their labor services to the highest bidder. Finally, producers must know costs as well as price in order to attain the most profitable rate of output.

The discussion to this point can be summarized by the following:

**Principle.**   Perfect competition is an economic model of a market possessing the following characteristics: each economic agent is so small relative to the market that it can exert no perceptible influence on price; the product is homogeneous; there is free mobility of all resources, including free and easy entry and exit of business firms into and out of an industry; and all economic agents in the market possess perfect knowledge. Furthermore, markets are free and firms attempt to maximize profits.

### Conclusion

Glancing at the requirements above should immediately convince one that no market has been or can be perfectly competitive.

Even in basic agricultural markets, where most of the requirements are frequently satisfied, the requirement of perfect knowledge is not met. One might therefore reasonably ask why such a palpably unrealistic model should be considered at all.

The answer can be given in as much or as little detail as desired. For our present purposes, it is brief. First, generality can be achieved only by means of abstraction. Hence, as we stressed in Chapter 1, no theory can be *perfectly* descriptive of *real-world* phenomena. Furthermore, the more accurately a theory describes one specific real-world case, the less accurately it describes all others. In any area of thought, a theoretician does not select assumptions on the basis of their presumed correspondence to reality. For example, physicists often assume away friction even though a frictionless world is incomprehensible; and chemists analyze, as a matter of course, the chemical reactions between two compounds without considering the role of impurities—even though impurities are always present. The conclusions of theory, not the assumptions, are tested against reality.

This leads to a second point of great, if somewhat pragmatic, importance. The conclusions derived from the model of perfect competition have, by and large, permitted accurate explanation and prediction of real-world phenomena. That is, perfect competition frequently works as a theoretical model of economic processes even though it does not accurately describe any specific industry.[2] The most persuasive evidence supporting this assertion is the fact that, despite the proliferation of more sophisticated models of economic behavior, economists today probably use the model of perfect competition in their research more than any other model.

## 8.4 DEMAND FACING A PERFECTLY COMPETITIVE FIRM

Recall from our previous analysis of consumer behavior that demand is a list of prices and the quantities demanded by a consumer or a group of consumers at each price in the list per period of time. The demand curves for products are generally assumed to be downward sloping. The entrepreneur or owner of an individual competitive firm sees the demand for the product produced by that firm in a much different way.

This difference follows from two of our assumptions about competitive firms—first, each firm produces a homogeneous product

---

[2] Furthermore, the assumptions do not imply that the model of perfect competition is not relevant in predicting the consequences of a disturbance in an economy containing industries that comprise a few interdependent firms (economists call such industries oligopolistic). The competitive model is a useful approach to many problems in which the conditions differ from the assumptions set forth here.

and, second, each firm is very small relative to the size of the total market for the product. Thus, since no firm, acting alone, can affect market price, each firm takes the market price, as set by total industry supply and demand, as given. Any firm can sell all it wants at the going market price. If the market price of the product is $10 each, the marginal revenue from each additional unit sold is $10. The marginal revenue curve is therefore a horizontal line at $10. Such a curve is shown in Figure 8–1; marginal revenue equals the price, $10, at any relevant output.

**FIGURE 8–1**
**Marginal revenue (demand) facing a perfectly competitive firm**

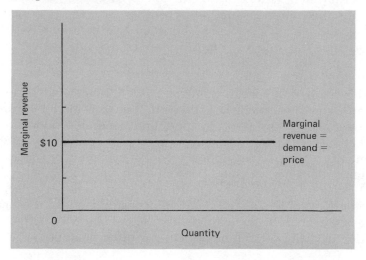

The horizontal marginal revenue curve at the market price is called the *demand* for the product of a perfectly competitive firm. This is the demand facing the firm, because each firm can sell all it wishes at the going market price. This conclusion follows even though the demand curve faced by the industry for the commodity is downward sloping.

We use Figure 8–2 to illustrate the entire process. Panel A shows equilibrium in the market. Equilibrium price is $p_0$ and quantity is $x_0$. The marginal revenue for every firm in the industry is therefore $p_0$. The demand curve for any firm in this perfectly competitive industry is shown in panel B. Each producer knows that changes in the firm's volume of output will have no perceptible effect upon market price. A change in the rate of sales per period of time will change the firm's revenue, but it will not affect market price.

The producer in a perfectly competitive market, therefore, does

**FIGURE 8-2**

Derivation of demand for a perfectly competitive firm

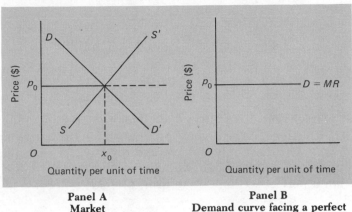

Panel A
Market

Panel B
Demand curve facing a perfect
competitor

not have to reduce price in order to expand the rate of sales. Any number of units per period of time can be sold at the market equilibrium price. If the firm charges a higher price, it could sell nothing. A lower price would result in a needless loss of revenue.

Since price remains constant, each additional unit sold increases total revenue by its (constant) price. Therefore, the demand curve and the marginal revenue curve are identical for a producer in a perfectly competitive market. For this reason, the curve in panel B is labeled $D = MR$. When the demand curve is horizontal, demand is said to be perfectly elastic.

Alternatively, recall from Chapter 2 that demand elasticity depends upon the number and closeness of substitutes. The product of a perfectly competitive firm has perfect substitutes—the products of all other firms in the industry. We would expect then that the demand elasticity for a firm's output would be infinite.

The results of this section may be summarized as follows:

**Relation.** The demand curve facing a producer in a perfectly competitive market is a horizontal line at the level of the market equilibrium price. The output decisions of the seller do not affect market price. In this case, the demand and marginal revenue curves are identical (that is, $D = MR$); demand is perfectly elastic, and the coefficient of price elasticity approaches infinity.

Frequently, the demand curve of a firm is referred to as an *average revenue curve*. This is true for perfectly competitive firms, as well as for firms that do not meet the requirements of perfect competition. At any price, say $p_0$, the demand curve tells a seller how much can be sold at that price, and, therefore, total revenue; i.e.,

$$TR = p_0 \cdot x_0.$$

Average revenue $(AR)$ is simply total revenue divided by total sales so

$$AR = \frac{TR}{x} = \frac{p_0 \cdot x_0}{x_0} = p_0.$$

Hence, average revenue is always equal to price. For any quantity, a demand curve reveals the highest price at which the entire amount can be sold. This is simply the average revenue for that quantity. Thus, a demand curve and an average revenue curve are the same thing. For a perfectly competitive firm, $D = AR = MR$.

## 8.5 SHORT-RUN PROFIT MAXIMIZATION

Let us turn now to the output decision of a firm in the short run. Recall from Chapter 5 that, in the short run, the firm has fixed costs, a fixed amount that must be paid regardless of output, and variable costs, which vary with the level of output. In the short run, the firm, given its production function and the prices of inputs, must make two decisions. The first decision is whether to produce or to close down; if the first decision is to produce rather than close down, the second decision concerns the proper level of output. We analyze these decisions first with a numerical example.

### Numerical example

Suppose a hypothetical firm faces the short-run cost situation shown in Table 8–1. Let the given market price of the firm's product be $42 per unit. Thus, the marginal revenue for each unit produced and sold is $42. From the marginal cost schedule, shown in column (7), we see that, if the firm produces at all, it will produce eight units of output. That is, each additional unit of output through eight units adds less to cost than the marginal revenue received for that unit. The firm would not produce the ninth unit, which adds $45 to cost but only $42 to revenue. The total profit is 8 times $42 = $336 minus a total cost of $210. This yields a profit of $126 for the period. Since the entrepreneur's opportunity cost is included in the total cost of production, the $126 represents an "above-normal" profit, sometimes, as mentioned above, called "pure" profit or "economic" profit. In any case, it represents a return over the opportunity cost. The reader should verify arithmetically that $126 is the maximum obtainable profit.

**TABLE 8–1**
**Short-run costs**

| (1) Rate of output and sales (units) | (2) Fixed cost | (3) Variable cost | (4) Total cost | (5) Average variable cost | (6) Average total cost | (7) Marginal cost |
|---|---|---|---|---|---|---|
| 0 | $30.00 | $ — | $ 30.00 | $ — | $ — | $ — |
| 1 | 30.00 | 5.00 | 35.00 | 5.00 | 35.00 | 5.00 |
| 2 | 30.00 | 15.00 | 45.00 | 7.50 | 22.50 | 10.00 |
| 3 | 30.00 | 30.00 | 60.00 | 10.00 | 20.00 | 15.00 |
| 4 | 30.00 | 50.00 | 80.00 | 12.50 | 20.00 | 20.00 |
| 5 | 30.00 | 75.00 | 105.00 | 15.00 | 21.00 | 25.00 |
| 6 | 30.00 | 105.00 | 135.00 | 17.50 | 22.50 | 30.00 |
| 7 | 30.00 | 140.00 | 170.00 | 20.00 | 24.29 | 35.00 |
| 8 | 30.00 | 180.00 | 210.00 | 22.50 | 26.25 | 40.00 |
| 9 | 30.00 | 225.00 | 255.00 | 25.00 | 28.33 | 45.00 |
| 10 | 30.00 | 275.00 | 305.00 | 27.50 | 30.50 | 50.00 |

Now let price fall to $33. Using the same method of increasing output as long as marginal revenue exceeds marginal cost, we see that the profit-maximizing output is now six units. With total revenue of 6 times $33 = $198 and a total cost of $135, the firm now earns a profit of $63. Again, it can be verified arithmetically that this output does, in fact, yield maximum profit when commodity price is $33.

Finally, let us assume that market price decreases to $12. Marginal revenue exceeds price for each of the first two units of production. The third unit costs $15 to produce but only yields $12. Therefore, if the firm produces at all, it will produce two units. Total revenue is $24; total cost is $45, resulting in a loss of $21. Should the firm produce at a loss? The answer is yes, because the $21 loss is $9 less than the $30 fixed cost that must be paid if the firm closes down in the short run. In other words, if the firm produces nothing in the short run, revenue is zero, and cost is $30. By producing two units and selling at $12 each, the $24 would cover all of the $15 variable cost, leaving $9 left over to apply to fixed cost. The net loss is $21, compared to a loss of $30 at zero production. The reader should verify that the $21 loss is the minimum loss possible at a price of $12.

To be sure, the firm would not and could not go on for a very long period of time suffering a loss in each period. In the long run, the firm would leave the industry if it could not cover costs, including opportunity cost at any level of output. Or it would change its short-run situation if all costs could be covered at some optimal level of output in the long run. We shall postpone long-run analysis until we analyze the short-run situation graphically.

## APPLICATION

### Decision making and marginal analysis

Many businesses are, from time to time, faced with the decision of whether to extend the number of hours that they operate during the week. Restaurants, once open only 16 hours a day, choose to stay open all night. Stores extend the number of evenings that they stay open. Service stations change the number of hours that they operate. What factors influence the decision to stay open additional hours?

The answer is simple. The manager compares the expected marginal revenue with the expected marginal cost of staying open. Fixed costs are not spread over the additional hours of operation. They are irrelevant in this type of decision. For example, the following problem was put to the readers of *Business Week* some years ago.[3]

Problem:  Should Continental Airlines run an extra daily flight from city X to city Y?

Facts:  Average total cost of the flight—$4,500.
Marginal cost of the flight—$2,000.
Marginal revenue from the flight—$3,100.

The decision should be to run the flight. Marginal revenue will add $1,100 more than marginal cost to Continental's income. Average cost is irrelevant in the decision, because the fixed costs of $4,500 − $2,000 = $2,500 must be paid whether the flight is scheduled or not. Regardless of the fixed cost, the marginal changes are all that matter. Fixed costs are ignored.

Decision makers in government should and do make decisions based upon marginal analysis, ignoring fixed costs. Even in the military, if a weapon or piece of equipment does not prove satisfactory in combat, the Pentagon is frequently quick to drop the defective equipment, ignoring the costs already sunk, and develop replacements. Two such examples are the M-14 rifle and the M-1 tank.

According to a column by Lynn Ashby,[4] the M-14 was a remarkable rifle on the firing range; "It could fire semi-automatically, automatically . . . shoot around corners, under rocks, [and] through walls." The problem was it could not function in combat. Any dampness or dust turned it into a good club. After discovering that the M-14 was too delicate for combat, the Pentagon junked millions

---

[3] "Airline Takes the Marginal Route," *Business Week*, April 20, 1963, pp. 111–14.

[4] L. Ashby, "Bellbottoms' Return May Ring in New Pentagon Era," *Houston Post*, 6 August 1981, p. 1B.

of them in favor of the M-16, which, unfortunately is so sophisticated that it breaks down even more easily.

According to Ashby, the M-1 tank can "roll, fire, turn around, leap, sleep five [people], and dance backward." It was a magnificent piece of equipment, except that its computers and calculators kept failing and the crews could not fix them. It was simply no good in a war and was, therefore, discarded in favor of another tank.

We might say that these mistakes should not have been made. But, once the mistakes are discovered, the governmental agency responsible should ignore the dollars already sunk in the project and decide what to do not on the basis of what is wasted, but on the marginal benefits and costs of future activities and undertakings. Once equipment is shown to be unsatisfactory, it might be more costly to remedy the existing problems than to develop new equipment. This was the choice faced by the military.

### Graphical exposition of short-run equilibrium

Figure 8–3 shows a set of typical short-run cost curves; marginal cost ($MC$), average total cost ($ATC$), and average variable cost ($AVC$). Average fixed cost is omitted for convenience and because it is irrelevant for decision making. The given market price is $p_0$. Therefore, marginal revenue is the horizontal line at $p_0$. The firm produces where short-run marginal cost equals marginal revenue,

**FIGURE 8–3**
**Short-run equilibrium**

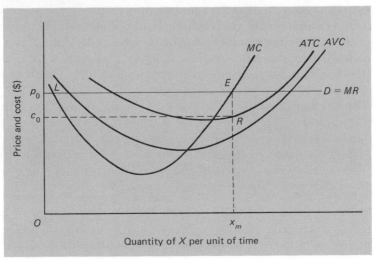

point $E$ at output $x_m$. Producing another unit would add more to costs than the firm would receive from the sale of that unit; $MC$ exceeds $MR$. The firm would not stop short of output $x_m$, however, since at lesser outputs, producing another unit adds more to revenue than to cost; $MR$ exceeds $MC$. Total cost is the area $Oc_0Rx_m$; total revenue is the area $Op_0Ex_m$; profit is the difference, the area $c_0p_0ER$. The firm makes a positive profit over and above opportunity cost.

Note that, at point $L$ in Figure 8–3, marginal cost also equals price. That is not, however, a point of equilibrium, since the firm would not choose to produce this output under the circumstances depicted. In the first place, average cost exceeds price at this output so losses would occur, whereas at some other outputs profits could be realized. Second, the firm could clearly gain by producing an additional unit. Price is greater than marginal cost; thus, the firm would be motivated to increase output.[5]

### Profit, loss, and the firm's short-run supply curve

The equality of price and short-run marginal cost guarantees either that profit is a maximum or that loss is a minimum. Whether a profit is made or a loss incurred can be determined only by comparing price and average total cost at the equilibrium rate of output. If price exceeds unit cost, the entrepreneur enjoys a short-run profit; on the other hand, if unit cost exceeds price, a loss is suffered.

Figure 8–4 illustrates four possible short-run situations for the firm. First, the market-established price may be $p_1$; the firm settles at point $A$ where $MC = p_1$, produces $x_1$ units, and, since $ATC$ is less than price, receives a profit. Second, market price may be $p_2$. $MC$ now equals price at point $B$; the firm produces $x_2$. Since $B$ is the lowest point on $ATC$, the firm makes neither profit nor loss, but it does cover opportunity cost, which is included in $ATC$. Third, if price is $p_3$, the firm produces $x_3$; price equals $MC$ at $C$. Because average cost is greater than price at the optimal output, total cost is greater than total revenue, and the firm suffers a loss. That loss is $CR$ times $x_3$.

When demand is $D_3 = MR_3$, there is simply no way the firm can earn a profit. At every output level, average total cost exceeds price. If output were either smaller or greater than $x_3$ units per period of time, the loss would be greater. As we noted above, the firm would not necessarily close down in the short run, even though losses result. Recall that a firm incurring a loss in the short run will con-

---

[5] Economists say that $MC = P$ is the *necessary*, or first-order condition for profit maximization and that the second-order condition is that where $MC = P$, $MC$ must be positively sloped. The two conditions together are *necessary* and *sufficient* for profit maximization.

**FIGURE 8–4**
**Profit, loss, or ceasing production in the short run**

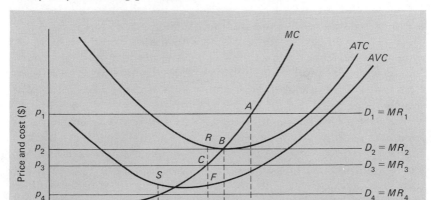

tinue to produce if, and only if, it loses less by producing than by closing the plant entirely. Remember there are two types of costs in the short run: fixed costs and variable costs. The fixed costs cannot be changed and are incurred whether the plant is operating or not. Fixed costs are unavoidable in the short run and are the same at zero output as at any other.

Therefore, at zero output, total revenue would be zero also and total cost would be the total fixed cost. The loss would thus be the amount of total fixed costs. If the firm can produce where $MC = MR$, and if at this output total revenue is greater than total variable cost, a smaller loss is suffered when production takes place. The firm covers all of its variable cost and some revenue is left over to cover a part of fixed cost. The loss is that part of fixed cost not covered and is clearly less than the entire fixed cost.

Returning to Figure 8–4, one can see more easily why the firm in the short run would produce at $C$ and not shut down. The firm loses $CR$ dollars per unit produced. However, variable cost is not only covered but there is an excess of $CF$ dollars per unit sold. The excess of price over average variable cost, $CF$, can be applied to fixed costs. Thus, not all of the fixed costs are lost, as would be the case if production were discontinued; the amount $CF$ times $x_3$ can be applied to fixed costs. Although a loss is sustained, it is smaller than the loss associated with zero output.

Suppose, however, that market price is $p_4$; demand is given by $D_4 = MR_4$. If the firm produces, its equilibrium would be at $T$ where $MC = p_4$. Output would be $x_4$ units per period of time. Here, the average variable cost of production exceeds price. Not only would the firm lose all of its fixed costs, it would also lose $ST$ dollars per unit on its variable costs as well. The firm could improve its earnings situation by producing nothing and losing only fixed cost. Thus, when price is below average variable cost at every level of output, the short-run equilibrium output is zero.

As shown in Chapter 6, average variable cost reaches its minimum at the point at which marginal cost and average variable cost intersect. If price is less than the minimum average variable cost, the loss-minimizing output is zero. For price equal to or greater than minimum average variable cost, equilibrium output is determined by the intersection of marginal cost and price. For a perfectly competitive firm we have:

**Principle.**  (1) Marginal cost tells *how much* to produce, given the choice of a positive output; the firm produces the output for which $MC = P$. (2) Average variable cost tells *whether* to produce; the firm ceases to produce if price falls below minimum AVC. (3) Average total cost tells how much profit or loss is made if the firm decides to produce; profit equals the difference between $P$ and $ATC$ multiplied by the quantity produced and sold.

Using the concepts just discussed, it is possible to derive the short-run supply curve of an individual firm in a perfectly competitive market. The process is illustrated in Figure 8–5. Panel A shows

**FIGURE 8–5**
**Derivation of the short-run supply curve of an individual producer in perfect competition**

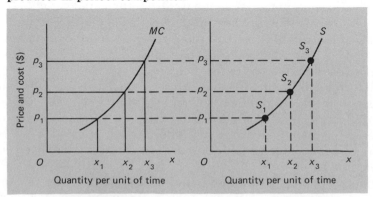

| Panel A | Panel B |
|---|---|
| Positions of short-run | Equilibrium quantities |
| equilibria for the firm | supplied by the firm |

the marginal cost curve of a firm for rates of output greater than those associated with minimum average variable cost. Suppose market price is $p_1$, the corresponding equilibrium rate of output is $x_1$. Now, find on panel B the point associated with the coordinates $p_1$, $x_1$. Label this point $S_1$; it represents the quantity supplied at price $p_1$.

Next, suppose price is $p_2$. In this case, equilibrium output would be $x_2$. Plot the point associated with the coordinates $p_2$, $x_2$ on panel B—it is labeled $S_2$. Similarly, other equilibrium quantities supplied can be determined by postulating other market prices (for example, price $p_3$ leads to output $x_3$ and point $S_3$ on panel B). Connecting all the $S$ points so generated, one obtains the short-run supply curve of the firm, the curve labeled $S$ in panel B. But by construction, the $S$ curve is precisely the same as the $MC$ curve. The following is thus established:

**Principle.** The short-run supply curve of a firm in perfect competition is precisely its marginal cost curve for all rates of output equal to or greater than the rate of output associated with minimum average variable cost. For market prices lower than minimum average variable cost, equilibrium quantity supplied is zero.

## APPLICATION

### Competitive firms and mineral extraction[6]

Now that we have established the profit-maximizing rule for a perfectly competitive firm, we can discuss the *rate* at which a price-taking firm will extract a depletable mineral resource like copper, coal, oil, etc. Recall that, in Chapter 7, we discussed how interest rates affect the decision to extract a natural resource. Our conclusion was that the owner of a mineral asset will extract if the price of the asset is expected to rise at a rate lower than the rate of interest. The firm could extract the mineral, sell it, then invest the returns at the market rate of interest and gain a larger return than would occur from appreciation of the deposit. We were unable to say anything about the rate of extraction, because we had not yet covered how firms maximize profits. This application explores the rate at which a competitive firm will extract a depletable resource once it has decided to sell some of the mineral.

---

[6] This application is based upon G. Anders, W. P. Gramm, S. C. Maurice, and C. W. Smithson, *The Economics of Mineral Extraction* (New York: Praeger Publishers, 1980), pp. 15–17.

Let us assume that the firm has a fixed quantity of a depletable resource and will sell it until the total amount is extracted. The firm maximizes the present value or discounted stream of profit:

$$PV = \sum_{t=0}^{H} \left(\frac{1}{1+r}\right)^{t} (TR_t - TC_t)$$

where

$r$ = rate of interest.
$H$ = the firm's planning horizon.
$TR_t$ = total revenue in period $t$.
$TC_t$ = total cost in period $t$.

The firm must realize that it cannot extract the mineral forever. The size of the mineral body constrains the total amount that can be extracted. In a sense, the mineral asset is like a piece of capital equipment: as capital is used, there is depreciation. Similarly, for minerals, as a firm extracts some of the substance from its mines or wells, there is depletion.

We will also assume that the prices in each period are known to the firm. With this information, the firm must decide the amount of resource to be extracted for each period 0 to $H$. Maximization of present value under these circumstances requires that the firm, in each period, extract the amount at which the discounted price equals the discounted marginal cost. Thus, for the $t$ periods, we would have

$$\left(\frac{1}{1+r}\right)^{t} (P_t - MC_t) = 0, \qquad t = 0, 1 \ldots H.$$

$P_t$ is the market price in period $t$. A competitive firm takes this as given. Marginal cost, though, is determined by the firm's technology and rate of extraction. To understand fully the profit-maximizing rate of extraction, we need to look closer at the makeup of marginal cost.

If the firm had an unlimited mineral deposit in the sense that it could not be exhausted during the time horizon of the firm, and if the rate of extraction during one period did not affect the cost of extraction in future periods, $MC_t$ would simply be $\Delta TC/\Delta X_t$. Marginal cost would be the change in total cost from extracting more of the resource at the given time.

However, extraction in the present makes extraction in the future more costly. For example, a mine must go deeper in later periods because of mining in earlier periods. Deeper mines are more expensive to operate. As a pool of oil is depleted, it becomes technologically more difficult to bring up additional crude. The technology is more expensive.

   Also, as the resource is depleted, the future value of the deposit declines. Just as machinery depreciates, the reduction in the quantity of the mineral available is a cost to the firm. This depreciation or depletion factor is generally referred to as a *user cost*. The user cost shows the opportunity cost of current extraction on future profit, because a unit of output extracted now cannot be extracted in the future.

   We show the makeup of the marginal cost of extraction for period $t$ in Figure 8–6. The lowest marginal cost curve, $MC_t$, is the per-

**FIGURE 8–6**
**The impact of the future costs of present output on present production**

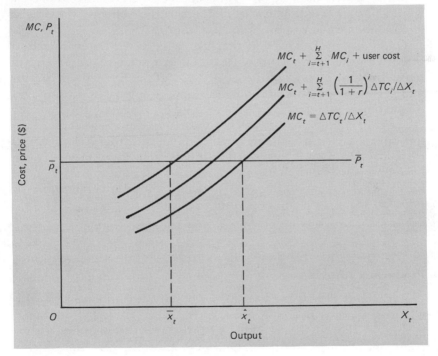

unit effect of extraction in period $t$ on cost in that period; this can be expressed as $\Delta TC_t / \Delta X_t$. As is usually the case, marginal cost increases with output over the relevant range. The second curve is $MC_t$ plus the discounted sum of the per-unit effects of extraction in all future periods until the end of the horizon, $H$. This part of marginal cost is expressed as the sum of $\Delta TC_i / \Delta X_t$, where the i-th period is each period beyond $t$ up to $H$. The highest marginal cost curve includes the opportunity cost, or user cost discussed above.

   Now let us discuss the effect of these additions to marginal cost on the firm's rate of output. Suppose the firm has no effect on the price of the mineral it sells. Also in Figure 8–6, assume that the price in period $t$ is $\bar{p}_t$. The firm would increase its rate of extraction as long as the price it receives for the mineral exceeds the marginal cost of extracting the mineral. It would not increase its rate of extraction if the marginal cost exceeds the price. Thus, in equilibrium, price equals marginal cost. In Figure 8–6, if only current marginal cost, $MC_t$, is considered, the firm would extract $\hat{x}_t$ in period $t$. But when all effects are considered in the marginal cost curve, output in the $t$-th period declines to $\bar{x}_t$. In other words, the effect of current extraction on future costs and future profits decreases current output below what it would be in the absence of these future effects, as would be expected. Because of these future effects, the firm is forced to conserve resources for the future.

One must note, however, that increases in the relevant rate of interest tend to increase present rates of extraction relative to future rates. That is, increases in the interest rate cause present profits, which can be invested at the higher rate, to increase in value relative to future profits, which are more heavily discounted. Therefore, the rate of exploitation of known deposits tends to be increased. On the other hand, exploration, development, and investment are affected by the rate of interest. For this reason, there may be some offsetting forces to the increased rates of extraction of known deposits. The direction of change depends upon the strengths of all forces.

### Producer's surplus

A concept closely related to consumer's surplus, discussed in Chapter 4, is *producer's surplus*. Put very directly, producer's surplus is the difference between price and the marginal cost of each unit of output sold, summed over all units. Algebraically

$$\text{Producer's Surplus} = \sum_{i=1}^{n} (P - MC_i),$$

where $n$ is the number of units sold by the firm. While consumer's surplus was defined as the difference between the willingness to pay and the market price, producer's surplus is the difference between price and a producer's "willingness to sell." Marginal cost is a firm's supply curve; it represents the lowest price at which $n$ units of output will be sold in the short run. Hence, marginal cost represents the firm's willingness to sell.

Geometrically, producer's surplus can be described in the following manner: suppose we have a grocer who sells apples. One of many sellers of apples in a market, the grocer takes the price of apples as given; at present, the price of an apple is 40 cents. At this price, the grocer maximizes profits by setting the marginal cost of selling apples equal to 40 cents. The grocer earns no producer's surplus on the *last apple* sold. But as Figure 8–7, panel A, illustrates, *all of the other* apples have $MC < P$, and a surplus is earned on these apples. Total producer's surplus is estimated by the shaded geometric area $ABC$ in Figure 8–7, panel A.

**FIGURE 8–7**
**Producer's surplus**

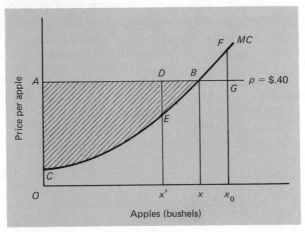

**Panel A**

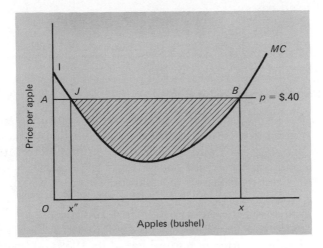

**Panel B**

Panel B in Figure 8–7 shows that for some apples ($x''$), marginal cost can be above price. The firm takes a loss on these apples and earns negative producer's surplus equal to the geometric area $AIJ$. But to earn any returns, these apples must be sold in order to move down the marginal cost curve. After $x''$ apples, $MC < P$ and the firm begins earning positive surplus. Surplus is maximized where $MC = p$ at $B$. Notice that, if the firm stopped producing at point $J$, it would have actually maximized its losses. The marginal cost curve must have a positive slope when the firm sets $p = MC$ to maximize profits. Total surplus in panel B is the shaded region minus area $AIJ$.

**Definition.**   Producer's surplus is the difference between price and marginal cost. It is estimated by the area between price and the marginal cost schedule. If price is greater than marginal cost, surplus is positive; if price is below marginal cost, it is negative.

You can easily see that, if a seller maximizes profits, producer's surplus is maximized. If, for instance, the grocer did not set $MC = p$, but instead sold $x'$ bushels of apples in Figure 8–7, there would be a loss of surplus estimated by the area $DBE$. Now, suppose the grocer mistakenly sells $x_0$ apples. We know that this output does not maximize profits because $xx_0$ apples are sold at a price below marginal cost. Area $ABC$ is earned as surplus, but area $BFG$ must be subtracted, since the grocer incurs a loss on apples sold beyond $x$.

We must be careful not to think producer's surplus is profit. It is not, because its definition ignores fixed costs. If we wanted to find the profit of a seller by using producer's surplus, we would need to subtract fixed costs.

## APPLICATION

### Federal regulation of natural gas

Consumer's and producer's surplus can be combined to analyze the effects of a price ceiling on natural gas. For illustration, we use the years between 1960 and 1973. For this application, suppose we have only one consumer and one seller of natural gas.

In 1938, Congress passed the Natural Gas Act which gave the Federal Power Commission (later called the Federal Energy Regulatory Commission) the right to set "just and reasonable" rates for interstate sales of natural gas. From 1960 to 1973, the commission froze the wellhead price of natural gas at its 1959–60 level. In real dollars, the price of natural gas to residential customers declined by almost 20 percent from 1960 to 1973.[7]

There is strong evidence that this price was below the market equilibrium that would have been established by the intersection of the supply and demand curves. Before the price of gas was fixed, the average number of wells drilled annually between 1948 and 1960 was 662. Between 1960 and 1973, the number fell to 641, and after 1973, when the ceiling was raised, the average number of wells drilled increased dramatically to 1,370 per year.[8] Furthermore, natural-gas suppliers were having difficulty meeting their contract obligations. Failure to supply the gas in amounts agreed upon was a *curtailment*. In 1970, curtailments represented .5 percent of total production; by 1974, they were 9.6 percent of production. Shortages were resulting from the price ceiling.

**FIGURE 8–8**
**Price ceilings on natural gas**

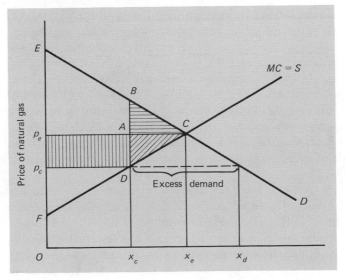

Figure 8–8 shows a familiar diagram. Price $p_c$ represents the price set by the Federal Power Commission; $p_e$ is the equilibrium price for natural gas. At first, $p_e$ and $p_c$ were probably about equal, but in the early 1970s, the size of curtailments indicates there was a

---

[7] *Annual Report to Congress*, vol. 2, (Washington, D.C.: Department of Energy, 1978), p. 85.

[8] Ibid., p. 27.

large excess demand at the artifically low price, $p_c$. The curtailments do not even include those contracts that might have been made if more gas had been available. At $p_c$, excess demand is the distance $x_d x_c$ in Figure 8–8.

Does a consumer or a producer benefit from a price ceiling? The question can be answered in terms of consumer's and producer's surplus.

Without the price ceiling, a consumer would have purchased $x_e$ natural gas and have paid $p_e$. Consumer's surplus would have been the area $ECp_e$. A price ceiling restricts the output of a producer to $x_c$; to produce any more means $MC > P$, which is not profitable. Under these conditions, surplus for the consumer becomes area $EBDp_c$. The consumer gains if $p_e ADp_c > ABC$ and loses surplus if $ABC > p_e ADp_c$. So, it is not clear whether the consumer gains or loses on balance from the ceiling.

A clearer answer emerges for the producer. Producer's surplus is the area between price and $MC$, which is the supply schedule. Before regulation, producer's surplus was $p_e CF$; afterwards, it is $p_c DF$. It is unambiguous that $p_c DF < p_e CF$. The producer loses area $ADC$. Hence, we do not know whether surplus for the consumer goes up or down; but for the producer, it goes down.

What about the combined consumer's and producer's surplus? In other words, what happens to total market surplus when a price ceiling is set? Before regulation, the sum of producer's and consumer's surplus was $p_e CE + p_e EC = ECF$. Once the price ceiling came into effect, it was $p_c DF + p_c EBD = EBDF$. We see that total surplus falls by the amount $BCD$. A price ceiling, in general, will reduce total surplus in a market.

Thus, we can see that, if the consumer gains surplus from the ceiling price, the result is a wealth transfer from the producer to the consumer. But, since there is a net *total* loss of surplus, both could be made better off if price was raised to the equilibrium, $p_e$, and the producer paid the consumer an amount that made this change desirable.[9] Suppose $p_e ADp_c - ABC = T$. This difference is the gain in consumer's surplus from the price ceiling. Then, if the producer paid the consumer slightly more than $T$, both would be willing to have prices at $p_e$. The producer could easily do this, since it gains all of area $p_e ADp_c$ and area $ACD$ when the price is raised to $p_e$. Of

---

[9] Such transfers may, in reality, be very difficult, if not impossible to make. The cost of making the payment could be more than the payment. See P. Joskow and R. Noll, *Regulation in Theory and Practice*, Massachusetts Institute of Technology Working Paper, no. 218, (April 1978), Boston: for a more thorough treatment of this problem.

course, if $ABC > p_eADp_c$, both the producer and consumer could be made better off without a transfer if the ceiling were removed.

### Short-run industry supply curve

In earlier chapters it was shown that market demand is simply the horizontal sum of the demand curves of all buyers in the market. Deriving the short-run industry supply curve is not always such an easy matter.

As you will recall from Chapter 6, the short-run marginal cost curve of a firm is derived under the assumption that the unit prices of the variable inputs are fixed; no change by the individual firm acting alone can change a factor's unit cost to the firm. This seems a reasonable assumption under perfect competition because one firm is usually so small, relative to all users of the resource, that variations in its rate of purchase will not affect the market price of the resource. In other words, many resource markets are more or less perfectly competitive, at least on the buying side. Thus, production, and therefore resource use, can frequently be expanded by one firm without affecting the market price of the resource.

But when *all* producers in an industry *simultaneously* expand output, there may be a marked effect upon the resource market. For example, one small cotton textile manufacturer could probably expand production by 10 percent or even 100 percent without affecting the world price of raw cotton. The few additional bales purchased would not have a significant effect on the total demand for raw cotton. If all textile manufacturers in the United States simultaneously attempt to expand output by 10 percent, however, the demand for cotton would probably increase substantially, and the resulting increase in the price of cotton would be significant. When all manufacturers attempt to increase output, raw cotton prices are bid up; and the increase in the price of a variable factor of production (raw cotton) causes an increase in all firms' cost curves, including marginal cost.

As a consequence, the industry supply curve usually cannot be obtained by horizontally summing the marginal cost curves of all producers. As industry output expands, some input prices normally increase, thereby shifting each marginal cost curve upward and to the left. A great deal of information would be required to obtain the exact supply curve. However, one may generally presume that the industry supply curve is somewhat more steeply sloped and somewhat less elastic when some input prices increase in response to an increase in industry output. In this case, the concept of a competitive industry supply curve is less precise. Nonetheless, doubt is not cast upon the basic fact that, in the short run, quantity supplied varies directly with price. The latter is all one needs to draw a positively sloped market supply curve. Finally, we should emphasize that price equals each firm's marginal cost at each and every point along a competive industry's supply curve, even though cost curves of individual firms do shift.

### Summary of firms in the short run

The firm operates in the short run, a period in which some costs are fixed regardless of the level of production. The firm will produce some positive output in the short run so long as price can cover all of average variable cost and at least some portion of average fixed cost. The price to the firm is its marginal revenue, because each unit sold adds its price to the firm's revenue. Equilibrium output is that output at which marginal revenue equals marginal cost. Therefore, the firm's short-run supply curve is its marginal cost above average variable cost.

If price equals marginal cost above average total cost, a pure profit above opportunity cost is earned. Profit is price minus $ATC$ times output. If price equals marginal cost between $ATC$ and $AVC$, the loss to the entrepreneur is $ATC$ minus price times output. If price falls below minimum $AVC$, the firm produces nothing and loses all of its fixed cost per time period.

Industry short-run supply is not necessarily the summation of the supply curves of all firms. Any firm can change output without changing the prices of inputs; all firms changing output together will probably affect the prices of some inputs. Thus, industry supply would probably be more inelastic than the horizontal sum of all firms' supplies.

We do not wish to give the impression that the marginal cost–marginal revenue analysis is applicable only to decisions directly involving revenues and costs. This decision-making rule applies to the allocation of any resource. For instance, our marginal analysis is quite applicable to crime prevention. Suppose a local government is interested in reducing criminal activity. The local government produces a product called "crime prevention." Clearly, the city government could spend nothing on crime prevention, or it could spend an inordinant amount, possibly putting two or three police officers on every corner, and decrease crime practically to zero. Obviously, there is an optimal situation somewhere between these extremes.

The scale of crime prevention produced by government should be set at a point at which the additional return from preventing crime (marginal revenue) is not less than the additional expenditure necessary to gain that return (marginal cost). In other words, society should not spend an additional $100 to prevent $50 worth of crime. On the other hand, if society wishes to spend an additional $100 preventing crime, it should spend it where the return in preventing crime is greatest, as long as the return exceeds $100.[10] While this analysis does not give the entire solution, this approach is the first step in a complete analysis.

The rule that marginal cost equals marginal revenue can also help you decide how much you should study. In Chapter 5 it was pointed out that a student should not stop studying simply because diminishing marginal returns were realized. The proper decision rule is to study as long as the marginal gain from studying is greater than the marginal cost. In this case, gains and costs are more subjective than they are for the business firm, but the decision framework remains the same. Benefits take the form of grades and future employment or graduate school opportunities, while the costs are clearly the forsaken alternatives to sitting down with the books.

## 8.6 LONG-RUN EQUILIBRIUM OF A COMPETITIVE FIRM

In the short run, the firm is limited by past decisions. In the long run all inputs are variable; the firm is not bound by the past. The long run may be the planning stage, prior to entry into the industry. Or a firm operating in the short run may be at a scale such that it is not obtaining maximum possible profits. It would then readjust its scale in the long run. Once the plans have congealed, the firm operates in a short-run situation again. It operates in the short run until it makes another long-run change in the scale of operation.

### Profit maximization in the long run

In the long run, just as in the short run, the firm attempts to maximize profits. We use exactly the same approach, except in this case there are no fixed costs; all costs are variable. As before, the firm takes a market-determined commodity price as given. This market price is also the firm's marginal revenue. As above, the firm would increase output as long as the marginal revenue from each

---

[10] Even the theft situation is complicated by the measurement problem. Theft does not necessarily mean a net loss to society. If I steal $100 from you, it is a transfer from you to me. I gain $100, while you lose the same amount. Unless one makes utility comparisons, society as a whole is no better or worse off. We return to this problem below. For an analysis of the economics of law enforcement, see G. J. Stigler, "The Optimum Enforcement of Laws," *Journal of Political Economy* 78, no.3 (May/June 1970): 526–36.

additional unit is greater than the marginal cost of that unit. It would not expand when marginal cost exceeds marginal revenue.

To illustrate, let us take the long-run situation shown in Table 8–2. In deciding the size plant to build, the entrepreneur attempts

**TABLE 8–2**
Revenue, cost, and profit

| Market price | Rate of output and sales | Total revenue | Total cost | Profit (TR − TC) |
|---|---|---|---|---|
| $5 .............. | 1 | $ 5 | $17.00 | −$12.00 |
| 5 .............. | 2 | 10 | 18.50 | −  8.50 |
| 5 .............. | 3 | 15 | 19.50 | −  4.50 |
| 5 .............. | 4 | 20 | 20.75 | −  0.75 |
| 5 .............. | 5 | 25 | 22.25 | +  2.75 |
| 5 .............. | 6 | 30 | 24.25 | +  5.75 |
| 5 .............. | 7 | 35 | 27.50 | +  7.50 |
| 5 .............. | 8 | 40 | 32.50 | +  7.50 |
| 5 .............. | 9 | 45 | 40.50 | +  4.50 |
| 5 .............. | 10 | 50 | 52.50 | −  2.50 |

to achieve maximum profit, which is the difference between the total receipts from selling the product (total revenue) and the total cost of producing it. The third and fourth columns of Table 8–2 show the long-run revenue and cost schedules of a hypothetical firm planning to enter an industry. Columns one and two show the market price and the attainable rates of output from which total revenue (price times output) is derived. Clearly, maximum profit is $7.50, attained at an output of either seven or eight units. The entrepreneur would build a plant to produce either output. The seeming indeterminancy of the rate of output is attributable to the discrete data used in this hypothetical example.

We can examine these relations using demand, long-run average cost, and long-run marginal cost. Table 8–3 shows the relevant schedules for the situation set forth in Table 8–2; it indicates the same profit-maximizing condition as before. (Any differences are because of rounding errors.) Maximum profit again corresponds to seven or eight units of output. Unit profit is maximized at seven units of output, but this is immaterial inasmuch as the entrepreneur is concerned with total profit. Equilibrium is clearly where marginal cost equals marginal revenue equals price.

So long as the firm can sell an additional unit for more than the marginal cost of producing that unit, it can increase profit by producing one more. If price is less than marginal cost, the firm should not produce that unit, because it costs more to produce than would be gained from its sale.

**TABLE 8–3**
**Marginal revenue, marginal cost, and profit**

| Output and sales | Marginal revenue or price | Marginal cost | Average cost | Unit profit | Total profit |
|---|---|---|---|---|---|
| 1............. | $5.00 | $17.00 | $17.00 | −$12.00 | −$12.00 |
| 2............. | 5.00 | 1.50 | 9.25 | − 4.25 | − 8.50 |
| 3............. | 5.00 | 1.00 | 6.50 | − 1.50 | − 4.50 |
| 4............. | 5.00 | 1.25 | 5.19 | − 0.19 | − 0.75 |
| 5............. | 5.00 | 1.50 | 4.45 | + 0.55 | + 2.75 |
| 6............. | 5.00 | 2.00 | 4.04 | + 0.96 | + 5.75 |
| 7............. | 5.00 | 3.25 | 3.93 | + 1.07 | + 7.50 |
| 8............. | 5.00 | 5.00 | 4.06 | + 0.94 | + 7.50 |
| 9............. | 5.00 | 8.00 | 4.50 | + 0.50 | + 4.50 |
| 10............. | 5.00 | 12.00 | 5.25 | − 0.25 | − 2.50 |

Let us examine these relations graphically. In Figure 8–9, $LRAC$ and $LRMC$ are the long-run average and marginal cost curves. The demand curve indicates the market price ($p_0$), which is marginal revenue. As long as price is greater than long-run average cost, the firm can make a profit above the opportunity cost. Thus, any output between $x_0$ and $x_1$ yields some profits.

Maximum profit occurs at point $S$ where marginal revenue equals long-run marginal cost. The firm would not, under these circumstances, try to produce at point $M$, the minimum point of long-run

**FIGURE 8–9**
**Profit maximization by the marginal approach**

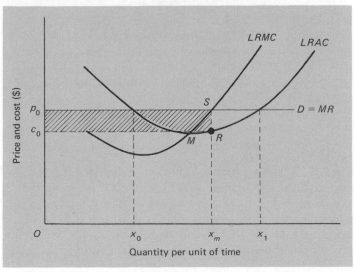

average cost. At $M$, marginal revenue exceeds marginal cost; the firm can gain by producing more output. In Figure 8–9, total revenue (price times quantity) is given by the area of the rectangle $Op_0Sx_m$. Total cost (average cost times quantity) is the area $Oc_0Rx_m$. Total profit $(TR - TC)$ is the shaded area $c_0p_0SR$.

To summarize, the firm will plan to operate at a scale or size such that long-run marginal cost equals price. This is the most profitable situation with the given market price. Of course, if market price changes, the point of long-run profit maximization will change also.

### Zero and negative profit situations

If firms in a competitive industry are, in fact, making above-normal returns, there is strong reason to believe that the price in the market will, in fact, fall. Profits attract new firms into the industry. This increased supply drives down price. Price may even be driven below long-run average cost, at least temporarily.

**FIGURE 8–10**
**Zero and negative profit situations**

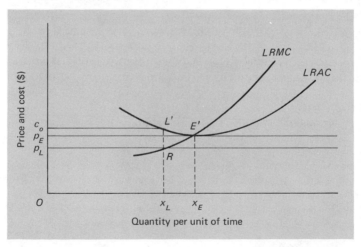

Figure 8–10 shows such a situation. Price $(p_L)$ lies below $LRAC$ at every output; no positive profit can result. The minimum loss at a positive output occurs at $x_L$, where $LRMC$ equals $p_L$. This loss is given by the area of the rectangle $p_Lc_0L'R$, the difference between total cost and total revenue. Firms would no longer wish to enter the industry under these circumstances. In fact, under the assumption

that all firms have similar cost curves, firms already in the industry would be induced to exit.[11]

If an increase in the number of firms increases supply and lowers price, a decrease in the number of firms must decrease supply and raise price. Firms would be motivated to leave the industry until market price rises sufficiently to eliminate losses. Let us assume that price rises to $p_E$ in Figure 8–10. After firms have had sufficient time to adjust optimally, all profit above opportunity cost is eliminated. Price equals marginal cost at $x_E$. At this output, price also equals average cost; hence, total cost equals total revenue. At any other positive output, average cost is above price, and losses result.

While no profit results at $x_E$, no firm is induced to leave the industry since each covers its opportunity cost—that is, the amount the entrepreneur could make in any alternative industry. Neither is any other firm induced to enter, since it would earn only its opportunity cost, which it presumably earns already. Each firm is in profit-maximizing equilibrium, since long-run marginal cost equals marginal revenue; of course, this maximum pure profit is zero. The industry is also in long-run equilibrium, because price equals long-run average cost for each firm. Since profit is zero, no firm is induced to enter and none is induced to leave.

**Principle.**  Long-run equilibrium of a competitive industry involves several equilibrium conditions. Each firm in the industry must be in long-run (and short-run) profit-maximizing equilibrium; marginal revenue equals long-run marginal cost. The entry or exit of firms must compete away all pure profit. Then, all firms must produce the quantity at which price equals the minimum long-run average cost.

### Graphical exposition of long-run equilibrium

Consider a firm in a short-run situation in which it incurs a loss. In looking to the long run, the entrepreneur has two options: liquidate the business and transfer resources to a more profitable alternative

---

[11] The student might note that we violate our assumption of perfect knowledge by positing that enough firms enter to drive the price down to $p_L$. Why would a firm with perfect knowledge enter knowing full well it would make losses? We could assume that demand suddenly falls and drives price to $p_L$. The explanation given, however, is more consistent with the model of long-run industry equilibrium, to be analyzed later in this chapter.

The reason we know all firms are making losses is that the firms in the industry are operating in the short run and, except for the one point at which they are equal, short-run average cost is everywhere greater than long-run average cost. Thus, if price is less than $LRAC$, it is also at least as far below $SRAC$, if not farther.

or construct a plant of a more suitable or profitable size and remain in the industry. Furthermore, even a firm in a profitable short-run situation may build at a more appropriate size in the long run in order to make even more profit. But, if profits are obtainable in the industry, new firms enter. This adjustment of the number of firms in the industry in response to profit motivation is the key element in establishing long-run equilibrium.

The process of attaining long-run equilibrium in a perfectly competitive industry is illustrated in Figure 8–11. Suppose each

**FIGURE 8–11**
**Long-run equilibrium adjustment in a perfectly competitive industry**

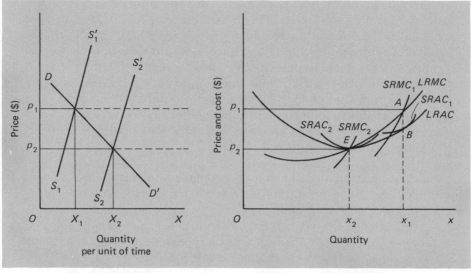

**Panel A**
**Long-run market equilibrium**

**Panel B**
**Long-run equilibrium adjustment**
**of a firm**

firm in the industry is identical. Its size is represented by $SRAC_1$ and $SRMC_1$ in panel B. The market demand curve is given by $DD'$ in panel A, and the market supply is $S_1S'_1$. Market equilibrium establishes the price of $p_1$ per unit and total output and sales of $X_1$ units per period of time. At price $p_1$, each plant is built to produce $x_1$ units (the output at which $p_1 = LRMC$) at least possible cost ($x_1B$). Each firm receives a profit of $AB$ per unit of output. The number of firms multiplied by $x_1$ (each firm's output) equals $X_1$ (total output). Although each firm is in equilibrium, the industry itself is not. As we saw earlier, the appearance of *pure economic profit,* a return in excess of that obtainable elsewhere, attracts new firms into the industry, expanding industry supply, say to $S_2S'_2$, and reducing market price. The process of new entry might be very slow, or it might be very fast. It depends primarily upon the liquid assets in other industries. In any event, as time elapses, new firms will enter the industry, thereby shifting the supply curve to the right.

When each firm adjusts optimally to the new market price, the output of each will be smaller. The larger number of firms accounts for the increase in output from $X_1$ in panel A. Now, all firms produce the output at which $p_2$ equals $LRMC$ at output $x_2$. The number of old firms plus the number of new entrants times $x_2$ equals $X_2$. Since the new price equals $LRMC$ and $SMRC_2$ at $E$, the minimum $LRAC$ and the minimum $SRAC_2$, neither profit nor loss is present for any firm. Both the industry and its firms are in long-run equilibrium.

The long-run equilibrium position of a firm in a perfectly competitive industry is explained by Figure 8–12. As we have seen, if price

**FIGURE 8–12**
**Long-run equilibrium of a firm in a perfectly competitive industry**

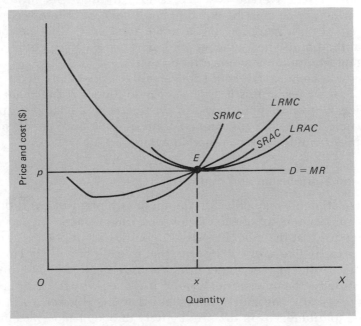

is above $p$, each established firm can adjust plant size and earn a pure profit. New firms are attracted into the industry, shifting the supply curve to the right. Price falls, and, hence, the horizontal demand curve facing each firm, old and new, falls also. All firms readjust. If "too many" firms enter, market price and each firm's horizontal demand curve may fall below $p$. Each firm incurs a loss.

As their plants and equipment depreciate, some firms will leave the industry, thereby causing the market supply curve to shift to the left. Market price and, accordingly, the horizontal individual demand curves rise.

So long as the cost curves do not change, the only conceivable point of long-run equilibrium occurs at point $E$ in Figure 8–12. Each firm in the industry receives neither profit nor loss. There is no incentive for further entry, because the rate of return in this industry is the same as in the best alternative. But for the same reason, there is no incentive for a firm to leave the industry. The number of firms stabilizes, each firm with a short-run plant represented by $SRAC$ and $SRMC$. Note, however, that the entrepreneur is covering opportunity costs, since these are included in the cost curves. We say the firm earns "normal" profit, but not pure profit.

Firms will enter or leave the industry if there is either pure profit or pure loss. Therefore, since the position of long-run equilibrium must be consistent with *zero* profit (and zero loss), it is necessary that price equal average cost. For a firm to attain its individual equilibrium, price must be equal to marginal cost. Therefore, price must equal both marginal and average total cost. This can occur only at the point where average and marginal cost are equal, or at the point of minimum average total cost.

The statement, so far, could conceivably apply to any $SRAC$ and $SRMC$. However, unless it applies only to the short-run plant that coincides with minimum long-run average cost, a change in plant size would lead to the appearance of pure profit, and the wheels of adjustment would be set in motion again.

### Long-run equilibrium and rent

Some students may object to the model of long-run equilibrium at the minimum point of each firm's long-run average cost curve on the grounds that the model is based upon the assumption that each firm is exactly like every other firm; that is, each firm's cost curve is the same as that of every other firm. We have made that assumption for simplicity; theory does not require it. To see why the assumption is not necessary, one must understand that any differences in cost are due to differences in the productivity of one or more resources. Assume that all firms except one are alike; that firm, because of (say) a more favorable location, has a lower cost curve. The owner of that location (who could be the owner of the firm) could raise the rent to the firm (if the person is the firm's owner, the opportunity cost would rise) up to the point at which the firm's pure profit disappears. The firm would be motivated to pay the rent, since the owner of the firm would continue making the equivalent of the best alternative. If the firm did not pay that rent, some other firm would.

Thus, the cost of the previously lower-cost firm would tend to rise because of increased rent. It would not, of course, rise above those of other firms, because any higher rent would occasion losses; hence, no firm would pay it. The same type of argument applies to the superiority of other specialized resources, including the superiority of management. If a superior manager, even a manager-owner, could lower the firm's costs, that manager could presumably lower the costs of other firms as well. The hiring price would be bid up, or, if the owner of the resource is the owner of the firm, the opportunity cost would rise. At equilibrium, all firms' long-run average cost curves would, therefore, reach their minimum points at the same cost (albeit not necessarily at the same output), and no firm would make pure profit or loss (although some might have differing factor payments or rents).

We might also note that firms with even higher cost structures are generally "waiting in the wings" to enter the industry if demand increases and drives up prices sufficiently to cover their costs. These higher-cost firms could cover opportunity cost only at a higher price. But if price increases enough to induce their entry, the owners of resources that cause the firms already in the industry to have lower costs than the new firms will receive increased rents. Or some firms that were just making normal profits prior to the increase in price may begin to enjoy above-normal profits, which will, in the long run, be dispersed as rents to the resources responsible for lower costs.

# APPLICATION

## Long-run profits in the defense industry

The theory developed in this chapter predicts that, when profit is "abnormally" high in one sector of the economy, firms will enter that business, drive down prices, and eliminate the above-normal profit, so long as entry is reasonably free. However, we frequently hear about the vast profits being made in some businesses over long periods of time even in the face of free entry. Admittedly, no industry exhibits all the characteristics of perfect competition, but the logic of the theory should fit much of the economy. Some major industries in which we hear of "excessive" or "exorbitant" profit over a long period are the defense industries. During times of war or preparation for war, the "war profiteers" are allegedly free from competition; otherwise, their profits would be competed away. On the other hand, possibly the defense industries do fit our theory.

When we hear of the profits in the defense establishment, we might wonder why investors, induced by these profits, do not change some of their capital from non-defense-oriented industry to defense. The resulting increase in capacity, according to our theory, would drive down prices and eliminate the excess profit. The defense industries allegedly have been prospering since World War II. Surely that is sufficient time for entry to have taken place. Only three explanations seem possible. First, entry into the industry is difficult. Second, risks are greater in the defense industry than elsewhere, and the larger returns are necessary to compensate for increased risk. Third, the allegation is not correct. Therefore, let us examine the evidence to obtain a solution.

In a paper by George J. Stigler and Claire Friedland, considerable evidence in this area was presented.[12] The first piece of evidence is the report of 40 major defense contractors on their rates of return from both defense and commercial or nondefense business. From 1958 through 1961, the average return from defense contracts exceeded the average return from nondefense. Furthermore, the average defense-oriented return was greater than the average return of the Federal Trade Commission–Securities and Exchange Commission listing of the returns for 3,500 companies. From 1962 through 1968, the average defense rate of return of the 40 defense contractors was less than both the return of these firms from commercial business and the average rate of return of the FTC–SEC 3,500 companies. In the last year of the sample, 1968, the defense return averaged 6.8 percent while the 3,500-firm average return was 10.2 percent. Note that the latter years included the period of the vast Viet Nam buildup.

The relative performances of all stocks and the stocks of the major defense contractors point in essentially the same direction. Investments in the defense contractors were almost twice as profitable as the average return from investment in all stocks on the New York Stock Exchange during the 1950s. During the 1960s, investments in the major defense contractors did approximately as well as the average investment in all stocks. Stock market performance shows a positive relation with the ratio of defense to total sales in the 1950s and no significant relation for the leading defense contractors of 1959 for the 1960s.

From the evidence, it appears that the profitability of defense industries was higher than normal in the 1950s but that entry (or something) competed away the above-normal profits in the 1960s. It seems that the defense industry has performed in somewhat the way

---

[12] G. J. Stigler and C. Friedland, "Profits of Defense Contractors," *American Economic Review* 61, no. 4 (September 1971): 692–94.

we would predict: early excess profits were competed away in the long run.

## 8.7 CONSTANT–INCREASING–, AND DECREASING–COST INDUSTRIES

The analysis thus far has been, in large part, based upon the tacit assumption of "constant cost," in the sense that expanded resource use by the industry does not entail an increase in resource prices. To carry the analysis further and to make it more explicit, constant-, increasing-, and decreasing-cost industries are examined in this section. We shall discover that a decreasing-cost industry leads to a downward-sloping supply curve. Such an industry is an empirical rarity.

### Constant-cost industries

Long-run equilibrium and long-run supply price under conditions of constant cost are explained by Figure 8–13. Panel A shows the long- and short-run conditions of each firm in the industry, while panel B depicts the market as a whole. $D_1D'_1$ and $S_1S'_1$ are the original market demand and supply curves, establishing a market equilibrium price of $\bar{p}$ dollars per unit. We assume that the industry has attained a position of long-run equilibrium, so the position of

**FIGURE 8–13**
**Long-run equilibrium and supply price in a perfectly competitive industry subject to constant cost**

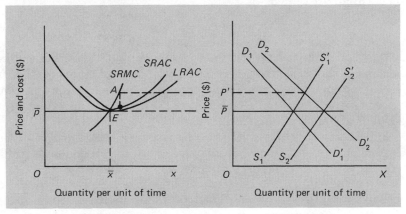

Panel A
Long-run equilibrium of the firm

Panel B
Long-run market equilibrium

each firm in the industry is depicted by panel A—the price line is tangent to the long- and short-run average cost curves at their minimum points.

Now suppose demand increases to $D_2D'_2$. With the number of firms fixed, the price will rise to $p'$, and each firm will move to short-run equilibrium at point $A$. However, at point $A$, each firm earns a pure economic profit inasmuch as price exceeds average cost. New entrants are thereby attracted into the industry; the industry supply curve shifts to the right. In this case, we assume that all resources used are so general that increased use in this industry does not affect the market price of resources. As a consequence, the entrance of new firms does not increase the costs of existing firms; the $LRAC$ curve of established firms does not shift, and new firms can operate with an identical $LRAC$ curve. Long-run equilibrium adjustment to the shift in demand is accomplished when the number of firms expands to the point at which $S_2S'_2$ is the industry supply curve with a given number of firms in the industry.

In other words, since output can be expanded by expanding the number of firms, each producing $\bar{x}$ units per period of time at average cost $\bar{p}$, the industry has a constant long-run supply price equal to $\bar{p}$ dollars per unit. If price were above this level, firms of the size represented by $SRAC$ would continue to enter the industry in order to reap the pure profit obtainable. If price was less than $\bar{p}$, some firms would ultimately leave the industry to avoid the pure economic loss. Hence, in the special case in which an expansion of resource use does not lead to an increase in resource price, the long-run industry supply price is constant. This is precisely the meaning of a constant-cost industry.

### Increasing-cost industries

An increasing-cost industry is depicted in Figure 8–14. The original situation is the same as in Figure 8–12. The industry is in a position of long-run equilibrium. $D_1D'_1$ and $S_1S'_1$ are the market demand and supply curves, respectively. Equilibrium price is $p_1$. Each firm operates at point $E_1$, where price equals minimum average cost—both long- and short-run cost. Thus, each firm is also in a position of long-run equilibrium.

Let demand shift to $D_2D'_2$ so that price rises to a much higher level. The higher price is accompanied by pure economic profit; new firms are consequently attracted into the industry. The use of resources expands, but now we assume resource-price increases with expanded resource use. The cost of inputs therefore increases for the established firms as well as for the new entrants. As a result, the entire set of cost curves shifts upward, say, to a position represented by $LRAC_2$ in panel A.[13]

Naturally, the process of equilibrium adjustment is not instantaneous. The $LRAC$ curve gradually shifts upward, as new entrants gradually join the industry. The marginal cost curves of all firms shift to the left, as new firms enter and bid up factor prices. Thus, two forces tend to work in opposite directions upon the industry's supply curve. Shifting marginal cost to the left tends to shift the industry's supply curve to the left. However, new firms enter the industry, and this entry tends to shift industry supply to the right. The forces causing a shift to the right (entry) must dominate those causing a shift to the left (rise in marginal costs); otherwise, total output could not expand as dictated by the increase in market price.

To see why supply must shift to the right after an increase in demand, let us assume that the opposite happens. In Figure 8–14,

**FIGURE 8–14**
**Long-run equilibrium and supply price in a perfectly competitive industry subject to increasing cost**

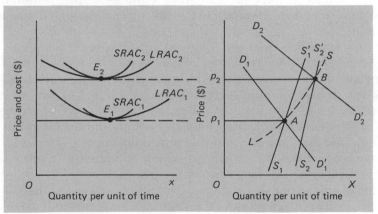

| Panel A | Panel B |
|---|---|
| **Long-run equilibrium of the firm** | **Long-run market equilibrium** |

demand, as before, shifts to $D_2D'_2$. In the short run, price and quantity increase along with profits. The profits attract new firms, which, upon entering, bid up resource prices. All cost curves rise, as indicated in panel A. Suppose, however, that the leftward shift in all

---

[13] As Figure 8–14 is constructed, the minimum point on $LRAC$ shifts to the left as $LRAC$ shifts upward. In fact, minimum $LRAC$ can correspond to either a smaller or a larger output. The analysis underlying the exact nature of the shift involves an advanced concept not treated in this text.

marginal cost curves dominates the tendency for an increase in supply caused by entry. Therefore, the new supply curve would lie somewhere to the left of $S_1S'_1$. If demand remains $D_2D'_2$, price must be greater than $p_2$; firms must be making pure profits; entry must continue. If the same process reoccurs, price will rise further, costs will rise, profits will continue, and entry will be further encouraged. Thus, a leftward shift in supply is not consistent with equilibrium. At some point, the entry of new firms must dominate the increase in costs, and supply must shift to the right, though not by as much as it would in a constant-cost industry, since under constant costs, no shift in marginal and average costs occurs.

The process of adjustment must continue until a position of long-run equilibrium is attained. In Figure 8–14, this is depicted by the intersection of $D_2D'_2$ and $S_2S'_2$, establishing an equilibrium price of $p_2$ dollars per unit. Each firm produces at point $E_2$, where price equals minimum average cost. The important point to emphasize is that, in constant-cost industries, new firms enter until price returns to the unchanged level of minimum long-run average cost. For industries subject to increasing cost, new firms enter until minimum long-run average cost shifts upward to equal the new price.

In the transition from one long-run equilibrium to the other, the long-run supply price increases from $p_1$ to $p_2$. This is precisely what is meant by an increasing-cost industry. In keeping with this, the long-run industry supply curve is given by a line, $LS$, joining such points as $A$ and $B$ in panel B. Thus, an increasing-cost industry is one with a positively sloped long-run supply curve. Alternatively stated, after all long-run equilibrium adjustments are made, an increasing-cost industry is one in which an increase in output requires an increase in long-run supply price.

Recall also in our above discussion of rents, we noted that, possibly because of scarce resources, industry expansion could take place only through the entry of higher-cost firms, perhaps because less productive resources are used. Until now, we have assumed all firms are alike, and the only reason for cost to rise is because resource prices are bid up. But, if expansion takes place through the entry of higher-cost firms, we have an increasing-cost industry as well. Demand increases; firms that would have been previously unprofitable enter. The lower-cost firms earn pure profits, which are competed away by rents to the scarce resources. The final equilibrium price is, therefore, higher than before, but each firm is operating at the minimum point on long-run average cost. The lower-cost firms have their cost curves pushed up by rents. For simplicity, without loss of analytical usefulness, economists generally assume, in the theory of perfect competition, that all firms are identical.

### Decreasing-cost industries

A decreasing-cost industry exists when the market price actually falls after the initial increase in demand. Oddly, the long-run industry supply is downward sloping.

Such an industry is graphically described by Figure 8–15. Firms begin in equilibrium in panel A at point $E_1$. Price is equal to $SRAC$ and $LRAC$; firms in the market make normal returns. The market price is determined by the intersection of supply and demand in panel B—that is, the intersection of $D_1D_1'$ and $S_1S_1'$ at $M$. Demand then increases so the new equilibrium is at $N$. At such high prices, firms make above-normal profits and entry takes place. So far, we have the same story as before.

The difference is that, as entry occurs, the cost of production falls. The long-run equilibrium of the firm is not restored until prices are lower than before the shift in demand, as shown in Panel A. We see, in panel B, that supply must have increased relative to demand, reaching a new equilibrium at $Q$. The long-run market price has fallen from $p_1$ to $p_2$, making the long-run supply curve, $LS$, downward sloping. Thus, a decreasing-cost industry is characterized by a long-run supply curve with a negative slope.

Decreasing-cost industries are not commonly observed, but they are conceivable. For example, increases in demand may encourage specialization in the industry and lower costs. As an illustration, in small towns, medical care can be relatively expensive when laboratory testing must be done out of town, but if the town grows and the demand for medical care increases, laboratories may be set up nearby, allowing tests to be done at a lower cost. As a result of the increase in demand, each doctor can charge patients lower prices for medical tests.

We must be very careful though about identifying a decreasing-cost industry. Everyone can think of many examples, over the past decades, of products that decreased dramatically in price while experiencing significant gains in sales and quality. One of the most recent examples is the hand-calculator industry. Prices dropped greatly as sales increased. The computer industry experienced the same phenomenon. Earlier, color TV sets dropped in price as sales increased; this was also the case with many household appliances.

These and other cases *are not examples of decreasing-cost industries* in the sense discussed above. In the case of decreasing-cost industries, an increase in output reduces the price of some inputs because of increased use. For such industries, we stress that costs fall because of reduced input prices, and a decreasing-cost industry results. This is not the case in the above examples. Technological change is the proper explanation in such cases.

**FIGURE 8–15**
Long-run equilibrium and supply price in
a perfectly competitive industry subject
to decreasing costs

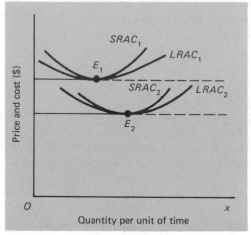

**Panel A**
**Long-run equilibrium of the firm**

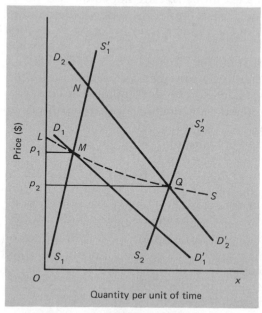

**Panel B**
**Long-run market equilibrium**

**FIGURE 8–16**
**Effect of technological change**

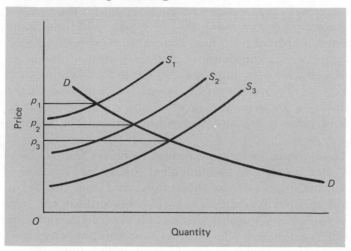

**Panel A**

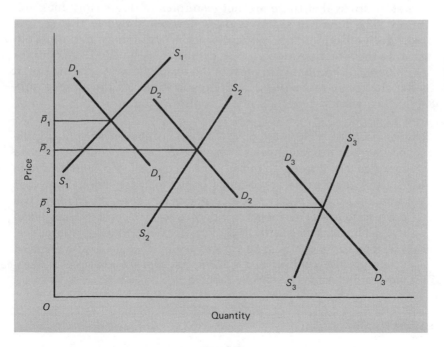

**Panel B**

Recall that technological change lowers firms' costs and, consequently, increases industry supply. Two possible situations are depicted in Figure 8–16. In panel A, the demand for the product, $DD$, remains constant over a reasonably long period of time. Begin with a long-run supply of $S_1$. Thus, a price of $p_1$ results. If technological change occurs, the isoquant map shifts toward the origin, causing a reduction in costs. Supply increases to $S_2$, lowering price to $p_2$. Clearly, equilibrium output increases. Technological change continues (induced, spontaneous, or otherwise), increasing supply to $S_3$, reducing price to $p_3$, and increasing output. The situation could continue.

In panel B, the demand for the product increases from $D_1D_1$ to $D_2D_2$ to $D_3D_3$. But, because of technological change, not because of a reduction in factor prices from increased factor use, supply increases even more, from $S_1S_1$ to $S_2S_2$ to $S_3S_3$. These shifts cause price to fall from $\bar{p}_1$ to $\bar{p}_2$ to $\bar{p}_3$. We note that output also increases in this case. Supply does not increase because of reduced input prices from increased use, but from technological change, which improves the production process and lowers costs; or, in some instances, the technological change could have occurred in the factor market, causing a reduction in the price of the input.

Let us stress that these are not examples of decreasing long-run supply. The long-run supply curves derived above in this section were derived under the assumption that technology remains constant. In the situations depicted in Figure 8–16 and in the examples given here, and probably in most of the examples you can think of, it is the change in technology that is responsible for the shift in supply. Thus, we have no theoretical contradiction.

**Relation.** Constant, increasing, or decreasing cost in an industry depends upon the way in which resource prices respond to expanded resource use. If resource prices remain constant, the industry is subject to constant cost; if resource prices increase, the industry has increasing costs; and if resource prices decrease, the industry has decreasing costs. The long-run supply curve for a constant-cost industry is a horizontal line at the level of the constant long-run supply price. The long-run industry supply curve under conditions of increasing cost is positively sloped, and the long-run supply curve for a decreasing-cost industry is downward sloping.

## APPLICATION

### Long-run effects of a price ceiling on coal

Suppose the demand for coal at the retail level is elastic over the relevant price range. Further, suppose the government feels that the price of coal is too high. It, therefore, places a price ceiling, or maximum on coal at the mine. What will happen to the price of coal at the retail level? Will total receipts of retailers increase or decrease?

As a first step, let us consider what happens at the mine (or mining area). Assume, for analytical purposes, that coal mining is a perfectly competitive, increasing-cost industry. Assume also that, before the imposition of the ceiling price, the industry was in long-run equilibrium; each firm produced the quantity at which $P = LRAC$ and, therefore, enjoyed no pure profit. Figure 8–17 shows the market demand and supply for coal at the mine. Demand $(D_m D'_m)$ is the demand curve of retailers for coal at the mine. It is derived holding the demand for coal from retailers and other factors constant. (We assume that individual consumers cannot purchase coal directly from the mine.)

**FIGURE 8–17**
**Supply and demand at the mine**

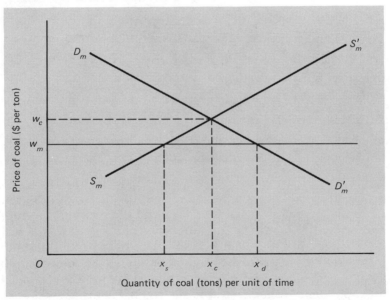

The long-run industry supply curve, $S_m S'_m$, is the type of supply curve developed above. It is the locus of long-run equilibria for the mining industry. Since we assume an increasing-cost industry, $S_m S'_m$ is upward sloping. The equilibrium price at the mine is $w_c$ and equilibrium quantity is $x_c$.

Figure 8–18 shows demand and supply conditions at retail. $D_r D'_r$ is the consumers' demand for coal. $S_r S'_r$, based upon a given

**FIGURE 8–18**
**Demand and supply at retail**

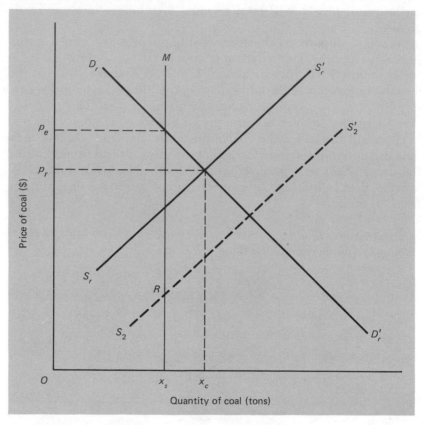

cost of coal at the mines to retailers (Fig. 8–17, $w_c$), is the retailers' supply curve. Since coal is an input for the retailers, the supply
curve for coal at retail should shift when the price of coal at the
mines changes, just as a change in the price of any factor of production changes the supply of the product produced. Specifically, when
the price at the mine falls, other things remaining the same, the
retail supply curve should shift to the right. That is, if retailers can
buy coal more cheaply, they would be willing and able to supply
more retail coal at every retail price. Begin with equilibrium in the
retail market occurring at a price of $p_r$ (given a price at the mine of
$w_c$) and a quantity sold of $x_c$, obviously the same as $x_c$ in Figure
8–17, because the retailers sell all that they buy.

Returning to Figure 8–17, assume that the government sets the
ceiling price $w_m$. Quantity demanded by retailers at the new price
is $x_d$. The new price is below $w_c$ (the price at which neither profit

nor loss occurs); thus, firms begin to make losses and some leave the industry. Since we assume that mining is an increasing-cost industry, the exit of firms and the decrease in quantity produced lower factor prices and, hence, lower the long-run average and marginal cost curves of the remaining firms in the industry. Figure 8–19

**FIGURE 8–19**
**Cost curve of a firm**

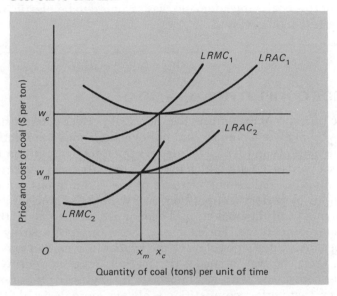

Quantity of coal (tons) per unit of time

shows the process. Long-run average and marginal costs fall from $LRAC_1$ and $LRMC_1$ to $LRAC_2$ and $LRMC_2$. The minimum point on $LRAC_2$ equals the ceiling price of $w_m$. Each remaining firm now produces $x_m$ (the new equilibrium output) rather than $x_c$, but there are fewer firms, none of which makes pure profit. The new quantity supplied by the industry, indicated in Figure 8–17, is $x_s$. Thus, a shortage (excess demand) of $x_s x_d$ occurs at the mines, since retailers now wish to purchase $x_d$, but the mines are only willing to sell $x_s$. The mining industry must find some method of allocation (rationing, first come–first served, favoritism, and so on) in order to determine which retailers get the available supply. In any case, only $x_s$ is available to the retailers.

Now, according to our analysis, the lower price of coal at the mine should cause supply at retail to shift to $S_2 S'_2$ (Figure 8–18). Retail price should fall, and the quantity of coal sold should increase as determined by the intersection of $D_r D'_r$ and $S_2 S'_2$. But remember that only $x_s$ is produced, so only $x_s$ can be sold. The curve $S_2S'_2$ specifies the quantities that retailers are *willing* to sell at the mine price of $w_m$; the vertical line $Mx_s$ indicates the maximum amount retailers are *able* to sell at that price. Thus, the curve $S_2RM$ shows the quantities that retailers are *willing and able* to sell at each retail price when the mine price is fixed at $w_m$.

The intersection of supply and demand now occurs at the price $p_e$, clearly higher than the old price. The quantity sold is $x_s$. After the ceiling price at the mine is imposed, consumers pay a higher price for less coal. Since demand was assumed to be elastic, retailers receive less total revenue.

## 8.8 PERFECT COMPETITION AS A GOAL

One purpose of presenting the theory of perfect competition is to show why many economists and policymakers make perfectly competitive markets an ideal. The model of perfect competition is often used as a yardstick with which to compare real-world markets. Most actual markets violate one or more of the assumptions underlying the model of perfect competition, but which assumption a market fails to meet tells lawmakers and economists how to make the market more competitive. For example, if the price of hearing aids is high because elderly people lack the proper information to compare prices, then the way to make the market more competitive is to provide consumers with the information they need. It is not clear, however, that perfect competition is always more desirable than are other market structures. This section briefly analyzes the desirable and possibly undesirable features of the model.

### Desirability of perfect competition

Foremost, perfect competition is viewed as a standard of market performance, because the assumptions underlying the model guarantee that a large number of producers operate at the lowest possible point on their $LRAC$ curve, and since $P = LRMC = LRAC$, consumers pay the lowest possible price for a good or service.

Perhaps equally important, in a perfectly competitive market, the fundamental forces of supply and demand determine who gets what and how it is produced. Goods are produced by the lowest-cost firms; as prices rise, less efficient firms may enter, but, if prices fall, it is these firms that exit first. Therefore, competition guarantees that the lowest-cost producers operate. This is the "how" of production. The "what" in production is established by demand. Consumers, not producers, decide this question. Cattle ranchers would like to see Americans eat more beef, but the decision is made by buyers. Consumers decide whether they want beef, pork, poultry, or even meat at all. Free entry into, and exit from, any industry lets consumers make this choice. Without this assumption in the model, it might be the case that beef is the only meat available now because of historical preferences. Finally, "who" gets what is produced is determined by the willingness and ability of consumers to pay. This, we know, is influenced by tastes, income, and other prices, but the market prevents people from buying a product if their willingness to pay is below the marginal cost of production. This would be a waste of resources which could be devoted to producing goods and services valued above their marginal cost.

Taking all of these features of perfect competition into consideration, probably the most important characteristic of competitive markets is that buyers and sellers are so small relative to the total market that anyone acting alone cannot affect market prices. We will see in the next two chapters that, because of economies of scale, a few or even one firm may have lower costs than would be the case with a large number of producers. These kinds of market structures give producers some control over price. Prices can be higher because consumers do not have as many substitutable products. What is produced and how to produce it are no longer determined by the impersonal interaction of supply and demand.

In fact, even when it is apparent that the overall cost of production is higher with many producers than with just a few firms, many economists would prefer more producers to fewer, because the *market* determines prices and output, rather than the *managers* of a few large businesses. In a 1945 court decision that eventually lead to a more competitive aluminum industry, Judge Learned Hand wrote in his court opinion:

> It is possible, because of its indirect social or moral effect, to prefer a system of small producers, each dependent for success upon his own skill and character, to one in which the great mass of those engaged must accept the direction of a few.[14]

It must be pointed out, however, that a large number of competing firms goes a long way toward explaining some undesirable aspects of the model of perfect competition.

### Incentive effects of being small

In making any decision, a firm or an individual weighs the marginal effect on the cost that must be paid to carry out an activity

---

[14] *U.S.* v. *Alcoa Aluminum*, 148 F. 2d 416 (1945).

against the marginal effect of that activity on revenue or benefit. It may be that the marginal increase in benefit is rather small, but, if the marginal effect on the total cost is smaller, the activity will be carried out. In the case of competitive firms, or of individuals acting alone, their actions would generally have no *perceivable* effect on the total benefit. For example, this characteristic of competitive behavior in large part explains why appeals for voluntary actions, supposedly in the public interest, but not necessarily in the interest of the firm or the individual, seldom accomplish what the appealer wishes, in the case of either competitive firms or individuals.

Consider the following example. Suppose that scientists discover that a certain insecticide used by most farmers is harming much of the wildlife in a particular state. As is frequently the case, the governor pleads for farmers to change to a brand of insecticide that, presumably, would not harm wildlife. Now, clearly, the original, harmful insecticide is more productive, i.e., leads to lower cost, or farmers would have been using some other brand voluntarily. The question is, would farmers have any reason to comply with the governor's request, even knowing that the original brand of insecticide harms wildlife? Probably not! Why not?

In the first place farmers must realize that each one, acting alone, probably has no effect, or an infinitesimal effect, on total wildlife killed or damaged, even though all farmers acting together would have an effect. Thus, no farmer would have the incentive to bear higher costs that have zero effect, even though each farmer deplores the fact that wild animals are being damaged or killed. Even if a farmer did decide to comply with the plea, the higher costs in the long run would drive the operation out of business. Furthermore, each farmer, being competitive, knows that the particular brand of insecticide used has no effect on the farm's sales or on the price that can be obtained for the product. The output of any one farm is indistinguishable from the output of any other farm. In this case, voluntary actions by any individual farmer would not help sales or the public. Either a tax would have to be levied or a law passed.

We can apply the same analysis to water or air pollution. If no one owns the water or air (we will return to the effect of property rights in the final chapter), any firm can pollute at zero cost. If each firm knows that there are so many firms polluting that its own polluting activity has practically a zero effect on total pollution, appeals for voluntary restraint would have little or no effect on the total. Every firm knows that reducing the amount of pollution would raise costs but would have no effect on the price of the product. Knowing the increase would have no effect on the price of the product, no firm would raise costs voluntarily. Therefore, no firm would have the incentive to reduce pollution voluntarily. (Again, if someone owned the water and could charge for polluting, firms would reduce pollution, but this is a problem that belongs in the section on property rights, and will be addressed in the final chapter.)

Similar analysis applies to the behavior of individuals in response to appeals for voluntary actions in the alleged social interest. Take, for example, the national reduction in the speed limit to 55 miles per hour. Would governmental appeals to reduce speed in order to conserve the nation's energy have worked? What do you think?

As you well know by now, time is valuable. You know that if we drive the largest "gas guzzling" automobile 24 hours a day all year at 90 miles per hour, it would have absolutely no effect on the nation's total gasoline consumption. For each individual, slowing down would merely cost valuable time but would have no perceivable effect on total consumption. There would be few volunteers. We see now, even with the law, the penalty for speeding is so small that the 55-mile-per-hour driver on the expressways of the nation is a rarity. There has been, thus far, only slight reduction in average speed.

What about appeals by the president to keep homes colder in winter and use less air conditioning in the summer in order to conserve the nation's gas and electricity? If all homes complied, certainly the total use would decline. But any household knows that the temperature of its home has absolutely no effect on national energy use. Why bear discomfort if the discomfort has no perceivable effect on the total? Frequently, during water shortages in cities (often caused by too low prices), city officials ask households to cut down water use voluntarily. Again, everyone knows that his or her own use of water has no effect on the city's water use, so why comply?

During World War II, the government imposed price controls and rationing in the case of many goods. National appeals were made to consumers not to deal with black markets in the nation's interest. Yet we are told there was considerable trade in black markets. Appeals to patriotism did not work well even when the country experienced the greatest period of national purpose and patriotism in its entire history. Why should appeals to national purpose work any better now?

In sum, if any competitive firm is doing a social "bad," whatever that is, it would have little incentive to cease doing "bad" if its actions alone have only an infinitesimal effect on the total amount of "bad" and zero effect on sales, but would raise costs. In fact, even if owners of the competitive firms are earning rents on some of their resources, and therefore would not be driven out of business by the increased cost, few owners would be willing to sacrifice income, knowing the sacrificed income has no effect on total "bad."

## Product variety

Another characteristic of perfectly competitive markets that may have undesirable consequences is a complete lack of product variety. Products must be homogeneous in competitive markets so that they are perfectly substitutable, thus insuring that no seller has any power to set prices. In some markets, this is not a bothersome imposition. Product variety is not important, for instance, in agriculture, steel production, and coal. But for other markets, homogeneity would make consumers very unhappy. Suppose there was perfect competition in the apparel industry. Homogeneity implies one color, one style, one fabric. . . . You can quickly understand why consumers would not want *perfectly* competitive markets in such cases.

As soon as noticeable quality differences are allowed between substitutable products the products become less substitutable. A Mercedes Benz is not readily substituted by a Ford. In fact, most consumers would not consider the two automobiles to be in the same market, even though Ford would like you to believe differently. Think about it yourselves; if you were seriously contemplating the purchase of a Ford, would you be thinking about buying a Mercedes Benz instead?

Product variety also leads to brand loyalties, which makes apparently very similar products unsubstitutable. For instance, firms like Levi Strauss & Co. and Coca-Cola sell products that have many substitutes, but because of strong brand loyalties among consumers, they dominate the markets in which they sell. So strongly do consumers identify with Levi Strauss & Co. and Coca-Cola that even substitute denim jeans and soft drinks are referred to by their respective registered brand names. It is difficult to say how these loyalties develop. There are actually many possible reasons, and it is not easy to identify one as being the cause in a particular case. Firms attract loyal customers by having a reputation for superior quality, by being the first in the market with a new product, through advertising and creating an image associated with the consumption of their product, by providing good service, and so on.

In any case, there is a cost connected with product variety. Product differentiation, whether real or created by advertising, gives a seller some control over price. Prices can be raised without the fear of losing all of the product's sales. In other words, the demand curve of the seller is no longer perfectly elastic. As a consequence, we will see in Chapter 10 that, if the cost curves are not different for perfectly competitive producers, prices and the average cost of production will be higher. This outcome is considered the cost of product variety.

## 8.9 SUMMARY

Perfectly competitive markets exist when there are a large number of buyers and sellers, identical products, easy entry and exit by producers, perfect information, and prices freely determined by the interaction of supply and demand. In the short run, the firm produces the quantity at which short-run marginal cost equals price, so long as price exceeds average variable cost. Therefore, marginal cost above average variable cost is the firm's short-run supply. If all input prices are given to the industry, industry short-run supply is the horizontal summation of all marginal cost curves. If the industry's (although not the individual firm's) use of the inputs affects the prices of some inputs, industry supply is less elastic than this horizontal summation. In the long run, the entry and exit of firms force each firm to produce at minimum $LRAC$, where $LRAC = LRMC = SRAC = SRMC$. Profit is zero at this output, although each entrepreneur earns opportunity cost. In a constant-cost industry, long-run industry supply is a horizontal line at the level of the firm's minimum long-run average cost. If the industry's use increases the prices of some inputs directly, the industry's long-run supply curve increases with output, and it is an increasing-cost industry. If input prices fall, the industry's long-run supply curve decreases with output, and the industry is a decreasing-cost industry.

Up to this point, the salient feature of perfect competition is that, in long-run market equilibrium, market price equals minimum average cost. This means that each unit of output is produced at the lowest possible cost, either from the standpoint of money cost or of resource use. The product sells for its average (long-run) cost of production; each firm, accordingly, earns the going rate of return in competitive industries, nothing more or less.

It should be emphasized that firms do not choose to produce the quantity with the lowest possible long-run average cost simply because they believe this level of production is optimal for society and they wish to benefit society. The firms are merely trying to maximize their profits. Given that motivation, the market *forces* firms to produce at that point. If society benefits, it is not through any benevolence of firms but through the functioning of the market.

Finally, it should be emphasized that the theory of perfect competition is not designed to describe specific real-world firms. It is a theoretical model that is frequently useful in explaining real-world behavior and in predicting the economic consequences of changes in the different variables contained in the model. The conclusions of the theory, not the assumptions, are the crucial points when analyzing economic problems.

## TECHNICAL PROBLEMS

1. Use the output-cost data computed from problem 1 (Technical Problems) in Chapter 6.
    a. Suppose the price of the commodity is $1.75 per unit.
       (1) What would net profit be at each of the following outputs?

           | | |
           |---|---|
           | 1,314 | 1,494 |
           | 1,384 | 1,534 |
           | 1,444 | |

       (2) What is the output that yields the greatest profit?
       (3) Is there any output that will yield a greater profit at any price?
       (4) How much more revenue is obtained by selling this number of units than by selling one fewer? What is the relation between marginal revenue and selling price?
       (5) If you are given selling price, how can you determine the optimum output by reference to marginal cost?
    b. Suppose price is 70 cents.
       (1) What would net profit be at each of the following outputs?

           | | |
           |---|---|
           | 410 | 945 |
           | 560 | 1,234 |
           | 700 | 1,444 |
           | 830 | |

       (2) Is there any output that will earn a net profit at this price?
       (3) When price is 70 cents, what is the crucial relation between price and average variable cost?
       (4) Consider any price for which the corresponding marginal cost is equal to or less than 70 cents. At such a price, what is the relation between marginal cost and average variable cost?
       (5) When the relation in (4) exists, what is the relation between average and marginal product?
       (6) What will the producer do if faced with a permanent price of 70 cents?
       (7) Why is it not socially desirable to have a producer operating when price is 70 cents?

    *c.*  Suppose price is 80 cents.
        (1)  What will the optimum output be?
        (2)  Can a profit be made at this price?
        (3)  Will the producer operate at all at this price?
        (4)  For how long?
    *d.*  Determine the supply schedule of this individual producer.

| Price | Quantity supplied |
|-------|-------------------|
| $0.60 | |
| 0.70 | |
| 0.80 | |
| 0.90 | |
| 1.00 | |
| 1.10 | |
| 1.20 | |
| 1.30 | |
| 1.40 | |
| 1.50 | |
| 1.60 | |
| 1.70 | |
| 1.80 | |
| 1.90 | |
| 2.00 | |

**2.**  Use Figure E.8–1 to answer these questions.
    *a.*  If price is $7 the firm should produce ———— units.
    *b.*  Since average total cost at this profit-maximizing output is
        $————, total cost is $————.

**FIGURE E.8–1**

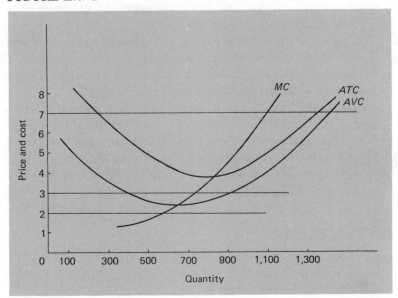

     *c.* Therefore, the firm makes a total profit of $_____.

     *d.* Price then falls to $3. The firm will produce approximately _____ units.

     *e.* Since average total cost at this output is $_____, total revenue less total cost is $_____.

     *f.* Total variable cost is $_____; thus, the firm's total revenue covers all of variable cost, leaving approximately $_____ to apply to fixed costs.

     *g.* If price falls to $2 the firm will produce _____ units. Why?

**3.** Draw precisely and label the following curves:

     Long-run average cost.

     Long-run marginal cost.

     Short-run average cost.

     Short-run marginal cost.

Let the short-run profit-maximizing output be greater than minimum long-run average cost.

The firm is a perfect competitor making short-run profits. It could, however, increase profits (maximize profits) by decreasing plant size.

     *a.* Show the current output price and profit.

     *b.* Show the profit that could have been earned and the optimal output if, at the same price, the firm was maximizing long-run profit.

     *c.* Show price and output of this firm after the industry goes into long-run equilibrium.

     *d.* Explain how this long-run competitive equilibrium situation is attained.

**4.** The supply of labor to all firms in a perfectly competitive industry is reduced. Explain the effects on the wage rate, the quantity of labor employed, total industry supply of the commodity produced, and the price of the product.

**5.** Explain how a perfectly competitive industry can have a horizontal (perfectly elastic) supply curve for its product when each firm in the industry is subject to increasing costs.

**6.** If price falls below average total cost in the short run, the firm, in the long run, will do one of two things. What are these, and under what circumstances will each be done?

**7.** Figure E.8–2 shows a graph of a perfectly competitive firm's short-run cost structure.

     *a.* Label the three curves.

     *b.* Show a price at which the firm would make a pure profit. Show the quantity it would produce at this price and the amount of pure profit earned.

FIGURE E.8–2

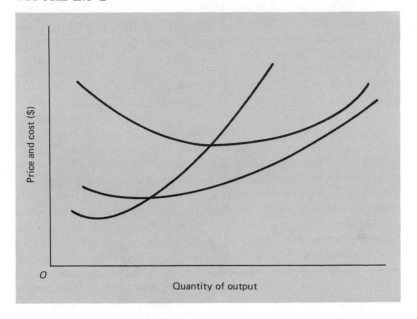

c. Show a price at which the firm would continue to produce in the short run but would suffer losses. Show the output and losses at this price.
d. Show the price below which the firm would not produce in the short run.

8. The marginal revenue of a firm operating under perfect competition is $5. The elasticity of marginal cost (supply) in the neighborhood of equilibrium is .25. What is selling price?

9. Show that a perfectly competitive firm would never produce an output at which marginal cost is falling. (*Hint:* Begin where $P = MC$, and examine what happens when one more unit of output is produced.)

10. The demand schedule for beer is $X_D = 25 - 1P$, where $X_D$ is the quantity demanded of beer in millions of barrels per year and $P$ is its price in dollars per barrel.
    a. If the supply curve for beer is $X_S = -20 + 4P$, what is the equilibrium price of a barrel of beer?
    b. What would be the effect on the price of a barrel of beer if a tax of $5 per barrel is imposed by the government?
    c. How much revenue does the government collect?
    d. What is the market benefit lost due to the tax? (*Hint:* use consumer's and producer's surplus and calculate a dollar amount.)

FIGURE E.8–3

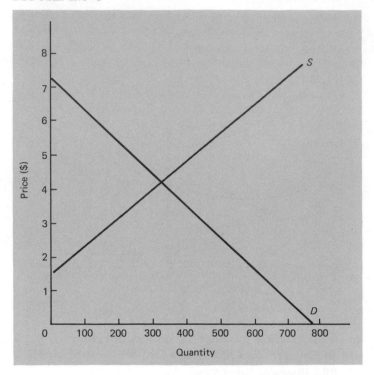

11. Use Figure E.8–3 to answer the following questions. Recall the area of a triangle is one half base times height.

   a. In equilibrium, consumer's surplus is $_____ and producer's surplus is $_____.

   b. Impose an effective ceiling price of $3 per unit. Consumer's surplus is now $_____, and producer's surplus is $_____.

   c. The total net loss is $_____.

12. Explain why producer's surplus is not necessarily equal to profit.

13. Explain why the short-run supply curve of a perfectly competitive industry is less if industry usage affects the prices of some inputs than would be the case if all input prices are given to the industry.

## ANALYTICAL PROBLEMS

1. Assume that the peanut industry is a constant-cost industry. Let society's demand for peanuts increase. Explain precisely the steps that must be taken for society to have more peanuts at

the same price. Suppose that government becomes alarmed at the first sign of rising peanut prices and imposes a ceiling price on peanuts at the original level. What will occur now? Explain. What will happen if the peanut industry is an increasing-cost industry? Does it matter whether the ceiling is imposed on the farmers' sales or the sales of retailers? Explain.

2. "Economists are silly to say that profits are competed away in the long run. No firm would operate unless it made profits." Explain.

3. "My overhead (fixed cost) at this car dealership is $2000 per day. So I figure that the best way to make the most money is to sell as many cars as possible, thereby spreading out the overhead so it is only a small part of the cost on each car sold." What is wrong with the reasoning of this person?

4. In the 1960s, hula-hoops were a popular toy, but in a short while, their novelty wore off and prices fell. However, after a few months, they were higher than ever. Given this description, trace out on a graph the fluctuations in supply and demand. What kind of long-run cost industry is this?

5. "In order to protect the poor, it is essential that the price of natural gas be kept low. Any increase in price would only go into the pockets of the rich." Comment using consumer and producer surplus.

6. If ceiling prices lead to lost total consumer's and producer's surplus, why are they imposed?

7. You own a deposit of a natural resource. The resource deposit is separated into two grades: (1) a high-quality, high-profit resource; (2) a low-quality, low- (but still profitable) profit resource. You extract either grade one or two. Which would you extract first? Why? (The price of neither is expected to change.)

8. Describe why, in the case of a decreasing-cost industry, one firm would have the incentive to buy up the competitive firms or to expand, under-price the competitive firms, and drive them out of business.

9. During the 1970s, much crude oil in the United States was subject to a price regulation much below the world price of oil. When the regulation was removed, most people predicted the price of gasoline would increase dramatically because the price of an ingredient input rose. Gasoline prices in the United States did rise a little at first, but then either fell or remained constant. Explain why predictions of sharply rising gasoline prices were not correct.

10. The beef market is competitive. During periods of rising prices, ranchers keep more heifers from market to breed them

and expand their herds rather than fattening them to slaughter weight for beef. It, of course, takes time for heifers to produce calves. Because of this, would you expect beef prices to fluctuate greatly or remain relatively stable? Explain your answer.

11.  In regard to the situation described in Question 11, a U.S. Department of Agriculture economist said that improved government information on cattle numbers and both domestic and export demand will help stabilize the situation. Using your knowledge of the theory of competition, explain why this economist is probably wrong.

12.  If all of the assumptions of perfect competition hold, why would firms in a real-world industry have little incentive to carry out technological change or much research and development? What conditions would encourage research and development in competitive industries?

# Chapter 9

## Theory of price under monopoly

## 9.1 INTRODUCTION

"Perfect competition" provides economists with a very useful analytical model, even though the exacting conditions of the model never hold entirely in the real world. The same statement applies to the model of monopoly. It is difficult, if not impossible, to pinpoint a monopolist in real-world markets. On the other hand, many markets closely approximate monopoly organization, and monopoly analysis often explains observed business behavior quite well.

A monopoly exists if there is only *one firm* that produces and sells a particular commodity or service and there are no good substitutes available. Since the monopoly is the only seller in the market, it has no direct competitors. Furthermore, no other sellers can enter the market, or a monopoly would not exist. Yet, as we shall see, monopoly does not necessarily guarantee success; it only guarantees that the monopolist can make the best of whatever demand and cost conditions exist without fear of new firms entering the market and competing away any profits.

While monopolists have no *direct competitors* who sell the same product, they do have *indirect competition*. In the first place, all commodities compete for a place in the consumer's budget. Thus, to a certain extent, the monopolist's product competes with all other goods and services in the general struggle for the consumer's dollar. Some goods, however, are closer substitutes for the monopolist's product than others. While there are no close substitutes for a monopoly product (otherwise a monopoly would not exist), a second source of indirect competition lies in the existence of imperfect substitutes.

For example, American Telephone and Telegraph is virtually the only firm providing long-distance telephone service in the United States. However, there are various substitutes that can be used: mail, messengers, personal visits, smoke signals. When the Aluminum Company of America (Alcoa) was the only manufacturer of aluminum (prior to World War II), it had no direct competitors, but it did have competition from producers of other metals that were imperfect substitutes. Until recently, International Nickel has been in a similar situation. Natural gas is a fairly good substitute for electricity, which usually has a regional monopoly. Any real-world monopolist, therefore, has competition to a greater or lesser degree, which, in some measure, tends to weaken the monopolist's position. There are, however, no other producers of the monopolist's specific product in the market.

To summarize:

**Definition.** A monopoly exists when there is only one producer in a market, and there are no good substitute products available to consumers.

### Monopoly and profit maximization

The theory of monopoly follows directly from the theory set forth in the introduction to Chapter 8. As was the case for the competitive firm, we assume that the monopolist wishes to maximize profit under the given cost and demand conditions. As you know from the preceding analysis, any firm can increase profit by expanding output so long as marginal revenue from the expansion exceeds marginal cost. The firm would not expand if marginal revenue is less than marginal cost. The basic principle that profit is maximized by producing and selling the output at which marginal cost equals marginal revenue is the same for the monopoly as for the competitive firm.

The fundamental difference is that, for the monopolist, the marginal revenue for additional units sold is less than the price at which these units sell. Unlike the competitor, the monopoly cannot sell all it desires to sell at the going market price. Since a monopolist is the only firm selling in the market, the market demand curve *is* the demand curve facing the monopolist. While additional sales by a competitive firm do not lower the market price, a monopoly firm can sell more only by lowering price. Therefore, the marginal revenue from additional units sold is the price of those units less the *reduction* in revenue from lowering the price of those units that could have been sold at the higher price. We will analyze this point in more detail later. Let us reemphasize, the basic principle of profit maximization is the same for the monopoly as for the competitive firm: *profit is maximized at the output at which marginal revenue equals marginal cost.*

The basic concepts to be learned in this chapter are

1. How to identify monopoly and monopoly power.
2. How equilibrium price and output are determined for a monopoly in the short run and the long run.
3. Why a monopolist has no supply curve.
4. How to determine the social cost of monopoly.
5. The conditions under which a monopolist would charge different prices for the same commodity.
6. Principles of monopoly regulation.

## 9.2 MONOPOLY POWER

The above definition of monopoly leads to a problem in identifying a monopolist, because we must determine the market in which a potential monopolist operates. This is not an easy task. While it is fairly easy to define industries and product lines, a definition of a market is elusive. For example, there is an aluminum industry which offers aluminum products. But the market for these products must include plastics, woods, and a number of other metals. There is a market for step ladders, for instance, that would include aluminum, wooden, metal alloy, and even durable plastic ladders. Markets cut across industries and product lines.

To identify a monopolist we must know whether there are good substitutes available for a commodity. There is only one Hershey's chocolate candy bar, but Hershey is a monopolist only if consumers do not think any other candy bar will do in Hershey's place—even if the Hershey bar gets more expensive than the other candy bars. The problem of identifying substitutes for a product is similar to the problem of defining a market. After all, products should be considered in the same market only if consumers see them as serving the same purpose and would switch to an alternative commodity if the price of the one they use now should rise relative to the others. The purpose of this section is to provide some basic tools that can help us overcome the problem of identifying monopoly.

### Cross-price elasticity of demand

It is more appropriate to discuss the degree of *monopoly power* a seller holds, rather than decide whether or not a seller is a monopolist. Monopoly power is the capability of a seller to increase prices without losing sales. The fewer sales lost after an increase in price, the more monopoly power the firm has. Nearly every seller has some monopoly power. The existence of a downward-sloping demand curve facing a firm is evidence of such power. Only when demand is perfectly elastic does a seller lose all sales with a price increase. Thus, any market that is not perfectly competitive is characterized by sellers with monopoly power. A firm can have so much monopoly power that it stands in danger of being labeled a monopolist by lawmakers and brought under antitrust action, but the point at which a firm with monopoly power is called a monopolist is arbitrary and has varied over the last hundred years.

We have strongly hinted that one way of testing for monopoly is to study how sensitive a firm's sales are to a price increase. If a small increase in price leads to a large reduction in sales, we can be confident that consumers are finding substitutes for the seller's product. Thus, a high price elasticity of demand signals little monopoly power. Conversely, the less elastic is a firm's demand schedule, the more monopoly power it possesses.

Another helpful measure of monopoly is *cross-price elasticity of demand*. This measure tells us directly which products are in the same market and, therefore, whether a firm's output has good substitutes. Cross-price elasticity measures the sensitivity of the quantity purchased of one good to a price change in another. Take two products, $X$ and $Y$; in terms of a ratio, cross-price elasticity is

$$E_{XY} = \frac{\text{Percent change in quantity of } X}{\text{Percent change in price of } Y} = \frac{\% \Delta X}{\% \Delta P_Y} = \frac{\Delta X}{\Delta P_Y} \cdot \frac{P_Y}{X}.$$

This ratio can be positive, zero, or negative. If $E_{XY} > 0$, then a rise in $P_Y$ leads to an increase in the amount of $X$ sold. Consumers switch from good $Y$ to good $X$; therefore, $X$ and $Y$ are *substitutes*. As $E_{XY}$ gets larger, the better substitutes the two goods are. It may be that when $P_Y$ rises, less $X$ is purchased. In this case, when consumers buy less $Y$, they also buy less $X$. The two goods are then, by definition, *complements*. Examples of goods with negative cross-price elasticities are automobiles and gasoline, bread and butter, shoes and socks, and so on. Finally, the price of $Y$ may have no perceptable effect on the amount of $X$ sold, in which case $E_{XY} = 0$; these goods are said to be *demand independent*.

Cross-price elasticity helps us determine whether two products are in the same market. A large positive elasticity means the goods are easily substitutable. Monopoly power is, therefore, likely to be weak. However, if a firm produces a product for which we cannot find any other products with a high cross-price elasticity, we can be reasonably sure that the firm is alone in its market, and there are no good substitutes available.

## APPLICATION

### United States v. E. I. du Pont de Nemours & Company[1]

On December 13, 1947, the Department of Justice brought suit against E. I. du Pont de Nemours & Company with the charge it had violated the Sherman Antitrust Act by monopolizing the sale of cellophane. Cellophane is a clear plastic wrap developed by Du Pont in the 1920s. The product was hailed as a major innovation in packaging. It was the only wrap "clear as plate glass, flexible, easily ripped open, [and] moisture-proof . . ."[2] By 1949, cigarette manufacturers would use nothing else, and 47 percent of all fresh produce, 35 percent of all meat and poultry, 34 percent of the frozen foods, and 27 percent of the crackers and biscuits were wrapped in the substance.[3]

Nevertheless, there were a number of other wrapping materials available in the post–World War II period. Some of the most popular were foil, glassine, paper, and films, such as Saran and polyethylene. Together, these alternative packaging substances were used more than 50 percent of the time by food processors.

The case was finally decided in 1953, six years after the suit was filed. Paul Leaky, chief judge of the United States District Court for the District of Delaware, wrote that the charge against Du Pont rested on two questions: "(1) does Du Pont possess monopoly powers; and (2) if so, has it achieved such powers by 'monopolizing' within the meaning of the Act . . ."[4] Only if the answer to the first question was yes should the second be answered. The Department of Justice argued that cellophane had no good substitutes, and since Du Pont produced and sold 75 percent of all the cellophane in the United States, it possessed an illegal amount of monopoly power.

[1] 351 U.S. 377 (1956).

[2] G. Stocking and W. Miller, "The Cellophane Case and the New Competition," *American Economic Review* 45, no. 1 (March 1955):52.

[3] Ibid., p. 53.

[4] 118 F. Supp. (D. Del. 1953) at 54.

Du Pont, on the other hand, claimed that all flexible wrapping materials should be included in the market because they were substitutes for cellophane. If the market was defined in this way, the company would have had only 14 percent of the market. Judge Leaky based his decision on the cross-price elasticity of cellophane with other packaging materials. He concluded that the "facts demonstrate Du Pont cellophane is sold under such intense competitive conditions, acquisition of market control or monopoly power is a practical impossibility."[5]

The Department of Justice, not satisfied with this decision, appealed the case to the Supreme Court. A decision was reached in 1956 upholding the District Court. A majority of justices defined the market broadly to include all flexible packaging material. The decisive evidence supporting the court's opinion was cross price elasticity of demand. In their written opinion:

> If a slight decrease in the price of cellophane causes a considerable number of customers of other flexible wrappings to switch to cellophane, it would be an indication that a high cross-elasticity of demand exists between them; that the products compete in the same market. The court below held that the "great sensitivity of customers in the flexible packaging markets to price or quality changes" prevented Du Pont from possessing monopoly control over price. . . . We conclude that cellophane's interchangeability with other materials mentioned suffices to make it a part of this flexible packaging material market.[6]

High cross-price elasticity with several other products implies that there are good substitutes available and that the product in question is not alone in the market.

## Lerner Index

A second way to measure monopoly power is to examine the long-run pure profits of a firm. We know that, in perfect competition, these profits should be zero. Therefore, competition is imperfect if firms in a market earn profits in the long run. In a roundabout way, the presence of excess profits tells us that there are no good substitutes for the seller's product. If the firm had rivals, it would have the incentive to lower price and attract business away from other firms in the market. Pure profits would be competed away. Also, potential entrants into the market could observe that sellers were earning above-normal returns. Entry would occur. Supply would increase, if

[5] Ibid., at 179–98.
[6] 351 U.S. 378 (1956).

the firms already in the market maintained their levels of production, and prices would fall. Thus, the persistence of profits indicates that the firm is alone in the market, and consumers have no ready substitutes.

Operating under the premise that monopolies earn above-normal profits, the most popular measure of monopoly power is the Lerner Index. The Lerner Index is defined as

$$L = \frac{\text{price} - \text{marginal cost}}{\text{price}} \geq 0.$$

Perfectly competitive firms set $P = MC$, so the Lerner Index is zero. As we shall see, firms with monopoly power set price above marginal cost, so $L$ is strictly greater than zero. The more monopoly power, the greater the difference between $P$ and $MC$; hence, the larger is $L$.

Why monopolists want to set price above marginal cost is understandable. The motivation to do so will presently be illustrated in a very simple diagram. A more formal treatment of a profit-maximizing monopolist is presented in the next two sections, but this example introduces you to the profit-maximizing problem a monopolist faces.

Suppose fixed costs are zero and variable costs are constant, so $MC = AC$, and a market is supplied by one firm, a monopolist. Figure 9–1 shows the market demand curve $DD'$ along with the cost curve. The monopolist could behave like a competitive indus-

**FIGURE 9–1**
**Monopoly price above marginal cost**

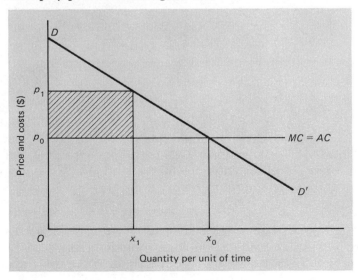

try and operate at the intersection of $S$ (or $MC$) and $DD'$. Output would be $x_0$, price would be $p_0$, and no profits would be earned. But notice what happens to profit when output is restricted to $x_1$ and price is raised to $p_1$. Profit becomes the difference between price and average cost for the all the units sold. It is the shaded region in Figure 9–1. By restricting output, a monopolist can earn pure profits. Competition would force the monopolist to set price closer to $p_0$, and this would cause the Lerner Index to get smaller. Thus, as the Lerner Index gets closer to zero, the more competitive is a market.

## 9.3 DEMAND AND MARGINAL REVENUE UNDER MONOPOLY

As we noted in the introduction, the fundamental difference between a monopolist and a competitor is the demand and marginal revenue curves they face. Let us use a numerical example to show the relation between demand and marginal revenue for a monopoly. Suppose a firm has the demand schedule shown in columns (1) and (2) of Table 9–1. Price times quantity gives the total revenue ob-

**TABLE 9–1**
**Monopoly demand and marginal revenue**

| (1)<br>Units of<br>sales | (2)<br><br>Price | (3)<br>Total<br>revenue | (4)<br>Marginal<br>revenue |
|---|---|---|---|
| 1 ............... | $2.00 | $2.00 | $2.00 |
| 2 ............... | 1.80 | 3.60 | 1.60 |
| 3 ............... | 1.40 | 4.20 | 0.60 |
| 4 ............... | 1.20 | 4.80 | 0.40 |
| 5 ............... | 1.00 | 5.00 | 0.20 |
| 6 ............... | 0.70 | 4.20 | −0.80 |

tainable from each level of sales. Marginal revenue, in column (4), shows the change in total revenue from an additional unit of sales. The only time marginal revenue equals price is for the first unit sold. That is, at zero sales, total revenue is zero; for the first unit sold, total revenue is the demand price for one unit. Thus, the change in total revenue is the same as price. Since the monopolist must reduce price to sell additional units, at every other level of output, marginal revenue is less than price.

This principle can be more concisely stated with the help of Figure 9–2. A monopolist is thinking about lowering price from $p_0$ to $p$; output will increase by one unit, from $x$ to $x + 1$. Marginal

**FIGURE 9–2**
**Marginal revenue when demand is downward sloping**

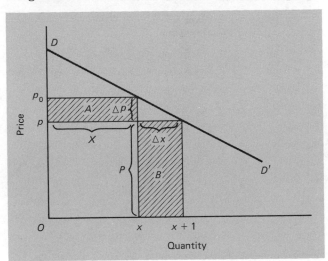

revenue, the change in total revenue, is the price the monopolist gets for the extra unit less area $A$ in the figure which is $\Delta p \cdot x$. Area $A$ is the revenue lost by selling the original $x$ units for less than $p_0$. Area $B$ is the revenue gained by selling one more unit at $p$. Marginal revenue ($MR$) may therefore be written as:

$$MR = \text{area } B - \text{area } A = p - \Delta p \cdot x. \qquad (9\text{–}1)$$

In Figure 9–2, we know $\Delta x = (x + 1) - x = 1$. It would not change the above equality to divide $\Delta p$ by $\Delta x$, since $\Delta x = 1$. Thus,

$$MR = p - \frac{\Delta p}{\Delta x} \cdot x. \qquad (9\text{–}2)$$

Either (9–1) or (9–2) tells us that marginal revenue is less than price.

**Relation.** Marginal revenue is the addition to total revenue attributable to the addition of one unit of output to sales per period of time. After the first unit sold, marginal revenue is less than price.

Figure 9–3 illustrates the relations between demand, marginal revenue, and total revenue for a monopolist with a linear demand curve. In panels A and B, the scales of the vertical axes differ, but the horizontal axes have the same scale. Total revenue (panel A) first increases when price is reduced and sales expand; it reaches a maximum at $x_0$ and declines thereafter. Panel B indicates the relations

**FIGURE 9–3**
Total revenue, marginal revenue, demand

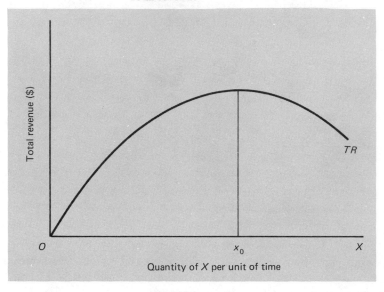

**Panel A**
**Total revenue**

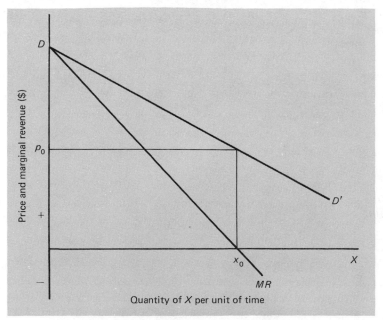

**Panel B**
**Demand and marginal revenue**

between marginal revenue (*MR*) and demand. As mentioned above, *MR* is below price at every output level except the first. (Since we have assumed continuous data, the two are equal infinitesimally close to the vertical axis.) The demand curve gives price at any output level; therefore, marginal revenue is always below the demand curve. Finally, when *TR* reaches its maximum, *MR* is zero (at output $x_0$, price $p_0$). At greater rates of output, *MR* is negative.

Equation (9–2) is correct in general for any small change in X. We may rearrange some terms and write the equation using the elasticity of demand. Recall that $E = \Delta x/\Delta p \cdot p/x$. Hence,

$$MR = p \left(1 - \frac{\Delta p}{\Delta x} \cdot \frac{x}{p}\right) = p \left(1 - \frac{1}{E}\right), \qquad (9\text{–}3)$$

where $E$ is the absolute value of demand elasticity at any quantity. From (9–3) it is apparent that when marginal revenue is negative, demand is inelastic ($E < 1$). When marginal revenue is positive, demand is elastic ($E > 1$). Finally, when marginal revenue is zero, demand has unitary elasticity ($E = 1$).

The relation between positive or negative marginal revenue and the elasticity of the demand curve is intuitively apparent. As you will recall from Chapter 2, changes in total expenditure are related to demand elasticity. When demand is elastic, an increase in quantity (decrease in price) causes an increase in total expenditure. Over an inelastic segment of demand, an increase in quantity occasions a decrease in total expenditure, while in the unitary portion, total expenditure remains unchanged. Since total consumer expenditure on a commodity is the same as the monopolist's total revenue, the relation of elasticity to marginal revenue follows directly from the above relations. If marginal revenue is positive (negative), a unit increase in sales leads to an increase (decrease) in total revenue. If marginal revenue is zero, a unit change in sales does not change total revenue. Therefore, a positive (negative) marginal revenue indicates that demand is elastic (inelastic) at that quantity. Zero marginal revenue means unitary elasticity. These relations are summarized in Table 9–2. They can be seen also in Figure 9–4, which shows a straight-line demand curve.

**TABLE 9–2**
**Relations among marginal revenue, elasticity, and changes in total revenue**

|  | (1) | (2) | (3) |
|---|---|---|---|
| Marginal revenue ................... | Positive | Negative | Zero |
| Demand elasticity ................. | Elastic | Inelastic | Unitary |
| Change in total revenue for an increase in quantity ......... | Increase | Decrease | No change |

**FIGURE 9-4**
**Relations among marginal revenue, elasticity, and demand**

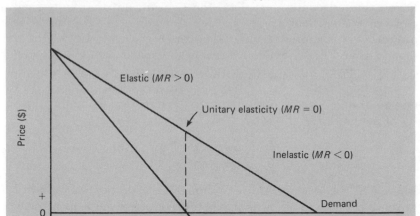

**Relation.** When demand is negatively sloped, marginal revenue is negatively sloped and is less than price at all relevant quantities. The difference between marginal revenue and price depends upon the price
elasticity of demand, as shown by the formula $MR = p(1 - 1/E)$. Total
revenue increases at first, reaches a maximum, and declines thereafter. The maximum point on the total revenue curve is attained at precisely that rate of output and sales for which marginal revenue is zero
and elasticity is unitary.

## 9.4 SHORT-RUN PROFIT MAXIMIZATION MONOPOLY

Monopoly analysis is based upon two of the important assumptions discussed in the theory of perfect competition: (1) the firm
attempts to maximize profit; and (2) the firm operates in an envi-
ronment free from outside control. Though certain other assumptions differ to some extent, as we have noted, the profit-maximizing
conditions are similar. We have already examined demand and marginal revenue conditions under monopoly. We will now analyze
short-run conditions under monopoly, then discuss in more detail
short-run equilibrium.

### Cost under monopoly

Short-run cost conditions confronting a monopolist are essentially
similar to those faced by a perfectly competitive firm. The theory of

cost follows directly from the theory developed in Chapter 6. Cost depends upon the production function and input prices. The chief difference for a monopolist lies in the potential impact of output changes on factor prices.

In the theory of perfect competition, we assume that each firm is very small relative to the total factor market and can therefore change *its own* rate of output without affecting factor prices, just as any one consumer can change the amount of a good purchased without affecting its price.

Recall, however, that, if *all firms* in the industry change output and therefore the use of all inputs, the prices of some of those inputs may change, unless, of course, the industry is a constant-cost industry. The output of the monopolist, the sole firm in the industry, is, accordingly, the output of the industry. Certainly a monopolist, just as a competitive industry, may be so small relative to the demand for all inputs that its input use will have no effect on the price of any input. To be sure, even a very large monopolist will purchase some inputs (such as unskilled labor) the prices of which are not affected by the monopolist's rate of use. On the other hand, there is a high probability that a monopoly will purchase certain inputs for which the firm's rate of purchase will have a definite effect on the prices of these factors of production. One would think that, in many cases, factor prices will vary with the monopolist's rate of use.

Notwithstanding the monopolist's possible effect upon factor prices, the cost curves are assumed to have the same general shape as those described in Chapter 6. The primary implication of rising supply prices of variable inputs is that the average and marginal cost curves rise more rapidly or fall less rapidly than they would if the input supply prices were constant. Thus, for example, marginal cost may rise not only because of diminishing marginal productivity, but also because input prices rise with increased use.

### Short-run equilibrium

A monopolist, just as a perfect competitor, attains maximum profit (or minimum loss) by producing and selling at that rate of output for which the positive (negative) difference between total revenue and total cost is greatest (least). This condition occurs when marginal revenue equals marginal cost (even though for the monopolist, $MR$ does not equal price). Using this principle, the position of short-run equilibrium is easily described. Figure 9–5 shows the relevant cost and revenue curves for a monopolist. Since $AVC$ and $AFC$ are not necessary for exposition, they are omitted. The profit maximizer produces at $E$ where $MC = MR$. Output is $x$, and, from the demand curve, we see that price must be $p$ per unit in order to ration the $x$ units among those who wish to buy the commodity. Total revenue is

$p \times x$, or the area of the rectangle $OpBx$. The unit cost of producing this amount is $c$. Total cost is $c \times x$, or the area $OcDx$. Profit is $TR - TC$, or the shaded area $cpBD$.

In the example of Figure 9–5, the monopolist earns a pure profit in the short run. This need not be the case, however; a monopolistic

**FIGURE 9–5**
**Short-run equilibrium under monopoly**

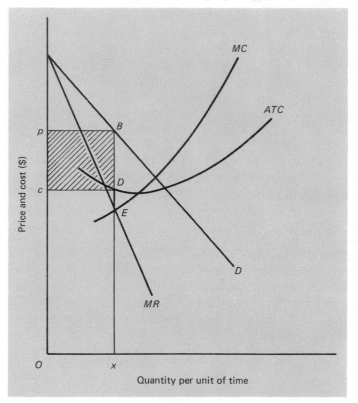

position does not ensure profit. If demand is sufficiently low, a monopolist may incur a loss in the short run, just as a pure competitor may. For example, Figure 9–6 shows a loss situation. Marginal cost equals marginal revenue at output $x$, which can be sold at price $p$. Average cost is $c$. Total cost, $OcDx$ exceeds total revenue $OpBx$; hence, the firm makes a loss of $pcDB$.

Note that the monopolist would produce rather than shut down in the short run, since revenue exceeds variable cost $(OvNx)$; there is still some revenue $(vpBN)$ left to apply to fixed cost. If demand

**FIGURE 9–6**
**Short-run losses under monopoly**

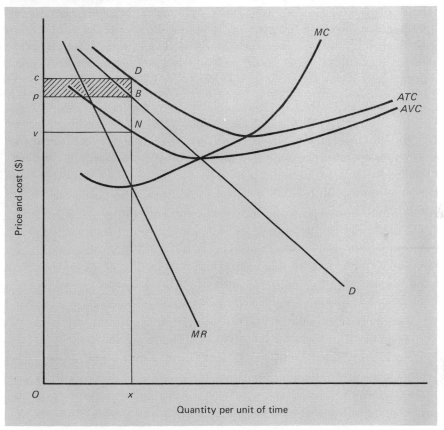

decreases so that the monopolist cannot cover all of variable cost at any price, the firm would shut down and lose only fixed cost. This situation is analogous to that of the perfect competitor.

In the short run, the primary difference between a monopolist and a perfect competitor lies in the slope of the demand curve. Either may earn a pure profit; either may incur a loss. Of course, in the long-run, another important difference is that the monopolist who earns pure profit need not worry about new firms entering the industry and competing away profits.

**Principle.** If a monopoly produces a positive output, it maximizes profit or minimizes losses by producing the quantity for which *MC* = *MR*. Since the monopolist's demand is above *MR* at every positive output, equilibrium price exceeds *MC*.

## Monopoly supply

The supply curve for a perfect competitor was the marginal cost curve. It is tempting to say the same is true for a monopolist, but a monopolist does not have a supply schedule.

To understand why, recall the definition of supply: a list of prices and the quantities that would be supplied at each price in the list per period of time. But, for a monopolist, any number of prices may be associated with a given level of output, depending upon the position of demand at that output level. An infinite number of prices can be associated with one level of output.

To illustrate this point, assume first that demand and the associated marginal revenue are $\overline{D}$ and $\overline{MR}$ in Figure 9–7. (Remember

**FIGURE 9–7**
**Why a monopoly has no supply curve**

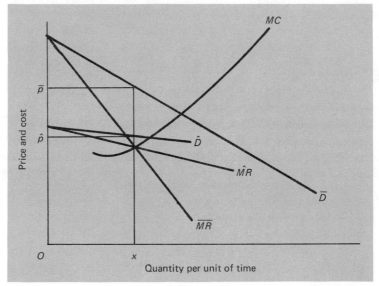

marginal revenue depends upon the elasticity of demand.) In this case, $\overline{MR}$ equals $MC$ at output $x$ and price is $\overline{p}$. Next, let marginal revenue and demand be $\hat{MR}$ and $\hat{D}$. While marginal revenue again equals marginal cost at $x$, in this situation, commodity price is $\hat{p}$. By changing the slope of the demand and, therefore, $MR$ curves, the same output, $x$, can be sold at an infinite number of prices. Thus, the monopolist has no supply curve.

## Numerical illustration

A numerical example can illustrate the principal points of this section. In Table 9–3, the demand schedule in columns (1) and (2) yields the total revenue schedule in column (3). We can simply subtract the total cost of producing each relevant level of sales from total revenue to obtain the profit from that output. Examination of the profit column shows that maximum profit ($4.50) occurs at 50 units of output. Marginal revenue and marginal cost, shown in columns (5) and (6), give the same result. The monopolist can increase profit by increasing sales, so long as marginal revenue exceeds marginal cost. If marginal cost exceeds marginal revenue, profit falls with increased sales. Hence, the monopolist produces and sells 50 units, the level at which marginal cost and marginal revenue are equal.

TABLE 9–3
Marginal revenue–marginal cost approach to profit maximization

| (1)<br>Output<br>and sales | (2)<br><br>Price | (3)<br>Total<br>revenue | (4)<br>Total<br>cost | (5)<br>Marginal<br>revenue | (6)<br>Marginal<br>cost | (7)<br><br>Profit |
|---|---|---|---|---|---|---|
| 5 | $2.00 | $10.00 | $12.25 | — | $0.45 | −$2.25 |
| 13 | 1.10 | 14.30 | 15.00 | $0.54 | .34 | −0.70 |
| 23 | 0.85 | 19.55 | 18.25 | .52 | .33 | 1.30 |
| 38 | .69 | 25.92 | 22.00 | .42 | .25 | 3.92 |
| 50 | .615 | 30.75 | 26.25 | .35 | .35 | 4.50 |
| 60 | .55 | 33.00 | 31.00 | .23 | .48 | 2.00 |
| 68 | .50 | 34.00 | 36.25 | .13 | .66 | −2.25 |
| 75 | .45 | 33.75 | 42.00 | −.03 | .82 | −8.25 |
| 81 | .40 | 32.40 | 48.25 | −.23 | 1.04 | −15.85 |
| 86 | .35 | 30.10 | 55.00 | −.46 | 1.35 | −25.10 |

## 9.5 LONG-RUN EQUILIBRIUM UNDER MONOPOLY

A monopoly exists if there is only one firm in the market. Among other things, this statement implies that "entrance" into the market is closed. Thus, whether or not a monopolist earns a pure profit in the short run, no other producer can enter the market in the hope of sharing whatever pure-profit potential exists. Therefore, pure economic profit is not eliminated in the long run, as in the case of perfect competition. The monopolist will, however, make adjustments in plant size as demand conditions warrant them, even though entry cannot take place.

A monopolist faced with the cost and revenue conditions de-

**FIGURE 9–8**
**Long-run equilibrium under monopoly**

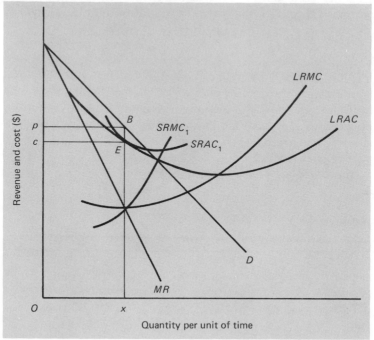

picted in Figure 9–8 would build a plant to produce the quantity at which long-run marginal cost equals marginal revenue. In each period, $x$ units are produced, costing $c$ per unit and selling at a price of $p$ per unit. Long-run profit is $cpBE$. By the now familiar argument, this is the maximum profit possible under the given revenue and cost conditions. The monopoly operates in the short run with plant size indicated by $SRAC_1$ and $SRAC_1$. New entrants cannot come into the industry and compete away profits.

But demand or cost conditions can change for reasons other than the entry of new firms, and such changes cause the monopolist to make adjustments. Assume that demand and marginal revenue change. At first, the firm will adjust without changing plant size. It will produce the quantity at which the new $MR$ equals $SRMC_1$, or it will close down in the short run if it cannot cover variable costs. In the long run, the monopolist can change plant size.

Long-run equilibrium adjustment under monopoly must take one of two possible courses. First, if the monopolist incurs a short-run loss, and if there is no plant size that will result in pure profit (or at least, no loss), the monopoly goes out of business. Second, if it suffers a short-run loss or earns a short-run profit with the original plant, the entrepreneur must determine whether a plant of different size (and, thus, a different price and output) will lead to a larger profit.

The first situation requires no comment. The second is illustrated by Figure 9–9. $DD'$ and $MR$ show the market demand and marginal

**FIGURE 9–9**
**Change in long-run equilibrium for a monopolist**

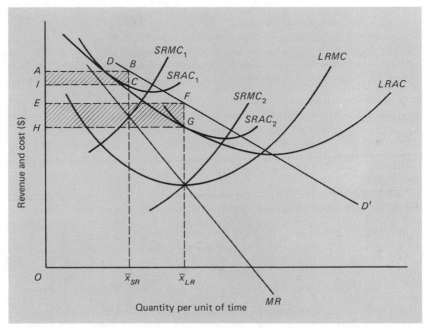

revenue confronting a monopolist. $LRAC$ is the long-run average cost curve, and $LRMC$ is the associated long-run marginal cost curve. Suppose, in the initial period, the monopolist built the plant exemplified by $SRAC_1$ and $SRMC_1$. Equality of short-run marginal cost and marginal revenue leads to the sale of $\bar{x}_{SR}$ units per period at price $A$. At this rate of output, unit cost is $I$; short-run monopoly profit is represented by the area of the shaded rectangle $ABCI$.

Since a pure economic profit can be reaped, the monopolist would not consider discontinuing production. But now the long-run marginal cost becomes the relevant consideration. The long-run profit maximum is attained when long-run marginal cost equals marginal revenue. The associated rate of output is $\bar{x}_{LR}$, and the price is $E$.

By reference to $LRAC$, the plant capable of producing $\bar{x}_{LR}$ units per period at the least unit cost is the one represented by $SRAC_2$ and

$SRMC_2$. Unit cost is accordingly $H$, and long-run maximum monopoly profit is given by the area of the shaded rectangle $EFGH$. This profit is obviously (visually) greater than the profit obtainable from the original plant.

Generalizing, we have the following:

**Principle.** A monopolist maximizes profit in the long run by producing and marketing the rate of output for which long-run marginal cost equals marginal revenue. The optimal plant is the one whose short-run average cost curve is tangent to the long-run average cost curve at the point corresponding to long-run equilibrium output. At this point, short-run marginal cost equals marginal revenue.

The profits reached by following the above principle are the highest the monopolist can attain; and they *can* be attained because, in the long run, plant size is variable and the market is effectively closed to entry.

## APPLICATION

### Analysis of effects of divestiture

An important question now being hotly debated is the issue of divestiture of some of the major oil companies. Some people (for example, certain members of Congress), allege that one of the problems of the oil industry is that some of the major oil companies have a large share of the market at more than one phase of the production process. Exxon, for example, owns refineries and also owns or leases service stations. Moreover, these critics suggest that certain firms with a large share of the refinery market are in the drilling phase also and are attempting to obtain a larger share of the pumping phase.

Proponents of divestiture argue that, if a company with a large share of the market in one phase of the production process has a large share of the market in another, price will be higher, output lower, and profits greater. In the extreme, they argue that, if a company has a monopoly in one phase, say refining, and then monopolizes another phase, say pumping, which had previously been competitive, this vertical integration will increase the price of the final product, decrease the output, and increase the profit of the firm that previously had the monopoly in the refining phase. Let us use some of the tools we have developed in this and the preceding chapter to analyze the situation. What would be the effect of forcing a company with a large share of the market in one phase of the production process to divest itself of its holdings in another phase?

For analytical simplicity, let us make a few assumptions. First assume that there are only two phases of production, refining and final sales, or pumping. Assume that, if either phase is operated competitively, the industry would be a constant-cost industry and the long-run industry supply would be a horizontal line. (Recall the discussion of constant-cost industries in Chapter 8.) Finally, assume that, if either phase of the process is monopolized—taken over by one company—this horizontal line would be the monopoly's long-run average cost curve. Since long-run average cost is constant (a horizontal line), average cost equals marginal cost in the long run.

**FIGURE 9–10**
**Monopoly in the gasoline market**

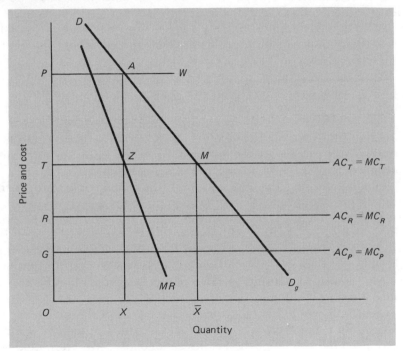

Figure 9–10 shows the situation graphically. The long-run average cost of the pumping industry, excluding the cost of gasoline from the refinery, is shown as $AC_p$. This would be long-run supply less the cost of gasoline, if the pumping industry is competitive. If the pumping industry is a monopoly, the average cost of pumping, $G$, is constant and $G$ equals marginal cost as well; in other words, $AC_p = MC_p$ is a horizontal line at $G$.

Moreover, refining is a constant-cost competitive industry, and long-run industry supply is $AC_R$. If the refining industry is monopolized, $R$ is the constant long-run average cost, which equals marginal cost; that is $AC_R = MC_R$. Let $DD_g$ be the final demand for gasoline and let a gallon of gasoline from the refinery equal a gallon sold at the pump. Thus, there is fixed-proportions production.

Assume, first, that each phase of production is organized competitively and transportation costs are zero. Thus, in the long-run, the supply at the retail, or pumping phase will be $G + R = T$. Demand equals supply, $AC_T$, at point $M$; price is $T$ (average total cost) and output is $\overline{X}$.

Next, let both phases of production be taken over by a monopolist. If there are no economies of integration, that is, no reduction in cost from having one firm control both phases of production, the monopolist's marginal cost is the line $AC_T = MC_T$. Marginal revenue equals marginal cost at $Z$. Price rises to $P$, and output falls to $X$, the output at which profits are maximized. These maximum profits are shown as the area $TPAZ$.

Next, let the refining phase be competitive while the pumping phase remains under control of the monopolist. Cost conditions remain the same. Since the refining industry is competitive, the price of gasoline to the monopolist in pumping is $R$. Marginal cost is, therefore, the same as before, $G + R = T = MR_T$. Since marginal revenue and marginal cost are unchanged, equilibrium price and output remain at $P$ and $X$, and profit is unchanged ($TPAZ$).

Finally, consider the case in which the monopolist controls the refining phase of production, but the pumping phase is competitive. Now, if gasoline were free from the refining phase to the pumping phase, long-run gasoline supply would be $AC_p$ and final price would be $G$. But the refining monopoly can cause the long-run supply in the final, or pumping, phase to be any horizontal straight line desired, simply by setting the price of gasoline from the refineries to the stations.

Clearly, it would charge a price above $OR$, or the total refining costs would not be covered. What would be the price that maximizes the profits of the refining monopoly? We know that the maximum profit possible when one firm controls both phases of production is represented by the area $TPAZ$. If the refinery monopolist imposes on the pumping industry a price that equals $(P - G) = GP$, the long-run supply price of the pumping industry will be the horizontal line $PW$. In this case, the demand for gasoline equals long-run supply at $A$. Price is $P$ and output is $X$. The refinery profit is $(P - G - R)$ times $X$, or the area ($TP$ times $X$) equals $TPAZ$. Thus, in this case, final price, final output, and monopoly profit are the same as when the monopolist controls both phases of production. Any price charged by the refinery to the pumping industry greater or less than PG would result in a final price greater or less than *P*. In either case, profit is less than the maximum profit, *TPAZ*.

Thus, under these assumptions, a monopoly at either phase of production, when the other phase is competitive, leads to the same equilibrium price, output, and profit that would result if the monopoly owned or controlled both phases. In other words, nothing changes if the monopoly is forced to give up one phase or the other in the production process, and that phase then becomes competitive. Moreover, if there are more than two phases, a monopoly at any one phase can extract all of the profit it could gain if it controlled all phases, if all other phases are competitive.

This analysis is not meant to imply that, if both phases are competitive, price might not be lower. This may or may not be the case, depending upon the cost structure of the industry. The analysis simply shows that divestiture would not lower gasoline prices under the above assumptions. Furthermore, we have analyzed the situations under the assumption of fixed proportions—a gallon of gasoline at the refinery becomes a gallon at the service station—and under the assumption that both phases are constant-cost industries. The assumption of increasing cost in either or both phases does not change the results at all. The assumption of variable proportions does make the analysis more complicated, but the conclusions do not change much.[7]

The situation would change somewhat if there are possible economies of integration when one firm owns both phases of production. These economies of integration could result because of decreased transaction costs or, possibly, decreased management costs, causing a higher price after divestiture than would result when both phases are controlled by the same firm. Thus, it may well be that an action designed to lower gasoline prices could raise prices.

## 9.6 MARKET EFFECTS OF MONOPOLY

Economists have done extensive research, both theoretical and empirical, on the costs and benefits of monopoly relative to perfect competition. By using consumer's and producer's surplus, it is theoretically possible to show, under stylized cost conditions, that there

---

[7] For an early analytical treatment of the subject, see J. J. Spengler, "Vertical Integration and Antitrust Policy," *Journal of Political Economy*, 68, no. 3 (August 1950):347–52. For a discussion of the difference made by assuming variable-proportions production and a review of some of the literature, see J. S. McGee and L. R. Basset, "Vertical Integration Revisited," *Journal of Law and Economics*, 19 (April 1976):17–38.

is a surplus loss as markets become monopolized. We will present some empirical evidence in this section estimating the surplus lost as a result of monopoly in the United States. However, once we remove ourselves from the familiar U-shaped average cost curves and allow a producer to experience pervasive economies of scale, it is not clear whether a market is better served by monopoly or by perfect competition. Lower costs of production may counterbalance the ability of the monopolist to set price. The monopoly price could be lower than price under perfect competition. Moreover, under some cost conditions, a product will not even be produced unless the market is monopolized. The choice is to go without the product or have it produced by a monopolist. Hence, perfect competition is not always a viable market structure.

## Comparison with perfect competition

The most common criticism of monopoly is that price is higher and output is lower than it would be in a perfectly competitive market. This assertion is based upon the following analysis. The monopolist depicted in Figure 9–11 produces $x_M$ per period of time

**FIGURE 9–11**
**Price and output comparisons**

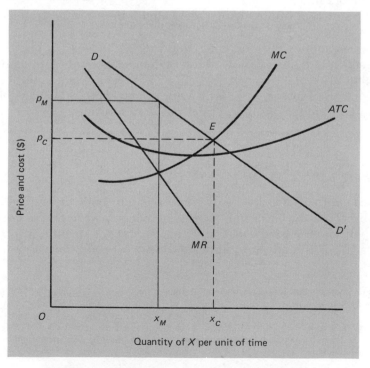

and sells at a price of $p_M$. If we can also assume that $MC$ represents competitive industry supply, supply equals demand at $E$. The perfectly competitive industry would sell $x_C$ at a price of $p_C$. There is reason to doubt, however, that $MC$ can represent the supply curve of a perfectly competitive industry. The sum of a large number of firms' marginal cost curves is not necessarily the marginal cost curve of a single, much larger firm. In any event, we see that a monopoly is more likely to earn a pure profit because it can effectively exercise some market control; output is restricted and prices are raised relative to perfectly competitive markets.

We can also say that, in long-run industry equilibrium under perfect competition, production occurs at the point of minimum long- and short-run average cost. The monopolist utilizes the plant capable of producing long-run equilibrium output at the least unit cost. Only under the extremely rare circumstances in which marginal revenue intersects marginal cost at the output associated with minimum long-run average cost would this plant be the one characterized by the absolute minimum cost.

### Surplus loss from monopoly

We have just shown that, while the perfect competitor produces at the point where marginal cost and price are equal, the monopolist's price *exceeds* marginal cost. Under certain conditions, demand represents the social valuation of the commodity. Similarly, long-run marginal cost, with some exceptions, represents the marginal social cost of production. Under monopoly, the marginal value of a commodity to a society exceeds the marginal social cost of its production. Society as a whole would, therefore, benefit by having more of its resources used in producing the commodity in question. The profit-maximizing monopolist will not do this, however, for producing at the point where price equals marginal cost would decrease profit. Alternatively, the perfect competitor in long-run equilibrium produces the quantity at which the marginal social cost of production equals the marginal social valuation, but does so not because of any innate social consciousness but because the market forces this situation.

We can illustrate the loss monopoly causes society by using the tools of consumer's and producer's surplus. Suppose perfect competition forces producers to operate where marginal cost for the industry equals demand. The monopolist, on the other hand, operates where marginal cost equals marginal revenue. In Figure 9–12, we show prices and outputs for both a monopolist and a perfectly competitive industry.

For the competitive market structure, total surplus is the sum of

FIGURE 9–12
Surplus loss from monopoly

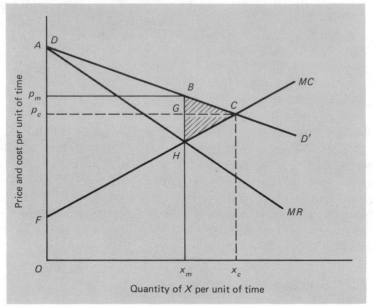

Quantity of X per unit of time

consumer's and producer's surplus, or $Ap_cC + p_cCF = ACF$. If a
monopoly operates in the market, the sum is $ABGp_c + p_cGHF =
ABHF$. Because monopoly restricts output, the shaded area $BCH$ in
Figure 9–12 represents a loss of both consumer's and producer's
surplus. The consumer's loss is $BCG$, while the producer loses
$GCH$. Also, by restricting output and raising price, there is a transfer
of surplus from the consumer to the producer. In total, the consumer
loses surplus represented by the sum of the areas $p_mBGp_c + BCG$.
Since the monopolist gains only area $p_mBGp_c$, area $BCG$ represents
the net market loss.

Observe that the monopolist is willing to forego the surplus represented by $GCH$ to obtain surplus area $p_mBGp_c$. It must be true
that, by setting $MR = MC$ to maximize profits, a monopolist
maximizes the difference between areas $GCH$ and $p_mBGp_c$. The
transfer in consumer's surplus $p_mBGp_c$, from higher prices is greater
than the loss of producer's surplus, $BCH$, from restricting output.

## APPLICATION

### Welfare loss from monopoly in the United States

In 1954, Arnold C. Harberger attempted to measure both the
total welfare loss (lost consumer's surplus) from all monopoly in the

United States, and the value of the resources that society would have to transfer from monopolized industries to competitive industries in order to make the economy fully competitive—that is, to eliminate all monopoly in the economy.[8] As in the model presented in this chapter, he assumed constant marginal and average costs, and that those industries with higher-than-average returns on capital have too few resources, and those yielding lower-than-average returns have too many. Because of the relative tranquility of the period and the availability of good data, Harberger used the years 1924–28 for his estimation.

Harberger found that $550 million in resources would have to have been transferred from low-return to high-return industries to eliminate excess profit during this period. Since only 45 percent of all companies were included in the sample, the estimate was raised to 1.2 billion. This transfer would have involved about 4 percent of all resources in manufacturing, or 1.5 percent of total resources.

He then estimated how much better off society would have been had the transfer of resources taken place by reducing monopoly price to average cost and increasing output. This figure would equal the sum of all increases in consumer's surplus due to changing monopolies to competition. This is the sum of the areas of all of the welfare loss triangles. The total welfare gain estimated from the resource transfer was $59 million, less than one 10th of 1 percent of national income. In terms of 1954 income, this averaged to less than $1.50 per person in the United States. When Harberger included certain intangibles in the data, the necessary transfer rose from 1.5 percent to 1.75 percent of national income, and the welfare loss rose to $81 million. (We might note that the welfare change does not consider the reallocation of income from the rest of society to the monopoly.)

In all the estimates, the total welfare loss came to less than one 10th of 1 percent of national income, and in most instances, Harberger used assumptions that biased the estimates upward. This extremely low estimate was startling at the time. Aside from the transfer of resources from consumers to monopoly, it appeared that the total welfare cost was quite small.

The estimates did not go unchallenged. Several economists made similar types of estimates of the welfare cost of monopoly for different industry classifications and for different time periods. Again, these estimates of loss were very small. Does this result indicate that, if we ignore pure transfers, monopoly has little effect on welfare?

---

[8] See A. C. Harberger, "The Welfare Loss from Monopoly," *American Economic Review*, 34, no. 2 (May 1954):77–87. For some additional insights into this question, see F. M. Scherer, *Industrial Market Structure and Economic Performance* (Chicago: Rand McNally, 1971), Chap. 17.

Gordon Tullock added a new insight to the discussion, comparing the welfare loss from monopoly to the economics of theft.[9] While it may be argued that, if one person steals $100 from another, the theft simply involves transfer of resources, the very *existence* of theft does have a large cost to society even though theft only involves interpersonal wealth transfers. In the first place, potential thieves would invest in resources—time, burglar tools, getaway cars, lookouts—until any additional resources would cost more than the marginal return in stolen assets from using these resources. (Even thieves can use a knowledge of economic theory.) Similarly, potential victims wish to protect their wealth. A potential victim would invest in preventive resources—watchdogs, locks, guns, etc.—as long as the expected marginal saving from such resources is expected to exceed their marginal cost. Furthermore, the return to resources used in theft depends upon the number of resources used in theft prevention, and vice versa.

In time, society would attain an equilibrium amount of theft, which would probably be positive, since the prevention of all theft would cost too much. But, even though the equilibrium amount of theft involves only transfers, the *existence* of theft costs society considerably. Those resources used to steal and to prevent stealing cost the individuals involved, and they cost society the use of those resources that could be used to produce other products. They are *completely wasted* from society's point of view. They are used only to cause or to prevent transfers of wealth, not to produce wealth.

Society generally attempts to prevent theft collectively. People find that enforcement of laws by courts and police are sometimes technologically more efficient in preventing theft than individual expenditures on resources. To the extent that collective expenditures are more efficient than private ones, the returns to theft are reduced, which in turn reduces theft. To be sure, public expenditure does not replace all private preventive expenditure. People still buy locks, hire guards, and keep dogs. Both the public and the private preventive expenditure costs society those resources used in prevention. The important point is not how societies allocate between public and private prevention, but that the existence of theft costs society resources that could be used to produce wealth.

Monopoly involves only a transfer of resources from the public to the monopolists plus an empirically insignificant welfare loss. According to Tullock's analysis, the welfare losses estimated using Harberger's technique underestimate the true welfare loss from monopoly. Because the return from establishing a *successful*

---

[9] See G. Tullock, "The Welfare Costs of Monopolies and Theft," *Western Economic Journal* 5, no. 2 (June 1967):224–32.

monopoly is so great, one would expect potential monopolists to expend considerable resources in attempting to form monopolies. In fact, entrepreneurs should be willing to invest resources in attempts to form monopolies until the marginal cost equals the expected discounted return. After a monopoly is formed, others will invest resources toward trying to break the monopoly, which in turn means that the monopolist must use additional resources trying to prevent the break. Just as successful theft encourages additional theft, successful monopoly encourages additional attempts to monopolize.

As Tullock noted, identifying and measuring the resources used to gain, break, and hold monopoly are quite difficult. But it appears that a large amount of the very scarce resource, skilled management, is used toward this end. In any case, the welfare triangle measurement ignores this cost and underestimates the social cost of monopoly. The monopoly question is still far from being settled.

## Monopoly and economies of scale

It is not always the case that a monopolist charges a higher price than would perfectly competitive firms. Costs may be so much lower for a single firm producing in the market that, even after the monopolist has set a profit-maximizing price, it is still lower than the price at which a perfect competitor earns normal profits. Economies of scale, where the $LRAC$ curve is sharply declining over a long range of output levels, can lead to prices lower under monopoly than under perfect competition.

The problem is that competitive firms have such a small share of the market that these economies cannot be fully realized. Figure 9–13 shows the situation. The $LRAC$ is declining at every level of output. If we let one firm operate in the market, profit maximization leads to output $x_m$ and price $p_m$. Suppose, though, that competition was desirable as an end in itself, and that the monopoly was divided into a large number of small firms, each producing output $x_c$. Then the lowest possible price they can charge at that output level without making economic losses is $p_c = LRAC$ at $x_c$. Profits are normal, but prices are higher in the market.

When economies of scale affect costs like this, it is very difficult to have a competitive market. In fact, competition could only exist if producers were strictly prohibited from expanding. Imagine what would happen if they were not. Every firm would have the incentive to expand and move down the $LRAC$ curve where unit costs would be lower, and, as a consequence, price could be lower. The larger firm could always undersell smaller firms and drive them out of

**FIGURE 9-13**
Monopoly and competitive equilibria with economies of scale

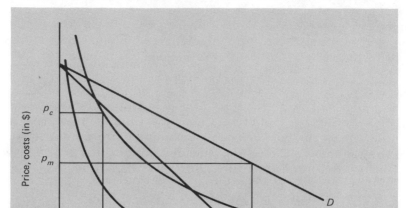

business. Bigger firms would continue getting bigger until only the largest firm remained. Hence, pervasive economies of scale not conducive to the existence of perfect competition. Profit-maximizing incentives naturally lead to monopoly. Frequently, when a monopoly exists because of economies, it is said to be a *natural monopoly*.

### Monopoly and fixed costs

Large fixed costs relative to variable costs can also lead to firms with monopoly power. Once again, the cause of monopoly power lies in the cost structure of production. To illustrate, let $MC = AVC$, so that average variable and marginal costs are constant. Fixed costs ($FC$) exist and are large. Figure 9–14 shows the cost schedule along with demand and marginal revenue. If the monopolist had to behave as a perfectly competitive firm and set $P = MC$, price would be $p_c$ and output would be $x_c$. Profits would be negative, because no producer's surplus is earned, but fixed costs must be covered. Thus, such behavior would continually cause losses and therefore the firm would not produce in the long run.

The only way a firm can manage to break even is if it has some monopoly power, or more precisely, the firm can raise price above marginal cost. If the firm behaves like a monopolist by setting $MR = MC$, then a surplus of $p_mABp_c$ is earned, and this may be enough to cover fixed costs. If profits are above normal and entry is easy, firms will enter the market until profits are normal. This occurs when $FC$ equals producer's surplus; the producer's surplus earned is just equal to fixed costs, and total revenue equals total cost.

You might be wondering whether it would ever be better to forego the product altogether rather than to have it produced by a monopolist. The answer is no, since total surplus in the monopolized market is positive. In Figure 9–14, total surplus before entry is

**FIGURE 9–14**
**Monopoly with fixed costs**

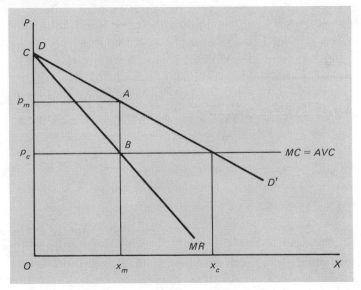

$CABp_c$. Part of this surplus covers fixed costs; however, consumer's surplus, $Cp_mA$ in particular, exists. Even though only $x_m$ is sold, at least some consumers are willing to pay more than $p_m$ for the product. As long as the price they are willing to pay is above the price they are charged, the product ought to be produced.

**Summary**

In a simple theoretical framework, it is possible to compare monopoly unfavorably to perfect competition. Relative to a perfectly competitive market, monopoly restricts output, charges a higher price, and does not operate at minimum long-run average cost. Furthermore, because monopoly does restrict output, we can show that there is a loss of surplus relative to perfect competition.

But the comparison between the two market structures is not so clear if production technology is characterized by continuous economies of scale in the long run or high fixed costs in the short run. For economies of scale, the profit-maximizing incentive encourages firms to become larger and, as a consequence, fewer in number. A large number of firms could be maintained by making it illegal for a firm to get large, but this has serious disincentive effects for the profit maximizer. More importantly, though, it is not clear that a few, or even a single firm producing the product is undesirable. Because of lower costs, a monopolist may charge a lower price than would competitive producers.

The presence of fixed costs in the short run can sometimes allow no choice in the market structure. Unless firms have monopoly power so that price can be set above marginal cost, the product may not be produced.

Thus, as a matter of public policy, economists cannot say that perfect competition is more efficient and, therefore, "more desirable" than a monopolized market structure. This judgment cannot be generalized. Moreover, if we extended our comparison to the issues of research and development, employment, and inflationary impact, the relative advantages and disadvantages of the two market structures would become even less clear-cut.

## 9.7 BARRIERS TO ENTRY

In general, the reason firms have monopoly power is that other producers cannot enter the market and make at least normal returns. They are blocked by *barriers to entry*. Although there is some controversy over what constitutes a barrier to entry, for purposes of discussion, we shall say that an entry barrier is any factor in the market that might prevent a firm from producing a particular product.

Economies of scale and fixed costs are two reasons monopolies exist in the real world. Monopoly power can therefore result from technical causes, for it is technology which leads to economies of scale in the long run and to fixed costs in the short run. Entry barriers are, however, not necessarily connected with the technology of production. We will describe causes other than technology that encourage monopoly in this section. It is also possible for firms to strategically erect barriers on their own. In particular, a monopolist may keep price below the point where marginal revenue equals marginal cost to forestall entry. This pricing strategy is discussed below.

### Possible barriers to entry

Barriers to entry are as diverse as the number of markets in an economy. We have no hope of enumerating every conceivable reason a potential producer might not be able to enter a market. What we shall do is provide several examples of how barriers have actually led to monopolies. You will then be able to identify barriers on your own as you consider other markets.

A most obvious entry barrier is government. Allocations, licensing, and franchises are ways monopolies are created by fiat. Allocations, for instance, are granted to growers of many agricultural commodities to prevent the free entry of farmers into the market. The allocation restricts output and raises the price of a foodstuff, and, in many cases, growers earn above-normal returns. Licenses are granted to radio and television stations by the Federal Communications Commission. Stations are not allowed to operate without the license. Locally, this tends to confer immense monopoly power on those stations that have licenses. Entrants can petition the FCC for a license to operate, but if those who are operating protest to the commission, the petition is usually denied.

Finally, exclusive franchises are frequently granted for city, county, and state services. For example, telephone and cable television utilities have ultimate monopoly power in that they are regionally the only producer of the product. By law, no other producer exists. However, utilities, e.g., the postal service, can raise prices enough so that substitute products outside their franchise become feasible substitutes. Then again, utilities may have limited monopoly power. There may be only one electric utility, but there is also a gas utility consumers can turn to for an alternative means of heating or cooling. A close substitute exists despite the franchise.

Another barrier to competition lies in the patent laws of the United States. These laws make it possible for a person to apply for and obtain the exclusive right to produce a certain commodity, or to produce a commodity by means of a specified process that gives it an absolute cost advantage. Obviously, such exclusive rights can easily lead to monopoly. E. I. du Pont de Nemours & Company enjoyed patent monopolies over many commodities, cellophane, discussed above, being perhaps the most notable. At one time, the Eastman Kodak Company enjoyed a similar position.

Despite many notable examples, holding a patent on a product or on a production process may not be quite what it seems in many instances. In the first place, like the exclusive owner of some necessary raw material, the holder of a product patent may choose not to exploit the monopoly position in the production of the product. If diseconomies of scale set in at a low level of production, the patent holder may find it more profitable to sell production rights to a few firms (in which case oligopoly results), or to many. Second, a firm that owns a patented lower-cost production process may have a cost advantage over competitors but may sell only a small part of the industry's total output at the equilibrium position. The new technique will lead to patent monopoly only if the firm can supply the market and still undersell competition. Third, a patent gives one the exclusive right to produce a particular, meticulously specified commodity, or to use a particular, meticulously specified process to produce a commodity others can produce. But a patent does not preclude the development of closely related substitute goods or closely allied production processes. International Business Machines has the exclusive right to produce IBM computers, but many other computers are available and there is competition in the computer market.

One of the most important bases of monopoly or oligopoly is the control of raw-material supplies. If one firm (or perhaps a few firms) controls all of the known supply of a necessary ingredient for a particular product, the firm or firms can refuse to sell that ingredient to other firms at a price low enough for them to compete. Since no others can produce the product, a monopoly or oligopoly results. For example, for many years, the Aluminum Company of America (Alcoa) owned almost every source of bauxite, a necessary ingredient in the production of aluminum. The control of resource supply, coupled with certain patent rights, provided Alcoa with an absolute monopoly in aluminum production. Indeed, it was only after World War II that the federal courts effectively broke Alcoa's monopoly of the aluminum market. The International Nickel Company enjoyed much the same position over a relatively long period.

Nonetheless, a firm's control of the source of raw-material supply does not guarantee that it will choose to exploit its opportunity to be a monopolist. If diseconomies of scale set in at a low level of output relative to demand, the firm may find it more profitable to sell the raw material to other firms. The number of firms that may enter the industry depends, in large part, on economies of scale. If economies of scale are only attainable at a relatively large level of output (but not the entire market output), few firms will enter, and oligopoly will result. If all economies of scale are attainable at low levels of output, more firms will enter. However, the sole owner of the raw material remains a monopolist in the raw-material market. Only if it is more profitable will the firm choose to be a monopolist of the product as well.

Another frequently cited barrier to competition is the advantage that established firms sometimes have over new firms. On the cost side, the established firms, perhaps because of a history of good earnings, may be able to secure financing at a more favorable rate than can new firms. On the demand side, older firms may have built up, over the years, the allegiance of a group of buyers. New firms might find these advantages difficult to overcome. Buyer allegiance for durable goods can be built by establishing a reputation for service. No one knows what the service or repair policy of a new firm may be. The preference of buyers can also be influenced by a long successful advertising campaign; this type of allegiance is also probably more prevalent for durable goods. Although technical economies or diseconomies of sale may be insignificant, new firms might have considerable difficulties establishing a market organization and overcoming buyer preference for the products of older firms. A classic example of how loyalty preserves monopoly power can be found in the concentrated-lemon-juice market. Realemon lemon juice has developed such strong brand loyalties among consumers that rival brands cannot sell in the market. The situation became so serious that the courts recently forced Realemon to license its name to would-be competitors.

We have by no means exhausted the list of possible barriers to entry. The point of this discussion is to expose you to several of the most common types of entry barriers and to illustrate the diversity of factors that prevent entry into a market and, consequently, foster monopoly power.

**Entry limit pricing**

Under some circumstances, a monopoly might charge a price below that at which short-run profit is maximized and, therefore, produce and sell an output greater than that at which marginal revenue equals marginal cost. One such circumstance would be the case of a monopolist that, facing *potential* competition, lowers price to block the entry of these potential competitors.

Figure 9–15 illustrates an example in which a monopolist might lower price to prevent entry. A monopolist's average and marginal costs are $AC_M$ and $MC_M$. Market demand and marginal revenue are $D$ and $MR$. The profit-maximizing price and quantity are $p_1$ and $x_1$. Assume that, for technological reasons, the most advantaged potential rival would have average cost curve $AC_C$. Even though the competitor does suffer a cost disadvantage, entry into the industry could be made at a price lower than $p_1$ but above $AC_C$; thus, some of the monopolist's business would be taken away. The monopolist would then be forced to lower price, because total market output would be higher. Price would have to fall in order to sell all that was produced.

The monopoly, however, can set a price slightly below the minimum point of the potential competitor's average cost curve. For the competitor to make any profit, its price must be above $AC_C$. If the

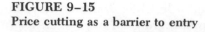

**FIGURE 9–15**
**Price cutting as a barrier to entry**

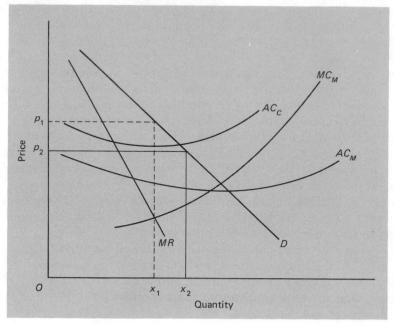

monopoly sets the price $p_2$ and sells $x_2$, the competitor will not be able to make profit and, hence, will not want to enter the market. The monopoly's profit, of course, will be lower in the long run but higher than if entry had actually occurred. If the threat of entry is not great, the monopolist may not wish to sacrifice the stream of higher earnings. But if entry is easy, the monopoly firm may well be satisfied with lower profit and the retention of its monopoly position. An analysis of this situation requires the monopolist to compare the discounted future streams of profit with and without entry.

The above example is not meant to suggest that the entrant must have a higher cost curve than the monopolist before a price can be set to block entry. We switch to the long run in Figure 9–16, and assume that all firms in the market can operate on the same *LRAC* schedule. The monopolist can prevent entry by producing at $x_m'$ and setting price below the profit maximizing price, $p_m$.

If an entrant wants to come into the market, it must produce at least $x_e$ units of output. Any amount less than $x_e$ means *LRAC* is above $p_m'$, and the entrant will not earn normal returns in the long run. But if the entrant produces $x_e$, total market output is $x_m' + x_e$; to sell this output, price, $p_{m'+e}$, must be below the long-run average cost schedule at every point. So there is no output at which the

**FIGURE 9–16**
**Entry limit pricing on common cost curves**

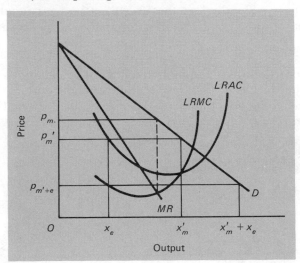

entrant could produce and break even. Entry is typically blocked in this situation. Notice that, if a firm did enter the market, both the entrant and the monopolist would earn below-normal profits. Sometimes an entrant will attempt to outlast the former monopolist. The losses cannot be sustained indefinitely, and if a monopoly eventually exits, it may be possible for the entrant to recoup the losses by raising prices to the pre-entry level.

These two examples illustrate how a monopolist can maintain its monopoly position in the market. Thus, monopoly does not necessarily exist because of market conditions outside a firm's control. Very often, monopoly is created as part of a firm's strategy to maximize long-run profits. Notice, however, that in these two examples, the threat of entry forces a monopolist to price closer to the point where $MC = D$, the price in a competitive industry. Hence, it acts as a force bringing monopoly prices closer to the competitive equilibrium.

## APPLICATION

### Entry limit pricing

As noted above, the decision to set price below the point corresponding to the intersection of the marginal revenue and marginal cost curves involves a choice between two discounted streams of profit. Profit maximization depends upon relative profits in each period and the discount rate. Let us consider an example.

Suppose we have a firm that is currently a monopolist in the production of some good. Assume, for analytical purposes, that the firm has a 10-year time horizon and it has a choice of two strategies. First, it can set prices to prevent entry and earn a steady stream of profits over its entire planning horizon. Or it can charge a price that earns higher profits at first, but later encourages entry. After entry, profits are reduced. Figure 9–17 shows the alternative profit streams.

**FIGURE 9–17**
**Entry limit profits and profits with entry**

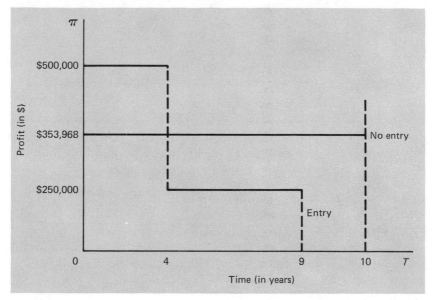

If the firm ignores the threat of entry, it can earn $500,000 a year during years 1 through 3. After entry takes place in year 3, it will earn $250,000 a year in years 4 through 8, and no pure profit in years 9 and 10. With a 12 percent interest rate, the present value of following such a strategy is

$$PV_1 = \sum_{t=1}^{3} \frac{\$500,000}{(1 + .12)^t} + \sum_{t=4}^{8} \frac{\$250,000}{(1 + .12)^t} = \$1,842,000.$$

Alternatively, the firm could set an entry limit price and earn $353,968 per year over the entire horizon. Using this strategy, present value is

$$PV_2 = \sum_{t=1}^{10} \frac{\$353,968}{(1 + .12)^t} = \$2,000,000.$$

Clearly, under these conditions, the firm would maximize profits, charging the lower price, which discourages entry and ensures the firm's monopoly position. Of course, a different interest rate or a different stream of income could make the first strategy more profitable. For example, if the stream of income under the entry limit price is $265,476 a year, the present value of the stream, using a 12 percent rate of interest, is $1.5 million. In this case, the firm would set a high price during the early years, letting entry drive it down in later years. Thus, you can see that the decision is not static; it involves a pricing decision over time. This discussion of entry limit pricing emphasizes the fact that high monopoly prices encourage the production of substitute products. Potential sellers observe above-normal profits in a market and look for a way to earn them; buyers who are paying high prices are searching for substitutes.

Even for monopolies in which direct entry into the market is illegal, high prices can encourage the development of substitutes which "indirectly" compete with a monopolist's product or service. Competition can come from products unknown before the monopoly prices became relatively high. An illustration of how entry is indirectly encouraged comes from the U.S. Postal Service. This illustration shows that the postal service did not protect its market by an entry limit pricing strategy.

The Postal Service is over 200 years old. It certainly has had as much protection as any monopoly over this period. During the great majority of this period, the general rule was good service and low prices. In 1883, you could send a letter coast to coast for 3 cents. In 1958, you could send a letter coast to coast for 3 cents. The price was down in real terms, and the letter got to its destination much more quickly.

But after 1958, service began to decline and prices to rise. First-class mail rose to 4 cents. In 1971, it was 8 cents; 1974, 10 cents; 1975, 13 cents; 1978, 15 cents; 1981, 20 cents. Now a price of 23 cents is expected in the near future.

Despite its monopoly power, the Postal Service is pricing itself out of the market. In the face of legal action from the postal service, old and new companies have begun to provide letter and package services. Some examples are Greyhound, Purolator, Federal Express, and United Parcel Service. But the mail of the future, and the mail that may in large measure replace the postal service, is electronic mail—unknown a few years ago.

Firms are now in the electronic mail service business, even though the technology is still in its infancy. But, as Sylvia Porter recently wrote:

By the dozens, newspapers, magazines and book publishing sub-sidiaries, units of network and cable TV systems, telephone companies, banks and merchants are either cooperating or competing to deliver a wide variety of data. The range goes from personal letters to giant ency-clopedias, latest news, product prices, even money (via electronic funds transfer).

As the technology is improved, as services are added, growing num-bers of post office customers will switch to the newer and faster "mail."

And prices for these electronic services will drop in the 1980s, just as prices for users of the U.S. mail dropped in the 1880s.

There'll be no need for the Postal Service. It will be your phone, your TV, or your computer that rings. The "operator" may say: "I have your *Satellite Morning Sun* for you," or a " 'Lectra-Card' ('Compu-Card')"—you'll be able to listen to it, see it on a TV screen, spray it on paper, or file it on a memory disc.

And your letter carrier? He'll be retired on a special pension that your last $1 stamp helped pay for.[10]

---

## 9.8 PRICE DISCRIMINATION

As early as 1920, A. C. Pigou realized that, if buyers could be separated into groups with different price elasticities of demand, the monopolist could charge different prices for the same product and raise profits.[11] In general, the more a seller knows about buyer preferences and the less easily buyers can trade among themselves, the greater the profits that can be made by asking a different price for the same good.

Price discrimination exists when buyers pay different prices for the same product, but the costs of producing and selling the product are identical. Sometimes sellers charge buyer groups different prices for the same product because of differences in the costs of selling to them. In this case, we do not have price discrimination unless prices differ by more than the difference in costs. For exam-ple, a firm producing in Pittsburgh might charge buyers in New York a lower price than it charges buyers on the West Coast because shipping costs are higher in the latter market. On the other hand, if a pharmacy gives senior citizens a discount on drugs while others receive no discount, this is price discrimination. Theaters discrimi-nate when they charge teenagers a lower price for tickets than they do adults for the same showing.

---

[10] Sylvia Porter, "Postal System Chaos Could Signal Boom in Electronic Mail," *Houston Post*, August 7, 1981, p. 5F.

[11] A. C. Pigou, *The Economics of Welfare* (London: Macmillan, 1920).

While it is certainly not necessary for a firm to be a pure monopolist in order to discriminate in price, it must have some degree of monopoly power in order to do so. Price differentials would be competed away in more competitive market structures.

The purpose of this section is to discuss the various types of price discrimination. We begin with an analysis of third-degree price discrimination, the most frequently encountered form. Under third-degree discrimination, sellers charge different prices in separate markets based upon the elasticities of demand in the markets. We then describe two more specialized forms of discrimination, commonly called first- and second-degree price discrimination.

## Price discrimination in theory—third degree

In order for a firm to discriminate, markets must be *separable*. If purchasers in the lower-price market are themselves able to sell the commodity to buyers in the higher-price market, discrimination will not exist for long. Arbitrage, or secondary trading between buyers, would soon restore a single, uniform price in the market. Goods that cannot be easily traded are more apt to involve discriminatory prices than are those that can be easily transferred. For example, a lower-price medical patient cannot resell his or her operation to a higher-price patient, but a lower-price buyer of some raw material could perhaps resell it to someone in the higher-price market. Discrimination would not be practical in the latter case.

As a first step in the analysis of discriminatory pricing, let us assume that a monopoly has two separate markets for its product. Demand conditions in each market are such that the marginal revenues from selling specified quantities are as given in Table 9–4.

**TABLE 9–4**
**Allocation of sales between two markets**

| Quantity | Marginal revenue market I | | Marginal revenue market II | |
|---|---|---|---|---|
| 1 .......... | $45 | (1) | $34 | (3) |
| 2 .......... | 36 | (2) | 28 | (5) |
| 3 .......... | 30 | (4) | 22 | (7) |
| 4 .......... | 22 | (6) | 13 | (10) |
| 5 .......... | 17 | (8) | 10 | (12) |
| 6 .......... | 15 | (9) | 8 | |
| 7 .......... | 10 | (11) | 7 | |
| 8 .......... | 7 | | 4 | |
| 9 .......... | 4 | | 2 | |
| 10 .......... | 0 | | 1 | |

Assume also that, for some reason, the monopoly decides to produce 12 units. How should it allocate sales between the two markets?

Consider the first unit; the firm can gain $45 by selling it in the first market or $34 by selling in the second market. Obviously, if it sells only one unit per period, it will sell in market I. The second unit per period is also sold in the first market since its sale there increases revenue by $36, whereas it would only bring $34 in market II. Since $34 can be gained in II but only $30 in I, unit three is sold in market II. Similar analysis shows that the fourth unit goes to I and the fifth to II. Since unit six adds $22 to revenue in either market, it makes no difference where it is sold; six and seven go to either market. Eight and nine are sold in I because they yield higher marginal revenue there; ten goes to II for the same reason. Unit 11 can go to either market, since the additional revenues are the same, and unit 12 goes to the other. Thus, we see that the 12 units should be divided so that the marginal revenues are the same for the last unit sold in each market; the monopolist sells seven units in market I and five in market II.

**Principle.** The discriminating monopolist allocates a given output in such a way that the marginal revenues in each market are equal. The firm sells any additional unit in the market with the higher marginal revenue.

Intuitively, one would predict that, if there are two separate markets and the firm price discriminates, the higher price would be charged in the market with the less elastic demand, and the lower price would be in the more elastic. Consumers in the more elastic market would have better substitutes; thus, price could be raised only at the expense of a large decrease in sales. In the less elastic market there are poorer substitutes; thus, higher prices bring less reduction in sales. The conclusion that the higher price is charged in the less elastic market and the lower price in the more elastic can be proved using the following method:

Let there be two distinct markets for one monopolistically produced good; call these markets $A$ and $B$. $P_A$ and $P_B$ are, respectively, the prices in markets $A$ and $B$. $MR_A$ and $MR_B$ are the marginal revenues, and $E_A$ and $E_B$ are the absolute values of demand elasticity. Recall from our discussion of marginal revenue that

$$MR = P\left(1 - \frac{1}{E}\right).$$

We can use this relation to prove that if $P_A > P_B$, $E_A < E_B$.

A discriminating monopolist divides output between the two markets so that the marginal revenues are equal in equilibrium.

Thus,

$$P_A \left( 1 - \frac{1}{E_A} \right) = P_B \left( 1 - \frac{1}{E_B} \right).$$

If $P_A > P_B$, then

$$\frac{\left( 1 - \dfrac{1}{E_B} \right)}{\left( 1 - \dfrac{1}{E_A} \right)} > 1.$$

Since the monopolist would never choose a point at which $MR$ is negative

$$\left( 1 - \frac{1}{E_B} \right) > \left( 1 - \frac{1}{E_A} \right).$$

Manipulation of this inequality yields

$$E_B > E_A.$$

Thus we see that, whenever $P_A > P_B$, $E_B > E_A$. The more elastic market has the lower price.

In order to analyze the situation graphically, assume that a monopoly can separate its market into two distinct markets. The demands and marginal revenues of each are shown in panel A, Figure 9–18. $D_1 D'_1$ and $MR_1$ are demand and marginal revenue in the first market; $D_2 D'_2$ and $MR_2$ are demand and marginal revenue in the second. Panel B shows the horizontal summation of the two

**FIGURE 9–18**
**Submarket and total market demands and marginal revenues**

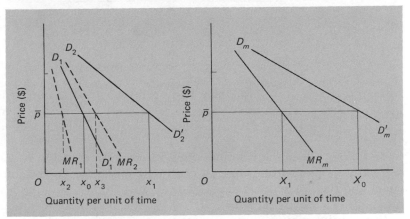

Panel A
Demand and marginal
revenue in submarkets

Panel B
Monopoly demand and
marginal revenue

demand and marginal revenue curves. For example, at a price of $\bar{p}$, consumers in market I would take $x_0$ and consumers in market II would take $x_1$. The total quantity demanded at $\bar{p}$ is, accordingly, $x_0 + x_1 = X_0$, shown in panel B. All other points on $D_m D'_m$ are derived similarly. $MR_1 = \bar{p}$ at output $x_2$; $MR_2 = \bar{p}$ at $x_3$. Therefore, in panel B, $MR_m = \bar{p}$ at a quantity of $x_2 + x_3 = X_1$. Other points on $MR_m$, the total market $MR$ curve, are derived similarly.

The demand and marginal revenue conditions depicted in panel A, Figure 9–18, are reproduced in Figure 9–19, along with average

**FIGURE 9–19**
**Profit maximization under price discrimination**

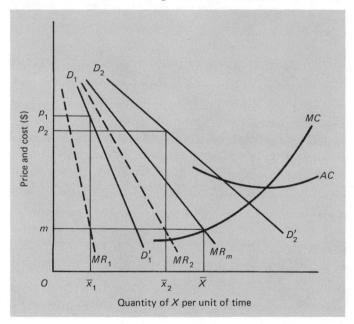

and marginal costs of production. The profit-maximizing output is $\bar{X}$, the quantity at which total market marginal revenue equals marginal cost. The marginal revenue (equals marginal cost) associated with this output is $m$.

The market allocation rule, previously determined, requires that marginal revenue be the same in each submarket. Since the total market marginal revenue is the added revenue from selling the last unit in either submarket, $MR_1 = MR_2 = m$. At a marginal revenue of $m$, the quantity sold in submarket one is $\bar{x}_1$; in submarket two, $\bar{x}_2$. Since $MR_m$ is the horizontal summation of $MR_1$ and $MR_2$, $\bar{x}_1 + \bar{x}_2 = \bar{X}$, the total output. Furthermore, from the relevant demand curves, the price associated with output $\bar{x}_1$ in market one is $p_1$, the price associated with $\bar{x}_2$ in market two is $p_2$. Because these prices clearly differ and the costs of production are the same, discrimination exists.

Summarizing these results:

**Principle.** If the aggregate market for a monopolist's product can be divided into submarkets with different price elasticities, the monopolist can profitably practice price discrimination. Total output is determined by equating marginal cost with aggregate monopoly marginal revenue. The output is allocated among the submarkets so as to equate marginal revenue in each submarket with aggregate marginal revenue at the $MC = MR$ point. Finally, price in each submarket is determined directly from the submarket demand curve, given the submarket allocation of sales.

## APPLICATION

### Some examples and analyses of price discrimination

The typical textbook example of price discrimination is the medical profession. Doctors frequently scale fees according to income. Economists say that this is done in order to increase income. The medical profession argues that doctors price discriminate in order to act as a collection agency for a medical charity. They charge high-income patients a high fee to finance the low fees charged low-income patients.

In a classic article on the subject, Reuben A. Kessel tested the hypothesis that doctors price discriminate because of charitable motives.[12] He asked why we do not observe parallel behavior in nursing and dentistry, or even by grocery stores since food is as "necessary" as medical care. The argument presented is that the state supplies food and shelter to the poor but not medical care; therefore, this type of charity is up to the medical profession.

According to Kessel, if the charity hypothesis is in fact correct, there should be no price discrimination among patients with the same income, even if some have medical insurance while others do not. On the other hand, if increased income is the reason for discrimination, those who have insurance should pay, on average, higher fees than do the uninsured. Insurance affects the *demand* for doctors but does not change the income of an individual. Those with insurance would, other things being equal, have a more inelastic demand than those without, and would pay higher fees. Holding income constant, the evidence cited by Kessel does show that medical fees are higher for the insured than for the uninsured. This evi-

---

[12] R. A. Kessel, "Price Discrimination in Medicine," *Journal of Law and Economics*, 1 (October 1958):20–53.

dence comes from unions and from the insurance industry. Kessel pointed out that the effect of insurance upon fees, abstracting out variations in income, suggests that fees are determined by "what the traffic will bear."

A second bit of evidence that profit, rather than charity, motivates price discrimination in medicine is the stand of the American Medical Association (AMA) on different types of insurance. The first type of insurance, cash indemnity plans, has not been opposed at all by the AMA or by local medical societies. Cash indemnity plans such as Blue Cross and Blue Shield allow doctors and patients to determine fees just as though there were no insurance. Doctors are, therefore, able to discriminate, and under such plans, the demand for medical care is increased.

In contrast, the AMA and local medical societies have strongly opposed prepaid plans that supply medical services directly to patients. Costs of such cooperative plans are independent of income, and, as such, represent a threat to doctors' ability to discriminate. These plans provide the means for extensive price cutting to high-income patients. The opposition of organized medicine to these types of plans is in strong support of the profit-maximizing, discriminating-monopolist hypothesis.

The two conditions necessary for firms to be able to price discriminate are met: differences in income would probably cause different price elasticities, and patients cannot easily sell medical services among themselves. That is, low-price patients cannot resell their operations to high-price patients. But doctors do not have a monopoly. Since there are many, many doctors, why do not some doctors break the agreement, causing the price for high-income patients to fall?

According to Kessel, the reason doctors do not attempt to cut prices individually is the extensive control of the AMA over medical education. Every doctor must undergo an internship administered by a hospital, and only hospitals approved by the AMA are sanctioned for internship and residency. Hospitals value intern and residency training, because they can provide medical care more cheaply with interns and residents than without them. Thus, the AMA controls an important resource for hospitals, and its "advice" that hospitals use only doctors who are members of their local medical society is almost always adhered to. Doctors who are "price cutters" can be removed from the local medical societies, and thus are denied access to hospitals. It would be supposed that any doctor who is denied hospital services finds the demand for his services substantially weakened. It, therefore, pays doctors not to lower prices.

What other kind of businesses can and do practice price discrimination? The many drug stores that offer discounts on drugs to persons 65 and over are one example. Thus, the drug stores discriminate in price. One would suppose that retired persons have a more elastic demand for drugs, because the market value of their time is lower. Thus, retired persons would tend to shop around more for lower prices, and differences in price among different age groups can be explained by different price elasticities, resulting from different evaluations of time.

But the other conditions are absent in the case of drugs. There are many drug stores that would be willing to reduce prices, and if the price differential becomes sufficiently large, older people would buy drugs and sell to younger persons. There may be some prevention of reselling because of prescription laws (not applicable in the case of toothpaste, aspirin, etc. How important these are is an empirical question.)

Movies, plays, concerts, and similar forms of entertainment involve price discrimination according to age. Generally, younger people pay lower prices. Supposedly, in this case, younger people have more elastic demands for such tickets, possibly because of the availability of more substitute forms of entertainment. (It is not correct to say that different ticket prices for afternoon and evening performances or for Tuesday and Saturday are evidence of price discrimination. These are different products in the eye of the consumer.)

Airlines have in the past discriminated between students and nonstudents and now vacation and business travel. The regulatory agency allowed these prices to be maintained. One would believe that students or vacation travelers would have a more elastic demand than business travelers, probably because the value of time in business travel is greater.

Other examples of price discrimination are electric companies that charge lower rates to industrial users than to households (although this may be due to differences in costs), and university book stores that charge lower prices to faculty than to students. Citizens of the United States vacationing in Mexico pay higher prices in restaurants than do Mexican nationals. Trucking companies frequently charge different rates for different goods when the distance and size of the goods are the same.

### First-degree price discrimination—perfect price discrimination

Under first-degree discrimination, the most extreme form of price discrimination, the firm would treat each individual's demand separately. That is, each consumer is a separate market. The firm then

**FIGURE 9–20**
First-degree price discrimination

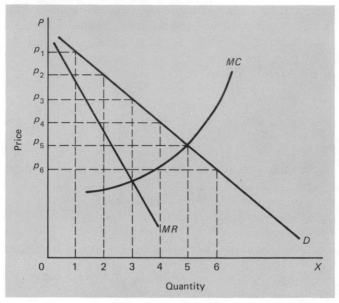

maximizes its profit for each individual consumer. In Figure 9–20, we have illustrated a consumer's demand function with its associated marginal revenue curve and the firm's marginal cost curve. Note that, in the normal case, the firm would maximize profit by selling that output at which $MR$ is equal to $MC$ (i.e., an output of three units at a price of $p_3$). However, with first-degree price discrimination, the firm can increase its profit. For the first unit of the product, the consumer is willing to pay $p_1$; so the firm makes a profit equal to the difference between $p_1$ and average cost at this output. For the second unit, the consumer will pay $p_2$, and so on. Thus, the firm charges the consumer a different price for each unit of output purchased. The firm will continue to sell to this consumer as long as the price the consumer will pay is greater than or equal to marginal cost. More specifically, under first-degree price discrimination, the firm will produce and sell to that level of output at which $P = MC$—that output at which the demand curve intersects the marginal cost curve. This is due to the fact that, in this case, price is equal to marginal revenue. Since the firm charges a different price for each unit consumed, the addition to revenue for a unit of the product will be the price charged for that unit. It will not sell the sixth unit, since the price the consumer is willing to pay ($p_6$) is less than the marginal cost associated with this level of production.

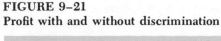

**FIGURE 9–21**
**Profit with and without discrimination**

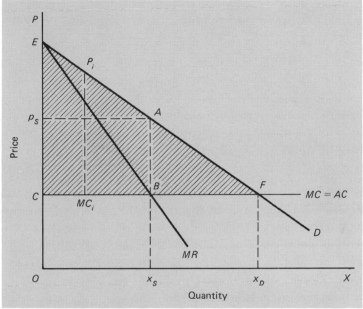

Figure 9–21 provides a comparison of profits with and without price discrimination. For simplicity, we assume that marginal cost is constant, so $MC = AC$. $D$ and $MR$ are the market demand and marginal revenue curves. Without discrimination, the firm will sell $x_s$ units at a price of $p_s$. Since average cost is constant, the firm's total profit is indicated by the rectangle $p_sABC$.

Next, let the firm practice first-degree price discrimination. We can analyze this situation also using Figure 9–21. Let $ED$ again be the horizontal summation of the demand of all consumers. With price discrimination, the firm will charge each consumer the maximum price he or she would be willing to pay for each unit purchased. Thus, each unit sells for the highest price that can be obtained for that unit. The firm will sell up to the point at which the price any consumer is willing to pay equals marginal cost; so, with price discrimination, the firm will sell $x_D$ units of output. For each unit, the firm charges the price on the demand curve, and profit is the difference between that price and the corresponding point on the marginal cost curve (e.g., $P_i - MC_i$). Thus, total profit to the discriminating firm is the shaded section $EFC$. Obviously, price discrimination leads to an increase in profits. While first-degree price discrimination could increase the firm's profits, it is very costly. Each individual consumer must be isolated and dealt with separately. Thus, perfect first-degree discrimination probably does not exist.

To the extent that first-degree price discrimination does exist, notice what happens to producer's and consumer's surplus. Returning to Figure 9–21, suppose the monopolist could only charge one price and would, thus, set it where marginal cost intersects marginal revenue. Price would be $p_s$ and output $x_s$. The surplus lost from such a move will be the area $ABF$, the oft-cited social cost of monopoly, because output is restricted. Perfect price discrimination, however, eliminates this loss; the monopolist sells $x_D$, the quantity associated with setting $D = MC$. Total surplus is maximized. Price discrimination gives monopolists the incentive to increase output and thus increases total producer's and consumer's surplus.

Consumers have good reason, though, not to favor discriminating strategies. First-degree price discrimination provides the most extreme support for their case. They receive no consumer's surplus from the market. All of it is extracted in the form of profit by the monopolist.

### Second-degree price discrimination

As we have noted, first-degree price discrimination is expensive to implement, since, at least in theory, the firm must determine each individual's demand function. Second-degree price discrimination is somewhat simpler because it requires the firm to consider groups of consumers. This form of discrimination can best be explained using Figure 9–22, in which we again employ the simplifying assumption that marginal cost is constant. With second-degree price discrimination, the firm would charge every buyer $p_1$ for the first $x_1$, units, but if consumers wanted to purchase more, they would receive discrete discounts. In Figure 9–22, for instance, the next $x_2x_1$ would cost $p_2$, then price would fall to $p_3$ for the next $x_3x_2$ units, and so on. In effect, buyers are receiving quantity discounts. The discounts are offered as long as the price consumers are willing to pay exceeds marginal cost. Thus, the firm will sell a total of $x_6$ units of its product. Total profit is again the shaded area. Note the similarity between this case and the profits in first-degree price discrimination. In essence, second-degree price discrimination is an approximation of first-degree discrimination.

It is particularly crucial for second-degree price discrimination that arbitrage does not occur between buyers. You can easily see that an enterprising consumer could buy cheap at $p_6$ and sell dear at $p_1$ or at any price above $p_6$. Before long, the monopoly would find itself selling only at $p_6$ and making smaller profits.

**FIGURE 9–22**
Second-degree price discrimination

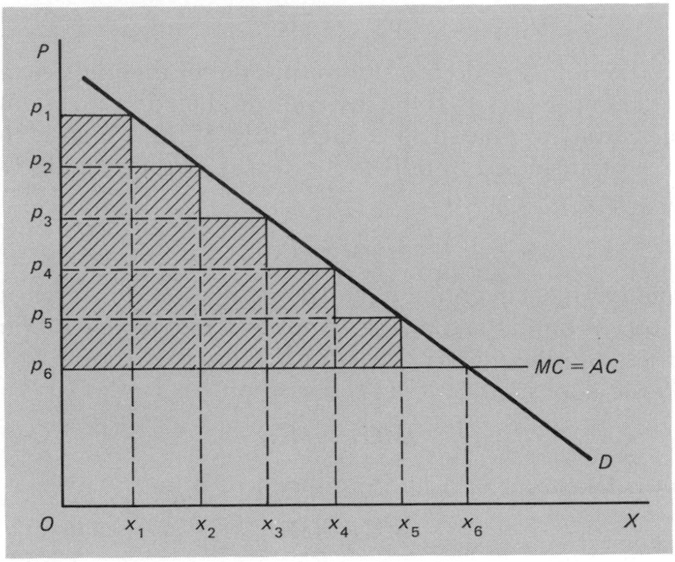

## 9.9 MULTIPLANT MONOPOLY AND MULTIPRODUCT COSTS

We will now explore the theoretical issues associated with a monopolist operating several plants but selling only one product; then we will examine the rapidly developing theory surrounding multiproduct production costs. The theory of multiproduct monopoly is, for the most part, too advanced for the level of difficulty at which this text is written, but it is possible to draw attention to the important issues without a complicated model.

### Multiplant monopoly

A situation quite similar analytically to the case of third-degree price discrimination is the situation of the monopolist that produces output in more than one plant, with different cost structures. As in the case of price discrimination, this situation has many interesting implications.

Consider first how a firm would allocate a given level of output among several plants. For simplicity, we use the case of only two plants. From our analysis of the discriminating monopolist, you have probably already deduced that the firm allocates a given output between two plants so that the marginal costs in both plants are equal.

Assume there are two plants, $A$ and $B$. Suppose, at the desired level of output, the following situation holds

$$MC_A < MC_B.$$

Clearly, the firm should transfer output out of the higher-cost plant $B$ into the lower-cost $A$. If the last unit produced in $B$ costs \$10, but one more unit produced in $A$ adds only \$7 to $A$'s cost, that unit should be transferred from $B$ to $A$. In fact, output should be transferred from $B$ to $A$ until

$$MC_A = MC_B.$$

We would suspect eventual equalization because of increasing marginal cost. As output is transferred out of $B$ into $A$, the marginal cost in $A$ rises, and the marginal cost in $B$ falls. It is simple to see that exactly the opposite occurs in the case of

$$MC_A > MC_B.$$

Output is taken out of A and produced in B until

$$MC_A = MC_B.$$

The total situation is pictured graphically in Figure 9–23. Demand for the product is $D$, and total marginal revenue for the firm is $MR$.

**FIGURE 9–23**
**Multiplant monopoly**

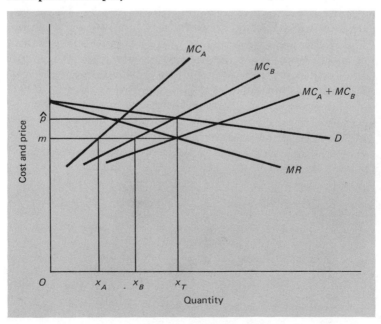

Total marginal cost for the firm, $MC_A + MC_B$, equals marginal revenue at output $x_T$. The product price is $p$, and marginal cost in each plant is $m$. Plant $A$ produces $x_A$ units; plant $B$ produces $x_B$ units. Because of the way in which the curves were derived $x_A + x_B = x_T$. Thus, the firm is in equilibrium. Exactly the same principles apply for firms producing in more than two plants.

Suppose the monopolist did not have the high-cost plant $A$. What would happen to prices in Figure 9–23? The intersection of $MR$ and $MC_B$ tells us that this price would have to be above $p$. Ironically, the expensive plant actually helps to keep the monopolist's price down.

## APPLICATION

### Nonconventional mineral extraction[13]

Presently there is a considerable amount of discussion about the implementation of new types of technology in mineral extraction, particularly in energy-related areas. The government has recently established a synthetic fuels commission to investigate new sources of energy and technology. But most discussions of these new technologies and new sources of energy make one fundamental mistake—they assume that the new, generally higher-cost technology will increase the price of the mineral.

Suppose a natural gas producer can pump gas from the Permian Basin in Texas at an average cost of $C_1$ per million cubic feet (MCF). The company also has some leases in the Rocky Mountains. But these mountain deposits are of such low permeability that the firm must use a more expensive, special type of stimulation—perhaps nuclear stimulation—in order to extract the gas. Suppose the average extraction cost for a certain quantity, using the new technology, is $C_2$ per MCF, where $C_2$ greatly exceeds $C_1$.

Now, suppose that gas from Texas and gas from the Rockies are mixed, then pumped through the same pipeline to the East Coast. Texas gas makes up 80 percent of the total and gas from the Rocky Mountains, 20 percent. The total cost of the gas is, therefore,

$$C = .8 \, C_1 + .2 \, C_2,$$

which is, of course, more than $C_1$, because $C_2 > C_1$. For this reason, people argue that the new technology must raise the price of the gas.

---

[13] S. C. Maurice and C. W. Smithson, "The Assimilation of New Technology: Economic versus Technological Feasibility," in *Advances in the Economics of Energy and Resources*, ed. J. R. Moroney (Greenwich, Conn.: JAI Press, 1980), pp. 173–98.

We can adapt our theory of the multiplant monopolist to show that this analysis is not correct. In doing so, we can show how a firm decides upon the proper mix of technology.

In Figure 9–24 panel A, let $MC_P$ be the firm's marginal cost of extraction in Texas. Given the demand and marginal revenue conditions, if the firm pumped only in Texas, it would sell $x_1$ MCF per

**FIGURE 9–24**
**The optimal use of technologies**

**Panel A**

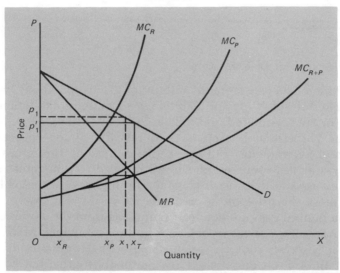

**Panel B**

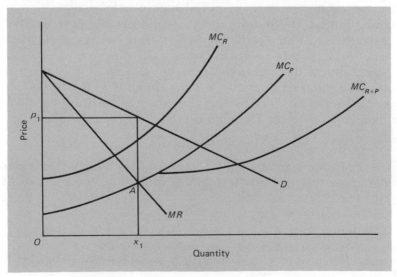

period at a price of $p_1$. The marginal cost of pumping gas in the Rockies using the more expensive technology is the curve $MC_R$. The horizontal summation is $MC_{R+P}$. Using the new technology, the firm produces and sells $x_T$ at a price of $p_1'$. The firm produces $x_P$ in the Permian Basin—a reduction from the previous amount—and $x_Px_T$ from the Rocky Mountains. It can easily be seen that, if the new technology is used at all, $MC_R$ must intercept the vertical axis below the value at which $MC_P$ intersects $MR$. Thus, the new, but more expensive, technology will not raise prices. This is the same as the above conclusion that, if a multiplant monopolist uses a more expensive plant, price must be lower.

In panel B, Figure 9–24, $MC_R$ intercepts the vertical axis above point A. Thus, the new portion of the marginal cost curve, $MC_{R+P}$, is not relevant for decision making, and all of the gas sold comes from the Permian Basin. For both fields of gas to be profitable, demand must increase.

## Multiproduct monopoly

When a firm produces more than one product and uses inputs in the production process that contribute simultaneously to the production of two or more goods, it is sometimes true that the total cost of producing the goods together is less than producing each separately. Examples of cases in which an input produces more than one product simultaneously are cattle used to make beef and leather, a well that pumps crude and natural gas, and trees that produce lumber and paper.

These are obvious examples of inputs that contribute to the production of more than one product. Less obvious examples arise from capital expenditures that contribute to the production of more than one product. Railroads, for instance, offer both freight and passenger transportation over the same tracks and between the same depots. These inputs are shared. The postal service shares its capital in sorting and delivering parcels and letters. Finally, telephone companies use the same lines and switching gear to place local and long-distance calls. In these instances, single investments contribute to the production of more than one product. This is a common phenomenon among multiproduct firms.

Whenever it is less costly to produce products together rather than separately, costs are said to *subadditive*. If we let $C(X)$ be the total cost of producing $X$ and $C(Y)$ be the cost of producing $Y$, then cost is subadditive if, for any amount of $X$ and $Y$,

$$C(X) + C(Y) > C(X,Y),$$

where $C(X,Y)$ is the cost of producing the goods together.

Subadditivity can lead to monopoly or, more generally, create barriers to entry. Suppose we have three products, $X$, $Y$, and $Z$, with the following costs of production for a specified number of units:

1.  $X$, $Y$, or $Z$ alone is $10.
2.  Any two product units is $16.
3.  All three product units is $23.

Thus we see that

$$C(X) + C(Y) + C(Z) = \$30$$
$$C(X,Y) + C(Z) = C(X,Z) + C(Y) = C(Y,Z) + C(X) = \$26$$
$$C(X,Y,Z) = \$23.$$

Costs are subadditive because it is less costly to produce two together rather than all three separately, and all three together rather than just two. Notice that the firm producing $X$, $Y$, and $Z$ together can undersell any firm that is not. For instance, the seller with a cost of $23 could set $p_X = p_Y = p_Z = \$7.99$ and not be undersold by anyone in the long run. Those producers making two or fewer products together will be driven out of business. A firm must produce all three products to enter any one market, and this creates a barrier to entry, since it is more costly to enter all three markets than to enter one.

Subadditivity can lead directly to monopoly. Consider three communities that all want equal amounts of electricity from a utility. Call the communities $X$, $Y$, and $Z$. To supply the communities through separate utilities costs $120,000 each. Any two supplied by one utility costs $190,000, and all three localities supplied by one firm have a total cost of $250,000. Note that electricity delivered to community $X$ is not the same as electricity sent to city $Y$. The destination of the electricity is an important product attribute which distinguishes the products. Clearly, the price of electricity in any one place will depend upon transport costs.

You can easily see that costs are subadditive. As a result, one firm willing to supply all three communities can underbid any other utility willing to serve fewer communities. A monopolist could offer a price per city of just below $95,000 and underbid any utility bidding on one or two contracts. When a multiproduct monopoly can set prices below what firms selling fewer products can charge, the monopoly is said to be *sustainable*.

Suppose, though, that the cost of selling electricity to all three locations at once is $300,000. Now

1.  $C(X) + C(Y) + C(Z) = \$360,000.$
2.  $C(X,Y) + C(Z) = \$190,000 + \$120,000 = \$310,000.$
3.  $C(X, Y, Z) = \$300,000.$

In case 2, any two cities can be supplied for \$190,000. Costs are still subadditive, and the least expensive way of supplying electricity to all three locations is monopoly. But, if a monopoly set prices to cover costs at, say, $p_X = p_Y = p_Z = \$100,000$, it would be possible for a utility to supply just two communities at a cost less than \$200,000. No matter how the monopoly sets prices, it could be undersold in one or more communities even though it has the least cost of supplying all three locations. In this case, the monopoly is said to be *unsustainable*.

Understandably, because total costs are less, there is reason to favor one firm supplying all three communities. If the monopoly is unsustainable, the cities could grant a franchise to a utility, requiring one electric company to provide all three communities with electricity. A word of warning must go with this plan. Although a protected monopoly in this example is able to provide the service at the lowest cost, this does not mean it will. A danger arises once protection is granted. Without the threat of entry, a monopolist no longer has the incentive to keep prices and costs down. With protection, there must often be regulation to guarantee that above normal profits are not earned.

## 9.10 MONOPOLY REGULATION

Since some of the social effects of monopoly behavior are thought to be "undesirable," governments from time to time attempt to regulate monopoly behavior by imposing price ceilings and by enacting certain forms of taxation. We can analyze some effects of such regulation upon the price-output behavior of monopolists.

### Price regulation

If government believes a monopolist is making "too much" profit, is charging "too high" a price, or is "restricting" output, it can set a price ceiling on the commodity. As you will recall from Chapter 2, a ceiling price under perfect competition causes a shortage, and some form of nonprice allocation of the good will evolve. This may or may not be the case under monopoly.

Consider, first, the situation in Figure 9–25. Under the cost and revenue conditions depicted, the nonregulated monopoly sells $x_m$ at a price of $p_m$; it obviously makes a substantial pure profit. Now let us assume that the government imposes a price ceiling (that is, a price less than $p_m$). Suppose $p_c$ is the maximum price allowed. The segment $p_c C$ becomes the new demand and marginal revenue up to the output $x_c$. The monopoly can sell any quantity up to $x_c$ at a price of $p_c$ because, over this range, actual demand lies above $p_c C$; it would certainly charge no lower price. Thus, over the segment $p_c C$, the monopolist's effective demand is a horizontal line, and $P = MR$. After $x_c$, the old demand and marginal-revenue curves become effective. The entire new demand is, therefore, the line $p_c CD'$. With the new demand curve, marginal revenue now equals marginal cost at $C$; the monopolist sells $x_c$ units per period at a price of $p_c$. Since $C$ lies on $DD'$, quantity supplied equals quantity demanded and the market is cleared. Price falls, quantity increases, and marginal cost now equals price. Profit clearly diminishes. Since $x_m$ and $p_m$ gave *maximum* profit, any other combination, including $p_c$ and $x_c$, must give less than maximum profit.

But in this case, price would be equal to marginal cost. If price represents the social marginal valuation of the commodity and marginal cost represents the social cost of the commodity, the two are equal. In other words, the consumer's and producer's surplus loss usually associated with monopoly pricing, area $H$, is eliminated. One of the results of perfect competition is obtained even though, in the long run, production need not take place at minimum average cost.

Other ceiling prices would not give this result. For example, at any ceiling price set between $p_m$ and $p_c$, price would equal $MC$ at an output greater than the quantity the market would demand at that price. Therefore, the monopolist sells the quantity given by the demand curve ($DD'$) at the ceiling price. Again, price falls from $p_m$ and quantity increases from $x_m$, but, in contrast to $p_c$, price exceeds the marginal cost of the last unit sold.

You may think, "If $p_c$ causes price to fall, quantity to rise, and profit to diminish, why not lower price even further, possibly to $p_e$?" True enough, at $p_e$ the monopolist could sell $x_e$ and still cover costs, since $ATC = p_e$ at $x_e$. Note, however, that the new demand and marginal revenue curve up to $x_e$ is $p_e B$; therefore, $MR = MC$ at $A$, and the firm would produce $x'_e$, which is *less* than $x_e$. Since quantity demanded at $p_e$ is $x_e$, a shortage of $x'_e x_e$ results. In this case, the monopolist must allocate by means other than price. In fact, any price below $p_c$ causes a decrease in quantity sold from $x_c$ and, hence, a shortage, inasmuch as quantity demanded exceeds quantity supplied at that price. The monopolist will produce quantities along the $MC$ curve over the portion $SC$; but the market demands a greater quantity at each of these prices. If price is set below minimum $ATC$ (point $S$), the monopolist will go out of business.

Under the conditions assumed in Figure 9–25, the greatest quantity is attained by setting the ceiling price so that the monopolist produces where $MC$ intersects actual demand. This result, however,

**FIGURE 9–25**
**Effects of price ceilings under monopoly**

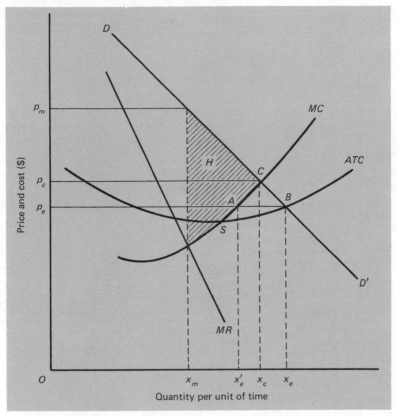

may not always be obtainable with a ceiling price. Figure 9–26 depicts such a case. The nonregulated profit-maximizing monopolist in Figure 9–26 sells $x_1$ units per period at price $p_1$. If the government sets a ceiling price of $p_3$, the price at which $MC$ crosses demand, the monopoly in the long run would go out of business; at this price, it could not cover total costs. In fact, the ceiling could be no lower than $p_2$ without forcing the firm to cease production. At $p_2$, the firm would sell $x_2$ units per period and make no pure profit. The monopolist would have to reduce price to sell a greater output and would, hence, make a loss. Therefore, at any ceiling price between $p_1$ and $p_2$, the firm sells the quantity given by the actual demand curve at that price; at any ceiling price below $p_2$ the firm eventually shuts down. Clearly, the conditions conducive to governmental price setting depend upon economies and diseconomies of scale.

**FIGURE 9–26**
**Effects of price ceilings under monopoly**

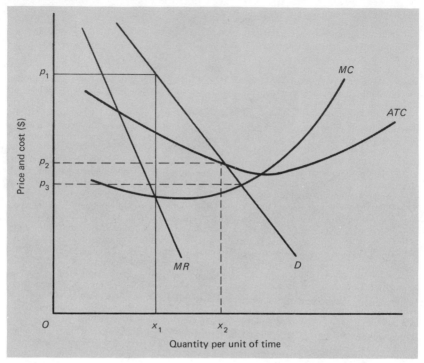

## Taxation

An alternative method of monopoly regulation is some type of special taxation. We examine here the effects of three common types: the excise or per-unit tax, the lump-sum tax, and the percentage-of-profits tax.

An excise or per-unit tax means that for every unit sold, regardless of price, the monopolist must pay a specified amount of money to the government. Assume that the monopolist, whose cost curves $ATC_0$ and $MC_0$ are shown in Figure 9–27, is charged a tax of $k$ dollars for every unit sold. Total cost after the tax is the total cost of *production* (presumably the same as before) plus $k$ times output; thus, average or unit cost must rise by exactly the amount of the tax, $k$ dollars. The aftertax $ATC$ in Figure 9–27 rises from $ATC_0$ to $ATC_1$, or by the vertical distance $k$. $MC$ also rises by $k$ dollars. If it costs $MC_0$ to produce and sell an additional unit of output before the tax, after the tax, it costs $MC_0 + k = MC_1$ to produce and sell that unit. This also is shown in Figure 9–27.

Before the tax is imposed, the monopolist produces $x_0$ and

**FIGURE 9–27**
**Effects of an excise tax under monopoly**

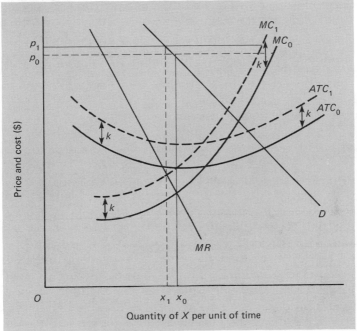

charges a price of $p_0$. After the imposition of the tax, the cost curves shift vertically by the amount $k$ to $ATC_1$ and $MC_1$. $MC_1$ now equals $MR$ at output $x_1$, so price rises to $p_1$. This effect, of course, differs completely from the effect of the ceiling price that causes price to fall and quantity to rise.

A lump-sum tax has a somewhat different effect upon price and quantity. Assume that, instead of imposing an excise tax on the monopolist, the government charges a license fee that remains the same regardless of quantity sold. The license fee is, therefore, a fixed cost to the monopolist. $ATC$ rises after the fee is imposed; at very small outputs, $ATC$ rises more than it does at larger outputs because, the larger the output, the more units the fee is "spread over." Once the fee is paid, however, no additional tax is charged for an additional unit of production per period. $MC$, therefore, remains unchanged. Since $MC$ and $MR$ do not change after the lump-sum tax, their point of intersection does not change, and, thus, price and quantity remain the same after the tax is imposed. The lump-sum tax, which does reduce profits, must not, of course, be so large as to drive $ATC$ above demand, consequently causing a loss and driving the monopolist out of business.

A percentage-of-profits tax, just as the lump-sum tax, does not affect quantity or price. Assume that a monopolist must pay $\pi$ percent of profit (regardless of the profit) as a tax. Since $\pi$ is presumably between 0 and 100, the monopolist retains $(100 - \pi)$ percent of profits after paying the tax. Revenue and cost curves remain the same. Before the tax is imposed, the monopoly chooses price and quantity so as to maximize profit. After the tax, it still chooses the same price and quantity so as to maximize before-tax profit, since $(100 - \pi)$ percent of the maximum profit is clearly preferable to $(100 - \pi)$ percent of some smaller amount.

Tax regulation, therefore, differs from price regulation in several ways, even though profits are reduced in all cases. In particular, taxation, in contrast to some price ceilings, cannot force the monopolist to set price equal to marginal cost.

Before we end this discussion, there is a caveat that should be attached to lump-sum and percentage-of-profit tax theory. Even though the tax, within limits, will not affect short-run profit-maximizing behavior, these taxes will have long-run effects. In the case of energy production, for instance, exploration and other forms of investment are undertaken in the hope of a future stream of profits. Firms would carry out exploration, for example, as long as the marginal cost of exploration exceeds the expected marginal return. Any tax that reduces the expected return consequently reduces exploration, and anything that reduces exploration reduces future resource extraction—in the case of natural gas, the output of gas would fall in the future. The situation is similar in the case of other forms of investment, which are carried out in the expectation of a stream of returns in the future. (Recall Chapter 7.) A tax that is expected to lower the stream of returns in the future lowers investment. Reduced investment causes a reduction in future output. Therefore, while the tax on profit would possibly not affect current output, such a tax would affect future output, possibly quite significantly.

## 9.11 SUMMARY

A monopoly exists if there is only one seller in a market and there are no close substitutes for the seller's product. Few monopolies exist in the real world. It is more appropriate to speak of firms with monopoly power. Monopoly power is the capability to set price above marginal cost. It is frequently assessed in terms of cross-price elasticity, which can measure the presence of substitutes in a market, and the Lerner Index, the ratio of $P - MC$ to $P$.

Marginal revenue is the addition to total revenue obtained from selling an additional unit of output. For a perfect competitor, marginal revenue is price. Since a monopolist must lower price to sell more output, marginal revenue is less than price. In particular, the relation is given by $MR = P(1 - 1/E)$, where $E$ is demand elasticity. If demand is elastic (inelastic), marginal revenue is positive (negative). Notice that a monopolist always maximizes profits on the elastic portion of demand. Since $MC > 0$, setting $MC$ equal to $MR$ requires $MR > 0$, which requires that $E$ be greater than one.

The monopolist chooses the output at which $MC = MR$. In contrast to perfect competition, the market does not force the monopolist in the long run to produce the quantity at which long-run $ATC$ is at its minimum and to charge a price equal to minimum long-run $ATC$ and $MC$. This does not necessarily indicate that price must be higher and quantity lower under monopoly than under perfect competition. Cost conditions may differ between the two forms of organization. We can only say that price under monopoly will not, in the absence of regulation, equal marginal cost and that the entry of competitors will not reduce pure profit to zero. Demand conditions certainly can change so as to eliminate profit, however, since a monopoly position does not guarantee pure profit.

In particular, we wish to stress that economies of scale and the presence of fixed costs in the short run give rise to monopoly power. The more pronounced are economies, or the larger are fixed costs relative to total costs, the stronger is monopoly power. In general, monopoly exists because there are barriers to entry. Entry barriers come from a wide variety of sources. They may exist for purely technical reasons, e.g., technological economies, or they may be created as part of a long-run profit-maximizing strategy, as in the case of entry limit pricing.

A discriminating monopolist maximizes profit by selling the output at which the market marginal revenue (the horizontal summation of all submarket marginal revenues) equals marginal cost. The firm allocates the output so that the marginal revenues in each submarket are equal. It charges the associated price in each submarket; the more inelastic the demand, the higher the price. For discrimination to continue, there cannot be reselling among submarkets. Governments can regulate monopoly by taxation or by setting price ceilings. Only in certain cases can price be made equal to marginal cost.

## TECHNICAL PROBLEMS

1. Assume a monopoly with the demand and cost curves shown in Figure E.9–1. It is in the short run with the plant designed to produce 400 units optimally.
   a. What output should be produced?
   b. What will be the price?
   c. How much profit is made?

**FIGURE E.9–1**

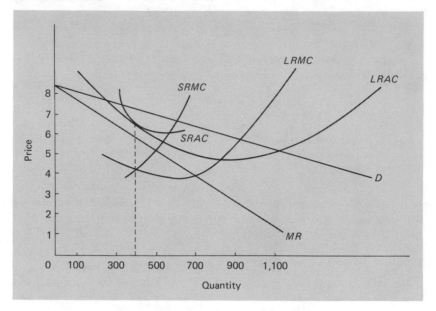

d.  If the firm can change plant size and move into the long run, what will be output and price?

e.  Will profit increase? How do you know?

f.  Draw the new short-run average and marginal cost curves for the new output.

2.  Explain why a percent-of-profits tax on a monopolist will change neither price nor output. Do the same for a lump-sum tax. Explain why either tax may affect future investment.

3.  When will a discriminating monopolist with two separate markets do the following:

a.  Charge the same price in both markets?

b.  Sell the same output in both markets?

4.  Explain why a profit-maximizing monopolist always (in theory) produces and sells on the elastic portion of the demand curve. If costs were zero, where would the monopolist produce?

5.  Compare the perfectly competitive firm and the monopolist as to how each makes the following decisions:

a.  How much to produce.

b.  What to charge.

c.  Whether or not to shut down in the short run.

d.  What happens in the long run if losses persist.

6. Assume that a monopolist can divide output into two submarkets, the demands and marginal revenues of which are shown in Figure E.9–2, along with marginal cost. $\Sigma MR$ is the horizontal sum of the two marginal revenue curves.
    *a.* Find equilibrium output and price in each market.
    *b.* Which market has the more elastic demand?
    *c.* What would be price and output if the monopolist could not discriminate?

    **FIGURE E.9–2**

    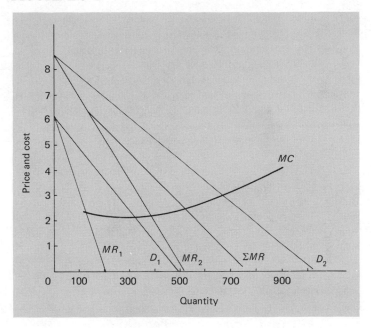

7. A monopolist's revenue and long-run cost curves are shown in Figure E.9–3.
    *a.* Output and price are _____ and $_____.
    *b.* A ceiling price of $_____ would eliminate profit.
    *c.* Output and price would change to _____ and $_____.
    *d.* An excise tax of $2 per unit would change price to $_____ and output to _____.

8. Draw demand, marginal revenue, marginal cost, average variable cost, and average total cost for a monopolist making short-run losses but continuing to produce. Label all curves and show output price and the amount of loss. What two options will the monopolist have in the long run?

**FIGURE E.9–3**

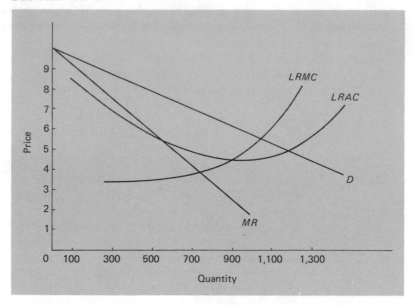

9. If a monopolist is not making enough profit, it can simply raise price until it does. Comment critically.

10. A monopolist takes over a perfectly competitive industry composed of many plants. There can be no entry now. How would the monopoly allocate output among the various firms? What happens to output? Does supply elasticity increase or decrease? (This last is tricky.)

11. There are two industries; one is composed of 1 firm, the other of 1,000 firms. At the point of equilibrium, the demand elasticity is 1.75 for one industry and .86 for the other. Which industry has which elasticity? Why?

12. Dr. Hood is a medical doctor who practices first-degree price discrimination. His prices rise with the income of his patients. He claims that everyone pays a reasonable price, and more importantly, the poor are helped. Assuming the rich are willing to pay more than are poor people for medical services, graphically show how this price discriminating strategy helps the poor. (*Hint:* Suppose the doctor could only charge one price, what would $x$ and $p$ be? Now let the monopolist first-degree price discriminate.)

13. The consumption of cigarettes is relatively insensitive to changes in price. In contrast, the demand for individual brands is highly elastic. In 1918, Lucky Strikes sold for a short time at

a higher retail price than Camel or Chesterfield and rapidly lost half their market. Explain why the demand for a particular brand is more elastic than the demand for all cigarettes. If Lucky raised its prices by 1 percent, what was its elasticity of demand in 1918?

14. Suppose we have a natural monopoly; recall that economies of scale are experienced over all ranges of output. Show *LRAC* and *LRMC* in a graph. Now add a demand curve and marginal revenue. At what output and price does a monopolist maximize profits? If the monopolist was forced to price and produce where *LMRC* = *D*, would it continue to operate? Show the profit or loss and, consequently, the subsidy a monopolist would need to operate at this point.

## ANALYTICAL PROBLEMS

1. Some people say that a per-unit excise tax has no effect on a monopolist, because the monopolist simply passes the tax along to the consumer, whereas the competitive firm cannot shift the tax. Show graphically that, with a given marginal cost and a given excise tax, the elasticity of demand determines the percent of tax that can be shifted to the consumer and the percent that is absorbed by the monopolist.

2. You are an adviser to a local government agency. The agency will grant a monopoly license to a firm to operate a profitable business. You are asked to set a price at which the government will grant the license. How would you advise setting the price?
   *a.* Assume you wish to maximize the government's revenue.
   *b.* Assume government will not set a monetary price. How would you make the decision as to who gets the license?

3. Some bars charge women half price for drinks. Is this consistent with profit maximization? Are all conditions of price discrimination met in this case? Is there an alternative explanation? Speaking of bars, many establishments have a "happy hour," meaning that in a certain time, say, 4 to 6 P.M., drinks are served at a reduced price. Is this consistent with price discrimination?

4. The patent system conveys monopoly rights to some good or process. It is often claimed to be beneficial to economic growth because it encourages research. But, in general, it is asserted that monopolies result in inefficient resource allocation. Discuss.

5. Suppose a monopolist made a certain product, say a tire, in two styles. The two styles of tire are *exactly* alike in every way

except one. One tire lasts *precisely* twice as long as the other
and costs exactly twice as much to produce. Will the longer-
lived tire sell for *exactly* twice the price of the shorter lived?
Explain your answer. (Ignore shopping time and recall our
discussion of discounting in Chapter 7.)

6.  Why do faculty get discounts from the university bookstore
    while students do not? (Don't just say price discrimination.)
    Why can price discrimination exist? Are *all* conditions neces-
    sary for price discrimination met? Discuss.

7.  Consider a monopolist with the labeled curves shown in Fig-
    ure E.9–4. Where would the monopolist produce and what
    output will be sold? Note that they need not be the same. Does
    the solution tell us anything about why economists do not even
    consider the case of decreasing total cost as production in-
    creases?

FIGURE E.9–4

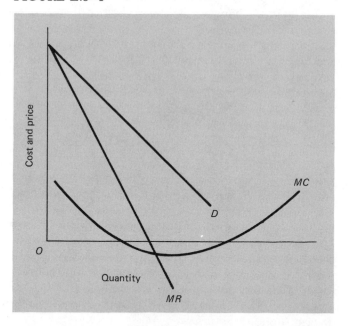

8.  In what sense is the only bank in a small town a monopoly? In
    what sense is it not? In what sense is GM or Exxon a
    monopoly? In what sense is it not? How about the U.S. Postal
    Service or your local electric company? If you were an adviser to
    a Supreme Court justice, how would you decide what does or
    does not constitute a monopoly? How could cross elasticity of
    demand help you decide?

9. In 1945, ALCOA was found guilty of attempting to monopolize the aluminum market. Up to that time, the company maintained low markups and had a modest profit rate. Ironically, if ALCOA had set high markups and realized a high profit rate before WWII, it probably would have not been found guilty. Can you explain why?

10. For many years, AT&T has claimed that it cannot provide overseas telephone service at reasonable rates unless it also provides domestic long-distance service at the same time. Justify this claim using the discussion of multiproduct monopoly.

11. Some economists argue that it is better to have a monopoly producing energy, because monopoly conserves more energy than does perfect competition. Do you agree?

12. Section two of the 1914 Clayton Act prohibits sellers from discriminating in price between different purchasers, except where differences in the grade, quality, or quantity of the commodity exist and the resulting lower prices make due allowance only for differences in the cost of selling or transportation, and are offered in good faith to meet competition. As an economist, evaluate this restriction on pricing.

13. Can a firm have any control over the cross elasticity of demand of its output with other products? To put the question another way, can a seller lower a high cross elasticity of demand? If so, how? Is your answer consistent with an entry limit pricing strategy?

14. In a market characterized by rapid changes in technology, e.g., calculators and computers, would there be less or more incentive to practice an entry limit pricing strategy? Explain your answer.

# Chapter 10

## Imperfect competition

## 10.1 INTRODUCTION

The two market structures we have analyzed thus far—perfect competition and monopoly—are extremely useful tools for analysis, even though neither accurately depicts real-world producers. While they are not designed to describe actual markets, they are able to explain many economic problems. Nonetheless, there are some discrepancies between the underlying assumptions and what happens in the real world. For instance, both models ignore the real-world situation of a large number of firms selling slightly different products. This kind of market structure is known as *monopolistic competition*. It is somewhat monopolistic because product differentiation provides a firm with some monopoly power; it is somewhat competitive because there are many firms in the market and entry is easy. There are many monopolistically competitive markets. Most consumer services, food products, apparel, and household appliances are produced by monopolistically competitive firms.

The assumptions of monopoly and perfect competition also fail to deal with a market structure in which a *few* firms sell either identical or differentiated products. This market structure is referred to as *oligopoly*. Oligopolistic firms characteristically have large amounts of monopoly power, but profit maximization is complicated by the fact that the actions of any firm affect the profits of the others. Many capital goods and refined commodities are produced and sold by oligopolistic firms. Automobiles, heavy machinery, sugar, and copper are typically characterized as oligopolistic industries.

How do sellers behave under these more realistic market structures? We shall discover that profit maximization does not confine itself solely to the simple formula of setting marginal cost equal to marginal revenue. This rule is certainly an important part of the story, but the recognition of competing products and market rivals complicates things considerably.

Before we proceed, we must stress that the distinction between monopolistic competition and oligopoly can become cloudy. The most obvious distinction between the two forms of market structure is that oligopolistic markets have a few firms, while monopolistically competitive markets have many. But how do we decide that a market has "many" or "few" firms? In terms of the number of firms in a market, we really do not know when market structures become less like monopolistic competition and more like oligopoly. So we cannot make a sharp distinction between these two market structures on this basis. However, whether a market is monopolistically competitive or oligopolistic depends less on the number of firms in a market and more on whether each firm recognizes that its actions will have a discernible impact upon other rivals. To put it another way, the difference between monopolistic competition and oligopoly is really determined by the degree to which sellers are interdependent. Even so, judging a market as oligopolistic or monopolistically competitive is still subjective. But the recognition that profit depends upon the actions of a producer's rivals is a critical turning point when moving from the theory of monopolistic competition to oligopoly.

This chapter takes the following approach: it first presents the theory of monopolistic competition and compares the results of the theory with the perfectly competitive model. Since both monopolistic competition and oligopoly frequently use nonprice competition to increase profits, we next discuss this type of competitive behavior. Oligopoly models are then presented, with emphasis upon why there is no general theory of oligopoly. The chapter ends with a discussion of collusion.

The basic concepts to be learned in this chapter are

1. How equilibrium is attained when there is a large number of firms producing closely related, but slightly differentiated products.
2. Why we have no *general* theory when there are a few firms producing a reasonably closely related product (oligopoly).
3. Why collusion among firms takes place, and why it generally breaks up.
4. How some aspects of imperfect competition can be used in analysis.

## 10.2 FUNDAMENTALS OF MONOPOLISTIC COMPETITION

One of the most notable achievements of economists who examine the middle ground between competition and monopoly was done simultaneously by an American economist, Edward Chamberlain, and a British economist, Joan Robinson.[1] They both contributed heavily to the modern development of economic theories of nonperfect competition.

At the time they published, neither economist knew of the other's work, but they both based their theories on a solid empirical fact: there are very few monopolies because there are very few commodities for which close substitutes do not exist; similarly, there are very few commodities that are entirely homogeneous. Instead, there is a wide range of commodities which have many good, but not perfect, substitutes.

Chamberlain, who developed the theory of monopolistic competition, noted that, because products are *heterogeneous* rather than homogeneous, perfect competition cannot exist. On the other hand, although heterogeneous, the products are only slightly differentiated. Each is a rather close substitute for the other. Hence, competition exists, but it is competition among rivals; unlike perfect competition, it involves sellers who are, to a greater or lesser extent, aware of each other, and buyers who can distinguish among sellers of similar goods.

It is important to note that the only difference between perfect competition and monopolistic competition is product differentiation. In the model of monopolistic competition, there remain large

---

[1] E. H. Chamberlain, *The Theory of Monopolistic Competition* (Cambridge, Mass.: Harvard University Press, 1933), and J. Robinson, *The Economics of Imperfect Competition* (London: Macmillan, 1934).

numbers of buyers and sellers, easy entry and exist into the market among sellers, and perfect information with respect to prices. We shall see, though, that this modest change in the assumptions underlying perfect competition has profound effects on the behavior of sellers in the market.

In contrast to perfect competition, when products are differentiated, the sellers in the market do not necessarily make up a specific industry. This is a point we made in Chapter 9, but it needs to be repeated. In some cases, an industry is much broader than the relevant market; in others, an industry is too narrow. For instance, within the automobile industry there exist markets for small cars, midsize cars, luxury cars, and so on. The industry encompasses several markets. On the other hand, there is a plastics industry in which many plastic products are easily substitutable with similar products made from glass and steel. The market is broader than the industry.

As we discuss the theories of imperfect competition, we must keep in mind the distinction between industries and markets. It is the market with which we are concerned. A market is made up of sellers of goods that are easily substituted for one another by consumers. More precisely, the market is defined by the set of goods that share high and positive cross-price elasticities. In the case of monopolistic competition, there is a large number of firms that sell easily substituted products.

### Demand under monopolistic competition

We can begin our discussion of demand for a monopolistically competitive firm by recalling that, in the theory of monopoly, one firm supplies the entire market; there are no good substitutes for the producer's product. The reason monopoly exists in the long run is that barriers to entry prevent other firms from entering the market and offering substitutes. We can arrive at the demand curve of a monopolistic competitor by allowing easy entry into a monopolist's market.

Let us begin by picturing the demand for a monopolist as $D_m$, the linear demand curve shown in Figure 10–1. The curve can be algebraically described by the equation for a straight line:

$$P = a - bX.$$

The elasticity of demand for the monopolist is the same as the elasticity of market demand. Note that $\Delta P / \Delta X$ represents the change in $P$ when $X$ changes by one unit. It is the slope of $D_m$ in Figure 10–1. Hence,

$$\frac{\Delta P}{\Delta X} = [a - b(X + 1) - (a - bX)]/1 = a - bX - b - a + bX = -b.$$

**FIGURE 10-1**
**Demand shift after entry**

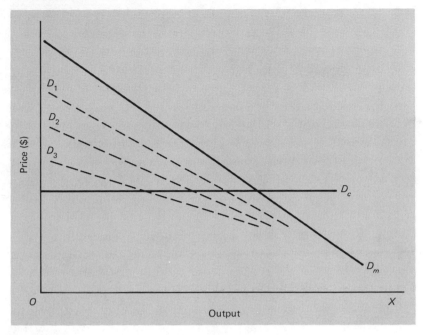

Thus, the slope of $D_m$ is $-b$. If we call the elasticity of demand in the market $E_m$, then

$$E_m = -\frac{\Delta X}{\Delta P} \cdot \frac{P}{X} = \frac{1}{b}\left(\frac{P}{X}\right).$$

Now, let a second firm enter the market. Both firms produce an amount, $x_i$, where $X = x_1 + x_2$. For the moment, let us assume that the products are alike. The sum of the amounts each firm produces is total market output; so price in the market becomes

$$P = a - b(X) = a - b(x_1 + x_2).$$

If either firm increases output by one unit $\Delta P/\Delta X = -b$, as before. Say the second firm expands, then

$$\frac{\Delta P}{\Delta x_2} = a - b[x_1 + (x_2 + 1)] - [a - b(x_1 + x_2)]$$

$$= a - bx_1 - bx_2 - b - a - bx_1 - bx_2 = -b.$$

We have assumed that the two products are such close substitutes that the same price is charged for each. Each firm in the market has elasticity $E_i$;

$$E_i = \frac{\Delta x_i}{\Delta P} \cdot \frac{P}{x_i} = \frac{1}{b}\left(\frac{P}{x_i}\right).$$

The ratio $x_i/X$ is the market share of the $i$th firm. It is the proportion of the total market supplied by a single firm. For convenience, we can let $s_i = x_i/X$. For a monopolist, $s = 1$, but as firms enter the market, $s_i$ becomes less than one. Under perfect competition, when there are many firms producing identical products, $s_i$ gets very close to 0. We know, therefore, that for imperfect competition, $s_i$ ranges between one and zero.

Using the ratio $s_i$, we may rewrite the elasticity of demand for the firm ($E_i$) in terms of the elasticity of demand at the market level ($E_m$). With some substitution we see that

$$E_i = \frac{1}{b}\left(\frac{P}{x_i}\right) = \frac{1}{b}\left(\frac{P}{x_1}\right)\frac{X}{X} = \frac{1}{b}\left(\frac{P}{X}\right)\frac{X}{x_i} = E_m\left(\frac{1}{s_i}\right). \quad (10\text{--}1)$$

We can verify this equality by supposing that only one seller operates in the market. Then $s_i = 1$, and $E_i = E_m$. The elasticity of demand for a monopolist is the market's elasticity. Suppose we have perfect competition and $s_i$ gets very close to zero. Then $1/s_i$ becomes very large, and this makes $E_i$ approach infinity. We know that, in perfect competition, the firm's demand curve is horizontal, which means the elasticity of demand is infinite. Such a demand curve is labeled $D_c$ in Figure 10–1.

Equation (10–1) tells us what demand looks like as a market becomes more competitive. At the extremes, we have $D_m$ and $D_c$ in Figure 10–1. If we allow entry into the market, then we know each firm supplies a smaller share of the market; that is, $s_i$ gets smaller. The firm's demand curve must shift to the left. We also know that the elasticity of demand increases. Hence, the firm's demand curve must, at the same time, be more elastic than $D_m$. Entry, therefore, shifts demand in a way illustrated by the dotted schedules, from $D_m$ to $D_1$, to $D_2$, etc. The more entry, the closer demand gets to the perfectly competitive schedule $D_c$.

However, product differentiation prevents the firm's demand curve from becoming perfectly elastic. Perceived differences between goods make them less than perfect substitutes. For instance, toothpastes taste different and presumably clean your teeth differently. Because consumers can identify these product characteristics with the producer, toothpastes are not perfect substitutes. This means that a seller's demand curve is not horizontal; some market power is possessed by sellers. What is more, because of product differences, firms capture different shares of the market. From Equation (10–1), this means firms face different elasticities of demand. Partly because of this, and partly because costs are different, we see different prices in monopolistically competitive markets. The effects of product differention will be discussed in more detail in Section 10.3.

### Short-run equilibrium

The theory of monopolistic competition is essentially a long-run theory. In the short run, there is virtually no difference between the analysis of monopoly and of monopolistic competition. Each producer of a product behaves so as to maximize profit. With a given demand curve and a corresponding marginal revenue curve, the firm maximizes profit or minimizes loss by equating marginal cost with marginal revenue.

So far as the short run is concerned, there appears to be very little *competition* in monopolistic competition. But when a longer view is taken, one essential element of monopoly is missing. In particular, a monopoly cannot be maintained if there is free entry. If pure profit is present in the short run, other firms will enter and produce the product, and they will continue to enter until all pure profits are eliminated.

### Long-run equilibrium

Using the above assumptions and analytical tools, we can proceed immediately to the analysis of long-run equilibrium in a monopolistically competitive market. Because of easy entry, all pure profit must be competed away in the long run. A zero-profit equilibrium is reached when price equals $LRAC$ and the firm cannot increase profits by raising or lowering price. This occurs when demand is tangent to $LRAC$. We can see from Figure 10–2 that, if demand intersected $LRAC$, there would exist prices that could be above average cost allowing firms to make above-normal profits. For instance, if the firm were a monopolist and had demand curve $D_m$, profits would be maximized at a price well above $LRAC$. In a monopolistically competitive market, entry would occur until the firm had a demand curve like $D_i$, just tangent to $LRAC$. Thus, long-run equilibrium must exist at a point like $A$ in Figure 10–2.

Equilibrium is depicted in Figure 10–2 with an $LRAC$ curve that has some economies of scale at first, but diseconomies over larger ranges of output. We know that demand for a monopolistic competitor is not perfectly elastic, which implies that the demand curve is never horizontal. Therefore, equilibrium cannot occur at the low-

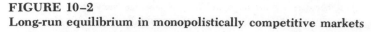

**FIGURE 10–2**
**Long-run equilibrium in monopolistically competitive markets**

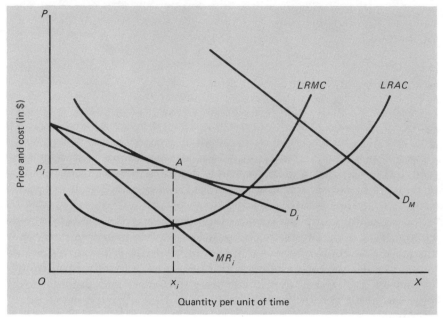

est point on *LRAC*, but must exist on the downward-sloping portion of *LRAC* before economies are exhausted.

Point *A* must also be described by the intersection of *LRMC* and $MR_i$, where the subscript $i$ is used to represent a typical firm in monopolistic competition. The profit-maximizing rule must lead a monopolistic competitor to the highest possible profit, given the demand curve. If the firm produced an amount of *X* different from $x_i$, price would be lower than average cost, and profits would be below normal.

**Principle.** Long-run equilibrium in a monopolistically competitive market is attained when the demand curve for a producer is tangent to the long-run average cost curve.

## Comparison of long-run equilibria with perfect competition

In long-run competitive equilibrium, total output is produced by a large number of small firms, each of which operates at long-run minimum average cost. The industry product is sold at a price equal to minimum average cost, and it should be remembered that long-run marginal cost equals both price and average cost at this point. If demand should either increase or decrease, in the long-run producers enter or exist, leaving each firm producing at the minimum point on its $LRAC$ curve. It is impossible for any firm to lower costs by either increasing or decreasing output. Thus, costs are minimized for any level of industry output.

A monopolistically competitive firm is like a monopolist in that it faces a downward-sloping demand curve. At the same time, it is like a perfectly competitive firm in that it faces market competition which competes away long-run excess profits. The differences between the model of perfect competition and monopolistic competition result solely from product differentiation. Putting the desirability of product differentiation aside for the moment, we can show that monopolistic competition compares unfavorably with perfect competition on two accounts.

First, since demand is less than perfectly elastic, marginal revenue is different from average revenue. Profit is maximized where $MR = MC$ in the long or the short run, and price is not equal to marginal cost. From our study of monopoly, we know this causes a loss of consumer's and producer's surplus; total surplus is not maximized. Figure 10–3 shows this loss as the shaded region between demand and marginal cost. Given the demand for the firm's product, the willingness to pay for the product is greater than the marginal cost of production for $x_e - x_m$ units. Since potential buyers value the product at more than the marginal cost of production, this reduction in output represents a loss to society. Obviously, a monopolistically competitive firm would never produce $x_e$ in the long run. At $x_e$, $LRAC$ is greater than $p_e$. The firm would need a subsidy to break even and continue production.

The second criticism of monopolistic competition is that the long-run average cost of production is higher than it would be under perfect competition. In equilibrium, a monopolistically competitive firm produces at point $A$ on $LRAC$ in Figure 10–3. A perfect competitor would produce at $B$ where $LRMC = LRAC$ and $LRAC$ is minimized. A monopolistic competitor, therefore, does not exhaust economies of scale in production like a perfect competitor does. The less important are economies, the less of a cost difference there is between producing at point $A$ or $B$. Frequently, monopolistic competitors are accused of having excess capacity, but this is not the real issue. The firm chooses the most efficient plant size, as described by the $SRAC$ curve in Figure 10–3. The average cost of producing quantity $x_m$ can be no lower whether the market structure is perfect competition or monopoly. The problem with monopolistic competition is that output is restricted, and, because of economies of scale, average cost is higher.

**FIGURE 10–3**
Monopolistic competition versus perfect competition

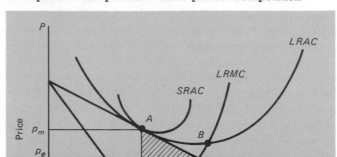

These two criticisms of monopolistic competition ignore product differentiation. There is something to be said about the desirability of differences in product characteristics. Although it cannot be measured, consumers benefit from product variety. A choice between styles, colors, flavors, and qualities is a very desirable feature of market structures. Some economists argue that the difference in the average cost of production and loss of surplus is the "price" society pays for product variety. The argument is that, if consumers did not wish to pay this price, then, because of free entry and exit in monopolistic competition, buyers would choose and producers would sell only one product type. Since product differentiation is so common, buyers in markets are, therefore, willing to pay the price for product variety. Hence, the social cost of monopolistic competition is possibly less than or equal to the social benefit.

## 10.3 NONPRICE COMPETITION

Imperfect competition is frequently characterized by competitive behavior not involving price changes. Some examples of nonprice competition are product quality changes and advertising. A perfectly competitive firm would have no reason to resort to nonprice competition, since it can sell all it wants to sell at the going market price. For different, but obvious reasons, a monopoly does not resort to nonprice competitive behavior. The product of a monopolist has no close substitutes. Thus, a firm with considerable monopoly power would have little reason to resort to any kind of competition, because it cannot attract customers from or lose them to other producers.

But firms selling in markets with differentiated products frequently do have the incentive to use methods other than price to increase profits. As we have seen, free entry drives profits to zero in the long run. Nonetheless, firms can sometimes delay or reverse this process by further differentiating their product from the products of competitors—possibly by advertising or some other marketing strategy designed to increase the demand for the product. If the strategy is successful, the firm will enjoy above-normal profits, at least temporarily.

As we shall see in the next section, in markets with few sellers, there is quite often a great deal of rivalry among firms. At times, because of strong interdependence among the firms, oligopolists hesitate to change prices frequently. Price changes can lead to very unprofitable price wars. Oligopolies, therefore, resort to nonprice rivalry to raise profits, but even this is not a safe strategy. As is discussed below, firms are sometimes forced by the actions of their competitors to make nonprice changes, such as expensive changes in styling designs, that they would not have undertaken if their rivals had not initiated the change. But, like price competition, nonprice tactics are a profit-maximizing tool.

Thus, product differentiation opens an entirely new dimension of competition, unavailable, by assumption, to perfect competitors. *Nonprice competition* makes products less than perfect substitutes. If successful, such competition increases the demand for the product and, at any given price, causes the elasticity of demand to fall, allowing firms to charge higher prices for their products. This section discusses how product differentiation is a competitive decision variable. Firms can distinguish their output in two basic ways: first, by the actual characteristics or qualities they attach to the good they sell, and, second, by advertising. Although discussed separately, these two means of product differentiation are not independent. Often, product differences are accentuated, and perhaps even created by advertising.

### Product quality

Products can be thought of as a collection of attributes. For example, an automobile can be described by its engine size, brakes, transmission, suspension, fuel efficiency, tires, head and trunk room, number of doors, color, and so on. These product features differ among automobiles and can be altered by the maker. How they are selected determines the product. Algebraically, product characteristics are variables $(a_i)$, which are *bundled* in certain ways to make a product, $X$. That is,

$$X = g(a_1, a_2, a_3, \ldots, a_n), \qquad (10\text{--}2)$$

where $n$ is the number of possible attributes a product may have. How a producer selects these attributes determines the quality and nature of the product and the product's substitutability with other products in the market. The decision of a manufacturer to give an automobile all the product attributes that characterize a Lincoln Continental will make the car an unlikely substitute for a Ford Mustang. In general, product differentiation determines the substitutability of products.

The idea that product attributes are a nonprice competitive tool is captured by letting all of the possible preferences consumers may have for a particular attribute be measured along a scale with endpoints 0 and 1, as shown in Figure 10–4. Let us say that this product attribute is sugar on breakfast cereal, then 0 is cereal with no sugar and 1 is cereal of virtually pure sugar cubes.

**FIGURE 10–4**
**Product quality measure**

Suppose that those who buy breakfast cereal are evenly distributed along this scale so that the number of individuals who want no sugar on their cereal is equal to the number who want their cereal half sugar and is equal to the number who want all sugar. In the case of the first firm to produce cereal, it does not matter how much sugar is put on its product. It is the only cereal consumers can buy. Thus, we arbitrarily locate firm $A$ on the scale. Since sugar is expensive, we place A on the lower end of the scale. We subscript the location because the firm may later want to change the sugar content of its cereal.

Things get interesting when firm B decides to enter the market. It knows the preferences of consumers, i.e., the scale in Figure 10–4, and how much sugar A has on its product. The question is, how much sugar should B use to capture the largest share of the market? Market share is very important to profit maximization. We know from Section 10.2 that the larger a firm's market share, the less elastic is demand and, consequently, the higher can be price. Also, if there are economies of scale, increased sales allow a producer to move down the *LRAC* curve and realize a lower average cost of production. Of course, at the margin, higher prices and lower production costs must be balanced against the marginal cost of increasing market share, which may, for example, involve advertising, or, in this case, putting more sugar on cereal.

In Figure 10–4, we can see that firm B could capture most of the market by using a little more sugar than A. The best thing for B to do is to enter with a product that is just to the right of $A_1$ in sugar. We label the point $B_1$. Firm B captures all of the market to the right of $A_1$.

Firm A will not tolerate this for long. Its market share has been reduced to a very small part of the total market. Only those buyers with preferences between 0 and $A_1$ remain loyal to A's cereal. The firm has to think about countering B's product by putting more sugar on its cereal. It can regain much of its lost market by moving to the right of B. But then B will move to the right of A again, and A will then move to the right of B a second time. The leapfrogging will continue until one firm drops out of the market, or both firms end up with equal market shares at the midpoint of the preference scale. After a large number of moves, we will find both firms putting approximately the same amount of sugar on their cereal and supplying the amounts desired by the average buyer.

The situation gets more complicated when a third firm enters the market. With a little experimenting, you will discover that firms will not find an equilibrium; they continually change the amount of sugar on their cereals. This is not so unusual in the real world, considering how many "new" and "improved" labels producers put on their products. Often these improvements are nothing more than a slight adjustment in a product attribute, a change marketers hope will increase their sales.

We have oversimplified things a great deal by allowing product differentiation for only one product variable. Equation (10–2) tells us that there are numerous product attributes for any one commodity. Realistically, there are all sorts of ways attributes can be mixed. Discovering the attributes that capture the largest share of the market requires sophisticated marketing techniques and, at times, just plain luck. The point of our simple model, though, is that product differentiation is a competitive tool that firms use to maximize profits. Differentiation can be as much a dimension of competition as price.

One further conclusion that we can draw from the discussion surrounding Figure 10–4 is that nonprice competition can lead to the *bunching* of product attributes. Referring to Figure 10–4, in the case of two firms, equilibrium occurred at the midpoint of the preference spectrum. Tastes could be better served if there was more product variety; say A moves closer to 0 and B closer to 1. Algebraically, it can be shown that, if consumers are evenly distributed along the scale, one firm should locate one quarter and the other three quarters of the distance between 0 and 1 to best serve consumer tastes in the market.[2] But there is no incentive for firms to behave this way. The incentive to give a product attributes close to those of a rival can be easily seen in the location of businesses, television programming, automobile styling, and fashion apparel. Nonprice competition leads to what economists call *excessive sameness* in the market. Sometimes, though, a lack of product differentiation is unavoidable. In some markets, there is little that can be done to change the product. There is, for instance, little or no product differentiation in the facial tissue or aspirin markets, yet these markets fit the monopolistic competition model well. Advertising is a device used to highlight slight differences and, in some cases, even create them.

## Advertising

Advertising is so diverse that it is nearly impossible to give it a definite description. Very broadly, advertising is a message about a particular commodity or service. Such messages are divided into two categories by economists: those that are intended to convey information and those that are intended to create an image. This breakdown should not give the impression that advertising conveys either information or an image. Usually it does both, but ads lean toward one purpose or the other.

Informative advertising is exemplified by the want-ad section in a newspaper. Generally, such ads convey price and pertinent quality characteristics. Catalogs are another example of advertising for information. They convey primarily price information and concise descriptions of the product.

Economists generally believe that such advertising is socially useful because it lowers search costs and decreases the dispersion, or variance of prices for similar products. When the prices of similar products differ, consumers search, or "shop around" for a lower price and more desirable features. Searching or shopping takes time, which, as we know from Chapter 4, is valued at what consumers would do with the time if it were not spent searching. The increased information makes consumers more efficient shoppers

---

[2] There are some special assumptions on the preference map. See H. Hotelling, "Stability in Competition," *Economic Journal* 39 (March 1929):41–57; F. M. Scherer, "The Welfare Economics of Product Variety: An Application to the Ready-to-Eat Cereal Industry," *Journal of Industrial Economics*, 28, no. 2 (December 1979):113–34.

and, hence, decreases the time they spend shopping. Furthermore, the additional information lowers the sales of higher-priced sellers and increases the sales of the lower-priced sellers. Thus, the higher-priced sellers must lower prices or go out of business. But if there is excess demand for the lower-priced products, these prices will be bid up, or sellers will enter and sell at the low price. In any case, price dispersion will decrease, and shopping costs will fall.

Advertising designed to create an image, on the other hand, does not directly convey information. Image advertising is most often found on television, billboards, and in magazines with wide circulations. To be sure, image advertising conveys some information. At the very least, it tells a consumer a product is available. However, the aim of all image advertising is to make individuals associate the advertised image with consumption of the product. For instance, Marlborough cigarettes attempted to create a rugged cowboy image for those who smoke the cigarettes by repeatedly showing a tough Wyoming cowboy smoking Marlboroughs. The intent of such ads is to make consumers think they are buying this image when they buy the product. The image, in a sense, is a product attribute created by advertising. Some other examples are the advertising of Calvin Klein jeans, which tries to give the image that Calvin Klein's make teenage girls sexy, or of Cadillac, which tries to give the image that Cadillacs make middle-aged men rich. Certainly, you can think of many other examples of image advertising. Image advertising has been and continues to be a subject of controversy among economists. In 1958, John Kenneth Galbraith argued that image advertising is socially wasteful. The central function of such advertising, according to Galbraith, is "to bring into being wants that previously did not exist."[3] The mere communication of information is not what Galbraith found disturbing, but, rather, advertising that instills a feeling of need in a consumer who appeared quite happy before the product came along. The implication of his arguments is that utility is lowered by image advertising if the product is not purchased. After the product is purchased, it is not clear whether utility is higher than it was before the product was introduced.

Other economists, for example Friedrich Hayek, are not as critical of image advertising.[4] Hayek argues that it is difficult to say an image for a product is not beneficial. Things are demanded because they instill feelings and emotions as much as because they satisfy an absolute need. To argue that a perceived product image does not

---

[3] J. K. Galbraith, *The Affluent Society* (Boston: Houghton Mifflin, 1958), p. 155.

[4] F. Hayek, "The Non Sequitur of the 'Dependence Effect'," *Southern Economic Journal* 27, no. 4 (April 1961): 346–48. For a complete survey, see F. M. Scherer, *Industrial Market Structure and Economic Performance*, 2d ed. (Chicago: Rand McNally, 1980, Chap 14.

provide a consumer with a net gain in utility is presumptuous. The image is literally a characteristic of the product, just as style, color, and size are. The image is part of the product package consumers can choose to go without. For example, people buy Rolex watches partly because of the image that successful, rich people wear these watches. If consumers are less interested in a status symbol, they have the option of purchasing a lesser-known brand. The Rolex status is a product attribute of the watch. Hence, image advertising that creates such product attributes is not necessarily socially wasteful.

Whether from the consumer's point of view, advertising is excessive or not is indeed arguable. But from the seller's viewpoint, rivalry can easily lead to advertising levels which, to them, are excessive. Specifically, if sellers could agree to restrict the amount of advertising they undertake—much of it done in response to a rival's ads in the first place—profits for sellers would rise. Hence, advertising is, to them, excessive because it is often a defensive tactic to maintain a seller's market share against the advertising of rivals. In many cases, it is a necessary cost of entry into a market, a cost that would be lower or even nonexistent if firms already producing in the market were not making heavy advertising expenditures.

How rivalry leads to unprofitable amounts of advertising can be illustrated by a model known as the *prisoner's dilemma*. The model is best described by the story for which it is named. Suppose a crime is committed and two suspects are apprehended and questioned by the police. Unknown to the suspects, the police do not have enough evidence to convict the suspects without at least one of them confessing. So the police separate them and make each an offer known to the other. The offer is, if one suspect confesses to the crime and turns state's evidence, the one who confesses receives only a 2-year sentence, while the other who does not confess gets 10 years. If both turn state's evidence, each receives a 2-year sentence. Of course, if neither confesses, the probability is very high both will go free. Thus, each could receive 2 years, 10 years, or go free, depending upon what the other does.

Figure 10–5 shows the four possibilities in the dilemma. The upper-left and lower-right cells show the results if both, respectively, plead innocent or guilty. The upper-right and lower-left cells show the consequences if one pleads guilty and the other innocent.

The problem is that the suspects cannot *collude* and decide to plead innocent. They must make their decisions independently. If either suspect pleads innocent, each stands a chance of 10 years in prison if the other confesses. The likelihood of this depends on the character of the other suspect and whether or not he or she really did

**FIGURE 10–5**
Prisoner's dilemma

|  |  | Suspect 1 | |
|---|---|---|---|
|  |  | *Innocent* | *Guilty* |
| Suspect 2 | Innocent | **A**<br>1: 0 years<br>2: 0 years | **B**<br>1: 2 years<br>2: 10 years |
|  | Guilty | **C**<br>1: 10 years<br>2: 2 years | **D**<br>1: 2 years<br>2: 2 years |

commit the crime. However, the worst that could happen if a suspect confesses to the crime is two years imprisonment regardless of what the other does.

Whether or not the crime was committed by these suspects, the less each knows about the other, the more likely he or she will confess to the crime. In other words, the less information these accused felons possess, the less certainty they have about going free—settling in cell A. One or the other wants to avoid cells B and C. Each can get two years in prison with certainty by confessing. Thus, the safest plea for both is guilty, and they end up in cell D.

Imperfect competitors are caught in a similar dilemma when it comes to nonprice competition. Suppose the choice is to advertise a little or a lot. The relative advertising outlays determine profits. Low advertising by rivals keeps profits relatively high; any single firm can increase profits at the expense of other firms if it advertises more while the others do not. As in many imperfectly competitive markets, the *total* amount of advertising by all firms hass little effect on *total* sales in the market.[5] That is, market demand is relatively inelastic with respect to advertising. But, if any firm does little or no advertising while the other firms advertise heavily, that firm loses a substantial share of the market.

To illustrate the situation, assume there are two rival firms. As with the prisoner's dilemma, there are four combinations of choices for the rival firms. In cells A through D in Figure 10–6, the profitability ($\pi$) of each combination is shown for the firms. If neither firm undertakes large amounts of advertising, profits are, say, $100 for each firm. They have equal costs and market shares. But you can see that there is a big temptation to increase advertising relative to that of the rival. Profits jump to $150, largely because the high advertiser attracts business away from the low advertiser, whose profits fall to

---

[5] See F. M. Scherer, ibid., pp. 384–93.

FIGURE 10–6
Advertiser's dilemma

*Firm 1*

|  |  | Low | High |
|---|---|---|---|
|  |  | **A** | **B** |
|  | Low | $\pi_1$: 100 | $\pi_1$: 60 |
|  |  | $\pi_2$: 100 | $\pi_2$: 150 |
| *Firm 2* |  | **C** | **D** |
|  | High | $\pi_1$: 150 | $\pi_1$: 80 |
|  |  | $\pi_2$: 60 | $\pi_2$: 80 |

$60. To a small extent profits also rise because the total market expands as a result of more total advertising. Cells B and C are not an equilibrium. The low advertiser can at least raise profits to $80 by following with a high advertising budget. In the long run, both firms end up with relatively higher advertising expenditures and lower profits. From the seller's perspective, there is too much advertising.

If firms recognize the long-run effects of high advertising budgets, they might tacitly agree not to increase expenditures. Such an agreement is much more likely to occur when firms recognize their interdependence than when there are many firms with small market shares. Thus, an oligopolistic market structure is more apt to prevent advertising excessiveness, as measured by profits, than is monopolistic competition. However, once a rival decides to increase advertising, it is very difficult, regardless of the market structure, to avoid cell D in Figure 10–6. And it is very unlikely that, without an explicit agreement, firms will return to cell A.

## APPLICATION

### Nonprice competition in the decaffeinated coffee market

The decaffeinated coffee market is characterized by few sellers. The three largest producers are General Foods, the Nestle Company, and Procter & Gamble. These producers are well acquainted with the products of the others and know their market actions are observed by their rivals. To say that the decaffeinated coffee market is oligopolistic would be a safe conjecture. Recent behavior in this market offers a showcase for nonprice competition.

To begin, even though there are three main producers, they market, under different names, more than five nationally known products. General Foods leads the decaffeinated market with its

Sanka and Brim brands. In September 1980, Sanka brand supplied 40.5 percent of the market. At the same time, Nestle had 17.0 percent of the market with its decaffeinated products, Taster's Choice and Nescafé, while Proctor & Gamble held 17.3 percent of the market after the introduction of its new brand—High Point.[6]

Why should firms introduce more than one brand of coffee? Automobile manufacturers sell more than one car model, tobacco companies market several brands of cigarettes, and cereal makers, one of which is General Foods, also sell a variety of brands in which the company's own products have high cross elasticities of demand. A major reason for what economists call *brand proliferation* is that producers are very uncertain about the product preference spectrum. Recall the product-quality scale in Figure 10–4. When a firm introduces a product, it may be at point $A_1$ or $B_1$ without knowing the rest of the scale. Consumers far away in their preferences could decide to forego decaffeinated coffee altogether rather than drink something that does not taste good to them; this could be the case for a significant number of potential decaffeinated coffee drinkers, if companies inadvertently located at one end of the scale. So companies explore the market by introducing new brands, hoping to find a flavor that carves out a new market niche.

Companies also introduce multiple brands to protect their established market shares. If a company's own brands are located sufficiently closely on the product scale, then another company may not be able to gain enough sales with a close substitute to enter profitably. Figure 10–7 helps explain such a marketing strategy. The sub-

**FIGURE 10–7**
**Product quality for coffee**

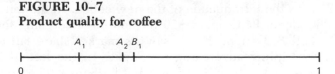

scripts in the figure represent brands of coffee. The scale represents a product characteristic of coffee, say bitterness. By introducing two brands, firm A protects some of its market. When $A_1$ and $A_2$ are located relatively close together, it is unprofitable for firm B to locate between 0 and $A_2$. Sales would not be large enough. The worst that can happen to A is for B to locate next to $A_2$. The firm loses the market between $A_2$ and 1, but it has kept its market share between 0

---

[6] These figures and those that follow are from "P & G's Campaign to Unseat Sanka," *Business Week*, 26 January 1981, p. 65.

and $A_2$. Thus, one reason a firm introduces multiple brands is to protect its market share against entry.

Before Procter & Gamble introduced its new High Point coffee, it had 11.8 percent of the decaffeinated coffee market. Its main rival, General Foods, had 49 percent of the market. P&G wanted more than 20 percent of the market with a second brand. To capture this much of the market, Procter & Gamble increased advertising. How would you expect General Foods to react after it sees its share of the market erode? The answer is obvious. It will also advertise more. General Foods is caught in a prisoner's dilemma, as shown below:

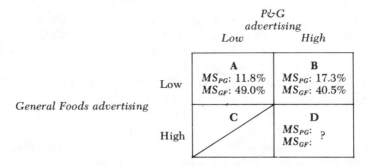

In the cells we indicate market share ($MS$) instead of profits, since profits are not reported for specific products. In cell A, High Point has not been introduced yet. Advertising by each of these two large household product firms was relatively low. After High Point was introduced, Procter & Gamble was reported to be spending at least $30 million on the introduction of the new coffee. In the third quarter of 1980 alone, P&G spent $10 million on advertising for High Point. In cell B, General Foods saw its market share fall and responded by tripling advertising for Sanka. In the last quarter of 1980, it spent $8.4 million on advertising for Sanka. The firms have moved to cell D in the above diagram. How the battle will end remains to be seen. The model would predict that neither firm will win—market shares will stay roughly the same, but profits will be lower because of the higher advertising expenditures.

## 10.4 OLIGOPOLY

In monopoly, only one seller is in the market; competition does not exist. Perfect competition and large-group monopolistic competition represent the opposite extreme. So many firms are in the market that the actions of each are thought to be imperceptible to the others. Oligopoly is said to exist when more than one seller is in the market, but when the number is not so large as to render negligible the contribution of each. A market has few enough sellers to be considered oligopolistic if the firms recognize their *mutual inter-dependence*. In monopoly and competition, firms make decisions and take action without considering how these actions will affect other firms and how, in turn, other firms' reactions will affect them. Oligopolists must take these reactions into account in their decision-making process.

When contemplating a price change, a design innovation, a new advertising campaign, and so on, Ford Motor Company must anticipate how GM and the Chrysler Corporation will react because, without doubt, Ford's actions will affect the demand for Chevrolets and Plymouths.

This, in short, is the oligopoly problem and the central problem in oligopoly analysis. The oligopolistic firm is large enough relative to the total market to recognize (*a*) the mutual interdependence of the firms in the oligopoly and (*b*) the fact that its decisions will affect the other firms, which in turn will react in a way that affects the initial firm. The great uncertainty is *how one's rivals will react*.

Since so many industries meet the general description of oligopoly, it would, at first glance, seem that a general theory of oligopoly would have been developed. The problem in developing an oligopoly theory, however, is the same as the oligopoly problem itself. Mutual interdependence and the resulting uncertainty about reaction patterns make it necessary for the economist to make specific assumptions about behavioral patterns; that is, specific assumptions about how oligopolists *believe* their competitors will react and about how their competitors actually react.

Therefore, as we shall see, the solution to the oligopoly model (that is, equilibrium price and output) depends critically upon the assumptions the economist makes in regard to the behavioral reaction of rival entrepreneurs. Since many different assumptions can and have been made, many different solutions can and have been reached. Thus, there is no "theory of oligopoly" in the sense that there is a theory of perfect competition or of monopoly.

A second complication encountered when modeling oligopoly is a fact noted in the introduction to this chapter: oligopolists can produce homogeneous or differentiated products. As noted in our discussion of monopolistic competition, product differentiation is a major determinant of demand elasticity. As a consequence, just as a single model cannot simultaneously describe perfect and monopolistic competition, one model cannot describe oligopolies produc-

ing identical or differentiated products. Let us turn to what economists *can* do to analyze oligopoly.

## Oligopoly traits

Broadly speaking, economists usually posit two contrasting patterns of behavior for oligopolists: they are assumed to be either
*cooperative* or *noncooperative.* Cooperative oligopolies tend to accommodate changes made by rival firms. For instance, if a rival should
raise price, a cooperative oligopolist would go along with the move
and raise price too. Noncooperative behavior, on the other hand,
does not accommodate such changes. If another firm raised price,
rivals would keep prices low in an attempt to attract sales away from
the higher-priced producer.

Because of the possibility of differentiated or identical products,
there are four general oligopolistic market structures. One structure
consists of a few *noncooperating* firms producing either (1) homogeneous or (2) different products. Alternatively, there may be a few
*cooperating* firms producing either (3) homogeneous or (4) differentiated products. If oligopolists produce the same products and do
not cooperate, the market resembles perfect competition. Each producer's demand elasticity will be high because there are very close
substitutes available. And, if each firm's output exhausts all economies of scale, price will be close to minimum long-run average cost.
Cooperating oligopolists producing identical products jointly behave much like a monopoly. For instance, firms tend to act as one
firm in the case of a price increase, and, since buyers cannot distinguish among products, it appears that industry price has risen because a monopoly controlled production.

Product differentiation makes cooperation more difficult, because
product differences allow firms to charge different prices, and firms
find it difficult to cooperate on anything except prices. Noncooperation would give an oligopolistic market the character of monopolistic competition, while cooperation would give an oligopoly traits
closer to monopoly. For example, cooperating oligopolists, despite
product differences, would go along with a price increase of another
rival even though prices are different.

Oligopoly behavior, in general, is determined by the threat of
entry. If entry is easy, prices must be kept low and output high or
new firms will enter the market, decreasing both market share and
price. Such behavior resembles a perfectly competitive market. But
if entry is difficult and oligopolists have relatively secure market
shares, it is much easier for them to cooperate or even collude.
Hence, a key to understanding and predicting oligopoly behavior

lies in an understanding of the existence and strength of barriers to entry.

### Barriers to entry

We have already discussed the important role of entry barriers in establishing monopoly. Essentially the same barriers that lead to monopoly give rise to oligopoly. These barriers are weaker in oligopolistic markets, because a few firms, as opposed to one, are able to overcome them. Thus, monopoly and oligopoly share the same causes; how much monopoly power entry barriers confer is a matter of degree. Why, in some industries, do the few largest firms produce a large percentage of total output, while in other industries no firm has a substantial share of the total market? Because entry is blocked. The reasons are numerous, but, historically, a few have dominated in the creation of oligopolies.

Perhaps the most important determinant of oligopoly lies in the existence of economies of scale. Economies may allow only a few firms to realize minimum long-run average cost in a market. For instance, Joseph Bain found economies were so prevalent in the automobile industry that many thousands of automobiles had to be produced to completely exhaust them.[7] Hence, price competition in the 1930s and 40s led to all but the largest and most efficient firms exiting from the market. Those firms that could increase output and lower average costs could undersell smaller rivals and drive them out of the market. Bain found similar economies in the production of typewriters.

Another important base of oligopoly is the control of a certain factor of production. If a few firms control all of the known supply of an ingredient necessary to a particular product, the firms can refuse to sell that ingredient to potential entrants at a price low enough for them to compete. Since no others can produce the product, an oligopoly results. For example, in the car rental industry, Hertz Corporation and Avis Corporation dominate rentals because they control crucial airport locations. Other companies have much lower market shares because they are unable to meet flights with offices next to baggage-claim terminals. Generally, they are forced to bus customers to their offices, which is a service disadvantage. In the long run, of course, we would expect rents at these preferred locations to be bid up, so that excess profits are eliminated. But because of limited locations, a few firms dominate rentals.

---

[7] J. Bain, *Barriers to New Competition* (Cambridge, Mass.: Harvard University Press, 1956).

A third barrier to competition, which has had a hand in creating oligopoly, is patents. As mentioned in Chapter 9, patents grant a right to produce a certain commodity, or to produce a product by means of a specified process that gives the firm an absolute cost advantage. Xerox is an example of an oligopolist based upon patent rights. Its strong market position today is largely attributable to a string of copier patents during the 1950s that prevented other firms from entering the market with the same technology. Polaroid and Eastman Kodak dominate the photography market because of patent protection.

Finally, advertising is a frequently cited source of oligopoly. New firms sometimes are unable to make the necessary expenditure required to overcome the brand loyalties and reputation of older firms. Often these loyalties are created by years of advertising. In a sense, advertising is an investment to create goodwill that is difficult for entrants to overcome. Consumers are reluctant to try new products when they are happy with established brands.

The role of advertising in fostering oligopoly has, however, been a source of controversy. Some argue that advertising acts as a barrier to entry by strengthening buyer preferences for the products of established firms. On the other hand, consider the great difficulty of entering an established industry without access to advertising. A good way for entrenched oligopolists to discourage entry would be, in fact, to get the government to prohibit advertising. The reputation of the old firms would enable them to continue their dominance. A new firm would have difficulty informing the public about the availability of a new product unless it was able to advertise. Thus, advertising may be a way for a new firm to overcome the advantages of older firms from being established. The effect of advertising on oligopoly remains a point of disagreement among economists.

### Tacit collusion

Cooperative oligopolies are often said to be *tacitly colluding.* Tacit collusion is agreement without communication. For instance, steel producers may restrict their sales to specified geographical regions without meeting and explicitly dividing a map into designated marketing areas. A firm's market is *understood* from the ongoing relations it has had with its rivals. As opposed to the formation of a cartel or a trust in an attempt to monopolize a market, tacit collusion is not per se, or categorically, illegal. However, evidence of agreement would quickly tip the legal balance against accused participants.

Examples of tacit collusion are evident among manufacturers of consumer durables. For instance, oligopolists will often act together by changing their models annually at almost the same time. Washing machines, refrigerators, cooking ranges, and lawn mowers have annual changes that are announced by manufacturers at nearly the same time. Without any known agreement, there is a surprising amount of uniformity in such behavior. The same holds true for fashions when spring and fall designs are announced. For another example, ask yourself why makers of soft drinks and beer all use the same sized cans and bottles, or makers of breakfast cereal package their product in the same size boxes. It is not that consumers all have a preference for the 12-ounce size. As far as anyone knows, cereal makers and bottlers have no explicit agreement that only this container size—along with a few others—is allowable. Probably the strongest evidence of tacit collusion comes from the prices oligopolists charge. In the service sector of our economy, there is a surprising amount of price uniformity, even though there is a wide variance in the quality of services. For instance, lawyers and real estate agents by and large charge the same prices for their services even though the quality of services varies from lawyer to lawyer or broker to broker. Explicit collusion is illegal in these industries and presumably does not take place, but a substantial amount of price uniformity exists.

How does tacit collusion arise? What makes oligopolists cooperate without an explicit arrangement? The answer lies in the consequences of noncooperation. When it comes to selecting competitive strategies, the main difference between a monopolistic competitor and an oligopolist is the realization that what an oligopolist does will cause rivals to react. The expected reaction is likely to leave sellers no better off than they were before the move. Oligopolists know that they are related to rivals in a prisoner's dilemma. A new style or a lower price may increase profits in the short run, but reduce them in the long run.

Thus, whether or not an oligopolist makes a change depends upon relative present values of making the change or leaving things as they are. Profits may increase substantially at first with a nonprice product change, but decrease in the long run after rivals react. How quickly rivals react in large measure determines how profitable a change will be. Moreover, each oligopolist knows that its rivals may have the same motivation to make a change, so that there is the temptation to move first.

To present a real-world example, several years ago there was suspicion that battery producers were withholding a battery that would outlast an automobile; tire manufacturers were supposed to have a tire that would triple the life of the best tires available, but these were suppressed. As it turns out, these inventions have, in fact, come onto the market; at the time of the rumors of suppression, these products were in the development stage, but were too costly to be profitable.

Unless there is out-and-out collusion, this suppression would be unlikely under oligopoly. The management of each company realizes that, if they have this product or have made this innovation, their rivals either have already done it or are on the verge of doing so. If they do suppress the product, there exists the uncertainty that other firms will not do so, even if suppression decreases the demand for the products currently being produced. This uncertainty about rival behavior makes it unlikely that an oligopolist can withhold an invention for very long. The new technology will either lower costs or broaden the oligopolist's market. In the former case, the firm can be made no worse off in the long run once prices fall, and if it is first with the new production technique, it can reap short-run profits. In the latter case, a waterless battery and radial tires will surely damage the market for conventional products, but if rivals introduce the invention first, the firm loses short-run returns. Because of the invention, long-run profits are questionable in terms of whether it should be introduced or not, but short-run returns are definitely lowered if it is not. Thus, there is very little incentive for oligopolists to cooperate tacitly on the introduction of new technology or new products.

But in the many cases in which the discounted stream of profits is expected to be less than what it would be without the change, patterns of behavior are established among rivals. Oligopolists cooperate because, given the expected reaction of rivals to another firm's attempt to raise profits, long-run profits are maximized by stable behavior. This is particularly true for behavior that, in the long run, will raise the costs of producers, because revenues are not likely to go up after rivals have adjusted.

### Competition in oligopoly

There is a certain amount of debate among economists as to the amount of competition in industries characterized by oligopoly. The discussion boils down to the extent of cooperation that exists in oligopolistic market structures. The less cooperation, the more price and nonprice competition there should be.

Oligopolists are profit maximizers, so even when there appears to be a great deal of cooperation among rivals in a market, there is an incentive to make competitive moves that are not easily observed by rivals. Price is probably the most obvious form of competition that exists. Generally, price is easily observed by rivals, so tacit understandings not to lower price often occur. But nonprice competition is not as easily noticed, and may be very difficult to emulate. Hence, oligopolists are usually more competitive with respect to nonprice variables. For instance, an oligopolist's advertising budget is not widely known; a firm can incrementally increase the budget without inducing a reaction from rivals. Oligopolists, therefore, do a considerable amount of advertising.

Even changes in product quality are often less perceptible than changes in price. A wine that is aged longer to give it a better taste, a few added inches between seats on an airplane, or fewer defective parts in a large shipment of equipment are quality changes not easily observed by rivals. Product-quality competition is particularly intense in service oligopolies, where product quality is difficult to judge. Doctors and dentists, for instance, do not usually compete over the prices they charge patients, but the quality of their services and the waiting time in their offices vary a great deal. These are the dimensions in which medical professionals compete.

## APPLICATION

### Nonprice competition in the beer industry[8]

Recent events in the beer industry illustrate how intense nonprice competition can become. While the brewing industry is composed of a large number of firms, a few large, national firms control most of the market. Behavior with respect to advertising and product development indicates that the largest firms recognize their rivals. Thus, the industry fits the oligopoly model. In 1980, the six largest brewers, ranked according to their share of total U.S. beer sales, were: (1) Anheuser-Busch, (2) Miller, (3) Schlitz, (4) Pabst, (5) Coors, and (6) Heileman.

In the 1950s, Schlitz was the nation's number one brewer. The company was still a strong second—to Anheuser-Busch—until the mid-1970s. In 1969, the tobacco conglomerate Philip Morris bought Miller and began to organize a strong, expensive marketing campaign. Miller aimed at the "beer belly" crowd instead of occasional sippers. Both its Lite beer and its regular beer advertising were designed to appeal to the big beer-drinking market—blue-collar workers from the late 20s to middle age. Miller tripled its sales in three to four years and moved into a strong number two position behind Anheuser-Busch, which, along with the other larger brewers, suffered a slump but, unlike Schlitz, managed to recover with the help of a massive advertising campaign. By 1979, Anheuser-

---

[8] This application is based on C. Cannon, "The Battle of the Beers Rages on as Anheuser-Busch Foams into Lead," *Los Angeles Times*, 4 May 1981, p. 13; and "What Schlitz Adds to Heileman's Formula," *Business Week*, 10 August 1981, pp. 24–26.

Busch was spending close to $200 million annually in advertising and promotion; Miller about $160 million.

In response to the surge of Miller, Schlitz changed both its brewing formula and its advertising policy, each of which was a dramatic failure. It dropped the previously successful "Gusto" and "You only go around once" advertising in favor of a very poorly received campaign featuring "characters threatening mayhem to anyone daring to replace 'my Schlitz' with any other brand."

By 1979, Schlitz was operating at only about half capacity, whereas in 1973 it was planning to increase its capacity greatly—more than 50 percent—within five years. Furthermore, by 1979 Busch and Miller outspent Schlitz in advertising by 50 percent.

The battle between Miller and Anheuser-Busch is a rivalry unknown to perfect competitors. Anheuser chairman August Busch openly spoke of Miller and its parent, Philip Morris, as "interloping Madison Avenue hucksters. . . ." John A. Murphy, president of Miller in the 1970s, kept a rug with the Anheuser-Busch symbol beneath his desk to wipe his shoes on. But 1981 has marked a watershed in the fight over market shares between the two large firms. First, after six years of television commercials and new product developments, the most important being light beers, Anheuser-Busch looked exceptionally strong. In 1981, Busch had 28.4 percent of the U.S. market, while Miller had 21.1 percent. While not a seemingly large difference in market shares, it is the largest gap between the number 1 and number 2 beer makers in U.S. brewing history.

Secondly, the ailing Schlitz Brewing Company became a takeover target for the smaller, but financially healthier, Heileman Brewing Company. The merger would move Heileman into a strong third-place slot. Nonprice competition has eliminated Schlitz as a strong market competitor. Just as a firm can make mistakes in pricing a product, Schlitz made errors in the advertising image it created and in attempts to speed up the brewing process.

The merger would help Heileman overcome barriers that have kept the firm from becoming a national beer maker. Until now, the company has been successful only at marketing several regional brands. It was not a national rival to Anheuser-Busch or Miller. In particular, Heileman would pick up a national distribution and brand network that would allow the brewer to enter markets in the fast-growing Sunbelt. Notable too, Heileman would gain cheap brewing capacity. Through the merger, Heileman would pay roughly $19 per barrel of brewing capacity while new construction costs $40 to $50 per barrel at this time. The company's chairman, Russell Cleary, freely admits that these are the two barriers to entry into national beer distribution. In his words: "The two key elements to this [merger] . . . are the capacity, which we couldn't afford to build, and the wholesale network already in place in the South that we probably could have never built."[9]

The stage is set for a new round of rivalry between the largest three brewers: Anheuser-Busch, Miller, and (potentially) Heileman. It is likely that nonprice competition will do nothing to change the market shares of these firms. One thing is certain, though, the competition will serve to cement their market shares relative to smaller beer makers. Because of the large advertising expenditures made in the 1970s, it will be very difficult for entrants to overcome the advertising barriers in the 1980s.

Certainly prices do fluctuate under oligopoly, particularly when it is noncooperative. But there is controversy over how much price flexibility exists among oligopolists in general. One thing is clear, however; there is more price flexibility under oligopoly than would exist if the market were monopolized. This point has been made by two studies.

In 1947, George Stigler, using industrial data from the 1930s, carried out tests to determine the relative flexibility of prices under oligopoly.[10] As a first piece of evidence, Stigler found that, in seven highly oligopolistic industries (cigarettes, automobiles, anthracite coal, dynamite, oil, potash, and steel), both price decreases and increases by firms in the industry were rapidly followed by other firms. In none of the seven industries was there any evidence of a lack of price flexibility.

Stigler then compared the flexibility of oligopoly price in many industries with that of prices in industries characterized by monopoly. Even though their outputs varied significantly—more than that of most of the oligopolistic industries tested—two monopolies (aluminum and nickel) were characterized during the period by significantly more price rigidity than was the case for the oligopolies. Furthermore, the oligopolists, who had periods of known explicit collusion, experienced extreme price rigidity during collusion. There was much more flexibility during periods of noncollusion.

Later Julian L. Simon tested the rigid oligopolistic price hypoth-

[9] *Business Week*, ibid., p. 26.

[10] G. J. Stigler, "The Kinky Oligopoly Demand Curve and Rigid Prices," *Journal of Political Economy*, 55 (October 1947): 432–49. Reprinted in G. J. Stigler, *The Organization of Industry* (Homewood, Ill.: Richard D. Irwin, 1968).

esis, using changes in advertising rates in business magazines for the period 1955–64.[11] His data indicated that monopolistic magazines, that is, magazines with no competitors in the same category, do not change rates any more frequently than do magazines with a few close competitors within their classification. In fact, Simon found that, with one exception, magazines in one-magazine groups change price less frequently than do magazines in multiple-magazine groups. Also, there was progressively more frequent price change in going from single-magazine to 10-magazine groups. The main results of the test show no evidence that oligopoly changes price less frequently than does monopoly.

## 10.5 OLIGOPOLY AND COLLUSION

Thus far, we have excluded to some extent a formal analysis of one possible form of oligopolistic behavior. The firms in an oligopoly may decide that competitive behavior is unprofitable and decide to collude or fix price explicitly. Explicit collusive behavior is illegal in the United States under the Sherman Act and other legislation. But antitrust litigations still flourish, indicating that such behavior continues.

### Cartels and profit maximization

A cartel is a combination of firms whose objective is to limit the competitive forces within a market. It may take the form of open collusion, the member firms entering into contracts about price and other market variables. On the other hand, the cartel may involve secret collusion among members. Or it can operate like a trade association or a professional organization. At this time, the most famous cartel is OPEC, a cartel of major oil-producing nations. Cartels may have an enforceable contract or they may not. We will speak of all such cases of organized collusion as cartels.

Let us consider an "ideal" case. Suppose a group of firms producing a homogeneous commodity forms a cartel. A central management body is appointed, its function being to determine the uniform cartel price. The task, in theory, is relatively simple, as illustrated in Figure 10–8. Market demand for the homogeneous commodity is given by $DD'$, so marginal revenue is given by the dashed line $MR$. The cartel marginal cost curve must be determined by the management body. If all firms in the cartel purchase all inputs in perfectly competitive markets, the cartel marginal cost curve ($MC_c$) is simply

---

[11] J. L. Simon, "A Further Test of the Kinky Oligopoly Demand Curve," *The American Economic Review* 59, no. 9 (December 1969): 971–75.

the horizontal sum of the marginal cost curves of the member firms. Otherwise, allowance must be made for the increase in input price accompanying an increase in input usage; $MC_c$ will stand further to the left than it would if all input markets were perfectly competitive.

In either case, the management group determines cartel marginal cost, $MC_c$. The profit-maximization problem is the simple one of determining the price that maximizes cartel profit—the monopoly price. From Figure 10-8, marginal cost and marginal revenue inter-

**FIGURE 10-8**
Cartel profit maximization

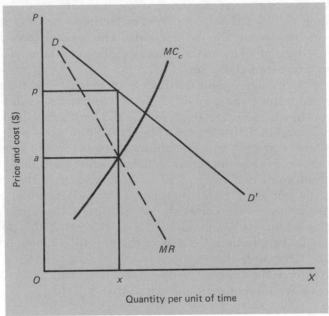

sect at the level $a$; thus, the market price $p$, is the one the cartel management will establish. Given the demand curve $DD'$, buyers will purchase $x$ units from the members of the cartel. The second important problem confronting the cartel management is *how* to distribute the total sales of $x$ units among the member firms.

### Cartel and market sharing

Fundamentally, there are two methods of sales allocation: non-price competition and quotas. The former is usually associated with "loose" cartels. A uniform price is fixed, and each firm is allowed to sell all it can at that price. Firms cannot reduce price but can compete by other means. For instance, in most localities, both medical doctors and lawyers have associations whose code of ethics is frequently the basis of a price agreement. Each person selects a doctor or lawyer on the basis of considerations other than price.

The second method of market sharing is the quota system, of which there are several variants. Indeed, there is no uniform principle by which quotas can be determined. In practice, the bargaining ability of a firm's representative and the importance of the firm to the cartel are likely to be among the more important elements in determining a quota. Beyond this, there are two popular methods. First, either the relative sales of the firms in some precartel base period or the productive capacities of the firms are used. As a practical matter, the choice of base period or the measure of capacity is a matter of bargaining among members. The second basis is a geographical division of the market. Many of the more famous examples involve international markets.

While quota agreement is difficult in practice, in theory some simple guidelines can be laid down. Consider the cartel solution that was shown in Figure 10–8. $MC_c$ is the horizontal summation of all firms' marginal cost curves. The cartel produces and sells the output level $x$ at a price $p$. The minimum cartel cost of producing $x$, or any other level of output, is achieved when each firm produces the output such that every firm's marginal cost is the same and equals the common cartel marginal cost and marginal revenue. Thus, each firm in the cartel shown in Figure 10–8 produces the output at which its marginal cost is $a$. Note that this solution is precisely that set forth in the case of the multiplant monopolist, discussed in Chapter 9 above.

To reinforce the analysis, suppose that two firms in the cartel are producing at different marginal costs; that is, assume

$$MC_1 > MC_2$$

for firms 1 and 2. In this case, the cartel manager could transfer output from the higher-cost firm 1 to the lower-cost firm 2. So long as the marginal cost of producing in firm 2 is lower, total cartel cost can be lowered by transferring production. Thus, in equilibrium, the marginal costs will be equal for all firms.

There still exists the problem of allocating the profit among firms. If the cost structure for all firms was alike, the firms could, of course, simply share profits equally. But if cost differences exist, the voluntary profit sharing would probably collapse. That, as we shall see, is what is most likely to happen to cartels.

### Short and turbulent life of cartels

Unless backed by strong legal provisions, cartels in the United States are very likely to collapse from internal pressure (before being found out by the Antitrust Division of the Justic Department). A few large, geographically concentrated firms producing a homogeneous commodity may form a very successful cartel and maintain it, at least during periods of prosperity. But the greater the number of firms, the greater the scope of product differentiation, and the greater the geographical dispersion of firms, the easier it is to "cheat" on the cartel's policy. In times of marked prosperity, profit may be so great that there is little incentive to cheat. But when profits are low or negative, there is a marked incentive; and when the incentive exists, enterprising entrepreneurs will discover what they believe to be ingenious methods of cheating.

The typical cartel is characterized by high (perhaps monopoly) price, relatively low output, and a distribution of sales among firms such that each firm operates at less than minimum unit cost. In this situation, any one firm can profit greatly from secret price concessions. Indeed, with a homogeneous product, a firm offering price concessions can capture as much of the market as desired, providing the other members adhere to the cartel's price policy. Thus, secret price concessions do not have to be extensive before the obedient members experience a marked decline in sales. Recognizing that one or more members are cheating, the formerly obedient members must themselves reduce price in order to remain viable. The cartel accordingly collapses. Without effective *legal* sanctions, the life of a cartel is likely to be brief, ending whenever a business recession occurs. If entry is relatively simple and there are no great economies of scale, the probability of collapse increases. If firms can produce relatively similar products and sell at lower prices, these entrants must be absorbed into the cartel, or the price-fixing agreement will break up. But entry will compete away all profits even with price fixing.

The incentives to cheat in a cartel can be explained by using a *kinked demand curve.* The kink in the curve comes from the incentive structure in a cartel. Suppose the collusive organization has fixed prices that maximize profit for the group. Once this is done, there is no incentive for one oligopolist to cheat by raising price, because the other producers would not follow, even if they knew about the infraction. The cheater is imposing a self-inflicted punishment. As its price rises, sales are rapidly lost to rivals. It is likely that demand is very elastic for a price increase, especially if the products are homogeneous.

There is an incentive for members of an oligopoly to cheat by lowering price. If rivals do not follow the price cut, the cheater quickly gains additional sales. Presumably, the firm has the productive capacity to sell the quantity demanded at the lower price. Figure 10–9 shows the situation for a member of a price-fixing cartel.

**FIGURE 10–9**
**The incentive to cheat in a cartel**

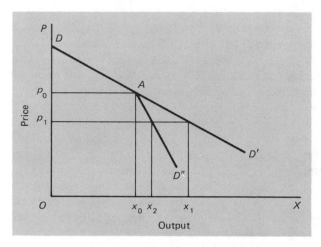

Assume the price is set at $p_0$; the oligopolist, in this case, sells $x_0$, but output may vary among members.

The demand facing the oligopolist, if other members do not follow either price increases or decreases, is the relatively elastic $DD'$. If a price decrease is not followed, a lower price substantially increases sales. But if members in the cartel discover that a rival has lowered price, a reasonable reaction would be to match the lower price. This would protect their market share and punish the violator by reducing the firm's sales. Observe that, if rivals match a price cut, the demand curve below $p_0$ would be the much less elastic segment $AD''$. Customers would have no cause to change sellers if all firms sell at the same prices.

Thus, if the cheater is discovered, the gain in sales from the price decrease is relatively small. Output rises from $x_0$ to $x_2$ rather than to $x_1$. This increase is due mainly to more total market sales because of the lower price charged by everyone in the cartel. Sales represented by $x_2x_1$ are those sales that could have been made if the price cut had gone undetected. These sales represent, then, the incentive of a cartel member to cheat on an agreement. The more elastic is $DD'$, the larger the difference between $x_2$ and $x_1$, and the greater the incentive to cut price.

Let us suppose that the amount $x_0 x_1$ is very small. The total market demand is so inelastic that total market sales increase very little after price is lowered to $p_1$. Then sales $x_2 x_1$, for the most part, represent business attracted away from rivals. If this is a noticeable amount, rivals will suspect that someone has lowered prices. Moreover, a substantial increase in the output of one firm while others are losing sales when prices are supposed to be fixed is another signal of cheating. Hence, a potentially large increase in sales from an undetected price cut is the incentive for cheating in a cartel, but, at the same time, it is the signal to other members that prices have been cut. The larger the increase in sales, the higher the probability of detection.

Of course, the smaller the number of firms in a price-fixing agreement, the easier it is to detect firms that break the agreement and reduce price. Thus, in the case of very few firms, the detection cost is low and the cartel is more likely to survive.

## APPLICATION

### An unsuccessful cartel in real estate[12]

A crucial ingredient for the success of a cartel is barriers to entry. As mentioned, if prices are set to give cartel members above-normal profits, unprevented entry will restore normal profits and result in excess production capacity. The post–World War II history of the real estate industry is a classic case study.

Most real estate agents are members of local real estate associations or boards, professional organizations with a state and a national office. The national association is known as the National Association of Realtors (NAR). Members of the organization (who subscribe to its Code of Ethics) are called Realtors®, a registered trade name. The stated purpose of the organization is to enhance the professional character of real estate agents by establishing and enforcing a code of ethics. Until 1950, real estate boards set commission rates at 6 percent of a residential sale price. Price competition was considered unethical. When the practice was legally challenged, organizations resorted to "recommending" the 6 percent commission rate. In the late 1970s, a number of antitrust suits found this practice illegal. Presently, the NAR and local boards are prohibited from mentioning any prices in their manuals. Nevertheless, surveys show that nearly 80 percent of the homes sold through real estate agents are exchanged at 6 percent commission rates.

---

[12] This application and data are taken from O. R. Phillips, *Residential Real Estate Markets in Texas: Prices, Quality, and Regulation*, Texas A&M Working Paper (College Station, Tex., April 1981).

**FIGURE 10–10**
Entry in the Texas real estate industry

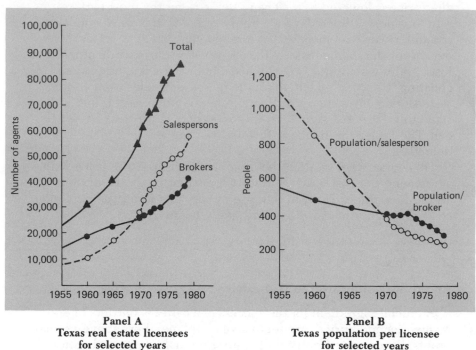

**Panel A**
**Texas real estate licensees**
**for selected years**

**Panel B**
**Texas population per licensee**
**for selected years**

Note: Salespersons are real estate agents who must work under the supervision of a broker.
Source: *Real Estate Atlas of Texas* (College Station, Tex.: Texas Real Estate Research Center, Texas A&M University, July 1979), sec. 7, p. 3.

For many years, the national association, along with local real estate boards, has acted as a cartel manager. A local board has wide latitude in disciplining members who violate the ethical code; measures range from a reprimand to expulsion, and if a member is expelled, he or she loses access to the board's multiple-listing service. This service collects in a catalog all of the available homes a realtor can show. Without the service, agents are at a severe disadvantage as compared to those who have the information. Thus, the cartel had the ability to punish those who cut prices. Historically, there exist numerous examples in which price cutters were discovered and expelled from the organization.

The cartel, however, has not been successful in raising the income of its members, because, as income rises, entry occurs. With entry, each Realtor, on average, sells fewer homes, and income—profit—is restored to a normal level. Data on the number of real estate agents in Texas illustrate the lack of success. Figure 10–10 shows the tremendous increases in agents both in total number and in per capita income between 1955 and 1980. Panel B, in particular, tells us that the number of agents has been increasing much faster than the population in Texas.

The cause of this influx has been fixed commission rates. As real housing prices increase, the amount an agent collects rises. For example, Realtors collect $3,000 on a $50,000 house at 6 percent commission rates, but $4,500 if the price is $75,000. In Texas, between 1973 and 1979, the average price of a house rose 17 percent each year, while the average annual rate of inflation was 8 percent. Thus, without entry, the real income of agents would have increased. Presently, the income of real estate agents, as reported by the Texas Employment Commission, is slightly below average for all service industries. This evidence indicates that there may be too many agents in the Texas industry. If this is true, the rate of increase should decline in the future.

### Price leadership in oligopoly

Another type of solution to the oligopoly problem is price leadership. This solution does not necessarily require open collusion, but the firms must at least tacitly agree to the solution. Price leadership has, in fact, been quite common in certain industries. It was characteristic of the steel industry quite some time ago. At times, it has characterized the tire, oil, and cigarette industries. At the present time, the most famous cartel characterized by price leadership is OPEC, although Saudi Arabia is presently being challenged. Smaller oil-producing countries are resisting the price changes made by Saudi Arabia.

Any firm in an oligopoly can be the price leader; while it is frequently the dominant firm in the oligopoly, it may be the most efficient firm or simply one with a past reputation for good judgment. The price leader sets a price that will maximize industry profits, and all firms in the industry compete for sales through advertising and other types of marketing. The price remains constant until the price leader changes the price or until one or more other firms break away.

Another form of price leadership occurs when there is one firm that has the capability of becoming a monopoly. The dominant firm sets a price at which the smaller firms behave as competitors and sell all that they wish at that price. The dominant firm will supply the rest of the quantity demanded at the market price. The dominant firm, therefore, sets a price that maximizes its own profit subject to the constraint that the fringe firms will supply the remaining portion of the market at that price. In the pre-World War II period, U.S. Steel was recognized as a price leader that allowed competitors to operate under its "price umbrella." The firm knowingly set prices that let less-efficient competitors operate in the market.

## 10.6 SUMMARY

Monopolistic competition and oligopoly are imperfectly competitive market structures that come from a change in the assumptions underlying the theory of perfect competition. Monopolistic competition is a result of product differentiation. There are a large number of buyers and sellers, easy entry and exit by producers, and market participants have perfect information.

Product differentiation confers a small amount of monopoly power on sellers. Because of these differences, the demand curve is less than perfectly elastic. However, since entry is easy, under the theory of monopolistic competition, pure profits are competed away. In equilibrium, the *LRAC* curve is tangent to the demand curve at a point above minimum average cost.

When products are differentiated, nonprice market strategies become an important competitive tool. Advertising and product-quality changes are the two most general means by which a firm can increase market shares and profits. The gains from such strategies are short run under monopolistic competition. In the long run, a successful move is generally matched, and profits in the market return to normal.

Because of interdependence, there is no complete theory of oligopoly. Oligopolies are characterized by few firms in a market. In contrast to perfect competition, there must exist barriers to entry. Also, oligopoly sellers may offer differentiated products. Behavior in oligopoly is determined by how well rivals recognize their interdependence with other oligopolists. Broadly speaking, an oligopolist can be cooperative or noncooperative with rivals. The degree to which oligopolists do cooperate determines, to a large extent, market prices and output. Oligopoly can closely resemble perfect competition, or monopolistic competition, if products are differentiated. But it can also approach monopoly if cooperation is close among sellers.

The most extreme form of cooperation is a cartel. Oligopolists explicitly agree on output, price, or both. In some cases, firms can be so well organized that behavior is closely akin to multiplant monopoly. But cartels are fragile, because incentives to cheat are inherent within any agreement. A cheater can gain at the expense of other members if the firm is not caught.

Little has been said conclusively about the desirability of

oligopoly for two reasons. It is difficult to be very precise about the welfare effects of oligopoly when there is no single theory of oligopoly. Certainly there is no reason to believe that oligopolists will produce at minimum long-run average cost. Thus, oligopoly requires more units of resources per unit of output than are absolutely necessary. Price is frequently higher than both average and marginal cost.

Furthermore, many resources can be devoted to nonprice competition under oligopoly, just as they can for monopolistic competition. If, as some say, many of these resources are "wasted," then too many resources are devoted to the effort. On the other hand, much advertising and quality and design differentials may be socially desirable. There is no clear evidence on either side. But the welfare criteria imposed are static. Dynamic considerations are also important.

Industrial research and development (R&D) has been essential in the development of our modern industrial economy and is essential to its continued viability and growth. Many argue, with considerable persuasiveness, that R&D usually thrives only in oligopolistic markets. Neither perfect competitors nor pure monopolists have the incentive; moreover, perfect competitors are usually not large enough to support research departments. Oligopolistic firms, on the other hand, always have the incentive. They want to improve the product or reduce its cost of production so as to increase profit relative to that of rivals. Furthermore, such firms are typically large enough to absorb the short-run cost of R&D in order to reap its long-run payoff. In short, all sorts of static welfare criteria may be violated, more or less with impunity, if the dynamic rate of growth is sufficiently rapid. Some economists, and all oligopolists, hold that oligopolistic market organization is essential for the dynamic growth of the economy.

## TECHNICAL PROBLEMS

1.  The smaller the seller's share in a cartel, the greater would be the temptation to cut prices in slack times. Why?
2.  Describe the major features of monopolistic competition:
    *a.* How is it similar to monopoly?
    *b.* How is it similar to competition?
    *c.* What characterizes short-run equilibrium?
    *d.* What is excess capacity under monopolistic competition?
3.  Assume that the bituminous coal industry is a competitive industry in long-run equilibrium. Now assume that the firms in the industry form a cartel.
    *a.* What will happen to the equilibrium output and price of coal? Why?

      *b.*  How should the output be distributed among the individual firms?

      *c.*  After the cartel is operating, are there incentives for the individual firm to cheat? Why or why not?

4. If you were attempting to establish a price-fixing cartel in an industry,

      *a.*  Would you prefer many or few firms? Why?

      *b.*  How could you prevent cheating (price cutting) by cartel members? Why would members have an incentive to cheat?

      *c.*  Would you keep substantial or very few records? What are the advantages and disadvantages of each?

      *d.*  How could you prevent entry into the industry?

      *e.*  How could government help you prevent entry and even cheating?

      *f.*  How would you try to talk government into helping? Under what conditions might this work?

5. Explain why we do not have a general theory of oligopoly. Given the absence of a general theory, what can we say about this type of market structure?

6. Advertising makes the demand curve faced by a seller less elastic. How might this fact be useful to a firm that desires to raise the price of a product without encouraging entry?

7. In many market structures, sellers behave alike without colluding. Use the prisoner's dilemma concept to explain apparent collusion.

8. The key difference between perfect competition and monopolistic competition is product differentiation. How does differentiation affect a market's structure?

9. According to some economists, there are too many gas stations and grocery stores. Is this in keeping with the theory of monopolistic competition?

10. Product variety is a desirable feature of markets, but it leads to market inefficiencies. Explain the costs of product variety.

11. Describe the difference between monopolistic competition and differentiated oligopoly. Do firms in each category behave differently?

12. During the Christmas holidays, the toy industry organized itself into a secret cartel. Use the kinked demand model to describe the incentive of each member of the cartel to cheat.

13. In the text, we noted that the decision concerning whether an oligopolist should break a price-fixing agreement or introduce a new product, knowing that the rivals will follow, is essen-

tially a present-value problem. To illustrate, consider the following case: a cooperating oligopolist is considering introducing a new product. It knows that if it does so, profits will be high at first, but after rivals adapt, the profits will be lower than they were prior to the introduction. If the new product is not introduced, profit will be $100,000 a year for the next 10 years—the length of the horizon. If the product is introduced, profits will be $150,000 in years 1 through 3. After the rivals adapt, profits will fall to $80,000 a year during the next seven years. The rate of interest is 10 percent. Should the firm introduce the new product? Explain.

## ANALYTICAL PROBLEMS

1. Explain in the terms of the kinked demand curve why cartels tend to break up.
2. "One sure test that an industry is competitive is the absence of any pure profit." Comment critically.
3. In antitrust suits, estimates of cross elasticities of demand have been of major importance. Why would such estimates be of importance?
4. Oil companies advertise that they are very pollution conscious. Beer companies do also. Why do not cotton farmers advertise that they use pollution-free insecticide?
5. By applying the prisoner's dilemma model to advertising, some observers argue that, to avoid the waste of resources on excessive advertising, some collusion should be permitted between firms. Comment.
6. A recent report shows that an aggressive advertising campaign by Pepsi has given the company an increased market share over Coca-Cola in food store sales. In essence, the "Pepsi Challenge" has lowered Coke's profits. Using the prisoner's dilemma model, show how Coke is likely to react to the challenge.
7. Television critics frequently argue that TV series are too similar—there is too little variety. Assuming they are correct, explain this phenomenon in terms of the analysis in this chapter.
8. Restaurants in large cities seem to fit the basic model of monopolistic competition. But we note that some restaurants are making substantial profits while others are going broke or barely breaking even. Is this consistent with long-run equilibrium? Why or why not?

9. In states in which insurance rates are regulated, how do rate increases affect the income of insurance agents in the short run and in the long run? How does this result differ from the consequences of rate increases for a privately owned municipal electric or gas company? What about a telephone rate increase?

10. Many economists argue that more research, development, and innovation occur in oligopolistic market structures than in any other. Why might this be true? (Consider perfect and monopolistic competition and monopoly.)

# Chapter 11

## Markets for production inputs

## 11.1 INTRODUCTION

We have now developed the neoclassical theory of value—a theory explaining the origin of demand, supply, and market price. A central part of this theory of value is the marginal cost of production and its possible reflection in the supply curve. Costs and supply, in turn, depend upon the technological conditions of production and the prices of productive services. So far, we have generally assumed that both are given. We will continue to assume that the physical conditions of production are technologically given and do not change over the time period relevant to our analysis. But now we must determine the prices of productive services.

Broadly speaking, the theory of input pricing does not differ from the theory of pricing goods. Both are fundamentally based upon the interaction of demand and supply. But there are important differences. Demand arises from business firms rather than consumers. The quantity of input used depends on the quantity of output sold by the firm. Sales, in turn, depend upon the size of the market and whether producers are perfect competitors or monopolistic. Thus, input demand is derived from and affected by conditions in the market for the commodity. Supply, at least the supply of labor services, arises from individuals who are not only sellers of labor time, but are also consumers. Furthermore, for the more interesting cases of capital and labor, one determines the price of using the resource for a stipulated period of time, not the price of purchasing the resource.

### Fundamentals of input demand

You have already been exposed to the fundamental elements of input demand in Chapters 5 and 7. In Chapter 5, we took a single variable input and showed why profit maximization occurs in stage II of the production function for a price-taking firm. Chapter 7 discussed how interest rates determined the most profitable level of investment. In both contexts, the theory of input demand was based upon marginal analysis.

It makes no difference whether the input is labor, capital, land, fuel, or something else. A firm increases its use of an input if the additional unit of input adds more to revenue than it adds to cost. If the additional unit increases cost more than it increases revenue, less of the input should be used. The basic theory is simple; but it is simple probably because you have already learned a great deal about marginal analysis—the economic way of thinking.

Recall, in Chapter 5, that we defined *marginal revenue product* ($MRP_i$) as the addition to total revenue attributable to the addition of one more unit of the $i$th input. That is,

$$MRP_i = \frac{\Delta \text{ Total revenue}}{\Delta \text{ Usage of } i \text{th input}} .$$

The amount that an additional unit of input adds to total cost is called *marginal factor cost* ($MFC_i$). Thus, for the $i$th input in general,

$$MFC_i = \frac{\Delta \text{ Total cost}}{\Delta \text{ Usage of } i \text{th input}} .$$

The basic rule for a particular input is, if

$$MRP_i > MFC_i,$$

the firm should add more of the input. If

$$MRP_i < MFC_i,$$

the firm should use less of the input. Equilibrium input use for a profit maximizer occurs when

$$MRP_i = MFC_i$$

for all inputs.

While the fundamentals are the same for a competitor or a monopolist, marginal revenue product for a monopolist differs from that for a competitive firm. Similarly, marginal factor cost can differ somewhat among different firms. We will analyze the various aspects of the theory in this chapter.

In this chapter you will study the following concepts:

1. The fundamental determinants of the demand for factors of production in the cases of a monopolist, a competitive firm, and a competitive industry.
2. How firms decide how much of an input to use.
3. What differences occur when a firm's input use has some effect on the price of that input.
4. How unions can affect wages and employment.
5. How the firm's investment decision is made.
6. What determines an input's price and amount of use in the market.

## 11.2 ONE VARIABLE INPUT AND PERFECT COMPETITION IN INPUT MARKETS

This section begins the theory of input markets with the simplest case. We assume that only one resource, or input is variable to the firm, and that the input is supplied by perfectly competitive agents. In particular, there are no quality differences in the factor supplied; neither are individual suppliers large enough relative to the total market to affect the price of the single input. On the other hand, we allow the demand side of the market to be, first, perfectly competitive and then monopolistic. The market structure affects the marginal revenue product of an input and, therefore, demand for the factor.

The theory developed here is applicable to any productive service, although the most natural application is to the demand for labor. Thus, when we speak of the demand for labor, the demand for any factor of production is implied.

### Demand of a perfectly competitive firm

As we stressed above, it is intuitively obvious that any firm would increase the amount of labor used if the additional labor contributes more to the firm's income than to its cost; that is, if the marginal revenue product exceeds the marginal factor cost. Consider the following example: a perfectly competitive firm sells its product at a market price of $1. It can hire one unit of the variable input, labor, at $10 per day. If increasing its labor force by one more worker adds more than 10 units of output per day, the firm would hire the additional worker.

Since each additional worker adds $10 to cost, the marginal factor cost in this case is the wage rate. Marginal revenue product is the amount each additional worker adds to revenue. In other words, marginal revenue product is marginal product times marginal revenue. Marginal revenue for the competitive firm is the commodity price, $1. Hence, the perfectly competitive firm maximizes profit by setting

$$W = MP_L \cdot P,$$

where $W$ is the wage rate and $P$ is the price of the firm's output. This profit-maximizing rule was developed in Chapter 5. In the case of a competitive firm, marginal revenue product has a specific name, *the value of the marginal product (VMP)*.

Let us consider another numerical example. A perfectly competitive firm sells a product for $5 and employs labor at a wage rate of $20 a day. Table 11–1 lists the daily total product, marginal product, and value of marginal product for zero through nine workers. Note that the value of the marginal product in the last column is simply $5 multiplied by marginal product. Under these conditions, the firm

**TABLE 11–1**
**Value of the marginal product (VMP) and individual demand for labor**

| Units of variable input | Total product | Marginal product | VMP |
|---|---|---|---|
| 0 | 0 | — | — |
| 1 | 10 | 10 | $ 50 |
| 2 | 30 | 20 | 100 |
| 3 | 50 | 20 | 100 |
| 4 | 65 | 15 | 75 |
| 5 | 75 | 10 | 50 |
| 6 | 80 | 5 | 25 |
| 7 | 83 | 3 | 15 |
| 8 | 84 | 1 | 5 |
| 9 | 81 | −3 | −15 |

hires six workers. It would not hire fewer than six, since hiring the sixth adds $25 to revenue but costs only $20, and the firm increases net revenue by $5. It would not hire seven workers, because revenue would increase by $15 while cost would increase by $20, thereby causing a decrease in net revenue of $5. If, however, the wage rate dropped below $15 (say to $14) the work force would increase to seven (an additional $15 revenue can be gained at a cost of $14). If wages rose above $25 but remained below $50, the firm would reduce the labor force to five.

**FIGURE 11–1**
**Proof of $VMP = \bar{w}$ theorem**

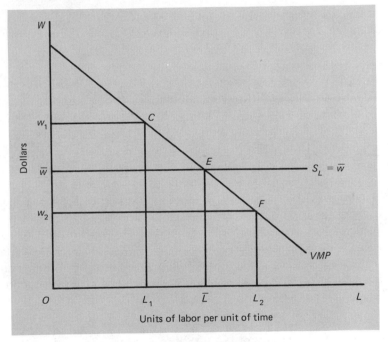

To make the theory more general, consider Figure 11–1. Suppose the value of the marginal product is given by the curve labeled *VMP*. The market wage rate is $\bar{w}$, so the supply of labor to the firm is the horizontal line $S_L$. First, suppose the firm employed only $L_1$ units of labor. At that rate of employment, the value of the marginal product is $L_1C = w_1 > \bar{w}$, the wage rate. At this point of operation, an additional unit of labor adds more to total revenue than to total cost (inasmuch as it adds the value of its marginal product to total revenue and its unit wage rate to cost). Hence, a profit-maximizing entrepreneur would add additional units of labor and, indeed, would continue to add units so long as the value of the marginal product exceeds the wage rate.

Next, suppose $L_2$ units of labor were employed. At this point, the value of the marginal product, $L_2F = w_2$, less than the wage rate. Each unit of labor adds more to total cost than to total revenue. Hence, a profit-maximizing entrepreneur would not employ $L_2$ units, or any number for which the wage rate exceeds the value of the marginal product. These arguments show that neither more nor fewer than $\overline{L}$ units of labor would be employed and that employing $\overline{L}$ units leads to profit maximization. The statements are summarized as follows:

**Principle.** A profit-maximizing competitive firm will employ units of a variable productive service until the point is reached at which the value of the marginal product of the input is equal to the input price.

In other words, given the market wage rate or the supply-of-labor curve to the firm, a perfectly competitive producer determines the quantity of labor to hire by equating the value of the marginal product to the wage rate. If the wage rate were $w_1$ in Figure 11–1, the firm would employ $L_1$ units of labor to equate the value of the marginal product to the given wage rate. Similarly, if the wage rate were $w_2$, the firm would employ $L_2$ units of labor. By definition of a demand curve, therefore, the value of the marginal-product curve is established as the competitive firm's demand curve for labor, when only labor is variable.

**Principle.** The competitive firm's demand curve for a *single* variable productive service is given by the value of the marginal-product curve of the productive factor. This is, of course, limited to production in stage II.

### Monopoly in the commodity market

The analytical principles underlying the demand for a single variable input are the same for perfectly and imperfectly competitive commodity markets. However, since commodity price and marginal revenue are different in imperfectly competitive markets, the marginal revenue product does not equal price times marginal product.

When a perfectly competitive seller employs an additional unit of labor, output is augmented by the marginal product of that unit. In like manner, total revenue is augmented by the value of its marginal product inasmuch as commodity price remains unchanged. When a monopoly employs additional labor (we restrict our attention to monopoly, since the principles are the same for all imperfectly competitive firms), output also increases by the marginal product of the additional workers. However, to sell the larger output, commodity price must be reduced; hence, total revenue is not augmented by the price times the marginal product of the additional workers. Instead $MRP = MR \times MP$, where $MR$ falls as output increases.

A numerical example might clarify this point. In Table 11–2, columns (1) and (2) give the production function when labor is the only variable input. Columns (2) and (3) show the demand for the commodity that is produced by labor. Column (4) is the total revenue (price times quantity) associated with each level of labor use, and column (6) is the marginal product of labor. The crucial amounts in the demand for labor are shown in columns (5) and (8). Column (5) shows the addition to total revenue (from column [4]) from increasing labor by one unit. These figures represent the marginal revenue product of labor. $MRP$ can also be computed by multiplying marginal product times marginal revenue, in this case the average, or per-unit-of-output marginal revenue as shown in column (7). For example, the average marginal revenue associated with changing from three to four units of labor is $350 (the additional revenue) divided by the change in total product, 15, or $23.33.

**Definition.** Marginal revenue product for a monopolist is the additional revenue attributable to the addition of one unit of the variable input. It is per-unit marginal revenue times marginal product.

Note that, in this case, marginal revenue product falls because both marginal revenue and marginal product fall. Marginal revenue product is the *net* addition to total revenue. For example, the gross addition to revenue from increasing the variable input from three to four units is 15 (the additional units of production) times $30 (the selling price) or $15 \times \$30 = \$450$. But to sell 15 additional units, price must fall by $20. Thus, the "lost" revenue from the price reduction is $5 \times \$20 = \$100$, since five units could have been sold for $50. This "loss" must be subtracted from the gross gain, or $\$450 - \$100 = \$350 = MRP$.

Columns (5) and (8) of Table 11–2 show the monopolist's demand for a single variable input. For example, if the daily wage is $25, the monopolist would hire eight workers. Each worker up to the ninth adds more than $25 (the additional daily cost per worker) to revenue. The ninth adds $13, and thus would cost the firm $25 − $13 = $12. If wages rise to $50 a day, the firm would reduce labor to six units. Both the seventh and the eighth add less than $50 to total revenue.

**TABLE 11–2**
Marginal revenue product for a monopolist

| (1) Units of labor | (2) Total product | (3) Commodity price | (4) Total revenue | (5) Additional total revenue per unit additional labor | (6) Marginal product | (7) Marginal revenue | (8) Marginal revenue product MR × MP |
|---|---|---|---|---|---|---|---|
| 3 | 5 | $50.00 | $250 | — | — | — | — |
| 4 | 20 | 30.00 | 600 | $350 | 15 | $23.33 | $350 |
| 5 | 30 | 25.00 | 750 | 150 | 10 | 15.00 | 150 |
| 6 | 38 | 22.00 | 836 | 86 | 8 | 10.75 | 86 |
| 7 | 44 | 20.00 | 880 | 44 | 6 | 7.33 | 44 |
| 8 | 48 | 19.00 | 912 | 32 | 4 | 8.00 | 32 |
| 9 | 50 | 18.50 | 925 | 13 | 2 | 6.50 | 13 |
| 10 | 51 | 18.00 | 918 | −7 | 1 | −7.00 | −7 |

To illustrate graphically, consider the marginal-revenue-product curve in Figure 11–2. It must quite obviously slope downward, because two forces work to cause marginal revenue product to diminish as the level of employment increases: (*a*) the marginal prod-

**FIGURE 11–2**
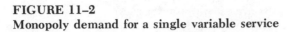
**Monopoly demand for a single variable service**

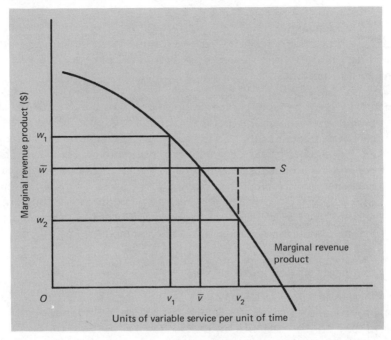

uct declines (over the relevant range of production) as additional units of the variable service are added; and (*b*) marginal revenue declines as output expands and commodity price falls. For the monopolist, marginal revenue product falls more quickly than it does for a perfect competitor. Under perfect competition, output price remains constant, so the only force causing **MRP** to decline is declining marginal product.

By assumption, the monopoly purchases the variable service in a perfectly competitive input market. Hence, it views its supply-of-input curve as a horizontal line at the level of the prevailing market price, $\overline{w}$.

Given the market price, $\overline{w}$, we wish to prove that equilibrium employment is $\overline{v}$. Suppose the contrary, in particular, that $v_1$ units of the variable service are used. At the $v_1$ level of utilization, the last unit adds $w_1$ to total revenue but only $\overline{w}$ to total cost. Since $w_1 > \overline{w}$, profit is augmented by employing that unit. Furthermore, profit increases when additional units are employed, so long as marginal revenue product exceeds the market equilibrium price of the input. Thus, a profit-maximizing monopolist would never employ fewer than $\bar{v}$ units of the variable service. The opposite argument holds when more than $\bar{v}$ units are employed, for then an additional unit of the variable service adds more to total cost than to total revenue. Therefore, a profit-maximizing monopolist will adjust employment so that marginal revenue product equals input price. If only one variable productive service is used, the marginal-revenue-product curve is, therefore, the monopolist's demand curve for the variable service in question.

**Principle.**   An imperfectly competitive producer who purchases a variable productive resource in a perfectly competitive input market will employ that amount of the service for which marginal revenue product equals market price. Consequently, the marginal-revenue-product curve is the monopolist's demand curve for the variable service when only one variable input is used. Marginal revenue product declines with output for two reasons: (1) marginal product declines as more units of the variable input are added, and (2) to sell the additional output, the monopolist must lower the commodity price.

### Determinants of demand

We should mention the variables that are assumed to be held constant when deriving the competitor's or the monopolist's demand for a single, variable input. Obviously, we hold the use of all other inputs constant; otherwise, it would not be the demand for a *single* variable input. Recall from Chapter 5 that, when the rate of use of another input changes, the marginal product curve of the other input shifts. Thus, if the use of another input changes, the *VMP* curve for a competitor, or the *MRP* curve for a monopoly would shift also, and neither would be the demand for the input. In the second place, technology is held constant, since technological change shifts the marginal product curves. Also, in the case of a competitive firm, the commodity price is held constant. Similarly, commodity demand remains fixed if the *MRP* curve is the monopolist's demand for a single variable input. Finally, until now, we have assumed that the wage bill is the *total* payment to the input; there are no additional or fringe payments, such as contributions to social security or to group insurance plans.

All of the conditions held constant except the last are quite apparent. The last point requires some discussion. If you are an employer, you would use the theory described above, but you might look at the wage rate or the price of an input in a slightly different way. In the real world, workers cost an employer more than simply the money wage rate. There are certain *additional* payments to workers required by law or perhaps paid by tradition. The most familiar legal requirement is the employer's contribution to social security. Firms also frequently make contributions to the employees' insurance policies or their retirement plans. There are other fringe benefits, such as improvements in working conditions, noise controls, lounge facilities, and so on.

All of these additional payments are not costless to the firm. Firms simply view the *total wage bill* as the market-determined wage plus the cost of the fringe benefits, such as the social security payment. Thus, at any market-determined wage, if additional payments are required, fewer workers are hired than would be hired in the absence of such payments. This is not to say, however, that the employer absorbs *all* of the cost of the benefits that are required. As we shall see, this is far from the case.

## 11.3 DEMAND FOR A PRODUCTIVE SERVICE: PERFECT COMPETITION IN INPUT MARKETS, SEVERAL VARIABLE INPUTS

When a production process involves more than one variable productive service, the derivation of input demand curves is more complicated. The value of the marginal product curve and the marginal revenue product curve are no longer the perfect competitor's and the monopolist's demand curves for an input. The reason lies in the fact that the various inputs are interdependent in the production process, so a change in the price of one input leads to changes in the rates of utilization of the others. As we noted previously, a factor's marginal product curve is derived under the assumption that the amount of other inputs remains constant. Therefore, changes in the rates of utilization of other inputs shift the marginal product curve of the input whose price initially changes. We now examine input demand when the use of more than one input is allowed to vary. From this point on, we shall, for the most part, refer to the firm's *MRP* curve and not distinguish a perfect competitor's marginal revenue product with the special term, value of marginal product.

### Adjusted demand in the commodity market

Consider Figure 11–3. Suppose that equilibrium for a perfectly competitive or monopoly firm initially exists at point $A$. The market wage rate is $w_1$, the marginal revenue product curve for labor is

FIGURE 11–3
Individual input demand when several variable inputs are used

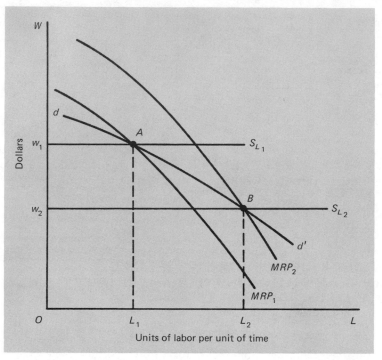

Units of labor per unit of time

$MRP_1$ when labor is the only input varied, and $L_1$ units of labor are employed. Now let the wage rate fall to $w_2$, so that the perfectly elastic supply curve of labor to the firm is $S_{L_2}$.

When the wage rate falls from $w_1$ to $w_2$, the use of labor expands. However, the expansion does not take place along $MRP_1$. When the quantity of labor used and the level of output change, the use of other variable inputs changes as well. Under these conditions, labor's marginal product curve changes.

Since the marginal revenue product is equal to marginal product multiplied by marginal revenue of the commodity, the marginal revenue product of labor curve must shift. Suppose it shifts to $MRP_2$. The new equilibrium is reached at point $B$. Other points similar to $A$ and $B$ can be generated in the same manner. Thus, the demand curve, $dd'$, can be determined from successive changes in the market wage rate and the marginal revenue product curve. The input demand curve, while more difficult to derive, is just as determinate in the multiple-input case as in the single-input situation.

The results can be summarized in the following important principle:

**Principle.** An entrepreneur's demand curve for a variable productive agent can be derived when more than one variable input is used. This demand curve must be negatively sloped. Even though the demand, when more than one input is variable, is no longer the marginal revenue product curve, we should stress that, at every point on the demand curve, the wage rate still is equal to marginal revenue product.

## 11.4 MARKET DEMAND FOR AN INPUT

The market demand for a variable productive service, in contrast to the firm's demand for a commodity, is not necessarily the horizontal summation of each producer's demand curve. In general, the process of addition for productive services is considerably more complicated, because when all firms in an industry expand or contract simultaneously, the market price of the commodity changes. Nonetheless, the market demand curve can be obtained.

The situation is analogous to the derivation of a perfectly competitive industry's supply curve from the firms' supply curves. Recall that any firm can change its level of output without affecting input prices. But, when all firms attempt to vary output together, input prices change and each firm's supply curve shifts. Therefore, industry supply is the horizontal summation of these "shifted" supplies. In the case of input demand, any perfectly competitive firm can vary its inputs, and thus its output, without effecting commodity price. When all firms respond to a change in the price of an input, commodity price does change. Since each firm's demand for the input is derived holding commodity price constant, all input demands shift when all firms change simultaneously.

To illustrate the process, assume that a typical employing firm is depicted in Figure 11–4, panel A. For the going market price of the commodity produced, $d_1 d'_1$ is the firm's demand curve for the variable productive service, as derived in Figure 11–3. If the market price of the resource is $w_1$, the firm uses $v_1$ units. Aggregating over all employing firms in the industry, $V_1$ units of the service are used. Thus, point $A$ in panel B is one point on the industry demand curve for the variable productive service.

Next, suppose the price of the service declines to $w_2$ (because, for example, the supply curve of the variable service shifts to the right). Other things being equal, the firm would move along $d_1 d'_1$ to point $b'$, employing $v'_2$ units of the service. But other things are not equal.

**FIGURE 11–4**
Derivation of the industry demand for a variable productive
service

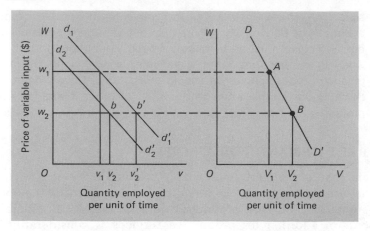

Panel A
The demand of a firm for a
variable productive service

Panel B
Industry demand for a
variable product service

When all firms expand their use of the input, total output expands.
Or, stated differently, the market supply curve for the commodity
shifts to the right because of the decline in the input's price. For a
given commodity demand, commodity price must fall; and when it
does, the individual demand curves for the variable productive service also fall.

In panel A, the decline in individual input demand attributable
to the decline in commodity price is represented by the shift leftward from $d_1d'_1$ to $d_2d'_2$. At input price $w_2$, $b$ is the equilibrium
point, with $v_2$ units employed. Aggregating for all employers, $V_2$
units of the productive service are used and point $B$ is obtained in
panel B. Any number of points such as $A$ and $B$ can be generated by
varying the market price of the productive service. Connecting
these points by a line, one obtains $DD'$, the industry demand for the
variable productive service.

If an industry is monopolized by a single firm, the monopoly
demand for an input is the same as the industry demand. If several
industries demand an input, the total market demand is the horizontal summation of every industry's demand, assuming, of course, that
we ignore the effect of changes in commodity price in one industry
upon commodity prices in other industries that demand the input.
There is some minor qualification in the case of oligopoly and
monopolistic competition. In these cases it must be considered that,
like perfect competition, when all firms attempt to expand output,
market price falls.

We can use the concepts of input demand under monopoly and perfect competition to make a crude comparison between industry employment under the two market structures. We know that, under the same cost conditions, a monopolist restricts output and charges a higher price relative to a perfectly competitive industry. It should, therefore, come as no surprise that, under the same condition, a monopolist hires less of an input relative to the competitive industry. Assuming the monopolist is unable to realize economies, the degree of "inefficiency" attributable to a monopoly employer can be observed by comparing employment at any given wage to that in a perfectly competitive industry.

To make the comparison, we use the following somewhat restrictive assumption. First, there is only one variable input, in this case, labor. As noted, we assume the same cost structure for both the competitive and the monopolistic structure. The same amount of labor is associated with a given amount of output in either case. And, at any given level of output and labor usage, the marginal product of additional labor is the same under each structure. This might be the case if the monopoly simply organized the firms into individual plants and allocated output among the plants in the same way output would have been divided among firms under competition.

Thus, for the monopolist, the demand for labor is marginal revenue times the marginal product of labor, shown as $D_m = MR \times MP$ in Figure 11–5. For the competitive industry, demand is price times marginal product, shown as $D_c = P \times MP$ in the figure. Since, at any level of output and labor use, marginal product and, hence, cost are

**FIGURE 11–5**
**A competitive industry and a monopoly employer**

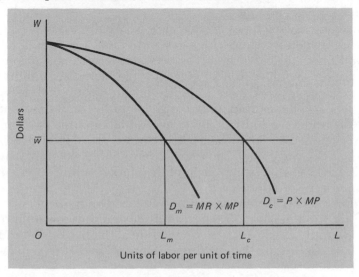

the same under either structure, $D_m$ lies below $D_c$ at every amount of labor. This obviously results from the fact that, with a given demand, $MR$ is less than price. At any given wage rate, say $w$, the monopolist will hire less labor, $L_m$, than would a competitive industry, which hires $L_c$.

The fundamental deficiency lies in the difference between price and marginal revenue. But when making such a comparison, recall the assumption upon which the analysis was based. If cost advantages were available to the monopolist but not to the competitive industry, more labor might be used by the monopolist at a given wage level.

## 11.5 SUPPLY OF A VARIABLE PRODUCTIVE SERVICE

All variable productive services may be broadly classified into three groups: natural resources, intermediate goods, and labor. Intermediate goods are those produced by one entrepreneur and sold to another, who in turn utilizes them in the productive process. For example, cotton is produced by a farmer and sold as an intermediate good to a manufacturer of fabric; the fabric, in turn, becomes an intermediate good in the manufacture of upholstered furniture. The short-run supply curves of intermediate goods are positively sloped because they are the *commodity outputs* of manufacturers, even if they are variable inputs to others; and, as shown in Chapter 8, short-run commodity supply curves are positively sloped.

Natural resources may be regarded as the commodity outputs (usually of extractive operations). As such, they also have positively sloped short-run supply curves. Thus, our attention can be restricted to the final category: labor.

There are several types of labor supply. We discussed one type in Chapter 4 when we showed how an individual's supply of labor is derived from indifference curves between leisure and income. In that chapter, we showed that, given a wage increase, an individual might choose to work more (sacrifice leisure) or to work less (take more leisure), depending upon the shape of his or her indifference map. Therefore, an individual's supply-of-labor curve may be positively sloped over some range and negatively sloped over other ranges of the wage rate. The crucial question, however, is how the sum behaves—what is the shape of the market supply curve of any specified type of labor.

A firm, monopolist or competitor, can face two types of supply for a specific kind of labor. In the cases discussed thus far in this chapter, the supply of labor is a horizontal line at the market-determined wage rate, indicating that the firm can hire all of that type of labor it wishes at the going market wage rate. In certain cases, firms have some effect upon the wage rate. In these instances, the firm faces an upward-sloping supply of labor, indicating that, in order to hire more of a specified kind of labor, the firm must pay higher wages. Under this set of circumstances, the firm is called a *monopsonist,* a situation to be analyzed theoretically below.

Next there is the situation in which one industry uses a specialized type of labor, specialized in the sense that the industry's use of the input affects that input's price. In the long run, the supply to the industry must be positively sloped because of labor mobility; an industry must bid away people from other occupations in order to get more of the specific type of labor or to induce people to enter that occupation. If there is a given number of people in a specific occupation and the firms in a particular industry desire more of that type, they must lure them away by paying higher wages.[1] The situation is similar when more than one industry uses a particular type of labor. If output is to be expanded in one or more of these industries, the employment of workers must increase.

---

# APPLICATION

### The shortage of nurses

Economic theory recognizes that people get different levels of utility from working in different occupations. Economists also observe that people are willing to make a trade-off between less desired occupations and increased incomes. Just as in the case of commodities, supply and demand determine relative wages and the relative numbers of employees in different occupations.

Let us analyze the following facts brought out in an Associated Press report made in February 1981.[2] The shortage of registered nurses is termed "serious to very critical" across the nation. Hospitals everywhere are on the "edge of unsafe situations." To avoid substandard care, hospitals in Boston, Atlanta, Baltimore, Detroit, Dallas, Milwaukee, and many smaller cities have left beds empty

---

[1] There are two possible exceptions, each of which leads to a horizontal industry supply-of-labor curve. First, if the industry is small or if it uses only very small quantities of labor, its effect upon the market may be negligible. That is, the industry may be to the market what a perfectly competitive firm is to the industry. Second, if there is unemployment of the particular type of labor under consideration, the supply of labor to all industries may be perfectly elastic up to the point of full employment. Thereafter, the supply curve would rise. The latter is a disequilibrium situation not encompassed in the analysis here.

[2] "Crisis in Nursing: Shortage Nearing Critical Point," *Houston Post,* 19 February 1981, p. 1N.

and sometimes closed entire units. The shortage of nurses is put at 100,000 by the American Hospital Association. Yet, of the nation's 1.4 million registered nurses, only 900,000 are employed, and 300,000 of these are part-time staff. There are at least 500,000 qualified nurses who are not working and 300,000 who could work more.

Most hospital administrators do not feel that higher salaries are the answer to the problem. Instead, many hospitals are spending millions on help-wanted advertising and recruiting gimmicks, such as new-employee bounties to anyone who recruits a nurse for their hospital. Nurses begin at $16,000 a year in a few cities, such as Houston; but the average nurse earned $13,000 annually in 1980. At the same time, the average salary of hospital laundry managers was $16,700 a year. Nurses earn less than the average unionized grocery clerk.

It is nonsense to assert that salary and fringe benefits are not the answer. If the hospital wants more nurses, or if employers of people in any occupation want more employees, the only way to get them is to bid them away from other locations. Or, in the long run, they must bid them away from other occupations. The higher bids can only be in the form of higher salaries and/or increased benefits. What else would attract more nurses? Of course, it may be that the hospital administrators do not want to pay higher salaries or to increase fringe benefits. In this sense, higher salaries and benefits may not be the answer for them.

In the story, it appears that nurses do not wish to work weekends and nights. They can work weekdays elsewhere. What is the problem? Clearly, hospitals are not paying a sufficient differential to attract nurses to the less desirable hours. If there are jobs with more desirable hours at the same rate of pay, nurses obviously would choose these. With all forms of labor, as with commodities, a shortage will continue in the long run if the wage is below equilibrium. To increase the number of people in a particular occupation or in a particular location, total wages, salary, and/or benefits must be increased.

It is interesting to note that, while salaries of nurses are just keeping pace with the rate of inflation, hospitals are taking steps to increase the fringe benefits of nurses—an implicit rise in payment. Some hospitals are giving cars to nurses who work the late-night shifts. For instance, Eisenhower Medical Center in Rancho Mirage, California, offered nurses use of a Chevrolet Chevette for commuting. Others are offering child care for nurses who work; those who work at night receive a 50 percent discount.

A big change has come in the flexibility of hours a nurse may work. For instance, an Alabama hospital allows nurses to take every other week off. Baylor Medical Center in Dallas has hired 100 nurses to work two 12-hour shifts on Saturdays and Sundays for a full week's pay so that the hospital's 1,000 full-time nurses can work Monday through Friday—an unusual schedule in nursing.

Much of the reason for disequilibrium in the nursing market is job dissatisfaction. Certainly dissatisfaction may be overcome with higher salaries. People will do almost anything for the right price, but hospitals have probably learned it would be much less expensive to eliminate the source of dissatisfaction, e.g., schedules, rather than increase compensation directly.

Let us return to the analysis of the determinants of the various supply curves of labor. As population increases and its age composition changes, as people migrate from one area to another, and as education and reeducation enable people to shift occupations, rather dramatic changes can occur in the supply of various types of labor at various locations throughout the nation. These changes represent *shifts* in supply curves and are quite independent of their slopes. To get at the supply curve for a well-defined market, assume that the following are held constant: the size of the population, the labor-force participation rate, and the occupational and geographic distribution of the labor force.

As was the case in the supply of products, the time period of adjustment is one of the most important factors influencing the elasticity of supply of a particular type of labor. If the salary in a particular occupation rises, people may choose to enter that occupation, but acquiring the needed skills takes time. However, given the necessary period of adjustment, an increase in the relative wages in a particular occupation will attract additional people into that occupation.

Thus, we can say almost unequivocally that, except for the case of an individual worker, the supply of labor to a specific occupation is upward sloping. This reflects the fact that, at least in the long run, higher wages or benefits must be paid in order to attract more persons into the occupation. The longer the time period of adjustment, the more people are induced to enter. The same thing applies to the supply of a particular type of labor in a specific area—city, state, region. When you hear people complaining that a city can't get enough teachers, or a county can't get enough doctors, or a college can't get enough professors, or a community can't get enough garbage collectors—and these are things we hear every day—you should be able to suggest a solution. This is not to say the solution will be acceptable to those paying the bill. What people who make such statements generally mean is they cannot get enough of a particular type of worker at a price low enough to suit themselves.

## 11.6 MARKET EQUILIBRIUM AND RETURNS TO INPUTS

The demand for and supply of a variable productive service jointly determine its market equilibrium price; this is precisely marginal productivity theory. In Figure 11–6, *DD'* and *SS'* are the

**FIGURE 11–6**
**Market equilibrium determination of the price of a variable productive service**

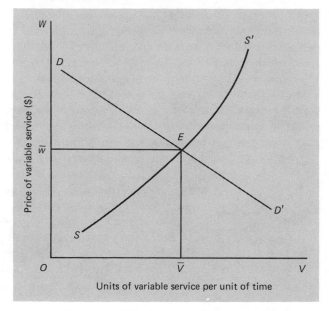

demand and supply curves. Their intersection at point *E* determines the equilibrium price, *w*, and quantity demanded and supplied, *v*, in a particular input market.

If the price of the variable input (say, labor) exceeds $\bar{w}$, more people wish to work in this occupation than employers are willing to hire at that wage. Since there is a surplus of workers, wages are bid down by the workers until the surplus is eliminated. If the wage rate is below $\bar{w}$, producers want to employ more workers than are willing to work at that wage. Employers, faced with a "shortage" of labor, bid the wage rate up to $\bar{w}$. The analysis is similar to that in Chapter 2. The only features unique to this analysis are the methods of determining the demand for variable productive services and the supply of labor services. The fact that input demand is based upon the marginal revenue product of the input gives rise to the label "marginal productivity theory."

Since all resources are variable in the long run, marginal productivity theory applies to all resources. However, in the short run, certain inputs are fixed; they cannot be varied, and hence a "marginal product" cannot readily be generated. The return to short-run fixed factors is called "quasi-rent." Quasi-rent is the difference between total revenue and total variable cost. It must always be nonnegative since, you will recall, the firm will shut down in the short run if it cannot cover all variable costs. Sometimes, when a pure profit is being enjoyed in the short run, quasi-rent exceeds fixed costs. Sometimes, when the firm operates at a loss in the short run, quasi-rent is less than total fixed cost, and some of the fixed cost must be paid by the entrepreneur, who suffers the loss. Quasi-rent is not profit and should never be confused with the return a firm earns. We can show quasi-rent using the conventional cost curves of the firm. Figure 11–7 illustrates the short-run equilibrium for a per-

**FIGURE 11–7**
**Quasi-rent for a perfect competitor**

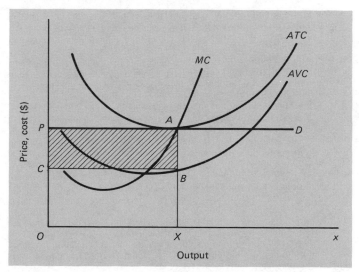

fectly competitive firm. The firm earns zero profits, but to cover fixed costs, there must be positive quasi-rents. Total revenue in the figure is area $OPAX$; total variable costs are represented by area $OCBX$. Therefore, by definition, quasi-rents are area $CPAB$, the shaded region in the diagram.

It should be emphasized that, in general, quasi-rent is a short-run phenomenon. In the long run, when all factors are variable, quasi-rent is eliminated. We might note, however, that contrived or sometimes natural barriers may lead to continued quasi-rent over a long period of time. There might be a natural barrier to entry—possibly the ownership of some specialized, highly productive resource that allows these rents to continue. Or the barriers may be artificially set by governmental licensing regulations. For example, in some cities, taxis are issued licenses which are given free or at a very low charge. But these licenses are limited in number. Therefore, entry is prohibited and quasi-rents can persist over a long period. Other businesses are licensed, leading to the effect of preventing or hindering entry. Some land has tobacco allotments, giving the owner the right to grow a certain amount of tobacco on that land. The holders of these licenses or permits can continue to receive quasi-rent so long as large numbers of additional licenses or permits are not issued.

Suppose that, in your city, one must have a city permit to operate a mortuary. There are only 20 mortuaries in operation, and in all likelihood the city will issue no more licenses in the near future. Each of the mortuaries is doing a thriving business because of the prevention of entry as the city grows. Now suppose you are a young mortician and one of the licensed mortuaries comes up for sale. The license goes with the business. If you purchase the mortuary, will you make positive quasi-rents over a reasonable period of time, because you hold a license to do business in a thriving industry in which entry is prevented?

Probably not. Why? Well, in the first place, other morticians will also be bidding for the licensed business. How high will the bidding go? In all likelihood the business will sell for the value of the equipment *plus* the amount of rent due to the ownership of the license. For example, if the license enables the mortuary to make $100,000 a year *additional,* or pure profit because of protection from entry, the discounted value of this stream of profit will be added to the selling price. In other words, when you buy a *business and a license,* you pay the value of the business *plus* the value of the license. Thus, you, as a new owner, will probably earn no quasi-rent because this rent would have to be paid to the original owner. Licenses only benefit those who receive them first from government, and only when there is a limit on the number of licenses.

Earlier in this chapter, we spoke of the effect of fringe benefits; either externally imposed benefits such as social security payments paid by employers, or voluntary benefits such as improved working conditions or low-cost group insurance plans. You will recall that employers simply considered the added cost of the benefits as an addition to wages, and they adjusted their use of labor accordingly.

In that analysis, we may have given you the impression that employers absorb the entire cost of such benefits—that the only effect on employees is that fewer workers are hired, but those hired receive higher *total* wage rates (that is, wages plus the value of the benefits). That is only one part of the story. We neglected the supply side of the market in that analysis.

Remember that demand and supply determine the wage rates in markets. If working conditions in a particular market improve, or if there are additional fringe benefits paid to workers in this market, jobs in that market become more desirable relative to jobs in markets in which conditions do not change. The increased desirability of jobs in that market will, at least in the long run, increase the supply of labor to that market. As we know, the increase in supply will drive down wages in that market relative to what they would have been in the absence of the increased desirability of the occupation. Thus, at least some of the cost of improved conditions is passed on to the workers involved. The proportion depends upon demand and supply elasticities and how the curves shift. A somewhat factual, analytical example, using the tools we have developed in this section, may give a more complete insight into the process.

## APPLICATION

### Effect of improved working conditions in mining industries

Let us consider the case of the northern Canadian mining and smelting industry. This industry mines and processes, among other things, zinc, nickel, gold, and lead. The mines and smelters are in rather desolate parts of the country, and the working conditions have historically been quite harsh. Thus, wages have had to be rather high to lure workers away from other more desirable areas.

Recently, laws have been passed to make working conditions more amenable. Such laws are pollution controls, dust and safety regulations in mines and smelters, and other types of regulations. Moreover, in order to attract labor, mining companies have voluntarily improved working conditions in other ways. These changes in working conditions took the form of improved housing, civic improvements, and so on. Now, as you know, these fringe benefits are added to the total wage income for each worker. But the question is what was the overall effect of the additional benefits? Who really paid for fringe additions to the wages?

We can use Figure 11–8 to analyze the effect. Let *DD* be the total demand for labor in the northern Canadian mining industry. This demand reflects the relation between *money wages only* and the

**FIGURE 11–8**
Effect of fringe benefits

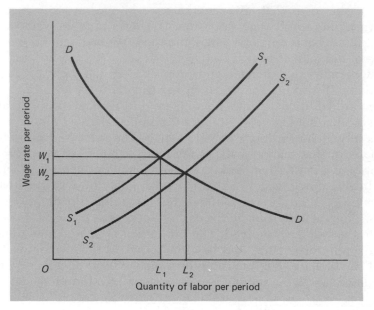

quantity of labor hired. That is, the wage rate on the vertical axis is the money wage rate and does not include the value of amenities. As we noted above, employers simply add the cost of fringe benefits to the market-determined wage rate in choosing the amount of labor hired.

Let $S_1S_1$ be the supply of labor to the industry prior to the imposition of additional benefits. Again, this supply is the relation between money wages and labor supplied; it is obviously upward sloping. Equilibrium wages and labor hired are, respectively, $W_1$ and $L_1$. Next, let fringe benefits be imposed. These would be improved environmental conditions, possibly added insurance benefits, improved housing, and so on. Suppose, to take the most farfetched example possible, that government absorbs all of the costs of such benefits. In this case, analysis would not be complicated by a downward shift in input demand.

But, because of improved working conditions, one would suppose that the supply would increase. That is, at each wage rate, more workers than before would be willing to work in the industry because of improved working conditions. Thus, even though government pays for all of the fringe benefits—absurd though it may be—the wage rate *falls* to $W_2$. Of course, the amount of labor increases to $L_2$. Thus, workers themselves absorb some of the cost of the benefits.

To be more realistic, if the companies themselves are forced to pay for most of the added benefits, they would be willing to hire fewer workers at each wage rate. That is, each worker costs more because of the added benefits. In this case, the demand for labor, $DD$, would shift downward and to the left, resulting in even lower wages than $W_2$ and in fewer than $L_2$ workers being hired.

Therefore, we can see that it is not necessarily the employer who absorbs the cost of any compulsory or voluntary fringe benefits. If the market works at all, the employees bear some part of the cost in the form of wages below the rate that would exist in the absence of regulations. The extent to which wages are reduced because of fringe benefits depends on several factors: (1) the valuation by workers of the fringe benefits, reflected in the extent to which supply increases; (2) the elasticity of supply for a given shift; (3) the extent to which demand decreases; (4) the elasticity of demand.

---

To some extent, the above application might explain why, in the absence of regulations and labor unions, wages differ from industry to industry. Other things being equal, if the wage rate for equal skill is higher in one industry than in another, workers would leave the low-wage industry and increase the supply of labor to the high-wage industry. In this way, wages would rise in the previously low-wage industry and fall in the previously high-wage industry, until wage rates were the same in both. Therefore, in the absence of external interference, the wages should be approximately equal in the two industries for equal skills. If, over the long run, one industry continues to pay higher wages than another, and there are no external interferences, then the working conditions for some reason or other—location, risk of danger, amenities, and so on—must differ between industries. Thus, the attractiveness of an industry relative to another affects relative wage rates for equal levels of skill.

## 11.7 EFFECTS OF LABOR UNIONS AND MINIMUM WAGES

The theoretical discussion thus far may seem far removed from the dramatic world of General Motors versus the United Automobile Workers. Indeed it is. A more complete understanding of such situations requires one or more *courses,* not chapters in a textbook. For example, there is a substantial body of theory concerning the collective bargaining process, but an understanding of labor markets also requires an extensive knowledge of the institutional framework within which labor unions and business operate. This type of knowledge must be acquired in "applied" courses or contexts, just as other applied courses supplement other portions of microeconomic theory.

This is not to say that we cannot gain considerable insight into the effect of unions on wages and employment by using our simple marginal productivity theory. The basic fundamentals of what unions can and cannot do are easily developed within our general framework. Furthermore, we can use our fundamental theory to analyze the effect of external interference in the labor market, such as the imposition of minimum wages. Much of the simple framework set forth here is used by professional economists to predict the effect of external interferences such as these on the market.

## Labor unions

Consider any labor market with a positively sloped supply of labor. If the workers in this market are unionized, the union bargaining representative has two powers to exert. First, the representative can set a wage rate above equilibrium and guarantee the availability of workers at this price (up to a limit) but also guarantee no workers at a lower price. Second, the union can limit membership in some way below the equilibrium number that would be hired in the absence of a union. This limitation, in effect, allows the market to raise wages above equilibrium.

Let us consider the first strategy. Suppose the labor market in question is perfectly competitive (large number of purchasers of this type of labor) and unorganized. The situation is depicted in panel A, Figure 11–9, where $D_L$ and $S_L$ are the demand for and supply of

**FIGURE 11–9**
**Effects of a labor union in a perfectly competitive labor market**

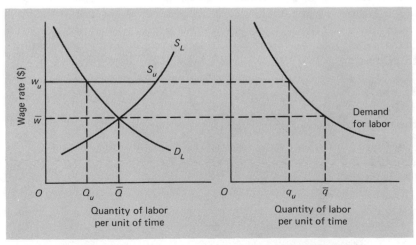

Panel A
The market

Panel B
The firm

labor, respectively. The market equilibrium wage rate is $\overline{w}$ and $\overline{Q}$ units of labor are employed. Each individual firm (panel B) accordingly employs $\overline{q}$ units. Next, suppose the labor market is unionized. If the union does not attempt to raise wages, the situation might remain as it is. However, scoring wage increases or other benefits is the reason for the existence of unions. Thus, suppose the bargaining agency sets $w_u$ as the wage rate. Firms can now hire all of the labor they want at the rate $w_u$, as long as the industry does not hire beyond the point $S_u$ on the labor supply curve. Thus, a total of $Q_u$ (where $w_u$ equals demand) units of labor are employed, each firm taking $q_u$ units. The result is an increase in wages and a decline in employment. The fact that the imposed increase in wages causes a reduction in the amount of labor hired does not necessarily mean a union cannot benefit its members. If the demand for labor is inelastic, an increase in the wage rate will result in an increase in total wages paid to the workers, even though the number of workers employed declines. If the union can somehow equitably divide the proceeds of $Q_u$ employed workers among the $\overline{Q}$ potential workers, all will benefit. Such a division is easy to achieve. Suppose $Q_u = \frac{1}{2}\,\overline{Q}$ and that a 40-hour week characterizes the market. Then $Q_u$ units of labor can be furnished by having $\overline{Q}$ workers work a 20-hour week.

The other side of the coin is worth examing, however. If the demand for labor is elastic, total wage receipts will decline, and the union cannot compensate the $Q_u\overline{Q}$ workers who are unemployed from the increase in wage rates.

The second option available for a union to raise wages is simply to limit the number of persons in an occupation. In terms of Figure 11–9, if the union could limit the number of union workers to $Q_u$ and somehow prevent nonunion workers from working in the industry, pure market forces would cause the wage rate to be bid up to $w_u$. Thus, limiting entry is an alternative way of raising wages. The problem here, of course, is that nonunion members can offer to work at lower wages and break the union. For this reason, the union must obtain, through threat of strike, boycott, or some other method, a contract with the firms preventing the hiring of nonunion labor. Or the union can get government to issue a limited number of licenses, thereby restricting entry. The more difficult and time consuming it is to get a license, the more entry is restricted and the higher are wage rates. But in either case, under reasonably competitive conditions, wage gains can be obtained only at the expense of reduced employment.

This analysis does not mean that unions deliberately set out to cause unemployment. Certainly they do considerable lobbying in Congress to restore full employment by expansionary monetary and fiscal policy. They continually support full employment as an economic policy. But the fact is that wage gains in a specific industry are frequently obtained at the expense of employment in that industry.

### Minimum wages

The effect of a minimum wage rate placed above equilibrium is similar to the effect of a union. Those who retain their jobs in industries covered by the minimum wages are better off with the higher wage. Those who lose their jobs (that is, the "surplus" labor) are worse off. They must find work in industries not covered by minimum wages. The supply of labor increases in these uncovered industries, and the wage rate there is bid down. Therefore, a minimum wage makes some better off and some worse off. The question is, who benefits and who loses?

We can show with a diagram that the equilibrium effects of a minimum wage are much like those of a union. An effective legal minimum keeps payments above the wage rate determined by the intersection of supply and demand; less labor is hired as a result.

The amount of unemployment caused by a minimum wage depends upon the elasticity of demand as it did for labor unions. To show this relation, let $D_1D_1'$ and $SS'$ in Figure 11–10 be, respectively, the demand and supply of labor. In the absence of a minimum wage, equilibrium would occur at a wage of $w_e$ with $L_e$ units

**FIGURE 11–10**
**The effect of a minimum wage**

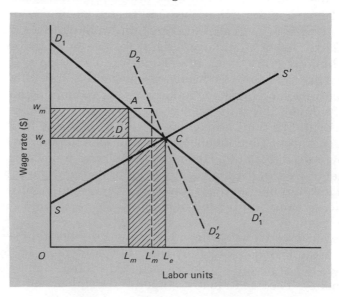

of labor employed. A minimum wage of $w_m$ reduces employment to $L_m$.

While there is unemployment, labor as a sector can gain from the minimum wage. In other words, it is possible for those who continue to work to receive total wages greater than before the minimum wage was imposed. Whether this happens or not depends upon the elasticity of demand for workers. Without the minimum wage, total wage payments are $Ow_eCL_e$. With the minimum wage, they are $Ow_mAL_m$. Wage payments increase if the area $w_ew_mAD$ is greater than area $L_mDCL_e$. But, from Chapter 2, we know that this is precisely what demand elasticity tells us. Demand is inelastic when $w_ew_mAD > L_mDCL_e$ and elastic if $w_ew_mAD < L_mDCL_e$. Thus, whether labor gains or loses as a group depends on the elasticity of demand for labor. It gains if demand is inelastic and loses if it is elastic. It is easy to see that, if we make demand more inelastic at point $C$, as shown by the dotted line $D_2D_2'$, employment would fall by only $L_m'L_e$, which is less than $L_mL_e$. Of course, even if the total wage bill does increase and labor as a sector is better off, those who are forced into unemployment are clearly worse off regardless of how much is gained by the ones working.

If all workers were homogeneous, as in our theory, the impact would be randomly distributed. If, as in the real world, workers differ in productivity and in employers' feelings toward them, the least productive workers and those most disadvantaged in their "reputation" with employers are released. While theory can say no more, we can examine a little empirical evidence for further insight into the problem.

## APPLICATION

### Effect of minimum wages: Some evidence

As noted above, an increase in the minimum wage causes some unemployment or shifting to industries not covered. In addition, because a minimum wage raises the relative wage of unskilled to skilled workers, there may be some shifting by employers from unskilled to skilled labor in the industries covered. The burden largely falls on those who are least skilled, least productive, or least desirable in the eyes of employers. Economists largely agree on this point. Any major disagreement concerns the magnitude of the unemployment effect. As was emphasized in the case of labor unions, the unemployment effect of an externally imposed wage increase can vary from negligible to substantial, depending upon the elasticity of the demand for labor.

A study by Thomas Gale Moore examined the impact of the minimum wage on disadvantaged classes of workers.[3] Moore notes that an increase in the minimum wage rate increases the wages of unskilled workers (those affected by the minimum wage) relative to the wages of those who have skills. Recall from Chapter 5 that changes in *relative* input prices cause substitution away from the relatively more expensive input. Since it takes time for employers to substitute capital and skilled labor for unskilled labor, the impact upon the unskilled increases over time. Thereafter, the impact gradually lessens as the *general* level of wages rises. Therefore, the unemployment effect of a specific increase in the minimum wage rate at first increases then decreases over time. Furthermore, the total unemployment effect should be greater the more extensive is the coverage. For example, if all industries were covered, anyone whose productivity was less than the minimum wage would be unemployed. If only a few industries were under the regulation, those unemployed in these industries would seek jobs in the uncovered industries, driving down wages there. But they would not be unemployed. The more extensive the coverage, the more difficult it is for the disadvantaged to find a job.

For the period 1954–68, Moore obtained the following results. The minimum wage rate as a proportion of hourly earnings was highly significant in explaining unemployment in all categories of teenagers. This variable was not significant in explaining unemployment for males between 20 and 25. The general unemployment level was the only significant factor explaining unemployment for this category. The percentage of workers covered by minimum wages was highly significant in explaining unemployment for males and females 16–19, and for males, 20–24. It was somewhat less significant for other categories. It appears that the burden of minimum wages is much less by the time a worker becomes 20. By then, the workers would have gained experience or undergone training and would no longer be disadvantaged. Moore points out that his results may understate the impact of the minimum wage. High unemployment can cause potential workers to drop out of the labor force. There is evidence that this has happened in the teenage labor force.

In 1969, the United States secretary of labor recommended making the minimum wage universal. Using the model, Moore estimated that this would raise nonwhite teenage unemployment an

---

[3] T. G. Moore, "The Effect of Minimum Wages on Teenage Unemployment Rates," *Journal of Political Economy* 79, no. 4 (July/August 1971): 897–902. The remainder of this application is based upon that paper.

additional 9.7 percent. He also showed that the secretary's proposal to increase the minimum wage rate would increase unemployment in all teenage categories.

This analysis is by no means meant to imply that administration officials, and particularly secretaries of labor, are ignorant of economics or are totally unfeeling about teenage unemployment. On July 29, 1977, the secretary of labor, Dr. Ray Marshall, a widely known labor economist, was quoted by UPI as saying that a proposed increase in the minimum wage to $2.65 an hour could cost the economy 90,000 jobs. Therefore, he certainly recognized the effect of an increased minimum wage on unemployment. But he also was quoted as saying that public service employment would create more jobs than those lost. Presumably, this meant that government would create jobs at the minimum wage or above for those workers who could not find jobs, because their value to privately owned firms is less than the minimum wage.

As an economist, one cannot say whether this is a good or bad policy; we cannot say whether or not society benefits by having more public service employees and fewer in the private sector. We only cite Secretary Marshall's statement to show that, if an increase in the minimum wage is not to cause unemployment, something else must be done to counteract an increase in the minimum wage; and we wish to indicate also that this topic will continue to be an important policy matter in the future.

Why, then, would the major labor unions, in which all members make much more than the minimum wage, be the major supporters of increases in the minimum wage and increases in the coverage of the minimum wage? Surely these union leaders are not unfeeling men who want to see teenagers, particularly nonwhite teenagers, unemployed.

But consider the fact that nonunion members can compete with union members for jobs. Furthermore, firms that have union contracts compete for business with firms that hire nonunion labor. Suppose, for example, New England textile mills hire all union labor. Southern textile mills use lower-cost nonunion workers. Other things being equal, the Southern mills could undersell the Northern mills, resulting either in some New England mills going out of business or moving to the South. In any case, the Northern union workers would be out of work, at least temporarily. In either situation, nonunion workers are competition to union workers. Do not forget that, in general, substitution is possible. If the minimum wage makes some nonunion labor less cheap, then there is marginally less competition for union members. Of course, this may not always be the only motive, but the higher the minimum wage, the less competition for union workers. This is not to deny that union leaders may have additional noneconomic motives. We only say there exist economic motives also.

## 11.8 MONOPSONY: MONOPOLY IN THE INPUT MARKET

Thus far, we have assumed that the price of an input is determined by supply and demand in the resource market. Entrepreneurs, whether perfect competitors or monopolists, believe they can acquire as many units of the input as they want at the going market price. In other words, no firm, acting alone, has a perceptible effect upon the price of the input. This obviously is not the case in all situations. There are sometimes only a few (and in the limit one) purchasers of a productive service. Clearly, when only a few firms purchase an input, each will affect input price by changing input use. We, therefore, need new tools to analyze the behavior of such firms.

For analytical simplicity, we consider only a single buyer of an input, called a *monopsonist*. However, the analytical principles are the same when there are a few buyers of an input, called *oligopsonists*.

### Marginal factor cost under monopsony

The supply curve for most productive services or productive agents is positively sloped. Since a monopsonist is the sole buyer of a productive service, the supply curve of the input is upward sloping. In order to hire more of an input, the monopsonist must raise the price of that input. Each unit of the input hired receives the same price. Therefore, in order to increase the use of an input, the monopsonist must pay *all* units an increased price. Thus, marginal factor cost is not, as above, simply the price of an additional unit of input, but is the *marginal expense* of purchasing additional units.

Table 11–3 might clarify this point. Columns (1) and (2) indicate the labor supply to the monopsonist. Column (3) is the *additional* expense of increasing labor by one unit. The firm can hire five workers at $10 an hour. To hire an additional worker, the wage rate must rise to $12 an hour. With five workers, the hourly wage bill is $50 an hour; with six, it is $72. Hiring the additional unit costs an additional $22 an hour, even though the wage rate rises by only $2. Hiring the additional unit costs $12, but increasing the wage of the previous five workers from $10 to $12 increases expenses an additional $5 \times \$2 = \$10$. We can use the same analysis to derive each entry in column (3). When we consider the addition of one unit of an

**TABLE 11–3**
**Input supply and marginal factor cost**

| (1)<br><br>Price | (2)<br><br>Quantity<br>supplied | (3)<br>Marginal<br>factor<br>cost | (4)<br>Marginal<br>revenue<br>product |
|---|---|---|---|
| $10 ................... | 5 | | |
| 12 ................... | 6 | $22 | $70 |
| 14 ................... | 7 | 26 | 50 |
| 16 ................... | 8 | 30 | 40 |
| 18 ................... | 9 | 34 | 36 |
| 20 ................... | 10 | 38 | 34 |
| 22 ................... | 11 | 42 | 31 |

input, the addition to total cost is the *marginal factor cost*. It includes the price paid to the additional unit *plus* the increase that must be paid to the units already employed. Therefore, for every unit except the first, the marginal factor cost exceeds price.

The supply curve of a variable input and the marginal factor cost curve are shown graphically in Figure 11–11. Since the price per unit rises as employment increases, the marginal factor cost exceeds supply price at all employment levels; and the marginal factor cost

**FIGURE 11–11**
**Marginal factor cost**

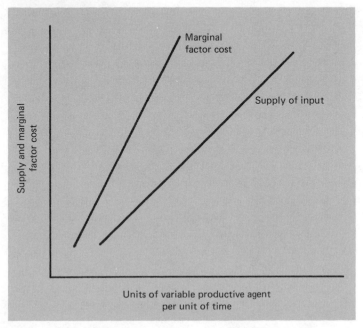

Marginal
factor cost

Supply of input

Supply and marginal
factor cost

Units of variable productive agent
per unit of time

curve is positively sloped, lies to the left of the supply curve, and typically rises more rapidly than the latter.

**Definition.** The marginal factor cost of an input to a monopsonist is the increase in total cost (and in total variable cost and in total cost of input) attributable to the addition of one more unit of the variable productive agent.

### Price and employment under monopsony

The relevant curves for price determination under monopsony are the *MFC* and the marginal revenue product curves, assuming one variable input. The firm is confronted with a positively sloped supply of input curve and the higher marginal factor cost curve. The situation is illustrated in Table 11–3 and in Figure 11–12. Using this table and graph, we will prove the following:

**Principle.** A profit-maximizing monopsonist will employ a variable productive service until the point is reached at which the marginal factor cost equals its marginal revenue product. The price of the input is determined by the corresponding point on its supply curve.

**FIGURE 11–12**
**Price and employment under monopsony**

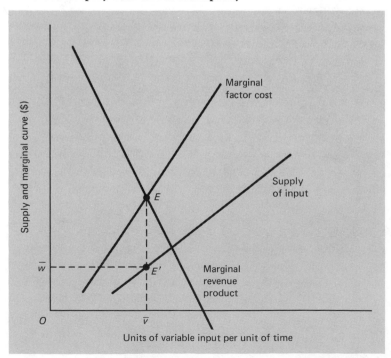

The proof of this principle follows immediately from the definitions of marginal revenue product and marginal factor cost. Marginal revenue product is the addition to total revenue attributable to the addition of one unit of the variable input; the marginal factor cost is the addition to total cost resulting from the employment of an additional unit. Therefore, so long as marginal revenue product exceeds the marginal factor cost, profit can be augmented by expanding input use. On the other hand, if the marginal factor cost of an input exceeds its marginal revenue product, profit is less or loss greater than they would be if fewer units of the input were employed. Consequently, profit is maximized by employing that quantity of the variable service for which the marginal factor cost equals marginal revenue product.

For example, assume only one variable input in Table 11–3. The marginal revenue product schedule for 6 through 11 workers is given in column (4). Each worker up through the ninth adds more to hourly revenue (*MRP*) than is added to hourly cost (*MFC*). Thereafter, the 10th and 11th add more to cost than to revenue. The firm hires nine units.

In the continuous case, the equality of *MRP* and *MFC* occurs at point *E* in Figure 11–12, and $\bar{v}$ units of the service are accordingly employed. At this point, the supply-of-input curve becomes particularly relevant; $\bar{v}$ units of the variable productive agent are associated with point *E'* on the supply-of-input curve. Thus, $\bar{v}$ units will be offered at $\bar{w}$ per unit. Hence, $\bar{w}$ is the equilibrium input price corresponding to market equilibrium employment $\bar{v}$. If the monopsonist is a perfect competitor in the commodity market, the situation is similar, except that the relevant curve is the value of marginal product curve. The firm employs the variable input until the value of marginal product equals the marginal factor cost of the input.

Recall from Section 11.3 that monopoly in the commodity market led to fewer resources being employed in the input market relative to perfect competition. Each productive service was paid its marginal revenue product, which was less than the value of its marginal product. It can now be shown that, when the demand side of the market is also a monopsony, still fewer resources are employed than would be if demand were competitive. Remember, we are dealing with only one input, and the monopoly faces the same cost curves as the competitive industry.

Figure 11–13 illustrates how monopsony on the demand side of the labor market reduces employment. Because $MR < P$, for any wage rate, $D_m < D_c$. Thus, when a monopolist maximizes profit by setting $MRP = w$, less labor is hired than would be employed by a perfectly competitive industry. The decrease is $L_pL_c$ in Figure 11–13. Now, suppose the monopolist is also a monopsonist. There is

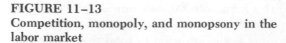

**FIGURE 11–13**
Competition, monopoly, and monopsony in the
labor market

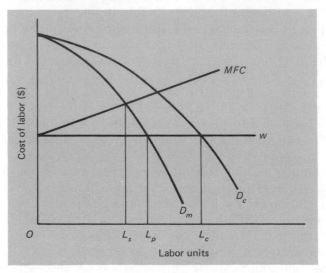

no longer a single wage rate at which all the labor a firm wants can
be hired, but there is an increasing marginal factor cost curve. This
curve intersects the $D_m$ schedule at a higher point. The profit-
maximizing level of labor is $L_s$. A monopoly that is a monopsony at
the same time hires less labor than a firm that is only a monopolist.

### Bilateral monopoly

An interesting aspect of monopsony behavior arises when the
seller of the input is a monopoly. The input market is organized so
that a single buyer of a resource—some form of labor, perhaps—
confronts a single seller of that resource, say, a union for that type
of labor. This situation, in which a monopsonist hires a resource
from a monopolist, is called *bilateral monopoly*. Examples of bilateral monopoly would be the United Auto Workers confronting
General Motors or, on a smaller scale, the only textile mill in a small
town bargaining with a local union. This market structure yields no
single equilibrium price or quantity. We can establish theoretical
bounds between which price and quantity will range, but the final
results depend on the bargaining and political powers of the
negotiating parties.

Figure 11–14 helps us establish the bounds within which price
and quantity will fall. To the union, the demand curve for its labor is
the *MRP* curve of the monopsonist. The union takes this as given.

**FIGURE 11–14**
**Bilateral monopoly**

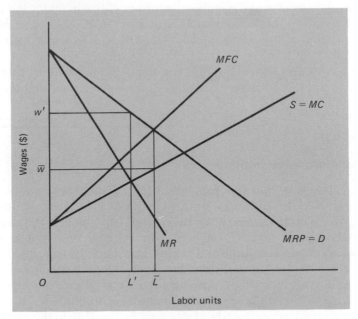

We have assumed that the *MRP* curve is linear for the sake of illustration. If this is the demand faced by the union, or labor monopolist, the marginal revenue curve can be easily derived. It is shown as *MR* in the figure. Suppose the union behaves as a profit maximizer and seeks to maximize returns to its organization, given its labor supply curve *S*,[4] which represents the marginal cost of hiring another worker. It sets *MR* = *S*, offers *L'* units of labor to the single employer, and asks for wage *w'*.

The monopsonist, on the other hand, we have already discussed. It maximizes profits where *MFC* = *MRP*; thus, it wants to hire $\overline{L}$ units of labor and pay a wage $\overline{w}$. The equilibrium wage rate will lie somewhere between $\overline{w}$ and *w'*, and the equilibrium amount of labor between *L'* and $\overline{L}$.

We can illustrate how bargaining eventually determines the equilibrium wage and employment level. In Figure 11–14, the bargaining could begin with the union refusing to supply more than *L'* units of labor and the employer refusing to pay a wage higher than

---

[4] In Chapter 9, we showed that a monopolist does not have a supply curve. We assume, in this case, that the supply curve is provided by its union members, and the union takes it as given. In other words, the supply curve is outside its control.

$\overline{w}$. Then, if the employer wants more workers, a higher wage must be paid as part of the bargain. Employment moves closer to $\overline{L}$ units for the employer, and the wage rate moves closer to $w'$ for the union. However, it might be the situation that $\overline{L} < L'$. That is, the monopsonist wants to hire fewer workers than the union wants to sell and wants them at a lower wage.[5] In this situation, the bargaining position of the union is weakened. It wants both more workers hired and higher wages. No longer is a quid pro quo exchange viable.

## APPLICATION

### Monopsony in the military

An employer that has monopsonistic characteristics and, until very recently, resorted to a draft in order to hire labor, is the military. While, at this time, the military draft is no longer used in times of peace, males turning 18 must now register with the selective service system. The draft can be brought back in time of national emergency. At the present time, however, the military must resort to a volunteer army and compete for labor in the open market.

We can use the theory established above to compare the social cost of an army conscripted in large part by drafting to the social cost of a volunteer army. While the military is by no means a monopsonist in the sense of being the sole buyer of a specific input, it must certainly face an upward-sloping supply of personnel classified as "suitable" for military service. Assume that $SS$ in Figure 11–15 represents this supply, showing the number of suitable personnel that would volunteer for military service at each wage rate in the list.

Now, if the military were a profit-maximizing monopsonist, it would equate its marginal revenue product curve to the marginal factor cost curve associated with $SS$ in order to choose the optimal number of personnel. It would pay the wage given by the corresponding point on the supply curve. But the military does not attempt to maximize profits and, therefore, operates under somewhat different principles.

First, assume the military resorts to a draft, as it did for so many years. Suppose the general staff decided it "needed" $L_1$ people in the services per year. If the military did not have the right to draft, it would have to pay a wage rate of $W_1$ in order to hire $L_1$ suitable personnel. This would cost society a total of $OW_1RL_1$ (excluding any fringe benefits) in money payments.

---

[5] This would happen if the demand curve in Figure 11–14 was more inelastic, the supply curve more elastic, or both.

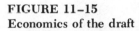
**FIGURE 11–15**
**Economics of the draft**

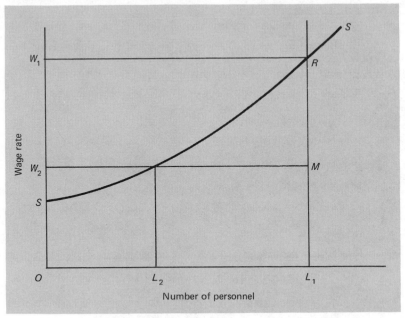

Suppose now that the military sets a lower wage of $W_2$. Clearly, in this model, only $L_2$ people would volunteer under the circumstances. If the military still "needed" $L_1$, it would have to draft the difference, $L_2L_1$, the shortage of personnel. Now society pays a money cost of $OW_2ML_1$, clearly a lower cost than before.

But as you probably realize already, this money cost does not represent the total cost to society. Suppose the yearly wage rate in the military for draftees is $8,000. Suppose also that a young man is drafted for two years. If that person could be making $15,000 a year in his chosen occupation, perhaps business, the opportunity cost to the person drafted is, therefore, $7,000 a year for two years. In fact, any young man drafted, whose supply price for volunteering for military service exceeds $8,000, pays an implicit tax of the difference between the supply price and $8,000. It is not just a matter of the draft costing society less than the volunteer army costs, it is simply that the tax burden under a draft is shifted from the older taxpayers to the young people who are drafted. Who pays the price does not change the cost.

It should be rather obvious why the young people were the leaders in the battle to abolish the draft. After all, they were the ones paying the implicit taxes.

We can use the model developed here to solve the following problem. Assume the army wishes to hire $X$ number of people. Assume that more than $X$ meet the army's standards. The army has three choices: (1) it can let supply and demand determine the wage that will attract $X$ people (assume an upward-sloping supply); (2) it can set wages below equilibrium and draft the number needed; or (3) it can set the wage below equilibrium, draft the number needed, but let people who are drafted pay others to serve for them if they wish and are qualified. We can analyze the costs to society, to those drafted, and to the army and compare the makeup of those who serve under the three choices.

**FIGURE 11–16**
**More economics of the draft**

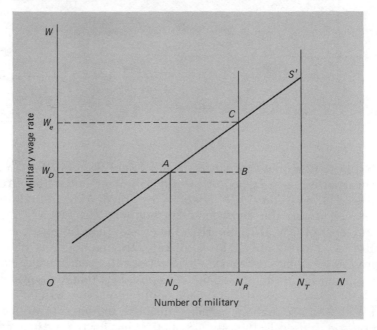

Let us analyze the problem with the aid of Figure 11–16. Assume that, from the total of the population that meets the military's criteria for duty ($N_T$), the military desires $N_R$. $SS'$ is the supply curve of the $N_T$ for military duty. The upward slope reflects the difference in taste for military duty and the differences in other opportunities. A market wage of $W_e$ would induce the required number, $N_R$, to volunteer. The total cost to society would be $OW_eCN_R$. If wages are set below $W_e$, say at $W_D$, $N_D$ would volunteer and $N_DN_R$ would be drafted. The wage cost to society would be $OW_DBN_R$. However, those who were drafted from the $N_DN_T$ people who did not volunteer would pay (in foregone earnings) the difference between their wage rate and their supply price. The drafted persons would be scattered randomly among the $N_D N_T$ group, if people could not pay others to serve. If draft notices were negotiable, the same people would serve as would be induced to enter by the equilibrium wage, $W_e$. Anyone who was drafted and had a supply price above $W_e$ would be induced to pay someone who was not drafted and had a supply price below $W_e$, the difference between that supply price and $W_D$. Society would still pay $OW_D BN_R$. Those who were drafted would pay $ACB$, the amount necessary to pay the market wage bill of $N_D N_R$ service people.

Once again, society as a whole shifts some of the military costs to those who are chosen by the draft. But notice that this system is less costly to society than is prohibiting substitution among draftees. When draftees can pay substitutes, the cost is $OW_D BN_R + ABC$; if they cannot, the cost is $OW_D BN_R$, but some of the draftees will come from the $N_R N_T$ pool, which has a relatively higher opportunity cost than has the $N_D N_R$ pool. Thus, non-negotiable draft notices makes society pay a higher cost for military service.

## 11.9 CAPITAL INPUT MARKETS

Although we have discussed input markets in terms of labor, we want to emphasize that the theoretical tools developed in this chapter apply to any input. Conceptually, the firm maximizes profits by setting $MFC = MRP$ across all inputs. This has always been the fundamental rule. The topics discussed in this chapter have essentially dealt with how either $MFC$ or $MRP$ is affected by monopoly in either the product or input markets.

We have already discussed the theory of investment and, hence, the demand for capital inputs in Chapter 7. We did this because a very important component of capital markets is the discount rate. The demand for capital equipment is determined by the present value of a stream of returns, and present values depend upon the discount or interest rate. In this section, we want to show that the theory of investment presented in Chapter 7 is consistent with the theory presented in this chapter. By expanding the analysis of Chapter 7, we will show that the dynamic nature of investment requires some special considerations.

### Demand for capital

We assume that a firm faces a given set of investment opportunities and can rank these according to the expected rates of return, from the highest to the lowest. The expected rate of return is the discount rate that makes the present value of a future stream of payments equal to its price. Suppose you are offered $110 next year for an investment of $100 now. Then the rate of return on your investment is the $r$, the *marginal return to investment* (MRI), that makes

$$100 = \frac{110}{(1 + r)}.$$

In this case, $r = .10$. More realistically, investments in machinery yield a periodic stream of returns $(R_t)$. The expected rate of return, $r$, is then the discount rate that makes this stream equal to the price $(P)$ of the investment. That is, we solve for $r$ so that

$$P = \sum_{t=1}^{n} \frac{R_t}{(1 + r)^t}, \tag{11-1}$$

where $n$ is the number of periods the machine is in use. By and large, this discussion is nothing but a review and minor extension of the discounting procedures learned in Chapter 7.

The expected rate of return is determined by the marginal revenue product of the machine each period it is in operation. After all, ignoring maintenance and depreciation, $R_t = MRP_t$. The income earned by the machine each period is, by definition, the machine's marginal revenue product. Thus, the expected rate of return reflects the discounted rate of capital. If the $MRP$ in each period is high, $r$ must be high to equate the right side of (11–1) to the left side, which is given by the market. If the $MRP$ is low, $r$ is low. Hence, there is a direct relation between $r$ and total discounted marginal revenue product.

It is much easier to discuss the value of investment in terms of its expected return rather than referring to its marginal revenue product. $MRP$ varies from period to period. And, because revenues are spread over time, it is cumbersome to compare them with another investment possibility without discounting. Therefore, when economists discuss the demand for capital, they refer to the *marginal return to investment* (MRI) rather than the marginal revenue product of capital.

Figure 11–17 shows the $MRI$ curve. Given this schedule, the firm purchases capital up to the point where the market rate of interest is equal to the marginal return to investment. The profit-maximizing amount of capital $\overline{K}$ in the figure. This is where $\overline{r}$, the market rate of interest, intersects the $MRI$ schedule. The firm is not maximizing profits if it uses less capital. At a capital use of $K_0$, the firm could borrow funds at the market rate, make the investment, and earn a net return equal to the difference $r_0 - \overline{r}$. If the firm used more than $\overline{K}$ units of capital, it would be earning a lower return on the amount

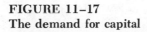

**FIGURE 11-17**
**The demand for capital**

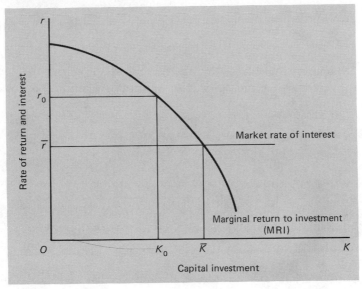

Capital investment

of capital beyond $\overline{K}$ than could be earned by not investing and putting the funds in a financial account earning $\overline{r}$. In essence, we have the following:

**Principle.** A firm's demand curve for capital is given by the marginal return to investment curve. The firm maximizes profits by equating *MRI* to the market rate of interest.

We should emphasize two points: (1) the rate of interest plays a very important role, and (2) capital is purchased in order to yield a discounted stream of income. Anything that alters the rate of interest or the discounted stream of income from potential investments changes the amount of investment. While we have not stressed this point, it should be understood that expectations by persons in business—admittedly difficult, perhaps impossible, to quantify—play a crucial role in determining the position of the demand for investment. If entrepreneurs forecast a gloomy future—gloomy in the sense of expectations of higher taxes, lower sales, higher wages, and so on—the expected flow of income from investment is reduced and the demand for investment declines. Investment is undertaken to yield returns far into the future. Since the future is so uncertain, the feelings of potential investors must play an important role in determining investment. The investor's confidence in the government and in other relevant institutions may play the most important role of all.

### Monopoly in capital markets

Of course, the market structure in which the purchaser of a capital input operates will have an effect on the shape of the $MRI$ curve. If the investor is a monopolist, the marginal revenue from selling more output is less than price. Hence, as the monopolist continues to invest in capital relative to a perfect competitor $MRP_K < VMP_K$ in each period and, as a result, future returns are less. This means that the marginal rate of return will be less for any given amount of investment. Thus, for the same reasons that $MRP < VMP$ for labor, $MRI$ is less for a monopolist than for a perfectly competitive industry. Graphically, the $MRI$ curve will have a steeper slope for the monopolist, assuming perfect competitors face the same technology as the monopolist, as shown in Figure 11–18. The competitive and monopoly $MRI$ curves are labeled $MRI_c$ and $MRI_m$, respectively.

For any market rate of interest, the monopolist maximizes profits by investing in less capital than does the perfect competitor. This conclusion is consistent with the theory developed in Chapter 9, which showed that a monopolist, in general, would produce less than a competitive industry.

**FIGURE 11–18**
**Imperfections in capital markets**

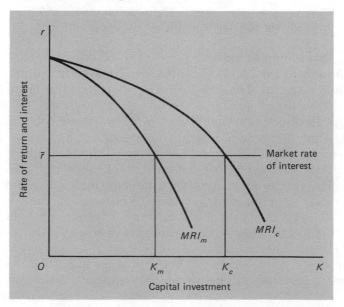

Capital investment

Monopsony in capital markets has no effect on the marginal price of capital. In contrast, recall that monopsony in labor caused the marginal price of labor to rise even faster than the slope of the supply curve for labor. The marginal factor cost of another unit of labor increased more quickly than did the marginal price, because it was assumed that all labor received the same wage. For capital, a monopsonist faces an upward-sloping supply curve, but there is no *MFC* schedule above the supply curve, as in Figure 11–11 for labor. A higher price for the marginal unit of capital does not necessitate paying a higher price for the units of capital already in use. Hence, the marginal factor cost of capital is the cost of the last unit purchased.

To summarize, we see that the theory of investment differs in some ways from the theory of labor, even though the basics are the same. The profit-maximizing criterion is, in essence, no different; the firm sets marginal factor cost equal to marginal revenue product. For capital, it is more convenient to make the transformation to rates of return, because the input yields a stream of marginal revenue products. Hence, the rule for capital is to equate the marginal return to investment to the market rate of interest. Monopoly affects *MRI* like *MRP*, but monopsony is conceptually different because capital does not receive a wage. As a consequence, a monopsonist in a capital market does not face a marginal factor cost curve that is steeper than the supply curve.

## 11.10 SUMMARY

We have covered many topics and developed many theories in this chapter. The more important points are the following principles:

**Principle.** When only one input is variable for the firm, the demand for that resource is its *marginal revenue product*. For the perfectly competitive firm, this is commodity price times marginal product, called the *value of marginal product*. For the monopolist, marginal revenue product is marginal revenue times marginal product. These curves represent the value of additional units of the resource to the firm. Since price exceeds marginal revenue for a monopolist, the value of marginal product exceeds the monopolist's marginal revenue product. When several resources are variable, these curves shift when the use of one input changes, but the resource still receives its *MRP* in equilibrium.

**Principle.** The demand for an input by a perfectly competitive industry is not the horizontal summation of each firm's demand. While any firm can change its level of output without changing commodity price, the industry as a whole cannot. Thus, in deriving industry demand, one must take account of the effect upon commodity price. The demand of a monopolist is the industry's demand, since the monopolist is the industry.

**Principle.** Input prices are determined in input markets by the interaction of supply and demand. The supply of an input is generally, though not always, upward sloping to an industry.

**Principle.** A monopsonist is a firm that is the only buyer for one or more inputs. It hires the quantity at which *MRP* equals the marginal factor cost. The input receives a lower price than its *MRP*. Bilateral monopoly exists when a monopsonist buys an input from a single seller of that input (a monopoly). In such cases, a determinant quantity-price equilibrium does not exist. Quantity and price depend upon the relative bargaining and political power of the two parties.

**Principle.** An investment is undertaken if the expected rate of return exceeds the interest rate. In the case of an industry, investment in a period will continue until the rate of return on the *marginal* investment equals the rate of interest.

We should end the summary of this chapter with a warning. Do not attach too much normative content to (make a value judgment about) the marginal productivity theory of wages and distribution. That is, do not simply draw the conclusion that marginal productivity theory says that all workers get what they "deserve" or what they "ought to get." The theory says no such thing. It is a positive predictive or explanatory theory. It enables us to predict the effect of a change in the minimum wage or the unionization of an industry. It enables us to explain differences in wage rates among occupations. It does not allow us to say whether such differences are desirable from a social point of view. It does not allow us to state that a distribution of income based upon marginal productivity is somehow more "just" than any other distribution.

Many decades ago, economists got something of a bad name because of such moral judgments. People begin with a specific amount of resources that they own—capital, labor skill, social position, and so on. Who is to say that the original distribution of resources is somehow more just than any other?

On the other hand, neither can we say that some other method of allocation or distribution may be more just, or may give people more closely what they deserve. We merely want to emphasize that marginal productivity theory does not say anything about deservedness. It simply explains to a great extent why people receive what they receive. We can only say that society, or some part of it, believes that the resources owned by individuals are worth a certain amount.

We frequently hear or read someone bemoaning that Sugar Ray Leonard does not deserve $10 million a fight; that Dr. J (Julius Erving), Tom Seaver, and other athletes do not deserve their huge salaries; that Robert Redford or Barbra Streisand should not get $3 million a movie; or that Professor X at the University of Y does not deserve his large salary because he teaches only a few students a year. We also hear and read that someone or some group deserves more income. Whether we feel this way or not, our theory, and we, as economists, can say nothing about deservedness. Barbra Streisand and others receive their income because someone thinks that the return from hiring them will be greater than the amount paid out. That is all we, as economists, can say.

## TECHNICAL PROBLEMS

1. Analyze some effects of a federal minimum wage. How do these effects differ from a state or local minimum wage?
2. Recall the definition of quasi-rent. Figure E.11–1 shows the short-run cost curves of a competitive firm.
   a. If price is $6, what is output?
   b. What is the amount of quasi-rent?
   c. How much of quasi-rent is attributable to the opportunity cost of the fixed inputs and how much is pure profit?
   d. Answer Questions a, b, and c in the case of a $4 price.

FIGURE E.11–1

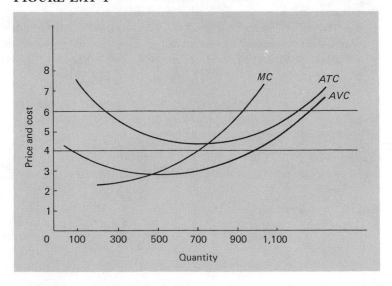

3. Consider a firm using one variable factor of production. The following table gives information concerning the production function [columns (2) and (3)], demand for output [columns (1) and (2)], and supply of labor [columns (3) and (4)] for the firm. Not all information will be used in each section of the problem. Add to the table any columns you wish.

| (1) P($ per unit) | (2) Q(units) | (3) L(units) | (4) w($ per unit) |
| --- | --- | --- | --- |
| 10.50 | 5 | 5 | 4.00 |
| 5.36 | 10 | 6 | 4.25 |
| 5.00 | 14 | 7 | 4.50 |
| 4.00 | 17 | 8 | 4.75 |
| 3.00 | 19 | 9 | 5.00 |
| 2.60 | 20 | 10 | 5.25 |

a. Suppose the firm is a perfect competitor in the output market and also a perfect competitor in the labor market. Draw a graph showing the demand for labor if the price of output is $3.50 per unit.

b. How much labor would the firm use if the wage is $10.50?

c. Suppose, instead, that the firm is a monopsonist in the factor market facing a supply curve for labor given in columns (3) and (4). This firm is a perfect competitor in the output market and the price of the output is $3.50 per unit. How much labor would be used? What would be the wage? Explain your answers and graph your solution, showing on the graph how you got your answers.

d. Now suppose the firm is a monopolist in the output market and a monopsonist in the input market where the demand for the output is given in columns (1) and (2) and the supply of labor is given in columns (3) and (4). What would be the profit-maximizing amount of labor used by this firm? And what would be the market wage? Explain your answer and graph your solution.

4. Consider the monopolist-monopsonist shown graphically in Figure E.11–2. Labor is the only variable input.

a. Show the equilibrium quantity of labor hired and the wage rate.

b. We emphasized in the text that, in a typically assumed case, a union that comes in and forces a wage increase will cause some unemployment. Suppose you represent such a union of this firm's employees. You can set any wage that you wish. In effect, you can simply set a wage and say to

**FIGURE E.11–2**

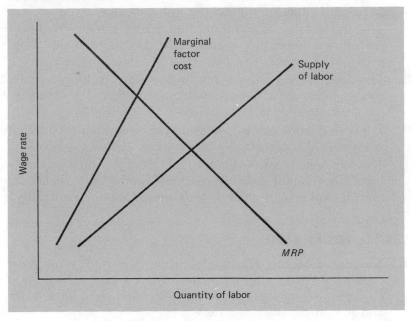

the firm, "You can hire all the labor you wish at this wage rate, but below this wage you get none." Thus, the wage is parametrically given to the firm by you.

(1) Show on the graph the *highest* wage that you can set and cause no *less* labor to be hired than was hired in part *a* of the question.

(2) Show how much labor would want to work for the firm at this wage but would not be hired.

(3) Show the wage that maximizes the amount of labor hired. (At this wage everyone who wants to work for this firm at the wage you set will be hired.)

Note:  This problem shows a minor exception to the point made in the text. The same thing could result from a minimum-wage law. But the analysis in the text generally holds.

5. Explain why the demand of a competitive industry for an input is less elastic than the sum of the demands of all the firms in the industry.

6. Monopolization of an industry will reduce the demand for an input but will not change wages unless the monopoly has monopsony power. Comment.

7. What would be the marginal product of an input that is free to a firm; that is, the input costs the firm nothing?

8. After the first unit of an input hired, why is the marginal factor cost of that input to a monopsonist greater than the supply price of the input?

9. The demand for a factor of production depends to some extent on the demand for the products produced by the input. Explain the connection.

10. "Unskilled workers have low wages because their productivity is low." Is this precise? Give a more complete explanation.

11. The wage rate is solely determined by the marginal productivity of labor. In any case, the marginal productivity theory says that all workers get what they deserve. Comment critically.

## ANALYTICAL PROBLEMS

1. You are attempting to get a labor union started. What conditions would make your job easier? What would make your job harder? Analyze the case of an individual firm, an industry, and an entire trade or profession.

2. Suppose that a particular firm in a competitive industry had a bigoted manager who refused to hire workers of a particular race even though these workers are as productive as those of other races.
   a. Under what conditions could the firm so discriminate?
   b. Under what conditions could it not?
   c. Would a monopolist be more likely to discriminate? Why or why not?

3. There is a proposal that government should provide an incentive payment to firms that hire unskilled handicapped workers. There would be a fixed amount per unskilled handicapped/hour used. How would this affect the wage and number of unskilled handicapped hired? If the payment is a lump sum regardless of the number hired, how would this affect your answer?

4. The fact that industries must pay a higher wage to get workers to work more means that none of these workers can have a negatively-sloped supply of labor. Analyze.

5. Theft is an occupation. How would each of the following circumstances affect the number of thieves and their remuneration. Think in terms of *MRP*.
   a. Higher minimum wages and broader coverage.
   b. Technological advances in the burglar-alarm industry.
   c. Longer sentences for theft.

     *d.* Economic prosperity.

     *e.* Recession.

     *f.* Laws restricting hours of work.

6. A member of Congress was quoted as saying that an increase in the minimum wage will not cause unemployment, since it will raise labor productivity. Comment critically.

7. There is a "shock theory" of minimum wage laws. They supposedly "shock" inefficient firms into becoming more efficient. The evidence is that, after increases in minimum wages, firms purchase new capital equipment to use with labor. Comment. (*Hint:* recall our theory of production.)

8. In many cities, the wages of school teachers are the same in any school for teachers with similar experience. Why do schools in the wealthier areas of the city generally get the best teachers?

9. A state government has recently spent $3 million of state funds to send units of the National Guard to a riot-torn city. What is the relevant economic cost of sending these troops? What other items should be included? (Recall our discussion of the draft.)

10. Go back to the exercise and solution about the draft associated with Figure 11–15. Analyze the possible differences in situations 2 and 3 as to their impact on the total output in the economy.

11. What discount rate makes the present value of $200 in one year equal to the $160 price of the investment now? What is the rate of return if the present price of the investment is $180?

12. Does it strike you as wrong that we do not compensate the brave men or women who climb a utility pole in a storm to restore electricity at least as much as we compensate the band leader on a television talk show? What about the nurses, paramedics, and enlisted military personnel who protect our lives and property? Are not these functions of more value to society? Comment.

13. Does Nolan Ryan, a well-known baseball pitcher, make more than a high school teacher because he has more talent?

14. Compare a person's decision to increase his or her human capital by obtaining additional education or training with a firm's decision to invest in physical capital.

15. Why might young Ph.D.s in economics choose to accept lower salaries to teach in prestigious departments, such as at Harvard or Stanford, knowing that the probability of tenure—a permanent position—is very low, rather than choose positions in government or business paying much higher salaries?

16. Professional football and basketball teams draft the top college seniors each year. If the drafted player wishes to play the sport—at least in the United States—he must sign with the team that drafts him. Most of the better players have agents. How does the theory of bilateral monopoly apply in this case? How are the beginning salaries determined? Would either party benefit if such a draft were declared illegal? Explain.

17. Some people say that, in general, firms do not spend enough training their employees because management believes the employees will be bid away by other firms at higher salaries after they have been trained. Thus, the training expenditure is allegedly wasted. Analyze this argument.

# Chapter 12

# Welfare and competition

## 12.1 INTRODUCTION

In the introduction to this text, we emphasized that economics is the study of choice. Because of scarcity, individuals must make decisions, and this involves choice. Economics is concerned with the way people make these choices and the results of such behavior. We can make predictions and explain economic phenomena using our theories about economic behavior.

Until now, we have been concerned with the decision-making or choice processes of *individuals*. Demand theory is based upon the theory of individual consumer behavior. To be sure, we combine these individuals into groups in order to obtain market demands, but these market demands result from the behavior or preferences of individuals or households.

Supply theory is likewise based upon the decision-making process of individual producers. Again, we combine producers into industries or markets, but behavior results from the decision making of the individual firms, not the group as a whole. We discussed briefly the fact that individual firms sometimes combine voluntarily

lowers the price of gasoline, while you oppose it because you place a higher value on your time. One person may feel that all pornography must be banned, whereas for other people reading pornography is their only leisure activity. Many faculty members think the university would be better off with more books and journals in the library at the expense of student study space. Students may think much more study space in the library would be better for the university. Who is the university? The faculty, the students, former students, the administration? In fact, could the entire student body speak as a unit?

Moreover, because actions taken by groups, or choices made by leaders of those groups, may harm some in the group and help others, we cannot say whether the group is better off or worse off. There is the further complication that we cannot compare changes in utility of different people. If you gain 10 hamburgers and someone else loses five six-packs of beer, we cannot compare your added utility with another person's loss in utility, because utility is neither measurable nor comparable. Even in the case of a social decision that takes $1,000 from you and gives it to a poorer person, one cannot say that society's utility increases. No one has ever proven that the marginal utility of income diminishes with increased income. Thus, in economics, we do not recognize the concept of a social utility function or a group preference ordering.

Any decision, whether the action of private producers or governmental decision makers, that benefits one group at the expense of another cannot be said to benefit or harm society, since we cannot compare changes in utility.[1] For the reasons given, it is virtually impossible to define social welfare accurately, and in particular, it is impossible to define *maximum* social welfare. Yet, almost daily, a society must make decisions that affect its welfare: *Should* we give foreign aid to underdeveloped countries? *Should* we tax the consumption of tobacco, alcohol, gasoline, jewelry, and so on? *Should* we give income to those households that cannot earn a specified level of income? There are many such questions that confront a society.

To specify maximum welfare or increases in welfare, we would have to specify a welfare function for society as a whole. Certainly, you might say, a society could vote upon all possible organizations and distributions, but even this leads to complications. Consider the following simple hypothetical case. There are three individuals in

---

[1] This statement is not quite accurate but is very close to being so. Say a social action harms one person and benefits another. If the one who is benefited is willing to bribe the one who is harmed sufficiently to compensate for the harm, both can be better off. This entire process is part of the subject matter in more advanced courses.

the society who will vote on three possible events, A, B, and C. The preference orderings of individuals 1, 2, and 3 are as follows:

1.  (ApB)(BpC)(ApC)
2.  (BpC)(CpA)(BpA)
3.  (CpA)(ApB)(CpB)

In the listing, (ApB) denotes that situation A is preferred to situation B. Note that each individual is rational in the sense that, if A is preferred to B and B to C, then A is preferred to C. If this three-person society voted upon events A and B, A would get a majority, as would B if they chose between B and C. But note that society would vote for C over A. This is inconsistent. If for society (ApB) and (BpC), then consistency would surely imply (ApC). But we see that this is not the case; this society might be said to be irrational. In any case, this simplified example shows that there can be inconsistency in determining social welfare by voting. Moreover, even with consistency in voting, we cannot say that majority rule must specify maximum social welfare. This method would involve interpersonal utility comparisons, and, as you know, economists cannot make such value judgments.

## Pareto optimality

Many, if not most, problems in public decisions, such as those discussed above, involve economic choices; so surely economists must be able to say *something* about them. Actually they can say very little. Economists cannot establish the goals of a society, nor can they say what is "good" for one person or for a collection of people. In general, economists can only determine the most efficient way to achieve a stipulated goal. Nonetheless, economists can make one prescriptive statement: If a change can be made such that one or more people are made better off and *none* worse off, the society's welfare will be increased if the change is made. We must first define "better off":

**Definition.** A person is said to be better off in situation A than in situation B if he or she gets as much of every good and service and more of at least one good or service in A than in B.

We can now define Pareto optimality.

**Definition.** A social organization is said to be Pareto optimal if there is no change that will benefit some people without making some others worse off.

This is admittedly a very weak concept of social welfare. To illustrate, suppose a new transcontinental highway is to be constructed. This will benefit millions of travelers. But it also forces the government to condemn (under the right of eminent domain) the home of a few families. These families, of course, are paid a "fair market price" for their property. However, some of the families may be unwilling to sell for a fair market price; yet they must by law, and they are made worse off. Millions may benefit and one may be harmed. Economists as economists cannot say that the new highway increases or decreases social welfare. For this reason, economists are primarily interested in Pareto optimality because it expresses efficiency and not because the concept is a social goal. Pareto efficiency is the major component of what economists call welfare economics.

To summarize the implications of the concept of Pareto optimally:

**Principle.**   (a) If a change will benefit one or more people without making *anyone* worse off, the change is socially desirable; (b) if a change helps some and hurts others—the *numbers* are immaterial—no conclusion can be reached by an economist.

### Consumer's surplus and Pareto efficiency

When economists analyze the effects of policy changes—for example, in cost-benefit analyses—they frequently find it impossible to use the Pareto rule. Unless consumers have identical preference patterns, in general, some benefit and some lose by these changes. As a substitute, the concept of consumer's surplus is used to determine whether or not a change, such as a change in price, is beneficial. Economists who compare consumer's surplus before and after the change say a price change benefits consumers if surplus increases and harms them if surplus falls.

Let us be more specific. Suppose a certain commodity has an effective price ceiling; i.e., price is set below the equilibrium market price. Panel A in Figure 12–1 illustrates the situation. With a price ceiling at $p_c$, consumer's surplus is $p_c nrt$. If prices were allowed to rise to the equilibrium price $p_e$, surplus would be $p_e nq$. Consumer's surplus would increase when prices rose if area $u$ is greater than area $v$, and fall if it is less.

The reason we cannot use the concept of Pareto optimality to analyze the results of eliminating the ceiling is because the ceiling causes shortages. Some consumers get the product at $p_c$, others do not. If the ceiling is eliminated, those who got the product at $p_c$ would be hurt, while those who could not buy it would be helped. On balance, it is impossible to use the Pareto criterion to say whether welfare rises if the ceiling is removed. Economists, however, frequently do compare areas $u$ and $v$ for the market demand curve, knowing full well that such a comparison is generally inconsistent with the definition of Pareto optimality.

The use of consumer's surplus is not always at odds with the definition of Pareto optimality, however. For instance, in panel B of Figure 12–1, we show a price floor at $p_f$. Consumer's surplus is the area $p_fab$ when prices are kept at $p_f$. If the floor is eliminated, price would fall to $p_e$, and consumer's surplus would be $p_eac$. Surplus rises by area $z$. In this case, since price is lowered for every con-

**FIGURE 12–1**
**Welfare consequences of a price ceiling and floor**

Panel A
Price ceiling

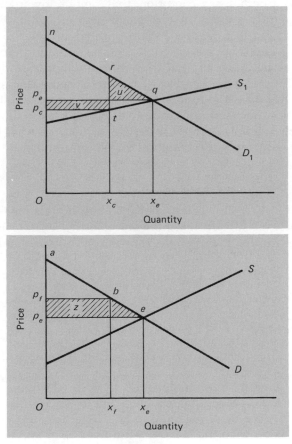

Panel B
Price floor

sumer, everyone who buys the product can buy more at the lower price. No consumer is harmed. Hence, the price decrease is also beneficial to consumers by the Pareto criterion.

Of course, in each diagram we have ignored whether producers are made better or worse off by the policy change. Thus, the use of consumer's and, for that matter, producer's, surplus requires great care at the market level. When surplus changes, frequently some gain and some lose—meaning we cannot determine whether welfare increases in the Pareto sense.

## 12.3 PERFECT COMPETITION AND PARETO OPTIMALITY

While the concept of Pareto optimality is a weak one, it does establish some useful boundaries for the role of economists in making welfare recommendations. We should emphasize that Pareto optimality is an efficiency condition, that a move toward Pareto optimality is simply a move to a more efficient allocation. An action that moves a group toward a Pareto optimal situation is the only condition in which we can say that a group is made better off. We must emphasize, however, that an infinite number of resource allocations can be said to be Pareto optimal, in the sense that no one can be made better off without making someone else worse off. None of these infinite number of allocations can be said to maximize social utility or to be socially preferable. In this section, we want to discuss how economists apply the notion of Pareto optimality.

### Edgeworth Box diagram

Markets exist in an economy because individuals have different marginal rates of substitution between goods. Let us consider the following example. Two people consume only two goods, an endowment of which they receive every week. These goods are hamburgers and milkshakes. Given preferences and the initial endowment, one person's marginal rate of substitution is three hamburgers for eight milkshakes. That is, the individual would be willing to exchange three hamburgers for eight milkshakes and remain indifferent. The second person's MRS is three hamburgers for six milkshakes. Thus, he or she would be willing to trade at the ratio of three to six.

Both can benefit from trade. One is willing to give up eight milkshakes to gain three hamburgers. The other requires only six milkshakes to give up three hamburgers. The first person gives up fewer milkshakes than the maximum number he or she would have been willing to trade in order to gain three added hamburgers. The person gains one more milkshake than he or she would have been willing to accept for the three hamburgers. Both make deals better than they would have been willing to make, and are therefore better off than they were before trade.

Or, put more realistically in money terms, McDonald's is willing to exchange hamburgers of a particular type for $1.95 each. If you are willing to trade more than $1.95 for a McDonald's hamburger, both you and McDonald's are made better off by the trade of $1.95 for one hamburger. The same analysis can be applied to any other type of exchange. Thus, markets occur when individuals' marginal rates of substitution are not equal. In fact, this is a major principle in economics.

**Principle.**  If two individuals have differing marginal rates of substitution, both can be made better off in the sense of attaining a more preferred level of consumption by exchange.

Economists frequently use a graphical method to analyze the above proposition, from which a certain amount of insight into the benefits of exchange can be gained. Assume only two people and only two goods. Each person has an *initial endowment* of each good, but each does not necessarily have the goods in the proportion that yields greatest satisfaction. To analyze exchange, we need to develop a graphical device known as the Edgeworth Box diagram, named for F. Y. Edgeworth, a famous British economist of the late 19th century.[2]

First, consider Figure 12–2. There are two consumption goods, $X$ and $Y$; these goods are available in absolutely fixed amounts. In addition, there are only two individuals in the society, A and B; they initially possess an endowment of $X$ and $Y$, but the endowment ratio is not the one either would choose if allowed to specify it. This problem is graphically illustrated by constructing an *origin* for A, labeled $O_A$, and plotting quantities of the two goods along the vertical and horizontal axes. Thus, from the origin $O_A$, the quantity of $X$ held by $A(X_A)$ is plotted on the horizontal axis and the quantity of $Y(Y_A)$ on the vertical axis. A similar graph for B, with origin $O_B$, may be constructed beside the graph for A. These two basic graphs are illustrated in panel A, Figure 12–2.

Next, rotate the B-graph 180 degrees to the left, so that it is actually "upside down" when viewed normally, as shown in panel B. The Edgeworth Box diagram is formed by bringing the two

---

[2] It has been pointed out to us by a reader of the manuscript, Professor Rodney Mabry, that Edgeworth had nothing to do with the development of the Edgeworth Box diagram; the true originator was V. Pareto. Not being historians of thought, we gratefully acknowledge this but yield to convention in naming the diagram.

**FIGURE 12–2**
Constructing the Edgeworth Box diagram

Panel A

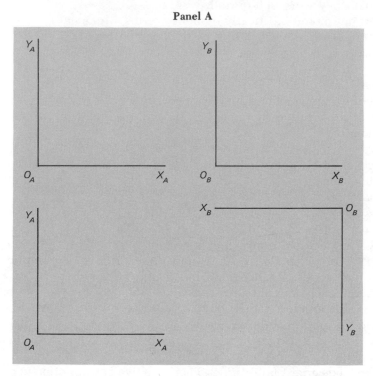

Panel B

graphs together. There could conceivably be a problem involving the lengths of the axes; if the $X$ axes meshed, the $Y$ axes might not. The problem does not, in fact, exist because of our assumption concerning fixed availabilities of $X$ and $Y$. $X_A + X_B$ must equal $X$, and $Y_A + Y_B$ must equal $Y$. The length of each axis measures the fixed quantity of the good it represents; when the two "halves" in panel B are brought together, both axes mesh. One thus obtains Figure 12–3.

Point $D$ in Figure 12–3 indicates the initial endowment of $X$ and $Y$ possessed by A and B. A begins with $x_A$ units of $X$ and $y_A$ units of $Y$. Since the aggregates are fixed, B must originally hold $x_B = X - x_A$ units of $X$ and $y_B = Y - y_A$ units of $Y$.

### Equilibrium of exchange

As a first step toward equilibrium analysis, consider an economy in which exchange of goods takes place. If you like, you may think of the problem in the following context. There exists a small country

**FIGURE 12–3**
Edgeworth Box diagram

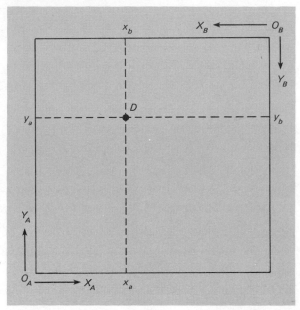

with only two inhabitants, A and B, each of whom owns one half the land area. A and B produce nothing; they merely gather goods of types $X$ and $Y$ that fall nightly. Each gathers only the goods that fall on his or her land; but the two types do not fall uniformly. There is a relatively heavy concentration of $Y$ on A's property and, consequently, a relatively heavy concentration of $X$ on B's land.

The problem of exchange is analyzed by means of the Edgeworth Box diagram in Figure 12–4. To the basic box diagram, the dimensions of which represent the nightly scattering of goods, we add indifference curves for A and B. For example, the curve $I_A$ shows combinations of $X$ and $Y$ that yield A the same level of satisfaction. As usual, $II_A$ represents a greater level of satisfaction than $I_A$; $III_A$ than $II_A$; and so on. Quite generally, A's well-being is enhanced by moving toward the $B$ origin; B, in turn, enjoys greater satisfaction the closer he or she moves toward the $A$ origin.

Suppose the initial endowment (the nightly fall of goods) is given by point $D$; A has $x_A$ units of $X$ and $y_A$ units of $Y$. Similarly, B has $x_B$ and $y_B$ units of $X$ and $Y$, respectively. The initial endowment places A on indifference curve $II_A$ and B on curve $I_B$. At point $D$, A's marginal rate of substitution of $X$ for $Y$, given by the slope of $TT'$, is relatively high; A would be willing to sacrifice, say, three units of $Y$ in order to obtain one additional unit of $X$. At the same point, B has a

**FIGURE 12–4**
General equilibrium of exchange

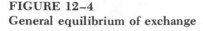
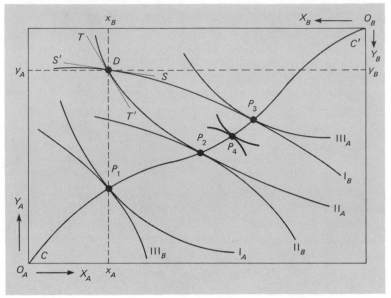

relatively low marginal rate of substitution, as shown by the slope of $SS'$. Or, turning it around, B has a relatively high marginal rate of substitution of $Y$ for $X$. Person B may, for example, be willing to forego four units of $X$ to obtain one unit of $Y$.

A situation such as this will always lead to exchange if the parties concerned are free to trade. From point $D$, A will trade some $Y$ to B, receiving $X$ in exchange. The exact bargain reached by the two traders cannot be determined. If B is the more skillful negotiator, B may induce A to move along $II_A$ to point $P_2$. All the benefits of trade goes to B, who jumps from $I_B$ to $II_B$. Or A might steer the bargain to point $P_3$, thereby increasing satisfaction from $II_A$ to $III_A$, B's utility level remaining $I_B$. Starting from point $D$, the ultimate exchange is very likely to lead to some point between $P_2$ and $P_3$, perhaps at a point such as $P_4$, at which two indifference curves are tangent. Both are therefore made better off by trade. But the skill of the bargainers and their initial endowments determine the exact location. In any case, one can be made better off without causing the other to become worse off, or both can become better off in the sense of attaining a higher level of utility.

One important thing can be said. Exchange will take place until the marginal rate of substitution of $X$ for $Y$ is the same for both traders. If the two marginal rates are different, one or both parties can benefit from exchange; neither party need lose. In other words, the exchange equilibrium can occur only at points such as $P_1$, $P_2$, $P_3$, or $P_4$ in Figure 12–4. The locus $CC'$, called the *contract curve*, is a curve joining all points of tangency between one of A's indifference curves and one of B's. It is thus the locus along which the marginal rates of substitution are equal for both traders. We accordingly have the following principle:

**Principle.** The general equilibrium of exchange occurs at a point where the marginal rate of substitution between every pair of goods is the same for all parties consuming both goods. The exchange equilibrium is not unique; it may occur at any point along the contract curve.

The contract curve is an optimal locus in the sense that, if the trading parties are located at some point not on the curve, one or both can benefit, and neither suffer a loss, by exchanging goods so as to move to a point on the curve. To be sure, some points not on the curve are more preferable to one or the other party than are some points on the curve. But, for any point not on the curve, one or more attainable points on the curve are preferable. The chief characteristic of each point on the contract curve is that a movement along the curve away from the point must benefit one party and harm the other. Every organization that leads to a point on the contract curve is said to be a *Pareto-optimal organization*.

**Definition.** A Pareto-optimal organization is one in which any change that makes some people better off makes some others worse off. That is, an organization is Pareto optimal if, and only if, there is no change that will make one or more better off without making anyone worse off. Thus, every point on the contract curve is Pareto optimal, and the contract curve is a locus of Pareto optimality.

To summarize, the economics behind all of the graphical analysis simply says that people will trade only if the trade makes the participants better off. Only if each person's MRS is the same will it be impossible to make both parties better off through trade.

## APPLICATIONS

### Uses of the theory of trade: Goods-in-kind and water rationing

We can use our concept of the Edgeworth Box to analyze the economics of government giving people goods-in-kind instead of money. Take food stamps, for instance. The government gives stamps that can be used to purchase food—in reality to purchase only certain kinds of goods—rather than money. If individuals pay a different price for food, there is motivation for exchange. Someone with food stamps pays a different price for food than someone without them. Or, possibly, we have two individuals both of whom receive food stamps and have other income. Unless the allocation of stamps and incomes between the two individuals is *precisely* on the contract curve, both individuals can be made better off by trade, in the sense of being able to reach higher indifference curves. Thus, trade will take place. But, to the extent that trade in goods—in this case food stamps—is less efficient than trade in organized markets because of transaction costs, there is waste involved in giving goods-in-kind.

"All well and good," some will say. Certainly there is waste involved in giving goods in kind rather than income, but if government gives income rather than goods, recipients will use some of the income to buy things that are not good for them, like liquor or drugs, and not buy desirable goods such as food for the family.

You can answer this question in the following way. Certainly income recipients may use some of the income to buy liquor or drugs, but if the government gives food stamps, the recipients can trade stamps for money in black markets. Since the transaction is illegal, food stamps yield a lower value. The stamp sellers then pay for the liquor or drugs with the money received. Since the market for stamps is less efficient than legal organized markets, the individual may give up more food to buy liquor than would have been the case if income had been given. The waste in the illegal transaction would have been the sacrifice of food.

Another application of the Edgeworth Box diagram is the analysis of water rationing. During the winter of 1976–77, a serious drought occurred in the Western United States, causing considerable decreases in the water supplies of many communities. In his *Newsweek* column of March 21, 1977, the famous economist, Milton Friedman, discussed the approach of one such community, Marin County, California, a prosperous bedroom community north of San Francisco.

In response to the drought, Marin County rationed water to 37 gallons per person per day for a household of four. Very stiff fines were imposed for exceeding this level. Furthermore, one household could not legally sell part of its water allocation to another household. Thus, no household would have the incentive to sacrifice or cut down and use less than 37 gallons of water.

We can analyze the situation with an Edgeworth Box diagram in Figure 12–5. Let A and B be any two individuals. The origins for A and B are at $O_A$ and $O_B$. The income of A is $I_A$; B's income is $I_B$. Each receives exactly the same amount of water; $W_A = W_B$. The

**FIGURE 12–5**
Trade in water

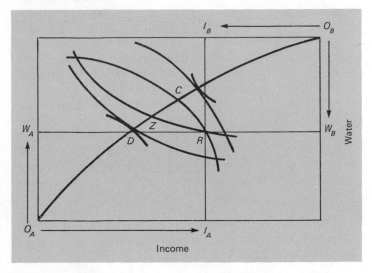

original allocation is shown as point $R$. The contract curve is $O_A O_B$, showing the locus of points of tangency between A's and B's indifference curves.

If trade were allowed, both individuals could be made better off than they were at point $R$. Their consumption sets would move to some point on the contract curve between points $Z$ and $C$. The only circumstances under which trade would not benefit both would be if the incomes of each were precisely such that point $D$, where the contract curve crosses $W_A W_B$, was the original allocation. This would appear to be a rather remote possibility. Otherwise trade would be preferable.

## Equilibrium of production

The analysis of the equilibrium of production is quite similar to that of the equilibrium of exchange. We can model production in the same way we did exchange. Suppose we have two firms producing two commodities with two inputs. We label the firms 1 and 2; commodities $X$ and $Y$ are produced using two inputs, $K$ and $L$, as shown in Figure 12–6.

We form an Edgeworth Box diagram similar to the diagram used to analyze exchange. Firm 1 produces good $X$. The origin of its

**FIGURE 12–6**
Pareto optimality in production

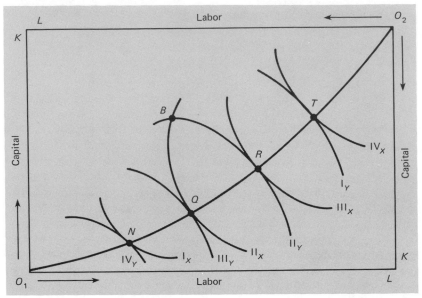

isoquant map is at $O_1$; a portion of the map is shown by isoquants $I_X$, $II_X$, $III_X$, and $IV_X$. Firm 2 produces $Y$. Its isoquant map is "turned around"; the origin is at $O_2$. The isoquant map is shown by $I_Y$, $II_Y$, $III_Y$, and $IV_Y$, and so forth. The total amounts of labor and capital available to the two firms are, respectively, $O_2L = O_1L$ and $O_2K = O_1K$; i.e., labor is plotted along the horizontal axis and capital along the vertical.

Equilibrium of production occurs at any combination of outputs at which the marginal rates of technical substitution between labor and capital are equal for the two firms. This means the isoquants must be tangent so that $MRTS_1 = MRTS_2$. To see why, suppose capital and labor are allocated between the two firms so that production takes place at point $B$. Firm 1 is producing the output given by $II_X$ and firm 2, the output given by $II_Y$. A reallocation of capital and labor between the two firms could move the production point to $R$—increased output for 1 with no decrease for 2—or to $Q$—increased output for 2 with no decrease for 1. Or both firms could increase output by moving to some combination between $II_X$ and $II_Y$, say to a point along the line $QR$. At any point at which the isoquants are not tangent, capital and labor can be reallocated so that one firm can increase its output without reducing the output of the other, or both can increase output.

The locus of points at which the isoquants are tangent is the *contract curve*. If the firms are at a point on the contract curve, one firm can increase production only at the expense of a decrease in production for the other firm. To see this point, assume that production takes place at a point such as $Q$. Next, move in any direction to a point either on or off the contract curve, and note that the output of one firm must fall while the output of the other must rise or remain constant if the movement is along an isoquant.

It is obvious that the production equilibrium is not unique; it can occur at an infinite number of combinations on the contract curve. But each point on this curve represents a Pareto-optimal equilibrium. Production along the contract curve means that all resources are being used and society is producing on its production-possibilities frontier. As you will recall, the production-possibilities frontier shows the opportunity cost of producing more of some good; that is, the rate at which some goods must be given up in order for society to have more of some other goods.

We can derive the production-possibilities frontier from the contract curve in Figure 12–6. It is a very simple transformation. Corresponding to each point on the production contract curve is a specific level of output of good $X$ and good $Y$. For example, at point $N$ in Figure 12–6, firm 1 is producing the amount of $X$ represented by isoquant $I_X$. The production of $Y$ is represented by isoquant $IV_Y$. A relatively large amount of labor and capital is used in the production of $Y$. These respective amounts of goods $X$ and $Y$ represent a point on the production-possibilities frontier. We call this point $N'$ in Figure 12–7. As we move to higher isoquants in the production of $X$, less $Y$ is produced. The isoquants tangent at $Q, R,$ and $T$ represent additional points on the production-possibilities frontier. They are labeled $Q', R',$ and $T'$. Society can choose any point on the frontier, all of which are Pareto optimal.

### General equilibrium

As was implied in the introduction to this chapter, we have thus far been concerned with conditions of partial equilibrium. These are equilibrium conditions for individual consumers, firms, industries, and markets. These conditions provide our basic decision-making tools in economics.

General equilibrium is concerned with the conditions under which all markets are in equilibrium. Given a set of commodity prices, consumers determine their demands by equating marginal rates of substitution with the corresponding commodity-price ratios. Given a set of input prices, producers determine supply by equating the marginal rates of technical substitution with the corresponding

**FIGURE 12–7**
**Derivation of production possibilities**

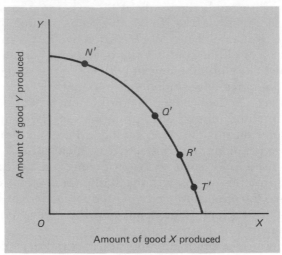

Amount of good X produced

input-price ratios. Finally, workers determine the supply of labor by equating the marginal rate of substitution of income for leisure with the wage rate. The *problem* of general equilibrium is as follows: can we find a set of prices at which the demands of consumers are voluntarily fulfilled by the supplies of producers who use all productive resources that are voluntarily supplied at the going set of prices? If so, a general equilibrium may exist.

Clearly, we could provide a fanciful example in which an auctioneer assembles all participants in the economy and "zeros in" on a set of prices in which all markets are in equilibrium. But this process is not even approximately descriptive of any real-world markets. However, competitive bids and counterbids in all markets do tend to push the economy *toward* a general equilibrium. Needless to say, such an equilibrium is never, in fact, even approximately attained. But there is a *tendency* toward it; and, at times, we can profitably analyze the situation that would exist if the general equilibrium existed. This is true for many problems, but it is perhaps most important in analyzing the social welfare results of various forms of market and economic organization.

General equilibrium occurs when we have equilibrium in both exchange and production. We can effectively combine the Edgeworth Boxes for production and exchange by placing the exchange box inside the production-possibilities frontier, which is derived from the production contract curve. Each point on the frontier is a point on the production contract curve. It determines what is

**FIGURE 12–8**

**General equilibrium in production and exchange**

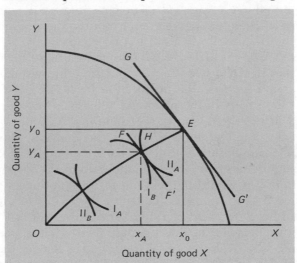

available for exchange in our two-good–two-consumer model. As Figure 12–8 shows, a tangent to the selected point on the frontier is the slope of the production-possibilities frontier. It is called the *marginal rate of transformation.* Hence, the slope of the tangent at $E$ represents the opportunity cost of producing another unit of $X$. More exactly, if $\Delta X = 1$, the slope $\Delta Y / \Delta X = \Delta Y$ is precisely how much of good $Y$ society must forego to have another unit of $X$.

Production at $E$ is Pareto optimal. Optimality in exchange comes from letting consumers A and B distribute the $x_0$ and $y_0$ output. Pareto efficiency, as we already know, exists along the exchange contract line. Let the Edgeworth Box for exchange be $Oy_0Ex_0$, with $x_0$ and $y_0$ being, from the production-possibilities frontier, the total amounts of $X$ and $Y$ available. The origin for the consumer with indifference map $I_A$ and $II_A$ is at $O$; the consumer with indifference map $I_B$, $II_B$ has the origin at $E$. Clearly, there are an infinite number of possible allocations along the contract curve. But general equilibrium occurs when the marginal rate of transformation $(MRT)$—the slope of the production-possibilities frontier—is equal to the marginal rate of substitution for both consumers. Because we drop the negative sign on the slope of the $MRS$, we do so also for the $MRT$. In Figure 12–8, general equilibrium exists at point $H$ when $x_0$ and $y_0$ are produced. It is here that $FF'$ and $GG'$ have the same slope. Consumer A gets $x_A$ and $y_A$ units of output; consumer B gets $(x_0 - x_A)$ and $(y_0 - y_A)$ units. The amount of labor and capital used in production at $E$ is found by going back to the point on the production contract curve. Of course, there could be other, perhaps many other, points on the contract curve at which the slopes of the indifference curves are equal to $FF'$ and $GG'$. The consumers will settle at such a point, but, if there are several such points, the one chosen will depend upon the distribution of the two goods.

Why must $MRS_A = MRS_B = MRT$ in general equilibrium? First, we know that if $MRS_A$ is not equal to $MRS_B$, individuals A and B could trade and increase the utility of at least one person without decreasing the utility of the other. So, whatever the output, $MRS_A$ must equal $MRS_B$. Next, suppose $MRS_A$ (or $MRS_B$) does not equal the $MRT$. For example, let the $MRS$ for either consumer be 2 and the $MRT$ be 3. Consumers are willing to take 2 more units of $Y$ for 1 unit of $X$, while producers can produce 3 more units of $Y$ if they produce 1 less unit of $X$. It would be possible for the producers to make 3 more $Y$, give 2 to consumer A (or B) for the $X$ lost to produce the extra $Y$, and have one unit of $Y$ left. The extra unit of $Y$ could be given to either person A or B to increase utility. Thus, welfare rises by the Pareto rule. Welfare can be improved as long as the absolute value of the slope of the production-possibilities curve is not equal to the common marginal rate of substitution in exchange.

### Equilibrium in perfect competition

Assume that there is perfect competition in every market. We shall show that the set of input and output prices that establishes a general economic equilibrium will also, in general, establish a Pareto-optimal organization for society.

Let us first consider consumers. If there is perfect competition, all consumers face the same set of commodity prices. Since each consuming unit sets $MRS$ equal to the price ratio, the $MRS$ of any one consumer is equal to the $MRS$ of *any other* consuming unit. Since all consumers are just willing to exchange commodities in the same ratio, it is impossible to make one better off without making another worse off. (That is, suppose the *common MRS* of X for Y is $3:1$. If someone is allowed to trade $2:1$, others must be *forced* to trade at a ratio at which they would not voluntarily trade.) Thus, a Pareto optimum is established among buyers.

Next, consider producers. In maximizing profit, entrepreneurs necessarily arrange the combination of inputs so as to minimize the unit cost of production. Under perfect competition, the factor-price ratios are the same to all producers. Since each producer equates $MRTS$ to the common factor-price ratio, the $MRTS$ is the same for all. Consequently, there is no reallocation of inputs that would increase one producer's output without reducing another's. Again we have a Pareto-optimal organization.

On the production side, the marginal rate of transformation represents the opportunity cost of producing another unit of either good. When perfectly competitive firms maximize profits, they set price equal to marginal cost or the opportunity cost of producing another unit. Notice now what the ratio of the marginal costs of two goods, $X$ and $Y$, tells us: $MC_X/MC_Y$ tells us how many units of $Y$ must be given up to produce another unit of $X$. For instance, if $MC_X = \$3$ and $MC_Y = \$1$, three units of $Y$ must be released at the margin to produce one more unit of $X$. Thus, $MC_X/MC_Y$ is equal to the slope of the production-possibilities curve. Under perfect competition,

$$\frac{MC_X}{MC_Y} = \frac{P_X}{P_Y}.$$

Since it is also true from the above that

$$MRS_{X \text{ for } Y} = \frac{P_X}{P_Y},$$

the marginal rate of transformation is equal to the marginal rate of substitution.

Finally, in this competitive general equilibrium, the number of hours of work voluntarily offered is exactly equal to the number of hours voluntarily demanded. An increase in wages would help some, but some others would be unemployed. That is, an increase in wages would make some better off, some worse off. A decrease in wages would cause an excess demand. Thus, a change in wages from the general equilibrium level will upset both Pareto optimality and general equilibrium.

Let us reemphasize that Pareto optimality does not necessarily indicate maximum attainable welfare or the maximum attainable level of utility for society as a whole. As we stressed above in this chapter, to specify maximum welfare, we would have to specify a welfare function for society as a whole. This we cannot do. Thus, perfect competition does lead to *some* final Pareto-optimal equilibrium point, but this is an arbitrary point because any other point on the production-possibilities frontier can also be Pareto optimal in the sense of being efficient.

The final point that is attained depends upon, among other things, the initial "starting point," or the initial distribution of income. Government may well become involved, and generally does become involved, in deciding what the initial distribution of income will be. But, while representatives may decide that the existing income distribution is preferable to any other, or that some other distribution is more preferred, the role of an economist is not to decide what distribution is best, even under perfect competition. An economist's role does include pointing out the economic consequences of changing the distribution. All an economist can say is that, if one or more people can be made better off by an action without anyone else being made worse off, the action makes the group better off.

## 12.4 PERFECT COMPETITION AND SOCIAL WELFARE

So far we have said that perfect competition will lead to a Pareto optimum, and this is the most economists can say. In certain cases, even this is not true. Either perfect competition may break down, or the results of perfect competition are not socially desirable in the sense of being Pareto optimal. We shall treat these cases briefly, with one important caveat. What we have to say is only an introductory statement. It requires a great deal of work to adequately treat the theory surrounding market failures.

There are several possible causes for market failure—failure in the sense that the existence of perfect competition does not lead to a Pareto-optimal situation. We will briefly discuss some of these in this section; then, in the next section, we study in more depth a very significant factor in market failure—property rights and externalities.

### Public goods

The first case to be discussed is that of public goods. A *public good* is a good for which consumption by individual A does not preclude its consumption by individuals B, C, D, and so on. An apple is a private good. If you consume an apple, no one else can consume the same one. While there is perhaps no good that precisely meets the definition of a public good, many goods exhibit some characteristics of public goods. Some examples may be open-air concerts or fireworks displays. Up to a point, as many people as desire can "consume" these goods. The same is true for public schools, libraries, roads, and so on. But after a point, a certain "crowding" effect sets in, and they are no longer public goods.

Perhaps a more illuminating way of describing a public good is to say a good is a public good if the marginal cost of letting an additional person consuming the good is zero once it is produced. National defense, parks, radio and television signals are examples of goods fitting this description. Generally, private markets provide too little of these goods. Since the marginal cost of letting another person consume the good is zero, the optimal price is zero. It costs society nothing for these "additional" consumers to consume the good. Thus, if these customers could consume the good at zero price, they would be better off and no one would be worse off, in the sense that none of society's resources would have to be used to add an additional consumer. But total costs are not zero. Private production must set a positive price to cover costs; hence, price will be greater than marginal cost, and a less-than-optimal amount of the good is consumed.

To summarize, regardless of the total consumption of the public good, the same amount of society's resources must be used to produce it. It is reasonable to assume that, for some consumers who elect not to purchase the public good, the marginal utility of the good is not zero. That is, even though for some consumers in the case of good $A$

$$\frac{MU_a}{p_a} < \frac{MU_b}{p_b} = \frac{MU_c}{p_c}, \text{ etc.,}$$

and $MU_a \neq 0$. Thus, if a zero price were charged these consumers, some would consume good $A$. If $A$ is a public good, they would be better off, and no one would be worse off because no more of society's resources are used when the good is consumed.

**Principle.** If the production of a public good is in the hands of private enterprise, social welfare is less than it would otherwise be because some consumers are excluded from the market when price is greater than zero. Since their consumption of the good is "free" to society in the sense that it entails no further resource sacrifice, society as a whole would be better off if these people were allowed to consume the good at zero price; but under free enterprise, they are not allowed to.

This is not an indictment of the market system. It is merely a recognition of the fact that there may be some goods that are not optimally consumed when price is set by the competitive market mechanism. It is for this reason that governments frequently supply public goods.

Analytically, the provision of public goods is different from the provision of private goods. Recall that market demand for a private good is found by horizontally adding the demand curves for each individual, as shown in Figure 12–9, panel A. We show two consumers, $A$ and $B$. Market demand is $DD'$, the horizontal sum of the two demand curves, $D_AD_A'$ and $D_BD_B'$. For instance, at $p_0$, $x_T = x_A + x_B$ or the sum of distances $p_0L + LM = p_0N$. A competitive market, then, operates at the intersection of market supply and demand. Public goods, however, are goods that can be consumed by different people at the same time. Hence, individuals can pay for a good that other individuals are also willing to pay for. Take, for example, public parks. What is the demand for public parks? Ignoring possible congestion, park land is shared; the market demand must therefore be the sum of each person's demand curve for the *same* land.

Consequently, in the case of public goods, demands curves must

be summed vertically because each person consumes the same
good. To see why, consider the situation shown in panel B, Figure
12–9. Two consumers, A and B, demand some public good; their
demands are, respectively, $D_A D'_A$ and $D_B D'_B$. Consumer A is willing
to pay $p_A$ to use $x_0$ of the public good $X$. Consumer B will pay $p_B$ for
the same amount $x_0$. Thus, the two consumers together will pay
$p_A + p_B = p_M$ for $x_0$. Summing the two demands over all amounts of
$X$, we obtain the market demand for the public good, $DD'$. For example, $x_0 t + tv = x_0 v$ yields market demand. The optimal price

**FIGURE 12–9**
**The market for private and public goods**

Panel A
Private goods

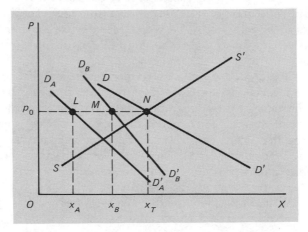

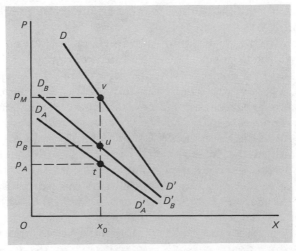

Panel B
Public goods

and amount of the good are determined by the intersection of marginal cost and market demand. Thus, price should be zero if the marginal cost of an additional unit is zero. But, as noted, this price would not cover total costs.

Thus, the problem is who should pay the initial cost of the public good? This is a question still open to debate and is an important topic in public finance. There is also the issue of whether or not there really exists such a thing as a pure public good. Frequently, the marginal cost of adding another consumer is not zero. Thus, the good is not a public good. In this case, there should be a positive price charged for the good. Still, total revenue may not cover the total cost of providing the good. Now the question is who should finance the deficit. Generally, if anyone does, government does. There are numerous examples of public goods in which we see consumers paying part of the cost of consumption, but not the whole cost. National parks are one example. Even though tourists are charged an entrance fee, national parks are subsidized by tax revenue. Gate fees do not pay the entire cost of the park.

A very closely related problem is that for some goods, exclusion from consumption is not technically feasible. Some examples are lighthouses, national defense, and dams. Suppose, for example, that 1,000 families live along a river that floods every few years and causes these people damage. An enterprising person could come along and offer to build a dam, charging each household an amount per year less than the expected value of the damage from flooding in the absence of the dam. Suppose you lived on the river; what would you say when asked to pay your share of the price? Probably, "Forget it." There would be no incentive to pay. How could a dam be built to protect everyone else's property but not protect yours? If one person had no incentive to pay, neither would anyone else. Thus, a dam that would benefit everyone more than it costs everyone would not be constructed because of the inability to exclude those who do not pay.

Or how could the nation defend itself from attack without defending St. Louis, Houston, or any other individual cities in which the citizens did not choose to pay for defense. While it may be technically possible to exclude nonpaying ships from the use of a lighthouse, it might be economically unfeasible to do so. Frequently, in such cases, people allow government the role of providing such services, for which there is this "free rider" problem.

### Imperfect competition

Another way in which the market mechanism may fail to provide a Pareto-efficient outcome is by a breakdown in competition itself. We know that, when there is imperfect competition, price is set above marginal cost. This, in general, violates the Pareto condition that requires for any two goods

$$\frac{MC_x}{MC_y} = \frac{P_x}{P_y}.$$

This condition was met under perfect competition, because competitive firms set marginal cost equal to price. Rearranging terms in the above equation we see that

$$\frac{MC_x}{P_x} = \frac{MC_y}{P_y} = 1$$

under perfect competition.

This last relation helps us understand why imperfect competition usually is not Pareto optimal, but, under special conditions, may be. Imperfect competition sets price above marginal cost, and the difference between them is almost never the same across industries. Hence,

$$\frac{MC_x}{MC_y} \neq \frac{P_x}{P_y}$$

under most circumstances for imperfect competition. However, it is not correct to say that imperfect competition categorically violates the Pareto rule. It could be true that for any two industries that

$$\frac{MC_x}{P_x} = \frac{MC_y}{P_y} < 1.$$

In other words, the Pareto-efficiency condition is not violated if the *ratio* of marginal cost to price is equal in each industry.

In reality, this is a very unlikely event. For one thing, the ratio depends upon the elasticity of demand faced by a firm. This varies a great deal from product to product and firm to firm. Secondly, marginal cost is determined by technology. Given different demand elasticities, production technologies would have to adjust marginal cost to just maintain the price–marginal cost ratio in other industries, and this is stretching the likelihood of such an event ever occurring.

In summary we have the following principle:

**Principle.** If there is imperfect competition, price is usually greater than marginal cost in equilibrium, and the market price mechanism will not, in general, allocate resources efficiently.

There is no uniform agreement among economists concerning the role of government in such cases. Some say, "Let it go; conditions are not perfect, but government would make it worse." Others say the government should carry out some form of regulation that forces firms to price close to marginal cost. There is no universal agreement, and the opinions are generally based on past observations and value judgments, and vary from industry to industry.

### Information

Most economists believe that market failure may also occur because of the absence of perfect knowledge among consumers. Perfect knowledge includes knowledge on the part of consumers of all benefits and hazards associated with a product. For the average consumer, this level of knowledge is a practical impossibility. Consumers, for instance, are often unaware of the side effects of chemicals in hair spray or floor wax; foods may contain harmful substances that are listed on the label, but mean nothing to the shopper; automobiles may have faulty designs that only an engineer can evaluate, and so on.

A lack of information distorts the preferences of consumers. When consumers are unaware of the full effects of dangerous products, they may be willing to purchase more of the commodity at the going price than they would under the condition of complete information. In other words, a lack of information causes misperceptions which affect the *MRS* between two products in a consumer's preference map. Better information would shift the contract curve in the Edgeworth exchange box. Hence, it could bring consumers closer to efficient exchange; distorted preferences lead to a distorted equilibrium.

In some cases, consumers agree to encourage specific governmental bodies such as the Food and Drug Administration (FDA) or the Consumer Product Safety Commission (CPSC) to provide information on products. For instance, the CPSC annually inspects children's toys and alerts consumers to potentially dangerous features. Beyond this, government agencies may even set standards that eliminate the danger. Usually, the danger involved is reduced, but the product is more expensive. For example, the CPSC has the authority to set product safety standards when they think the need arises. All products sold must meet these standards. In the mid-1970s, the commission determined that baby cribs were unsafe because infants could slip through the crib bars. So it set a maximum distance between the bars of cribs. Manufacturers as a group had to place bars closer together, and cribs became more expensive.

To the consumer, safety standards involve a trade-off. While standards usually relieve buyers of evaluating the hazards of products, they also make manufacturers conform to designs that restrict product variety. For instance, in the case of baby cribs, safety standards prevented consumers from buying less expensive cribs that were undoubtedly not as safe as those that conformed to the CPSC guidelines, but nevertheless may have suited a consumer's purposes and budget.

Whether a lack of information necessitates regulation is debatable. Many economists would argue that the market failure requires only additional information, not regulation. On the other hand, more is involved than simply acquiring a publication or reading a more informative description of a product. Once information is acquired, it must be studied, and if it is complicated or technically sophisticated, the costs associated with digesting the information can be high. Under these circumstances, many economists argue that safety and quality regulation are legitimate functions of government.

## 12.5 OWNERSHIP EXTERNALITIES

We have covered very briefly some circumstances in which markets may not necessarily provide a Pareto-optimal equilibrium. In these cases, many arguments have been made for some type of governmental intervention.

Quite possibly, a much more important problem of the market concerns the question of externalities, where the marginal private cost or benefit of some activity does not equal the marginal social cost or benefit of that activity. A very large part of the problem of externalities is closely related to the incomplete assignment of property rights.

For the most part in this text, though certainly not always, we have simply assumed away the problem of externalities and incomplete assignment of property rights. In this section, we will examine some aspects of these problems. While these are complex and far-reaching problems, here we are able to merely touch upon the major issues involved.

### Definition of externalities

An *external economy* is said to exist when marginal social cost is less than marginal private cost. Thus, when marginal private cost equals marginal social benefit, marginal social cost is less than marginal social benefit. More resources *should* be allocated to producing the commodity in question, but they are not. On the other hand, an *external diseconomy* exists when marginal social cost exceeds marginal private cost. At such a point, marginal social benefit is less than marginal social cost. An undesirably large amount of resources is allocated to producing the commodity in question.

> **Definition.** An external economy (diseconomy) exists when marginal so-
> cial cost is less than (greater than) marginal private cost.

At this stage, it is quite reasonable to ask *how* marginal private
cost and marginal social cost can diverge. One of the chief answers
is "by the existence of ownership externalities." Briefly, this means
that there is some scarce resource owned by a person, but for some
reason the owner cannot charge a price for the use of this resource.
And when prices cannot be charged, misallocation of resources results.

The now classic example of ownership externalities was first
brought up by the economist J. E. Meade in 1952.[3] A beekeeper
raises bees for honey. The ideal location for beehives is in fields
with lots of spring blossoms. While bees make honey, they also
pollinate blossoms, which, say for apple orchards, generates more
fruit in the fall. Hence, both the beekeeper and the apple farmer
benefit by being located close to one another. The beekeeper benefits because the apple blossoms are a source of nectar for bees,
and the apple farmer benefits from having the blossoms pollinated.
But these benefits are not necessarily paid for in the market. Hence,
for both the beekeeper and the farmer, private costs are greater than
social costs. Too few bees and too few trees exist as a result.

An example of an external diseconomy, when marginal social cost
exceeds marginal private cost, might be pollution. Suppose a commercial fishing industry exists at the mouth of a river. Let a factory
locate upstream. The factory dumps its waste into the river, killing
some of the fish downstream and, consequently, lowering the
amount of fish caught each day. Since the private cost to the factory
does not include the resulting reduced incomes of the downstream
fishermen, social cost is less than private cost. Too much factory
output is produced. There are many other examples of such external
diseconomies—some as simple as this, others much more complex.
The remedy is usually difficult.

## APPLICATION

### Externalities and urban renewal[4]

Based on our economic theory, we would expect that an individual who owns a piece of property would keep the property devel-

---

[3] J. E. Meade, "External Economies and Diseconomies in a Competitive Situation," *Economic Journal* 62, no. 245 (March 1952): 54–67.

[4] This section is based upon a paper by O. A. Davis and A. B. Winston, "The
Economics of Urban Renewal," *Law and Contemporary Problems* 26, no. 1 (Winter
1961): 105–117.

oped and repaired so long as the marginal benefits exceed the individual marginal costs of such repairs. There should be no reason for more than the optimal amount of "urban blight" under these circumstances. But, with certain ownership externalities, completely rational people may well allow their property to deteriorate under these conditions.

Note first that the value of a piece of urban property—houses, apartments, and so on—depends to some extent on the condition of other property in the neighborhood. Suppose there are only two properties, one owned by owner A, the other by owner B. Each is attempting to decide whether or not to make an added investment in repair. Both are reaping some return from the property. Each owner has made an initial investment and has an additional sum invested in bonds. Each is making an average return of 4 percent from the property and the bonds, and this return is expected to continue, even if no money is taken out of bonds and put into property repair.

If both owners take their money out of bonds and invest in property repair, each will make a return of 7 percent. Clearly, each will be better off. There is a problem, however. Suppose one owner invests the bond money in repairs while the other does not. One property is improved and the other remains run down. The owner who improves the property gives up the return from the bonds, but the property return does not increase much because it remains next to a deteriorated property. In this case, the improving owner's total return falls to 3 percent. The loss of bond income more than offsets the increase in income from improving the property.

On the other hand, the owner who did not improve the property retains the bond income and, in addition, finds that the return on the unimproved property increases because of being next to an improved piece of property. Perhaps the total return from property and bonds increases to 10 percent. These changes in return result no matter who does the repair and who does not. The owner who does not repair the property keeps the bond return and benefits from the better neighborhood.

Suppose both owners know the expected return but do not know what the other will do. If owner A decides to invest, it will be to owner B's advantage not to invest—a 10 percent compared to a 7 percent return. Owner A knows this and, therefore, knows that the investment will cause a decrease in total return from 4 to 3 percent. Owner B knows the same conditions apply to his or her own investment decision also. Therefore, neither invests. However, if both invest, each would be better off.[5]

---

[5] Such analysis is closely related to the prisoner's dilemma discussed in Chapter 10.

As the authors of the paper that set forth this example noted, the "neighborhood" effect must be strong enough to get the results set forth. They also noted—and you probably have already deduced it—that there is a solution to the problem. One owner can simply buy out the other owner and improve both properties. Each would be made better off.

But if there were many such properties in the area, the transactions cost, or the cost of "putting the deal together" might very well outweigh the benefits from one individual buying up all of the property. In any case, one owner of a small piece of property might hold out for so large an amount as to thwart the deal.

There is the danger of attributing too many problems to ownership externalities and saying simply that the competitive marketplace does not allocate efficiently. One may or may not be happy with the results of competition, but market failures as a result of these externalities when property rights are well defined are not all that easily come by. Moreover, the "solution" of government intervention may be no more satisfactory than the market solution.

We could, and many do, carry the externality problem to the extreme. Certainly, if a large group of people drive big fast cars, the price of gasoline rises. Some benefit; some lose. Selling wheat to Russia may increase the price of bread; again, some benefit, some lose. If I burn coal, the world has less coal. These externalities are not what we mean by market failure or the problems of competition. In these cases, government intervention makes some better off and some worse off. The decision simply involves interpersonal utility comparisons, a domain in which the economist does not belong. What we have stressed thus far are cases in which competition may not be Pareto optimal. To intervene or not to intervene is a decision for government. Economists can only point out the potential results, theoretical and historical, of such intervention.

### Property rights and externalities[6]

Up to now in the discussion of externalities, the property rights of resource owners were fairly well defined. Problems would arise only because the production or investment or even consumption decisions of some affected the incomes or utilities of others. The

---

[6] This section is in large part based on S. Pejovich, *Fundamentals of Economics* (Dallas, Tex.: The Fisher Institute, 1979), chapter 2.

problem of externalities becomes more serious when property rights are not well defined or when no one has property rights in the case of some scarce resources.

The most complete concept of property rights, and that which we have used throughout the text, is that of ownership of one's property. One can use the property in any way, subject to laws concerning injury to other parties. A less complete right is the right to use the property of someone else and to gain benefits from its use, but not to sell it or alter its form. Most rental properties and community-owned properties fall into this category, as do your classroom, our offices, and some government properties, such as national parks. Finally, there is the right to hold a good but not to use it, change it, or sell it.

There are many shades between the various forms of property rights, but these are the principal categories. Furthermore, even the right of ownership is not unrestricted. You may own a good but not be able to sell it above a governmentally fixed price. You may own land but not be permitted to build a swimming pool on it unless you build a fence.

As it turns out, most of the problems of externalities result from two situations. The first is incomplete or communal assignment of property rights or even no assignment of property rights. The second problem results when certain uses of one's fully owned property have harmful effects on someone else's property.

### Nonowned or community-owned property

A scarce resource that is not owned is both overused and underproduced. Early settlers in the United States had no incentive to postpone chopping down trees or to plant forests. If one group did not do it, others would. Forests were destroyed. Buffalo, which were not owned, were practically wiped out, while cattle, which were owned, were not. Rivers, which were not owned, were polluted. No one owned the valuable whales, and they practically disappeared when whale oil was the major source of light and lubrication. Neither perfect competition nor human greed was the problem. The problem was that no one had the incentive to kill fewer whales so that the whales could reproduce at a rate sufficient to maintain the population. Similarly, no one has the incentive to produce goods that they cannot own and, hence, realize returns from them. There is no point in individuals planting trees on publicly owned land. No one can reap the economic benefits from keeping publicly owned beaches clean. This is not to say that some people will not refrain from littering out of civic-mindedness; there is no economic incentive to do so, however, if there is no cost. People do not normally throw beer cans in their own yards, but many do so along the roadside.

As we have implied, publicly owned property gives rise to problems similar to those with nonowned property. A government- or community-owned property may not be used efficiently. Suppose a community owned a large piece of property that is better suited for growing vegetables than for cattle grazing. If anyone can use the property, it will probably be used for cattle grazing, because if anyone can harvest the vegetables, growers would have to expend added resources to protect their crops. Cattle owners can drive their cows home from the community property at night.

The point is that publicly owned property may not be put to its most efficient use. This may not be bad for the society. The society may wish to have free beaches and parks rather than have private ownership of these scarce resources. People may prefer overcrowding to paying for the use of the facilities. We only wish to stress that publicly owned resources will be put to uses different from those that would result from private ownership.

## APPLICATION

### A common property problem

Petroleum technology is such that, for a given pool of oil, there is a particular rate of extraction that maximizes the total amount of oil that can be extracted.[7] This rate, to be sure, is the *technically* optimal rate and not necessarily the *economically* optimal rate. But suppose, for a given pool, that the technically optimal rate is the same as the economically optimal rate. Suppose that the pool of oil is so large that many people own pieces of land over the pool, and, therefore, many people can pump oil from the pool. Suppose also that the amount pumped from this particular pool does not affect the world price of crude oil.

If one person owned all of the land over the pool, oil would be pumped at the profit-maximizing optimal rate. But if many people can pump from the pool, there is no incentive to pump at the optimal rate. Any single extractor would have no incentive to cut back. In fact, each landowner would have the incentive to pump as rapidly as possible in order to get as much as possible before the other

---

[7] For a complete discussion of the economics of petroleum extraction, see P. Davidson, "Policy Problems of the Crude Oil Industry," *American Economic Review* 53, no. 1 (March 1963): 85–108.

landowners get it all. If one person cuts back on extraction, it simply means others get more. Thus, oil is pumped at a rate that is greater than is economically optimal.

Again, one person or group could buy up all the pumping rights and make everyone better off, but, with a very large number of owners, the transactions cost may be too high. Some argue that this is a case for state interference; others argue that the state should simply operate the field as a cartel. We will not go into the problem here, beyond stating that this is an example of ownership externalities.

Note that this is not the same as the situation in which a group of formerly competitive firms collude to fix prices. Competition still exists in both this and the above example. But even in the case of competition, Pareto optimality does not exist.

### Private ownership and externalities

One of the fundamental problems of economics is the legal assignment of property rights when the marginal social cost of some activity exceeds the private social cost. A factory or group of factories pollutes a publicly owned river. As noted, the owners of property along the river downstream are damaged by this externality. Or we could have the same problem with air pollution.

Now, as we have mentioned previously, the polluting factories do not pay the full cost of pollution. The social cost is the total private cost plus the cost of the pollution to the property owners downstream. Or the full cost of production of a factory that is polluting the air is the total private cost of production plus the lowered values of the other people's property that is damaged by the smoke. We can think of many other cases; for example, noise pollution from a factory, oil spills from offshore drilling, even the pollution caused by people smoking in a crowded room. There are such externalities all around us; externalities caused by the production of firms and externalities caused by the consumption patterns of individual households.

In all the examples, the marginal private cost of polluting—dumping waste into rivers, belching smoke into the air, and so on—is quite small. The marginal social cost is greater because of the resources required to eliminate or reduce such pollution. No one owns the rivers or the air, only the land adjacent to the rivers or under the air. Thus, no one sets a price on this scarce resource. In the absence of well-defined property rights, there is no automatic corrective device built into the competitive market mechanism.

## Some solutions

The "solution" that says some sort of external control is necessary gives the impression that the only solution is for government to forbid the polluting firms from discharging waste into the river, smoke into the air, or noise into the ears. You know by now that this type of control may not be socially optimal.

In the first place, the market may well have already "solved the problem." Recall the example of the beekeeper and apple farmer. Both provided each other with an externality in the story. The bees pollinated the apple blossoms, and the blossoms allowed the bees to make honey. Once it is understood by the' farmer or the beekeeper that their work provides the other with a valuable benefit, there is an incentive to *internalize* the externality. The beekeeper, for instance, might begin a pollination service and offer to locate bees close to apple orchards for a fee, or might offer to pay the apple farmer for the right to keep bees near the trees if the beekeeper benefits more from the arrangement than does the farmer. Presently, pollination services do exist and flourish, for example, in the state of Washington.[8] Thus, contractual arrangements can eliminate externalities and a source of market failure.

Or government could redefine property rights in the case of rivers. The river owner (owners) might charge the factories for polluting if the downstream landowners own the river and, in this way, make up the loss in property value. Alternatively, if the factory is given property rights in the river, the downstream owners could bribe the factories to reduce the amount of pollution. Clearly, in either case, there would not be zero pollution. In the case of bribery, if the factory owners owned the river, the downstream landowners would bribe the factories until the marginal cost of an additional bribe equals the value of the marginal reduction in pollution to the downstream landowners. If property rights were assigned downstream and a charge set to the factories per unit of pollution, the factory would pollute until the marginal cost of polluting one more unit equals the marginal return from polluting.[9]

As you have perhaps already recognized, the efficiency of such a solution depends upon the number of parties involved. If 1,000 factories are damaging 10,000 fishermen downstream, it would be very

---

[8] S. N. S. Cheung, "The Fable of the Bees: An Economic Investigation," *Journal of Law and Economics* 16, no. 1 (April 1973): 11–34.

[9] In a very famous article by Ronald Coase, "The Problem of Social Cost," *Journal of Law and Economics* 3 (October 1960): 1–44, it was shown that, if one party is damaging another through its productive activity, the optimal amount of damage is the same regardless of the party to whom property rights are assigned, given zero transactions cost.

difficult and expensive to work out a transaction. Even if an *outside party* owns the river, the policing costs may outweigh the potential returns. Or, if 9,999 downstream property owners agree to bribe the factories not to pollute and one party does not agree, how could the nonpayer be excluded from the benefits? In the case of one damager versus one damagee, the solution would be simple if property rights are assigned. But the more parties involved, the greater the cost of making the transaction.

Another option, of course, is for government to force a "solution" by charging the damagers and compensating damagees. Again, there is the question (moral or economic?) of compensating those who acquired property at a lower cost because of the damage. A further question in the case of government control is how much pollution to permit. Surely a goal of zero air and water pollution is ridiculous. If there are diminishing marginal benefits and increasing marginal costs from reducing pollution, surely the solution is to have pollution at some optimal, but nonzero, rate. It is frequently the task of economists and engineers to determine that rate. Marginal costs are not easily measured, and, in the absence of a social utility function, marginal benefits are generally impossible to measure.

We have merely touched upon the problem of external ownership effects. Many more examples and solutions could be discussed. The economics profession is certainly not in agreement about the problem or the solution. Neither is the legal profession. The sole purpose of this discussion is to make you aware of the problem and some possible solutions. We want you to think about the problem of externalities in economic terms.

## 12.6 SUMMARY

Theoretically, perfect competition by means of the price mechanism leads to a Pareto-optimal allocation of resources. This allocation is optimal in the sense that it is efficient. It is not optimal in the sense that society's welfare or utility is maximized, because economists cannot define a social utility function. When government makes choices about allocation in order "to make society better off," it is generally making (implicitly) interpersonal utility comparisons. Economists as economists cannot do this.

In practice, for some cases of the type mentioned in this chapter, competition does not lead to an efficient allocation. It is impossible to determine empirically just how important these are. Certainly most economists would agree that, in any economic society, there is some role for government control or regulation in such cases. There is disagreement over how great a role government should play.

Again, probably the majority of economists would agree that government control should not extend to arbitrary controls over markets where demand and supply are an efficient allocative device. This may seem to be a weak conclusion, but, in fact, it is not. A function of microeconomic theory is to determine the relative efficiency of various types of market organization. The major conclusion is that competition can be efficient. The purpose of these last few sections is simply to show that there are some situations, the importance of which cannot be determined, in which competitive markets may not be efficient. Generally, however, competitively determined prices in competitive markets allocate resources in something like a Pareto-optimal way.

## 12.7 EPILOGUE

In the introduction to each chapter, we included an outline setting forth what you will learn in that chapter. After coming this far, you have learned, we hope, a great deal. Certainly you have learned the basic tools of microeconomic theory—marginal revenue, marginal cost, opportunity cost, supply and demand, marginal product, equilibrium, and so forth. You have also learned the fundamental determinants of many equilibrium situations—consumer equilibrium, the equilibrium of competitive firms and industries, wage equilibrium, the equilibrium of individual markets for goods, and some equilibrium conditions for a society (although the last situation was much less thoroughly covered). You are familiar with the determinants of demand and supply in both commodity markets and markets for factors of production, as well as with the importance of the interest rate in discounting streams of income over time.

We have also tried to make you well aware of some things that economists cannot do, for example, define a social welfare function for a group of people. Economists frequently cannot say that one set of circumstances is better than another, since they cannot make interpersonal utility comparisons. They can, of course, show the costs of various decisions or alternative solutions. They can compare the results of solutions that would occur under free-market determination with the results of governmentally determined solutions. They usually cannot say which is better; they can only say who benefits and who loses under each solution.

Economists have had little success in developing a general theory of market situations between competition and monopoly, particularly in the case of oligopoly, when there are a few closely interdependent firms in the industry. They have had the most success in using competitive or monopoly theory in predicting and explaining some results in these "imperfect" market structures.

Perhaps the most important thing you have learned, and one of our basic points of emphasis in this text, is how to use economic theory to solve real-world problems. By now, you are probably thinking like an economist. That is, in analyzing problems you immediately think in terms of marginal analysis, comparing marginal benefits with marginal costs. Fixed costs are generally irrelevant, and there are generally no "all or nothing" situations. Most decisions are made at the margin.

You should now be able to question and to comment critically on most of the economic analysis you hear on TV, read in newspapers or magazines, and hear from politicians. You are now able to predict the economic consequences of government decisions or activities at all levels of government. Possibly most important, we feel, you can use your economic expertise to aid in your own professional, business, and personal decision making.

Many of you are economics or agricultural economics majors. We hope and we believe that the tools and methods you learned here will be useful in your future courses and your careers as economists. Others of you who are not economics majors may wish to take additional economics courses. Those interested in the effects of government policies, control of the money supply, inflation, or taxation, may wish to take courses in macroeconomics or public finance. These are useful for people planning a career in government service. A course in industrial organization, or an equivalent course, will give you a slightly different and interesting insight into market structures. This course and a course in law and economics or government and business will be useful for those planning a business career or career in law, as would a course in managerial economics. Labor economics would be useful in many careers in business, government service, unions, or work with nonprofit organizations.

For many of you, perhaps the majority, this will be your last economics course. Do not let it be the last time you use economic analysis in decision making. You will find such analysis useful no matter what career you choose.

## TECHNICAL PROBLEMS

1. Explain why equality of marginal rates of substitution between any two goods for any pair of consumers implies that no consumer can be made better off without making some other consumer worse off. Why does perfect competition guarantee this result?

2. Assume two firms, each using capital and labor to produce two goods. The marginal rates of technical substitution between capital and labor are the same for each firm. *Total* capital and

labor are fixed in amount. Explain why one firm cannot increase output without causing the other to decrease output.

3. Explain why there can generally be no social welfare function or social preference ordering.

4. Why would a commonly owned forest be depleted more rapidly than a privately owned forest?

5. Explain in what sense a national park is a public good and in what sense it is not.

6. Is your school library a public good? Could the time of the year affect your answer?

7. There are two individuals, A and B, who consume two goods, X and Y. Consumer A's marginal rate of substitution between goods X and Y is 2X for 1Y. B's MRS is 3X for 2Y. In what direction will trade take place and between what two ratios?

8. In the Edgeworth diagram in Figure E.12–1, point R represents the original allocation of goods X and Y between individuals A and B. Indicate:

   a. The feasible region of exchange and why this range is feasible.

   b. All points unacceptable to A and why.

**FIGURE E.12–1**

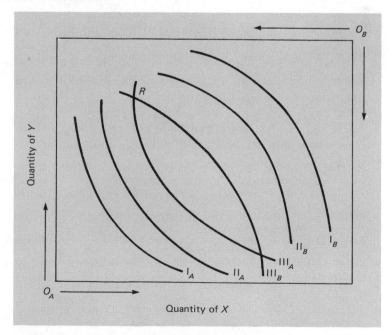

9. Explain how the production-possibility frontier is derived from the production Edgeworth Box.

10. Firm 1 produces good $X$ and firm 2 produces $Y$. Both firms use labor ($L$) and capital ($K$) in the production process. For firm 1, $MP_L = 10$ and $MP_K = 15$. For firm two $MP_L = 6$ and $MP_K = 12$. What should the firms do from a social point of view?

11. Why is perfect competition desirable according to the Pareto optimality rule in welfare economics? Explain.

## ANALYTICAL PROBLEMS

1. Suppose the social return to education is 8 percent and the return to other investment is 10 percent. This shows too many resources are being used in education. Comment.

2. Suppose from time to time a certain theater has long lines for a particular movie and sometimes has to turn away customers. Is this evidence of market failure? Why or why not?

3. Suppose your professor sets forth the following class policies. Identify those which would make the *class* unequivocally better off, those which would make the class worse off, and those for which the conclusion is indeterminate. Explain.
   a. There will be no final exam. Everyone receives as a final grade his or her present average.
   b. The final is optional. You may take your present average or take the final.
   c. The final is mandatory but it only counts if it improves your average.
   d. There will be a final, but points will be taken from the high-grade students and given to the low-grade students until everyone has the same grade.
   e. The professor gives everyone an A, regardless of average.
   f. The final is mandatory, but there will be a makeup final if a student is not satisfied with his or her final grade.

4. Suppose there are two classes made up of very similar students. In one class, each student receives the grade made on each test. In the other class, each student receives the class average on each test. These policies are known by all. In which class would you expect the higher average grade? Explain in terms of externalities, or the free-rider problem.

5. In the state of Texas, the state owns all the beaches. Analyze the following statements and determine whether they are true or false.
   a. If private individuals owned the beaches, poor and middle-income people would be denied access.

    *b.*   Since the state can afford to clean the beaches, there is less litter than if they were privately owned.

    *c.*   Since the state can regulate the beaches, it can keep off sleazy merchants, and the people using the beaches are better off.

    *d.*   Since the state owns the beaches, more people use them, and the people are better off because a beach is a public good.

6. Frequently people talk about the goals of a city.

    *a.*   Can a city have goals? Why or why not?

    *b.*   Under what circumstances could you state unequivocally that a city was made better off by a particular activity?

    *c.*   Suppose someone says the "goal" of a city should be to force the downtown merchants to beautify the downtown area. Can you see any possible trade-off or contradiction?

7. The federal government is very much involved in redistributing income. Programs that transfer income are welfare, social security, and unemployment compensation. Pareto optimality takes the distribution of income as given. Discuss the rationale for income redistribution in light of the Pareto criterion.

8. If bridges and highways are public goods, why do we see private enterprise building them and charging a toll? Do toll roads and bridges maximize consumer's and producer's surplus? Is a toll road or a toll-free publicly financed road better? (In your answer, consider the problem of congestion and the argument that "those who use the road should pay.")

# Index

## A

AAA corporate bond rate, the, 303
Ad valorem tax, 56, 60–61
Advertising, 238 n, 260, 460–64, 484; *see also* Consumer information
  in beer market, 473–75
  and buyer allegiance, 411
  in decaffeinated coffee market, 464–66
  excessive, 462, 464
  image-creating, 460–61
  informative, 460
  and oligopolies, 464, 473–75
  and price, 130–31, 461
  and sales, 463
  social usefulness of, 460–62
  as a source of oligopoly, 470
  two categories of, 460
Afford a good, unable to, 96
Agricultural agents and constrained optimization, 199
Agricultural methods, French versus American, 210
Air Force, U.S., 238

Airlines, 328
  and price discrimination, 423
Allocation
  government, as barrier to entry, 409
  of income, 70, 279–82
  of money income, 91–92, 108
  and Pareto optimality, 548
  of resources; *see* Resource allocation
  sales, 477
  of shortage, 363
Aluminum Company of America (ALCOA), 378, 410
Aluminum industry, 265, 410
  as a monopoly, 378, 475
American Hospital Association, 506
American Medical Association (AMA), 422
  control of medical education by, 422
American Telephone and Telegraph, 378
Anheuser-Busch, 473–75
Antitrust action, 380; *see also* Sherman Antitrust Act
Antitrust Division, Department of Justice, 479
Antonelli, G. B., 74

**583**

*This book has been set in 10 and 9 point Caledonia, leaded 2 points. Chapter numbers are 36 point and chapter titles are 24 point Serif Gothic Bold Outline. The size of the text page is 26 by 47 picas.*